Manuscript Poetics

THE WILLIAM AND KATHERINE DEVERS SERIES IN DANTE AND MEDIEVAL ITALIAN LITERATURE

Zygmunt G. Barański, Theodore J. Cachey, Jr., and Christian Moevs, editors

RECENT TITLES

VOLUME 22
Manuscript Poetics: Materiality and Textuality in Medieval Italian Literature
• Francesco Marco Aresu

VOLUME 21
Dante's Multitudes: History, Philosophy, Method
• Teodolinda Barolini

VOLUME 20
Dante's "Other Works": Assessments and Interpretations
• Edited by Zygmunt G. Barański and Theodore J. Cachey, Jr.

VOLUME 19
Liturgical Song and Practice in Dante's Commedia
• Helena Phillips-Robins

VOLUME 18
Dante and Violence: Domestic, Civic, and Cosmic
• Brenda Deen Schildgen

VOLUME 17
A Boccaccian Renaissance: Essays on the Early Modern Impact of Giovanni Boccaccio and His Works
• edited by Martin Eisner and David Lummus

VOLUME 16
The Portrait of Beatrice: Dante, D. G. Rossetti, and the Imaginary Lady
• Fabio A. Camilletti

VOLUME 15
Boccaccio's Corpus: Allegory, Ethics, and Vernacularity
• James C. Kriesel

VOLUME 14
Meditations on the Life of Christ: The Short Italian Text
• Sarah McNamer

VOLUME 13
Interpreting Dante: Essays on the Traditions of Dante Commentary
• edited by Paola Nasti and Claudia Rossignoli

VOLUME 12
Freedom Readers: The African American Reception of Dante Alighieri and the Divine Comedy
• Dennis Looney

VOLUME 11
Dante's Commedia*: Theology as Poetry*
• edited by Vittorio Montemaggi and Matthew Treherne

VOLUME 10
Petrarch and Dante: Anti-Dantism, Metaphysics, Tradition
• edited by Zygmunt G. Barański and Theodore J. Cachey, Jr.

VOLUME 9
The Ancient Flame: Dante and the Poets
• Winthrop Wetherbee

VOLUME 8
Accounting for Dante: Urban Readers and Writers in Late Medieval Italy
• Justin Steinberg

VOLUME 7
Experiencing the Afterlife: Soul and Body in Dante and Medieval Culture
• Manuele Gragnolati

VOLUME 6
Understanding Dante
• John A. Scott

VOLUME 5
Dante and the Grammar of the Nursing Body
• Gary P. Cestaro

VOLUME 4
The Fiore *and the* Detto d'Amore*: A Late 13th-Century Italian Translation of the* Roman de la Rose, *Attributable to Dante*
• Translated, with introduction and notes, by Santa Casciani and Christopher Kleinhenz

VOLUME 3
The Design in the Wax: The Structure of the Divine Comedy *and Its Meaning*
• Marc Cogan

MANUSCRIPT POETICS

Materiality and Textuality in Medieval Italian Literature

FRANCESCO MARCO ARESU

University of Notre Dame Press

Notre Dame, Indiana

Published by the University of Notre Dame Press
Notre Dame, Indiana 46556
undpress.nd.edu

Published in the United States of America

Library of Congress Control Number: 2023937774

ISBN: 978-0-268-20648-2 (Hardback)

ISBN: 978-0-268-20649-9 (Paperback)

ISBN: 978-0-268-20650-5 (WebPDF)

ISBN: 978-0-268-20647-5 (Epub)

ABOUT THE WILLIAM AND KATHERINE DEVERS SERIES IN DANTE AND MEDIEVAL ITALIAN LITERATURE

The William and Katherine Devers Program in Dante Studies at the University of Notre Dame supports rare book acquisitions in the university's John A. Zahm Dante collections, funds a visiting professorship in Dante studies, and supports electronic and print publication of scholarly research in the field. In collaboration with the Medieval Institute at the university, the Devers program initiated a series dedicated to the publication of the most significant current scholarship in the field of Dante studies. In 2011 the scope of the series was expanded to encompass thirteenth- and fourteenth-century Italian literature.

In keeping with the spirit that inspired the creation of the Devers program, the series takes Dante and medieval Italian literature as focal points that draw together the many disciplines and lines of inquiry that constitute a cultural tradition without fixed boundaries. Accordingly, the series hopes to illuminate this cultural tradition within contemporary critical debates in the humanities by reflecting both the highest quality of scholarly achievement and the greatest diversity of critical perspectives.

The series publishes works from a wide variety of disciplinary viewpoints and in diverse scholarly genres, including critical studies, commentaries, editions, reception studies, translations, and conference proceedings of exceptional importance. The series enjoys the support of an international advisory board composed of distinguished scholars and is published regularly by the University of Notre Dame Press. The Dolphin and Anchor device that appears on publications of the Devers series was used by the great humanist, grammarian, editor, and typographer Aldus Manutius (1449–1515), in whose 1502 edition of Dante (second issue) and all subsequent editions it appeared. The device illustrates the ancient proverb Festina lente, "Hurry up slowly."

Zygmunt G. Barański, Theodore J. Cachey, Jr.,
and Christian Moevs, editors

DANTE

alla mia famiglia, nonostante tutto

CONTENTS

PLATES

ACKNOWLEDGMENTS

Remo Ceserani is the first to whom I owe thanks, not least for his early suggestion that a brief essay on Francesco Petrarca's double sestina could develop into a broader reflection about materiality's effect on the aesthetic process. It grieves me that I cannot now present this book to him, *mas trop suy vengutz als derriers*. This first acknowledgment is a humble record of Ceserani's *humanitas* and a heartfelt act of gratitude to a teacher, who, for me, will forever represent an unequaled model of academic conduct.

Wayne Storey's teaching on the relationship between materiality and textuality in medieval literature forms the foundation on which this book was built, and the tools he gave me are the first I reach for when I approach the *gliuommeri* of manuscript culture. Jeffrey Schnapp has been a cherished mentor and an imaginative reader of my work. I owe my finest academic momentum to him, and I will happily recognize this obligation for many years to come.

Audiences at the European Society for Textual Scholarship, the Northeast Modern Language Association, Yale University's Dante Studies Workshop, James Madison University, Trinity College (Hartford, CT), Fordham University, the University of Connecticut, the Center for Medieval and Renaissance Studies at SUNY Binghamton, Harvard University, Columbia University, and Wesleyan University all responded to work in progress. I am especially grateful for the invitation from Eva Del Soldato and John Pollack to share my work at the University of Pennsylvania's Kislak Center for Special Collections, Rare Books and Manuscripts, and for the vibrant scholarly environment into which they have continued to welcome me.

For their feedback as readers and in conversation, I thank Beatrice Arduini, Dario Calimani, Marco Cursi, Francesco Erspamer, Elsa Filosa, Marisa Galvez, Olivia Holmes, Christopher Kleinhenz, Isabella Magni, Martina

Mazzetti, Gabrielle Ponce-Hegenauer, Marco Romani-Mistretta, Massimo Scalabrini, Paul Schleuse, Maddalena Signorini, and the two anonymous reviewers for the University of Notre Dame Press. Laura Banella and Rhiannon Daniels deserve special mention for the attention they dedicated to my work and for their depth of insight, constructive criticism, and good advice.

For an additional dimension of amity, support, and patience—and for countless hours spent encouraging me—I especially thank Giorgio Alberti, Biliana Kassabova, Katharina Loew, David Yagüe Gonzáles, and Simon Zenios. My Wesleyan University colleagues Roger Grant, Paula Park, and Jeff Rider were exceptionally supportive throughout the writing process. And they helped me keep my sanity.

Sarah Axelrod and Michael Wyatt shared the dubious privilege of proofreading an earlier version of this work when it was only a dissertation draft. My copyeditor Sean Manning turned my Anglo-Sardinian lingo into a more legible and idiomatic English. Without their help this book would have been completed later and with more imperfections. My editor Julia Boss turned the book manuscript upside down and inside out. She helped me find a more precise and clearer version of my voice. Thanks to her I am twice the writer that I was.

For all flaws and lacunae in the work, I alone am to blame.

This book would not have been possible without the help and expertise of librarians, conservators, and technicians at the Biblioteca Medicea Laurenziana, the Archivo y Biblioteca Capitulares in Toledo, the Biblioteca Apostolica Vaticana, the Bibliothèque Méjanes of Aix-en-Provence, the Kislak Center for Special Collections, Rare Books and Manuscripts at the University of Pennsylvania, the Veneranda Biblioteca Ambrosiana, the Hanna Holborn Gray Special Collections Research Center at the University of Chicago Library, the Houghton Library at Harvard University, the Beinecke Rare Book and Manuscript Library at Yale University, and the Olin Library at Wesleyan University. To all of these I offer my most sincere appreciation.

I am grateful to Zygmunt Barański, Theodore Cachey, Christian Moevs, and Editor in Chief Eli Bortz for welcoming this book into the William and Katherine Devers Series in Dante and Medieval Italian Literature at the University of Notre Dame Press. This book was also made possible by generous subventions from the Thomas and Catharine McMahon Memorial Fund at Wesleyan University.

This work is dedicated to my family, still and all. And I would not have it any other way.

Cartula, perge cito pelagi trans aequora cursu.

ON EDITIONS AND CITATIONS

Of the three main works discussed in this book—Dante Alighieri's *Vita nova*, Giovanni Boccaccio's *Teseida: Delle nozze d'Emilia*, and Francesco Petrarca's *Rerum vulgarium fragmenta*—the following editions and translations are used throughout. Other editions and translations of primary sources are listed in the notes. Fuller bibliographic information can be found in the bibliography.

All citations of the *Vita nova* indicated by Arabic numerals—preceded by the abbreviation *VN*—are from Carrai, ed., *Vita nova.* Carrai's edition follows Gorni's paragraphing in Gorni, ed., *Vita Nova*, but consistently adopts the *lectio* of MS Chigi L.VIII.305 of the Vatican Library. In Roman numerals, in square brackets (or parentheses in running text), I indicate the corresponding chapters in Barbi, ed., *La Vita Nuova* (1907). I also made extensive use of the following editions and commentaries: De Robertis, ed., *Vita Nuova*; Gorni, ed., *Vita Nova*; Rossi, ed., *Vita Nova*; Colombo, ed., *Vita Nuova*; and Pirovano, ed., *Vita nuova.* Unless otherwise indicated, all translations are from Frisardi, trans., *Vita Nova*, with minor adjustments to punctuation (Frisardi translates Gorni's critical text). For the sake of clarity, I occasionally refer to the prose translation of the poems provided in "Appendix A" (59–92) of Frisardi's translation: importantly, in "Appendix A," Frisardi reproduces and translates the poems according to Barbi, ed., *La Vita Nuova* (1932). For the intense critical debate on the text of the *Vita nova*, see, among others, including for additional bibliography, Gorni, "Per il testo"; Cervigni and Vasta, "From Manuscript"; Gorni, "'Paragrafi' e titolo"; Gorni, "Il 'copyright'"; Cervigni, "Segni paragrafali"; Gorni, "Ancora sui 'paragrafi'"; Trovato, *Il testo*; Gorni, "Per la *Vita Nova*"; Malato, *Per una nuova edizione*, 12–40; Bellomo, "Problemi"; Carrai, "Quale lingua"; Rea, "La *Vita nova*"; Pirovano, "Per una nuova edizione"; and Pirovano, ed., *Vita nuova*, "Nota al testo," 37–75 (esp.

37–54). Whereas I consistently refer to Dante's *libello* as *Vita nova* (following Carrai's edition), I respectfully preserve other scholars' preferences when I cite (and translate) them.

All citations of the *Teseida* are from Agostinelli and Coleman, eds., *Teseida*, with minor adjustment to the punctuation (e.g., dots of subpunction are always omitted). For lack of a more dependable English translation, I rely on and cite from McCoy, trans., *The Book of Theseus*, except when otherwise indicated.

All citations of the *Rerum vulgarium fragmenta* are from Santagata, ed., *Canzoniere*. In addition to Santagata, I consulted these commentaries: Mestica, ed., *Le Rime*; Carducci and Ferrari, eds., *Le Rime*; Chiòrboli, ed., *Le Rime*; Dotti, ed., *Canzoniere*; Bettarini, ed., *Canzoniere*; and Vecchi Galli, ed., *Canzoniere*. All translations are from Durling, ed. and trans., *Petrarch's Lyric Poems*, with minor adjustments in punctuation. For the *RVF* concordances, see *Concordanze*.

Introduction
Materiality and Method

Per noi non si dà teoria senza esperienza storica.
—Gianfranco Folena, *Volgarizzare e tradurre*, ix

"I like a poem"

In a 1973 lecture at the Pratt Institute in Brooklyn, architect Louis Kahn famously invited his student audience to dialogue with a brick: "You say to brick, 'What do you want, brick?' And brick says to you, 'I like an arch.' And you say to brick: 'Look, I want one too, but arches are expensive and I can use a concrete lintel over you, over an opening.' And then you say, 'What do you think of that, brick?' Brick says, 'I like an arch.'" It is imperative, Kahn continued, to honor the material that one uses: to honor and glorify the brick, rather than shortchanging it.[1] This book is about honoring and glorifying the materiality of literary texts and the material forms that literature is made of.

Literary texts come to us in multiple material forms. In classical antiquity, texts were inscribed on a diverse range of material supports: metal, stone, clay, wood, ivory, palm leaves, papyrus, parchment, wax, and more. In ancient Greece and Hellenized Egypt, fragments of broken pottery called *ostraca* often served as material supports for inscriptions. Since the material was cheap and easily accessible, inscriptions on *ostraca* were generally ephemeral: private messages, votes, receipts, prescriptions, recipes, school exercises.[2] In some cases, however, surviving *ostraca* reserve notable surprises. In 1937, papyrologist Medea Norsa published a text deciphered and transcribed from an *ostracon* acquired in Egypt and now conserved in a velvet case, like a relic, in the Biblioteca Medicea Laurenziana in Florence. This potsherd dates back to the third or second century BCE and transmits seventeen lines of a hymn by Greek poet Sappho (ca. 630–ca. 570 BCE) describing a shrine to Aphrodite. Modern scholars had previously known only a few lines of this poem, some cited by grammarian Athenaeus of Naucratis and others by rhetorician Hermogenes of Tarsus. The cursive script and the many mistakes and omissions in the text have suggested that the *ostracon* transmits a dictation exercise, and they have revealed to scholars the student-transcriber's limited familiarity with the Eolic dialecticisms of Sappho's verse.[3] The combined analysis of material and textual aspects of this sherd allows us to form hypotheses about the modalities of reproduction, transmission, circulation, and reception of the text itself. And if you asked *ostracon* the same question Kahn asked brick—What do you like, *ostracon*?—*ostracon* would say to you: "I like a poem."

Like most medieval songbooks, the autograph of Francesco Petrarca's *canzoniere* displays the fourteen hendecasyllables of each of its sonnets on seven lines, with two hendecasyllables on each line. The reading proceeds first horizontally—from the odd verse on the left to the even verse on the right—and then vertically. Following textual styles codified in Renaissance *canzonieri*, modern editions present instead Petrarca's sonnets in the thoroughly vertical layout—one verse per line—to which we are now accustomed. But with sonnet 25—"Amor piangeva, et io con lui talvolta" (Love, from whom my steps have never strayed, used to weep)—a thoroughly vertical layout dismantles the acrostic structure of the poem: a structure that forms the word *Amore*, also the sonnet's incipitarian word, with the opening letters of the odd hendecasyllables of the sonnet's *fronte*. A reading of sonnet 25 that disregards its layout in the autograph fails to recognize Petrarca's project of transcribing texts in meter-specific spatial formations. It fails to recognize that different meters may *like* different material presentations. A material awareness of the text—from its physical support to its visual and spatial design on the folio façade—often helps us shed light on the poetics, compositional techniques, scribal conventions, and editorial strategies behind its creation. And it affects its perception.[4]

Materiality influences creative endeavor, affects reception, shapes meaning. The brick from Kahn's apologue *decides* the creative operation and the form of architecture that should result from it; it implicitly *declares* itself innately suitable for arch-making. The potsherd preserving Sappho's text reveals itself to be just the right size for holding a short hymn, learning a poem, practicing a style; its disposability is intrinsically useful to, or even determinative of, those actions. The medieval authors discussed in this book honor and glorify the material forms that embody their works by writing literature that *likes*—that predicts, responds to, and absorbs—the physical features of those material forms.

Manuscript Poetics

Manuscript Poetics: Materiality and Textuality in Medieval Italian Literature is both an investigation into the material foundations of literature and a reflection on notions of textuality, writing, and media in late medieval and early modern Italy. It practices, and advocates for, a literary criticism that engages—and begins—with the book-objects of manuscripts and early printed editions, asking questions about the material conditions of production, circulation, and reception of literary works. The material turn in literary studies has taught us that the material forms in which texts are embodied affect how texts are produced, transmitted, and interpreted. It has taught us that looking at how and where words appear on the manuscript folio can better inform our understanding of what those words mean, or could have meant, for their author and audience.[5] This book invites scholars to reconcile reading with seeing and touching, to recognize the affinity—the *liking*—that by Dante's time parchment and paper folios had developed for poetry, and to challenge our contemporary presumptions about technological neutrality and the modes of interfacing/reading to which we are most accustomed.[6]

Manuscript Poetics examines the correspondences and interactions between textuality and materiality, message/form and medium, visual-verbal discourse and its physical support through readings of three works by medieval

Italian authors: Dante Alighieri's *Vita nova*, Giovanni Boccaccio's *Teseida*, and Petrarca's *canzoniere* (*Rerum vulgarium fragmenta*). Each of these literary texts is read here as an interaction between conceptual, linguistic, rhetorical, and material elements. In a manuscript poetics, the container and the content, the book and the text, share a material and symbolic solidarity. The book represents the primary idea of the text, and the text, conceptually, assumes the material shape of a book. A manuscript poetics informed the *Vita nova*, the *Teseida*, and the *Rerum vulgarium fragmenta*: operating within the manuscript culture of late medieval Italy, Dante, Boccaccio, and Petrarca evaluated and deployed the tools and strategies of scribal culture to shape, signal, and layer meanings coextensive to those they conveyed verbally in their written texts.

In Nelson Goodman's classification of artworks, literary texts are allographic rather than autographic: the material changes they undergo in their transmission history leave their essential properties unaltered. A manuscript poetics instead reclaims for medieval literary texts in their material presentation Goodman's own notion of the artwork's autographic qualities, *pace* Goodman and regardless of the actual autography of these texts. For the literary texts discussed in this book, the history of production is integral to the works, the distinction between original and copy (and forgery) is significant to them, and the material changes they undergo affect their meaning.[7]

Manuscript Poetics proposes that we reexamine medieval texts in which authors are known to have played (or simulated) a significant scribal role, bringing questions about the manuscripts as objects into dialogue with questions deriving from other interpretive approaches, such as narratology, reception and reader-response theory, and rhetorical and stylistic analysis. When we integrate these multiple modes of inquiry, we come to understand narrative as emerging from—and unfolding in—both the syntax of plot elements and the material arrangement of sentences and paragraphs on the folio façade. We observe how various enunciative instances and narratorial modes—however concealed within the linguistic sequence that constitutes a literary text—incarnate or manifest in the material surface of the medium that preserves that text. We recognize that the specific scribal decisions authors made—about support, *mise-en-page*, *mise-en-texte*, script, illustration, and more—encouraged certain readings of texts and certain modes of reading those texts.[8] We see that poetry articulates, and merges, metrical techniques and rhetorical strategies into material forms through scribal conventions: we realize, in short, that the material presentation of a poem is mimetically and stylistically motivated.

Textuality and materiality were integrated into a common project of creating meaning and seeking to shape reception. This perspective—which medieval texts, crafted in the context of centuries-old scribal cultures and in dialogue with multiple text technologies, are uniquely positioned to provide—is foundational to the theoretical understanding of new forms and materials in our media-saturated contemporary world.

The contentions expressed above resonate with other recent contributions in the field of medieval Italian literature that have emphasized the corelationship of materiality and textuality and the complementary potential value of combining literary criticism and material philology. Rhiannon Daniels has studied the materiality of manuscripts and printed books preserving Boccaccio's works to trace a cultural and socioeconomic history of his readership. Martin Eisner has examined a single autograph by Boccaccio—transmitting his transcriptions of Dante, Guido Cavalcanti, and Petrarca—to show how Boccaccio authorized a literary tradition in the vernacular. Jelena Todorović has explored notions of poetry and genre in Dante's *Vita nova*, examining the relationship between texts and material supports within a broader framework of intercultural exchange among the various literary traditions of medieval Italy. Laura Banella has provided a philological analysis of the *Vita nova*'s circulation in the fourteenth and fifteenth centuries, focusing on Boccaccio's editorial interventions in Dante's prosimetrum. And Beatrice Arduini has investigated the manuscript and early print tradition of Dante's unfinished treatise *Convivio*, showing how literary works can be reappraised for cultural use beyond the author's original project.[9]

Manuscript Poetics shares with these works—and others emerging from the material turn in literary studies—an attention to the material dimension of oral and written texts. Like these works, it considers the material history of texts, but it attempts to move this consideration a step further to highlight the hermeneutical implications of material variation. It underlines the interaction of diverse scribal cultures in late medieval Italy and the diversification of the reading audience, but simultaneously addresses material, textual, and literary implications of that audience diversity. This study traces the history of empirical readers but also highlights their theoretical similarities to and distances from the texts' implied reader. Furthermore, by working across the manuscript traditions of three texts, authored by three influential writers, the project extends its scope beyond a single codex (Eisner), a single author (Daniels), or a single text (Todorović, Banella, and Arduini).

This book inscribes the concrete particularity of three case studies within a theoretical frame that serves as method for the simultaneous analysis of the material features of textual artifacts and the literary aspects of the texts preserved in those artifacts. The three case studies presented in this book follow a chronological order. They also follow a methodological order: Part I raises questions upon which parts II and III elaborate. Some of the questions addressed are these: What is the relationship between the book's inside (the narrated space of its imaginative world) and its outside (its physical features, but also the events that lead to the book's production)? How does the material dimension of the book shape authority and condition reception and reproduction? What is the impact of the book as material object on the author's poetics? *Manuscript Poetics* considers how the mutual (and nondeterministic) interplay between textuality and materiality, between literary texts and the media that form and formalize them, affects three different aspects of literary textual communication: the substance of the work's utterance (the form and content of the enunciated, the *énoncé* of Émile Benveniste) in the chapters on Dante; the textual manifestations of the enunciator (the originator of the utterance, the *énonciateur*) in the chapters on Boccaccio; and the very act of the enunciation (the act of enunciating as is performed by the enunciator, the *énonciation*) in the chapters on Petrarca. As Algirdas J. Greimas and Joseph Courtés observed, the notion of enunciation implies the production process of the utterance; the enunciated, in turn, is the utterance resulting from the enunciating act. Here, the actualization of virtual structures into actual forms of literary discourse is intended as entailing both textual and material forms. The transition from virtual to actual, in other words, involves the tangible forms of a text's materiality.[10]

As Michele Barbi pointed out, every text presents unique problems that accordingly require unique solutions.[11] For the study of Boccaccio's *Teseida* and Petrarca's *Rerum vulgarium fragmenta*, we can rely on autographs: manuscripts copied by their authors.[12] But even without an autograph of Dante's *Vita nova*, we can still reflect critically on the materiality of Dante's books by investigating the metatextual indications embedded within his texts and their material renditions in the earliest copies of his works. More about methodology will be discussed later in this introduction, but it seems appropriate here to introduce the book-objects *Manuscript Poetics* focuses on and the three parts of this book that in turn revolve around them.

The book's examination of Dante's *Vita nova* (part I: chapters 1, 2, and 3) assesses how the materiality of manuscript culture intersects the narrative of Dante's work: it shows that the story narrated in the text—the very substance of the *Vita nova*'s utterance—coincides with the material dynamics of its composition, circulation, and reception. The *Vita nova* is a metanarrative that theorizes the grounds for vernacular narrative by means of dramatizing its own creation, describing its own materiality, and conveying information on its anticipated book form, typology of expected readership, and visual rendition of the expository order of the text. The early manuscript tradition of the *Vita nova* often reflects the self-contained quality, paragraphing, and visual articulation detailed in the prosimetrum, material and textual features intended for the text and described within the text. And it shows that Dante's compositional technique and strategy of textual control were deeply rooted in medieval Italian scribal culture and were based on knowledge of specific book forms.

The chapters (4 and 5) on Boccaccio show how, in the autograph of his epic poem *Teseida*, he made the most of the medium's materiality to simulate multiple simulacra of his role as enunciator: scribe, commentator, author. He employed his expertise in making books to shape a plural authorial identity and condition the reception of his poem. By exploring the editorial and intertextual relationships between Boccaccio's autograph of the *Teseida* and several exemplars of the poem produced between the fourteenth and fifteenth centuries, the book's part II argues that the material configuration of the autograph and the complex system of authorial personae that Boccaccio stages are intended to anticipate and sanction multiple readings for his work. The manuscript tradition shows that his readers recognized their options and made choices according to their situations. We see both a *leisure* production—copied on paper without illustrative and commentative apparatus, and facilitating reading the text as a work of entertainment—and a courtly and scholarly production executed on parchment with elaborately illuminated initials and a detailed commentary.

The chapters (6 and 7) on Petrarca focus on the material and textual treatment of his sestinas in the autograph of his *canzoniere* (*Rerum vulgarium fragmenta*) and explore his editorial project of associating the poet's activity with the scribe's in an ideal coincidence of literary expression and inscription, text and book. These chapters demonstrate that, in Petrarca's autograph, the interactions between the sestinas' visual presentation, subject matter, and rhetorical articulation make these sestinas the designated poetic form to reassess and discuss (in metaliterary terms) the poetic and existential experience portrayed in the *canzoniere*. In the autograph of the *Rerum vulgarium fragmenta*, the sestinas produce meaning in the modes and forms of visual poems, thus functioning textually and materially as the poetic and ideological core of Petrarca's songbook.

As posited by Maurice Merleau-Ponty, verbal communication is determined by the physical interaction of one's body with its surroundings.[13] And Roger Chartier has emphasized how "reading is not only an abstract operation of the intellect: it puts the body into play and is inscribed in a particular space, in a relation to the self or to others."[14] To put it differently, texts, like words, do not exist in the abstract: writing and reading involve handling tools and manipulating materials; writing and reading get your hands dirty. *Manuscript Poetics* makes a series of interpretive claims regarding the specific texts examined—about metatextuality in Dante's *Vita nova*, about Boccaccio's authorship and authority, about Petrarca's poetics—but first and foremost it articulates a larger claim of method and procedure. Since texts do not exist in the abstract (and even more so in a manuscript culture where each exemplar is a unique object), since literary composition is an intellectual and material act that is modeled on and executed in exact book forms, and since consumption and interpretation are inscribed in time and space—they involve body and mind—the analysis of literary texts must bring together investigative tools and frames of reference that consider what is legible and what is visible, what is verbal and conceptual and what is material and spatial.

Studies in material philology, manuscript studies, and book history rarely theorize the theoretical foundations and implications of their approach to literary texts.[15] This book proposes that we fill this lacuna by bringing together materiality and theory. In so doing it approaches medieval literature through both *etic* and *emic* categories (in the terms proposed by Kenneth Pike and productively applied to art history and literary studies by Carlo Ginzburg): it applies the interpretive categories of the observer (etic) to understand the words of the actors (emic); it asks the defamiliarizing or even ostensibly anachronistic questions of contemporary theoretical approaches to highlight less apparent aspects of medieval textuality and literature.[16] Without claiming any radical innovation in methodology, we may now productively bridge between two existing approaches to medieval texts. The chapters that follow encourage scholars who favor more theoretical interpretive approaches to recognize the contingent nature of the texts they are studying and the role of the material text object(s) in articulating that contingency, and they invite scholars who are more familiar with the influence of the material on meaning to investigate further the interpretive and theoretical implications of their work: seeing how the close attention to variations in material exemplars they study especially for purposes of establishing the accuracy of texts and their history can also contribute productively to conversations about narrativity, poetics, reader response, and reception among critics who have not hitherto confronted the text as manifested in a specific material object.

What follows in this introduction serves as both heuristic preface and contextual framework for the literary works examined in this book. On the one hand, it explains the book's theoretical coordinates and situates its scope in relation to the broader fields of literary criticism and manuscript studies. And on the other hand, it draws a (necessarily succinct) outline of Italian manuscript culture between the thirteenth and the fourteenth centuries to help the reader position the book-objects discussed here within the context of their production, circulation, and consumption.

Materiality and Textuality

In this book, the quality of textuality is attributed to inscriptions provided with meanings, which can be deciphered and interpreted, and whose existence in relation to their reading audience coincides with the materiality of their physical forms. Peter L. Shillingsburg has provided a useful definition of what he calls material text: "the union of *linguistic text* and *document*: a *sign sequence* held in a medium of display."[17] According to Shillingsburg, material texts produce meanings additional, and perhaps complementary, to linguistic texts. Here we attribute a radical meaning to Shillingsburg's notation of "union" and posit therefore the coincidence of text and material, while also avoiding the implications that the linguistic and the material levels of meaning are added to, rather than inhere in, one another. If for Jacques Derrida "there is no linguistic sign before writing," here we conceive of materiality and textuality as the ontological and hermeneutical ground of possibility for each other.[18]

The notion of materiality referred to in this book involves the physical aspects of the book as object, the know-how and instruments employed for its creation, and the material conditions of its production, circulation, transmission, reception, consumption, and commodification. *Manuscript Poetics* reads the apparently unmediated immanence of the book-object with a focus on the cultural mediations and constructions behind its production history (and behind the very perception and recognition of the book as object and commodity). It also reads the material features of the book-object in their bijective relationship—that is, in a relationship of mutual correspondence—with the literary codes of the texts the book transmits. Broadly intended, the notion of materiality engages both with the codicological makeup investigated by material philology and with notions of historical materialism that focus on the materiality of human experience. On the one hand, materiality refers to the tangible and measurable aspects of the book-object. It tackles its visual and spatial features: size, format, number of leaves, fasciculation, size of written space, number of lines, ruling, layout, script, marginalia, illuminations, binding, and more. On the other hand, it interrogates the plurality of agencies—authorial intentions, readers' expectations, scribal conventions, compilers' agendas, patrons' commissions, scholars' interpretations—that come together to produce books and negotiate their meaning.[19]

The reference to authorial intention as decisive agency in the production and negotiation of meaning does not intend to repropose outdated or reactionary forms of intentionality and metaphysical origin. Rather, the stress on human agencies intentionally curtails posthermeneutical notions of technological determinism, one for which, in Friedrich Kittler's much debated terms, media would *determine* our situation.[20] The stress on human agencies—on both the authorial and the readerly side of the literary system—emphasizes the project behind the product, underscores the transactional and communicative quality of literary works, and privileges the experiential quality of literary phenomena for their readers. The reference to an authorial project coexists with the tenet that texts may signify different and equally legitimate meanings for authors and readers.

The goal here is to equilibrate the relationship between two conceptual domains—mind and matter, thought and thing, symbolic and physical, ethereal and corporeal, transcendent and immanent—rather than reinforcing their mutual opposition and irreducibility. The terms of this book's subtitle, "materiality" and "textuality," do not merely complement each other: in rhetorical terms, the *dicolon* they form may be best intended as hendiadys ("materiality and textuality" mean "material textuality") or as the expression of a hypostatic union (in which materiality and textuality are different modes and manifestations of a unique substance).[21]

Manuscript Poetics lies at the intersection of medieval Italian literature, literary theory and criticism, material philology, manuscript studies, and book history. This book enters into dialogue with a number of methods from these disciplines, but grounds its theoretical framework on and engages most specifically with—even where it does not address them explicitly—four theoretical principles and the pioneering work of the scholars who proposed them: (1) Donald M. McKenzie's contention that all aspects of a book's material and sociohistorical dimensions—not just its verbal components—bear a semantic value; (2) Jerome McGann's notion that both a text's presentational features and its linguistic substance constitute meaning; (3) H. Wayne Storey's concept of visual poetics as the interconnectedness between poem and layout on the manuscript folio; and (4) the idea of "rapporto di scrittura" (writing relationship) outlined by Armando Petrucci to indicate the author's participation in the material production of his or her work.[22]

Both McKenzie's sociology of texts and McGann's socialization of text describe books as the products of a collaborative process and point toward the abovementioned plurality of agencies involved in constituting and reconstituting meaning over time, space, and media. McKenzie's model of textuality rejected the traditional distinction in Anglo-American textual criticism between substantial (intrinsic) and accidental (extrinsic) data, asserting that in the study of a codex it is impossible "to divorce the substance of the text on the one hand from the physical form of its presentation on the other."[23] For McKenzie, the material form of the book itself expresses and constitutes meaning; and material changes in, as well as migrations through, the media that embody literary texts reconstitute meaning. Like McKenzie, McGann has emphasized how literary works do not function on purely linguistic terms: "Every literary work that descends to us operates through the deployment of a double helix of perceptual codes: the linguistic codes, on one hand, and the bibliographical codes on the other."[24] The material presentation of a work, in other words, is codependent on its poetics and aesthetic purpose. We will see how the very perception of the literary genre of Dante's *Vita nova*—poetic anthology, literary "autobiography," or treatise on the art of poetry—is a function of its material presentation. And we will observe how, in Boccaccio's *Teseida*, meaning and functionality are constituted and reconstituted through the various material forms the poem assumes in time and space.

In his seminal work on the visual semantics of early Italian lyric, Storey has described how authors integrated codicological principles, such as layout and fasciculation, into their poetry and poetics. He has therefore advocated for editorial solutions and interpretive approaches that are respectful of medieval scribal norms. The present book has taken Storey's lesson on Petrarca's visual poetics to heart: the chapters on the sestinas in part III could be considered—if a McLuhanesque moment is allowed—as a footnote to Storey's observations on Petrarca's compositional and editorial practices.[25] Where Storey focuses on the optical and graphological conceptualization of meters and genres, in a closer look at the sestinas we observe the interaction between their visual-spatial, rhetorical, and thematic components as that interaction affects the reader's experience of the autograph of the *canzoniere*.

Petrucci defined the notion of "writing relationship" as "the level of direct—that is, properly graphic—participation of the author in the written registration of their work in any phase of its composition, from preparatory materials to first tracing, to drafts, through the final version."[26] Classical authors offer precious testimonies on autography in the Greek and Roman world—Catullus laments that the autograph *codicilli* of his poems' first drafts were stolen (*Carmina* 62.11)—but no autograph of a classical text has come down to us.[27] Autographs begin to proliferate at the twilight of the Middle Ages, and they have survived in greater numbers.[28] These late medieval autographs are generally related to marginal figures in literary history and often limited to subscriptions or signatures in public records. As we have seen with *ostraca*, however, there can be notable exceptions. If the velvet pouch storage of the Sappho *ostracon* at the Biblioteca Medicea Laurenziana suggested a relic, that analogy is yet more apt for the small sheet of parchment that preserves Francis of Assisi's autograph of his *Laudes Dei altissimi*.[29] And notable exceptions are the autographs of Petrarca and Boccaccio, who conceived literary composition as a combination of both discursive and material components and progressively assumed the functions of copyists of their own texts. Of the *tre corone* of Italian literature, only Dante leaves no autographs. Reconstructing what the autographs of the *Vita nova* and the *Commedia* might have looked like can be attempted only in a virtual sense, by comparing what the early exemplars of Dante's works tell us about the context of their production with what the texts tell us about their own intended materiality.

This crucial material difference between the textual traditions of *Vita nova*, *Teseida*, and *Rerum vulgarium fragmenta* is also reflected in this book's methodology and procedure. Whereas the sections on Boccaccio and Petrarca address materiality directly—and they each begin with a book-object—the chapters on Dante approach instead the materiality of the text *obliquely* via the text's narration of its material construction and anticipated material future. In so doing, the chapters on Dante rely on the interpretive tools that scholars in the German new wave of narratology (particularly Ansgar Nünning and Monika Fludernik) have devised to examine the act of narration and its metanarrative corollaries.[30] The examination of Dante's *Vita nova*, in other words, begins by closely reading sites where the text narrates moments or events in its composition, textual constitution, physical construction, and visual organization on the folio, it looks at moments in the text that reflect scribal conventions and at references to the text's intended design that suggest effort to control reception, and it verifies in extant copies of the prosimetrum whether and how readers and scribes received the messages on the *Vita nova*'s implied materiality conveyed in the text.

Manuscript Cultures

The three works discussed in this book—Dante's *Vita nova*, Boccaccio's *Teseida*, and Petrarca's *Rerum vulgarium fragmenta*—require no presentation.

But to recognize the multiple relationships of *liking* between literary texts and material forms that were possible in thirteenth- and fourteenth-century Italy as well as the potential for multiple audiences that Dante, Boccaccio, and Petrarca will exploit—but also, in some cases, dismiss—we have to consider the emerging reading audiences of the period and the specific book forms and models of production that evolved in late medieval Italy to meet their multiple reading needs.[31]

In the course of the thirteenth and fourteenth centuries, the expanding bureaucratic and administrative structures in the richest among the central and northern Italian *comuni* and courts drove the development of a professional class of notaries and administrators. And the artisanal, commercial, and financial activities of the economically thriving mercantile classes required alphabetization and technical training for a progressively larger part of the *popolo*. A privately based (and diversely specialized) system of elementary education was implemented to meet the increased need for literacy and also the cultural and professional needs of the mercantile classes. The diversification of literacy and readerships found its material counterpart in the development of different scripts and book products. The chancery minuscule used for documentary and notary purposes became the standard script for the usual writing of cultivated people. An elegant stylization of this script was also used as a book hand in urban ateliers for the transcription of nonecclesiastical literary texts.[32] Merchants and artisans also devised a professional script—the *mercantesca*—which was used to impart a vocational education and transact business. We generally find the *mercantesca* in ledgers, account books, and technical treatises, but this script was also used to transcribe popular texts for leisure or entertainment reading.[33] The majority of the extant manuscripts of the *Teseida*, for instance, adopt *mercantesca* and chancery cursive scripts rather than the elegant book hand Boccaccio used in the poem's autograph. And they bear witness to the poem's wide diffusion and circulation among the new lay literates.

The progressive transformation of religious and cathedral schools into universities over the course of the twelfth century generated an increase in the demand for books. With the rise of universities emerged a qualified microcosm of book specialists—tanners, parchmenters, quill-makers, rubricators, scribes, illuminators, bookbinders—who gathered into urban ateliers and brought about a professionalization of expertise, with workers salaried and subject to precise regulations. Intermediaries (booksellers, stationers) centralized demand and offer. The growth of university libraries rationalized the access to texts and socialized it, reducing the financial burden of book production and acquisition for many new readers. In the first half of the thirteenth century, first in Paris and then in Bologna, universities developed the *pecia* system of producing and reproducing books: authenticated exemplars stored in official ateliers were made available to students in unbound quires (*peciae*) in order to maximize opportunities for transcription and facilitate the rapid turnover of texts.[34] We will see that Petrarca was blatantly skeptical of these kinds of "automized" and fragmented transcriptional practices: his new manuscript poetics and book aesthetics—which center on the unity of artistic control and the material and textual accuracy of the final product—are also a reaction to these and similar scribal conventions.

The transformation of book production, distribution, and demand in the period from the twelfth to the fourteenth century affected the material presentation of the codex. According to Erwin Panofsky, Gothic manuscripts—like Gothic cathedrals—materially implement, and visually manifest, two major structural principles of scholasticism: elucidation and clarification.[35] Didactic and homiletic praxes necessitated the easy browsing, accessibility, and usability of the immense repository of knowledge stored in university books. The attempt to order and organize these materials required formal and graphic devices to facilitate the location and retrieval of information. The material articulation of the codex into divisions and subdivisions reflects the ambition to achieve, within the covers of the codex, a comprehensive, explicit, and hierarchized order. This search for order implies both a scheme of literary presentation and a knowledge design aimed at optimizing the reading and studying experience. The presentation of written information on the folio façade, in other words, is methodically ordered through optical expedients. We will observe how Dante fabulates the material configuration and knowledge design of Gothic codices into elements of the *Vita nova*'s narrative. We will analyze how Boccaccio pursues his promotion of vernacular literature—and self-promotion of his work—by transcribing vernacular texts in the material forms generally reserved for the official academic culture in Latin. And we will read Petrarca's disparaging comments on the alleged lack of harmony of the Gothic scripts as a theoretical prerequisite of his innovative manuscript poetics.

To approach the late medieval manuscript culture in which Dante, Boccaccio, and Petrarca operated, we will often turn to Petrucci's lucid taxonomy of the various book forms of late medieval Italy: the courtly book of the aristocratic courts of northern Italy, written in textual Gothic, richly decorated, transmitting Occitan and Old French poetry, destined for recreational reading; the university desk (or lectern) book, instrument of the official culture in Latin, written on parchment, in *litterae scholasticae* (university Gothic scripts), in two columns with ample margins for annotations, visually organized to facilitate the retrieval of information; and the register-book, written in cursive scripts (chancery minuscule or *mercantesca*), provided with minimal ornamentation and no commentary, increasingly transcribed on paper, often binding together several texts of disparate nature, and further subdividable into the deluxe register-book (commissioned by patrons) and the hodgepodge book (*zibaldone*) of lower manufacturing quality.[36]

The late thirteenth century also witnessed a proto-humanistic interest in late Carolingian codices—dating to the tenth and eleventh centuries—and the first attempts by early humanists and scholars to produce or commission manuscripts that reproduced their features.[37] This "archeological" interest and the imitative practice that followed from it influenced the new manuscript poetics (and aesthetics) promoted by Petrarca and would culminate in the production of the first prototypes of humanistic books, with their recognizable centered text (with small margins), their frequent choice of small or medium book sizes (in-quarto or in-folio), and their preference for scripts and ornamentation inspired by Carolingian models.

The choice of a book form implies preliminary hermeneutical considerations regarding the text to transcribe on behalf of the copyist or the commissioner. And existing typologies of book forms also affect—and are appropriated to the service of—products that are not yet known to readers. When Boccaccio elects Statius's *Thebaid* as the classical text to model his own pioneering epic in the vernacular, he also imitates the codicological features and visual aesthetics of the manuscripts through which the *Thebaid* was available to him. Intertextuality, imitation, and allusive practices, in short, involved both the discursive aspects of literary texts and the material presentation of the books in which those texts were embodied. Readers and patrons, however, often determined book forms more than authors did. Only a limited number of exemplars of Dante's *Commedia*, for instance, conform to the university desk book form that Dante had anticipated for his poem and metatextually referenced in the poem: instead, the most diffuse book form for the *Commedia* in the first half of the fourteenth century, *pace* Dante, was the register-book developed by notaries (and merchants) for professional purposes.

The undisputed protagonist of this book is the codex. In Dante's *Vita nova*, the codex as inscription technology will be at the core of the prosimetrum's narrative. And codices feature as prominent characters in Petrarca's and Boccaccio's epistolaries. But if a steady rise in literacy and book production characterizes the thirteenth and fourteenth centuries, nevertheless orality—with its correlate phenomena of formularity, ritual, performance, and mnemotechnics—still plays a fundamental role in late medieval literature and in the works we are about to discuss.[38] In the Middle Ages, the practice of writing down a literary text in one's own hand coexisted with dictating a text to a secretary or a professional scribe. Delegating the material production of fair copies to scribes was still common in the thirteenth century.[39] Textualization (if not composition proper) was often dictation-based: *dictare* ("to dictate") designated the act of composing more often than *scribere* ("to write").[40] Orality could also affect the production and "publication" of practical nonaesthetic texts—such as legal texts, which could be recited before an audience—or philosophical works. Thomas Aquinas, for instance, would first write his notes in his notoriously cacographic *littera illegibilis* (unreadable script), a type of shorthand that still stymies modern paleographers. He would then summon his secretaries, who would take turns writing down what Thomas read aloud.[41] The intersection between oral and written communication characterizes the production and performance of lyrical texts (whether or not accompanied by music), religious poetry (the *laude*), narrative texts (the *cantari*), homilies, and academic lectures. We will glimpse elements of residual (if perhaps formulaic) orality in the lyric poems preserved in the *Vita nova* and in the description Dante provides of those poems' initial circulation and consumption. We will see how the inspiration for and textual tradition of Boccaccio's *Teseida* are intertwined with those of popular, anonymously transmitted *cantari*. And we will surprise Petrarca as he admittedly pronounces his poems to himself to verify the sonority of a turn of phrase. Materiality conditions expressive functions, even when the material support—in this case, the voice—is at its most "immaterial" and is not provided for us to see and touch.

When we consider the variety of book forms described above and the signals coded in the material books, we must recognize that matching text form and book form was a carefully considered process involving authors, scribes, compilers, and commissioning patrons in multiple decisions. We have to recognize, in other words, that each kind of book might *like* a certain kind of text. The choice of a book form, more precisely, depended on the nature of the text to transcribe and on the typology of the exemplar from which the text was transcribed (its antigraph, or antegraph). Different book typologies would also correspond to different commissions for different reading audiences, each characterized by specific reading habits, competences, and needs. And modes of textual and material presentation depended on and affected compositional and interpretive strategies.

Book Materials

This book is materially articulated into three parts. Part I, "Materiality as Narrative in Dante's *Vita nova*," is divided into three chapters (1, 2, and 3). It explores the intersections between narrative, textuality, and materiality within Dante's *Vita nova*, tackling materiality and textuality at the level of the text's utterance (the content and form of the text's enunciated). It explains how the material dynamics of composition, circulation, and reception of literary works in late medieval Italy shaped the subject matter of Dante's prosimetrum and structured its plot: the story narrated in the *Vita nova* coincides with the account of the material making of the book itself. Faced with the task of developing a love narrative and his own *biographia literaria* without consistent textual and material models in the vernacular, Dante turns to the story's developmental process itself—its conceptual design and material production—as content substance for this narrative. We do not see Dante's autograph of the *Vita nova*. What we do see is the composition of the prosimetrum's poems, their circulation and reception, and their (self-) exegesis turned into episodes in a narrative that culminates in, and coincides with, the *Vita nova*'s text itself. Dante also fixes specific parameters for the physical container of the narrative—its fasciculation, its *mise-en-texte*—and finds in the material form of the book the appropriate textual technology to frame, compose, and discuss the story of his sentimental and poetic apprenticeship. He exploits both the perceived shortcomings of manuscript culture (the uncontrolled proliferation of variants, nonauthorial reordering of textual sequences, extraction of texts from their discursive context, misattributions) and its resources (the material hierarchization of information, paragraphing, fasciculation) to maximize his intellectual and literary project of selecting, ordering, resemanticizing, and materially securing his poetic production and the overall meaning he attributed to it.

Chapters 1 and 2 detail the *Vita nova*'s metanarrative and self-reflective expressions, including the text's imagery of books, book production, literary composition, writing, and reading: these first two chapters show how Dante's innovative approach to narration and storytelling was programmed in concert with specific material features (such as fasciculation, rubrication, and *mise-en-texte*) to guarantee the semantic coherence and textual integrity of that narration. More specifically, chapter 1, "*Scriptor in Fabula*," is a narratological analysis of the *Vita nova*'s metanarrative statements and references to its own composition (and to writing in general). It demonstrates that the *Vita nova*'s metanarration is both an "incident" embedded in the narrative and a discursive function inherent to the act of narrating. The *Vita nova*'s metatextual references establish the theoretical foundations for an innovative first-person narrative in Italian that articulates—and interprets allegorically—Dante's parable of erotic and poetic apprenticeship. Chapter 2, "The Author as Scribe," underlines the material and context-specific aspects of the *Vita nova*'s self-description as material artifact. It investigates the material and historical foundations of the prosimetrum's self-reflexivity and unveils Dante's relationship to medieval Italian scribal culture: Dante translated the material and textual models he availed himself of—and the codicological features of the codices he was familiar with—into elements of the prosimetrum's story and discourse. Chapter 3, "The Scribe as Author," traces the effect of the *Vita nova*'s references to its own textuality and materiality on the early manuscript tradition of the prosimetrum. It compares some of the material references and interpretive guidelines embedded in the text with their actual rendition in four of its earliest transcriptions to determine the extent to which Dante's compositional strategies were successful in conditioning the reception of his work. The textual transmission of the *Vita nova* shows that professional and highly trained scribes—among whom, remarkably, Boccaccio—responded differently to the metatextual references encoded in the prosimetrum, thus opting for different transcriptional and textual styles. Part I ends with an appendix, "*Pulcra metaphora de quaterno et volumine*," which investigates in Dante's *Commedia* similar relationships between metanarration, self-reflexivity, and materiality.

Part II, "Materiality and Authority in Boccaccio's *Teseida*," is articulated in two chapters (4 and 5). It focuses on how the materiality of the medium interacts with the various roles Boccaccio performs, impersonates, and stages—scribe, commentator, author—as enunciator in the autograph of his epic poem *Teseida*. Boccaccio fragments the enunciator (the actual subject of the enunciating act) into several mutually complementary authorial roles (the grammatical subjects of the enunciation in the autograph). By detailing this fragmentation and by tracing, in the textual and material tradition of the poem, the often diverging itineraries these subjects subsequently follow (and even the emergence of nonauthorial paratexts and commentaries competing with Boccaccio's own for popularity and readers' attention), part II exposes the material foundations of Boccaccio's notion of authorship and authority and their implications for his apologia and promotion of vernacular literature.

Chapter 4, "Picture-Book (without Pictures)," argues that the textual and material strategies Boccaccio implements in the autograph diversify the semiotic functions of the enunciator into multiple authorial identities. His editorial choices furnish the autograph with the material trappings—parchment support, formal book hand, illuminations, illustrations, commentary—that were generally reserved for authoritative texts, thus inscribing the *Teseida* within the canon of cultivated texts. At the same time, his use of a popular meter and the circulation of uncommented exemplars preserve the potential for a wider, less scholarly, and more informal reception. Chapter 5, "The Textual Proliferation of the *Teseida*," explores how the editorial and marketing strategies implicit in Boccaccio's autograph compare to the rationale behind material and textual features of subsequent editorial artifacts transmitting the *Teseida*. It shows that the multiple opportunities of consumption encoded in Boccaccio's work are reflected in the various strains of manuscript production—for the courts but also for literate merchants—that emerged for (if not necessarily *from*) his work. Readers, patrons, and scribes perceived those multiple options of reading and often produced new manuscripts consistent with (and further contributing to) that mode. Part II, in other words, reveals the various outcomes of Boccaccio's farsighted endeavors to exert strategic control over his work that he hoped would extend beyond the work's publication.

Part III, "Materiality and Poetics in Petrarca's Sestinas," is also composed of two chapters (6 and 7). It examines Petrarca's material and textual treatment of the sestinas in the autograph of his *canzoniere* (*Rerum vulgarium fragmenta*) as an entry point into his manuscript poetics. It argues that Petrarca intended poetry—the very act of his textual enunciation—to be an indissoluble unity of scribal and discursive practices.

Chapter 6, "Materiality and Meter," shows that Petrarca's material choices, which isolate the sestinas and give them visual prominence in the autograph, and the specific ways he elects to facilitate the interaction of layout, meter, rhetorical articulation, and subject matter, define the sestinas as a coherent semantic unit. The choices Petrarca makes as intellectual originator and vigilant supervisor of (if not always actual copyist for) the *Rerum vulgarium fragmenta* as a physical container thus direct the reader to attend to the sestinas as to the "spine" of the autograph, which Petrarca materially, and also thematically and rhetorically, singles out as the *canzoniere*'s privileged space for recapitulating, reassessing, and reflecting (in metaliterary terms) on the poetic and existential itinerary he portrays in the *canzoniere*. Chapter 7, "*Carmina Figurata*," explores the intersection between material, metrical, rhetorical, and semantic elements within the mini-corpus of the sestinas. It argues that the sestinas function as visual poems, where the visual presentation of the sign contributes to determine the figurative meaning of the poems: the presentational format of the sestina, which underscores retrogression over progression, makes this genre particularly suitable to function as retroactive reflection on and reconsideration of the narrative and poetics of the *Rerum vulgarium fragmenta*. At the level of the poem—and even at the level of the manuscript as the reader must occasionally flip pages to experience the sestinas' retrogressive rhyme scheme—the sestinas direct the reader to a nonprogressive reading experience that mirrors the poet-protagonist's ethical paralysis and nonlinear itinerary of spiritual conversion.

This book concludes with a brief afterword that discusses some of the challenges of integrating multiple fields of scholarship and suggests topics for further investigation. But following the natural order, as the Philosopher states in the beginning of the first *Poetics* (1447a), we shall first commence with the first things.[42]

PART I

Materiality as Narrative in Dante's *Vita nova*

CHAPTER ONE

Scriptor in Fabula

Noi siàn le triste penne isbigotite,
le cesoiuzze e 'l coltellin dolente.
—Guido Cavalcanti, *Rime* 18.1–2

Probationes Pennae

The first document of Italian literacy and the first book of Italian literature, *si parva licet*, thematize writing as technology and engage in self-reflection on (and of) their own materiality and textuality. The Italian vernacular is, in fact, first recorded in a riddle about writing. In the upper margin of a folio contained in an eighth-century Mozarabic orational for Spanish Christians in Muslim Spain, a ninth-century scribe tries out his pen jotting down two lines of text in an "intermediate register" between Latin and vernacular:[1]

Se pareba boves, alba pratalia araba
albo versorio teneba, negro semen seminaba.[2]

(He led oxen ahead, he plowed white fields,
he held a white plow, he sowed a black seed.)

This so-called Veronese riddle—a version of a riddle that traveled widely in late antique and medieval literature—owes its name to Verona's Biblioteca Capitolare, where the codex that contains it is preserved. Historian and paleographer Luigi Schiapparelli made note of the text in 1924 but could not clarify its enigmatic content.[3] Later, philologist and glottologist Vincenzo De Bartholomaeis included it in a school anthology of oral poetry.[4] First-year Romance-philology student Lina Calza eventually solved the enigma. Retrieving a popular riddle from her rural north Italian hamlet, she suggested that the subject of the action, the plowman, might in fact be a metaphor for the writer. His fingers (the oxen) draw a white feather (the white plow) across the page (the white fields) and leave black ink marks (the black seed).[5] The text recording the first written occurrence of an Italian vernacular is thus a metatextual and metagraphical description of the writing process. The Veronese riddle simultaneously portrays, executes, and gives form to the act of writing in its material trappings. The conceptual framework of its textuality is formed and formalized by the material aspects of the technology of writing.

The material and textual hints of the Veronese riddle suggestively prefigure the discourse of "the first book" of Italian literature.[6] Dante Alighieri's *Vita nova* (ca. 1292–96) is an account of his amorous and poetic apprenticeship, a self-selection of his early poetry, a critical interpretation of contemporary poetic production in the vernacular, a figural history of poetic forms and *topoi* of love poetry in the Romance sphere, a narrative of its very own creation, and a guidebook for its interpretation and transmission.[7] In the terms proposed by the formalists of the Prague linguistic circle, in the *Vita nova* the *rhema* becomes the *thema*: the comment (what is being said about the topic) becomes the topic (what is being talked about).

The *Vita nova* has been called "an insidious book": its genre is difficult to grasp.[8] It is a prosimetrum (a combination of poetry and prose) that integrates *canzoniere*, commentary, poetic autobiography, and allegorical narrative.[9] Steven Botterill semiseriously described its combination of lyric texts and prose in terms of a "uniquely constructed variant on a venerable, if not archetypal, narrative paradigm (boy meets girl; boy loses girl; boy decides to console himself by writing about girl)."[10] Presented as a little book transcribed from the author's memory, itself presented as a book, the prosimetrum consists of a selection of thirty-one poems in various metrical forms.[11] This selection includes some of Dante's early compositions and also poems written ad hoc for the prosimetrum. The lyrical texts are encapsulated by prose sections, which are also ad hoc creations: the retrospective prose narrative of the situations that allegedly occasioned them (their *ragioni*) and an exegetical analysis of their content (their *divisioni*).[12] Poems and prose present the narrator's erotic and poetic education. Dante's preoccupation with his beloved Beatrice marks the prosimetrum's beginning and closure. Her epiphany—and her signature number, *nove* (nine)—sets up the narration proper (after the proem), while Dante's close to ecstatic vision of Beatrice's assumption into heaven is the *Vita nova*'s final event (before the explicit). Dante's preoccupation with literature also stands out in the beginning and ending of the prosimetrum. The proem to the self-styled *libello* (booklet) portrays Dante's writing of the *libello* (*VN* 1.1 [i]). Its explicit (*VN* 31 [xlii]) is Dante's announcement of a new literary project in which he will write about Beatrice "più degnamente" (more worthily).

This case study of the *Vita nova* explores the intersection between narrative, textuality, and materiality in Dante's prosimetrum. It provides—in chapters 1 and 2—narratologically and materially informed considerations on the *Vita nova*'s metanarrative statements and references to its own composition, and it traces—in chapter 3—their influence on the early manuscript tradition of the *libello*.[13] By systematically detailing a *catalogue raisonné* of the *Vita nova*'s imagery of books, book production, literary composition, writing, and reading, and by investigating the material and historical foundations of the prosimetrum's self-reflexivity, these three chapters will expose the literary project behind the *libello* and Dante's relationship to medieval Italian scribal culture. Faced with the task of developing a "love story" in the vernacular, both erotic narrative and retrospective appraisal of his *biographia literaria*, in the absence of consistent textual and material vernacular models, Dante turns to the story's developmental process itself—its conceptual design and material production—as content substance for this narrative, while also fixing specific parameters for the narrative's physical container. Dante was certainly aware of the material dynamics of book production and reproduction.[14] He also became aware of the interpretive and textual consequences of his poems' widespread circulation, possibly distrusting the potentially unlimited results of hermeneutical methods wherein multiple senses can lead to contradiction and deception.[15] As Walter J. Ong pointed out in an essay on the fictionalization of audiences, "readers' reactions are remote and initially conjectural."[16] As though suspicious of potentially inappropriate reception for his work, Dante took measures in the composition of the *Vita nova* against such risk. By exploiting both the perceived shortcomings of manuscript culture (uncontrolled proliferation of variants, nonauthorial reordering of textual sequences, extraction of texts from their discursive context, misattributions) and the resources of that manuscript culture (material hierarchization of information, paragraphing, fasciculation), Dante maximized his intellectual and literary project of selecting, ordering, resemanticizing, and materially securing his poetic production and the overall meaning he wanted readers to attribute to it.

When we compare the material references and interpretive "guidelines" embedded in the text with their actual rendition in the earliest transcriptions of the *libello*, we realize that Dante in fact shared with various writer figures—scribes, compilers, commentators—a notion of textuality intimately consistent with materiality and informed by the specific codicological models of medieval Italian manuscript culture. And we better understand to what extent Dante's compositional strategies were successful in conditioning the textual dissemination, circulation, and reception of his work.

Engaging in the challenging, if not unprecedented, project of compiling a coherent and teleologically oriented story of his literary self in the vernacular, Dante finds in the book, in its material form, the appropriate textual technology to frame, compose, and discuss that story. In manuscript culture, the materiality of the medium pervades all aspects of literary communication; in the *Vita nova*, materiality affects and reifies the very substance of the enunciated. By combining the study of a literary work's textual and material features with narratological analysis, this chapter and the next argue that, in the *Vita nova*, the story narrated in the text coincides with the material making of the book itself.

Metatextuality and the *Vita nova*: The Critical Debate

That Dante's works carry a strong metatextual component has long been recognized.[17] The self-reflexive features of Dante's texts are not the products of twentieth-century theory retroactively applied, a practice that has been discouraged, and even stigmatized, by scholars in the field.[18] It is instead Dante's own self-anthologization (*Vita nova*, *Convivio*) and self-exegesis (*Vita nova*, *Convivio*, *De vulgari eloquentia*, *Commedia*, and the disputed epistle to Can Grande della Scala) that clearly signal an authorial strategy aimed at conditioning future hermeneutics by offering authoritative interpretations, from a privileged authorial and authoritarian position.[19] As Albert Ascoli has argued, Dante believed the modern poet must be able to interpret his work, "must be able to demonstrate authoritative control over the informing intention of that work."[20]

Rather than a modern superimposition on the text, the metatextual reading of Dante's work was common practice among his first commentators.[21] Fourteenth-century scholars such as Jacopo della Lana and Benvenuto da Imola interpreted Dante's journey in the *Commedia* as a metaliterary representation of his poetic itinerary, an interpretation that Benvenuto conveys, for instance, when he glosses Dante's question to Virgil (*Inferno* 9.16–18) on whether any pagan descended from Limbo to Lower Hell: "et vult dicere: si aliquis poeta paganus descripsit unquam infernum, sicut ipse christianus facere intendebat" (And what he means is: whether any pagan poet ever described Hell, the way he, as Christian, meant to do).[22] When seven centuries later Saverio Bellomo stated that, in the *Commedia*, "the poet represents himself in the act of writing through a journey that is a metaphor of writing," he was thus following a hermeneutical perspective that dates back to the earliest Dante scholars.[23]

Modern scholars have especially observed metaliterary considerations in the *Vita nova*. Barbara Reynolds pointed out that "the *Vita Nuova* is a treatise by a poet, written for poets, on the art of poetry"; Giuseppe Mazzotta described the *Vita nova* as "a parable of a poetic apprenticeship"; for Edoardo Sanguineti, the *Vita nova* "is not a long tale, but rather a historical argument on the idea of poetry"; María Rosa Menocal asserted that "what we call the metaliterary is, in the case of this text, the plainly literary as well, the story at the surface as well as just below it"; for Winfried Wehle, the *Vita nova* is "a work of poetry but is at once poetry on poetry—poetry and metapoetics in one"; and for Jelena Todorović, the *Vita nova* "is an exercise in self-hermeneutics that at times reads like a manual for writing poetry."[24] This diffuse critical awareness has not, however, led to a comprehensive study of Dante's booklet as metanarrative. Zygmunt Barański recently observed an as yet unmet need to examine systematically the *Vita nova*'s "reflections on literature."[25]

The *libello*'s continuous self-reflexivity has, to date, mostly been examined with regard to its autoexegetical sections. Scholarship has focused on the models for Dante's commentative prose (scholastic *divisiones*, Occitan *razos*, *Glossa ordinaria*, Brunetto Latini's *Rettorica*), on the form and substance of the *divisioni*, on the relationship between self-exegesis and authority, and on the explicitly metaliterary section on poetry and poetics (*VN* 16 [xxv]).[26] Prior inquiry into Dante's self-exegesis has also addressed the relationship between prose and poetry and the literary precedents for the conjugation of poems and commentary. Sources and models have been variously identified in annotated scriptural texts (e.g., Song of Songs, Psalms, Lamentations, Ezekiel, Revelation, accompanied by their respective commentaries), classical texts with glosses (most prominently Ovid's *Remedia amoris*), late antique prosimetra (e.g., Martianus Capella's *De nuptiis Philologiae et Mercurii*, Boethius's *De consolatione philosophiae*), medieval prosimetra (e.g., Bernardus Silvester's *Cosmographia*, Alanus's *De planctu naturae*), and also, more generally, Latin poetry as it is presented in glossed manuscripts (with or without a relative *accessus ad auctorem*), to name just a few. In the Romance sphere, suggestive parallels have been drawn between the *Vita nova* and the Occitan chansonniers that associated poems with their prose *razos* and authors' *vidas*. The manuscript of Guittone d'Arezzo's alternated poems and prose texts has also been suggested as a plausible model for the *Vita nova*.[27]

Most studies specifically dedicated to the *Vita nova*'s metatextuality, furthermore, have focused on the text's explicitly metapoetic and autoexegetic passages: the paragraph entirely dedicated to poetry and poetics (*VN* 16 [xxv]) and the commentative sections in which Dante provides the analysis of a poem (its *divisione*). This focus privileges metatextual references at the highest level of textual enunciation, that is, at the level of discourse. It keeps us looking primarily at the exegetical glosses to the poem and the metatextual comments explicitly uttered by the *Vita nova*'s authorial narrator-as-commentator. Similar attention has not been paid to the metatextual references that emerge from the lyrical, narrative, and argumentative unfolding of the text.[28] A partial exception concerns the incipitarian metaphor of the book of memory. But studies on this metaphor have again mostly dealt with its intertextual stratigraphy—its sources and Dante's original rewriting of them—rather than with the characterization of its materiality as it relates to framing the prosimetrum's narrative.

Scholars have indeed addressed materiality in relation to the manuscript tradition of Dante's works: as will emerge more clearly in chapter 3, material-textual-codicological work recently published in medieval Italian studies has predominantly focused on the *Vita nova*. But the *Vita nova*'s self-references to materiality, the nonmetaphorical aspects of those references, the metanarrative traits of the prosimetrum, and the various modes in which metanarrative and materiality intersect in the *libello* have yet to be studied in detail.[29] This lacuna is partially because of the more general lack of coherent theoretical models for studying metanarrative devices. In spite of, or because of, an aggressive process of *Meta-ization*, the boundaries between notions of metalanguage, metadiscourse, metareference, metatext, metaliterature, metanarrative (and metanarration), and metafiction are often blurred.[30]

This chapter and the next fill the metanarrative lacuna in the critical literature on the *Vita nova*, while also drafting a chapter, or, at least, its prolegomena, of a much needed and as yet unwritten material history of metanarrations. If the first text of an Italian vernacular recorded a metaphor of writing, here we see the first book in the vernacular elect as its subject matter the textual and material ground of possibility for its own writing and integrate its own etiology into its actual *fabula*.

Metanarrative Models and Method

The pages that follow will propose a reexamination of the metanarrative elements of the *Vita nova*, building on crucial work by narratologists such as Monika Fludernik, Birgit Neumann, Ansgar Nünning, and Werner Wolf.[31] Recent theoretical studies in narratology have for the most part neglected the act of narration and its metanarrative corollaries;[32] the works of these scholars in the German new wave of narratological studies are a notable exception. The categories that derive from their theoretical protocols were, of course, unknown to medieval authors. There is risk in applying these theories to medieval texts: the double risk of anachronism and hyperaestheticized formalization (the text is reduced to dealing only, and rather insipidly, with its own textual process). And yet a meticulous classification of metanarrative strategies—in medieval works as in later productions—allows for their detailed description. Such a description enables a better understanding of how and why the *Vita nova* turns to itself, thematizes its own textuality, and manifests this thematization in specific material forms. A grammar of metanarrations is the prerequisite for a study of their material implications and pragmatics.

This subsection maps the metanarrative features of the *Vita nova* onto the typologies and categories that were elaborated by Nünning in his work on the English novel and further discussed by Fludernik in her theoretical studies in narratology. Nünning offers a rigorous, if at times idiosyncratic, terminology for describing the neglected metanarrative and metafictional components of narrative texts. "Metanarratives" (metanarrations) describe the narrative's capacity to reflect (on) the act and process of narration; "metafiction" concerns comments on the fiction's own status as fiction and thematizes the narrative's constructedness as fictiveness. Both terms include self-reflexive and self-referential utterances. Fludernik further implements and clarifies Nünning's classification: "While metanarrative statements need not have any distancing effect on the aesthetic illusion projected by the narrative, metafictional statements . . . do seriously impair the mimetic effect."[33] Metafictional statements, more exclusively, refer to the domain of *fictum* (constructedness as inventedness; artifactuality as fictiveness; imaginary references of the story); metanarrative strategies involve aspects of *fictio* (constructedness as compositional process; artifactuality as *inventio* and *dispositio*; fictionalization as narrative technique).

Based on Nünning's taxonomy and Fludernik's revisions, we can describe the *Vita nova*'s self-reflections as, for the most part, metanarrative rather than metafictional. The *Vita nova* thematizes its nature as a written narrative text, dramatizes its own writing, and includes reflections on its status as a literary artifact. However, it neither poses nor elicits questions on its own truth, as a postmodern fiction might do. Rather, it discusses its own narratorial language and plot construction as well as the conditions for its production and reception.

The *Vita nova* consistently provides comments on the act and process of narration, chronicles its own compositional history, "topicalizes" the internal structure of the text, offers stage directions for the reader (for instance, references to previous or subsequent sections in the narrative), represents its own communicational scenario, and, often expanding on the apostrophe to his various addressees within the poems included in the prosimetrum, textualizes Dante character's interactions with his audience.[34] Importantly, metanarrative statements can be explicit (and uttered by the first-person narrator) or implicit. In the latter case, the protagonist, another character, or (quite excitingly) the plot itself does the thematizing. With few possible exceptions, however, the *Vita nova*'s narrative is self-reflexive rather than self-conscious: to put it differently, the prosimetrum's observations on its own structure and compositional history are integrated into the narrative to explain the creative process rather than disrupt the aesthetic illusion.

Drawing upon Wolf's groundbreaking work on anti-illusionist elements in narrative, Nünning grounds his survey of metanarrations on four types (*Arten*)—relative to form, structure, content, and function—further subdivided into a number of often overlapping analytical criteria and parameters. Based on this fourfold interpretive model, consequently, Nünning classifies metanarrative statements into predominantly formal, structural, content-related, and reception-oriented.[35] The sections that follow will use Nünning's criteria and terminology—form, structure, content, and function—to identify various types of metanarratives in the *Vita nova* and explain their functions. Because the well-known excursus, or digression, on poetry and poetics in *VN* 16 (xxv) has been the primary focus of scholarly work on the metaliterary features of the *Vita nova* and because it displays various types of metanarratives, this passage will be discussed in particular (albeit briefly) in the section titled "The Digression on Poetry and Poetics (*VN* 16 [xxv])." Chapter 2 will complement this survey of the multiple types of metanarratives in the *Vita nova* with observations on the literary-historical and material context of Dante's prosimetrum.

Form

In Nünning's framework, form-related criteria for identifying formal types of metanarratives include the textual levels wherein the text is discussed, crossovers between levels of story and discourse, modes of mediation, and linguistic forms (metaphoric or nonmetaphoric) that articulate the metanarrative statements. In the *Vita nova*, formal types of metanarration show Dante's plural authorial identities—across various levels of textual discourse—as they authenticate his narratorial function, orient the prosimetrum's narrative, articulate (and validate) its allegorical sense, and premise its interpretation on the materiality of the *libello*.

Textual Levels

The first formal criterion questions "what kind of textual speaker self-consciously discusses the process of narration and on which level of communication this discussion can be situated."[36] In the *Vita nova*, this aspect is made more problematic by the proliferation of Dante's polymorphous literary personae: *auctor* and *agens* (the latter term was already used to indicate the *Commedia*'s protagonist in the disputed epistle to Can Grande della Scala); or *poeta* (poet: "the subject of poetic activity") and *personaggio* (character: "the subject of moral activity, of praxis").[37]

In the theoretical terms proposed by Gérard Genette and productively applied to the *Commedia* by Giuseppe Ledda, the *Vita nova*'s narrator is homodiegetic (autodiegetic, in fact) in his relationship to the story. With respect to the narrative level, he is instead extradiegetic.[38] As an extradiegetic narrator, he is somewhat omniscient (at least in relation to the events exposed in the *libello*): he tells the process of his ethical growth and poetic apprenticeship retrospectively. In the *Vita nova*, Dante *auctor* (and commentator) discusses biographical, textual, and literary matters at the highest narrative level. On the one hand, there is the extradiegetic narrator (Dante *auctor*), who comments on issues of poetry and poetics. On the other hand, there is the protagonist and autodiegetic narrator of the *fabula* of the prosimetrum (Dante *agens*), who is himself a poet with strong ties to other poets of the literary milieu in Florence. In addition to this, several other figures from Florentine literary circles participate in the debates on poetry and poetics that are part of the *Vita nova* itself. The audience, the addressees, and the commissioners of Dante *agens*'s poetry appear as characters in the *Vita nova* and engage in literary conversations with him. Wayne Booth's notion of "*self-conscious narrators* . . . aware of themselves as writers" applies in various degrees to both the narrator and the protagonist of the *Vita nova*.[39] By the end of the *libello*, Dante *agens* has proclaimed numerous accomplishments (technical skills, a corpus of "published" poems, public recognition). He has also become an *auctor* who is aware of the poetic, intellectual, and moral progress he has yet to pursue. Upon writing the *libello*, Dante *auctor* can profess to have become privy to the authentic metaphysical signification of the events (in textual form) that make up the *libello*. In the hermeneutical terms he probably borrows from Hugh of Saint Victor's *Didascalicon de studio legendi*, Dante *auctor* can therefore reveal the *sentenzia* (Latin *sententia*) of these textualized events (*VN* 1.1 [i]): their "profundior intelligentia, quae nisi expositione vel interpretatione non invenitur" (deeper understanding which can be found only through interpretation and commentary), as opposed to merely articulating their *littera* (their linguistic construction) or explaining their *sensus* (the grammatical, literal meaning).[40]

Hypodiegetic narratives also point toward the constructedness (as *fictio*) of the text.[41] Dreams and visions inserted into the main narrative, for instance, can be interpreted as markers of metatextual awareness in that they construct an inside frame and embed a secondary narrative sequence within the main storyline. As Steven Kruger has observed, "The dream fiction, by representing in the dream an imaginative entity like fiction itself, often becomes self-reflexive. Dream vision is especially liable to become metafiction [metanarrative, in Nünning's and Fludernik's terminology], thematizing issues of representation and interpretation."[42] The account of Dante's second dream vision (*VN* 5.9–16 [xii 2–9]) further amplifies this self-reflexive effect. In the Middle Ages, dreams were understood as external messages that carried a meaning to decipher. And yet, by formulating a vision *en abyme* of Dante sleeping and being observed by a hypostasis of Love, the prosimetrum enhances a fascinating kaleidoscopic effect (*VN* 5.10 [xii 3]):

> Avenne, quasi nel mezzo del mio dormire, che mi parve vedere nella mia camera lungo me sedere un giovane vestito di bianchissime vestimenta, e pensando molto, quanto a la vista sua, mi riguardava là dov'io giacea e, quando m'avea guardato alquanto, pareami che sospirando mi chiamasse, e diceami queste parole: "Fili mi, tempus est ut pretermictantur simulacra nostra."

> (About halfway into my sleep I seemed to see in my room, seated beside me, a young man dressed in the whitest of vestments, who, with an anxious expression, watched me where I was lying. And after he had looked

at me for a while, it seemed that he sighed and called me, saying: "Fili mi, tempus est ut praetermictantur simulacra nostra.")[43]

The metatextual effect of this passage is furthered by the use of the Gallicism *riguardare* (Old Occitan, *reguardar*; Old French, *regarder*), where the prefix *ri-* seemingly conveys an idea of repetition and reciprocity besides intensifying the verb's meaning ("to watch with attention"):[44] we watch Dante sleep, Dante watches himself and Love in the dream, and Love watches Dante. Rather than being set aside ("pretermictantur") as per Love's recommendation, the *simulacra* (simulations, fictions) structure the whole episode.

The self-citational articulation of the prosimetrum, its self-transcriptional nature, further contributes to disclosing its own literariness.[45] The poetic texts of the *Vita nova* constitute, and simultaneously (if diffractively) reflect, the substance of the narrative through a duplication of the fiction, provided both in the poems themselves and in the prose that (re-)contextualizes and comments on them. This doubling of the *Vita nova*, indicated by the *libello*'s denunciation of itself as an artifact copied from the book of memory, further exposes the text's materially coded nature as a written work.

The *Vita nova* also includes interior forms of reduplication, which duplicate the narrative and present it as a story told. The last section of the *libello* (*VN* 28–31 [xxxix–xlii]), for instance, includes a brief account of the events narrated in the whole text—it is "almost a 'vita nova' in the *Vita Nova*," in Guglielmo Gorni's words—thus reenacting Beatrice's story from her apparition and reconsecrating the text to her.[46]

In addition to involving the different levels of *diegesis* proper, metanarrative references can affect the level of the paratext in the forms of verbal and visual editorial materials. In this case, as Nünning posits, "the act of narrating is not discussed on the level of story or discourse but on the level of a fictive editor, by means of frames, chapter headings or other paratextual devices."[47] Here in the text of the *Vita nova*, as we will observe more closely in chapter 2, what we would generally consider paratext—editorial devices such as rubrics and titles, but also more intrinsically authorial features such as dedication and self-exegetical notes—is subsumed, more or less metaphorically, into plot. We see this, for instance, in the integration of the incipitarian rubric (*Incipit vita nova*), the dedication (to Guido Cavalcanti), and the prose commentative sections (the *divisioni*) into the plot.

Transgressions

A second formal criterion deals with the possible crossovers between levels of story and discourse. Genette designates these crossovers as metalepses.[48] An example in the *Vita nova*—albeit partial and heterodox according to strictly narratological categories of discourse levels—is the shift from past to present in the final paragraph of the prosimetrum, where the *auctor* and the *agens* of the narration are reunited in one authorial persona (*VN* 31.1–2 [xlii 1–2]):

> Appresso questo sonetto apparve a me una mirabile visione, ne la quale io vidi cose che mi fecero proporre di non dire più di questa benedetta infino a tanto che io potessi più degnamente trattare di lei. E di venire a ciò io studio quanto posso, sì com'ella sa, veracemente; sì che, se piacere sarà di Colui a cui tutte le cose vivono che la mia vita duri per alquanti anni, io spero di dire di lei quello che mai non fue detto d'alcuna.
>
> ---
>
> (After writing this sonnet a marvelous vision appeared to me, in which I saw things that made me decide not to say anything more about this blessed lady until I was capable of writing about her more worthily. To achieve this I am doing all that I can, as surely she knows. So that, if it be pleasing to Him who is that for which all things live, and if my life is long enough, I hope to say things about her that have never been said about any woman.)

Fludernik maintains that in this type of metalepsis there is a "temporal parallelization of the act of narration with the story."[49] Here that parallelization occurs in the simultaneous textual presence of protagonist and narrator and results in the transfer of authority from *auctor* to *agens*. The recomposition of multiple authorial identities enhances here, in Genette's terms, the "*testimonial function*, or function of *attestation*," of the first-person narration.[50] Whereas in postmodern fiction this type of metaleptic shift destabilizes the diegetic illusion, in the *Vita nova* it produces an authenticating effect and enriches Dante's narratorial self-characterization.

Mode of Mediation

A third formal criterion relates to the degree of explicitness in the metanarrative comments. Explicit analeptic or proleptic "directing functions," flashbacks, and prophecies give the text coherence and draw the reader's focus from the narrated to the narration: in *VN* 10.1 (xvii 1), Dante openly thematizes the necessity to "ripigliare matera nuova e più nobile che la passata" (take up new and nobler subject matter than that of the past); and in *VN* 19.8 (xxx 1), he signals that the use of a biblical citation (Lamentations 1:1) functions "quasi come entrata de la nova materia che appresso viene" (like a preamble to the new material that follows).[51] Implicit or covert metanarrative hints can also orient the plot for the reader and direct its interpretation. In *VN* 1.2 (ii 1), Beatrice is referred to as "la gloriosa donna de la mia mente" (the glorious lady of my mind); at the very onset of the *libello*, for the benefit of the reader, an omniscient narrator (or, at least, an ex post narrator) is implicitly anticipating Beatrice's paradisiac destination: as Teodolinda Barolini puts it, "Beatrice is thus dead before she has even begun to live."[52] We could describe Dante's opaque plot spoiler here as the determination through which, in Fludernik's theoretical terms, "by metacompositionally referring to his proleptic faculties, the narrator thematizes his role as omniscient narrator."[53]

The narrative orientation of the plot is still possible when our formally omniscient narrator eventually reveals himself as being partially uninformed on future events (namely, the exact nature of the "literary sequel" to the *Vita nova* wished for in the *libello*'s closing paragraph) or professes his inability to adequately pursue the praise of the ineffable Beatrice.[54] We see this profession of inadequacy, for instance, in the threefold excuse the narrator makes for not dealing with Beatrice's death (*VN* 19.2 [xxviii 2]):

> E, avegna che forse piacerebbe a presente trattare alquanto de la sua partita da noi, non è lo mio intendimento di trattarne qui per tre ragioni. La prima è che ciò non è del presente proposito, se volemo guardare nel

> proemio che precede questo libello; la seconda si è che, posto che fosse del presente proposito, ancora non sarebbe sofficiente la mia lingua a trattare come si converrebbe di ciò; la terza si è che, posto che fosse l'uno e l'altro, non è convenevole a me trattare di ciò, per quello che, trattando, converrebbe essere me laudatore di me medesimo, la qual cosa è al postutto biasimevole a chi lo fae, e però lascio cotale trattato ad altro chiosatore.

> (And though it might be desirable at this point to say something about her departure from us, it is not my intention to write about it here, for three reasons. The first is that it is not part of the present topic, if we look back at the proem that precedes this little book. The second is that, supposing it were part of the present topic, my language would not yet be capable of treating it as the subject demands. The third is that, supposing these two conditions were met, it is not appropriate for me to write about it, since such writing would put me in the position of singing my own praises, a thing which is after all reprehensible, whoever does it: and thus I leave this subject to another commentator.)

The explanation Dante *auctor* provides to his readers for such an unexpected and egregious omission is, at the very least, enigmatic.[55] In spite of Dante's confident (if possibly tongue-in-cheek) reliance in the third excuse on the critical skills of future glossators, the unexplained connection between writing about Beatrice's death, the dangers of boastful or inflated talk, and the perceived risk of vainglory still puzzles scholars. An observation can, however, be made regarding the first excuse and how its metanarrative content aims to orient the plot and condition interpretation. By referring back to the *libello*'s proemial considerations and terminology, the first excuse represents the narrator's invitation to reread. As Donato Pirovano remarks, "From this central point on, Dante invites the reader to go over the *Vita nuova* again, holding the narrated events under a new light; and he does this by recommending an ontological interpretation of the *libello*'s dominant number."[56] The indication to read the *Vita nova* recursively is an alert to the reader: in the prosimetrum, *tout se tient*; in the *libello*, the book form is what holds everything together.

Metaphoric versus Nonmetaphoric

The fourth of Nünning's formal criteria denotes metanarrations based on the metaphoric or nonmetaphoric linguistic forms in which they are realized. Wehle has provided several examples of how, in the *Vita nova*, love poetry is used to outline a metaphorical representation of itself. Wehle ultimately (if, at times, overdeterministically) institutes an ideal correspondence between *ars amandi* and *ars scribendi*: for instance, he interprets the narrative interactions between characters as an allegorization of the intertextual relationships in Dante's poetry; he associates Dante *agens*'s encounters with various female figures with as many stages in Dante *auctor*'s poetic development; and, intriguingly, he proposes the notion that the microanthology of three sonnets commissioned from Dante (*VN* 30.1 [xli 1]) constitutes the objective correlative of an internal *tenzone* between various models of love poetry practiced by Dante in his career.[57] This suggestion will be of interest to us in chapter 2, as we consider the reference to that microanthology as a hint to the various stages of the prosimetrum's compositional process and selection mechanism.

As we here reexamine the *Vita nova* with special attention to its self-reflexivity, metaphorizations of the plot remain relevant, as we will see in chapter 2 ("Book and Booklet") in analyzing the overarching metaphor of the book of memory from which the *libello* is transcribed, or Beatrice's dual role as character (*materia, subiectum*, "subject matter") and poetological *figura* (*maniera, modus tractandi*, "style"). But we must not lose sight of the concrete quality of the literal language that gives shape to the book metaphor, the material details that punctuate the *Vita nova*'s representation of the modes of composition and circulation of literary texts (and even figurative art, in *VN* 23.1 [xxxiv 1]), the references to the various occasions when the poems were actually consumed, and the characterization of the poems' communicative scenarios. This concreteness is all the more notable since it stands in stark contrast to the evanescence of the prosimetrum's spatial and evenemential coordinates: its urban environment is barely evoked—Florence is never called by name—and the sequence of events it recounts is connected through generic expressions of abstract formularity (e.g., *poi che*, "after").[58]

The study of the prosimetrum's metanarrative elements is fascinating precisely because of this continuous overlapping between literal sense and metaphorical implication, between narrative and poetics: the plot itself in its literal sense (not just its allegory) performs a literary-critical and exegetical function by narrativizing a discourse on literature.

Structure

Structure-related parameters, which Nünning uses to identify structural types of metanarratives, concern the quantitative and qualitative relationship between metanarrative expressions and nonmetanarrative parts of the text. Structural parameters include the position (marginal vs. central), degree of integration, and contextual plausibility of the metanarrative comments, as well as various other quantitative notions, such as frequency, regularity, and extent. Structural parameters highlight the pervasiveness of metanarrative statements in the *Vita nova*: they show how central the book imagery is for the prosimetrum's coherence and allegorical reading.

Position and Frequency

In the *Vita nova*, metanarrative hints are not limited to paratextual or conventional sections, such as opening and closure. Reflections on the poems' selection and order postillate the booklet's various *paragrafi*. The strictly metaexegetical sections of the *divisioni* accompany twenty-four of the prosimetrum's thirty-one poems. And the metaphor of the book of memory is retrieved through references to details that either articulate it or derive from it: for instance, the references to the *paragrafi* that constitute it (*VN* 1.11 [ii 10]) or to the *libello* transcribed from it (*VN* 1.1 [i], 5.24 [xii 17], 16.9 [xxv 9], 19.2 [xxviii 2]).

Integration versus Isolation

The syntagmatic relationship between the text and the metatextual is a further structural parameter: it concerns "the degree of integration or isolation of the metanarrative expressions vis-a-vis the narrated story."[59] As the narrative account of its own conception and *mise-en-livre*, the *Vita nova* displays no clear separation between the narrative and the metanarrative: metareferences form an indissoluble bond with both discourse and story. The *Vita nova*'s peculiar nature of "text in the process of its own writing" and its autodiegetic narration (where the protagonist ultimately coincides with the narrator) also control the degree of contextual plausibility between the narrated and the metanarrative.[60] In the *Vita nova*, the action of the story itself—the composition, collection, transcription, and exegesis of poems; the "invention" of a new poetic diction; the celebration of Beatrice through this innovative poetry—offers, to put it in Nünning's theoretical terms, "a plausible reason for the fact that a narrator or a narrating character reflects about problems of narration."[61] The protagonist is, after all, a poet who is compiling an anthology of his poems.

This contextual plausibility of the *Vita nova*'s metanarrative statements, notably, fulfills the theoretical propositions on which Lucien Dällenbach premises his investigation of textual self-reflexivity. Dällenbach bases his study of the *mise-en-abyme* (a metatextual sequence that is supposed to contain a mirror image of the work that contains it) on two criteria. First, in order to give a metatextual value to a textual sequence, this value must be authorized by the text as a whole. Second, a study of self-reflexivity is plausible only in texts in which reflexivity is thematized and guarantees a certain degree of systematicity. The work's turning toward itself is not sufficient on its own. As Dällenbach argues, for the relationship between text and its mirror image to have aesthetic and hermeneutical relevance, "one has to contrive to ward off the very otherness of the fictive character, and, in order to do so, to impose sufficient constraints on oneself: in other words to create it in one's own image, or, better still, to make it engage in the very activity that one is oneself undertaking in creating it—the writing of a novel . . . or the telling of a story."[62]

The degree to which the metanarrative digresses from the narrative distinguishes between (1) highly integrated, brief explanations of the way the narration is proceeding, such as, in the *Vita nova*, references to the inclusion or exclusion of poems, analeptic references to the content of the *proemio*, and, more thematically, proleptic references to Beatrice's glorious ascension aimed at promoting a specific reading of the *libello*'s narrative; (2) longer, parenthetical notes on the structural organization of the prosimetrum, as when Dante explicitly defers confuting possible readers' objections, displacing that work to a dedicated section in the *libello* (*VN* 5.24 [xii 17], "e però dico che questo dubbio io lo 'ntendo solvere e dichiarare in questo libello ancora in parte più dubbiosa"; "And so I say that I still intend to resolve and clarify this ambiguity in an even obscurer section of this little book"); and (3) proper digressions such as all the self-contained *divisioni.*

Content

Nünning's differentiation of various types of content-related metanarrative expressions is based on the object of the self-reflexive statement but also involves selection mechanisms, referential parameters, scope of reference, questions of genre and text type, and narratorial competence assessment, to name just a few. When it comes to content-related types of metanarration, Nünning warns, "the possibilities of differentiation are almost endless": there is potential to discuss "in a self-reflexive way" nearly any feature or problem of narrating.[63] And in the *Vita nova* the possibilities are, in fact, nearly endless and worthy of thorough consideration. Here we will specifically consider the narrator's statements on the prosimetrum's compilatory rationale and compositional process, his critical remarks on classical and vernacular literatures, and his considerations on audience and readership.

Selection and Order

Content-related metanarrative statements include reflections on the *forma tractatus* (expository order, division into sections and subsections), the selection of the materials (which poems are included), and reasons for omissions (why poems are excluded). In the *Vita nova*, the narrator states, as early as in the booklet's proem, his *intendimento* (intention) to collect a selection of poems. Over the course of the narration, the reader finds out more about the selection criteria. In the legendary episode of the first screen lady (*VN* 2.6–18 [v–vii]), the protagonist fosters the Florentines' misunderstanding that sees him in love not with Beatrice, but rather with an anonymous gracious woman whom he makes a "schermo de la veritade" (screen for the truth) (*VN* 2.8 [v 3]). The narrator reports (and possibly mystifies) that, for a number of years, the young Dante *agens* repeatedly pretended to write poems for the woman who, in reality, was probably one of his "sensual crushes."[64] From *VN* 2.9 (v 4) the readers learn that the *libello* excludes "certe cosette per rima" (certain little rhymes) composed for the first screen lady, but includes those that can be resemanticized for his praise of Beatrice. And in *VN* 2.11 (vi 2), the readers are made aware that the prosimetrum also excludes a not otherwise known "pìstola sotto modo di serventese" (epistolary poem in the form of a *serventese*) about the sixty most beautiful women in Florence, which allegedly had included the appropriately ranked names of both Beatrice and the first screen lady.[65]

Content-related forms of metanarrations also include reflections on the relationship between narrative prose, poems, and commentative prose; references to the relationship between the time of the story and the time of the narration; and the thematization of beginnings and ends. The exegetical *divisioni*, for instance, describe the metrical form of the poems. The manifesto *canzone* "Donne ch'avete intelletto d'amore" (Women who understand the truth of love) programmatically defines its own *maniera* (poetic diction) of praising Beatrice through the adverbial expressions "non . . . sì altamente" (not . . . so loftily) and "leggeramente" (lightly) (vv. 9 and 11, respectively).[66] The thematization of beginnings affects the prosimetrum on both a macro- and a microtextual level. On a macrotextual level, the rubrication and intitulation of the *Vita nova*—*Incipit vita nova*—take the form of a metareflection on the *libello*'s incipit. On a microtextual level, the notion of *cominciamento* (beginning) and the act of *cominciare* (to begin) assume the technical meaning of beginning a poetic composition, while also evoking the absolute novelty of Dante's poetry. On the one hand, the marked meaning of *cominciare* clearly comes in view when the verb is used in a polyptotic series as in *VN* 1.20 (iii 9): "E *cominciai* questo sonetto lo quale *comincia* . . ." (And I started composing this sonnet, whose incipit is . . .); or when the verb is associated with its deverbal *cominciamento* as in *VN* 10.14 (xix 3): "*cominciai* una canzone con questo *cominciamento* . . ." (I composed a *canzone* with this incipit . . .).[67] On the other hand, the implications of poetic innovation emerge from the modesty *topos* (*VN* 10.11 [xviii 9]): "sì che non ardia di cominciare, e così dimorai alquanti dì con disiderio di dire e con paura di cominciare" (and I didn't dare to begin. And I lived that way for several days, wanting to write but afraid to start); and from the role played by divine grace in inspiring the *cominciamento* of the manifesto *canzone* (*VN* 10.13 [xix 2]): "Allora dico che la mia lingua parlò quasi come per se stessa mossa e disse 'Donne ch'avete intelletto d'amore'" (Then, I tell you, my tongue uttered words as if it moved of its own accord, saying: "Women who understand the truth of love").[68]

Scope and Reference Point

Content-related metanarrative reflections can be further subdivided, classified based on the breadth and scope of the metanarrative indications: in the *Vita nova*, metanarrative statements comprehensively affect the very conception of the *libello* but also discuss in detail the act of narration and the vast majority of the poems. Content-related metanarrative reflections can involve the reference point, including statements on the narrator's own literary practice (proprio-metanarration), other authors' characteristics (allo-metanarration), or poetic diction, storytelling, and literature in general (general metanarration).[69] Proprio-metanarrative statements can either be intratextual (for instance, the *Vita nova*'s autoreferential comments on the process of its own transcription) or intertextual (the elusive references to Dante's poetic production prior to the first sonnet included in the *libello* in *VN* 1.20 [iii 9] or, from a different perspective, the remarks on the *Vita nova* formulated in *Convivio* 1.1.16). Examples of allo-metanarrations include the following: in *VN* 1.20–2.2 (iii 9–iii 15), the narrator's implicit dissatisfaction with the insufficient hermeneutical depth in some of the poems sent by "molti . . . famosi trovatori" (several . . . well-known poets) in response to his sonnet "A ciascun'alma presa" (To all besotted souls); or, in *VN* 10.33 (xix 22), the dismissive remarks on its possibly inadequate readership; "ma tuttavia chi non è di tanto ingegno che per queste [*sc.* divisioni] che sono fatte la [*sc.* canzone] possa intendere a me non dispiace se la mi lascia stare" (However, it does not bother me if anybody who is not insightful enough to understand the poem by using the divisions already provided leaves off trying).

Story and Discourse

Content-related metanarrative considerations also involve the levels or aspects addressed by metanarrative expressions. Nünning further differentiates them into story-oriented and discourse-oriented. Story-oriented self-reflexive expressions deal with the contents of the narrated story; discourse-oriented statements thematize aspects of the compositional process and the presentation of the narrative. Discourse-oriented statements can be further classified into the often overlapping categories of expressive, phatic, and appellative statements. Expressive statements are speaker-oriented: they are the narrator's statements on the narrator. For instance, the first two explanations for omitting the account of Beatrice's death (*VN* 19.2 [xxviii 2]) indicate that this self-evidently unordinary event transcends the narrator's mnemonic, linguistic, textual, and scribal abilities. However, these explanations more generally imply that the medium is incapable of expressing ineffability: they can be interpreted as phatic, channel-related statements. Appellative statements are reader-oriented, such as the various forms of addressing an audience that prominently feature in the prosimetrum (and in Dante's opus in general).[70]

Content-related statements focused on discourse also include genre- or text-type specific markers, of which the *Vita nova* offers a wide range: for instance, the taxonomic classification of each poetic form it anthologizes and the references to its own textual organization. Since the *Vita nova* presents its own textuality in material terms from the very incipit—which attributes to the text the material features of a book (or booklet)—the preposition *sotto* ("below") in syntagms such as "sotto la qual rubrica" (under this heading) and "sotto maggiori paragrafi" (under larger paragraphs) suggests a textual organization that is understood and phrased in spatial terms (*VN* 1.1 [i] and 1.11 [ii 10], respectively). *Sotto* may further prescribe the respective position of poetry and prose in the *libello* when it is used adverbially in expressions such as "ordinata nel modo che si vedrà di sotto ne la sua divisione" (ordered as we shall see below in its division) (*VN* 10.14 [xix 3]).[71] The same argument can be applied—by analogy—to the deictic marker *sopra* ("above"), used adverbially or as a preverb in compounds, in syntagms such as "sopra ragionate" (explained above), "nella soprascritta rima" (in the above poem), "questa soprascritta stanzia" (the above stanza), or "questo soprascritto sonetto" (the above sonnet) (*VN* 9.11 [xvi 11], 12.1 [xxi 1], 19.1 [xxviii 1], and 22.2 [xxxiii 2], respectively). If *sopra* (and *soprascritto*) may usually indicate generic precedence to something written previously, in the *Vita nova* they assume a more defined spatial connotation through their complementary and contrastive relationship to *sotto* (and compounds thereof): the spatial semantics of *sotto*, in other words, invests *sopra* (and compounds thereof) with material connotations from, and because of, *sotto* in the privileged function of proemial image that we have seen above. Rather than providing a vague "see *supra*" textual indication, these markers use the sustained coreference of materiality and textuality to remind readers that poems and prose form a textual and visual continuum and thus that the prose of the *Vita nova* should not be displaced. The deictics *sotto* and *sopra*, in short, define and visualize a specific kind of *mise-en-texte*, and they confirm the inchoate presence of materiality in Dante's textuality.[72] In chapter 3, we will see how these hints at the prosimetrum's visual argumentation contrast with the codicological solutions implemented by Giovanni Boccaccio, the *libello*'s most illustrious copyist.

Assessment: Affirmative versus Undermining, Critical versus Noncritical

Content-related comments involve the "narrator's assessment of his/her narrative competence, resulting in the differentiation between affirmative and undermining metanarration."[73] The *Vita nova* often refers to the protagonist's artistic hesitations, for instance, when it implicitly exposes the uncertainty of his (and others') oneirocritical skills (*VN* 2.2 [iii 15]) or when, more or less genuinely, it points to the protagonist's self-consciousness regarding the inadequacy of his poetic diction (*VN* 31.1 [xlii 1]):

> Appresso questo sonetto apparve a me una mirabile visione, ne la quale io vidi cose che mi fecero proporre di non dire più di questa benedetta infino a tanto che io potessi più degnamente trattare di lei.
>
> ---
>
> (After writing this sonnet a marvelous vision appeared to me, in which I saw things that made me decide not to say anything more about this blessed lady until I was capable of writing about her more worthily.)

Finally, content-related comments involve forms of critical assessment of the thematized modes of narration, contemplating whether or not the narrator distances himself from literary conventions (narrative and/or poetic). The references to the prosimetrum's *novitas* can be included in this category, from its eponymous rubric "*Incipit vita nova*" to its insistent reference to the election of "matera nuova e più nobile" (new and nobler subject matter) in *VN* 10.1 (xvii 1) and "nuova materia" (new material) in *VN* 19.8 (xxx 1).[74]

Function (and Reception)

Nünning's fourth typology involves reception-oriented and functionally determined forms of metanarrations. Parameters to identify and describe this fourth typology include the medial simulation of orality or literacy, strategies for reducing or enhancing distance between the narrator (or the narration) and the reader, and degrees of compatibility with aesthetic illusion. When we read Dante's prosimetrum against these parameters, we better understand how Dante inscribes the *Vita nova* within the hybrid communicational scenario—oral and written—of medieval Italian literature. And we see more clearly how references to the contextual situation of the prosimetrum's reception contribute to authorize Dante as *auctor* and authenticate the revisionist account of his poetic apprenticeship.

Orality and Literacy

The first parameter regards the narrative's simulation of orality or literacy. On the one hand, the *Vita nova* exploits the potentiality of writing as technology in manuscript culture, makes continuous references to its own writing, and exposes its existence as a written artifact. On the other hand, the *libello* thematizes the oral circulation and performative aspects of the poems of which it is a transcription. For instance, in *VN* 5.15 (xii 8), the text makes reference to the musical accompaniment (a "soave armonia," "sweet harmony") for the *ballata* "Ballata, i' vo' che tu ritrovi Amore" (Ballad, I wish you'd find where Love has gone), and to its intended recitation before Beatrice.

Diegetic Illusion

A second reception-oriented parameter distinguishes metanarrative references that are compatible with the diegetic illusion from those incompatible with it. Whereas metafictional references often unveil (*only* unveil, for Fludernik) the inventedness of their narration and denounce it as fictive, metanarrative references enhance the narrator's claim to truth by underscoring his or her autoptic approach to the narrative. They can be part of an authenticating strategy, give coherence (with ensuing plausibility) to the narration, and fulfill a mnemotechnical function.

We saw earlier that metanarrative references can be compatible with diegetic illusion and may not reveal the text's nature as literary fiction. This is especially true for a narrative such as the *Vita nova*'s, which is presented to the reader as "autobiographic" while, at the same time, claiming for itself higher, spiritual senses.[75] The metanarrative references in the *Vita nova* serve to uphold the plot's continuity and the character's consistency. This is particularly relevant to the multistylistic and experimental features of Dante's early production as well as the probably chaotic "publication" and dissemination of his poems before their inclusion in the prosimetrum. These metanarrative references produce a trust- and sympathy-inducing effect in the readers and contribute to authenticating the documentary value of the beloved's hagiographic praise, by presenting the narrator's testimony as the account of personal observations. They authorize Dante as *auctor* by providing a commentary on the *agens*'s literary apprenticeship and also by justifying and integrating it into a history of poetic progress. They resemanticize poems originally written for other purposes, to other addressees, with different meanings, according to a different chronology, sometimes with different textual variants.[76] They stage authorship and give authority to Dante's ethical and poetic didacticism.

Even if metanarrative utterances mostly accentuate what we could, with conscious anachronism, describe as its I-narrative's "confessional increment,"[77] the *Vita nova* also presents metafictional innuendoes that implicitly (and perhaps unintentionally) question its narratorial consistency or even expose its nature as *fictum*. These comments on discourse would, in Seymour Chatman's words, "undercut the fabric of the fiction"; and here in the *Vita nova*, they undermine its rhetorical claim to *veritas*.[78] The text of the *Vita nova* reveals Dante's mystifying editorial practice on at least two occasions. In *VN* 2.9 (v 4), the narrator declares that he will omit transcribing the poems dedicated to the first screen lady unless they can be reused in praise of Beatrice:

> Con questa donna mi celai alquanti anni e mesi e, per più fare credente altrui, feci per lei certe cosette per rima, le quali non è mio intendimento di scriverle qui, se non in quanto facesse a trattare di quella gentilissima Beatrice; e però le lascerò tutte, salvo che alcuna cosa ne scriverò che par che sia loda di lei.

> (I concealed myself by means of this woman for a number of years and months. And to make others even greater believers, I wrote certain little rhymes for her which I do not intend to write down here if they don't relate in some way to that most gracious lady, Beatrice. And so I will leave out all of them other than something I will write down that plainly is in praise of her.)

The *Vita nova,* thus, shows a clear repurposing of—and revisionist approach to—Dante's own poetic corpus in order to serve the teller's narrative purpose.

A more sophisticated example of the same strategy occurs in *VN* 21.2 (xxxii 2), where Dante recounts receiving a commission from an unspecified relative of Beatrice's (generally identified with her brother) to write a poetic homage for an unspecified dead woman (who, Dante protagonist immediately realizes, is in fact Beatrice herself):

> E poi che fue meco a ragionare, mi pregò ch'io li dovessi dire alcuna cosa per una donna che s'era morta, e simulava sue parole acciò che paresse che dicesse d'un'altra, la quale morta era cortamente: onde io, accorgendomi che questi dicea solamente per questa benedetta, sì li dissi di fare ciò che mi domandava lo suo prego.
>
> ———
>
> (After he had been talking with me for a while, he pleaded with me to write something for him about a woman who had died; and he faked his words, so that it seemed that he was talking about another woman who had died suddenly. And realizing that he was simply talking about the blessed one, I told him that I would do as he requested.)

The poem that Beatrice's relative commissions is to be written "per lui" (in his name, or in his stead) (*VN* 21.3 [xxxii 3]).[79] The sonnet resulting from this commission, "Venite a 'ntender li sospiri miei" (Come and take notice of my every sigh), is exposed as a double dissimulation of both author (Dante, not the relative) and theme (Beatrice, not another woman). On the one hand, Beatrice's relative explicitly requests a poem for "un'altra" (another woman). On the other hand, Dante accepts the simulation in order to be able to give vent to his sorrows and perhaps continue with an updated version of the fiction of the screen ladies, previously described as "simulato amore" (fictional love) in *VN* 4.6 (ix 6). The episode can be read as a theoretical statement on the frequent practice—by medieval poets including Dante—of imposing an altered meaning onto texts originally composed for other purposes and circumstances. At the same time, the selection and order of the poems included in the *libello* assumes an *ordo artificialis* that reflects a transcendental schema functional to a discourse of poetic apprenticeship and to a palinode of Dante's earlier literary production, both of which underscore a teleological itinerary of poetic and moral self-actualization.[80] As Michelangelo Picone showed, this itinerary calls for the transcription of relevant texts, their reordering in terms of narrative effectiveness, the rewriting of texts that may contain ambiguous contents or conflicting data, the elimination of nonpertinent texts, and the underscoring of the prosimetrum's global meaning.[81]

The Digression on Poetry and Poetics (*VN* 16 [xxv])

Among the most discussed sections of the *Vita nova* is the digression (or excursus) on poetry and poetics (*VN* 16 [xxv]). Placed at the very center of the *libello*, this long paragraph is also its theoretical core. The digression is entirely dedicated to discussing the *Vita nova*'s own vernacular poetics in the context of more general issues of rhetoric, hermeneutics, and literary history and criticism. We could thus assign the digression to Nünning's endlessly differentiable category of content-related metanarratives: the paragraph can be variously described as general metanarration (as it defends the legitimate use of prosopopoeia by vernacular poets), proprio-metanarration (as it zeroes in on the exclusively erotic theme of the poems included in the *libello*), or allo-metanarration (as it offers critical notes on classical and modern poets).

Despite these relationships to metanarrations, the excursus also stands as the most clearly isolated metaliterary section in the *Vita nova* and, as such, has often been perceived as disrupting the flow of the prosimetrum's plot. The eminently theoretical and seemingly nonnarrative nature of the passage transpires most immediately from the sustained employ of rhetorical terms and even scholastic terminology, such us "sustanzia" (a substance) and "accidente in sustanzia" (an accident in a substance): in *VN* 16 (xxv), Dante *auctor* noticeably claims the podium; he speaks to his readers *ex cathedra*. Or rather, following Nünning's formal categories, Dante's statements on poetry and poetics throughout *VN* 16 (xxv) are situated at the highest level of discourse: the extradiegetic level of Dante *auctor*. The digression is the first of many militant essays in literary history and criticism that Dante constructs and inserts into his works throughout his literary career and to which he authoritatively assigns normative significance. It is in this paragraph that Dante associates himself for the first time with the *bella scola* ("lovely school") of five classical poets—Homer, Virgil, Horace, Ovid, and Lucan—whom he will "physically" encounter in *Inferno* 4.70–106.

Dante's authoritative and authoritarian stance in *VN* 16 (xxv) and his programmatic take on crucial questions of poetics have determined that scholarship on the metatextual aspects of the *Vita nova* would focus primarily on this paragraph. And the perception of the paragraph's textual insulation—of its excursive property—has led scholars to attend to its general metaliterary content rather than its specific metanarrative scope with regard to the *libello* and its plot.[82] The paragraph's metaliterary component, as mentioned earlier, has thus ended up catalyzing scholarly attention more than the metanarrative comments integrated in, and disseminated throughout, the text (and the plot) of the *Vita nova* in its entirety. Readers have generally noticed the digressive nature of this paragraph and labeled it "excursus" or "digression."[83] The digression's apparently tangential relationship to the plot has even led some to propose that it could be a later addition.[84] Aligning with a long-standing critical tradition, we have continued to reference *VN* 16 (xxv) as excursus and digression throughout this chapter, and with good reason. In Nünning's structural approach to metanarrative—considering position, degree of integration, and contextual plausibility of a metanarrative element—we could describe the digressive nature of *VN* 16 (xxv) in terms of an ostensibly low degree of integration in the narrated story. At the very beginning of the excursus, after all, Dante signals its digressive nature directly, with a remarkable example of what Nünning generally designates as "metadigressive metanarration": the excursus is in fact introduced by a self-reflexive statement on the excursus itself, *VN* 16.1 (xxv 1): "Potrebbe qui dubitare persona degna da dichiararle ogni dubitazione . . ." (Here, a person worthy of having every doubt clarified might be doubtful . . .), and *VN* 16.3 (xxv 3): "A cotale cosa dichiarare, secondo che è buono a presente . . ." (To account for such a claim in the present context . . .).

And yet, despite the somewhat low degree of integration acknowledged above, the digression's metaliterary discourse is also intrinsically metanarrative: it concerns the prosimetrum's own artistic process and the very substance of its plot. By situating the origin of vernacular poetry "sociologically" in the need to reach out to an audience of women untrained in Latin, for instance, the excursus provides a prequel to, and a justification for, the *libello* (*VN* 16.6 [xxv 6]): "E 'l primo che cominciò a dire sì come poeta volgare si mosse però che volle fare intendere le sue parole a donna, a la quale era malagevole d'intendere li versi latini" (And the first one who started to write poetry in the vernacular started to do so because he wanted to make his words comprehensible to women, who found it difficult to follow Latin verses). The excursus, to put it differently, connects the erotic aspects of the prosimetrum's *fabula* with the rhetoric of, and rhetorical discourse on, its expression.

The excursus, additionally, directs its discourse on rhetoric to characterize the atmosphere of intellectual—and often polemical—exchange between poets that ultimately constitutes the prosimetrum's narrative background, as in Dante's tirade against poets unable to interpret the figurative language of their own work (*VN* 16.10 [xxv 10]): "però che grande vergogna sarebbe a colui che rimasse cose sotto vesta di figura o di colore rettorico e poscia, domandato, non sapesse denudare le sue parole da cotale vesta in guisa che avessero verace intendimento" (For it would be shameful for one who wrote poetry dressed up with figures or rhetorical color not to know how to strip his words of such dress, upon being asked to do so, showing their true sense). This polemical kind of allo-metanarration evokes the poetic correspondences and *tenzoni*—"domandato" (upon being asked to do so)—that have also marked Dante's own entry into Florence's literary society in *VN* 1.20–24 (iii 10–13). The ensuing reference to Dante's "primo amico" (best friend) and fellow-poet-turned-character Guido Cavalcanti—one of five such references, as will be discussed in chapter 2—links poetics to personal allegiances, transfigures cultural sodalities into literary characters, and fabulates the communicational scenario of medieval poetry into the prosimetrum's plot. Despite its declared and well-established digressive nature, the excursus acquires contextual plausibility with regard to the narrated story: it recodes metaliterary annotations as a driving force of the *Vita nova*'s *fabula*. The excursus, in other words, works as a *narrative* digression rather than—or as well as—a metaliterary digression from the narrative.

Nonnarrative Self-Reflexivity

Nünning's and Fludernik's models also include self-reflexive devices that are not narrative (in some cases, not even verbal), such as *mise-en-abyme*, metaleptic plot configurations, and illustrations (which include various forms of visual apparatus). In such cases, the self-reflexive device is not metanarrative, in that it references neither the narrative act nor the narration process. The identification of such implicit (and nonnarratorial) metatextual devices is more a matter of interpretation than one of classification. Igor Candido formulated the exciting hypothesis that the *Vita nova*'s first dream vision (*VN* 1.12–24 [iii 1–13]) could, in fact, contain a *mise-en-abyme*. Drawing persuasive parallels between Dante's *libello* and John's book of Revelation, Candido cautiously suggested that the mysterious object Beatrice feeds on in Dante's dream vision could be a book (as for John in Patmos) and not a heart (as traditionally interpreted), or rather, that the heart could allegorically stand for the book of the poet's memory mentioned in the proem.[85] The book of Dante's memory would thus include the *Vita nova*, which would then record this inclusion by reflecting it allegorically within itself.

We might take Candido's intuition one step further to describe the image of the book/heart in terms of Dällenbach's *mise-en-abyme* of the code,[86] which generally consists of some specular form of composition within the text: a work of art, a fabric, a machine, and so forth. Trying to find other such examples of inside representations within the *Vita nova* would be risky: an attempt to comply with Dällenbach's *esprit-de-système* can easily turn into a hunt for (or invention of) an inside composition where none actually exists. Examples of *récits spéculaires* (self-reflexive narratives) and *enchâssement* (embedding) are, however, anything but uncommon in medieval texts.[87] And even the most rigorous and cautious philologists have read the volume into which the unsewn quires of the universe are bound in the final canto of *Paradiso* (33.85–87) as both the symbolic representation of the ordered unity of the creation and the embedded image of the *Commedia* itself (and of the *Commedia* qua book).[88]

When so many textual signals point toward the prosimetrum's self-awareness, it is difficult to resist looking for self-reflexive representations within the *libello*. In *VN* 29.1 (xl 1), Dante comes across a group of pilgrims traveling to Rome to worship the veil of Veronica (*sudarium*), an icon (more specifically, an image on a fragment of cloth) allegedly bearing the likeness of Christ's face:[89]

> Dopo questa tribulazione avenne, in quel tempo che molta gente va per vedere quella imagine benedetta la quale Gesù Cristo lasciò a noi per essemplo de la sua bellissima figura (la quale vede la mia donna gloriosamente), che alquanti peregrini passavano per una via la quale è quasi mezzo della cittade ove nacque e vivette e morio la gentilissima donna.
>
> ---
>
> (After this tribulation, at that time when many people go to see the blessed image that Jesus Christ left us as an imprint of his beautiful visage, which my lady sees in glory, it happened that certain pilgrims were passing along a street that runs virtually straight through the middle of the city where that most gracious of women was born, lived, and died.)

The episode's lexical context alludes to Dante's beloved *gentilissima*, Beatrice. Dante had previously used the term *imagine* to refer to his mental representation of Beatrice from her first epiphany, in a context that stressed her divine nature by means of an indirect Homeric citation (*VN* 1.9 [ii 8]). Furthermore, *benedetta* (blessed) is an epithet that Beatrice shares with the "Christian pantheon."[90]

But it is the semantic archipelago of the keyword *figura* that especially sustains this series of correspondences. In the broad terms described by Erich Auerbach, the notion of *figura* entails, on the one hand, a form of symbolic realism with which the medieval imagination understood the relationship between history and the otherworldly, between the visible and the invisible. On the other hand, as Mary Franklin-Brown notes, the term *figura* was used in Medieval Latin both to describe the overall visual appearance of the manuscript folio (its material organization and aesthetics) and to designate a narrative program of manuscript painting, in alternation with the term *historia* and, remarkably, with the term *imago*.[91] Additionally, the term *essemplo* refers to a copy (an apograph, in philological terms) transcribed from another (its antigraph); the activity of *assemplare* is the one in which Dante the copyist of the *libello* self-declaredly engages when he transcribes from the book of his memory. In this case, the Veronica represents the transcription into images of a superior reality and para-etymologically exposes its own nature as a reliable copy (*vera-icona*, "true image"). The Veronica appears as a codified system of signs and discloses its own articulated composition in its manifestation as artifact or, rather, as *acheiropoieton*: the product of divine craft (literally, "something made without using hands"). Pirovano writes, "Whereas they [*sc.* the pilgrims] will find the most desired relic of Christ's face in Rome, in his poetry Dante has found Beatrice's relic, which he had vainly tried to reproduce as a drawing (xxxiv) and which he had thought to glimpse in the face of the compassionate gracious lady (xxxvi)."[92] Furthermore, the icon institutes a series of hypostatic correlations wherein the *libello* is to Beatrice what the Veronica is to Christ. This *mise-en-abyme* of the code would suggestively confirm Beatrice's Christological features and also the scriptural and hagiographic legacy in the *libello*.

We might also hazard a comparable relationship of specularity and intersemiotic *enchâssement* between the *libello* as an angelology of Beatrice and the drawing of an angel's *figura* inspired by the anniversary of Beatrice's death (*VN* 23.1 [xxxiv 1]). The assimilation of Beatrice to angels (e.g., *VN* 17.2 [xxvi 2]) and her description in terms of angelical attributes (e.g., *VN* 1.9 [ii 8]) are justified by the idea that both angels and Beatrice proceed as direct emanation from the Trinity. The notion of Beatrice's unmediated relationship with the Trinity is exposed in the doctrinal explanation of her analogical coincidence with her own distinctive number nine: "questo numero fue ella medesima, per similitudine" (she herself was this number, she bore a resemblance to it). This explanation is unexpectedly given in lieu of the omitted account of her death in *VN* 19.3–6 (xxviii 3–xxix 3).[93]

Novitas

With various degrees of explicitness, metanarrative and self-reflexive statements are situated at all textual levels of the *Vita nova*'s narrative. Applying models derived from contemporary studies in narratology, we have been able to see more clearly that in the *Vita nova* metanarration is both an "incident" embedded in the narrative and a discursive function inherent to the act of narrating. In other words, it is both a narrative object and a discourse on the various aspects of the linguistic representation of that object. We have also recognized that the *Vita nova* potentially engages in nonverbal forms of self-reflection and *mise-en-abyme*, which embed anamorphic images of the prosimetrum into the text. And this anamorphic image—because it is providentially inscribed in its story—is intended to confirm the nonliteral sense of the *Vita nova*, while also providing the reader with cues for interpreting the text: it reflects the narrative that contains it and bends its interpretation.

Dante's pioneering literary work and intellectual *novitas* lent themselves to presenting his creative process, challenges, and achievements in theoretical and self-referential terms. As Auerbach pointed out regarding unprecedented syntactic and semantic turns in the vernacular diction of the *Commedia*, we often come to the conclusion that Dante "used his language to discover the world anew."[94] The metatextual references disseminated in the *Vita nova* are set to establish the theoretical foundations for an innovative first-person narrative in Italian that can develop its coherent argument—Dante's parable of sentimental and poetic apprenticeship, but also the report of its higher signification—beyond the limits imposed by the *formae breves* of the Romance tradition well known to him (*exempla*, *fabliaux*, *vidas*, *razos*, etc.). The *Vita nova* is a narrative that also defines the condition of its coming into existence as a narrative.

As we better understand the workings of metanarrative in the *Vita nova*, we might also consider Dante's metanarrative approach in its broader late medieval context. It is worth noting here that the prose frame that holds together the coeval *Libro di novelle e di bel parlar gentile* (generally known as *Novellino*)—the first organic collection of *novelle* in a Romance vernacular—is also commentative and metanarrative rather than narrative: as Dante *auctor* similarly does in the *libello*, the anonymous compiler of the *Libro di novelle* chronicles and stages its compositional history and invests its readers with the task of transmitting the collection. In the fourteenth century, Giovanni Boccaccio and Francesco Petrarca will also confront the compositional issue of writing a love narrative in the vernacular. And they will both confront Dante's *Vita nova* and his prosimetrical solutions. Whereas in his transcriptions of the *libello*—as we shall observe in chapter 3—Boccaccio will take a clear stance on the subsidiary role of the prose (or at least of some sections of the prose), in the *Elegia di Madonna Fiammetta* (*The Elegy of Lady Fiammetta*) he suppresses the poems altogether and opts for a narrative entirely in prose. Petrarca, in the material and textual modes of his partially autograph *canzoniere*, will instead control and regulate all aspects of narration, including the metaliterary discourse on the act of narrating, through the strategic interaction of the verbal and visual codes of exclusively poetic texts.[95]

Chapter 2 will explore the *Vita nova*'s metanarrativity with regard to, and as a function of, the material dynamics of production, circulation, and reception in medieval Italian literature. Rather than referring to abstract and intangible entities, Dante's references to writing and to books express and signify well-defined material forms, which in turn determine the connotative functions that control the very modes in which those references, and their tropes, operate to produce meaning. Rather than proceeding mechanically with a systematic incorporation of the *Vita nova*'s material references into this chapter's narratological investigation, chapter 2 will show how Dante's innovative approach to narration and storytelling is programmed in concert with specific material features to guarantee the semantic coherence and textual-material integrity of that narration.

CHAPTER TWO

The Author as Scribe

> Si nimius videor seraque coronide longus
> esse liber, legito pauca: libellus ero.
> —Martial, *Epigrammata* 10.1.1–2

The Textualization of Materiality

Metanarrative devices—from statements on the poems' production and reception history to comments on the visual argumentation and material form of the *libello*—feature extensively in the *Vita nova*. Their structural presence reveals Dante's project of outlining an oriented compositional history of the prosimetrum and a revisionist "genetic criticism" of his poetic corpus. The ad hoc reordered sequence of the poems included in the *Vita nova* is intended to articulate a symbolic narrative. The order of the poems and the legitimacy of this narrative are reaffirmed (and textually safeguarded) by the exegetical prose sections that follow and then, after Beatrice's death, precede the poems. The cohesion and the self-contained quality of the narrative are enhanced by the *libello*'s self-description as a material artifact: the text presents the *Vita nova* as a materially coded written work in the process of being written. In doing so, it also announces—and, in fact, recommends—the various instances of, and hermeneutical norms for, its intended reception. The composition of the text—its constitution through the process of selection, order, and explanation of the poems—provides parameters, if not guidelines proper, for its interpretation, transcription, and integral transmission. The prosimetrum's metanarrative references render its occult mechanisms visible. These references are not limited to establishing the various readings and readers of the text. They imply a more wide-ranging contemplation of how narrative functions, of what makes reading possible, and of the text's nature as a material artifact, textual event, and *fictio*. The genetic history of the text coincides with the story in the text. The narrative gives form to its own etiology, and the text answers the question that is implicitly posed, as Lucien Dällenbach argues, in all narratives of narratives: "For how has it come to exist, in this form?"[1] In directing this question to the *Vita nova*, chapter 1 showed that the *Vita nova*'s metanarrative devices elect the *libello* as the specific material form for the prosimetrum's production, transmission, and reception. The exhibited presence of metanarrative references, in other words, points toward the material aspects of the writing of the *libello* as uniquely interwoven with the unfolding of its narrative.

N. Katherine Hayles asserts in her theorization of contemporary literature in electronic form that "when a literary work interrogates the inscription technology that produces it, it mobilizes reflexive loops between its imaginative world and the material apparatus embodying that creation as a physical presence."[2] The *Vita nova* similarly interrogates its own inscription technology. The writing of the *libello* and the description of its production process, material form, and textual components represent, in fact, the content substance of the *libello* itself. The literary project of the *Vita nova* is consubstantial with its self-contained (and self-proclaimed) book form (or rather, we could say, booklet form). Whereas in chapter 1 we exposed the pervasiveness and extensiveness of the *Vita nova*'s metanarrativity and self-reflexivity and provided a "grammar" of the prosimetrum's metanarrative and metatextual expressions—their morphology, semantics, and pragmatics—here we approach those expressions from a more context-specific angle. When we explore Dante's metanarrativity as it depends on and relates to medieval Italian manuscript culture, we see more clearly that Dante inscribed the textual and scribal practices of that culture and the codicological features of Gothic codices into the narrative of the *Vita nova*. Dante fabulated the material and textual models he was familiar with, and availed himself of, into elements of the prosimetrum's story and discourse.

Book and Booklet

From its very textual thresholds—*rubrica* and proem—the *Vita nova* is presented as book-object: a *libello* (booklet) extracted from the book of the author's memory and, as scholars have argued, the memory of himself.[3] On the one hand, the prosimetrum defines its narrative, metanarrative, and metaphorical features in the material terms of manuscript culture. And on the other hand, it integrates compositional and transcriptional practices based on specific textual and codicological models as narrative devices *into* the story—the composition, selection, transcription, exegesis, and reception of Dante's poems ultimately being the events that the *fabula* tells—and adopts those practices and models as metatextual tropes on the level of discourse to achieve coherence and boundedness, impose meaning, direct the reader's response, and secure textual integrity for his work.

Proem

The materiality of the *Vita nova* as physical artifact (as *libello*) is thematized very early in the text and retrieved regularly throughout it.[4] It is well established in Dante studies—one could call it, in fact, a scholarly *topos*—that the incipit of the *Vita nova* is situated in the context of Italian scriptoria. The proem is articulated around a cluster of images that denote the world of books and book production (*VN* 1.1 [i]):

> In quella parte del libro de la mia memoria dinanzi a la quale poco si potrebbe leggere si trova una rubrica la qual dice: *Incipit vita nova*, sotto la qual rubrica io trovo scritte le parole le quali è mio intendimento d'assemplare in questo libello; e se non tutte, almeno la loro sentenzia.
>
> ---
>
> (In the book of my memory—the part of it before which not much is legible—there is the heading *Incipit vita nova*. Under this heading I find the words which I intend to copy down in this little book; if not all of them, at least their essential meaning.)

The proem displays a high degree of self-reflection. On the one hand, the incipit explicitly describes the incipit itself. On the other hand, it implicitly denotes its paradoxical status as secondary incipit. Monica Farnetti has pointed out that "the incipit-book . . . is already a further book, a book that presumes another one and itself originates from a pre-writing."[5] By functioning as proem to a booklet drawn from a preexisting and more comprehensive book, to put it differently, the incipit excludes any referentiality to the non-textual: it immediately parades its own metatextual character, while also exposing the *Vita nova*'s nature as material object. The closing of the *Vita nova* similarly implies a certain degree of paradox, in that it brings about the much debated "proleptic announcement" of a new literary enterprise.[6] The proem and the conclusion, in sum, situate the incipit and the explicit *en abyme*, pointing toward a citational (and intertextual) notion of literature and deferring the perception of the prosimetrum's origin to other pretexts.

The metaphor of memory as writing is fairly conventional in classical and medieval texts.[7] A critical tradition that goes back to the positivist scholars of the Italian *Scuola storica* has progressively unveiled more or less probable sources for the phrase "book of memory."[8] The list of sources has grown long and distinguished, even if the availability of those sources to Dante remains difficult to prove. The critical attention to the intertextual sedimentation of Dante's book of memory has yet, however, to yield to an extended consideration of the exact material dimension behind the metaphor.[9] In an influential reading of the *Vita nova*, Charles Singleton focused on the prosimetrum's book metaphorics, underlining the connections between the *Vita nova*'s book of memory and its various instantiations in the *Commedia*.[10] Singleton asserted that the book of memory ultimately relates to the legibility of the world, is a facet of the more comprehensive symbolism of the creation as a book, and is implied by the very book of which God is the author—the Holy Scriptures. In spite of reading the *Vita nova* as a codex and using medieval categories of writing, Singleton was more interested in the tenor of the book metaphors than in the material trappings of their vehicle.[11]

And yet, references to texts in Dante's corpus always maintain a certain degree of materiality. For instance, Dante's keen competence with respect to Virgil's texts assumes the material form of leafing through and attentively perusing the latter's books (*Inferno* 1.83–84): "vagliami 'l lungo studio e 'l grande amore / che m'ha fatto cercar lo tuo volume" (let my long study and great love avail me, that has caused me to search through your volume).[12] For the proemial passage of the *Vita nova*, the concurrent mention of *rubrica* and *libello* as well as the allusion to the quantity of text that was omitted are conducive to an image of the book made of leaves, with an actual physical consistency. Several passages in the *Commedia* similarly indicate the measuring of textual quantities "by the leaf": for example, Virgil's mention of Dante's copy of Aristotle's *Physics* in *Inferno* 11.101–2 ("e se tu ben la tua Fisica note, / tu troverai, non dopo molte carte" (and if you take good note of your *Physics*, you will see, after not many pages); or Dante's reference to the book of Ezekiel in *Purgatorio* 29.103: "e quali i troverai ne le sue carte" (and as you find them [*sc.* the four animals] in his [*sc.* Ezekiel's] pages).

The book as a metaphor always coexists with the book as a material object. Marco Santagata proposed that the book of memory mentioned in the *Vita nova*'s proem could refer to an actual material exemplar: "a collection of poems, ordered in a way not dissimilar from the book's . . . a pre-existing organism, already selected and ordered."[13] Maria Giovanna Tassinari also contemplated the possibility that Dante "actually had a *book*—the fact that he was a writer allows us to think so—(book, or scattered leaves, or piled volumes, this is irrelevant) in which he had taken notes not only of events pure and simple, but also of the poetic compositions that he would put forward throughout the *Vita Nuova*."[14] Even without postulating an actual antigraph from which Dante would transcribe the booklet of the *Vita nova*, the materiality of Dante's editorial lexicon presupposes familiarity with specific book forms behind this imagery.

The book and the text, the container and the content, share, according to Lucia Battaglia Ricci, "a real physical and symbolic solidarity."[15] What is more, the continued analogy between memory and book implies that the material aspects of the book—layout, fasciculation, graphic rendition of the expository order—are the technological elements over which the organization of the subject matter is mapped. The codex, then, is the figure the author chose to epitomize the act of articulating his memory. What is more, the act of composing is conceived and visualized as the process of copying. The prosimetrum is presented as a material object, not as a text in abstract. Poetic memory is visually represented as the extraction of a booklet from a book. The *libello* is a booklet with its relative set of material elements (initials, rubrics, paragraphemic signs). The *Vita nova* clearly shows how Dante conceives of a piece of textual datum and a material unit as constituting one holistic entity. The act of composition is an intellectual act—and a material fact—that is modeled on exact book forms. The book represents the primary idea of the text. The text, conceptually and objectually, assumes the shape of a book. Furthermore, by presenting his authorial persona as the copyist of his own work—something not necessarily expected in the thirteenth century, when *dictare* (literally, "to dictate"), more often than *scribere* ("to write"), described literature's compositional mode—Dante asserts he alone is the originator and guarantor of the authoritative version of the *Vita nova.*[16]

Remembrance, as we have seen in the opening lines of the prosimetrum, takes the visual form of a material book from which a booklet may be drawn. As Warren Ginsberg asserts, "Dante presents his 'libello' as a tactile counterpart to the intellectual experience it records."[17] The metaphor of memory as a book generates a semantic constellation around which the whole proem is structured.[18] It brings about an alignment between the process of remembrance and the writing of literature as text forms and book forms. It reflects, as Marziano Guglielminetti remarked, a double process of literary reduction from what is experienced through what is remembered (and memorized) to what is transcribed.[19] From the more immediate image of finding written words (*VN* 1.1 [i]: "trovo scritte") to the use of technical terms such as *rubrica, assemplare,* and then *essemplo* and *paragrafi* (*VN* 1.11 [ii 10]), we see a specific representation of objective reality (through recollection), its textual dimension, the material dimension of the text, and its compositional history.

The thrift of Dante's writing makes the proem a compelling read. That same thrift also produces, however, the semantic ambiguity of some lexical items. Dante scholars have long debated which meaning to assign to the term *parole* ("words"). *Parole* clearly extends the book metaphor and connotes memories; evidently, the specific word choice (no pun intended) also implies the verbalization and textualization of these memories. But the dialectical correlation between *parole* and the technical *sentenzia* (deeper metaphysical sense of a text) makes it unclear if it is only the prosimetrum's verse—or also the prose sections—that the author as scribe transcribes directly from the book of memory. Dante's determined use of *parole* covers a wide semantic spectrum, which includes nonspecific and also technical acceptations.[20] But the very notion of selecting words and making them the focus of hermeneutical practice seemingly underlines a term suffused with meaning and designates words that have undergone intense stylistic elaboration: therefore, poetic words. As Domenico De Robertis asserted, in the prosimetrum "*parlare* [to speak], *dire* [to say] and *parole* [words] . . . mean above all to speak in verse, to compose poetry, poems."[21] And the question of whether Dante's *parole* means merely "words" or specifically "words of poetry" is not immaterial, as we shall see. It shapes the type of relationship the prosimetrum institutes between verse and prose. Ultimately, it affects their material organization as to their *mise-en-texte* (and, indirectly, *mise-en-page*).

Rubrica

We will observe in the next subsection of this chapter that, in Occitan chansonniers, the rubrics introducing poems or compilations of poems—such as Guiraut Riquier's *libre*—could assume a narrative character: in addition to providing the poem's authorial attribution and metrical genre, they could develop a basic story. We see a comparable phenomenon in the *Vita nova*, in which what is presented as the Latin rubric of the *libello*—*Incipit vita nova*—is included within the narration proper and is assigned various orders of signification, both material and metaphorical.[22] Kenneth P. Clarke states that "the rubric's ability to draw together both *incipit* and *titulus* is what makes the opening of Dante's *Vita nuova* so compelling."[23] From a textual point of view, the formula indicates the title of the prosimetrum. Similarly, in the disputed letter to Can Grande della Scala, we read (*Epistles* 13.10): "Libri titulus est *Incipit Comedia Dantis Alagherii*" (The title of the book is Dante Alighieri's *Commedia*).[24] From a codicological perspective, the rubric signposts the material beginning of the prosimetrum (or even the booklet's first quire) within the codex.

The *rubrica* performs various tasks. It marks the incipit, indicates the title, and establishes a formal boundary for the text. It is part of what Marco Pacioni describes as the "*libello*'s internal map," built in to preserve the uncorrupted textual transmission of the prosimetrum.[25] In conjunction with the explicit, in fact, the *rubrica* also safeguards the prosimetrum's cohesiveness and protects the wholeness of the work.

The *rubrica* is also rich in symbolic connotations that extend beyond the editorial practices it denotes, thus offering hermeneutic suggestions for an allegorical interpretation of the text. It reiterates the analogy between the *ordinatio* of a codex and the mnemonic *loci* that give memory its structure. As Mary Carruthers has shown, the classical and medieval tropes likening reminiscence to a writing and reading process indicate that "the ancients and their medieval heirs thought that each 'bit' of knowledge was remembered in a particular place in the memory, which it occupied as a letter occupies space on a writing surface."[26] To put it differently, mental representations that are made readable are also more memorable. The book of memory—and the prosimetrum as booklet extracted from it—owes its mnemotechnical properties to the visual and spatial features of the book-object that represents it and materially reifies it.

Furthermore, the *rubrica* institutes a series of relationships between the *libello* and Dante's life and works, by metaphorically marking the new phase of Dante's authentically Christian life—according to the well-known model of Augustinian conversion—and the ensuing correspondence between *vita nova* and *canticum novum* (new song).[27] Moreover, the semantic (and visual) implications of the color red stemming from the etymology of the word *rubrica* (red ochre) establish—as cursorily brushed over by Ginsberg[28]—a symbolic connection between the red ink used by the *rubricator* and the clothes that Beatrice wore upon first meeting Dante (*VN* 1.4 [ii 3]): in her first Vitanovan epiphany, she appears "vestita di nobilissimo colore, umile ed onesto sanguigno" (dressed in a very stately color, a subdued and dignified crimson). And crimson red punctuates the narration of the *Vita nova*, with evocative Christological implications emanating from the lexicality of the color itself (*sanguigno*, "blood red"). Red appears again in Dante's first dream of Beatrice (*VN* 1.15 [iii 4]) when her almost naked body is barely covered by a "drappo sanguigno" (crimson silken cloth) and again in her posthumous epiphany (*VN* 28.1 [xxxix 1]) when she is dressed in "vestimenta sanguigne" (crimson clothes).[29] In significant consonance with the oriented project of the *libello*, the prose account of the first dream (*VN* 1.13–19 [iii 2–8]) features analogous chromatic details, which are lacking in the sonnet: "di fuoco" (fiery) is the color of the cloud in which Dante discerns the intimidating figure of a lordly man, and fiery red seems the only possible color for the burning heart on which Beatrice feeds. In chapter 3, we will observe how this chromatic detail can assume material evidence in the earliest transcriptions of the *libello*, where the *rubrica* is extrapolated from the narrative continuum and given the prominent position of textual threshold.

Both Dante's *Vita nova* and his new life begin with a chromatic reference to Beatrice and hypostatically coincide with the *gentilissima*.[30] This dual order of signification (material and metaphorical) also characterizes the built-in explicit of the *libello*. The conventional final formula in the name of Christ "qui est per omnia secula benedictus. Amen" (who is blessed forever and ever. Amen) functions as closure and continues the series of correspondences between the booklet, Beatrice as a character of the *libello*—she is epithetized *benedetta* (blessed) twice in the last paragraph of the prosimetrum—and Beatrice as *figura Christi* (who is also blessed, "per omnia secula benedictus," unto the ages of ages).[31] The aforementioned dual order of signification, material and metaphorical (or even metaphysical), may in some ways be associated with the miraculous thaumaturgic effect of the material objectuality of Gautier de Coincy's *Miracles de Nostre Dame*. As Valeria Bertolucci Pizzorusso notes, Gautier's "book acquires the miraculous virtue of a holy relic, which heals the sore body of its author after having been applied to it (*Miracles* 209)."[32] In the *Vita nova*, similarly, we see Beatrice's miraculous effects on Dante—her "healing" effect on him and her agency in his *renovatio*—inscribed in the material features of the *libello*, as these features are explicitly announced in metatextual and metanarrative terms. If the prosimetrum's narrative associates a Christian relic (the veil of Veronica) with Dante's verbal iconization of Beatrice (*VN* 29 [xl]), as we have observed in chapter 1, the chromatic correspondence between the *rubrica* (as the textual threshold of Dante's parable of renovation) and the presentation of Beatrice (as the actual *dea ex machina* of that renovation) incorporates the latter's miraculous presence into the anticipated materiality of the *libello*.

Libello

The diminutive *libello* is the term used throughout the prosimetrum to indicate the *Vita nova* (*VN* 1.1 [i], 5.24 [xii 17], 16.9 [xxv 9], 19.2 [xxviii 2]).[33] Rather than being an endearing hypocorism (as Andrew Frisardi's above-cited translation may suggest), the term underlines the nature of the prosimetrum as a material artifact. H. Wayne Storey has illustrated the technical-editorial use of *libello* in the context of medieval scribal practices.[34] In using the term *libello*, Dante would materially refer to certain codicological units somewhere between single quires and compact codices.[35] These units were semantically self-sufficient (unlike the university *peciae*) and produced as autonomous entities that could circulate independently. Storey even hypothesizes the possible original dimensions of the *Vita nova*: "If the earliest copies of the work are reliable for their layout of the *libello*, the little book would have consisted materially of no more than two quinternions (10 bifolia/20 *chartae*) or perhaps even two quaternions (8 bifolia or 16 *chartae*)."[36] The scarcity of attestations to the term *libello* and the notorious lack of uniformity in medieval critical terminology make it difficult to certify a rigorous codicological acceptation on behalf of Dante. It is clear, however, that *libello* refers to a self-contained material form.[37]

The mention of a physical entity—the *libello*—evokes the type of codicological references that Dante uses as indications of material boundary in the *Commedia*, namely, as a metatextual clue for closure at the end of *Purgatorio*, and as an appeal to give material cohesion to the whole poem at the end of *Paradiso*. Dante seals the second canticle by referencing a rigorously planned correlation between material units and textual units, while also implying the textual and codicological caesura between canticles (*Purgatorio* 33.136–41):

> S'io avessi, lettor, più lungo spazio
> da scrivere, i' pur cantere' in parte
> lo dolce ber che mai non m'avria sazio;
> ma perché piene son tutte le carte
> ordite a questa cantica seconda,
> non mi lascia più ir lo fren de l'arte.
>
> ———
>
> (If, reader, I had more space to write, I would continue to sing in part the sweet drink that could never satiate me, but because all the pages are filled that have been laid out for this second canticle, the bridle of art permits me to go no further.)

Here Dante institutes a dual correlation: between *dispositio* (the rhetorical organization of the text's arguments) and planning of the manuscript's material components; and between literary unit (the canticle) and codicological structure (the number of folios and their fasciculation, their gathering into quires).[38] In the last canto of the third canticle, the bookbinding metaphor we cursorily observed in chapter 1—and to which we will return in the appendix to part I—performs a similar function (*Paradiso* 33.85–87):

Nel suo profondo vidi che s'interna,
legato con amore in un volume,
ciò che per l'universo si squaderna.

(In its depths I saw internalized, bound with love in one volume, what through the universe becomes unsewn quires.)

As John Ahern has cogently argued, Dante institutes here a series of analogies between God, Dante, and the reader/copyist of the *Commedia*, in their respective roles as writers of heavenly books (*libri coelestes*)—whether these be metaphysical or physical—because of the polysemy of the term *volume* ("book volume," but also each of the *revolving* heavens in the Ptolemaic cosmological model): God creates the elements of the universe, and then "binds them, metaphorically, into a book"; Dante *agens* experiences those elements in their singularity, and then "beholds a vision of them in their unity"; Dante *auctor* (and *scriptor*) transcribes that experience in his *quaderni*, and then "binds them, in principle, into a single volume"; the reader/copyist reads and copies those *quaderni*, and then "has them bound together—an act that parallels the effort to grasp the poem's aesthetic unity."[39] In the *Vita nova*, the term *libello* performs functions—cohesion and completion—similar to those at the end of *Purgatorio* and *Paradiso*, and from a similarly privileged position (the proem). The term *libello*, in other words, announces (and perhaps materially prescribes) the compactness and discreteness of the *Vita nova*. If the reference to a heading materializes its beginning, the implication of a specific codicological unit implies (and foresees) its closure.

At the time Dante wrote the *Vita nova*, authorial self-contained books of poems in the vernacular were still a novelty in Italy. In southern France, as Gustav Gröber conjectured in a seminal work on Occitan poetry, troubadours used to compose their poems in written form (as their elevated technical and formal accuracy indicates) and then had them transcribed in loose sheets (*Liederblätter* in Gröber's terminology, also referred to as rolls or *rotuli*) that would function as mnemonic aid for jongleurs and performers. Troubadours and their admirers started compiling anthologies of poems, moving from scattered leaves (*Liederblätter*) to more organic books (*Liederbücher*), which would become the material base for poetic anthologies (*Liedersammlungen*) at the twilight of Occitan poetry.[40] Only a few of these *rotuli*—

discovered after Gröber originally conjectured their existence—were rescued from what has been described as the manuscript tradition's "general shipwreck."[41] The manuscript tradition has handed down, for instance, a *rotulus* with a chronologically ordered collection of sixteen poems by Peire Vidal that can be traced back to an authorial project or, at least, to the initiative of an informed compiler. Miquel de la Tor also assembled an anthology of *sirventes* by Peire Cardenal. The copyist of Guiraut Riquier's *libre* professes his dependence on the chronological (and genre-informed) order allegedly imposed on the poems in the autograph by the author himself.[42] Guiraut's *libre*, in its turn, was probably inspired by Alfonso el Sabio's organizational strategies for the latter's *Cantigas de Santa Maria*. Troubadours probably considered these collections, Henry J. Chaytor pointed out, instrumental for securing monopoly of their corpora, establishing authoritative versions of their work, and protecting it from the piracy of other jongleurs (often explicitly shamed as "incompetent bunglers").[43] Other notable *rotuli* include one transmitting seven *cantigas* by Martim Codax and, in Italy, another preserving ten *laude* attributed to Jacopone da Todi as well as a parchment leaf transmitting the first stanza (with music notations) of a *planh* for Joan de Cucanh.[44]

An authorial book project seemingly lies behind Guittone d'Arezzo's garland of sonnets *Del carnale amore* (*Of Carnal Love*).[45] Its sonnets describe the miniature of Love, meant to fill in the empty space around which the sonnets are arranged on the folio of the *codex unicus* that transmits them.[46] This layout would have enacted an intimate intersemiotic and transmedial dialogue between word and page that could hardly be attributed to a mere compiler.[47] Moreover, the orchestration of the Guittonian sections of MS Redi 9 of the Florentine Biblioteca Medicea Laurenziana—produced toward the end of the thirteenth century—indicates that an earlier Guittone *Liederbuch* may have shaped the compositional syntax of this anthology.[48] And Benvenuto da Imola, in the second half of the fourteenth century, could still read an actual *liber* (a book) of Guittone's works.[49]

Statements from other authors suggest that textual references to books could be more broadly recognized as gestures toward material objects. We see that both Giacomino Pugliese (at the itinerant court of Frederick II) and Monte Andrea (in Florence) mention a book of their poems *in* their poems. Monte's reference is further confirmed by Terino di Castelfiorentino's responsive poem.[50] Furthermore, in the contrast canzone "Donna, di voi mi lamento," Giacomino's *libro* is explicitly associated with memory in the sarcastic words of his nonreciprocating beloved (vv. 68–72):

> poi che m'ài al tuo dimino
> piglia di me tal vengianza
> che lo libro di Giacomino
> lo dica per rimembranza,
> amore.[51]

> (since you have me in your power
> take such vengeance upon me
> that Giacomino's book
> may declare it by remembrance,
> love.)

Scholars have not come to an agreement on the exact nature (material or metaphorical) of these references.[52] Guglielmo Gorni, additionally, formulated the hypothesis that a materially preserved sequence of nine sonnets by Guido Cavalcanti—the "ennead of the dumbfounded poet," as Gorni designated it—may have built on a preexisting authorial project.[53]

When we move from this broader textual and material context back to our specific case study, we see, for instance, that Pio Rajna considered Bertran de Born's Occitan "operetta" (small work) of twenty *sirventes* and *cansos* alternated with prose to be a possible antecedent of Dante's prosimetrum.[54] And we can find analogies between the exegetical and narrative sections of the *Vita nova* and the metaliterary content of the more articulated rubrics of Guiraut's *libre* as this is transmitted in Occitan chansonnier *C*.[55] Textual entities such as Guiraut's *libre* share an organizational syntax and "a material and eminently visual factor, the 'space' of the book, which makes its marking possible and available," affirms Bertolucci Pizzorusso.[56] In Dante's case, the book project of the *Vita nova* and the book-object within the *Vita nova* depend on and exploit the grounds of creative possibilities offered by that materially and visually marked "space" of the book. To put it differently, the space of the book turns out to coincide with the space narrated in the book, while also constituting the *Vita nova* as book product.

It is hard to know what Dante knew of Guiraut's contemporary experiment of writing a *libre*. But Dante was certainly well acquainted with Guittone's and the Guittonians' production. And various parallels can be established between the *Vita nova* as self-styled book form and the material and textual aspects of the collections of poems discussed above: for instance, the translation of the paratextual into the textual, and the urge for a narrative parable whose semantic articulation and integrity in transmission are guaranteed by a discrete, self-contained, and cohesive textual sequence.

Selection Mechanisms and Organizational Syntax

A cohesive booklet-anthology offered Dante the material form to structure and resemanticize his poetic production by selecting, ordering, emending, curating, and securing poems otherwise dispersed orally or disseminated in scattered leaves and mini-collections. The *Vita nova* tells more than just "the story of Dante's discovery of narrative time, over against lyric time" or of Dante's learning "to play narrative time and lyric time against each other."[57] The booklet provided Dante with the material support and the writing technology to produce and preserve a self-anthologization and to infer from (or impose onto) this process of self-anthologization the allegorical reading—the *sentenzia* mentioned in the proem—of his sentimental and poetic parable. That is why the *libello* as material form plays such a prominent narrative role from the very start and through the end of the prosimetrum. That is also the reason why such codicological notations as the structuring of the book of memory into paragraphs, the relative positions of the *libello*'s sections, the exact placement of the *divisioni*, and the consecutive position of poems and prose are referred to in spatial and visual terms throughout the prosimetrum: "*trapassando* molte cose le quali si potrebero trarre de l'essemplo onde nascono queste, verò a quelle parole le quali sono scritte nella mia memoria *sotto* maggiori paragrafi" (*passing over* many things that could be copied from the same source, I come to words written in my memory *under* larger paragraphs) (*VN* 1.11 [ii 10]); "se volemo *guardare* nel proemio che *precede* questo libello" (if we *look back* at the proem that *precedes* this little book) (*VN* 19.2 [xxviii 2]); "E acciò che questa canzone *paia* rimanere più vedova *dopo lo suo fine*, la dividerò *prima* che io la scriva; e cotale modo terrò *da qui innanzi*" (And in order to make this canzone *appear* more widowed when it is done, I will divide it up *before* I write it down; and I will maintain this method *from this point on*) (*VN* 20.1 [xxxi 1]); "e compiuta n'avea questa *soprascritta* stanzia" (and had completed the *above* stanza) (*VN* 19.1 [xxviii 1]) (all emphasis mine).[58] The compactness and boundedness of the booklet and the ease of reference that its self-described textual and visual argumentation affords also facilitate parallelisms and symmetries between poems and also the cohesion these connections provide.

Resemanticization

In *VN* 2.9 (v 4) Dante explicitly admits to recycling poems originally written for the first *donna schermo* and resemanticizing them in praise of Beatrice. The *Vita nova* provides several examples of this resemanticization strategy, to the point that it often poses questions about the general veracity of Dante's statements. After all, as Ernst Robert Curtius confided to Gianfranco Contini, reportedly with some irritation, "Dante was a huge mystifier."[59] Such resemanticization can entail textual variants and the disambiguation of the poems' polysemic language through the ad hoc creation of their alleged occasions in the prose.

The *Vita nova*'s prosimetrical structure certainly contributes to resemanticization by inscribing the poem within a narrative a posteriori. The material cohesion of the booklet and the ease of reference allowed for by the visual rendition of its intended *ordinatio* significantly enhance this resemanticizing strategy.[60] The material and visual properties of the book form intended for the prosimetrum—cohesion, "usability," structuring organization—explain, once again, the coherence of the book imagery and the *libello*'s insisted-upon reference to its own antigraph's alleged paragraph division. As we shall see in chapter 3, the early transcriptions of the *Vita nova* offer various renditions of the material cues these references implicitly provide.

In his lifelong examination of the manuscript tradition of Dante's poems, which culminated in the monumental edition of Dante's lyric poetry (three *volumi* in five *tomi*), De Robertis traced a first redaction of thirteen poems of the *Vita nova* prior to their inclusion in the *libello*.[61] The narrative and exegetical prose that accompanies these poems in the prosimetrum often reorients their meaning or fails to notice discrepancies between verse and prose.

The option of giving new meanings to poems originally composed for a different occasion was inherent in medieval love poetry. On the one hand, the concept of a prosimetrical *libello* further actualized and enhanced this possibility by providing the poems with a compositional context (not necessarily corresponding to reality) and a narrative order (not necessarily respecting an authentic chronology): Manuele Gragnolati states that "Dante's *libello* does not discover or describe the true meaning of the poems originally written as free-standing *rime*, but rather creates new poems which did not exist before and now exist alongside the originals."[62] On the other hand, the prosimetrum fixed the material disposition of the poems to preserve that order.

The narrative opportunities provided by a collection of poems in book form maximized the possibility of recycling texts that had previously circulated autonomously and of making them relevant to the *libello*'s *fabula* by integrating them into an oriented prose context. This is the case, for instance, of the verses allegedly dedicated to Beatrice within the sonnet for the first screen lady (*VN* 2.14 [vii 3]): "O voi che per la via d'Amor passate" (O all ye passing by along Love's way).[63] The sonnet is a *sonetto rinterzato*, that is, a sonnet with heptasyllables added after every odd line in the quatrains and after the first two lines in each tercet.[64] This type of sonnet is generally associated with Dante's early literary apprenticeship.[65] Teodolinda Barolini noticed how the placement of the sonnet at the beginning of the prosimetrum and its close vicinity to another metrically archaic *sonetto rinterzato* are intended to outline in the *libello* "a metapoetic trajectory" leading Dante through various stages—courtly, Guittonian, Cavalcantian, Guinizzellian—of poetic apprenticeship toward defining his own new style.[66] In other words, Dante strategically inserts the sonnet into a teleology—and a textual sequence—of erotic and poetic path to perfection.

The sonnet describes a conventional situation: a Love-induced state of fluctuation between joy and despair. From the prose preceding the poem, we learn that Dante is pretending to love another woman to protect Beatrice's reputation from the same *lauzengiers* ("malicious eavesdroppers") who populate the world of Occitan poetry. From the prose (*VN* 2.13 [vii 2]), we also learn that the sonnet is included in the prosimetrum because Beatrice "fue immediata cagione di certe parole che nel sonetto sono, sì come appare a chi lo 'ntende" (was the direct source for certain words in the sonnet, as is plain to anyone who understands it). Foster and Boyde underscored, however, that "there is nothing in the poem itself to confirm this account. It is purely conventional and there is no need to assume a 'real' or biographical origin of any kind."[67] The prose information, with its distinctive metatextual lexicon (*cagione*, *parole*, *[i]ntendere*), evokes the Occitan poets' practice of concealing (*celar*) the beloved's name. The verses would indeed be very effective if their purpose was to hide an alleged, hardly recognizable reference to Beatrice (vv. 7–12):

> Amor, non già per mia poca bontate,
> ma per sua nobiltate,
> mi pose in vita sì dolce e soave
> ch'i' mi sentia dir dietro spesse fiate:
> "Deo, per qual dignitate
> così leggiadro questi lo core ave?"
>
> ———
>
> (Not, surely, by my merit's meager sway:
> by Love's nobility,
> Love placed me in a life so sweet and sane,
> I often heard behind me others say:
> "How did he earn to be
> so weightless in his heart—please, God, explain?")

The coincidence between the hypostasis of Love and the beloved is rather common in troubadour poetry, where it is also favored by the feminine grammatical gender of the noun indicating Love in Old Occitan (*amor*)—with that Love exclusively (and unsurprisingly) favoring heterosexual liaisons. This strategy of assimilating Love to the beloved was passed on to Italian poetry, and Dante explores here its semantic capacity. As Gorni observed, "Beatrice's name, at one point in the *Vita Nuova*, becomes Love because of the grace and will of the *Segnore de la nobilitade* [Lord of nobility] himself."[68] But the sonnet lamenting the departure of the first screen lady probably had little to do with the elaborate covering described by Dante in the prose or with a passion allegedly simulated in order to protect Beatrice's virtue and good name. It is the poem's resituation in the narrative continuum of the prosimetrum and in the material context of the *libello*—rather than anything intrinsic to the text—that effectively makes this poem about Beatrice.

In the previous example, we have seen how the narrative context in the prose can rewrite conventional materials and make them pertinent to the prosimetrum's *fabula*. It is the material decision to place the poem within the physical boundaries of the book—along with, as Barolini suggests, the location in which it is placed within the text—to "create" its relationship to Beatrice, a relationship that is not in fact produced or evidenced textually within the poem itself. In our next example, we see how the etymological and typological interpretation provided in an especially exegesis-oriented *ragione* integrates a poem—it deliberately overreads and repurposes the poem, one might hazard—into the *libello*'s militant history of vernacular poetry. In *VN* 15 (xxiv), the sonnet "Io mi senti' svegliar dentr'a lo core" (I felt, awakening in my heart one day) describes an epiphany of Beatrice in the company of Cavalcanti's beloved Giovanna, referred to here, hypocoristically, as Vanna (vv. 9–11):

> io vidi monna Vanna e monna Bice
> venire inver lo loco là ov'io era,
> l'una appresso dell'altra maraviglia;
>
> ———
>
> (I made out Lady Joan and Lady Bea,
> moving along in my direction there—
> one miracle behind the other came.)

In the prefatory *ragione* (*VN* 15.3–4 [xxiv 3–4]), the polysemy of the preposition *appresso* ("after," but also "beside") is resolutely and repeatedly elucidated so as to indicate Giovanna proceeding *before* Beatrice. Furthermore, the sonnet is accompanied by a pseudo-etymologic explanation of Giovanna's *senhal* Primavera, an epithet attributed to her by Cavalcanti in his poetic work (*Rime* 1.2): Primavera is thus named because *prima verrà* (he or she will come first).[69] The prose then institutes a further series of analogies between Giovanna coming before Beatrice, John the Baptist coming before the Christ, and, at this point quite uproariously, Guido Cavalcanti coming before Dante.[70] De Robertis observed that "the sonnet does not seem to bear the burden of responsibility the prose attributes to it."[71] On the one hand, the *ragione*'s rewriting of "Io mi senti' svegliar dentr'a lo core" confers Christological attributes on Beatrice. On the other hand, it partakes in instituting Dante's preferred version of literary history and consigns Cavalcanti to a mere stage in the teleology of poetic progress that reaches its zenith—unsurprisingly—in Dante.[72]

In *VN* 18 (xxvii), a mono-stanzaic *canzone*—"Sì lungiamente m'à tenuto amore" (Since Love took hold of me it's been so long)—is presented as the fragment of a pluristrophic *canzone*, whose completion was interrupted by Beatrice's death. Dante *auctor* authoritatively informs the readers of the dynamics of the *canzone*'s composition. Within the narrative of the prosimetrum, the decision to present this isolated stanza as a *canzone* (so defined in *VN* 18.2 [xxvii 2] and 19.1 [xxviii 1]) that was left interrupted makes perfect sense: it gives a visual and textual correlative of Beatrice's death. In the same way, the decision to place the *divisioni* before each poem (from *VN* 20.2 [xxxi 2] on) is explicitly intended to give a sense of emptiness after the poem. The prose scenario explains the metrical features of "Sì lungiamente" with the narrative unfolding of the prosimetrum. The manuscript tradition of this poem seems to confirm the explanation offered in the accompanying prose: the *canzone*, in fact, is only transmitted with the *Vita nova* or within the corpus of poems excerpted from the *Vita nova.*

The prose scenario, however, omits mentioning that mono-stanzaic *canzoni* exist outside the *Vita nova*; Dante himself authored two other such *canzoni* within the corpus of nine extant transmitted.[73] The *canzoni* of this small corpus share formal and thematic features. In seven cases, they share some rhymes (an element that often indicates, and helps detect, genetic and intertextual relationships in early Italian lyric poetry). Furthermore, the authors of this corpus (Guido Cavalcanti, Dante, Cino da Pistoia, Lapo Gianni, Lemmo Orlandi) are all connected, more or less tightly, to the same literary milieu. According to Maria Clotilde Camboni, Guido Cavalcanti's (*Rime* 11) "Poi che di doglia cor conven ch'i' porti" (Since I must carry pain within my heart) could be the hypotext of a monogenetic corpus of monostrophic *canzoni*, which all explore the metrical implication (compositional interruption) of the poem's content (the impossibility of continuing to write about love). Within this corpus and without the prose of the *libello*, Dante's "Sì lungiamente" shows no signs of incompletion. Furthermore, modern commentaries generally agree on the poem's archaic, Cavalcantian traits.[74] We do not know, Marco Grimaldi observes, "whether Dante chose to place a more archaic text in this section of the *Vita nuova* in order to show the impossibility of returning to an already surpassed phase of his poetic experience or he really continued, at that time, to move between various expressive registers."[75] What we do know here is that Dante endows a legitimate metrical genre with a meaning specific to the narrative structure and the material form of the *libello,* which only the prose texts of the *libello* allowed. The *Vita nova* makes the mono-stanzaic *canzone* exploit and maximize its semantic and material potentials as interrupted pluristrophic *canzone*, and also shape the plot of the prosimetrum, using its metrical features and material presentation to act upon the narrative.

The prose of the *libello* (*VN* 28 [xxxix]) inscribes the third-to-last sonnet, "Lasso!, per forza di molti sospiri" (Alas, by force of all my many sighs) within the narrative of Dante's parable of temptation and redemption with regard to the infamous episode of the *donna gentile*. The sonnet itself holds no reference to Dante's moral backsliding. Barolini focused on the role of the prose in forging the poem's meaning: "The manipulations of the plot are particularly explicit, as indicated by the fact that Dante himself provides the gloss to the opening exclamation 'Lasso!,' telling us that it indicates shame."[76] The sonnet was probably far too compatible with the prosimetrum's narrative (and serviceable for the *libello*'s agenda) to be dismissed (vv. 12–14):

> però ch'elli ànno i ·llor (li dolorosi)
> quel dolce nome di madonna scritto
> e de la morte sua molte parole.
>
> ———
>
> (because inside those multitudes of pain
> the sweet name of my lady's written out,
> and there's no dearth of words about her death.)

The sonnet retrieves the proem's book metaphor. The name of the lady and many "words about her death" are written on the poet's heart. The sonnet "Lasso!, per forza di molti sospiri," in sum, could be easily subsumed under the metaphorics of the book of the heart and the poetics of the book of memory, thus fulfilling a mnemotechnical purpose and establishing cohesion between various sections of the *libello*.

Symmetries

A cohesive anthology-booklet enhances an ease of reference that in turn highlights parallelisms and internal echoes between early poems and poems likely composed ad hoc for the *libello* or edited for it. Such intratextual correspondences increase the consistency of the narrative, validate the order of the poems within the prosimetrum, and emphasize the providential plan that has Dante *agens* as protagonist. The *libello* offers several examples of this organizational syntax reinforced by its self-styled material organization in book form, intended to reflect the sections and subsections of its antigraph (the *paragrafi* of the book of memory referred to in *VN* 1.11 [ii 10]).

The *canzoni* that introduce the prosimetrum's second section (after the "invention" of the new style) and third section (after Beatrice's death)—respectively, in *VN* 10 (xix) "Donne ch'avete intelletto d'amore" (Women who understand the truth of Love), and in *VN* 20 (xxxi) "Li occhi dolenti per pietà del core" (My eyes, in sorrow for my heart's torment)—engage in a well-known structural and thematic dialogue.[77] The proemial stanza of the latter *canzone*, for instance, explicitly refers to the proem of the former and to its election of an audience as well as to its context within the narrative of the *libello* (vv. 7–11):

> E perch'e' mi ricorda che io parlai
> de la mia donna mentre che vivea,
> donne gentili, volontier con voi,
> non vòi parlare altrui
> se no a cor gentil che in donna sia.
>
> ———
>
> (And since I well remember the details
> I spoke about my lady while she lived,
> my gracious women, willingly to you,
> I'll speak to no one new,
> save to the open heart that women give.)

Intertextual practice sustains the narrative discourse: the storyline is driven by poetic memory and the memory of poems allegedly composed in the past.[78] The proems of the two *canzoni* share rhymic echoes, such as the marked Sicilian rhyme *voi : altrui*, lexical features, such as *[i]sfogare* (to vent), and the synonymic series *dire/ragionare*, as well as syntactic-rhetorical elements, such as the vocative as verse incipit.[79] These echoes are certainly common in medieval Italian poetic diction, but more crucial symmetries affect structural and thematic elements. For instance, such symmetries involve and fulfill heaven's want and desire of Beatrice as expressed in "Donne ch'avete intelletto d'amore" (v. 29),

> Madonna è disïata in sommo cielo
>
> ---
>
> (My lady is desired in paradise)

by transfiguring it into Beatrice's actual ascension to heaven in "Li occhi dolenti per pietà del core" (v. 15),

> Ita n'è Beatrice en l'alto cielo
>
> ---
>
> (Departed is she, Beatrice, she's gone
> to heaven's realm.)

The correspondences between the two *canzoni* are further highlighted by the prosimetrum's narrative proper. Because of their perceived craftsmanship, both *canzoni* contribute to the public affirmation of Dante as a poet. And both *canzoni* beget the commission of a new poetic composition: a friend requests a theoretical sonnet on the definition of Love (*VN* 11.1 [xx 1]); and Beatrice's brother bespeaks a funeral poem for the death of an unspecified woman, whom Dante determines to be Beatrice (*VN* 21.2 [xxxii 2]). These parallelisms thus reinforce the idea of Dante *agens*'s ongoing public affirmation and self-authorization: they confirm, in other words, the idea of the *Vita nova* as Dante's ideal literary profile and portfolio.

Such symmetries elicit the rereading of the prosimetrum (and the reshuffling of the *libello*) according to a teleological narrative. Analogously, various types of parallelisms and linguistic echoes connect the sonnets "Con l'altre donne mia vista gabbate" (With other women you mock my distress) in *VN* 7 (xiv) and "Sè tu colui c'ài trattato sovente" (Are you that man who's often liked to write) in *VN* 13 (xxii): contextual-interactional (the "altre donne" mentioned in the former sonnet are seemingly the same women who address the poet in the latter); lexical ("rassembri"/"risomigli"; "figura nova"/"figura . . . d'altra gente"); and metrical (the Sicilian rhymes *voi : altrui* and *noi : lui*). These correlations invite the reader to connect the various steps of the poet's public emotional crisis and locate them within the superior (and revisionist) order of an ex post perspective. And it is worth pointing at a textual variant between the first redaction of "Con l'altre donne mia vista gabbate" before its inclusion in the *libello* (in the so-called *extravagante* tradition) and the redaction included in the prosimetrum (v. 2):[80] "risembro" becomes "rassembri," thus instituting a sort of distant *homoeoteleuton*, and additional factor of cohesion, with respect to "risomigli" in "Sè tu colui c'ài trattato sovente."

Daniela Shalom Vagata has argued that textual variants between the original redaction of the poems and the redaction included in the prosimetrum point toward a search for cohesion and therefore further stress the coherence of the *libello*: "The readings of the organic tradition reveal the poems' strict adherence to the narrative framework, made explicit and justified by the prose, and exhibit a deeper semantic and stylistic-linguistic coherence."[81] A textbook model of this strategy is provided by the textual variants De Robertis enumerated in comparing the *Vita nova*'s version of the sonnet (*VN* 17 [xxvi]) "Tanto gentile e tanto onesta pare" (So open and so self-possessed appears) to the first redaction of that sonnet before its inclusion in the *libello*.[82] By substituting the first redaction's first-person singular of *credere*, "credo" (I believe), with the impersonal and apodictic use of *parere*, "pare" (it appears manifest), the *Vita nova*'s version of the sonnet endows Beatrice's epiphany with a higher degree of objectivity (vv. 7–8):

> e par che sia una cosa venuta
> dal cielo in terra a miracol mostrare.
>
> ---
>
> (. . . appearing manifest
> from heaven to show a miracle on earth.)

The prosimetrum's variant provides, according to Contini's magisterial reading of the sonnet, the theoretical enunciation of "an incarnation of celestial entities."[83] If by means of this variant Dante rewrites Beatrice's epiphany in terms of a universal event beyond his individual experience, through this textual innovation he also integrates the event more organically into the *libello*'s narrative and poetic discourse.

Refunctionalizations

Dante situates literature at the confluence of textuality and materiality. In the *Vita nova*, as the previous sections have demonstrated, materiality informs the language of metanarrative and self-reflexive statements (*libello*, *rubrica*, *paragrafi*, etc.). The prosimetrum's self-description in material terms—as *libello*—is functional to outlining, and giving form to, a coherent and oriented presentation of Dante's poetic production. In other words, this thematization of materiality, and of the *Vita nova* as book project and book product, pursues the authentication, partial resemanticization, and authorization of Dante's work. The poems' *divisioni* and *ragioni* further show that Dante intends exegetical and compositional principles (such as the *forma tractatus*, i.e., the expository order) in both textual and material terms. Contextually, he refunctionalizes and converts scribal codes such the *mise-en-texte* into narrative expedients, editorial devices to prevent textual "tampering" (corruption and fragmentation), and hermeneutical strategies to condition reception and establish authority.

Divisioni

The *divisioni*—the analyses of the poems' structure—are often considered an exegetical tool with little relevance to the narrative of the *Vita nova*. This critical approach goes back to Boccaccio, who considered these sections merely reiterative "dichiarazioni per dichiarare" (explanations for the sake of explaining).[84] Steven Botterill observed, however, that "Dante only feels compelled to defend his compositional practice when it ceases to be one, that is, when he omits a *divisione*."[85] To put it differently, the presence of the *divisioni* in the *libello* is structural and, we shall see, has momentous implications for the *Vita nova*'s narrative.

The *divisioni* contribute to the general signification of the text. They convey, Antonio D'Andrea puts it, "the writer-protagonist's creation of a complex and elusive image of himself, continuously in-progress."[86] The *divisioni*, in other words, delineate the image of Dante *agens*'s fragmented persona and his attempt to conciliate his conflicting and often mutually exclusive thoughts, what in Petrarchan terms we could describe as the scattered fragments of Dante's soul ("sparsa anime fragmenta"; *Secretum* 3.18).[87] This characterization technique is most readily apparent in the exegetical apparatus placed before the sonnet "Gentil pensero che parla di voi" (A gentle, gracious thought that speaks of you) (*VN* 27.5 [xxxviii 5]): "In questo sonetto fo due parti di me secondo che li miei pensieri erano divisi" (In this sonnet I represent two parts of myself, echoing the way in which my thoughts were split). The *divisione* of the poem is lined up to mirror the dividedness of Dante's self.

The *divisioni* increase the semantic weight of the poems both visually and textually. Mary Franklin-Brown observes in her work on scholastic encyclopedias that "the gloss displaces its object. And, contrary to common assumptions about the derivative nature of commentary, medieval glosses became spaces for invention—scientific, philosophical, rhetorical, or artistic."[88] Quite literally in the *Vita nova*, we see a visual example of how this displacement enhances the text's inventiveness in the sudden change, as we reach the prosimetrum's *in morte* section, in positioning of the *divisioni*: all at once they are relocated to precede the poems, instead of following them. Commenting on this unforeseen shift—"an unexpected correlation of form and theme," according to John Kleiner[89]—Dante explicitly states that it will help convey the sense of despair and loneliness that he and the whole city of Florence are experiencing after Beatrice's death (*VN* 20.2 [xxxi 2]): "E acciò che questa canzone paia rimanere più vedova dopo lo suo fine, la dividerò prima ch'io la scriva; e cotale modo terrò da qui innanzi" (And in order to make this canzone appear more widowed when it is done, I will divide it up before I write it down; and I will maintain this method from this point on). Materiality, narrative, and hermeneutics intersect: the *mise-en-texte* of the *divisioni* functions as the codicological correlative of the text's content form.[90] In addition to their conventional exegetical quality, the prosimetrum's *divisioni*—by means of their intended expository and material order—also assume the less-anticipated fictional properties that Wolfgang Iser associates with fictional texts. The *divisioni* are not signifiers that designate a signified concept; they designate, instead, "*instructions* for the *production* of the signified."[91]

In *VN* 3.12 (viii 12), the well-structured *divisione* of the sonnet "Morte villana, di pietà nemica" (Barbarous Death, compassion's enemy) shows how the *divisioni* reveal both the theme and the structural features of the poem:

> Questo sonetto si divide in quattro parti: nella prima parte chiamo la Morte per certi suoi nomi propi; nella seconda, parlando a lei, dico la cagione per ch'eo mi movo a blasimarla; nella terza la vitupero; ne la quarta mi volgo a parlare a indifinita persona, avegna che quanto al mio intendimento sia diffinita. La seconda comincia quivi: *poi ch'ài data*; la terza quivi: *e s'io di grazia*; la quarta: *Chi non merta salute.*
>
> ———
>
> (This sonnet is divided into four parts. In the first part I call upon Death using some of her various names; in the second, speaking to her, I explain why I am moved to blame her; in the third I admonish her; in the fourth I address an unspecified person, even though in my own mind that person is quite specific. The second part begins, "since you're my suffering heart's"; the third, "And if I want to give you infamy"; the fourth, "And one can't hope.")[92]

This *divisione* provides a brief list of the poem's contents, its expository order (its *forma tractatus*), and an implicit, basic indication of its argumentative scheme. According to Storey, *divisioni* were intended to alert the compiler and the copyist in advance—even when repositioned after the poems they comment on—regarding what transcriptional format to use for each poetic composition and thus how to organize the layout and ruling of the folio.[93] By describing the typology of metric composition and the lines corresponding to the interstrophic subdivision—the title line having been provided, in this case, in the preceding *ragione* (*VN* 3.3 [viii 3])—the *divisione* also helps to curb the poem's textual instability (its *mouvance*), protecting its integrity and correctness against scribal interpolations and corruptions.[94] The classificatory nature of the *divisione*, in other words, makes intentional adulterations of texts extremely burdensome. The correctness of the *Vita nova*'s textual tradition would appear to confirm the effectiveness of Dante's expedient, especially if compared with the textual tradition of Francesco Petrarca's *canzoniere*—variously reshuffled and frequently flawed by misordered stanzas within single lyrics or alterations in the order of poems within the collection.[95]

Ragioni

The *ragioni*—the retrospective accounts of the poems' genesis—provide further evidence of the indissoluble bond between the *Vita nova*'s narrative, the discursive and scribal practices of manuscript culture, and the textual and material integrity of the *libello*.[96] The negotiation between the poems and the prose establishes and secures the correct sequence of the former. Any altering of the sequence would imply a heavy intervention at the level of the story line. Through their interaction with the narrative and exegesis of the prose sections, the poems are granted authorial legitimacy. The fiction itself as it takes form in the concatenation of prose and poetry works as an embedded strategy of editorial authentication.

Dante's compulsive attempt to protect the textual integrity of the *libello* and to condition its general interpretation shows an awareness of the risks of fragmentation, misattribution, and ideological misappropriation that medieval texts could experience during the process of transcription and anthologization. The compilers' and patrons' heterogeneous interests and limited access to reliable (or even complete) antigraphs could result in miscellanies of dubious quality. Uneven preparation and interventional proactiveness could unfortunately coexist in the same copyist. As Roberto Leporatti has pointed out, Dante was barely able to exercise his transcriptional and interpretive control even with his exclusive circle of friends and selected correspondents.[97] Justin Steinberg, furthermore, induced Dante's probable dissatisfaction with the critical response to his work: the early reception of his texts "reveals a striking contrast between how he imagines the materiality of his texts and the historical reality of extant transcriptions."[98] And if we are to believe Franco Sacchetti's fourteenth-century *novelle* that have Dante as protagonist (*Le trecento novelle* 114 and 115), Dante could easily rage against the extemporaneous and inaccurate executions of his work by amateur performers, such as blacksmiths and mule drivers.[99] In short, Dante's concern for the correctness of the textual transmission of, and interpretive approach to, his poems was well justified. As we shall see in chapter 6, disquieting thoughts on the textual integrity of his own work would also weigh heavily on Petrarca's mind.

Knowing how easily texts could be reordered or given a newly made-to-measure meaning likely influenced Dante's choice to provide a deeper metaphysical meaning for the events rather than leave these as unmediated accounts. Articulating the "sentenzia" of the "parole"—whether these include only the poems or also the prose sections—rather than merely their direct transcription may indicate this awareness of texts' ready mutability. The reader of the prosimetrum is thus explicitly told that the narrative is the authorially mediated reconstruction of the events and the meaning of the poems is updated to the new poetics (and the new medium) of the book.

Variorum

It is tempting, albeit speculative at best, to make out in *VN* 23 (xxxiv) further traces of codicological and material features that have been refunctionalized to serve as narrative strategies. With the double beginning of the sonnet "Era venuta ne la mente mia" (She had just come into my memory) and the narrative *ragione* before it, Dante seems to thematize what Byzantinist Alphonse Dain described as the "manuscript eclecticism" of *editiones variorum.*[100] Well known to philologists looking for horizontal contamination, an *editio variorum* is a manuscript that collects textual variants from various witnesses. While transcribing a text in a scriptorium (or in an urban atelier), a copyist could consult several manuscripts in addition to the principal antigraph he was copying from. Occasionally, he could include alternative variants from those manuscripts into his apograph's marginal and interlinear space. Dante narrativizes the editorial practice of materially juxtaposing alternative textual variants and embeds it into the prosimetrum's *fabula.*

In the sonnet's *ragione*, engrossed in drawing the figure of an angel "sopra certe tavolette" (on some boards), Dante realizes that several people have gathered around him. After they leave, Dante composes a poem about thoughts on Beatrice that occurred to him while he was being observed. The *libello* transmits the sonnet with two beginnings, that is, two different versions of the first quatrain (vv. 1–4):

Primo cominciamento:
Era venuta ne la mente mia
la gentil donna che per suo valore
fu posta dall'altissimo Signore
nel ciel de l'umiltate, ov'è Maria.

Secondo cominciamento:
Era venuta ne la mente mia
quella donna gentil cui piange Amore,
entro 'n quel punto che lo su' valore
vi trasse a riguardar quel ch'i' facia.[101]

(First Beginning:
She had just come into my memory,
that gracious one whose virtue's true reward
was to be stationed by the highest Lord
with Mary, in the heaven of humility.

Second Beginning:
She had just come into my memory,
that gracious lady Love is weeping for,
the moment that her virtue's great allure,
where I was working, made you look to see.)

The sonnet "Era venuta ne la mente mia" is an exceptional text for at least two reasons. First, it is the first anniversary poem ever composed for the death of a poet's beloved: in the lyrical tradition before Dante, anniversary poems would generally remember the day the poet fell in love.[102] Second, the *libello* includes (and authorizes) authorial variants from two redactions of the same sonnet, further authenticated and certified by a double *divisione* for the first quatrain. What is unusual is not the existence, in itself, of authorial variants. Poets would often use stock materials and could modify their poems based on the specific occasion or the change of addressee. Exceptional here, as Claudio Giunta has noted, is that Dante explicitly provides his audience with alternative versions of the same poem: instead of choosing between variants, he shares his indecision with his readers.[103]

Whereas the *extravagante* tradition of the sonnet—the tradition of the sonnet before its inclusion in the *libello*—only transmits the second *cominciamento*, the prose explicitly identifies the first *cominciamento* as composed, in fact, first (*VN* 23.4–6 [xxxiv 4–6]):[104]

> Dico che secondo lo primo [*sc.* cominciamento], questo sonetto à tre parti. Nella prima dico che questa donna era già nella mia memoria. . . . Per questo medesimo modo si divide secondo l'altro cominciamento, salvo che nella prima parte dico quando questa donna era così venuta ne la mia memoria e ciò non dico nell'altro.
>
> ———
>
> (Now, in terms of the first beginning, this sonnet has three parts. In the first part I say that this woman was already in my memory. . . . The sonnet is divided the same way according to the other beginning, except that in the first part I say when this woman had come into my memory, something I do not mention in the first beginning.)

Trusting the manuscript tradition against Dante's artifactual reconstruction in the prose *divisione* cited above, several commentators sustain the priority and chronological precedence of the latter *cominciamento* over the former.[105] The first *cominciamento*, then, would have been composed ad hoc for the *libello*. The noncoincidental arrival of the bystanders is inscribed within the miraculous effects that Beatrice exercises on her neighbors: it consolidates the *Vita nova*'s hagiographic component, for the greater glory of Beatrice. Within the context provided by the prose, in the first *cominciamento* the term *valore* (v. 2) assumes the broad metaphysical implications of Beatrice's supernatural power; in the second *cominciamento*, instead, *valore* (v. 3) more limitedly indicates the ethical acceptation of virtue and worth. The first *cominciamento* complies with the allegorical narrative of the *libello*, whereas the second alludes more to the erotic lexicon of the courtly tradition and, therefore, to the early phases of Dante's poetic apprenticeship.[106]

By transmitting the two *cominciamenti* juxtaposed, the *libello* regulated, formalized, and legitimized what was in all probability an existing situation. The original sonnet—with the second *cominciamento*—had probably gone through a successful circulation prior to the literary project (and the figural narration) of the prosimetrum. By recycling that poem in its nonspecifically

Vitanovan redaction, Dante builds on the popularity of the sonnet and vindicates the legitimacy of his poetic career, without missing the material opportunity to outline its ideal trajectory more clearly by exploiting the scribal codes he was familiar with.

History and Chronicle of the *Libello*

We have observed in the previous sections that the protracted presentation of the *Vita nova* as a self-contained material unit is met with, and given specificity through, the thematization of textual codes and material conventions of medieval Italian manuscript culture. The *libello*'s metatextual references to its material condition—and to the visual articulation and presentation of its textual components—describe, confer on the prosimetrum, and inscribe in its enunciated momentous features such as boundedness, sequential order, and self-conclusion that maximize the literary potential of the *Vita nova* as oriented poetic portfolio and coherent, self-authorizing story of Dante's literary persona.

Yet there is still more. Not only does the *Vita nova* maximize the literary potential offered by the material features of the booklet, it also chronicles its constitutive process and details the contextual situation for this process. Adelia Noferi wrote that the *Vita nova* is "the story of an event that already took place and, at the same time, is demanded to produce itself, without which the story could not begin, but which only occurs in the story: constitutive event of subject and sense."[107] In addition to producing its subject and sense ontologically and textually, the *Vita nova* also stages the phases of its constitution as material artifact: it describes the progression and intermediate stages from scattered compositions and oral performance to a single materially self-contained and textually self-concluded entity; it narrativizes the reception history of the poems it contains; it dramatizes its own communicational scenario; it includes commissioners and readers as characters into the *fabula*; and it encloses the prosimetrum's dedication in the prosimetrum's narrative continuum. The composition and reception history of the poems included in the *Vita nova*, in short, is fabulated as contextual and foundational antefact for the composition of the artifact—the *libello*—and is subsumed within the prosimetrum's narrative.

Commissions

With the writing down of the words programmatically avowed in the proem, Olivia Holmes affirms, "a transition takes place from their memorial preservation to visual and material transmission, and this transition can stand for . . . the widespread movement from orality to literacy taking place at that historical time."[108] The very plot of the *Vita nova* mirrors this progression from the oral recitation and circulation of single poems to the compilation and dissemination of more organic multitext poetic sequences. The *Vita nova*, in other words, makes note of the intermediate steps that have led to the completion of the *libello*. The narrative within the prosimetrum provides an explanation for the origin of the *libello*. In *VN* 30.1 (xli 1), for instance, Dante sends upon request a micro-anthology of three sonnets to two unnamed *donne gentili*:

> Poi *mandaro* due donne gentili a me pregando che io *mandassi* loro di queste mie parole rimate, onde io, pensando per la loro nobilità, propuosi di *mandare* loro e di fare una cosa nuova la qual io *mandassi* a loro con esse, acciò che più onorevolmente adempiessi li loro prieghi. E dissi allora un sonetto lo quale narra del mio stato e *manda*'lo a loro col precedente sonetto acompagnato e con un altro che comincia *Venite a 'ntender*.
>
> ---
>
> (Then two lovely women *sent* me a request that I *send* them some of my rhymes. Taking their nobility into account, I decided to *send* some poems to them and to compose something new, which I would *send* along with the other rhymes to more worthily satisfy their request. Then I composed a sonnet that tells of my state, and *sent* it to them with the foregoing sonnet and with another sonnet that starts, "Come and take notice.") (Emphasis on the conjugated forms of the verb *mandare* are mine.)

The noble women's request is referenced in the partitive—"di queste mie parole rimate" (some of my rhymes)—which seemingly implies a selection from a richer poetic corpus. Rather than underlining the women's "prayer and the importance of this poetic submission" as indicated by Donato Pirovano, the polyptotic insistence on the verb *mandare* seems instead to enhance a textual rendition of the material back-and-forth communication between artist and commissioners.[109] For Santagata, this episode is "a precious testimony that Dante, occasionally, would circulate small florilegia of his rhymes."[110] Additionally, it is also a testimony that the *libello* had potential to add new meanings to Dante's production. The micro-anthology consists of "Venite a 'ntender li sospiri miei" (Come and take notice of my every sigh), "Deh peregrini, che pensosi andate" (Oh, pilgrims walking by oblivious), and "Oltre la spera che più larga gira" (Beyond the sphere that turns the widest gyre). The first poem was written as a *planh* (a dirge), yet not for Beatrice.[111] Dante's funeral lament changes in meaning between the time of its composition and when it was transcribed into the booklet. The micro-anthology would probably not fill an entire *Liederbuch* but could certainly circulate on a *Liederblatt*. This micro-anthology features some of the characteristics outlined by Walter Meliga for identifying authorial sequences in troubadour chansonniers. Besides Dante's more or less reliable pronouncement, the three sonnets have in common rhyme scheme, structural elements (an apostrophe), contents (the death of a woman, if not of the same woman), and keywords, such as *peregrino*, and, remarkably, the very name of the beloved.

We do not find a material confirmation of Dante's account in the manuscript tradition of these poems. Only one codex from the Biblioteca Ambrosiana in Milan transmits the three sonnets together, but they are transcribed on different folios.[112] A thorough search for similar sequences in the manuscript tradition, however, remains to be undertaken and might offer exciting clues on mini-collections for specific, intermediate interlocutors. Paola Allegretti underscored, for instance, that the two sonnets allegedly composed for the death of Beatrice's friend (*VN* 3.2–3 [viii 2–3]) appear, introduced by a short *ragione*, within a sequence of ten sonnets transmitted by five manuscripts grouped together by Barbi under the heading "40. Frammento di § VIII."[113]

The episode of the two women's request builds on the narrative of Dante's public recognition. For Pirovano, "the climactic sequence also leads one to think about—now that the story will soon end and the I-*agens* will reunite with the I-*auctor* (see xlii 2)—progressive and subsequent steps leading to the birth of a book of poems precisely like the *Vita nuova*."[114] The micro-anthology for the two women is the third commission Dante receives in the prosimetrum, after the sonnet on the nature of Love asked for by an unspecified acquaintance (*VN* 11.1 [xx 1]) and the funeral poem requested by Beatrice's brother (*VN* 21.2 [xxxii 2]). Even in the absence of material confirmation for Dante's staged compilational process, the narrative account of its stages, the dramatization of the commissions within the narrative, and the integration of the commissioners as *dramatis personae* into the prosimetrum show Dante's aesthetic sensibility toward collecting and recycling materials to produce updated meanings through semantically coherent—or coherently resemanticized—textual series. The account of this single intermediate stage provides, in short, an embryonic version of the larger production history of the *libello*. And it shows how Dante took measures against, and even took advantage of, the risks—intellectual appropriation, incorrect attribution, fragmentation, nonauthorial recycling, "piracy"—which were inherent to the dynamics of production, circulation, and consumption of medieval literature.

Communicational Scenario

An aspect of Dante's marketing strategy and an illustration of his commitment to self-promotion, the prosimetrum's portrayal of its own communicational scenario is also aimed at presenting the composition and "publication" of discrete poems as partial accomplishments within a larger history of the book's writing. "A ciascun'alma presa e gentil core" (To all besotted souls, my counterparts) is the first poem of the *libello* (*VN* 1.21–23 [iii 10–12]). This sonnet is an example of verse epistolography and retains features of both orality and writing. In the fiction of the *libello* (*VN* 1.20 [iii 9]), Dante *agens* sends the poem to "molti li quali erano famosi trovatori in quel tempo" (several of the well-known poets of that time). The poem consists of an account of a dream vision and a request for its interpretation.[115] Its rhetorical structure, accordingly, is articulated into a salutation (*salutatio*, vv. 1–2 and 4), a request proper (*petitio*, v. 3), and a narrative account of the events (*narratio*, vv. 5–14):

> A ciascun'alma presa e gentil core
> nel cui cospetto ven lo dir presente,
> in ciò che mi rescriva in su' parvente,
> salute i·llor segnor, cioè Amore.

(To every in-love soul and noble/open heart into whose sight the present poem comes, in order that they write back to me their interpretation of it, greetings in the name of their lord, namely Love.)[116]

Focusing on the audience, the long two-verse incipitarian indication of the addressees mimics a dialogic situation. The sonnet's material nature as a written text, on the other hand, is implied by the term *cospetto* (< Lat. *conspectus*, from *conspicio*: "I gaze upon"), whose preverb *co*-etymologically suggests the bringing together of several entities, and seemingly, for the intended audience, the physical presence of the text to read (further alluded to by the descriptor *presente*) and its autoptic reading.[117]

The object of Dante's request is an interpretation (*parvente*). The hermeneutical implication of this request also seems to demand a written mode of expression: *rescriva* points, in fact, to a written response.[118] The manuscripts transmit three poetic replies to Dante's sonnet, with identical rhyme scheme yet very different content. Dante recognizes the various outcomes of his fellow poets' attempts at oneirocriticism. The *Vita nova* even quotes one of those replies by its incipit (*VN* 2.1 [iii 14]): significantly, Guido Cavalcanti's "Vedesti, al mio parere, onne valore" (You saw, it seems to me, the whole of worth).[119]

The narrative context and the textual form of "A ciascun'alma presa e gentil core" exemplify the very modes of publication of a single poem, while also showing Dante's awareness of the unconstrained domain of literary interpretation. Steinberg underlined that "the frequent references in the self-commentary as to what someone or a certain person might think about his poetry demonstrate the degree to which Dante had internalized his empirical readers."[120] On the one hand, Dante dramatizes the dynamics of composition, circulation, and reception of a literary text: in the prosimetrum, the self-anthologization and self-exegesis of his poems parallel the narrativization of their reception history, and the recipients of those poems are characters in his anthology. On the other hand, by encapsulating the poem within the material, narrative, and exegetical container of the collection, Dante claims for himself the authority of an ideal reader.[121] Whereas "several well-known poets" (including Dante *agens*) were not able to ascertain the sonnet's true meaning at the time of its circulation, Dante's readers can now take advantage of the enlightening narrative of the progressive revelation of its metaphysical *sentenzia* (*VN* 2.2 [iii 15]): "Lo verace giudicio del detto sogno non fue veduto allora per alcuno, ma ora è manifestissimo a li più semplici" (The correct interpretation of my dream was not understood by anyone at first, but now it is clear to even the most simple-minded).[122]

In chapter 4, we will observe Boccaccio's sophisticated strategy of pursuing authority through distinguishing, impersonating, and performing the role of multiple scribal identities. Conversely, by conflating different degrees of authorship and authority—copyist, poet, commentator—into one literary persona, Dante claims for himself legitimacy as *auctor* and, ultimately, as the interpreter of his own work.

Dedication

Guido Cavalcanti's responsive sonnet "Vedesti, al mio parere, onne valore" is the only non-Dantean poem in the vernacular that the prosimetrum explicitly mentions and whose incipit it cites verbatim. The page of Dante's book of memory already bears a Cavalcantian watermark. The language of the overarching metaphor of the book of memory from which to copy echoes the *envoi* in Cavalcanti's *canzone* "Io non pensava che lo cor giammai" (I did not think my heart could ever be) (*Rime* 9.43–44): "Canzon, tu sai che de' libri d'Amore / io t'asemplai . . ." (My song, you know that from the books of Love / I copied you . . .).[123] Intertextual references to Cavalcanti's poems punctuate the *Vita nova*. Guido is also the dedicatee of the *libello*, even if, at times, this dedication reads more like Dante's agonistic recognition of his own superiority.

The dedication, if not an actual submission, to Cavalcanti is an additional example of Dante's thematization and narrativization of both the communicative scenario and what we would now call the paratext. In medieval literature, a work's dedication would be enacted in the actual presentation of a manuscript to a patron. In the *Vita nova*, by contrast, the dedicatee is implicated in the *fabula* itself. The position of the dedication marks this innovative shift. As Brugnolo and Benedetti note, the dedication occurs "over the course of the work and almost in passing and not in a position that is acknowledged or liminal."[124] Cavalcanti is never called by his name: Dante only designates him through various periphrases. For Marco Pacioni, "what we improperly name 'dedication' is more than anything a tangency nominally left unspecified which interacts 'with' Dante without a direct allocution."[125] And yet, this evanescent simulacrum of a dedicatee is evoked five times in the prosimetrum.[126] Friendship and poetry characterize the first reference to him as the author of a responsive sonnet to "A ciascun'alma presa e gentil core" (*VN* 2.1 [iii 14]): he is described as "quelli cu' io chiamo primo delli miei amici" (somebody whom I consider my best friend). We could describe the second and third references to Cavalcanti—"primo mio amico" and "mio primo amico" (my best friend) (*VN* 15.3 [xxiv 3] and 15.6 [xxiv 6], respectively)—with the same words that Giovanni Cappello uses to characterize the prosimetrum's dedication to Guido: "antiphrastic and almost parodic."[127] In *VN* 15 (xxiv), in fact, Dante records his friendship with Cavalcanti in the same itinerary of literary progression that connotes Beatrice's succession to Giovanna. As Roberto Rea underscored, a hierarchical presentation of Guido's and Dante's beloved is also the figurative expression of a value judgment on their respective poetics and poetry.[128] Friendship and literary allegiance also characterize the fourth implicit reference to Cavalcanti in the final statement of the digression on the legitimate use of rhetoric by poets in the vernacular (*VN* 16.10 [xxv 10]). Cavalcanti, Dante alleges, shares Dante's opprobrium for poets unable to interpret the tropes they use in their own poems: "E questo mio primo amico e io ne sapemo bene di quelli che così rimano stoltamente" (My best friend and I are only too well acquainted with poets who write in such a stupid manner). The fifth mention is the closest to a formal dedication and involves Guido in the *Vita nova*'s exclusive choice of poems in the vernacular (*VN* 19.10 [xxx 3]): "E simile intenzione so ch'ebbe questo mio primo amico a cui io ciò scrivo, cioè ch'io li scrivessi solamente in volgare" (And I know that my best friend, for whom I write this, had the same idea—that I would write only in the common tongue).[129]

By the time of Dante's dedication to Cavalcanti, Rea suggests, Guido had in turn dedicated himself to philosophy.[130] He had abandoned his writing tools, "le triste penne isbigotite, / le cesoiuzze e 'l coltellin dolente" (the sorry quills bewildered, hurt / the penknife and the little scissors), that take the floor in one of his sonnets and speak in the first person about the poet's fragmented and quasi-moribund persona (*Rime* 18.1–2).[131] But if Cavalcanti's doctrinal *canzone* "Donna me prega" (A lady bids me) and scolding sonnet "I' vegno 'l giorno a te 'nfinite volte" (When countless times I come to you each day)—*Rime* 27 and 41, respectively—were ultimately a direct response to the prosimetrum, one could probably hazard that disdainful Guido felt a certain irritation at being implicated in a love doctrine that resolved the tensions at the core of his poetry, that he scorned being indicated as a transient figure in a literary history written by Dante for Dante, and that he rejected being framed as the dedicatee of an organic book project the like of which he could not (and would not) boast in his own poetic archive.[132]

Audience and Readership

The narrative of the first circulation of "A ciascun'alma presa e gentil core" further illustrates how the material existence of the text is thematized. The *Vita nova* subsumes its own audience within the story and portrays them as characters. Dante places the enunciatees of the poems into the substance of the prosimetrum's enunciated. Franz H. Bäuml underscores that the creation of a fictional narrator parallels the appointment of a fictional public: in written narratives, "just as the author is absent from the public, which must 'constitute' a narrator on the basis of the text, and an 'author' implied by the text, the public is absent from the author, who must 'constitute' the public whom he addresses in his text."[133] The *Vita nova* constitutes its public by involving its own historical audience in the plot. In other words, the *Vita nova* selects its audience by repeatedly representing figures of intended readers as characters in the prosimetrum's narrative.

Leggere (to read) is the first verb with full semantic weight in the *libello*. The *Vita nova* repeatedly stages figures of readers, starting with Dante *auctor* himself, who reads the book of his memory and transcribes from it. This is also notable since, Selene Sarteschi underlines, "*lector*, in the Middle Ages, indicates both reader and commentator."[134] The inside recipients of the *Vita nova*'s poems and, more broadly, the recipients designated internally—within the *fabula*—include the various categories outlined by Giunta: dedicatees, explicit addressees, defined but nonspecific recipients (both individual and collective), fictitious recipients (or rather: addressees who are occasional pretexts rather than actual interlocutors).[135] In the prosimetrum, these figures include, in order of appearance: Guido Cavalcanti and the addressees of the first sonnet (and, implicitly, their later simple-minded counterparts, "li più semplici"), repeatedly addressed as "fedeli d'Amore" (Love's faithful) over the course of the prosimetrum (*VN* 1.20 [iii 9], 2.18 [vii 7], 3.7 [viii 7], 21.4 [xxxii 4], and, in the singular, 7.14 [xiv 14]); the first screen lady (*VN* 2.9 [v 4]); the choir of women addressed in the context of Dante's new poetics (*VN* 10.9 [xviii 7], 10.12 [xix 1]); the friend who asks for a poem on the nature of love (*VN* 11.1 [xx 1]); the choir of women with whom Dante simulates a poetic correspondence (*VN* 13 [xxii]); the compassionate lady who attends to Dante when he is sick (*VN* 14 [xxiii]); the hypothetical "altro chiosatore" (another commentator) who should tackle the topic of Beatrice's death (*VN* 19.2 [xxviii 2]); the "principi della terra" (rulers of the land) to whom Dante *agens* sends a letter in Latin—not included in the *libello*—to mourn the death of Beatrice (*VN* 19.8 [xxx 1]); Beatrice's brother (*VN* 21–22 [xxxii–xxxiii]); the honorable passersby (poets, according to Wehle's suggestive hypothesis),[136] who interrupt Dante while he is drawing angels (*VN* 23 [xxxiv]); the gracious lady who led Dante astray (*VN* 24–25 [xxxv–xxxvi]); the pilgrims to Rome (*VN* 29 [xl]); the two women who commission an anthology of Dante's poems (*VN* 30.1 [xli 1]); and, of course, Beatrice.[137]

The prosimetrum's internal audience—the characters to whom the poems are addressed—is subject to continuous oscillation: on the one hand, there is the extreme elitism of an audience selected on the basis of intellectual sensitivity and noble disposition of the soul and, on the other, the appeal of (and to) a broader readership.[138] The manifesto *canzone* "Donne ch'avete intelletto d'amore," for instance, is intended only for a choir of women (*VN* 10.12 [xix 1]); a further limitation expects that they be "coloro che sono gentile e che non sono pure femine" (not just . . . any women but . . . those who are noble and gracious). The *envoi* of the canzone, however, mitigates this limitation and includes both women and men, provided they are noble-spirited (vv. 64–68):

E, se non vuoli andar sì come vana,
non restare ove sia gente villana,
ingegnati, se puoi, d'esser palese
solo con donne o con uomo cortese,
che ti menranno là per via tostana.

(And if you do not want to go [there] without results, do not stay where the base people are: arrange, if you can, to show yourself only with noble-spirited women or men, who will guide you to her without delay.)[139]

This split between the apostrophe's specific addressees and the *envoi*'s more inclusive audience reflects what Elena Lombardi explains as "the tension between the desire of popularization and that of keeping control over his own texts."[140] The *divisione* of the poem confirms these systolic and diastolic phases of the poem's fictionalized reception (*VN* 10.33 [xix 22]):

> Dico bene che, a più aprire lo 'ntendimento di questa canzone, si converrebbe usare di più minute divisioni, ma tuttavia chi non è di tanto ingegno che per queste che sono fatte la possa intendere a me non dispiace se la mi lascia stare, ché certo io temo d'avere a troppi comunicato lo suo intendimento pur per queste divisioni che fatte sono, s'elli avenisse che molti le potessero udire.
>
> ---
>
> (I will add, nevertheless, that to further clarify the sense of this canzone it would be necessary to use still subtler divisions. However, it does not bother me if anyone who is not insightful enough to understand the poem by using the divisions already provided leaves off trying, since in fact I fear I have already communicated its meaning to too many people simply by analyzing it as I have—assuming, that is, it should ever have a large audience.)

The *Vita nova* is constantly striving to forge its own audience and elect an idealized type of reader. In Pacioni's words, "the void left by the addressees, now turned into characters, leaves room for ambition to address an audience as a cluster of possible readers."[141] With its self-directed alternation between internal addressees, the text progressively expands its intended readership (with the proviso of a constant hermeneutical monitoring by the author-commentator). The "compagnia di molti" (a large group of people) of *VN* 4.2 [ix 2] alternates with a selected audience able to understand Dante's "dubitose parole" (the obscurity of the words) in *VN* 7.14 [xiv 14]. On the one hand, the prosimetrum draws upon forms, motifs, and devices connected to the public and oral dimensions of medieval poetry. These range from whole compositions, such as the funeral eulogetic poems, to simple deictics that mimic the context of a public performance, such as the pronoun *voi* in "Voi che portate la sembianza umile" (You whose expressions are so meek and low). On the other hand, the *libello* envisions an audience made of cultivated literates who can move objections to Dante's poetry on the basis of their rhetorical training. Such is the case of the articulate excursus on poetics (*VN* 16 [xxv]), which opens with an eloquent prebuttal—in rhetorical terms, a *procatalepsis*—of possible opponents' arguments.

The tension between an elitist circle of readers and a more inclusive audience partially reflects the dialectic between Dante's drive to condition interpretation and the release of textual and hermeneutic control, between the uninterrupted commentative and imitative practices and the *libello*'s material dissemination necessary for his self-promotion. As Ascoli points out, "Dante's simultaneous occupation of the roles of commenting *lector* and commented-upon *auctor* hastens along the authorizing process by modeling it for future readers."[142] In *VN* 19.2 (xxviii 2), this dialectic between hermeneutic control and the release of such control is personified in the cryptic reference to the "altro chiosatore" (another commentator, but also, by extension, interpreter of the events) who is entrusted with the spin-off "trattato" (in the generic sense of treatment of a subject) on the omitted topic of Beatrice's death.[143] This presumably cultivated reader/writer might very well be a further distinction in, and different instantiation of, Dante's authorial personae, but also another unspecified author such as the even "più sottile persona" (subtler person) who would see a "più sottile ragione" (subtler reason) in Beatrice's elective affinity with her distinctive number nine; even subtler, that is, than the not-too-dull astrological and Trinitarian reasons already provided by Dante *auctor* (*VN* 19.7 [xxix 4]).[144]

The prosimetrum parallels two audiences: an audience within and an audience without. According to Judson B. Allen, "a poem fully understood is larger than its textuality, and includes, by assimilation, its audience and its commentary as well, by which and because of which it functions as part of the system of parallel systems of which the world is composed."[145] The possible reading audience outside the *libello* progressively overtakes and includes the partial receivers of the individual poems inside.

THE *VITA NOVA*'S "IMPLIED BOOK"

Looking on narrative theory from a media studies perspective, Christine Putzo conceptualizes the "implied book" as the "author's historically assumable, not necessarily conscious idea of how his text, which is still in the process of creation, will be dimensionally created and under these circumstances visually absorbed."[146] The implied book, in other words, represents the material form anticipated for the textual form and whose characteristics the text reflects. The implied book assumable for the *Vita nova* would be historically reconducible to the codicological features of the book forms Dante was familiar with and likely predicted his work would resemble. In the *Vita nova*, the implied book is also "explained" by the prosimetrum's metalanguage: it is explicitly made to assume the material characteristics assigned to the *libello* in the text.

The implied book of the *Vita nova* is a foundational aspect of the prosimetrum's composition. As such, it also contributes to shaping the text and structures its narrative. The macro-prospective of the *libello* illustrates—and is inscribed with—the coherence of the protagonist's developmental trajectory. The material configuration intended for the prosimetrum, and described in the prosimetrum, highlights the cross-references and echoes among poems. The cohesion of the narrative allows for the resemanticization and emendation of earlier compositions and also for the seamless insertion of ad hoc newly composed poems into the prosimetrum. And the organic distribution of verse and prose in a materially self-contained structure describes the protagonist's sublimation of erotic desire through poetry, while also indicating the appropriate hermeneutical itinerary for the reader.[147]

Chapter 1 argued that the *Vita nova*'s metanarrative statements provided a theoretical method for narrativity itself. Chapter 2 has now outlined how Dante detailed the material resources he would avail himself of for writing a narrative that could both control its own meaning—*littera* through *sententia*—and display its textual self-sufficiency through its self-declared codicological autonomy.

But the history of the social diffusion of Dante's work often shows, as Giuseppe Petronio pointed out, a dialectic between "the work's intentional destination, that is, the one its author intends, and its effective destination or diffusion, the one it successfully attains."[148] In chapter 3, we will observe that this dialectic also includes the material modes—intended vis-à-vis effective—of such destination and diffusion. By exploring this dialectic in four of the earliest complete transcriptions of the *Vita nova,* we will see how other literary figures and actors who shared many codes and conventions of Dante's own manuscript culture received the prosimetrum. And we will see to what extent the *Vita nova*'s self-referentiality left its traces in the manuscript tradition of the *libello.*

CHAPTER THREE

The Scribe as Author

> Quegli che queste cose così non essere state dicono, avrei molto caro che essi recassero gli originali.
>
> —Giovanni Boccaccio, *Decameron*, IV, "Introduzione"

Material Discourse

A document providing valuable testimony on the early circulation of the *Vita nova* recently resurfaced from the depths of the Archivio di Stato in Bologna. Luca Azzetta tracked down a scrap of paper, dated to 1306, transmitting the theft charges that Bolognese notary Iacopo di Domenico Mascarone pressed against Pietro (aka Petruccio) di Zaccaria da Musignano.[1] Allegedly, Petruccio "had violently, premeditatedly, maliciously, furtively, and evilly stolen from him a parchment book titled *Vita nova* and some other registers bound with it through two wooden boards, valued (book and registers) at an estimated fifteen *lire* of *bolognini*."[2] The exact content of this bound volume is difficult to determine. Guido Zaccagnini, who first referenced the notary deed transmitted in the scrap of paper in 1918, thought the *rationes* bound together with the *Vita nova* were likely *razos*—narrative texts in prose like the prosimetrum's *ragioni*.[3] Focusing on the notarized diversity between those *quedam alie rationes diverse* and the *liber* of the *Vita nova*—though *diverse* could arguably here describe generic multiplicity—Azzetta excludes the possibility that the *rationes diverse* could have contained literary materials and posits instead that they might be accounting ledgers. The disputed book could thus be a "libro di famiglia" (family book)—a book of memory of a sort—and represent a unique such case in the *libello*'s manuscript tradition.[4] Unfortunately, we have no other record of this allegedly purloined book, and there is no manuscript matching this 1306 description among the forty-three extant manuscripts in which the *Vita nova* has been preserved. Yet those dozens of surviving manuscripts do allow us to see how the earliest copyists of the *Vita nova* interpreted and materially executed some of the metatextual references integrated in the prosimetrum (and examined in the previous chapters). This chapter describes the dialectics between the *libello*'s references to its own materiality and textuality and their various effects on the *libelli* that historically transmitted it.

When we work on medieval textuality, we must necessarily engage with the simultaneous study of both the discursive and the material dimensions of literary texts. We must account, as Martin Irvine asserts, for both "the systems of literary or textual language that formed the archive of discourse for medieval textual communities" and "the material or physical form of texts in actual manuscripts."[5] To put it differently, the production and interpretation of meaning happen at the confluence of literary codes and conventions (tropes, motifs, genres, meters, styles) and material supports and techniques (fasciculation, *mise-en-page*, script). The study of the material aspects of Dante's works, however, is notoriously complicated by the absence of autographs—an absence that, at least for one of Dante's works, stands in stark contrast to the plethora of extant manuscripts.[6] The tradition of the *Commedia* alone consists of about 850 manuscripts, fragmentary or complete, textually corrupted and contaminated as a result of the poem's early, widespread circulation (often in single canticles or groups of cantos).[7]

Despite the lack of autographs, however, we can still provide a critical reflection on the materiality of Dante's book by exploring how the metatextual references integrated in the *Vita nova* were understood and implemented in four of the earliest complete transcriptions of the prosimetrum (with occasional hints at other early codices).[8] The purpose here is neither the improbable reconstruction of a virtual autograph of the *Vita nova* from the textual and material references disseminated into its *fabula*, nor the evaluation of the copyists' accuracy in interpreting and deterministically executing the transcriptional and hermeneutical guidelines embedded in the *libello*.[9] Rather, when we investigate the metatextual references integrated in the prosimetrum vis-à-vis their material renditions in the earliest copies of the *libello* we better understand—we *see* more clearly—that Dante and the copyists who would transcribe his works shared textual and codicological models and a concept of textuality coextensive with materiality. The literary project of Dante's *Vita nova* described in the prosimetrum's metanarrative statements is set to exploit material conventions of medieval Italian scribal cultures. The self-contained quality of the book form of the *libello*, and the functional organization and visual presentation of its *ordinatio*—as they are metatextually outlined in the *Vita nova*—reference actual forms and codes that we find in the manuscript tradition of medieval Italian texts, including, at least partially, in the manuscript tradition of the *libello*. In the self-concluded quality and visual features that the *libello* ascribes to itself we recognize, in other words, a material intentionality that parallels and embodies the literary aspects of self-authorization, resemanticization, militant orientation, and artifactual order of prose and poetry that we see in the prosimetrum. Modeled on the codicological forms familiar to Dante, the material properties signaled in the *libello*'s metanarrative statements were programmed in concert with its literary innovations to control future copying and interpreting of the text. By inscribing the making of the *Vita nova* in the text itself, then, Dante attempted to create a work that would be stable and recognizable in its future material iterations.

And yet, when we examine the material "afterlife" of the *Vita nova*'s metanarrative expressions—which ones the copyists attended to and which ones they neglected—we also see that the codicological self-sufficiency and visual argumentation Dante had devised for the *libello*, and inscribed in the *libello*'s enunciated (in the *libello*'s utterance), were only partially executed in the manuscripts that preserve the earliest complete transcriptions of the prosimetrum. Copyists could adulterate, modify, recodify, restructure, and reorder texts, often in spite of or against the material and textual instructions embedded in the exemplars from which they transcribed. Similarly, Dante's implicit aspiration that the *Commedia* be copied as a university desk book

(*Paradiso* 10.22–23) was not uniformly received in the early textual tradition of the poem.[10] Patrons and scribes often determined book forms more than authors did when they elected their intended readership.[11] If Dante's misconceptions about manuscript culture led him to imagine an improbable scholastic book form for the *Commedia* (as Armando Petrucci maintained), similar misconceptions deluded him into thinking that his metatextual directions for an unprecedented work such as the *Vita nova* would be unambiguously understood and dependably applied.[12]

Writing the Booklet

The manuscripts preserving the *Vita nova* that we examine in this chapter date from the first half of the fourteenth century (with the exception of MS Chigi L.V.176, dated to the second decade of the second half).[13] These are their current shelf marks (in parentheses, their *sigla* in Barbi's edition):

> Florence, Biblioteca Medicea Laurenziana, MS Martelli 12 (*M*)
> Toledo, Archivo y Biblioteca Capitulares, MS Zelada 104.6 (*To*)
> Vatican City, Biblioteca Apostolica Vaticana, MS Chigi L.V.176 (K^2)
> Vatican City, Biblioteca Apostolica Vaticana, MS Chigi L.VIII.305 (*K*)

Each of the four codices occupies a prominent position in the textual tradition of the *libello*. Manuscript Martelli 12 is the earliest preserved copy of the *Vita nova*. Manuscript Chigi L.VIII.305 is considered the most reliable witness of the *libello* (both textually and "ideologically"). Manuscripts Zelada 104.6 and Chigi L.V.176 are Giovanni Boccaccio's autographs and established the vulgate version of the prosimetrum for more than four centuries.[14] Importantly, all manuscripts transmitting the *libello* associate the *Vita nova* with other texts. Multitext and multiauthor compilations were often, in the Middle Ages, the product of circumstantial rather than semantic decisions. Compilers might have had limited options for materials to choose from, and scribes not otherwise explicitly instructed would often comply with the characteristics of the antigraph on their bench. The study of textual and material associations within the manuscript, however, can often provide valuable insight on the ideology behind a codicological project.[15]

MSS Martelli 12 and Chigi L.VIII.305

If that paper scrap from the Archivio di Stato in Bologna, in the course of documenting its theft, bears witness to the presence of the prosimetrum—and, it has been recently argued, of Dante himself[16]—north of Florence in 1306, then MS Martelli 12 (hereafter, *M*) offers a precocious testimony of the *libello*'s early circulation south of Florence. It also shows an interesting responsiveness to some of the metatextual references encoded in the prosimetrum.

M is a parchment codex of medium-small format begun in Gubbio (Umbria) during approximately the first quarter of the fourteenth century and completed in Florence by the first half of the fourteenth century.[17] It is the *Vita nova*'s most ancient complete witness and, quite exceptionally, was probably copied when Dante was still alive. *M* is a composite, miscellaneous codex written by six different hands and preserves very heterogeneous materials: in prose and poetry, in Latin and the vernacular, from chivalric tales to dream books.[18] The scribe usually indicated with γ (or C) is the copyist of a selection of poems (fols. 25–32) by Guido Cavalcanti and Dante—separated by a *ballata* by the less remarkable Caccia di Castello—and also the *Vita nova* (fols. 35–51). Sandro Bertelli proposed that γ be identified with Pietro Berzoli, the second scribe of the Occitan chansonnier *P*, completed on March 28, 1310.[19] The material and intertextual relationship between chansonnier *P*, Dante's *Vita nova*, and manuscript *M* extend further. According to D'Arco Silvio Avalle—who built on Salvatore Santangelo's crucial work on Dante and Occitan poets—chansonnier *P* or a closely related anthology was at some point on Dante's "desk," since it probably was the source of information on Occitan poetry for Dante's *De vulgari eloquentia*.[20] As Todorović posits, chansonnier *P* adopts peculiar material choices for the distribution of poems, *vidas*, and *razos*, thus creating mini-prosimetra.[21] Furthermore, according to Paolo Trovato (after Arrigo Castellani's observation that the Umbran and Florentine sections of *M* were bound together in Florence by the mid-fourteenth century), it is possible that *M* briefly passed through Boccaccio's hands when *M* was in Florence: Boccaccio might have consulted it before putting forth his own "edition" of the *Vita nova*.[22]

Scribe γ copies the *Vita nova* in two columns in a sober *littera textualis* (Gothic book hand). A series of paragraphemic notations marks the internal articulation of the prosimetrum. The scribe applies the same transcriptional criteria to the poems of the *Vita nova* as those he uses for the selection of poems that precedes it. Each poem starts with a filigreed capital, alternately blue and red, corresponding to two lines of text.[23] The transcription of the poems follows the same format throughout the text. Sonnets are transcribed vertically in one column, as is the only *ballata*. *Canzoni* are transcribed continuously, as prose, and paragraph signs indicate strophic divisions (see pl. 3.1).

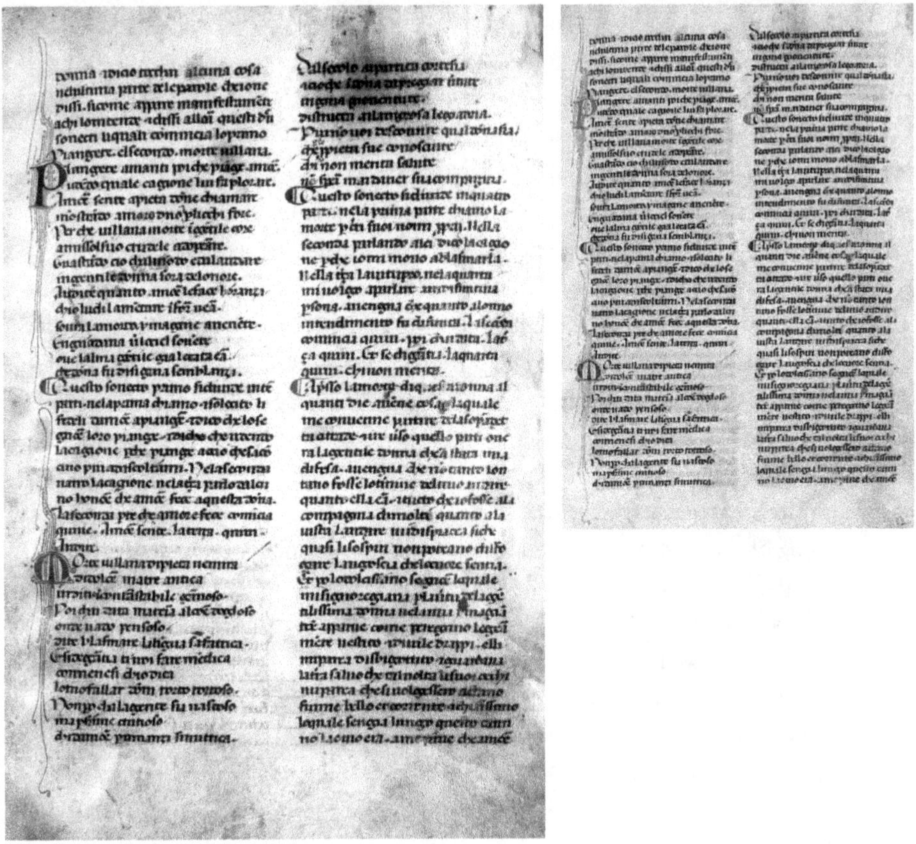

Plate 3.1. Florence, Biblioteca Medicea Laurenziana, MS Martelli 12, fol. 37r. The color image shows the filigreed blue and red initials marking the incipits of the poems. By permission of the MiC (Ministero della Cultura). Further reproduction in any medium is forbidden.

The copyist transcribes poems and prose without interruption. The prose sections are introduced by paragraph signs, placed at the left margin of the column. Alternating blue and red paragraph signs regularly mark the *divisioni* after each poem before Beatrice's death and, accordingly, the *divisioni* before the poems in the section after her death. The same paragraph notations variously subdivide the narrative prose of the *ragioni*.[24]

The copyist gives clear precedence to the poems over the prose: with the exception of the actual incipit of the proem, filigreed initials only mark poetic compositions. Dante scholars disagree on whether the *parole* mentioned in the proem designate only the prosimetrum's poetry or the prose also. Scribe γ would seem to adhere to the former position and follow an acceptation of the term authorized by the *Vita nova* itself. The codicological features of *M*, in fact, suggest that scribe γ intends the prosimetrum to be first and foremost a poetic anthology with commentary.[25]

The early date around which scribe γ operates (optimistically, less than twenty-five years after the composition of the *Vita nova*) makes *M* a unique witness to the early circulation, reception, and reproduction of the *libello*. Moreover, scribe γ shows a subtle understanding of, and an interesting response to, the material implications of the metatextual references provided by the text within the story and at the discourse level—in the substance of the enunciated and by the subject of the enunciating. In *M*, the *Vita nova* is preceded by a rubric in red (fol. 35r): "*Incipit vita nova*."[26] In the context of medieval manuscripts, this notation signposts—prior to any symbolic implications of regeneration through the experience of love—the material beginning of the work and the indication of its title. As such, in *M* it assumes the clear position of a title in the upper margin of the folio, heading the text proper (see pl. 3.2).[27]

An apparently similar type of rubrication opens the *Vita nova* in a Tuscan manuscript from the middle of the fourteenth century, the so-called MS Strozziano (indicated with the *siglum S* by Barbi): "Incipit il libro della nuova vita di Dante" (fol. 4r).[28] The relationship between literary texts and the media that give form to them is rarely deterministic. However, the use of the vernacular (instead of Latin) and the specific labeling of the *Vita nova* as *libro* (despite the presence of the term *libello* in the text seven lines below) may reveal a less subtle interpretation and more naïve material rendition of

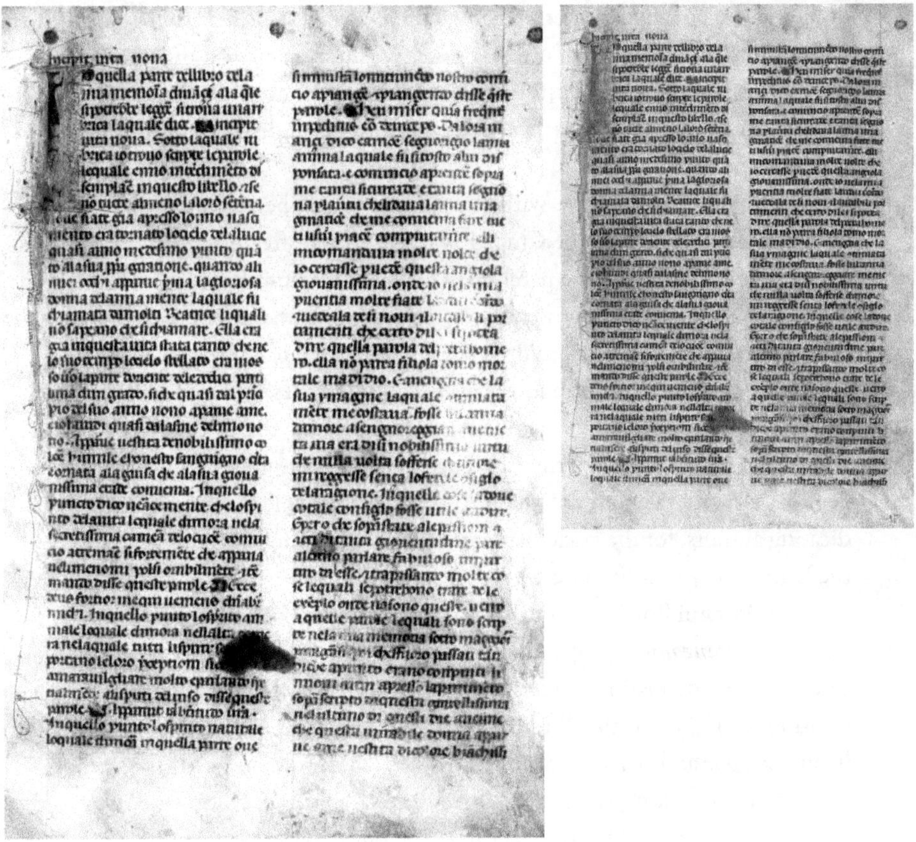

Plate 3.2. Florence, Biblioteca Medicea Laurenziana, MS Martelli 12, fol. 35r. The color image shows the red rubric opening the *Vita nova*. By permission of the MiC (Ministero della Cultura). Further reproduction in any medium is forbidden.

the *libello*'s metatextual references. It is only in *M* that an identical *rubrica* is first used as a heading and then in fact mentioned in the text as a structuring metaphor, creating a peculiar negotiation between the text and its material threshold: the prosimetrum interpolates and thematizes what we would now call a paratextual feature within the narrative, while the manuscript extrapolates the rubric from the text and assigns it to the paratext. Along the same lines is the colophon "*Explicit liber. Deo gratias, amen.*," which in *M* immediately follows the blessing formula that closes the prosimetrum (fol. 52r). We do not know how many intermediate manuscripts (*codices interpositi*) separate *M* from the archetype of the *Vita nova*. We do see, however, that the earliest witness of the prosimetrum preserves a material execution of the text that shows the copyist's awareness of the interpretive guidelines embedded in the substance of its *fabula*.

A simplified red rubric with the indication of the author opens the prosimetrum in manuscript Chigi L.VIII.305 (hereafter, *K*): "Dante Alaghieri" (on fol. 7r).[29] *K* is a parchment codex of medium-large format produced in Tuscany in the second quarter of the fourteenth century. The codex is a *canzoniere* of almost six hundred poems, attributed to approximately one hundred poets, copied continuously over sixteen fascicles.[30] The anonymous, professionally trained scribe (scribe A) responsible for the vast majority of the texts (534 out of 543) writes full-page in chancery minuscule. This "diligent copyist and talented calligrapher" is also responsible for the rubrics indicating authors, for the fasciculation instructions, and for the translations of the Latin passages of the *Vita nova*.[31]

As Giovanni Borriero has demonstrated, what had been in the past considered the *canzoniere*'s apparent "huge mess" expresses instead a sophisticated double articulation.[32] Texts are first organized based on a metrical opposition, or rather on the different prestige of different meters: on the one hand, *canzoni* and *ballate*, and on the other hand, sonnets (with *tenzoni*). This metrical ranking is repeated three times—enacting "a sort of *climax*, which is both descending and cyclical"—and outlines a critical-aesthetic orientation.[33] Major poets of the Stilnovo (with Dante) are followed by minor Stilnovisti, and, finally, by other Sicilian and Tuscan poets (with a further marginalization of realistic, comical, and burlesque poetry). The repeated scheme and dialectic correlation between form and author show a specific ideology behind the manuscript's structure. *K* is generally considered "the *Dolce stil novo* manuscript according to Dante's perspective."[34] It represents the material formalization of Dante's new poetics and poetic canon.

Scribe A transcribes *canzoni* and *ballate* continuously, like prose, with various types of paragraphemic signs indicating the end of each verse. Sonnets are transcribed horizontally, two verses per line. The Gothic initials of the poems vary: large blue and red filigreed initials mark the first poem at the beginning of sections dedicated to major Stilnovisti, and medium monochromatic (alternating blue and red) filigreed initials correspond to the in-

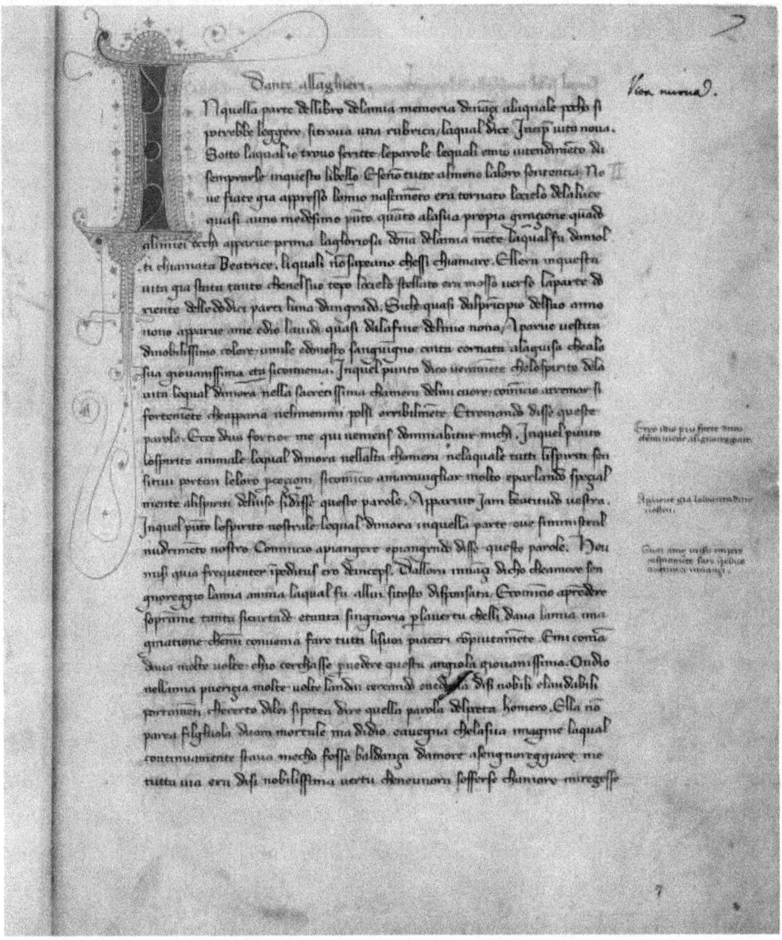

Plate 3.3. Vatican City, Biblioteca Apostolica Vaticana, MS Chigi L.VIII.305, fol. 7r. By permission of the Biblioteca Apostolica Vaticana.

cipit of the poems within each section. Alternating blue and red paragraph signs indicate strophic units within the poems.[35]

In the first cluster of *canzoni* and *ballate*, fascicles i–iv transmit the *Vita nova* (fols. 7r–27v). Devoid of its self-styled codicological autonomy, the *libello* is transcribed in material continuation and fascicular solidarity with an anthology of poems. On fol. 7r, a larger than usual filigreed blue and red capital also opens the prosimetrum (see pl. 3.3). Much as we have observed in *M*, the poems of the *libello* in *K* follow the same transcriptional norms as the other poems of the songbook and are marked by the same initials. In the *mise-en-page* of the *Vita nova*, Donato Pirovano concludes, "scribe A shows a general tendency to highlight poetic compositions for the reader with signs similar to those used in the other lyrical sections of the Chigi chansonnier [*sc. K*]."[36] With the exception of the prosimetrum's incipit, the prose sections are not granted a distinctive initial. A paragraph sign indicates the return of the prose following the poems (*divisioni* in the section *in vita*, *ragioni* in the section *in morte*). In spite of the *libello*'s own metareference to the paragraphs in its antigraph (the book of Dante's memory), *K* presents no systematic subdivision for the prose. The *ragioni* and the *divisioni* are not differentiated from each other. Despite its prose accretions, the *Vita nova* in the quintessential *Dolce stil novo* manuscript is presented as a poetic anthology.

Giovanni Boccaccio's Transcriptions

It is a common (and intuitive) opinion that authors make books. As Roger Chartier and Peter Stallybrass maintain, however, the opposite can also be true: "Books create authors when scribes, editors, or publishers bring together a range of texts under an authorial name."[37] Noteworthy in regard to the second set of manuscripts we will examine below is the role played by their copyist in shaping the *Vita nova*'s textual tradition and the early canon of Italian literature (its "invention," according to Martin Eisner); our copyist is none other than Giovanni Boccaccio.[38] From the 1350s on, Boccaccio devoted much of his intellectual efforts to the celebration of Dante as *auctor*, possibly well aware of the positive repercussions for his own literary career.[39] We have two extant copies of Boccaccio's transcription of the *Vita nova*, transmitted in two manuscripts that represent the matrix of the so-called *b* branch of the α family of Barbi's *stemma codicum*.[40] These are MS Zelada 104.6 (1348–55) of the Biblioteca Capitular in Toledo (hereafter, *To*), and MS Chigi L.V.176 (ca. 1363–66), preserved in the Biblioteca Apostolica Vaticana (hereafter, K^2).[41] With regard to the *Vita nova*, K^2 is a *descriptus* of *To* (a manuscript derived from *To*) but presents original features in the material execution of the *libello*.[42] The comparative study of *To* and K^2 shows Boccaccio's search for textual and codicological solutions suitable for Dante's prosimetrum—and for the macro-prosimetra that *To* and K^2 ultimately are—and his continuous confrontation with the *libello* foreshadows his active engagement with the prosimetrum as form in his own literary production.[43]

The contents of the two manuscripts and their material presentation reveal Boccaccio's distinctive and evolving interpretation of Dante's work. *To* is Boccaccio's first formal compilation of Dante's texts.[44] It is a parchment codex of medium-small format in Boccaccio's characteristic book hand. It preserves the first redaction of the *Trattatello in laude di Dante* (Life of Dante), the *Vita nova*, the *Commedia* with the *Argomenti* in *terza rima* (also known as *Brieve raccoglimento*, "brief synthesis"), and Dante's fifteen *canzoni distese* (i.e., polystrophic *canzoni*).[45] In short, it transmits Boccaccio's edition of a strictly Dantean anthology—a "tutto Dante" (everything Dante), in Domenico De Robertis's words—with Boccaccio's own prefatory and paratextual apparatus.[46] K^2 is also a parchment codex of medium-small format. Battaglia Ricci described it as "Boccaccio's autograph ideal library of vernacular texts."[47] K^2 currently contains the following: the second redaction of the *Trattatello in laude di Dante*; the *Vita nova*; Guido Cavalcanti's doctrinal *canzone* "Donna me prega" (A lady bids me), accompanied by physician Dino del Garbo's Latin commentary; Boccaccio's hexametric *carmen* "Ytalie iam certus honos" (Already certain honor of Italy), addressed to Francesco Petrarca to accompany the gift of a copy of Dante's *Commedia*; Dante's fifteen *canzoni distese*; and Petrarca's *Fragmentorum liber* (*Book of Fragments*), the so-called Chigi form of the *Rerum vulgarium fragmenta*.[48] Through the compilation of K^2, Boccaccio translates into codicological forms the heartfelt plea that closes "Ytalie iam certus honos," an invitation to Petrarca to join the latter's own works to Dante's *Commedia*: v. 38, "iunge tuis . . . [*sc.* operibus]" (attach this work to yours). It is worth noting that a Petrarchan section also closes the aforementioned manuscript *K* (MS Chigi L.VIII.305): in the last quarter of the fourteenth century, an anonymous scribe (not scribe A) added a binio transmitting seven sonnets and one *canzone* by Petrarca (fols. 120r–121r), further evidence of the early institution of a Dante/Petrarca teleology among medieval readers.

In *To*, the *Vita nova* occupies fols. 29r–46v. The prosimetrum starts on a new leaf (fol. 29r) and corresponds to an independent subunit of three quires within the codex (fascicles v–vii, two quaterniones and a binio). In his scribal practice, Boccaccio used different transcriptional techniques.[49] We see an example of split transcription at work here: codicological units are made independently and then composed into one book project. Practical reasons, such as having access to discrete unbound—or temporarily bound—texts and the work-in-progress nature of this anthology, could certainly explain *To*'s fasciculation.[50] But the *Vita nova*'s codicological self-sufficiency in *To* reflects, and de facto complies with, the notion of *libello* as a self-concluded codicological unit. The prosimetrum's material autonomy from the preceding *Trattatello* is further suggested by the removal of fol. 28, in all likelihood a leaf left blank to signal closure or to separate the two works. On fol. 29r, Boccaccio heads his transcription with the prosimetrum's title in the form of a red Latin rubric: "Incipit *Vita nova* clarissimi viri Dantis Aligerii Florentini." Boccaccio deduces the *titulus* from the *rubrica* mentioned within the narrative and restores (an amplified version of) it to the prosimetrum's threshold.[51] Boccaccio's augmented *rubrica* highlights both Dante's great fame (*clarissimus*) and—something the two had in common—illustrious Florentine origin (*Florentinus*) (see pl. 3.4).

In transcribing the *Vita nova*, Boccaccio opts for a single column of text with ample margins. The transcription presents centralized poetic texts and narrative prose units, with marginalized exegetical *divisioni*. A large blue initial *I* with red filigree (corresponding to approximately eight lines of text) opens the *libello*. The poems and ensuing narrative sections are marked by filigreed red and blue initials. The verses of the poems are transcribed continuously like prose and separated by a *coma*, "a dot beneath a comma with a swash leaning right."[52] The closure of the poems is indicated by a *periodus* (similar to a semicolon). Distinctive majuscules also indicate the interstrophic divisions in the *canzoni* and the two tercets in the sirma of the sonnets.[53] Paragraph signs and yellow majuscules open the *divisioni*, which are transcribed in the margins in a smaller module. On fol. 41r, a single blank line separates what we generally refer to as sections *in vita* and *in morte* of Beatrice. The citation from Jeremiah's Lamentations (*VN* 19.1 [xxviii 1]) is marked by a blue initial *Q* (with red filigree) of larger module (corresponding to three lines of text, but smaller than the incipitarian *I* that opens the *libello*).

We have seen how *To* accurately preserves the codicological autonomy of all textual units: the beginning of each work coincides with the beginning

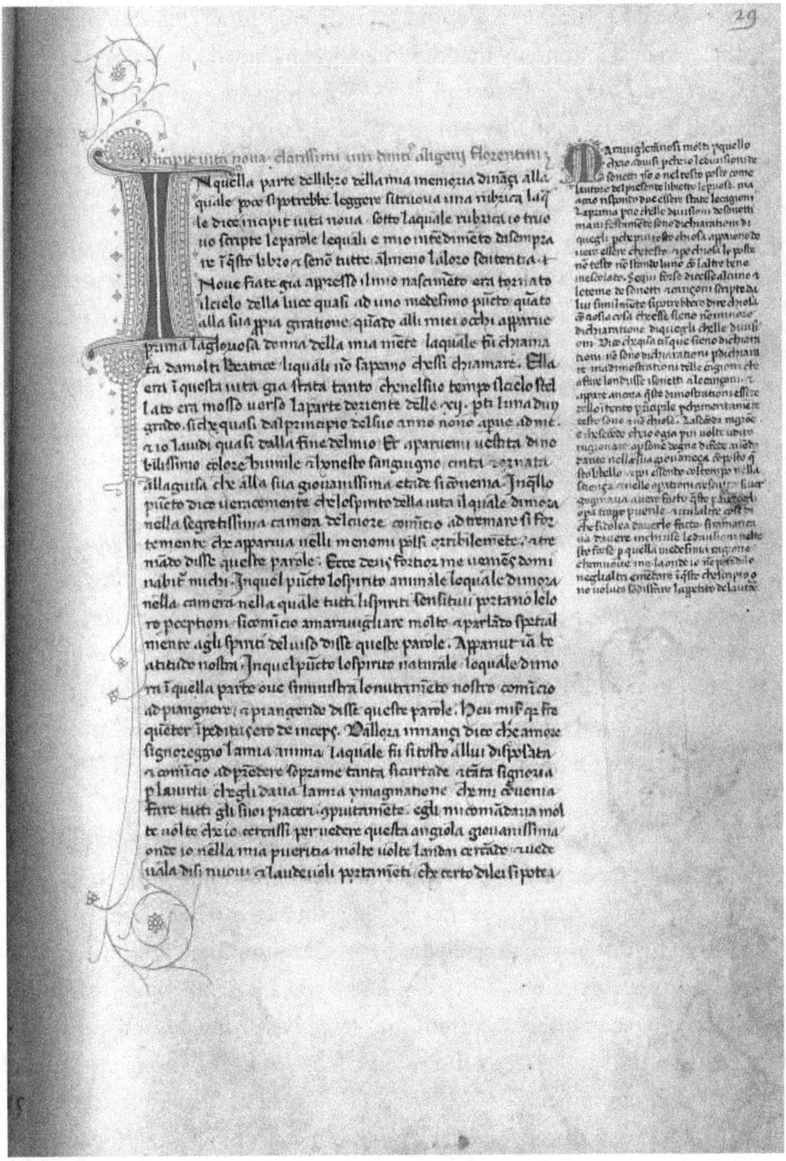
Incipit uita noua clarissimi uiri danti aligery florentini
IN quella parte dellibro della mia memoria dinazi alla
quale poco si potrebbe leggere si truoua una rubrica laq
le dice incipit uita noua · sotto laquale rubrica io truo
uo scripte le parole lequali e mio intendimento diasempra
re i qsto libro e se no tutte almeno la loro sententia ·
Noue fiate gia appresso il mio nascimento era tornato
il cielo della luce quasi ad uno medesimo puncto quanto
alla sua ppia giratione quando alli miei occhi apparue
prima la gloriosa donna della mia mente laquale fu chiama
ta da molti Beatrice liquali no sapeano chessi chiamare. Ella
era i questa uita gia stata tanto che nel suo tempo si lcielo stel
lato era mosso uerso la parte doriente delle · xij · pti luna duy
grado · sicche quasi dal principio del suo anno nono apue ad me ·
e io la uidi quasi dalla fine del mio · Et apparuemi uestita dino
bilissimo colore humile et honesto sanguigno cinta e ornata
alla guisa che alla sua giouanissima etade si conuenia. Inqllo
puncto dico ueracemente che lo spirito della uita ilquale dimora
nella segretissima camera del cuore comincio ad tremare si for
temente che apparia nelli menomi polsi orribilemente · e tre
mando disse queste parole · Ecce deus fortior me ueniens domi
nabitur michi · Inquel puncto lo spirito animale loquale dimora
nella camera nella quale tutti lispiriti sensitiui portano le lo
ro perceptioni si comincio amarauigliare molto e parlando spetial
mente agli spiriti del uiso disse queste parole. Apparuit iam be
atitudo nostra · Inquel puncto lo spirito naturale loquale dimo
ra i quella parte oue si ministra lo nutrimento nostro comincio
ad piangnere e piangendo disse queste parole. Heu miser quia fre
quenter impeditus ero de incepts. Dallora innanzi dico che amore
signoreggio la mia anima laquale fu si tosto allui disposata
e comincio ad prendere sopra me tanta sicurtade e tanta signoria
p la uirtu che gli daua la mia ymaginatione che mi conuenia
fare tutti gli suoi piaceri compiutamente. egli mi comandaua mol
te uolte che io cercassi per uedere questa angiola giouanissima
onde io nella mia puerita molte uolte landai cercando e uede
uala di si nuoui e laudeuoli portamenti che certo di lei si potea

Plate 3.4. Toledo, Archivo y Biblioteca Capitulares, MS Zelada 104.6, fol. 29r. By permission of the Archivo y Biblioteca Capitulares, Catedral de Toledo.

of a new fascicle. Boccaccio's second transcription in K^2, instead, dismisses the codicological autonomy that the *Vita nova* metatextually claims for itself (its self-styled *libello* form) (see pl. 3.5). Not only is the prosimetrum transcribed in fascicular solidarity with the *Trattatello*, but on fol. 13r the explicit of the latter and the incipit of the former are also integrated into a single *rubrica* in vernacular (vis-à-vis *To*'s option for Latin):

> Qui finiscie *Della origine, vita et studij et costumi di Dante Alighieri poeta chiarissimo et dell'opere composte da lui*. Et comincia la sua *Vita nuova*: nella quale esso in sonetti, ballate et canzoni distese discrive come di Beatrice s'innamorasse; et del suo amore et li accidenti mentre ella visse; et appresso quanta et quale fosse la sua amaritudine dopo la partita di Beatrice dalla presente vita.
>
> ———
>
> (Here ends *Della origine, vita et studij et costumi di Dante Alighieri poeta chiarissimo et dell'opere composte da lui* [*Of the Origin, Life, Studies, and Manners of the Most Famous Poet Dante Alighieri and of the Works Composed by Him*]. And begins his *Vita nuova*: in which he describes how he fell in love with Beatrice in sonnets, ballads, and polystrophic *canzoni*; and his love and the events while she was alive; and then how much and how deep his despair was after Beatrice's parting from this life.)[54]

In K^2, the *Vita nova* occupies fols. 13r–28v. K^2 presents a set of paragraphemic and diacritical signs similar to those used in *To*.[55] As in *To*, the *divisioni* are transcribed in the margins in a smaller module. Even more so than *To*, K^2 institutes a materially dramatic separation between the sections *in vita* and *in morte*: on fol. 24r, a blank line and a four-line-high red initial with blue filigree mark the citation from Jeremiah's Lamentations, enhancing what Gorni defined a re-rubrication of the *libello*.[56] The ensuing prose ("Io era nel proponimento . . ."; I was still engaged . . .) is not marked (see pl. 3.6). Boccaccio dismisses the *Vita nova*'s metatextually sanctioned division into three narrative sections (punctuated by the explicit references to the taking on of new materials: *VN* 10.1 [xvii 1] and 19.8 [xxx 1]). He enacts, instead, a thematic/narrative dichotomy that underlines Dante's itinerary of erotic sublimation after the death of the beloved. Accordingly, he also emphasizes the parallelism between the Latin incipit, the Latin explicit, and the

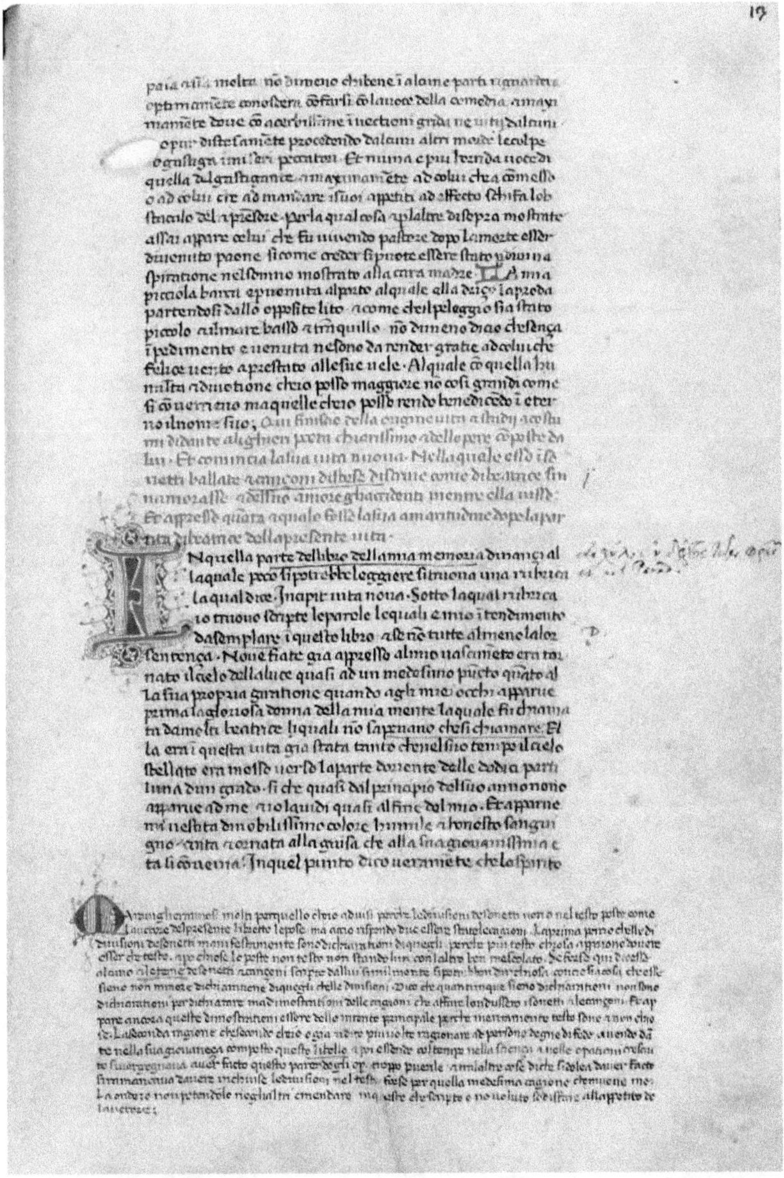

Plate 3.5. Vatican City, Biblioteca Apostolica Vaticana, MS Chigi L.V.176, fol. 13r. By permission of the Biblioteca Apostolica Vaticana.

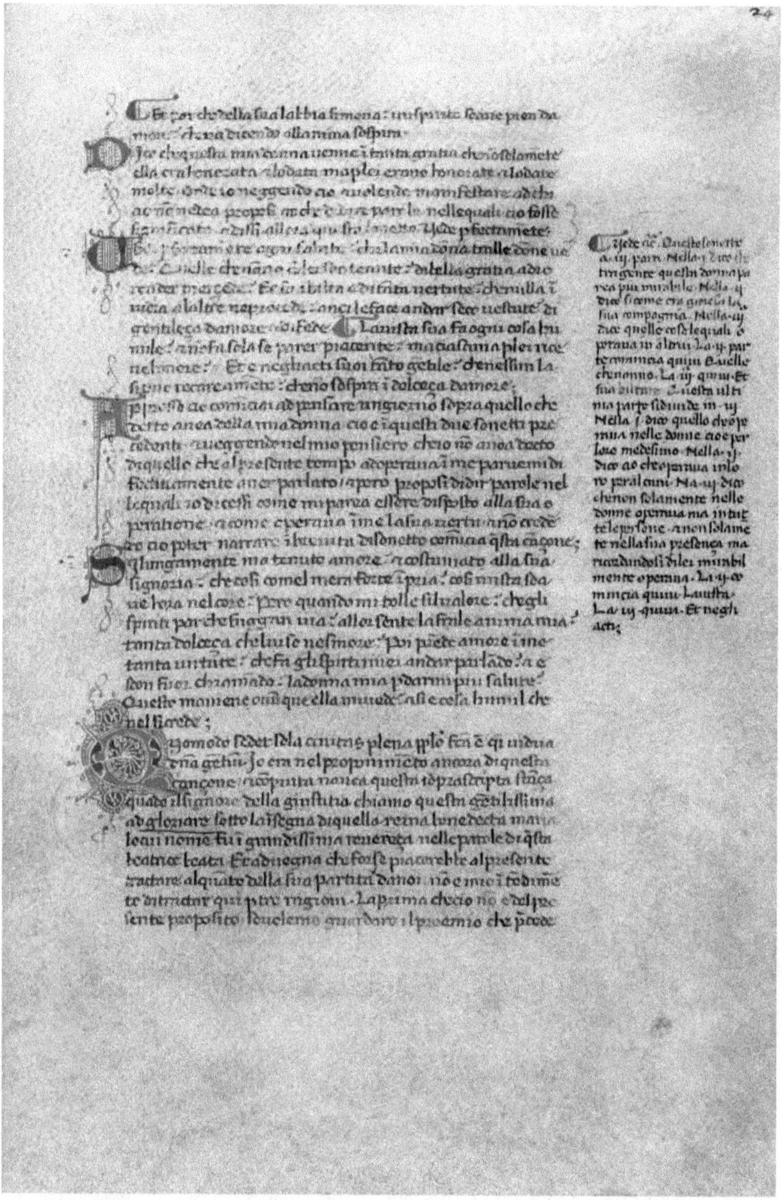

Plate 3.6. Vatican City, Biblioteca Apostolica Vaticana, MS Chigi L.V.176, fol. 24r. By permission of the Biblioteca Apostolica Vaticana.

new *proemio al mezzo* (proem in the middle) signposted by the Latin citation from Lamentations 1:1, whose proemial function Boccaccio could possibly infer from its alleged incipitarian position in Dante's untransmitted (if, indeed, ever written) letter to the "principi della terra" (rulers of the land) as well as in Dante's materially documented (and well known to Boccaccio) *Epistle* 11.[57] It has been observed that this noteworthy accentuation of a bipartite structure of the *Vita nova* through a corresponding material division reflects the treatment reserved for Petrarca's *Liber fragmentorum* (transmitted on fols. 43v–79r of K^2): fol. 72rv of the *Liber fragmentorum* is left blank after the sonnet "Passa la nave mia colma d'oblio" (My ship laden with forgetfulness passes). The *Vita nova*'s bipartite structure could thus be a backformation modeled on Petrarca's *canzoniere* and date back to Boccaccio's authoritative edition of the prosimetrum.[58] In chapters 6 and 7, we will return to this narrative and material fracture to observe how Petrarca handles it in the autograph of the *Rerum vulgarium fragmenta.*

The textual transmission of the *libello* shows how professional and highly trained scribes interpret the textual form of the prosimetrum and opt for different textual styles and *mise-en-page*. In doing this, each scribe tackles the prosimetrum's unexplained (if not wholly unprecedented) self-exegetical apparatus and attempts to solve the transcriptional aporia of the arrangement of poems, *ragioni*, and *divisioni*: distinctive features that still puzzle modern critics.[59] We have seen how *M* and *K* transcribe poems and prose sections continually as one compact block of text and institute a hierarchy of verse over prose by means of distinctive initials and paragraphemic signs.[60]

In the first redaction of the *Trattatello*, upon mentioning the tripartite articulation of the "volumetto" (little volume) into poems, *cagioni* (Dante's alternative term for *ragioni* in *VN* 7.13 [xiv 13]), and *divisioni*, Boccaccio explicitly, if not entirely accurately, refers to their mutual arrangement on the page: "di sopra da ciascuna [*sc.* operetta per rima] partitamente e ordinatamente scrivendo le cagioni che a quelle fare l'avea[n] mosso, e di dietro ponendo le divisioni delle precedenti opere" (each of these compositions was prefaced with an explanation of the motives which had moved him to compose them, and after each one he analyzed the work's divisions).[61]

Boccaccio's transcriptions of the *Vita nova*, however, extrapolate the exegetical sections from the textual and narrative continuum and marginalize them. Boccaccio's layout entails an active editorial process of expunging sections of Dante's prose from the center of the folio and ascribing them to the margins as gloss. Boccaccio's sensibility to and awareness of these layout and textual styles emerge clearly from the editorial note in which he justifies this innovation in *To* (fol. 29r, outer margin) and again, with negligible orthographic variants, in K^2 (fol. 13r, *bas-de-page*): "Maraviglierannosi molti, per quello ch'io advisi, perché io le divisioni de' sonetti non ho nel testo poste, come l'autore del presente libretto le puose" (A great many will wonder, I believe, why I have not placed the divisions of the sonnets in the text as the author of this little book placed them) (see pls. 3.4 and 3.5).[62] Laura Banella underlines, "Boccaccio, in his role as editor, assumes for himself . . . functions proper to the author."[63] Boccaccio establishes a structural and codicological hierarchy between *ragioni* and *divisioni*. He reduces the *divisioni* to gloss (rather than text): mere "dichiarazioni per dichiarare" (explanations for the sake of explaining). Instead, he "promotes" the *ragioni*, hereby referred to as "teme" (themes), since they are "dimostrazioni delle cagioni" (demonstrations of the reasons) behind the composition of the poems. This hierarchy, however, is only partially plausible for Dante's text, where the *divisioni* often perform a distinct narrative function (at least in the characterization of Dante *agens*) and where *divisioni* and *ragioni* are explicitly made to switch position over the course of the narration, with clear semantic repercussions. Boccaccio frames his peculiar decision in a discourse of accuracy and alleged restitution of Dante's "final authorial intention," an intention made known to Boccaccio through multiple reports of unspecified "persone degne di fede" (trustworthy people):[64]

> avendo Dante nella sua giovanezza composto questo libello [*sc.* the *Vita nova*], o poi essendo col tempo nella scienza e nelle operazioni cresciuto, si vergognava avere fatto questo, parendogli opera troppo puerile; e tra l'altre cose di che si dolea d'averlo fatto, si ramaricava d'avere inchiuse le divisioni nel testo, forse per quella medesima ragione che muove me; là ond'io non potendolo negli altri emendare, in questo che scritto ho, n'ho voluto sodisfare l'appetito de l'autore.[65]
>
> ---------
>
> (Dante having composed this little book in his youth and then grown in knowledge and works, he was ashamed of having done this, since it appeared to him too childish a work; and among the other things he re-

> gretted having done, he complained about having included the divisions in the text, perhaps for that same reason that moves me; and so, being unable to emend any of the other copies, in the one I have written I have endeavored to satisfy the author's desire.)

It is unclear whether Boccaccio was unable to access Dante's *Convivio*—a work only mentioned en passant in the *Trattatello*—or deliberately ignored the passage in the *Convivio* (1.1.16–18) wherein Dante describes the *Vita nova* as the literary endeavor of his fervid and passionate youth but refuses to *derogare* ("dismiss/depart from") any of it.[66]

In spite of his declared author-centric project to establish an "ideal copy" of the *libello*, one that would account for Dante's change of heart and restore his final intention, Boccaccio's transcriptions provide instead a paradigmatic example of an early "socialization" of Dante's text and a case study for the generative process of textual works intended as social, participated-in events. His transcriptions offer an exemplary case study for how textuality and materiality depend on several textual agencies and lie at the intersection of authorial projects, transcriptional models, professional backgrounds, commissioned requests, and scholarly interests. The texts and the material artifacts in which they are embodied are contingent on editorial and hermeneutical negotiations alike between authors, copyists, patrons, readers, and scholars.

In K^2's material organization, it has been contended, the codicological and textual suture of the two works, their agglutinated *rubrica*, and the expunction of the *divisioni* from the textual continuum show Boccaccio's intention to present the *Vita nova* as the autobiographical counterpart to the biographical *Trattatello*.[67] It has also been argued that the *Vita nova* reads like a continuation and an appendix to the *Trattatello*.[68] The observations on the codicological and textual affinity between the two works are certainly valid. Furthermore, the use of the same distinctive initials and paragraph signs in K^2 enhances an aesthetic and visual uniformity between the *Trattatello* and the *Vita nova*.[69] Certainly, Boccaccio's editorial approach to the *libello* should be studied with an eye on his exegetical and biographical work on Dante, especially in light of the material contiguity between the *Trattatello*, the editorial note to the prosimetrum, and the material form of the prosimetrum proper.

And yet, Boccaccio's life of Dante culminates in the critical catalogue of Dante's texts: the narrative of Dante's life serves as an introduction to, and is functional to the understanding of, Dante's works. The prefaced work is never subordinated to its introduction. Boccaccio's biographies of poets and the various chapters of his own intellectual autobiography (disseminated throughout his works) are narrative especially insofar as they are critical-exegetical.[70] Billanovich asserted that "the choral theme in the *Trattatello* is the exaltation of the harsh defense with which Dante heroically stayed loyal to his vocation as scholar and poet against the impediments of a destitute life."[71] Both the original Latin title and the vernacular translation of what we, after the author himself, commonly refer to as the *Trattatello* show that Boccaccio's portrait of Dante is a *vida* (*De origine, vita, studiis et moribus viri clarissimi Dantis Aligerii florentini, poete illustris*) in that it is an *accessus* (*et de operibus compositis ab eodem, incipit feliciter*).[72] Even anecdotical elements are intended to establish a continuity between classical *auctores* and Dante and can be traced back, for the most part, to classical sources, such as Suetonius-Donatus and Servius.[73]

The *Trattatello* details Dante's ethical and intellectual growth (setbacks, hurdles, backslidings included) and outlines his teleological itinerary to become an *auctor*, thus more broadly authorizing literature in the vernacular. Both *To* and K^2 present a progression from prose to poetry. Whereas *To*'s selection outlines an increase of stylistic and thematic *gravitas* within Dante's corpus, K^2 establishes Dante's work as foundational for a vernacular canon and casts Dante's long shadow over subsequent literature in the Florentine vernacular. A common Florentine origin is the explicitly asserted linguistic-literary correlative to the material association of the second sylloge's texts.[74] Additionally, the marginalization of the *Vita nova*'s *divisioni* does not necessarily translate into augmented narrativity for the prosimetrum. The autobiographical continuum does acquire material and textual cohesion with the expunction of the strictly exegetical *divisioni*, but the reduplication of the verses' content in the prose—however resemanticized and reoriented that content—delays and dilutes the narrative sequence rather than heightening it. If anything, the *ragioni* elicit a recursive reading of the poem rather than the appreciation of the narrative sequence proper.

The *ordinatio* of the text through distinctive initials and paragraph signs, the ample margins reserved for curatorial practice, and the "adscript" *divisioni* give Boccaccio's Vitanovan transcriptions their scholarly (and scholastic) appearance. The visual consistency of their *mise-en-page* and *mise-en-texte* dovetails with a distinctly Gothic coherence evoked by Corrado Bologna.[75] More than the prosimetrum's narrative and autobiographical component, Boccaccio's transcriptions enhance—and translate into material forms—his idealized presentation of Dante as a vernacular *auctor*.

Boccaccio's project of authentication and institutionalization of Dante's work goes so far as to overshadow what the prosimetrum tells about its own textuality and intended material form. Boccaccio's editorial approach to and codicological choices for the *libello* indicate that Dante's concern for the correct interpretation and transmission of the *prosimetrum*—meticulously detailed in the *Vita nova*'s metanarrative and self-referential statements—was not misplaced or overly suspicious: rather, it may demonstrate that Dante was overly confident in the possibility of exerting hermeneutic and transcriptional control by means of metatextual cues. Petrarca similarly worried over how to maintain control over his materials: we will observe in chapter 6 how he more or less successfully attempted to condition the correct reproduction of his works by circulating authoritative versions of them among colleagues and admirers for transcription and divulgation.

Boccaccio's authority among scribes, literati, and scholars controlled the *Vita nova*'s peculiar reception through the centuries until Barbi's magisterial 1907 edition. As Storey observes, Boccaccio virtually obliterated "the *Vita Nova*'s unique and often intricate narratives which interweave episodes with notes on *how* and *why* the poems were composed, *how* they should be read, and *how* they should be copied and ordered by the private reader."[76] The copies of the *Vita nova* stemming from Boccaccio's transcriptions reflect his editorial reshaping of the prosimetrum.[77] And the *editio princeps* of the *libello* (Florence: Sermantelli, 1576)—following a copy of Boccaccio's "edition"—completely obliterates the *divisioni* by omitting them altogether, thus confirming their editorial and critical eclipse for the following three and a half centuries.[78]

Scholars have differed in their responses to Boccaccio's explicit statement of why he dismissed the implicit guidelines embedded in the *Vita nova* and chose to move the *divisioni* to the margins. Susan Noakes argues that Boccaccio aimed to establish a hierarchy between text and gloss and institute the author's central role at the readers' expense. Boccaccio, in her reading, advocated for the textual stability of the *Vita nova*, which the medieval readers' proactive role in establishing textual meaning and their practice of interweaving reading with writing could have endangered. Jason Houston reads Boccaccio's practice as an attempt to shape Dante's poetry "so that it could compare with Latin authors whose dominating presence in Italian humanism was threatening to stunt the nascent vernacular literature." Boccaccio's presentation of the *divisioni* as glosses, Eisner maintains, materially enhances Dante's implementation for vernacular texts of exegetical (and transcriptional) practices generally applied to classical texts: "Boccaccio visually manifests Dante's own scholastic strategy." Banella underscores the innovative (and militant) codicological perspective of Boccaccio's codices, where "the texts in question are literary classics: not only to read, but also to study."[79] For Banella, then, like Eisner, Boccaccio's intervention asserts the *Vita nova*'s equality to established authoritative texts. If Dante devised the prosimetrum's structural alternation of verse and prose, its self-exegetical apparatus, and its methodical metatextual references to its own formal architecture as textual devices to pursue authority (and authorization) and guarantee textual stability (and authenticity), Boccaccio's textual choices regarding the *libello*'s commentative sections and his material presentation of those sections distinctly prioritized the authoritative feature of Dante's strategy.

Boccaccio was certainly working with an audience in mind, not just to augment his manuscript collection. In the note "Maraviglierannosi molti" (A great many will wonder), as Giuseppe Vandelli underlined, "*molti* indicates the audience of readers for whom the new editor wants to preemptively motivate the novelty."[80] Boccaccio's version of the prosimetrum ultimately complies with, and intends to affirm, a distribution between commentary and poetry that characterizes the relationship between an authoritative text and its exegetical apparatus in scholastic university desk books and glossed manuscripts of classical literature. This is the case—as we will see in chapter 4—of Boccaccio's own transcriptions of Aristotle's *Nicomachean Ethics* with Thomas Aquinas's commentary, Apuleius's works, and Statius's *Thebaid*.[81] Boccaccio's transcription of the *Vita nova* materially crafts and institutes Dante's first work as an *auctoritas*, a text deserving and demanding an exegetical apparatus. In the *Trattatello*, Boccaccio explicitly thematized the continuity between the most eminent Greek and Latin poets and Dante, between classical poetry and vernacular poetry, "la quale, secondo il mio giudicio, egli [*sc.* Dante] primo non altramenti fra noi Italici esaltò e recò in pregio, che la sua Omero tra' Greci o Virgilio tra' Latini" (which, in my opinion, he exalted to prestigious heights among us Italians, just as Homer had done among the Greeks or Virgil among the Latins).[82]

Sandro Bertelli and Marco Cursi's discovery in *To*'s final leaf has recently provided the iconographic counterpart to Boccaccio's endorsement. With the help of a Wood's lamp, Bertelli and Cursi detected the profile portrait of a laureled poet on fol. 267v. A heading above the portrait spells out in capitals the Dantean words (*Inferno* 4.88): "Homero poeta sovrano" (Homer, the supreme poet). Stefano Martinelli Tempesta and Marco Petoletti later deciphered and interpreted the Latin subscription in Greek characters below the portrait: "Ioannes de Certaldo p[inx]it" (Giovanni from Certaldo [*sc.* Boccaccio] painted [me]).[83] The portrait and the heading seal the collection of Dante's texts under the aegis of Homer's and Dante's poetry, an association that the *Trattatello* endorsed and theorized. Four centuries later, Giambattista Vico would still refer to Dante as "the Tuscan Homer," an ideal genealogy that Dante himself had promoted and outlined in *Inferno* 4.[84] Chapter 4 will show how Boccaccio's editorial and critical approach to Dante's texts strategically relates to the authorization (and canonization) of the former's own production in the vernacular.

Novus Libellus

A book metaphor opens Dante's first "organic" work in the vernacular. A metaphorical representation of the act of writing also opens Dante's last work (*Ecloga* 2.1–2):

> Vidimus in nigris albo patiente lituris
> Pyerio demulsa sinu modulamina nobis.
>
> ---
>
> (We saw in letters black, supported by the white, the modulations
> milked for us from the Pierian breast.)[85]

The two Latin hexameters combine the distinctly Dantean image of the Muses' milk with an elegant variation on the *topos* of the materiality of writing, here conceptualized in terms of the color white (metonymically standing for the clean sheet) absorbing the letters' black.[86] This incipit opens the first of two metrical letters in Latin (*Ecloge* 2 and 4), written in bucolic form in response to two poems (*Ecloge* 1 and 3) by Giovanni del Virgilio, a rhetorician, Latinist, and Virgilianist at the Studium in Bologna. In the *Ecloge*, Dante respectfully (if inflexibly) rejects Giovanni's request that Dante compose an epic in Latin for a scholarly audience (the "carm[en] vatison[um]" [bard-like song] evoked in *Ecloga* 1.24) as well as Giovanni's offer that Dante be crowned with the poetic laurel in Bologna. Dante "published" his *Ecloge* between 1319 and 1320 in Ravenna, where he was a guest of Guido Novello da Polenta. While composing the last ten cantos of *Paradiso*—the "decem . . . vascula" (ten measures) filled with the Muses' milk promised to Giovanni in *Ecloga* 2.64—Dante also found the time to engage in a polite literary controversy and to bring new life to pastoral poetry in Latin. Dante's final apology for a literature in the vernacular, his confident expression of poetic dignity, his inclination to literary experimentation, and the proud defense of his life choices are premised on, and framed by, the notion that literature exists in, and consists of, material forms.

Books are recursive figures in Dante's opus. The semantic domain of writing marks the beginning of his literary career and ideally seals its end. The book metaphor that opens the *Vita nova* has its own "internal history" in Dante's corpus of poems written before the prosimetrum and not included in it.[87] In the early *canzone* (20 [lxvii, 10]) "E' m'incresce di me sì duramente" (I feel such deep compassion for myself), Dante employs the book metaphor to articulate a retrospective analysis of the first phases of his relationship with Beatrice. Like the *Vita nova*, the *canzone* is also a "first attempt at a complete history of an experience."[88] Dante first reads of the exceptional trauma he suffered the day Beatrice was born in this initial actualization of the book of memory: v. 59, "nel libro della mente che vien meno" (according to the book / of memory that falters more and more), and v. 66, "e se 'l libro non erra" (and if this book is right). The metaphor is sustained through the additional occurrences of the term *mente* (vv. 20, 44, and 87), pseudo-etymologically related to *memoria*.[89] Remembrance, Mary Carruthers has pointed out, is a reenacting procedure "analogous to reading letters that 'stand for' sounds (*voces*) that 'represent' things in a more or less adequate, fitting way."[90] The mind, like memory, is legible.

With its inclusion in the *Vita nova*, the book of memory receives a more detailed and concrete characterization—and references to books, writing, and textuality thereafter retain a high degree of material denotation throughout Dante's corpus.[91] In the prosimetrum, the book metaphor is the first of several references to the world of books, writing, and literature to assume metanarrative connotations. Its material trappings become the foundation of the prosimetrum as a written artifact: they generate the structural notion that the latter is given in the form of a *libello*. From the very proem, as we saw throughout chapters 1 and 2, the *Vita nova* turns to itself, its metanarrative references entailing various orders of signification. The reconstructed history of the events that led to the writing of the poems establishes the prosimetrum's etiology. The details about the poems' communicational contexts describe their modes of circulation and outline an intended audience. The thematization of the constitutive alternation of verse and prose fixes the expository order and suggests an intended—or, at least, anticipated—*mise-en-texte*. In sum, the *Vita nova* explains its own composition in a specific textual and material form: it stages its own *mise-en-livre* while also bending its own interpretation.

The book form intended *for the text* is described *within the text*. It is posed as the prerequisite for its reception and interpretation—and, in fact, for its actual textualization. It has been persuasively argued that the title *Vita nova* indicates both Dante's itinerary of personal renovation and the work's literary innovation. Michelangelo Picone, for instance, read the title to be the prosimetrum's self-referential presentation as a new type of troubadour *vida*, one which goes beyond the superficial account of the poet's life and works and discloses, instead, the true teleological sense of his poetic and amorous experiences.[92] Zygmunt Barański identifies the *Vita nova*'s self-styled novelty in the malleable and versatile hybridity of its textual form, which elides the hierarchical differences between poetry and prose to adapt to and integrate "the density of the real."[93] This first case study has sought to extend the rich metatextual implications of the title *Vita nova* to include the materiality of the innovative, if not wholly unprecedented book form—this *novus libellus*—that the prosimetrum is specifically and explicitly made to adopt.

But the manuscript tradition of the *Vita nova* would only partially reflect the novelty of the textual and material program exposed in the prosimetrum.

If the reexamination of the earliest complete transcriptions of the prosimetrum demonstrates that Dante's strategy of textual control was deeply rooted in the scribal practices he was familiar with, that examination also shows that Dante was excessively optimistic about its outcome. And it shows that, in the end, *habent sua fata libelli*: books (and booklets) have their own destiny. Or we might say rather that their fates depend on—and are shared with—their readers (*pro captu lectoris*).[94] The actual translation of the *libello* into its historically preserved material forms—into actual *libelli*—was the result of a negotiation between what the text reveals about itself and the various agencies of manuscript culture: not only authorial intentions (*pace* Dante) but also readers' expectations, scribal conventions, compilers' agendas, and patrons' commissions.

APPENDIX TO PART I

Pulcra metaphora de quaterno et volumine

> Revolventes et poetarum et aliorum scriptorum volumina, quibus mundus universaliter et membratim describitur . . .
>
> —Dante, *De vulgari eloquentia* 1.6.3

A map of the *Commedia*'s metanarrative strategies is certainly a desideratum in Dante studies: the *Commedia* is at once a *summa* and encyclopedic synthesis of narrative forms and an as yet uncharted constellation of metanarrative statements and references to the materiality of writing.[1] Such a mapping, well beyond the aspirations of this project's investigation, would show Dante's uninterrupted attention to, and metatextual reflection on, all aspects of textuality and materiality. This appendix merely begins the exercise by illustrating similarities and consistency between the metanarrative strategies of the *Commedia* and those we observed earlier in the *Vita nova*. These cursory observations suggest the intellectual and figurative coherence of the book metaphoric across Dante's literary production, highlighting the progressive broadening, deepening, and diversification of that metaphoric's connotative reverberations.

The *Commedia*'s accomplished characterization of the protagonist as a writer, Dante's allusions to and interactions with fellow poets (which turn the mountain of *Purgatorio*, in Justin Steinberg's words, "into a literary anthology, a living *compilatio*"[2]), and the citational—and in three prominent cases, explicitly *self*-citational nature of these interactions—result in highly integrated metanarrative statements.[3] Metacritical passages also include intersemiotic and multimedial argumentations: for instance, in the dialogue between Dante and the illuminator Oderisi da Gubbio (*Purgatorio* 11.73–117), and in the technically phrased, self-reflexive translations into text of the divinely inspired didacticism of figurative and plastic arts in *Purgatorio* 10–12.

The narrative proper—its forms and contents—often lends itself to an allegorical description of the poem's narration. In the infernal cantos dedicated to thieves (*Inferno* 24–25), the intertextual plundering and metamorphosed rewriting of the sources seem to reflect the sin and its punishment, while also embedding them into the fibers of the text. Similarly, the rhetorical superfetation of Geryon—"sozza imagine di froda" (filthy image of fraud) (*Inferno* 17.7)—and the fact that its sinister illative motion is indispensable for the continuation of Dante's journey institute disturbing correspondences between truth, narrative, rhetoric, prophecy, and deceit. Even the theological complication of Beatrice's characterization in the *Commedia* does not eclipse the Vitanovan poetological innuendos of her figure, if the triumphal return of her name in *Purgatorio* 30.73—"'Guardaci ben! Ben son, ben son Beatrice'" ("Look at us well! Truly I am, truly I am Beatrice")—is indeed marked not only by a paronomasia but also by an amphibology (*son*: I am/I sound). In the fascinating interpretation advanced by Roger Dragonetti, on top of truly being herself, "she sounds well" too.[4]

The narrator's thematization of incipits, the "apostilling technique" of his narration,[5] his agonistic statements toward illustrious predecessors, and his assertions on the poem's *novitas* constitute as many occasions for metaliterary (and metanarrative) reflections. The expository order of the narrative is also thematized in the analeptic or proleptic references spoken by the poem's characters. This is the case in the anticipation, deferral, and fulfillment of the explanation for the obscure *post eventum* prophecies regarding Dante's future—for instance, *Inferno* 15.88–89: "Ciò che narrate di mio corso scrivo, / e serbolo a chiosar con altro testo" (What you narrate about my path I am writing down and keeping to be glossed, with other texts); and *Paradiso* 17.94–95: "Poi giunse: 'Figlio, queste son le chiose / di quel che ti fu detto'" (Then he added: "Son, these are the glosses on what was said to you").

The order of discursive elements is also exhibited in the narrator's "stage directions," often expressed in technical terms, as in *Paradiso* 5.138–39, introducing Justinian's canto-long monologue of *Paradiso* 6: "e così chiusa chiusa mi rispuose / nel modo che 'l seguente canto canta" (thus, all enclosed, it answered me in the mode that the following canto sings). The use of critical terminology in the context of Dante's highly condensed poetic diction can also generate peculiar short circuits between referential and self-referential use of the language. The term *canto*, a one hundredth unit of the poem, also describes, and often coincides with, the content (and perhaps the meter) of the blessed souls' paradisiacal singing (*their* canto). And even Beatrice, ineffable as ever, seems at liberty to float gracefully across heavenly spheres and the poem's structural units alike, at least in the compendious, polysemic, and debated hendecasyllable (*Paradiso* 5.16): "Sì cominciò Beatrice questo canto" (Thus Beatrice began this canto).

The narrator's addresses to his narratees provide guidelines for interpretation—and transcription—and even describe the specific intellectual skills of an ideal audience (*Paradiso* 10.22–23):

> Or ti riman, lettor, sovra 'l tuo banco,
> dietro pensando a ciò che si preliba.
>
> ———
>
> (Now stay there, reader, on your bench, thinking back on your foretaste here.)

The anticipated *lettore prelibante* ("foretasting reader") who studies the poem on a materially encoded university desk book—as Armando Petrucci posits—is a scholarly trained reader and a direct descendant of the *altro chiosatore* ("other commentator") to whom the treating of Beatrice's death is hypothetically assigned in the prosimetrum (*VN* 19.2 [xxviii 2]).[6]

In the metanarrative references that punctuate the *Commedia*, discursive features often form an indissoluble bond with (broadly intended) material traits, much as we saw in the *Vita nova*'s structuring image of the book of memory from which the *libello* is transcribed. Writing can be described with reference to the materiality of its process and through the tools of the trade that give shape to it: folios, stylus, ink. In the purgatorial terrace where lust is purged, Dante addresses his cherished precursor Guido Guinizzelli and explains in material terms the reason for his own filial affection toward him (*Purgatorio* 26.112–14):

> E io a lui: "Li dolci detti vostri,
> che, quanto durerà l'uso moderno,
> faranno cari ancora i loro incostri."
>
> ---
>
> (And I to him: "Your sweet poems, which, as long as modern usage lasts, will make precious their very ink.")

In an eminently metaliterary conversation where most terms refer to literature, to the literary production of the two conversing characters, and to the style in which the conversation itself is being had, Guinizzelli's poetry, the reason for Dante's affection, is referred to in its objectual manifestation: Guinizzelli's poems will make the inked papers on which they are preserved dear to readers for as long as vernacular poetry exists. In the same canto, upon presenting himself to Guinizzelli, Dante had asked for the former's identity in order to include him as a character in the *Commedia*, which reminds us of similar textualizations of Dante's fellow poets as characters of the *Vita nova*. In disclosing his role as author-in-progress of the poem to Guinizzelli in canto 26, Dante describes himself in scribal terms and represents himself in the material process of writing on folios (*Purgatorio* 26.64).[7]

Material details often give an unexpected twist to common metanarrative *topoi*. In the sphere of the fixed stars, for instance, the soul of St. Peter dances thrice around Beatrice while singing a song of which Dante can preserve no memory. Dante uses strictly material references to thematize ineffability and the associations it generates between remembrance (or oblivion), ingenuity, poetic inspiration, rhetorical skills, and writing. The depth of the paradisiacal experience is such that memory cannot fathom it and quills cannot articulate it in writing; even the representational shortfalls of the materials used in figurative arts are marshaled in a criticism of the human imagination as it fails in the task of textualizing the otherworldly (*Paradiso* 24.25–27):

> Però salta la penna e non lo scrivo:
> ché l'imagine nostra a cotai pieghe,
> non che 'l parlare, è troppo color vivo.
>
> ---

(Therefore my pen leaps over and I do not write it, for our imagining has colors too unsubtle for such folds, let alone our speech.)[8]

In the *Vita nova*, Dante had already faced the limits, across different media, of referential language. The unfinished drawing of angels and the concluding sonnet "Oltre la spera che più larga gira" (Beyond the sphere that turns the widest gyre) are self-professed failed attempts to represent Beatrice in either pictures or words (in *VN* 23 [xxxiv] and 30 [xli], respectively). The ineffability of his heavenly experience frustrates all efforts at multimedial and transmedial expression.

In the *Commedia*, even metaphysical books are connoted by material details. In *Paradiso* 15.49–52, Dante's ancestor Cacciaguida reveals that he has long waited for his descendant after reading the record of his grace-induced arrival in the "magno volume" (great volume). Enrico Fenzi has recognized in this volume an instantiation of the biblical *Liber vitae* (Book of Life), that is, "the list or registrar of the blessed souls . . . that has forever been in God's mind, and is, therefore, broadly speaking, the very divine mind considered in its infinite foreknowledge."[9] Despite its metaphysical nature, the *Liber vitae* exhibits distinctly physical features. Its immutable script acquires the chromatic concreteness and visibility of the brown ink on white leaves (*Paradiso* 15.51): in the Book of Life "non si muta mai bianco né bruno" (white and black are never changed).[10]

In the purgatorial terrace where gluttons are gathered, the materiality of writing is thematized to describe the penitent's emaciated face (*Purgatorio* 23.32–33): "chi nel viso de li uomini legge 'omo' / ben avria quivi conosciuta l'emme" (those who read *omo* on the human face would have recognized the *M* there clearly). As already noted by early commentators, the Gothic execution of the word *omo* with the two *o*'s inscribed in the empty spaces between the *M*'s minims form a graphic image of the penitents' shrunken aspect and eye sockets—an ideal subject, one could add, for the historiation of the initial *M* that opens the canto: "Mentre che li occhi" (While I was probing my eyes).

In *Paradiso* 18.70–114, the blessed souls of the Heaven of Justice sing the first verse of the book of Wisdom in the Latin text of the *Vulgata*: "Diligite iustitiam qui iudicatis terram" (Love justice, you who are the judges of the earth). Meanwhile, they also compose themselves to form each letter (in sequence) of the graphic transcription of that verse. The language of the passage is decisively metadiscursive: *favella, segnare, segno, figura, vocale, consonante, verbo, nome, vocabolo* ("speech," "to make a sign," "sign," "figure," "vowel," "consonant," "verb," "noun," "word"). Also the verb *rilevare* ("to set forth") indicates the recomposition of the whole word after its letters have been signed, spelled out, and spaced out by punctuating silences.[11] The final letter *M* of the scriptural pericope does not vanish, but rather remains as a golden letter on the silver leaf of the sphere/volume of Jupiter (v. 96: "pareva argento lì d'oro distinto," "appeared there silver of gold adorned"). An author, a scribe, and a skilled illuminator, God himself arranges the souls to form the letter *M* (vv. 109–111).[12] He further metamorphoses the letter, he illuminates it into the figure of a lily, and then he gives it the form of a heraldic eagle. God's Holy Book is materially transcribed into God's book of nature: the notion of justice dispensed in the former historically translates into the symbol of Dante's favored political institution in the latter. Readers of the *Commedia* will—by the time they reach *Paradiso* 18—be well accustomed to the textual presence of both biblical citations and biblical characters. But there they find Dante *agens* himself in the very presence of the signifier of the scriptural text: a material object with spatial features, not a mere linguistic phenomenon. As David Orbson puts it, it would seem "as though the pilgrim—and, by extension, the reader—is, so to speak, inside a manuscript."[13] If the execution of the word *omo* in Gothic epigraphs could suggest the subject for a historiated capital hypothetically opening *Purgatorio* 23, then in *Paradiso* 18 Dante's encounter with the Holy Book's letters divinely transcribed into the book of creation that he is navigating seemingly evokes the illuminative practice of including the author's figure within the historiated initials of a text's incipit.[14] But if we might still reduce the metaphorization of the script's materiality in *Purgatorio* 23 to a clever pertinentization of the *topos* of the legibility of all world's creatures—"Quasi liber, et pictura" (as if each were a book and a painting), as Alanus de Insulis writes—in the thematization of the script's materiality in the sphere of Jupiter we see instead the expansion of the metaphorical and the metanarrative into the metaphysical.[15]

Metanarrative references with a focus on the materiality of the medium, as we noted in chapter 2, also indicate the text's material boundaries in order to underline its integrity of codicological unit. The *libello* of the *Vita nova* is intended as a self-contained, autonomous booklet, and the closure to *Purgatorio* is effected in the discursive terms of compositional propriety (*Purgatorio* 33.141: "non mi lascia più ir lo fren de l'arte," "the bridle of art permits me to go no further") and by referencing the materiality of the writing support (*Purgatorio* 33.139: "piene son tutte le carte," "all the pages are filled"). Also, Dante's dialectic vision of the unsewn quires and the bound volume in *Paradiso* 33 signifies the unity and multiplicity of the cosmos, while also recommending to posterity, John Ahern explained, that the unbound fascicles transmitting the three canticles of the *Commedia* be bound in one single codex, a physical book form that their wandering author might never have held in his hands.[16]

The *volume* in *Paradiso* 33 retains its metanarrative value and bridges the distance between the *agens* and the *auctor*: the former foresees the material product of the journey as it has been textualized by the latter. The return of the image of the *volume* also entails the widening of its symbolic scope. Charles Singleton argued that what Dante reads in the book of his memory in the *Vita nova* is a limited but complementary version of the signs he can read in the books of which God is the author: the book of nature (i.e., the creation as book) and the Holy Book. Dante's allegorical and symbolic modes of writing are intended to imitate "God's ways of writing."[17] In Andrea Battistini's words, "the book, most apt symbol of the creation conceived as a perennial and inexhaustible epiphany, surges then as a vehicle of an all-encompassing semiotic system with which to certify both the unity of creation and the indissoluble nexus between natural and moral orders."[18] The *volume* asserts the notion of the world's legibility and intelligibility, conceived of as a system of divinely written, providential signs.

But there is more. At the climax of Dante's oneiric-visionary experience, and at the apogee of manuscript culture, the codex (and the *Commedia* qua codex) becomes the instrument designated to express the coherence of God's plan of creation and to represent Dante's contemplation of that creation through writing (*Paradiso* 33.85–87):

> Nel suo profondo vidi che s'interna,
> legato con amore in un volume,
> ciò che per l'universo si squaderna.

(In its depths I saw internalized, bound with love in one volume, what through the universe becomes unsewn quires.)

The four-layered track of signification—material, metatextual, metaphorical, metaphysical—generates a form of comprehension irreducible to paraphrase and *logos*. The verb *internarsi* ignites here the vertiginous polysemy of the tercet, variously explained by the *Commedia*'s earliest commentators. In correlation with the *verbum videndi* ("vidi," "I saw"), *s'interna* describes the narrator's visual penetration into the gutter of the codex and, in turn, the gathering and encasing of the scattered quires into one volume before his eyes (*uno* retaining its etymological meaning of only one, single). The creation's substances, accidents, and their modes appear metaphysically recomposed in the unity of God's design (*Paradiso* 33.88–89); the cantos already in circulation are presented in the intended formal and codicological unity of the poem. If in the tercet cited above Benvenuto da Imola stresses the notion of compenetration, Francesco da Buti evokes the Trinitarian mystery as matrix of the cosmos: "*che s'interna*; cioè lo quale profondo è Trinità, cioè tre persone in una sustanzia, Padre, Figliuolo e Spirito Santo" (*che s'interna*, that is, whose depth is the Trinity, that is, three persons in one substance, Father, Son, and the Holy Ghost).[19]

The *hapax squaderna* displays a similarly complex interplay between material, metatextual, and metaphorical levels of discourse. On the one hand, it connotes the constitutive elements of the created universe, which unfold in their multiplicity, are perceived as unsewn quires in the sensory world, but exist together in the creator's mind in one bond of love ("legato con amore"); and on the other hand, *squaderna* mirrors the original, scattered circulation of the *Commedia*.

Dante envisions God's creation as including the book by which it is represented symbolically and into which it is reported textually. In its turn, the book recognizes this inclusion by mirroring it within itself. From the privileged position of verse clause, the rhyming of *s'interna* and *squaderna* integrates the narrative progress of Dante *agens*'s journey (his final vision), the codicological features of the volume Dante *auctor* is almost through with composing, the intellectual intuition of the unity of the cosmos's phenomena, and the all-pervading Trinitarian mystery of the one Christian God in three consubstantial persons, whose symbolic manifestation in abstract geometrical forms Dante *agens* will contemplate nine tercets later. If *s'interna* paronomastically resonates with the Trinitarian mystery (*s'inTERna*)—at least if interpreted as a distinctly Dantean parasynthetic verb—the signifier and the etymon of *squaderna* evoke the quadrangular shape of the codex (*sQUADerna*).[20]

Like one of Hans Blumenberg's absolute metaphors, the book metaphor of *Paradiso* 33 has the irreducible capacity of a nondeducted, nonconceptual paradigm: it rejects literal paraphrase while still expressing a tangible (and material) form of knowledge.[21] The accuracy of the visual and tactile denotation of the book metaphor is paradoxically counterbalanced by the intangibility of its ontological reverberations. The richness of the metaphor's semantic ramifications compensates its resistance to an exact literalization. As Osip Mandelstam put it, "the reading of Dante is an endless labor, for the more we succeed, the further we are from our goal."[22] If the metaphor of the (opened) book of memory at the very opening of the *Vita nova* indicated the legibility of a concluded experience in Dante's intellectual biography and designated the self-contained material form for the memorial articulation of that experience, then the book metaphor in the ending of the *Commedia* discloses the revelation of the multiplicity and unity of God's creation (and of human history) aoristically—in "un punto solo" (one point alone), *Paradiso* 33.94—only to enclose that revelation in itself immediately after, as the heavens will be rolled together as a scroll in the end time, according to Isaiah (34:4): "et complicabuntur sicut liber caeli" (and the heavens shall be rolled together as a scroll).[23]

PART II

Materiality and Authority in Boccaccio's *Teseida*

CHAPTER FOUR

Picture-Book (without Pictures)

"And what is the use of a book," thought Alice, "without pictures or conversations?"

—Lewis Carroll, *Alice's Adventures in Wonderland*, chap. 1, 7

Habent Sua Fata Libelli

The scholar who studies Giovanni Boccaccio's *Teseida: Delle nozze d'Emilia* faces a challenging epic poem that readers and critics have received with mixed appreciation. The *Teseida* (ca. 1340) consists of twelve books written in octaves, a strophic form that Boccaccio adopted from *cantari* (narrative poems performed in public) and whose rhyme scheme he regularized into the form's definitive ABABABCC pattern.[1] The poem takes its cues from the closure of Statius's *Thebaid*, a twelve-book Latin epic on the fratricidal war between Oedipus's sons Eteocles and Polynices. In its first two books, the *Teseida* focuses on Athenian "duke" Theseus's victory over Hippolyta, queen of the Amazons (whom he then marries), and over Creon (king of Thebes). It continues with the Theban warriors and prisoners Arcita and Palemone and their competing love for Emilia, Hippolyta's younger sister. Theseus instigates a duel between Arcita and Palemone for Emilia's hand. The duel results in Arcita's victory, but Palemone survives. After marrying Emilia, Arcita dies of wounds from the duel. Funeral honors are duly performed, and Theseus determines that Palemone and Emilia should marry. Or, in Robert Hollander's laconic summary of the poem, "boys meet girl, but only boy gets girl."[2] Influential readers of the *Teseida* have agreed on its experimental nature and commended Boccaccio's scholarly efforts. They have generally expressed, however, a negative evaluation of its aesthetic value and literary technique.[3] The shadow of artistic failure still haunts this peculiar attempt at a poetry of arms in the Italian vernacular.

The scholar who approaches the *Teseida* has, however, the extraordinary privilege of access to Boccaccio's autograph transcription of the text and, as we shall see, also the paratext. In 1929, Giuseppe Vandelli authoritatively confirmed the Boccaccian autography of MS Acquisti e doni 325 in the Florentine Biblioteca Medicea Laurenziana.[4] Vandelli also recognized Boccaccio's hand in the interlinear and marginal commentary. And yet, scholars have only recently begun to capitalize on the exceptional insights this manuscript affords, and to pay critical attention to crucial nonverbal data that show Boccaccio working at the confluence of textuality and materiality.

The object of this case study is thus Boccaccio's more or less successful effort to "determine" and condition the reception of his work—the readers' situation—by assigning agency to the materiality of the work's medium. This chapter and the next inquire into the literary, textual, material, and editorial connections between the poem's autograph, five manuscript copies, and an incunable as multiple book-objects that transmit the *Teseida*.[5] When we examine the mutual interplay between the *Teseida* as multilayered literary construct involving poetry and exegesis and the *Teseida*'s autograph as material container that forms (and transmits) that construct—between the textual and paratextual aspects of the poem/commentary and the visual and codicological features of the book—we have a better understanding of Boccaccio's intellectual project of advancing vernacular culture and promoting his own literary production. Boccaccio's editorial choices (which provide the autograph with the material trappings generally reserved to authoritative texts) and the textual and material strategies he implements (which diversify the semiotic functions of the enunciator into multiple authorial identities) inscribe the *Teseida* within the canon of cultured texts while also preserving its potential for a wider, less scholarly, and more relaxed reception.

Umberto Eco indicated that "*a text is a product whose interpretative destiny must be part of its own compositional mechanism*; composing a text means enacting a strategy of which the expectations of another person's moves form a part."[6] This chapter reveals Boccaccio's material and textual endeavors to anticipate his readers' moves and exert strategic control over his work, even beyond its "publication," that is, its release and circulation in manuscript form susceptible to reproduction by others. It shows, in other words, the author's attempt to condition the *Nachleben* of his poem, its afterlife and survival, even after his own Barthesian death. If in the *Teseida*'s autograph Boccaccio strongly signals a classicizing and scholarly reading of the poem via material and textual features, such as parchment support, formal book hand, sophisticated system of decoration, and "academic" commentary, conversely he also invites leisurely approaches to the poem—and thus other future visual manifestations and expressions for its text form and book form—through the very choice of a popular meter (*ottava rima*), the anonymity and deferred release of that commentary, and the prior or subsequent circulation of uncommented and unornamented copies.

When we consider, as we shall do in chapter 5, how the editorial and marketing strategies implicit in Boccaccio's autograph compare to the reasoning behind the material and textual features of subsequent editorial artifacts transmitting the *Teseida*, we find that the plural mode of consumption encoded in Boccaccio's work is reflected in the multiple strains of manuscript production that emerged for (if not necessarily *from*) his work in the autograph. Readers, patrons, and scribes perceived the multiple modes of reading that are also implied in the autograph and produced new manuscripts that were consistent with (and further contributed to) those diverging modes.

This case study takes its cues from, and enters into dialogue with, four fundamental contributions to the study of the *Teseida*'s materiality: Edvige Agostinelli's description of the poem's manuscript tradition, Francesca Malagnini's work on the autograph's illustrative program, Rhiannon Daniels's analysis of the *Teseida*'s reading audience, and Martina Mazzetti's investigation into the visual components of the autograph.[7] With these scholars it shares an interpretive approach—informed by the principles of bibliography and material philology—that highlights the physical dimension of the poem's autograph, the material execution of its articulation into sections and subsections (its *forma tractatus*), and its rich visual-verbal paratext.[8] But following the line of inquiry outlined in the introduction, the focus of this study is not the material per se but the material as it interacts with the textual and the literary, that is, on the modes of interaction between, and mutual enhancement of, those material features and the literary elements—epic conventions and *topoi*, intertextual dynamics, applied exegetical strategies, and more—of the text embodied and preserved in the autograph. In the pages that follow, this bifocal perspective will, in turn, not only shed light on Boccaccio's more or less successful project of self-authorization but will also illuminate aspects of the *Teseida*—such as its commentary, ekphrastic features, and classicizing practice—that have often been overshadowed.

In the first case study in chapters 1, 2, and 3, we observed the interaction between the materiality of manuscript culture and the *fabula* of Dante's *Vita nova*: we examined, that is, the effect of materiality at the level of the prosimetrum's enunciated and the impact of its textuality on the manuscript tradition of the *libello*. By detailing Boccaccio's fragmentation of the enunciator—the actual subject of the enunciating act—into the mutually complementary grammatical subjects of the enunciation in the autograph of the *Teseida* and by tracing the often diverging itineraries these multiple subjects subsequently follow in the textual and material tradition of the text, this second case study will demonstrate the material foundations of Boccaccio's authorship and authority and their implications for his apologia and promotion of vernacular literature.

Scribal Practice

The *corpus* of Boccaccio's autographs reveals the multiplicity of his textual interests, the variety of his material choices, and the extent of his codicological competence. The autographs predating the autograph of the *Teseida* include transcriptions—in both Latin and vernacular—of Boccaccio's own texts and of other writers' works. These autographs show Boccaccio's attention to devising specific material presentations for the most diverse literary genres: historical, philosophical, exegetical, and biographical prose; epic, lyric, and dramatic poetry. These autographs also preserve Boccaccio's work as illustrator. The autograph of the *Teseida* reflects and condenses Boccaccio's decades-long scribal and literary training. The autograph's aniconic ornamentation, illustrative apparatus, and scribal styles provide tangible evidence of Boccaccio's textual and material versatility. By inscribing the *Teseida*'s autograph in the history of Boccaccio's material apprenticeship, this section explains this autograph's elevated standard of execution as a significant component of Boccaccio's intellectual project of—and marketing strategy for—promoting vernacular literature and diversifying his poem's audience.

Autography

That Boccaccio paid great attention to the relationship between textuality and materiality, between text form and book form, is made clear by his informed choices of different editorial and codicological solutions for different literary and textual genres. Furthermore, Boccaccio engages—to use Armando Petrucci's interpretive category—in an active "writing relationship" with his works: he actively participates, in other words, in the material registration of his texts and in the various phases of book production.[9] We possess twenty-three manuscripts—including the one transmitting the *Teseida*—in which Boccaccio's complete or partial autography has been identified.[10] We also have eleven additional manuscripts that transmit Boccaccio's annotations. This rich, heterogeneous corpus reveals a broad knowledge of books and book models: regarding the choice of literary genre and codicological form, Boccaccio always displays his "encyclopedic taste, . . . genius of the experimental and the composite."[11] Boccaccio exhibits, in other words, an exceptional command of various types of *mise-en-texte*, *mise-en-page*, and *mise-en-livre*.

Six of Boccaccio's autographs predate the transcription of the *Teseida* (which Marco Cursi has argued likely took place ca. 1348).[12] By the time he transcribed the poem, Boccaccio had already acquired significant skills as a copyist of different textual genres in different scripts and book forms:[13] historical and moral treatises in the so-called *Zibaldone Laurenziano*; the transcription, in the form of marginal glosses, of Thomas Aquinas's commentary on Robert Grosseteste's Latin translation of Aristotle's *Nicomachean Ethics*; a portion of his personal copy of Statius's *Thebaid*; the whole corpus of Terence's comedies with glosses and figurative marginalia; and the rare poetic collection *Carmina Priapea*.[14] Cursi writes, "For the realization of such heterogenous book projects, Boccaccio had resorted to various graphical and codicological solutions for the layout of the text on the page."[15] Moreover, not long after producing his autograph of the *Teseida*, comes the first result of Boccaccio's editorial and critical work on Dante Alighieri: the production of MS Toledo Zelada 104.6, which contains the first redaction of the *Trattatello in laude di Dante*, the *Vita nova*, the *Commedia*, and the fifteen *canzoni distese*.[16] Boccaccio's commitment to and zeal for manuscript production extended beyond mere transcription and composition to embrace a varied use of diacritical marks and *maniculae* (pointing hands as attention marks); an interest in drawings, illustrations, and illuminations; and an active role for Boccaccio as copyist in the restoration of a manuscript by supplying missing folios (as in the case of one of his copies of the *Thebaid*).[17]

MS Acquisti e doni 325 (*Aut*)

Boccaccio most probably composed the *Teseida* between 1339 and 1341, between Naples and Florence.[18] He reworked the *Teseida* over the course of the following decade, during which he also elaborated a sophisticated commentary in the forms of marginal and interlinear glosses. The autograph transcription of the *Teseida* dates to a decade after the poem's composition: its multilayered construction reflects this reelaboration and gradual accretion.

The autograph of the *Teseida* is a hybrid codicological project that conjugates features from the various typologies of book form outlined by Petrucci: from the "libro cortese" (courtly book), it inherited its writing support (parchment), sophisticated system of decoration (if only partially executed), and formal book hand; from the "libro registro di lusso" (deluxe register-book), it derived its format and thickness; and the "libro da banco universitario" (university desk book) inspired the material presentation of its egregiously academic commentary (including a "mild," user-friendly abbreviation system for the marginalia).[19]

The autograph of the *Teseida* (hereafter, *Aut*) is a manuscript of medium-small format (275 x 195 mm).[20] The material support for its 144 leaves is high-quality parchment. Coherently with the status of dedication or presentation copy implied for *Aut* in the dedicatory preface to Fiammetta—on which more below in the section titled "Materiality, Paratext, and Fiction"—two ornamental elements indicate an ambitious program for the manuscript: a system of decorated initials (and paragraph signs) and a planned iconographic apparatus, which would be executed only in part.

Aut displays, in fact, a set of (hierarchically differentiated) initials: two large red initials on a blue background, with tempera phytomorphic decorations corresponding to the preface incipit (fol. 1r) and the incipit of book 1 (fol. 3r); eight large filigreed red and blue initials (with inverted blue and red geometric decoration) for the incipits of books 3–7, 9, and 11–12 (on fols. 30v, 40r, 50r, 62v, 70r, 100r, 122v, and 133r); three large blue initials with red filigree for the incipits of books 2, 8, and 10 (on fols. 18v, 86r, and 109v); alternating blue and red medium filigreed initials for the first line of the octave immediately following a rubric and for the incipit of the synoptic sonnets (on which, more below in the subsection titled "Preface"); and small initials overlaid in yellow at verses 1 ("outdented") and 7 of all remaining octaves or immediately following large and medium initials (see pls. 4.1 and 4.2).[21]

The small initial that opens each octave gracefully extends into the margin (within two vertical ruling lines), underscoring the poem's strophic structure. The decorated initials variously mark important structural and metrical subdivisions of the text. A similar structuring function has been assigned to the paragraph signs—128 in all, alternating red and blue—that precede the first line of octaves between rubrics, each tercet of the sonnets, and several marginal glosses. Francesca Malagnini attributes the paragraph signs in the octaves to "the emphasizing of some narrative stages," namely, progress in the action, characters' reactions, physical descriptions, and direct discourses.[22] In the sonnets, the paragraph signs indicate the strophic division. Additional metrical markers include dots of subpunction to correct the prosodic scansion in hypermetric verses by expunging a syllable.[23]

In Sandro Bertelli's words, *Aut* displays "an extraordinary ability to visualize the page, in which all elements (text, paratext, writing, and decoration) are arranged so as to create a substantial balance, a sought-after harmony among parts, clearly the product of a very decided expertise."[24] The *mise-en-page*'s elegant distribution of textual and paratextual elements and the meticulous use of initials and paragraphemic signs demonstrate all that Boccaccio had learned from copying different literary genres using genre-specific transcriptional forms. *Aut* also shows undeniable evidence that Boccaccio planned a sophisticated and rich series of illustrations. The manuscript presents one executed, but now severely damaged, watercolor illustration (fol. 1r): a man offering a red book to a woman. According to Maria Grazia Ciardi

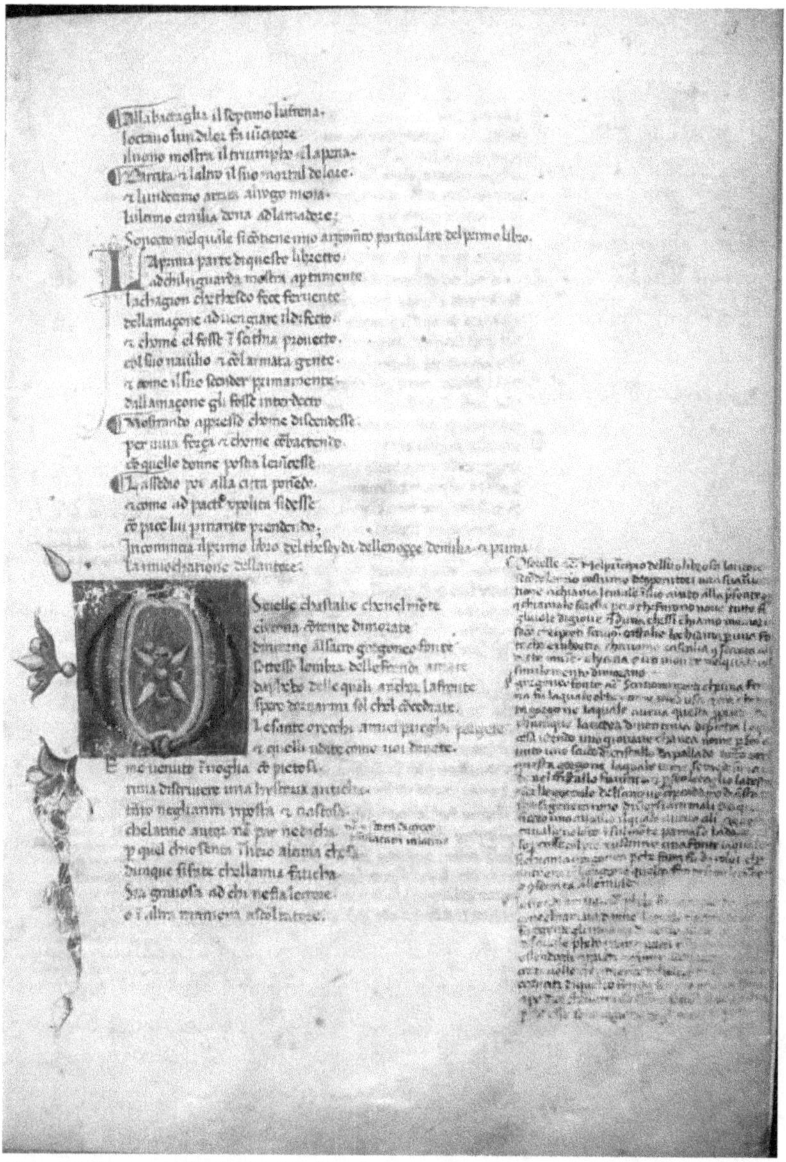

Plate 4.1. Florence, Biblioteca Medicea Laurenziana, MS Acquisti e doni 325, fol. 3r. By permission of the MiC (Ministero della Cultura). Further reproduction in any medium is forbidden.

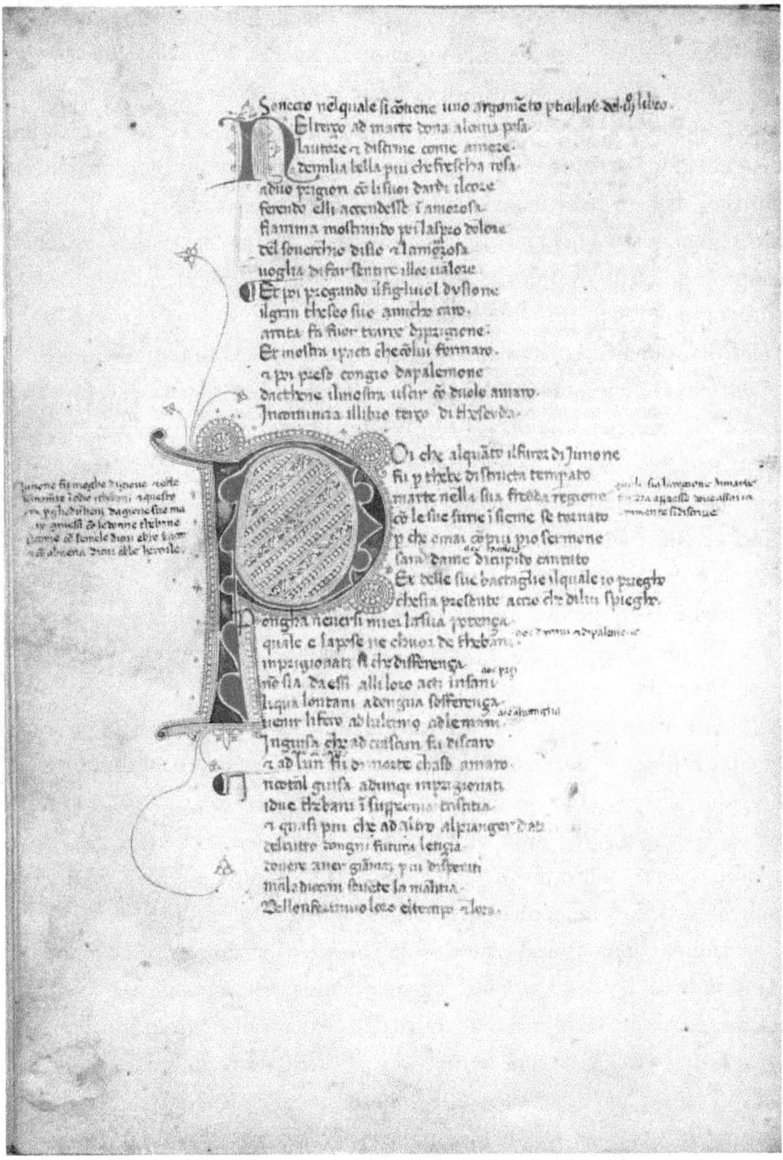

Plate 4.2. Florence, Biblioteca Medicea Laurenziana, MS Acquisti e doni 325, fol. 30v. By permission of the MiC (Ministero della Cultura). Further reproduction in any medium is forbidden.

Dupré Dal Poggetto, Boccaccio himself is the author of this illustration.[25] Additionally, *Aut* presents fifty-eight blank spaces, located on lower and upper margins and intruding into the frame of the octave text (in twenty-five cases, intersecting the octaves). With all probability, these blank spaces were designated for as many illustrations—to be executed by a professional miniaturist—that would visually complement the text of the preceding or following octaves.[26] This hypothesis is supported by the illustrative apparatus transmitted by an extant manuscript—presumably copied from a now lost autograph of the poem—preserved in the Biblioteca Oratoriana del Monumento Nazionale dei Gerolamini in Naples.[27] Copied in the mid-fifteenth century in Florence, the Oratoriana *Teseida* presents thirty-five drawings and blank spaces for an additional twenty-five drawings. Agostinelli and Coleman estimate regarding the relationship between the Oratoriana manuscript and *Aut* that "42 (70%) of the drawings and drawing-spaces in the text-blocks of the two manuscripts were intended to illustrate the same event in the narrative."[28] Malagnini's more cautious estimate of a 50 percent coincidence between the two manuscripts—twenty-nine out of fifty-eight cases in which drawings or drawing-spaces correspond to those in *Aut*—also supports the hypothesis of a planned illustrative apparatus.[29]

From these brief notes of codicological analysis one can infer some notable aspects of *Aut*'s typology. The autograph, via material support and program of illustration, is presented as an exemplar to invest in. From its preparatory stages, the autograph is consequently already intended as worthy of long-lasting transmission and circulation. Furthermore, *Aut*'s elegant codicological features situate the *Teseida* in proximity to a prestigious circle of culturally momentous literary works. Boccaccio's choices regarding material support and ornamentation suggest an audacious attempt to pass off an *ottava rima* epic—a pioneering vernacular text by an emerging author—as an already established authoritative work, one that can compete with classical and Christian *auctoritates*, at least in terms of its material trappings. Before the *Teseida* achieved what we might now perceive as status of "classic" by merit of wide distribution, we see Boccaccio's choice to endow it with the material features of a literary and cultural masterwork, presented as a notable text to imitate, reproduce, and circulate.

The choice by later actors—patrons, purchasers, scribes, and readers—to make or commission paper copies of the poem thus presents an apparent inconsistency to modern readers. On the one hand, the survival of these paper copies—all dating several decades after *Aut*'s production but not necessarily deriving from it—suggests that there was widespread diffusion of the text; on the other hand, the materially diminished quality of these copies shows an apparent discrepancy between the authorial project of the *Teseida* (literarily executed as highly allusive elevated epic poetry and materially embodied in an elegant codex) and the effective reception of the poem as "popular fiction," as *Trivialliteratur*, by its actual audience. On this note, it is also relevant to point out the more properly paleographic element of the *Teseida*'s manuscript tradition: its various script typologies. Whereas *Aut*, for the most part, displays Boccaccio's elegant book hand, the majority of the extant transcriptions of the *Teseida* adopt the more common (and popular) *mercantesca* and chancery cursive scripts.[30] On the one hand, there is *Aut*, an expensive codex whose evident high value signals Boccaccio's expectation—or, at least, his aspiration for his text—that the work would be preserved and communicated to a highbrow or sophisticated audience; on the other, there is a series of less expensive paper exemplars that effectively reveal the *Teseida* to have been a breakout book (and popular success), since these paper copies both allowed for and demonstrate wide circulation and dissemination.

As we shall observe in chapter 5 ("The Textual Proliferation of the *Teseida*"), our present understanding of the textual history of the *Teseida*—and of *Aut*'s exact position in that history—is still imperfect. And we cannot postulate that the whole manuscript tradition of the poem originated directly from the autograph. We cannot exclude, in other words, that exemplars of the *Teseida* transcribed on paper in *mercantesca* or chancery script originated from copies (or even autographs) circulating in the approximately ten years between the composition of the *Teseida* and the production of *Aut*, or that patrons and scribes subsequently rejected certain features of *Aut*.

And yet, the material inconsistency outlined above could indicate only a superficial discrepancy: it does not necessarily show that Boccaccio attempted—but failed—to market his work to a cultivated audience able to appreciate his classicizing project. Boccaccio might well have initially predicted a dual textual (and material) itinerary for his poem. Or he might have retroactively recognized—only after re-presenting the *Teseida* in the classicizing and authoritative materiality of *Aut*—that the first epic in the vernacular could exist in two forms and circulate in two modes: either as a scholarly text accompanied by commentary and rich ornamentation or as an uncommented work of entertainment that might circulate in unpretentious exemplars among literate merchants. As we shall observe more specifically below (in the sections "Materiality and Exegesis" and "Dissimulations, Omissions, Generative Potentials"), the delayed addition of an authorial (but anonymous) commentary to the poem a decade after the composition of the octaves suggests that the *Teseida* existed in an ongoing relationship with readers through time.

Materiality, Paratext, and Fiction

The *Teseida*, as it is transmitted by *Aut*, is a multilayered aesthetic product. Its autography certifies the semantic capacity of the mutual correspondence and interaction of its textual and material components: it certifies, in other words, the artistic intentionality of its project. In other of his works, Boccaccio makes explicit, if fictionalized, mention of a mutual correspondence between material container and textual contents: the choice of a specific book form has semantic motivations and implications. Boccaccio's *Elegia di Madonna Fiammetta* (*The Elegy of Lady Fiammetta*), for instance, is metatextually prescribed to be contained in a "piccolo . . . libretto" (little book).[31] And its protagonist Fiammetta, addressing her own diary-booklet (9.4–5), demands that it assume a modest form, congruous with the genre and the text's elegiac content:

> e però non ti sia cura d'alcuno ornamento, sì come li altri sogliono avere: cioè di nobili coverte di colori varii tinte e ornate, o di pulita tonditura, o di leggiadri minii, o di gran titoli: queste cose non si convengono alli gravi pianti li quali tu porti: lascia e queste e li larghi spazii e li lieti inchiostri, e le impomiciate carte alli libri felici.[32]

> (Therefore, do not concern yourself with any ornamentation such as other books are accustomed to have, namely, with elegant covers, painted and adorned with various colors, with clean-cut pages, pretty miniatures, or grand titles; such things do not suit the grave lamentation

you bear; leave these things to happy books, and with them the broad margins, the colorful inks, and the paper smoothed with pumice.)

This classicizing address *ad libellum*—modeled on Ovid's *Tristia* 1.1—explicitly reconfigures the rhetorical principle of correspondence between style and subject matter (the *conveniens*, or *aptum*) to include the material aspects of composition and presentation.[33] Even in the absence of an autograph of the *Elegia*, we can assume that for Boccaccio the textuality of his works implies their codicology.

Preface

The felicitous preservation of an autograph of the *Teseida* allows for a more direct inquiry into the relationship between materiality, textuality, and *fictio*. In *Aut*, the poem is accompanied by a rich verbal and visual apparatus that we would now label paratextual. The poem is preceded by a dedicatory preface to the beloved Fiammetta and by a sonnet introducing the work as a whole. Each book of the *Teseida* is also headed by a synoptic sonnet. Two caudate sonnets close the work (Vandelli calls them "ultrafinali"):[34] an invocation to the Muses, and the Muses' response. Rubrics articulate the poem into narrative subunits, and an intricate system of majuscules and paragraphemic signs further enhances these subdivisions. The poetic text proper—the octaves—is accompanied by Boccaccio's marginal and interlinear commentary. And various types of commentaries (by Boccaccio or others) appear in about one-third of the sixty-eight preserved manuscripts.

The preface to Fiammetta herself creates a fictionalized dedication, endows the work with an aura of authenticity, anticipates the poem's allegorical content (or, rather, the declared need to interpret its content allegorically), institutes a correspondence between the *persona loquens* and an unspecified character in the poem, and delegates its interpretation to Fiammetta's keen intelligence.[35]

In the preface, the *persona loquens* indirectly presents himself as a compiler, a label that has important implications not only in relation to the text composition but also for the material presentation of that textual content: "Et che ella da me per voi sia compilata . . ." (. . . that I have composed this for you).[36] Medieval literary jargon—including the vernacular jargon—is notoriously unsystematic in nature, intimidating in magnitude, and, in consequence, understudied. As a result, then, of its inherent complexity—and especially in the absence of a systematic study of medieval literary language to turn to—a modern reader encountering these terms struggles to infer the level of consciousness with which Boccaccio used this terminology and precisely where the boundary exists between original contribution and reuse of ancient materials: the phrase *opus compilatum per*—and the Italian verb *compilare*—can indicate various degrees of authorship.[37] The notion of *compilatio* can generically refer to the composition of a work. It can imply the intertextual weaving or juxtaposition of different source materials. Here in the *Teseida* (and in *Aut*), it may also indicate the coordinated transcription of poem and commentary.[38] In Bonaventure's well-known classification of writing figures, the *compilator* is one who adds texts (not his/her own) to texts (also not his/her own): a definition that also evokes the features of visual and argumentative presentation common to the scholastic encyclopedic organization of knowledge.[39] The concept of *compilatio* also proves consistent with the diffraction of Boccaccio's authorial voice into multiple authorial *personae*.[40] And one may even argue that, in *Aut*'s fiction, the poem's author referred to in the commentary to the *Teseida* is the author of preexisting source materials. The *compilator* himself makes reference to a preexisting source he has allegedly rearranged and adapted—"ridocta"—to vernacular verse:

> Trovata una antichissima hystoria et alle più delle genti non manifesta, bella sì per la materia della quale parla, che è d'amore, et sì per coloro de' quali dice, che nobili giovani furono et di real sangue discesi, in latino volgare et per rima, acciò che più dilectasse, et maximamente ad voi che già con sommo titolo le mie exaltaste, con quella sollecitudine che conceduta mi fu da l'altre più gravi disiderando di piacervi, ò ridocta.[41]

> (Having found a very ancient tale and one not known by most people, beautiful indeed for the matter which it treats, which is love, and for those of whom it speaks, who are noble youths descended of royal blood, I have rewritten it in the vernacular and in rhyme for your delight, and with the care acquired from other weightier works, so as to give greater pleasure to you who have already praised them in the loftiest terms.)

The sonnet to the Muses makes another reference to the notion of *compilatio*, seemingly (if metaphorically) implying the assembling and connecting of various preexisting sources or textual components (vv. 9–11):

> io ò ricolte della vostra mensa
> alcune miche da quella cadute,
> et come seppi qui l'ò compilate;

> (I have collected some crumbs fallen from your table and I have compiled them here to the best of my ability.)[42]

This self-styled compositional practice is further evident in the glosses—written, as we shall see, in the person of a commentator—which often work as narrative digressions: they recall previous episodes and mythical "prequels" or disclose events to follow and "sequels." These sections of the commentary are parallel to the poem's main *fabula*: as Susan Noakes has suggested, glosses can "contribute to the illusion of multiplication of the narrative's temporal sequence by making explicit a subtheme that is only implicit in the text."[43] Such temporal multiplications function as *paralipomena*: narrative and motivic expansions that offer a further perspective on Boccaccio's compositional skills. And they are consistent with the proliferation of, and mutual interaction between, Boccaccio's authorial voices in the *Teseida*: the *Teseida*'s commentator has an individual authorial identity, and under that identity he often writes as a *compilator*.

The preface, in its dual nature of fiction and paratext, thematizes the dedication of the poem to the author's beloved. Appropriately, the only illustration executed in the autograph in all probability depicts an author—likely Boccaccio himself—in the act of giving a book to his lady. Whether or not this dedicatee actually existed historically, the material features of *Aut* turn this fictional author–dedicatee relationship into a physical dedication or presentation copy. The material, paratextual, and thematic levels all concur and mirror each other in their insistence on the poem's literary exceptionality. The status of dedication or presentation copy signals that the text preserved in the codex should be deemed of a high quality and held in high esteem. The dedication-copy framing—also in light of its reference to the poem's ancient sources—and its material presentation in *Aut* are intended to promote the *Teseida* as classicizing text in the vernacular and to assert its equality (including in terms of its transcriptional worth) beside similarly framed texts from classical antiquity.

Aut also presents the *Teseida* as a text to study—a presentation that is confirmed by the material articulation of its textual subdivision (its *ordinatio*), which is in turn informed by the principles of scholastic book culture.[44] Didactic and homiletic practices required an easy access to the immense repository of knowledge accumulated through the Middle Ages. The attempt at synthesizing this knowledge was expressed in formal and graphical devices that facilitated the retrieval of information. The *ordinatio* of a text/book entailed the mutual reinforcement of visual-spatial presentation and argumentative process. This reinforcement determines that the material articulation of the textual content functions both as a heuristic principle and as a hermeneutical hypothesis. Boccaccio would likely have wanted to provide a similar paratextual apparatus, investing his book with the authority of a text to be studied, and instituting a specific interpretive itinerary—a sort of user's guide—in order to do so. Approximately 200 prose rubrics invite this scholarly oriented approach to the poem.[45] They can be classified into two groups: rubrics marking the incipit and the explicit of each book of the poem, and rubrics dividing each book into sections and cataphorically revealing the content of the octaves that follow. These rubrics elicit what Malcolm Parkes illustrates as the "more ratiocinative scrutiny of the text and consultation for reference purposes" of the scholastic *lectio* (as opposed to the monastic *lectio*).[46] They briefly explain the text, coordinate its interpretation, and make it more cohesive through a sophisticated set of cross-references. They impose, in short, a hermeneutical schema onto the text.

Ekphrasis

The autograph's paratextual elements (dedicatory preface, sonnets, rubrics, commentary) and its visual components (program of illustrations, system of decorated initials) establish an interaction, or even a coincidence, between *forma tractandi* (literary style), *forma tractatus* (the expository and narrative organization of the text), and material solutions (*mise-en-page*, visual markers, aniconic decoration, principles of codicological organization).[47] The visual articulation that materially characterizes the codex mirrors and reinforces the textual order and literary structure of the poem. Malagnini has suggested that "it is as if Boccaccio had planned the codex and its macrostructure and had then hidden its very structure in the container."[48] Building on Malagnini, Martina Mazzetti has described these features of the *Teseida*/*Aut* system in terms of "figuralità" (figurality) and pointed to their exegetical rather than decorative function.[49]

We can build further on these scholars' observations to suggest that the visual-verbal schema also intersects and affects the content of the poem. A first example of this can be found in the text's digressive sections, such as book 7's digression on the temples of Mars and Venus. On the one hand, these conform to the ancient epic's convention of *ekphrasis*. On the other hand, they inscribe this coincidence of expository order and material apparatus within the poem's storyline. Boccaccio's treatment of the temples of Mars and Venus represents a descriptive excursus in compliance with his epic models. Additionally, however, it offers an allegorical interpretation of the poem, explained through an extremely articulate form of architectonic and figurative mimesis. Notably, the temple of Mars is described (7.36, 1–2) as "tutto istoriato / da sottil mano et di sopra et di sotto" (all storied by a clever hand, above and roundabout): this description could be aptly used to designate the illustrative program intended for *Aut*.

A second example is offered by the description of the temple dedicated to Arcita, erected by Palemone (11.71–88). The historiated walls of the temple tell the story of Theseus, Arcita, and Palemone, as it is narrated in the *Teseida* itself. They re-present this story and summarize the *fabula* of the poem *en abyme*. The repeated use of verbs of visual perception (*verba videndi*), the polyptoton of the verb *vedere* (to see) in its various verbal forms, the obsessive glossing of the verb *vedere* with the appropriate forms of the predicative participle *dipinto* (painted) in the interlinear space, and the reiterated synaesthetic transitions underline a diffused sense of visuality and materiality:

Et per li monti *si vedean* fuggire
le dolorose madri co' figliuoli;
pareanvisi le voci ancor sentire
de' lor dolenti et dispietati duoli;
et *vedeansi* le donne achive gire

> nell'alte torri, con diversi stuoli,
> et ardere ogni cosa, poscia ch'esse
> ebber le corpor' nelle fiamme messe.
>
> ———
>
> (And figures *could be seen* fleeing through the mountains, sorrowful mothers with their children, and *it seemed* that their wailing and bitter laments could still be heard. The Argive women *were shown* going in and out of the high towers in different groups, burning everything, after they had consigned the corpses of their men to the flames.)
> (11.74, 1–8; emphasis mine)

In this passage, Boccaccio's ekphrastic technique underscores the relationship between image and word by framing the presence of sound and movement within the image.[50] The description of the historiated walls offers a rich phenomenology of the physical mechanisms of visual observation: (1) looking left and right, proceeding sequentially (11.76, 4–6: "et rimirando un poco più avante, / in prigion si vedeano, et l'amoroso / giardino ancora a·llato a·lloro stante," "By looking a little further on, one could see them in prison, and the amorous garden near their room, too"); (2) zooming from long shots to close-ups (11.72, 4–6: "et similmente si vedeva il sito / di Thebe qual el fu né più né meno, / e ' monti ancor donde era circuito," "The setting of Thebes just as it was, neither more nor less, and the mountains which surrounded it were portrayed"); and (3) concentrating the eyesight to distinguish the details of what one sees (11.73, 4–6: "et quale era valente / et qual codardo assai bene advisati / eran da chi mirava fisamente," "and anyone who looked at it for a long time could detect very well which men were valiant and which cowardly"). The reader's experience of ocular and cognitive disorientation in switching from master text to commentary is metaphorically reenacted by the viewer's sequential observing of the walls in Arcita's temple.[51]

When describing Boccaccio's ekphrastic technique and its summarizing and duplicative aspect, Johannes Bartuschat hinted at its implications as metacritical discourse on the intersemiotic relationships between media: "The poem is implicitly compared to a figurative work because of its monumentality, that is, its ability to transmit the memory of heroes to future generations."[52] In short, the ekphrastic device is structural to the text's narration, and it also raises questions of visuality and representation in a book that makes constant use of visual aids as a means to condition the consumption of the poem.

Boccaccio attempts to conjugate the pictorial and the poetic, to inscribe the presence of language within images, to provide a language to talk about visual arts, and to scrutinize the linguistic and sensorial issues of poetic mimesis. The coincidence between content, *forma tractatus*, *forma tractandi*, and materiality now assumes a clearer physiognomy. At the material level of the manuscript, the reader comes into contact with the codex's spatial and formal strategies of articulation, visual order, and reprise of the poem's textual contents: Mary Carruthers argues that "marginal notations, glosses, and images are an integral part of the *painture* of literature, addressing the ocular gateway to memory and meditation."[53] At the level of textual content, the reader is exposed to the narrative continuum in the form of visual re-presentation.

This inextricable connection between the visual and the verbal, between the material and the textual, was never fully accomplished in *Aut*: the autograph's program of illustrations was never executed.[54] However, the mere arrangement of the blank spaces for those illustrations shows that *Aut* was conceived in textual and visual form. Illustrations are not systematically assigned to fixed areas of the folio (upper or lower margins, historiated initials, etc.). Their collocation varies and often breaks the metrical cohesion of the stanza in order to accomplish an ideal correspondence between word and image.[55]

Intertextuality and Materiality

Boccaccio's "archeological" project of an epic poem in the vernacular can be ascribed to the broader cultural project of authorizing and canonizing vernacular literature. This project—which includes Boccaccio's editorial and exegetical promotion of Dante's work—is informed by "classicistic" principles and citational practices. It aims to institute a relation of continuity and equality between vernacular texts and classical texts, by providing the former with the same aura of authority (and even antiquity) as the latter. Boccaccio's *imitatio*—his active rewriting of antiquity—involves both the literary aspects of his classical models and the physical features of the manuscripts that contained them. If in the *Teseida* he reproduces epic codes and conventions from his principal epic model, Statius's *Thebaid*, then in *Aut* he specifically replicates the material characteristics—marginal and interlinear apparatus, *mise-en-page*—that he found in the manuscripts of Statius's works he could procure for himself. Boccaccio's intertextual practice, in short, cites, manipulates, and appropriates both textual and material forms of classical literature (or that transmitted classical literature).

Epic

The *Teseida*'s concluding stanzas (12.84–86) are introduced by the rubric "Parole dell'autore al libro suo" (Words of the author to his book). Among these, the antepenultimate stanza has been almost unanimously perceived as a Dantean allusion. In the *De vulgari eloquentia* (2.2.8), Dante famously complains about the absence of martially themed poetry in the Italian vernacular: "Arma vero nullum latium adhuc invenio poetasse" (As for arms, I find that no Italian has yet treated them in poetry).[56] By having it sing the labors endured for Mars "in Italian" (12.84, 8: "nel volgar latio"), Boccaccio expects the *Teseida* to fill this void.[57] We can read this poem as part of Boccaccio's lifelong attempt to create a canon of vernacular texts and thus institute a vernacular *auctoritas*, an undertaking that is also manifest in his curatorial-editorial intervention in Dante's oeuvre we discussed in chapter 3.[58] It can be associated, in Martin Eisner's words, with "Boccaccio's larger strategy of authorizing himself by canonizing others."[59] We saw in chapter 3 that, from the 1350s on, Boccaccio devoted much of his intellectual efforts to the celebration of Dante as *auctor*. This made Boccaccio (possibly alongside Dante's own sons, Jacopo and Pietro) the most competent and enthusiastic Dante scholar of the fourteenth century. Boccaccio was well aware of the positive repercussions of this critical strategy for his own literary career.

Significant analogies can be observed between the material setting of *Aut* and Boccaccio's editions of Dante's "epic" text. We have three extant copies of Boccaccio's transcription of the *Commedia*, transmitted in three manuscripts: MSS Toledo Zelada 104.6 (ca. 1350), Riccardiano 1035 (ca. 1360), and Chigi L.VI.213 (ca. 1363–66). We do not have the antigraphs from which Boccaccio transcribed his copies. In the extant witnesses of the *Commedia* produced in Florence in the fourteenth century, we recognize a regular and uniform presentation, which resembles Petrucci's definition of the deluxe register-book: parchment support, large format, text in two columns, and minuscule chancery script.[60] For his own transcriptions of the *Commedia*, Boccaccio ostensibly rejects this model and chooses in its stead a different codicological form, opting for a medium format, a formal book hand, and a single column of text with ample margins. Coherent with this editorial project, his transcriptions of Dante's *Vita nova* present a similar layout: centralized poetic texts and marginalized *divisioni*. In the *Vita nova*, this form entailed an active editorial process of expunging sections of Dante's prose from the center of the folio and placing them in the margins as commentary. Boccaccio's sensibility to *mise-en-texte* and *mise-en-page* is clearly indicated in the editorial note to the *Vita nova* in MS Toledo 104.6 (fol. 29r) in which he justifies this innovation, and again in MS Chigi L.V.176 (fol. 13r). Although he was not advancing a specifically epic agenda in the *Vita nova*, Boccaccio was pursuing "classicizing" goals that he pushed yet further in his transcriptions of the *Commedia* and in his own *Aut*.

The convergence between Boccaccio's treatment of Dante's texts and his codicological choices for the *Teseida* in *Aut* is evident for us modern readers, but not historically obvious or predictable. Boccaccio's material presentation, in each instance, reveals an attempt to create a series of authoritative texts in the vernacular in dialogue and/or in rivalry with classical texts. The autograph of the *Teseida* also presents a single column of text—with four octaves on each side of the folio—and ample margins. The beginning of each book never coincides with the upper margin of a folio or with a new quire. This highly consistent approach to beginnings indicates an attention to the integrity of the poem as a whole, in competition with the discrete measure of books and subsections. This codicological solution might even allude to—and materially translate—the classical notion of *carmen continuum* (i.e., undivided poem) alongside the meticulous system of divisions and subdivisions.[61]

With the *mise-en-page* of *Aut*, Boccaccio pursued what Jeffrey Schnapp described as "the antiquity effect," which Boccaccio associated with the manuscripts that preserve and transmit classical poetry, manuscripts visually characterized by the placement of a master text in a single centered column for each side of the folio, with ample margins for annotations.[62] This textual style was most common for the long sequences of dactylic hexameters in epic poetry. And among the manuscripts transmitting hexametric poetry in Latin, those of the *Thebaid* seem to have played a dominant role in Boccaccio's literary project for a vernacular epic.[63]

Teseida and *Thebaid*

John W. Mackail was the first to note that the *Teseida* exactly replicates the number of lines of Virgil's *Aeneid.*[64] But among the texts on Boccaccio's desk, Statius's *Thebaid*—not the *Aeneid*—was the closest literary model for the *Teseida.* Schnapp characterizes the *Teseida* as "a sort of vernacular commentary on Statius's *Thebaid,* inasmuch as Boccaccio's continuation surrounds and supplants the very poem from which it claims to derive and in whose name it presumes to speak."[65] Boccaccio's poem can be seen, then, as both an epigonal continuation and an original expansion of Statius's plot.

Statius's *Thebaid* was a cornerstone of medieval education. The anonymous commentary known from its incipit as the *In principio*, composed in northern France in the twelfth century within the circle of Anselm of Laon, ranks Statius immediately after Virgil as a model of elevated style.[66] In his studies on the reception of classical texts up to the twelfth century, Birger Munk Olsen includes Statius in the canon of eight most copied *auctores.* Without counting its presence in excerpts and *florilegia*, Statius's *Thebaid* is preserved by more than 250 manuscripts, a noteworthy eighty-five of which were transcribed between the ninth and the twelfth century.[67] Of these eighty-five, only four transmit the poem without an exegetical apparatus. Medieval readers such as Boccaccio could potentially have approached the poem with the aid of a rich set of paratextual devices: *accessus ad auctorem*, late antique and medieval continuous commentaries, *argumenta* in verse and prose, *epitaphia*, marginalia, and interlinear glosses.

In the letter (*Epistole* 4) "Sacre famis et angelice viro dilecto forti" (To the beloved man of holy and angelic fame)—composed in Naples in 1339 and autographically preserved in the so-called *Zibaldone Laurenziano*—Boccaccio asks an anonymous friend for a copy of the *Thebaid* with a commentary, possibly by Lactantius Placidus.[68] In this letter, Boccaccio explains that the copy of the poem he has recently acquired lacks an exegetical apparatus: he finds it extremely difficult to read Statius "sine magistro vel glosis" (without a teacher or notes). As Giuseppe Billanovich suggested, this epistle reads as a *dictamen*: a conventional rhetorical exercise in letter form without a real addressee.[69] The request for a copy of the *Thebaid* with which the epistle ends might also be a conventional *petitio.* Even as he wrote the letter (coeval to the composition of the *Teseida*), Boccaccio had probably already procured that copy for himself. The statement that a commentary is indispensable for fully understanding an authoritative text—and a classical *auctoritas* in particular—is likely conventional.[70] The conventional assumption that commentary is indispensable to text helps to understand that Boccaccio's promotion of vernacular literature necessarily entailed for the *Teseida* an exegetical apparatus and, above all, the aura this apparatus would confer.

We have one manuscript of Statius's poem that unquestionably belonged to Boccaccio: MS Pluteo 38.6 of the Biblioteca Medicea Laurenziana in Florence.[71] We also know of two additional manuscripts of the *Thebaid* that were at some point in his possession.[72] Moreover, we have indirect proof that Boccaccio used at least one further manuscript of the poem: David Anderson has identified conspicuous references in the *Teseida* to the aforementioned *In principio* commentary, which is not transmitted by any of the *Teseida* manuscripts we know Boccaccio had access to.[73]

When describing Boccaccio's relationship to Statius's poem, we can consider the former's literary activity as an example of that ideal (and material) continuation between sources and of the kind of creative writing that characterized medieval cultural models of literary composition, where the practice of reading and the practice of writing flowed seamlessly into each other. Scholars and cultivated readers read to write and read while they were writing: as Petrucci pointed out, a scholar would read "to compose a text of his own that was largely made up of the citations of others; he read by writing, because he continuously annotated books in the margins and between the lines."[74] Boccaccio's reading of the *Thebaid* thus flows seamlessly into—and perhaps occurs simultaneously with—his writing of the *Teseida.* The *Thebaid* is first and foremost a textual and literary model for the *Teseida*. Whereas Boccaccio's practice of actively rewriting his sources often makes it difficult to detect the *Thebaid*'s presence in the octaves of the *Teseida*, Statius's poem, as Punzi has argued, "is instead recuperated in the commentary as reference background in which to insert his own poetic inventions."[75] The extensive gloss (at *Teseida* 3.5) summarizing the plot of the *Thebaid* confirms the attention Boccaccio allocated to the audience's exact comprehension of the subtle references to structural elements and specific passages in the *Thebaid.*

Boccaccio's rewriting of the *Thebaid* into the commentary of the *Teseida* shows the eminently citational nature of his "scholarly" approach to classical literature. It also inscribes in *Aut*'s *mise-en-page* the relationship of textual and material continuity between reading and writing described by Petrucci. And by integrating into *Aut*'s materiality the Statian sources of the *Teseida*—the layers of the poem's intertextual stratigraphy—he demonstrates that the commentary is an essential part of understanding the octaves and that vernacular texts, like classical literature, cannot be fully experienced "sine magistro vel glosis."

Imitatio

The practice of active and eclectic *imitatio* of classical models features consistently in Boccaccio's literary production. And a shared knowledge between author and audience is the foundation of the "social" aspect of his intertextuality. By alluding to or explicitly imitating episodes and *topoi* of Statius's *Thebaid*—and, more generally, of classical epic—Boccaccio is giving his audience what they expect to find in an epic poem: invocations to the Muses, catalogues, orations, arming scenes, scenes of heroes at their finest in battle, funeral games, digressions, sacrifices to the gods, divine interventions *ex machina*, theomachies—to name a few.

Boccaccio's *imitatio* is not limited to the linguistic and literary aspects of the *Thebaid*. He alludes to classical epic in the forms in which it is materially transmitted. The material presentation of the *Teseida* in *Aut*, in other words, alludes to the codicological features of the exemplars of Statius's *Thebaid* that Boccaccio had in various moments on his desk. As Robert R. Edwards has indicated, "Boccaccio reproduces the apparatus of a classical poem as read in a manuscript culture."[76] And Patrizia Rafti reminds us that Boccaccio the scribe is deeply influenced by the visual aesthetics of the model from which he transcribes and whose overall arrangement and presentation he intends to reproduce.[77] The *Thebaid* is never, for Boccaccio, a text in the abstract: it is always linked to, and embodied in, the concrete codices that preserve it. Boccaccio's intertextuality, in other words, involves both textual and material forms.

This material intertextuality can become actual codicological "mimicry," as Boccaccio's skillful restoration of MS Laurenziano Pluteo 36.8 of the *The-*

baid well exemplifies. In this restoration, dated between 1340 and 1345, Boccaccio integrates four missing folios and transcribes the missing portions of text and commentary in compliance with the general material features and visual aesthetics of MS Pluteo 36.8. Furthermore, he provides the poem with his own marginalia, which he models after those of Lactantius Placidus.[78]

The reproduction in *Aut* of specific material components of the Statian manuscripts provide further evidence of Boccaccio's imitative and allusive skills. Anderson has pointed out that the dicolic title *Teseida: Delle nozze d'Emilia* reproduces the two-membered *titulus* of the *Thebaid* as it appears in MS Pluteo 38.6 (fol. 1r): "*Statius Thebaydos ystoria destructionis thebarum.*"[79] Vandelli indicated, furthermore, that the introductory sonnets heading each book of the *Teseida* resemble the summarizing *argumenta* at the beginning of the books of the *Thebaid* and occupy the same positions that the *argumenta* hold in several medieval codices of the *Thebaid.*[80] And we could add to this list Boccaccio's interlinear annotations in the text of the *Thebaid*, which reproduce, and are echoed in, the interlinear annotations that we see in *Aut.* But it is above all the material and morphological similarities between Lactantius Placidus's commentary to Statius as it appears in MS Pluteo 38.6 and Boccaccio's marginal self-commentary in *Aut* that most clearly demonstrate Boccaccio's citational approach to the material features of the manuscripts on his desk.[81]

Materiality and Exegesis

By providing his poem with a commentary, Boccaccio outlined an ambitious and complex book project that relocates the reading experience of classical epic to the vernacular.[82] Boccaccio also enjoyed a uniquely privileged position of controlling the architecture of the space of the book, the geometry of the page, and the density of information. Whereas a scribe would often have to copy a commentary from an antigraph that had material features quite different from those of the codex that conveyed the primary text, Boccaccio could undertake a project that a priori maximized space and the relationship between text and commentary. And yet, even in their most charitable approaches to the *Teseida*, scholars have largely overlooked the textual and material features of Boccaccio's commentary and the literary project they entail. By conducting a coordinated analysis of the codicological and exegetical features of the commentary to the *Teseida* in *Aut*, this section argues that Boccaccio's material and textual distinction between—and mutual implication of—author and commentator creates a multilayered and polysemic book-object open to further and diverse levels of consumption. Rather than delivering *the* reading of the *Teseida*, Boccaccio's commentary authorizes others to read the *Teseida*, and not necessarily in the way that Boccaccio would. The *Teseida* as presented in *Aut*, in other words, is a work that competes with classical and Christian authorities and also participates in the status of those works as infinitely subject to further interpretation, new or different commenting, or—as we will observe in chapter 5—the selective/entire removal of commentary by new readers and copyists.

Critical Fortune

Whether or not the *Teseida* instantiates a poetry of arms in the vernacular, the issue of its genre, the allegedly unbalanced ratio between the martial theme and the erotic matter, the technical aspects of its *ottava rima*, and its relationship to oral poetry are all vexed questions that have catalyzed critics' attention and have resulted in a certain antipathy toward the poem. Vittore Branca, following closely on Benedetto Croce's idealism, critiqued Boccaccio's prosodic immaturity, lexical imprecision, artistic insensitivity, pedantic erudition, and petty bourgeoisification of the poetic life of the *cantari*.[83] Alberto Limentani dispraised the mechanical juxtaposition of chivalric and classical elements and their failed integration into a harmonic whole.[84] Piero Boitani lamented the lack of consequentiality among the poem's narrative components and exposed Boccaccio's "strange mixture of naïveté, self consciousness, love of erudition and mania for displaying the interior mechanism of his poem" as disruptive features for the literary plausibility of the *Teseida*.[85] Winthrop Wetherbee underscored "the incongruity of Boccaccio's pseudo-classicism" and the burden of conventional and decorative elements.[86] The *Teseida*'s versification technique has also received less than gratifying remarks: Salvatore Battaglia talked about "violence to the rules of traditional versification"; Limentani complained about "actual metrical wedges"; and Arnaldo Soldani deplored in Boccaccio's *ottava* "a certain lack of an accomplished awareness of the expressive means."[87] Francesco Bruni and, more recently, Lucia Battaglia Ricci have expressed more positive remarks in their evaluation of Boccaccio's work as a whole. Bruni has described the *Teseida*'s allegedly unresolved dualism of epic and romance in the more flattering terms of "double inspiration."[88] Battaglia Ricci has stressed the coherence and continuity between the poem and the other texts of Boccaccio's corpus.[89]

With few exceptions, this most recent positive reevaluation of the *Teseida* has not involved its commentary as it is presented in *Aut*. The presence of that commentary has elicited minimal interest among Boccaccio's readers. Vandelli had made short work of it: by describing the glosses as being "not without numerous abstrusities and excesses" and "very peculiar," he contributed to the idea that the commentative apparatus was merely a frivolous literary divertissement.[90] More harshly, Limentani liquidated the long allegorical glosses in book 7 as "a confused and absurd allegorical analysis."[91] For Hollander, 1,000 of the roughly 1,200 glosses "have little interest for one who would find some indications, in the author's own hand, of his eventual purpose in writing the *Teseida*."[92] Even Francesca Malagnini's and Martina Mazzetti's recent work on the relationship between visual presentation and verbal apparatus in *Aut* mostly focused on Boccaccio's illustrative project. Furthermore, Malagnini broadly excluded the commentary as "ipotesto aggiuntivo" (supplementary hypotext), not text, maintaining that "the glosses, as witnessed by the manuscript tradition, . . . are not strictly necessary to the work," as opposed to the rubrics that are intrinsically part of the text and not specific to *Aut*.[93] That a scholar—and a rigorous one—in the first decade of the twenty-first century could dismiss the commentary altogether as "not strictly necessary" indicates that significant work remains in recuperating this textual apparatus, and Boccaccio's material presentation of this apparatus, into our understanding of this work.

Materiality and Glosses

Paul Oskar Kristeller described commentaries as the most distinctive kind of literary production in the Middle Ages.[94] And Paul Zumthor argued that "all medieval poetry appears on the one hand as continuation and on the other as commentary."[95] Consistent with this recognition of commentaries' significance to medieval literary production, we can see in *Aut*'s marginal and interlinear commentary the most ingenious aspect of Boccaccio's editorial strategy.[96] If we agree with Cesare Segre's general assessment that "the commentary inserts itself as code breaker between sender and receiver" and bridges an "epistemic distance" between them, the *Teseida*'s simulated distinction between author and commentator assumes a strategic role in the history of the poem's reception: it pretends to broaden that epistemic distance.[97] In the terms proposed by Eco, the *Teseida*'s commentary camouflages the *intentio auctoris* (the empirical author's project) into an allegedly more objective *intentio operis* (the work's signification system through its textual and material articulation) in order to orient the *intentio lectoris* (what the reader makes of the text).[98] Readers are expected to approach the *Teseida*'s central text as an authoritative text, a "classic in the vernacular," because Boccaccio effectively deployed his commentary—its material presentation more so than its hermeneutical method proper—to signal the *Teseida* as requiring the mediation of an exegetical apparatus as classical texts also do.

The material characteristics and positioning of the commentary offer valuable insights into the literary strategy that *Aut* embodies. Battaglia described the marginal glosses very briefly in his critical edition of the poem: "extended and organic commentary that deals with the content of the poem by integrating, expanding, and paraphrasing it; it positions itself along all four margins of the page, around the poetic text, but with regular and beautiful symmetry."[99] Battaglia's description has often been cited. When we reexamine *Aut*'s *mise-en-page*, however, we see that the commentary does indeed consistently occupy the lateral margins of the poetic text, does run below the last horizontal line delimiting the lower border of the writing frame (but not above the upper border), but never surrounds the octaves (with the sole exception of fol. 41v). The commentary's material presentation variably corresponds to what Gerhardt Powitz describes as *Zwei-Spalten-Typ* ("two-column type") and, less frequently, *Drei-Spalten-Typ* ("three-column type"): in the former, the main text and the commentary are laid out in two columns (with the commentary generally on the outer margin); in the latter, the commentary is placed in two columns on both sides of the main text.[100]

Powitz's classification is useful for describing the immediate appearance of the commentary on the folio façade (its *figura*, in medieval terms), but it does not address the relationship between text and commentary.[101] In a seminal article on manuscripts containing texts with a commentary, Marilena Maniaci has offered more sophisticated guidelines for the material description of glossed manuscripts, focusing on the dynamic interactions between text and commentary rather than their mere presentation on the page.[102] Her protocol of analysis includes distribution of space between text and commentary, preparation of the page, form of connection between text and commentary, strategies of dissimilation between text and commentary, and temporal sequence of transcription. Maniaci's protocol thus allows for a more detailed description of the commentative apparatus. And if we apply her theoretical model to *Aut*, our manuscript's sophisticated editorial project becomes readily visible. First, the writing space for the verse is framed by two double vertical lines and two single horizontal lines; the commentary never intersects with the octaves. Second, where the main text is distributed over forty hard point ruled lines with a distance between lines of 5 mm, the distance between lines in the space dedicated to the commentary narrows down to 2.5 mm. Third, text and commentary blocks are generally juxtaposed: that is, a mostly unambiguous parallelism occurs between poem and relevant gloss. The connection can also materialize (sometimes redundantly) through additional verbal and symbolic strategies: repetition within the gloss of the words of the poem commented upon, the indication *nota* (abbreviated *no*), alphabetic symbols, paragraph signs, silcrows, and line fillers. Fourth, the gloss script is the same book hand as the verse, but reduced in module, presenting a slightly higher degree of cursivity, and featuring more frequent abbreviations. In a few glosses (e.g., fol. 42r) the script assumes occasional *mercantesca* traits.[103] Fifth, the space between words in the gloss script is in some instances reduced to match the quantity of space available: in *Aut*, in fact, the inner margin of the folio is always narrower than the outer margin, meaning that the script of inner-margin glosses is typically more condensed than that of outer-margin counterparts. And sixth, valuable as we assess the temporal modality of transcription of text and commentary, recent linguistic analysis by Francesca Faleri persuasively highlights different orthographic practices between the poem and the commentary, confirming Vandelli's hypothesis that Boccaccio wrote (and transcribed on *Aut*) the marginal glosses *after* the main text, if only shortly after.[104]

The material distinction between interlinear glosses and marginal glosses corresponds to a rhetorical one: the interlinear glosses are mostly limited to paraphrasing single lemmas, while the marginal glosses provide a more extensive expansion on the poetic text. This commentative subdivision complies with the hermeneutical categories of *littera*, *sensus*, and *sententia* exposed by Hugh of Saint Victor in the *Didascalicon de studio legendi*.[105] Boccaccio's apparatus evidently applies to the poem the traditional exegetical practices used for sacred texts and for (typologically interpreted) classical literature.

The border—textual and material—between poem and commentary is often porous and permeable: text and paratext closely interact. We can see clearly, however, Boccaccio's attempt to distinguish the main text from the commentary, and to keep their respective writers separate. The *mise-en-texte* and *mise-en-page* of octaves and marginalia show a strategic distribution and hierarchization of text space, commentary space, and blank space. The visual architecture of the page reflects a specific knowledge design. Poetry and commentary are kept distinct to comply with the fictitious distinction between the personae of the author and the interpreter. The centrality of the octaves aims to institute the *Teseida* as a unique, stable, and definitive classic. The organization of the glosses in the margins presents the commentary as a much-needed instrument of interpretation. However, the decentralized and peripheral collocation of the glosses implies the notion of commentary as a fluid and constantly evolving text. This dual relationship of distinction and implication of author and commentator is coherently maintained through the use of identical script, but that script is hierarchically reduced in size for the commentary. This effect of dissimilation is counterbalanced by the close juxtaposition of the two texts, aimed at minimizing the reader's visual itinerary between main text and ancillary text.

Sub cortice fabularum

A key issue in evaluating the commentary is its authorizing and ennobling function as part of Boccaccio's classicizing project. Hollander argued that "to herald the rebirth of epic in a modern tongue it was only fitting that the instant classic be born *cum commento*."[106] And Schnapp similarly associated the writing of the commentary with Boccaccio's project of dignifying vernacular literature after Dante's magisterium (but also beyond the latter's towering presence).[107]

This strategy of authentication and authorization of vernacular culture engages several aspects of the commentary. We can approach the exegetical practices provided in the commentary to the *Teseida* by referring to the later, monumental conceptual system of the *Genealogie deorum gentilium* (*Genealogies of the Gentile Gods*), where Boccaccio will give a precise (and explicit) theoretical foundation to these practices while outlining his apology for literature.[108] By clarifying unusual or obsolete words and interpreting tropes and figures, for instance, the *Teseida*'s glosses of linguistic and rhetorical content explain the excellence and necessity of poetic *ornatus*: plain truth gives no pleasure and is easily forgotten (*Genealogie* 14.12).[109] And through the notes of allegorical inspiration, the commentary sustains an apologia for poetic fiction. This aspect of the commentary can be inscribed within the general predisposition for *allegoresis* that characterizes most of Boccaccio's literary criticism, including his exegesis of Dante's *Commedia*. Allegorical commentaries are for Boccaccio the instruments through which the Holy Scriptures reveal the inscrutabilities of the history of salvation. Similarly, through *allegoresis*, poetic fiction acquires a truthful foundation that discloses the effects of vices and virtues. Commentaries are presented as unavoidable supporting instruments (*subsidia*) for the interpretation of poetic *fictio* (*Genealogie* 15.6.13).[110]

The meaning of the text, in sum, is not limited to the explanation of its own plot: under its outer layer—"sub cortice fabularum" (beneath the surface of their fictions) (*Genealogie* 14.10)[111]—the text offers a meaning whose ultimate goal is the spiritual elevation of the reader. And this hermeneutic practice affects theology and poetry alike. The extensive marginal note that accompanies on fols. 75v–77v the digression on the temple of Venus in the poem's book 7, for instance, implies a resemanticization of the nature of love and an innovative twist from the tradition of the troubadour and Tuscan erotic poetry. The note provides an explanation of the soul's concupiscible appetite by referencing the twofold nature of Venus:

> La quale Venere è doppia, perciò che·ll'una si può et dee intendere per ciascuno honesto et licito disiderio, sì come è disiderare d'avere moglie per avere figliuoli, e simili a questo; et di questa Venere non si parla qui. La seconda Venere è quella per la quale ogni lascivia è disiderata, et che volgarmente è chiamata dea d'amore.
>
> ———
>
> (This Venus is twofold, since one can be understood as every chaste and licit desire, as is the desire to have a wife in order to have children, and

> such like. This Venus is not discussed here. The second Venus is that through which all lewdness is desired, commonly called the goddess of love.)

By giving primacy to married love over passionate love, the note rejects the courtly notion of erotic—and extramarital—vassalage in favor of monogamy and marriage (also alluded to, after all, in the title of the poem).[112]

Significantly, the *commentator* always presents himself as a different persona than the *auctor* (with one ambiguous exception, as we shall see). We can also notice how the figures of *auctor* and *commentator* seem to diverge with respect to their specific intertextual competence and strategies. Whereas the *auctor* explicitly mentions the antiquity of his source, the *commentator* is open to contemporary medieval literary production. The gloss on the temple of Venus directly quotes Guido Cavalcanti's *canzone* "Donna me prega" (A lady bids me). The mention of physician Dino del Garbo's scientific commentary on Cavalcanti's poem further broadens the chain of intertextual references and increases the authority of Boccaccio's epos.[113] If we turn again, incidentally, from the specific context of the *Teseida*'s glosses to the general model for interpretation provided in the *Genealogie*, we find a later theoretical confirmation of this openness to using nonancient texts for exegetical purposes. The indispensable aid to interpretation that commentaries offer, in fact, legitimates the extreme solutions of resorting to little known ancient and even modern authors (*Genealogie* 15.6.14).[114]

The enunciator's simulation of a plural identity can be further seen in the paratextual fiction of the dedicatory preface to Fiammetta, where the *compilator* (as the *persona loquens* implicitly describes himself) subliminally intimates his own uncertainty in matters of the poem's interpretation, indirectly revealing a discrepancy between the *intentio auctoris* (the author's intended meaning as explicitly stated) and the *intentio operis* (the work's meaning as emerges from its signification system). As Victoria Kirkham has observed, Fiammetta provides "more penetrating" insight and, importantly, the dicolic title itself (as reported in the concluding sonnet, v. 12).[115] The *persona loquens* of the preface, in other words, identifies Fiammetta as the reader in charge of deciphering the "chiuso parlare" (figurative speech) of the octaves. On the one hand, the dedicatory preface to Fiammetta presents the poem as the lover's attempt to seduce the beloved: "Et tanto m'ànno oltre ad questo le cose traverse di conoscimento lasciato, che io sento che per humiltà ben servendo ogni durezza si vince et merita buono guiderdone" (And besides this, adversities have schooled me so well, that I feel that a man can triumph over every form of harshness and win his prize by humble devotion).[116] On the other hand, the dedication invests its titular dedicatee with the hermeneutic skills to read beyond the literal meaning and discern the text's own purpose. The author almost declares himself incompetent at recognizing and stating the true essence of his work beyond, of course, the immediate goal of his erotic gratification.[117] As Janet Smarr has suggested, we have a separation here not only between poet and commentator, but also between poet—who "pretends to miss the point of his own book"—and lover.[118] The lover, in other words, becomes the implicit target of a belittling strategy enacted by the *persona loquens*, who paradoxically coincides with the lover himself. On the one hand, this mythopoetic writing is the literary transfiguration of the author's personal elegy, as stated in the dedication preface addressed to Fiammetta:

> ciò che sotto il nome dell'uno de' due amanti et della giovane amata si conta essere stato, ricordandovi bene, et io ad voi di me et voi ad me di voi, se non mentiste potreste conoscere essere stato decto e facto in parte: quale de' due si sia non discuopro, ché so che ve ne advedrete.[119]

> (if you remember well, you will be able to recognize in what is related of one of the lovers and of the young lady who is loved, things said and done by me to you and by you to me, if you were not false. Which of the two it is, I will not reveal because I know that you will discern it.)

On the other hand, the poem's "chiuso parlare" implies deciphering a message deeper than the mere recognition of the *persona loquens*'s literary identity behind one of the poem's characters (alluded to in the passage cited above). In this case, the poem's meaning involves the essence of erotic feelings. As her proposed book title will confirm at the end of the poem—at the end, that is, of her reading of the poem—Fiammetta will inscribe the *Teseida* within an inquiry into the nature of love, where Love is reread in a "moralizing" manner and the poem's courtly combination of love and arms is resolutely unbalanced toward the former in spite of the poem's self-styled epic subject matter.

Authorizing Strategies

To gauge the true hidden meaning of the text—to elucidate poetic obscurity—one needs a specific doctrinal competence. This is provided (and exhibited) in the apparatus of poetic and critical texts that surrounds the poem with a scholarly cultural context. By referencing these texts, the marginalia de facto position the poem within a canon of authoritative works. Schnapp has argued that a scholarly commentary was probably a precautionary measure against the *profanum vulgus*, suggesting that Boccaccio joined Dante in rejecting the values of the recently enriched mercantile class.[120] And we saw above that Hollander dismissed 1,000 of the approximately 1,200 marginal and interlinear glosses as irrelevant for interpretation, saving only those of allegorical content or those showing Boccaccio's proto-humanist expertise: the main purpose of these texts, in Hollander's reading, is "to create an atmosphere around the poem, to lend to it the status of 'instant classic.'"[121] Hollander also adopted a somewhat condescending tone in his comments on the glosses, undermining the effectiveness of Boccaccio's strategy: "One smiles at Boccaccio's little game somewhat sadly: Had he revealed himself publicly as his own glossator his exertions would have seemed the self-loving effort of a nervous father."[122] And yet the commentary—all the commentary, and not just a small fraction of it—is certainly relevant. It shares with the octaves a critical and editorial project, aimed at inscribing the poem within the vernacular literary canon; or rather, aimed at instituting this canon of vernacular texts. The poem's antepenultimate octave makes explicit reference to this project, most probably alluding to Dante's well-known complaint in the *De vulgari eloquentia* (2.2.8) on the absence of epic poetry in Italian vernacular. The *Teseida* is ostentatiously proposed to its readership as a commented text because it is conceived as a text open to commentary, or rather, as a text that *must* necessarily be commented upon. Carruthers maintains that Boccaccio bases the production of a literary work—including the specific case of the *Teseida*—on the never-ending interaction between texts and readers in the texts' margins: "By giving his new work all the trappings of a glossed book,

Boccaccio was claiming for it the immediate institutional status of an *auctor*."[123] Boccaccio's commentary, to put it differently, should not be invoked as an absolute model for the hermeneutics of the poem. And a serious consideration (and material description) of Boccaccio's self-exegesis does not necessarily conflict with the Barthesian notion of the "death of the author" as precondition for readerly and interpretive practices.[124] In the case of the *Teseida*, the crucial presence of the commentary is more important than the effectiveness or reliability of that commentary in elucidating a correct—because authorial—interpretation. The commentary does not convey *the* correct and authentic interpretation of the text, authoritatively imposed by the author. The relevance of the commentary does not preclude—and, historically, it did not preclude—the poem's openness to alternative readings.[125] These readings may be even more persuasive or refined than those provided within Boccaccio's work, at least if we recall how the preface explicitly invests Fiammetta—the dedicatee of the *Teseida*—to detect the allegorical meaning beyond the letter of the poem's text. We often have the paradoxical impression that Boccaccio is not the most convincing interpreter of his own work, or, rather, that he enjoys being deliberately misleading about it, thus inviting, or even challenging, his readers to come up with alternative readings: in this, Boccaccio's glosses differ from Dante's explicitly authorial (and therefore authoritative) commentary in the *Vita nova*.

But the authorization and canonization of vernacular literature do not exhaust Boccaccio's intellectual project of advancing vernacular culture. Boccaccio's editorial project is subtler than his critics are inclined to concede, and it certainly included an openness to a large and growing section of the readership—literate merchants—into which he himself was born. Both the Neapolitan court and the readers Boccaccio would find in Florence were eager to be exposed to tales set in antiquity, as the coeval proliferation of *volgarizzamenti* ("vernacular translations") of classical texts also indicates.[126]

Authorship and Authority

The notion of authorship that permeates the *Teseida* is specific to the century of its composition. As Boccaccio writes his poem, in the fourteenth century, the perception of authorship, authenticity, and authority is mobile and ambiguous. To approach authorial functions as Boccaccio likely did, a modern reader might look back to Bonaventure of Bagnorea's fourfold classification of the ways of making a book (*faciendi librum*), to which as many writing figures correspond: *scriptor*, *compilator*, *commentator*, *auctor* (scribe, compiler, commentator, author).[127] The *scriptor* is the copyist, the scribe, the individual who materially transcribes someone else's text. The *compilator* is one who adds texts together (that are not his or hers). The *commentator* supplements primary texts with a written commentary. And the term *auctor* conceptually indicates the intellectual producer of his or her own texts but also refers more generally to the authoritative texts themselves. Although Bonaventure's terms and their cognates reassuringly occur in the various layers of the *Teseida*, the notorious inconsistency of the vernacular literary-critical lexicon should, again, dissuade us from instituting a deterministic correspondence between Bonaventure's categories and Boccaccio's authorial identities. Bonaventure's classification, additionally, reflects an attempt to systematize an evolving and more fluid scenario, where author, scribe, commentator, and compiler have mutually permeable borders: at the end of the thirteenth century, for instance, Florentine judge Bono Giamboni rewrites Lothar of Segni's *De contemptu mundi* in vernacular without mentioning his source text, thus presenting his *volgarizzamento* as a genuinely authorial primary text.[128] In a scenario like this, the notion of authorship could often conflate the intellectual originator of a text (the "inventor") with its material executor. The latter often has the capacity (and, in fact, the opportunity and recognized legitimacy) to modify or integrate the text he or she is copying, consequently taking possession of its authorship, signing it, and circulating it as his or her own.[129] Bonaventure's classification, however, gives valuable insight on the multiplicity of authorial figures in Boccaccio's time. In the *Teseida*, Boccaccio certainly plays with the writer figure's polyonymy and pseudonymity—or even anonymity—and exploits the variability of this theoretical frame. And in *Aut*, he materially maximizes the authorizing potentials of the various literary identities he impersonates and stages.

Anonymity

Though Vandelli established with the highest degree of completeness that *Aut* is Boccaccio's autograph, the manuscript itself stands in equally complete anonymity, with neither a signature nor a subscription. This anonymous presentation is consistent with Boccaccio's general tendency to leave his autographs unsigned. Cursi has indicated that only three autographs out of twenty-two present a subscription (all of them with Boccaccio's forename in Latin: *Iohannes*).[130] Agostinelli and Coleman read Boccaccio's signature or, rather, his "self-identifying mark" in "two arbitrarily capitalized and painted two-line capitals: A at I.13 and G at I.36," which would possibly stand for *Autore* and *Giovanni*.[131] The same arbitrary capitalization occurs in the corresponding *loci* of the aforementioned illustrated manuscript of the *Teseida* preserved in the Biblioteca Oratoriana in Naples.[132] Malagnini recently proposed an alternative interpretation, according to which the two capitals instead stand for *Arcita* and *Giovanni*, solving the enigma of the dedicatory preface concerning which protagonist should be associated with the compiler of the poem.[133] This mark does not constitute for the reader, however, an immediately legible sign. Moreover, it is often the case that medieval manuscripts transmitting classical texts bear no indication of author. The work often comes to be identified with the title. According to Violetta de Angelis, an explicit mention of both author and title is, for medieval manuscripts of classical texts, extremely rare.[134] Thus the omission of author identification would further conform with Boccaccio's editorial project of endowing *Aut* with the literary and material features of a classical text.

Authorial Figures

In the previous pages, we have observed in the *Teseida* and in *Aut* a proliferation of authorial identities and their mutually complementing production of meaning. The *auctor* of the *Teseida* derives his authorship from, and builds his authority on, the various material and textual contributions of the multiple literary personae Boccaccio stages in *Aut*: in Bonaventure's terms, the *scriptor* executes an elegant and "classicizing" codicological product; the *commentator* provides an authoritative apparatus and, above all, an aura of authority for the manuscript; and the more ambiguous figure of the *compilator* connects and arranges the various textual components into one multilayered cohesive work. Moreover, the *auctor* of the *Teseida* can dispose of this acquired authority—as we shall see in chapter 5—in light of Boccaccio's predetermined distinction and implication of those personae.

The term *auctor* conceptually indicates the intellectual producer of one's own texts but can also refer to authoritative texts themselves. The name of an *auctor*, in short, does not necessarily indicate a physical person. It may instead be metonymically perceived as a text, or a corpus of texts, whose authority is granted by a tradition: either a direct manuscript tradition, or, indirectly, a tradition in terms of citations and allusions. *Auctoritates* are, in fact, the Holy Scriptures, the Church Fathers' texts, or classical texts typologically (figuratively) reinterpreted. Even if authoritative texts bore the proper names of specific human beings, Albert Ascoli writes, "these texts had been proven to have transcended the limitations of the inevitably fallible men who wrote them and to bear truths that exceeded the limitations of historical contingency—being valid in any time and any place."[135] Ascoli clarifies here that a key aspect of this textual authority was its existence through time. The notion of *auctor*, in other words, entailed a transhistorical reliability that transcends individuals. By means of the material and textual multiplication of his literary identities, Boccaccio makes the relatively unprecedented move of (self-)appointing a vernacular poet with the title of *auctor*, thus bypassing—or rather, compressing—the centuries-long process of authorization through selection generally effected by manuscript tradition and exegetical practice through time.[136]

In the autograph of the *Teseida*, Boccaccio resolves all aspects of literary composition and exegetical practice within the material and institutional frame of the writing process: Gianfranco Alfano has argued that "Boccaccio's Angevin writings show that he tried to establish a sort of equivalence between existence of the book and recognition of an author function."[137] By translating the porousness and mutual permeability of the authorial distinctions into textual and material terms, Boccaccio furthers (or, rather, contributes to the institution of) the modern notions of author and authorship.[138] The numerous Latin and vernacular commentaries that had immediately followed the circulation of Dante's *Commedia* undoubtedly helped Boccaccio shape a new definition of "author," one that entailed both a rejection of a depersonalized figure and the eclectic manipulation of the four levels of writing described by Bonaventure.[139] This paradoxical activity of distinction and synthesis is particularly evident in the *Teseida*'s different textual roles, kept separate and yet executed by the same biographical figure (the *empirical* author). In chapter 6, we will see to what extent Francesco Petrarca performs and embodies this same conflation in an attempt to condition reception and prevent textual *mouvance* (the sprouting and propagation of widely divergent manuscript versions of a given text).

"Che sono io"

In a typical instance of this distinction between authorial identities, the *persona loquens* of the marginalia refers to the poet of the octaves as *autore*. The formulas of these references are rather homogeneous, as in the gloss to *Teseida* 1.14: "Vuole in questa parte l'autore mostrare, poeticamente fingendo, . . ." (In this section the author wants to show by a poetic fiction . . .); or the gloss to *Teseida* 2.10, "Poscia che l'autore à dimostrato di sopra, nel primo libro, . . ." (Since the author has shown in the first book . . .). At a macrotextual level, this strategy exercises a double effect. On the one hand, it confers on the poet the title of *auctor*, of authoritative and authorized litteratus, able to rival classical authors. On the other hand, by playing with the ambiguity of the medieval concept of authorship and the mutual porousness of the notions of *scriptor*, *compilator*, *commentator*, and *auctor*, it enhances the textual distinctiveness of both commentator and author. Consistent with this diffraction of multiple writing personae, in the *Teseida* the *persona loquens* is implicitly referenced as *compilator* twice: in the preface to Fiammetta and in the Muses' responsive sonnet to the author.

Other details show a clear attempt to give the persona of the *commentator* a proper individuality. The *commentator* speaks in the first person in three instances (glosses to 1.8; 2.10; and 12.86), thus explicitly distinguishing himself as one who presents the author's interpretation: "come di sopra ò mostrato . . . così l'autore . . ." (As I demonstrated above . . . Thus the author . . .).[140] The whimsicality of some notes (linguistic, mythological, antiquarian, etc.) that are not strictly pertinent to the sections they gloss further contributes to the persona of the commentator as trustworthy exegete and erudite, who is further distinct from the author also in terms of cultural background.

In one instance, however, these distinctions fade and *commentator* and *auctor* seem to coincide in an enigmatic authorial self-denunciation. This occurs on fol. 34r of *Aut*, in an interlinear (if marginally displaced) note to an octave that deals with the effects on Arcita and Palemone of their love for Emilia (3.35, 1–8):

> Et da' sospiri già ad lagrimare
> eran venuti, et se non fosse stato
> che 'l loro amor non volean palesare,
> sovente avrian per angoscia gridato.
> Et così sa Amore adoperare
> ad cui più per servigio è obligato:
> colui il sa che talvolta fu preso
> da·llui et da cota*li* dolori offeso.[141]
>
> ———
>
> (Now from sighing they advanced to weeping, and if it were not for the fact that they did not want to reveal their love, they would have frequently cried out in their anguish. This is how Love treats those to whom He is most obliged for service. Whoever has been captured by Him at some time and afflicted with similar pangs knows this.)

On the outer margin of v. 7, just above the word "preso" (captured), a gloss explicitly connects commentator and author with a deictic and peremptory personal pronoun: "che sono io" (who I am).[142] Scholars have recognized here Boccaccio's self-disclosing signature. Vandelli considered this a *sotto voce* revelation, "as if these were words meant to reveal as little as possible, almost a secret confidence."[143] Cursi further elaborated on this, focusing on the paleographic features of the annotation. The note is not in the usual gloss script of the rest of the manuscript (similar to Boccaccio's book hand but reduced in module). On the contrary, it is an example of what Cursi calls a "scrittura *sottile*" (*thin* script).[144] Even if this script can be found elsewhere in *Aut*—in editorial revisions and in interlinear notes explaining obscure or obsolete words—it is more often connected to "personal reflections in which the author gives a hint of an interior dialogue between his text and himself."[145] Thomas Stillinger argued that "the gloss mimics the gesture of an author stepping forth from behind his text, yet it preserves an impenetrable anonymity."[146] Worth further attention here is *Aut*'s diachronic script variance (including this "scrittura *sottile*" or the *mercantesca* traits on fol. 42r).

This variance is related to Boccaccio's sequential apostillation of the codex, but also provides material evidence of the authorial voice's diffraction into multiple personae of writers and readers. Boccaccio's maneuver here recalls the unexpected revelation that closes the allegorical poem *Caccia di Diana* (*Diana's Hunt*), where that work's purportedly extradiegetic narrator proves in fact to be one of the characters; or to the splitting of the authorial voice into two pastoral characters in the tenth eclogue of the *Buccolicum carmen*; or to the overlapping between the author's biographic persona and the protagonist's vicissitudes in the *Filostrato* (with allegorical implications and striving for erotic fulfilment similar to those of the *Teseida*).[147] And yet, rather than a dramatic agnition and revelation addressed to the reader, this unexpected identification reads like a self-contented and ludic note from an author well acquainted with multiple literary personae that often cross textual frames. Rather than an author coming onto the stage, we see here the *auctor* sit in the audience and engage in a gallant role reversal with the *lector*—or, perhaps, the *spectator*.

Dissimulations, Omissions, Generative Potentials

Scholars have found the interpretation conveyed by Boccaccio's autocommentary to be broadly unsuccessful:[148] the commentary might have achieved greater success if Boccaccio had not been so overly cryptic in assuming a split identity of *auctor* and *commentator*. Only one-third of the extant manuscripts of the *Teseida* accompany the poem with a commentary.[149] What is more, the choice of which commentary to transcribe does not always privilege Boccaccio's. Nonauthorial commentaries, such as the anonymous commentary in MS Par. Ital. 582 in the collection of the Bibliothèque nationale de France in Paris, or the better-known commentary by Ferrarese proto-humanist Pietro Andrea de' Bassi, competed with Boccaccio's for popularity and readers' attention.[150] Interpretations engender interpretations, writing commentaries brings about new commentaries. In the words of the Ecclesiastes (12:12), "of making many books there is no end."

Scholars of medieval rhetoric have often underscored the generative and transformational potentials of medieval commentative practices. Carruthers has emphasized the role of readers (vis-à-vis writers) in establishing authority.[151] And Rita Copeland has indicated the crucial role of commentaries in re-creating meaning and even rewriting authorial intention: in spite of being addenda to the text, these commentaries can engage in "a primary productive character" and thus refashion the text.[152] In the autograph of the *Teseida*, on the one hand, we see a manuscript that pursues authority by eliciting other commentaries and by instigating a continuous hermeneutic process in the modes Carruthers described. And on the other hand, the relative independence of the poem from its authorial (but anonymous) commentary, a deferred circulation for the commentary (composed for *Aut* a decade after the composition of the poem), and the circulation of the poem without the commentary—as we shall see in chapter 5—allowed for a more ephemeral and relaxed use of the *Teseida* as a form of popular and entertaining genre fiction. In the case of the *Teseida*, in other words, the same refashioning and productive character that Copeland observed in medieval commentaries will be also achieved through the admissible omission of the commentary, which Boccaccio—in dissimulating his plural enunciative position—had anticipated for the ground of textual and material possibilities of the poem.

CHAPTER FIVE

The Textual Proliferation of the *Teseida*

> In getting my books, I have been always solicitous of an ample margin.
>
> —Edgar Allan Poe, *Marginalia*, 1

Materiality and Reception

The autograph of Giovanni Boccaccio's *Teseida* (*Aut*), as we have observed in chapter 4, is a multilayered artifact that institutes a causal nexus between material container and textual contents. The active scribal role played by Boccaccio in the composition of *Aut* implies that all features—both textual and material—of this book-object are functional to his artistic project of authorization and canonization of vernacular literature. The material presentation of poem, paratext, and commentative apparatus—which reproduces the codicological features of manuscripts transmitting classical and authoritative texts—parallels the "classicizing" project of writing an epic poem in the vernacular. The citational modes of Boccaccio's creative process (his *imitatio*) concern both literary forms and book forms.

The relationship of Boccaccio's autograph with the rest of the extant manuscript tradition—sixty-eight exemplars—is still a topic for discussion.

As we shall briefly review in the pages that follow, we cannot a priori assume *Aut*'s centrality and originating status in the production history of the *Teseida*. Where *Aut* certainly enjoyed strong prestige and a power of attraction—as an "author's book" often did within the early textual and visual tradition[1]—the production history, textual transmission, circulation, and reception of the poem show a very heterogeneous scenario. The appeal of manuscript copies of the *Teseida* to multiple audiences across social classes has been established, but, Rhiannon Daniels has pointed out, this diversity of audience has not resulted in consistency of material variations between manuscripts.[2] The analysis of the *Teseida*'s afterlife also shows that the poem could actually be perceived and transcribed as both a text to study (and comment) and a more relaxed form of literary entertainment, its author being associated with both *auctoritates* (Christian and classical) and more popular forms of oral poetry.

This chapter considers the cultural and artistic complexity that inheres in the apparently incongruous textual tradition of the *Teseida* by comparing exemplars selected to illustrate two complementary and opposite cases: first, two Florentine manuscripts that transmit the poem without Boccaccio's commentative, paratextual, and visual apparatus; and second, three manuscripts (and an incunable) produced in Ferrara in which the poem is accompanied by a nonauthorial commentary. These exemplars represent only a sample of the *Teseida*'s manuscript tradition, but a detailed, autoptic study of their materiality updates work done by Edvige Agostinelli and William E. Coleman, and by Daniels to highlight ways in which specific material traits intersect with (and evidence) the multiple modes of engagement with Boccaccio's work that emerged over time and space. The current shelf marks of these exemplars—and the incunable's short title—are, in order of appearance:[3]

Philadelphia, University of Pennsylvania, MS Codex 254 (*Ph*)
Aix-en-Provence, Bibliothèque Méjanes, MS 180 (*Ai*)
Milan, Biblioteca Ambrosiana, MS Cod. D, 524 inf. (*MA*)
Chicago, University of Chicago Library, MS 541 (*Ch*)
Cambridge, Massachusetts, Houghton Library, MS Typ 227 (*CaM*)
Teseide, Ferrara: Augustinus Carnerius, 1475

By examining the literary/editorial similarities and differences between these exemplars and *Aut* as book-objects transmitting the *Teseida*, this chapter proposes that *Aut*'s material and textual presentation authorizes (by proactively originating it) or epitomizes (by retrospectively recognizing it) the dual scholarly/leisurely reception mentioned above. That this chapter proposes possibilities rather than arguing conclusively—if, indeed, firm conclusions are ever within our reach—depends not least on our present understanding of the textual tradition of the *Teseida*, regarding which many questions remain unresolved. Given what we know—and what we do not know—about *Aut*'s "genealogical" relationship to the extant nonautograph manuscripts of the *Teseida*, we begin from two interpretive options. One of these takes *Aut* as the starting point of the manuscript tradition and assumes that later readers and copyists had access to *Aut*—or to manuscripts copied from *Aut*—and thus made informed choices about its textual contents and material features. The other option reads *Aut* as what Boccaccio expected, or hoped, would become the reference point—that is, a representation of his text that could control future reception—but also recognizes that the choices expressed in later copies may reflect broader cultural directions and/or access to other versions of the *Teseida*, rather than explicit, direct readings of *Aut* itself.

Jerome McGann argues that "various readers and audiences are hidden in our texts, and the traces of their multiple presence are scripted at the most material levels."[4] This chapter contends that variations and differences in readership were inscribed in the literary project of Boccaccio's autograph. In fact, and regardless of the actual position of *Aut* in the *stemma codicum* of the *Teseida*—whether it enacts or records difference—its material features seem to take into consideration different itineraries for the text's reception and consumption. The playful dissociation of the author from the commentator that Boccaccio signals by assigning them different paleographic traits and distinct grammatical identities not only authorized the proliferation of other commentaries but also anticipated the readers' greater freedom to interact with the text in a more informal and spontaneous manner, often void of allegorical or scholarly preoccupations. The presence of a commentative apparatus does not impose a definitive interpretation of the poem; rather, it confers an aura of authority aimed to elicit further scholarly work. The deferred addition, the anonymity, and the affected nonauthorial presentation of the commentary, on the other hand, pave the way for—or reflect—the potential omission of the commentary and, consequently, these endorse alternative modes of consumption of the poem.

Textual Tradition: An Overview

This chapter is thus not intended as a systematic survey of the *Teseida*'s manuscript tradition, rather, it investigates how variance in the material presentation of selected manuscripts relates to, if not necessarily derives from, *Aut*'s multifarious artistic project. Any material investigation into the transmission and reception of the *Teseida* must, however, consider the stemmatic position of the poem's extant witnesses—all produced several decades after *Aut*, but most likely not directly derived from *Aut*—and their relationship to *Aut*.

If in studying the materiality of Dante's works we immediately confront the obstacle of the lack of autographs, Boccaccio's corpus presents here a different challenge. The felicitous preservation of autographs is paralleled by the existence of multiple redactions, even multiple autograph redactions, of a single text: a total of nine redactions, for instance, in the extreme scenario of the *De mulieribus claris* (*Famous Women*).[5] When it comes to Boccaccio's works, as Giorgio Padoan explained, we should expect "neither an 'original' from which the whole manuscript tradition mechanically derived, nor only just several originals to which the manuscript traditions of the various redactions go back. Instead, we should think of a range [literally, "a fan"] of autographs, some of which are situated within the stemma of the same redaction"—and these autographs might in turn be based on transcriptions that Boccaccio would commission from professional scribes.[6] Even when there is no material trace of them, multiple redactions inevitably haunt the *stemmata* of Boccaccio's works with the prospect of undetectable horizontal contaminations.

In 1938, Salvatore Battaglia established the first critical edition of the *Teseida*.[7] Prior to Giuseppe Vandelli's identification of Boccaccio's autography of *Aut* in 1929, Battaglia had conducted the *recensio* of about half of the manuscripts we now know (thirty-three out of sixty-eight) and had outlined a bipartite stemma. He distributed the witnesses of the *Teseida* into families α (more textually reliable, subdivided into κ and ζ) and β (consisting of a subgroup χ and the single codex P^2). Witnesses from family α have a homogenous text and lack Boccaccio's commentary (except for five codices transmitting an abridged version of the commentary). Some of the manuscripts from family β have the commentary, but their only common element is that they agree with the readings of *Aut* whenever they disagree with α. After Vandelli's discovery, however, Battaglia based his edition exclusively on *Aut*, emphasizing its extraneousness to either family, highlighting its rather isolated position within a highly corrupted corpus of manuscripts, and suggesting that both α and β originated from two additional lost autographs.[8] Both Aurelio Roncaglia's (1941) and Alberto Limentani's (1964) commented editions reproposed Battaglia's text with minimal emendations.[9] Both philologists, however, more or less explicitly expressed the necessity of reassessing Battaglia's *stemma* in light of several newly discovered manuscripts.

More recently, William E. Coleman has expanded on some elements of criticism from Gianfranco Contini's early response to Battaglia's edition, which had uncovered some fallacies in its *stemma*. Coleman has developed Contini's intuition of a tripartite *stemma* for a first redaction of the poem: in addition to families α and β, the first redaction would include the third branch γ, uniquely represented by MS Palatino 352 of the Biblioteca Nazionale Centrale in Florence (P^2 of Battaglia's *stemma*).[10] Abridged versions of the self-commentary exist in a total nine exemplars from the three branches of this newly articulated *stemma*.[11] Coleman has also hypothesized that a second and a third redaction of the *Teseida* would be respectively represented by *Aut* and by another autograph now lost of which the aforementioned *Teseida* manuscript in the Biblioteca Oratoriana in Naples would constitute an apograph.

Agostinelli and Coleman's recently published edition of the *Teseida* is also based on *Aut*. It is not, strictly speaking, a critical edition of the poem—at least not one based on Lachmann's method—since it does not undergo a systematic *recensio* of the manuscript tradition.[12] Compared to its predecessors, however, Agostinelli and Coleman's edition restores, if only partially, many of Boccaccio's linguistic peculiarities and scribal resolutions (e.g., Tuscanisms and Latinisms), his material choices (dots of subpunction, rubrication in the original layout, drawing-spaces, paragraph signs), and his own original *lectiones* under the overtracing of a later scribe.[13] Martina Mazzetti has recently proposed *Aut* as the actual archetype in the *stemma codicum* of the *Teseida*, but disagreement remains.[14]

Epos and *Cantari*

The material realities of manuscripts contribute to construct its meaning: they affect and reflect the interpretation readers derive from and impose on texts. Wolfgang Iser points out that "the potential text is infinitely richer than any of its individual realizations."[15] Material variations suggest there are multiple realizations of a given text. The manuscript tradition of the *Teseida* includes codices that omit—or dismiss—the commentary and the visual-verbal paratext we find in *Aut*. These manuscripts suggest a nonscholarly consumption of the poem, in line with the tradition of the *cantari* (oral narratives) and the popular origin of the *ottava rima*. Importantly, these manuscripts were produced several decades after *Aut* but cannot be aprioristically assumed to derive directly—to be transcribed—from *Aut*.

The two codices addressed in this section—MS Codex 254 of the University of Pennsylvania and MS 180 of the Bibliothèque Méjanes in Aix-en-Provence—were transcribed, however, by a copyist very close to Boccaccio's cultural milieu. The material features of both manuscripts—paper, *mercantesca* script, and lack of ornamentation—suggest that the *Teseida* appealed to the new literate merchants more than scholars and indicate a consumer-reader's perception of the poem as popular literature for entertainment. The absence of any commentary in MS Codex 254 further confirms a leisure or entertainment reception of the poem. The presence of an authorial (if perhaps only indirectly authorial) commentary in MS 180, however, shows that the same reader/scribe could be aware of the existence of—and possibly have access to—a commentary without necessarily seeking it out or deeming it indispensable to the poem's consumption.

Philadelphia, University of Pennsylvania, MS Codex 254

The University of Pennsylvania MS Codex 254 of the *Teseida* is a manuscript of medium-large format (295 x 220 mm).[16] It is a paper manuscript, as with the vast majority (85 percent) of the extant sixty-eight exemplars of the poem. The autoptic consultation of the manuscript confirms the thoroughness of Coleman's analysis of the watermarks and suggests that the codex should be dated to the last quarter of the fourteenth century.[17] The codex presents many of the codicological features of what Armando Petrucci describes as a "register-book."[18] A register-book generally preserves texts in the vernacular, its physical support is paper, it is written in a cursive script (either chancery minuscule or *mercantesca* minuscule), it does not present any apparatus or commentary, it lacks decoration and ornamentation (with few exceptions), it is written directly by a consumer-reader for personal use, and it often preserves multiple texts.

The script of MS Codex 254 (henceforth: *Ph*) is a *mercantesca*, a cursive script that merchants transferred from their professional documents to various codices mostly preserving literature in the vernacular (see pl. 5.1).[19] A further element that *Ph* has in common with register-books is a very limited decoration. The presence of blank spaces (accompanied by guide letters) in correspondence to the incipits of books 2–12 reveals that a minimal program of decorated initials had been planned. Of this seemingly unpretentious program, however, very little was executed: two simple colored initials—marking the octaves after the rubrics at 1.37 (fol. 1v [4v]) and at 1.40 (fol. 2r [5r])—most probably completed by the copyist himself, using a different ink, rather than a *rubricator*; and touches of unrefined filigrees in the initials of each octave. Even if blank spaces could still function as markers, Daniels argues that they indicate a typology of readers not especially interested in orientation and "perhaps preferring to proceed through the text in the linear fashion characteristic of leisurely reading, rather than jump from section to section according to the dictates of learned enquiry."[20] Boccaccio's program of rubrics is only minimally executed. The main scribe maintains it until book 2.1 and leaves blanks thereafter. A second scribe, instead, sometimes indicates the space for the rubrics with a *punctus* (a dot).

Two primary hands are recognizable in *Ph*. The first scribe is responsible for the majority of the transcription, whereas the second hand copied four folios that were implemented later (fols. 51r–52v [54r–55v] and 57r–58v [60r–61v]).[21] It is hard to know if the second scribe is also responsible for materially finalizing this implementation, in part because of a modern rebinding that damaged the gutter and virtually obliterated the original sewing. The editor/compiler also redacted the text in cases where the added

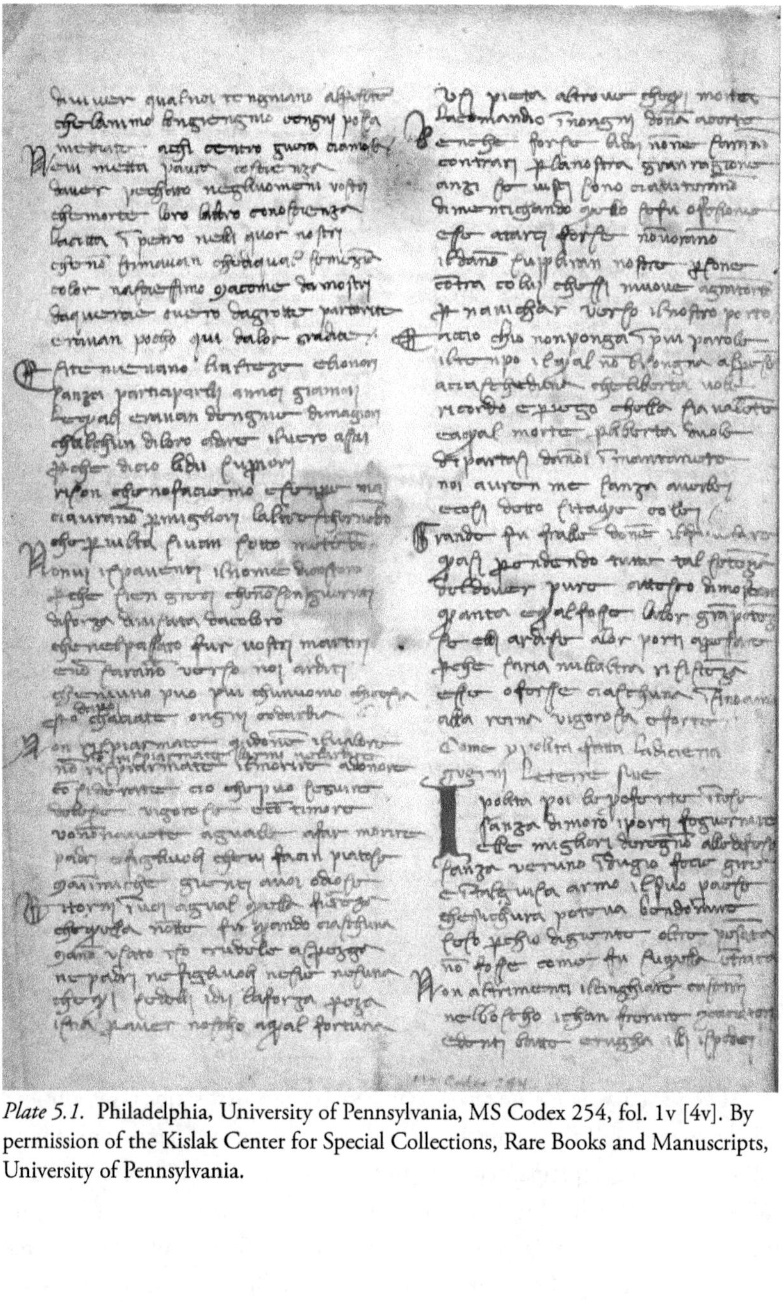

Plate 5.1. Philadelphia, University of Pennsylvania, MS Codex 254, fol. 1v [4v]. By permission of the Kislak Center for Special Collections, Rare Books and Manuscripts, University of Pennsylvania.

folios and the original manuscript overlapped, literally scoring through the repeated stanzas. We might be witnessing here the activity of at least three different individuals.

Ph is preserved anonymous and acephalous: three folios are missing from the beginning of the codex. The text concludes at 12.83 (like four other manuscripts of the same branch of the *stemma*), omitting the last three stanzas and the concluding sonnets, thus lacking the title of the work in its full form and Boccaccio's proud claim that the *Teseida* is the first epic in the vernacular. *Ph* is, therefore, also an epigraphic (without indication of the title), even if a title can be inferred from the rubric to book 2.1 (fol. 7v [10v]), where the poem's title is given in the form *Tesaida*.

Ph contains no trace of Boccaccio's extensive commentary. Boccaccio's material differentiation of the author from the commentator allowed readers greater freedom to interact with the text. As Mazzetti maintains, the transmission of the *Teseida* wiped out "what was too expensive (parchment, illustrations, decorated initials) or too time-consuming (the transcription of the self-commentary) for the social class that mostly received it: the mercantile class."[22] That copyists felt entitled to omit the commentary in its entirety rather than abridging or copying selectively, however, may also indicate that the omission was not exclusively a matter of time-saving or parsimony and suggest that readers sensed that the poem was afforded multiple options for consumption and transmission.

The textual tradition of the commentary seems to confirm this double editorial direction and dual critical itinerary for the text. The composition and transmission of the commentary, just like those of the poem, were characterized by multiple redactions. Kenneth P. Clarke has remarked, "The margins of Boccaccio's *Teseida* were for him a space of constant process, of re-reading and re-interpretation."[23] This unresolved commentative practice and the anonymity of the paratext proper (at least in the extant exemplars) could partially explain the frequency with which the octaves are not accompanied by the commentary (either interlinear or marginal). A second reason is probably the perception of the *Teseida* as "popular literature." The combination of the chivalric and epic elements and the use of a metrical form—the *ottava rima*—that had become the common mode of expression of oral narrative poetry inevitably enhanced the perception of the poem as literature for entertainment and nonscholarly consumption. Readers approaching the text from this nonscholarly angle probably made up the majority of the poem's audience, if we rely on the corpus of extant manuscripts and the majority of their subscriptions and notes of possession. This kind of audience neither needed luxurious codices nor wanted high-priced copies.[24]

The register-book form rarely presents comments or reader's notes. In *Ph*, marginalia, interlinear glosses, and scribal interventions on the text are extremely rare. This lack of reading traces does not necessarily imply that the text was not read; rather, it may indicate its readers' lack of familiarity with writing (implying a form of passive literacy) or, more coincidentally, suggest that the reading of the manuscript happened away from any writing equipment.

There are, however, two notable exceptions to this absence. The first exception is a subscription on fol. 66r [69r]: "Questo Libro è di Bartolomeo di Tomaso, choluj che se lo amore fossi ispiento lo ritrovorne solo per amore di suora [*rasura*] e di suora China e della piacente suora Isabetta tuta piena d'amore" (This book belongs to Bartolomeo di Tomaso, who, though love had faded, found it again only for the love of sister [erasure], sister China, and the delightful, love-filled sister Isabetta).[25] We do not know whether Bartolomeo is the editor/compiler of our manuscript (the one who supplied the missing folios or had them supplied) or a new individual—that is, a fourth person, after the three described above, possibly connected to the production of this manuscript—whose precise identity remains to be determined. But the script of the subscription, an unrefined *mercantesca*, points toward the recently educated mercantile society.

A Fragment of the *Guerra di Troia*

The second exception to the absence of reading traces—one of those "odd things you don't expect to find," to use Stephen Knight's words—is pertinent to the history of this specific artifact and also relevant for its literary-historical implications (see pl. 5.2).[26] On fol. 66v [69v], a subsequent hand, possibly datable to the first half of the fifteenth century, jots down a couple of lines in a very cursive (or even *currens*) *mercantesca*:

> Talamo dis[s]e: "E[h] nobile barone,
> se voi avete di me tal teme[n]za,

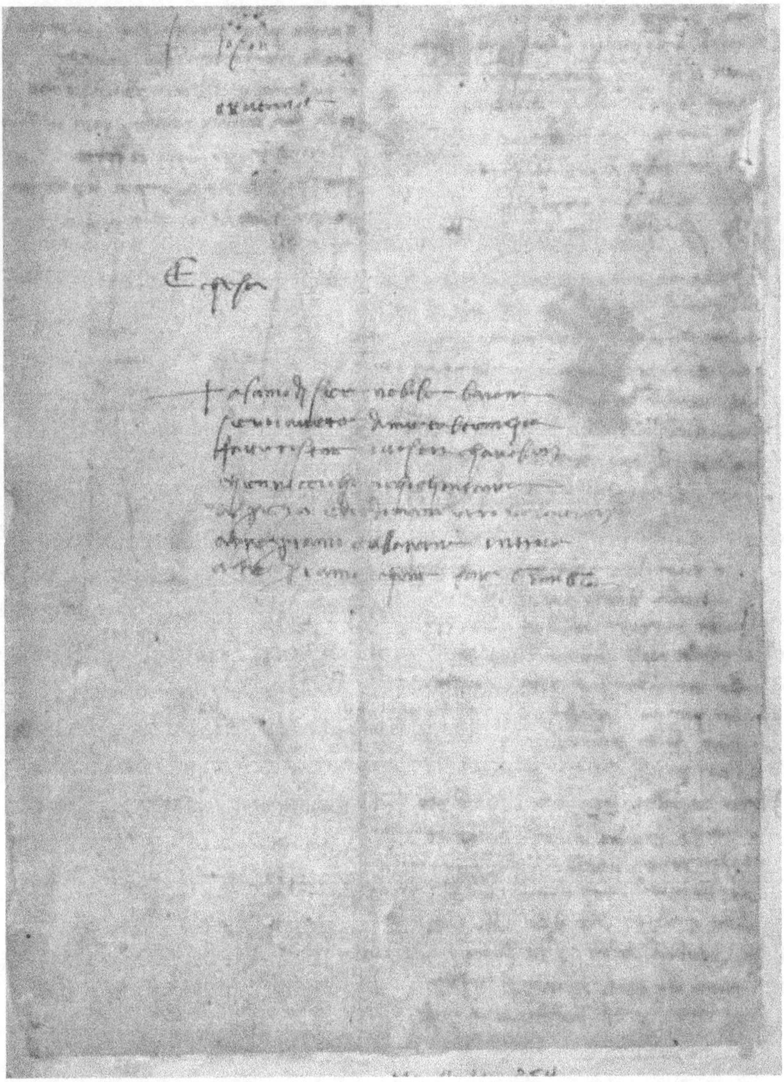

Plate 5.2. Philadelphia, University of Pennsylvania, MS Codex 254, fol. 66v [69v]. By permission of the Kislak Center for Special Collections, Rare Books and Manuscripts, University of Pennsylvania.

faite ristare i vostri chavalieri,
che nno cci cha[c]ci cho chontanta
aspreza, e di domani verò volontieri
a·rre Priamo e alla reina in Troia,
a re Priamo che ne farà gran gioia."[27]

(Telamon said: "Noble baron, if you are so intimidated by me, halt your knights, so that they not chase us so ferociously, and I will gladly come to King Priam and the queen in Troy, to King Priam who will be delighted.")

This passage represents, to my knowledge, the fourth extant testimony of a Tuscan *cantare* on the Trojan War: the anonymous *Guerra di Troia*. A *cantare* is a narrative poem in octaves whose origin and nature are oral and performative. As Domenico De Robertis indicated, the transcription of such *cantari* tells us something about their original producers but also something of the reader/listener who has chosen to transcribe them.[28] The text of the *Guerra di Troia* dates back to as early as 1369, the date of the earliest manuscript in which it is preserved.[29] According to Dario Mantovani, its most recent editor, only two other manuscripts preserve the full series of *cantari* of the *Guerra di Troia* and, therefore, also this octave, which is part of Cantare 2.[30] To these manuscripts one should add a few fragmentary testimonies (like the one preserved by *Ph*).[31] Among these testimonies, MS Tempi 2 (housed in the Biblioteca Medicea Laurenziana in Florence) is particularly relevant, because it preserves the whole text of Cantare 2 (fols. 161r–164r) and an autograph transcription of the *Libro di varie storie* by Antonio Pucci (1310–88), himself composer, performer of *cantari*, acquaintance of Boccaccio, and thus a linking figure between orality and writing in the early modern literature of Florence.[32]

From a strictly textual point of view, the fragment of the *Guerra di Troia* copied in *Ph* partially transmits octave 48 of the second *cantare* and combines (and closes) it with the last verses of octave 49. The result is an anisometrical "octave" (of only seven lines). This ephemeral testimony of textual instability might be the inaccurate transcription of a scribe who did not pay much attention to the integrity of the text. It could also be referred to as what Vittore Branca defines as "transmission by memory": the scribe is possibly citing from memory a passage he or she knows by heart but recalls incorrectly.[33] The fragment would represent a typical memory lapse and an ensuing attempt to fill the void with pertinent material.

The Trojan War, however, is an atypical *cantare*. It occupies an intermediate position between strictly performative forms of oral poetry and more literary-oriented poems in *ottava rima*, such as Boccaccio's own *Teseida* and *Filostrato*.[34] It conjugates traditional aspects of orality (preference for coordination over subordination, use of formulas, repetitive vocabulary) with intertextual references to a higher and more cultivated written tradition (classical texts, chivalric romances, historiographical narrations).[35] The combined presence of the *Teseida* and the *Guerra di Troia* in *Ph* materially shows that vernacular literature written in *mercantesca* existed at the intersection of cultivated poetry and more popular expressions of oral traditions.[36] The presence of this octave in *Ph* is also material evidence of the intertextual dynamic between *cantari* and Boccaccio's poetic works, which is the critical consensus of modern philology, but was clearly a material reality even for an early modern audience.

Aix-en-Provence, Bibliothèque Méjanes, MS 180

Adriano de' Rossi (died 1400) has been recently recognized by Giuseppina Brunetti as the main scribe of our codex *Ph*.[37] A friend and neighbor to Boccaccio and Pucci (in the Santa Felicita neighborhood in Florence), Adriano was also the author of a short "canzonieretto" (small songbook) of ten sonnets.[38] *Ph* thus represents the product of a reader who knew Boccaccio directly and can be assumed to have actual knowledge that a commented version of the *Teseida* existed. Brunetti's recognition was made possible by the existence of another codex of the *Teseida* (Aix-en-Provence, Bibliothèque Méjanes, MS 180), which was transcribed, signed, and dated (1394) by Adriano (on fol. 1r, then again with a similar formula in the colophon on fol. 64r): "in nome di dio amme[n] a dì 19 di luglio nel 1394 Adriano de' Rossi chominciò a scrivere questo libro" (in the name of God, amen: on July 19, 1394, Adriano de' Rossi started writing this book).

Manuscript 180 of the Bibliothèque Méjanes (hereafter, *Ai*) also presents, like *Ph*, several features of a "libro-registro" (register-book):[39] paper, medium format, minimal textual markers (use of paragraph signs for important rubrics, capitalized initials for the strophes of octaves and sonnets), and no illustrative apparatus. In contrast to *Ph*, however, *Ai* offers a rudimentary form of glosses, transcribed on the final folios of the manuscript (fols. 64v–66r): "Queste qui appresso sono le chiose a questo libro nel quale à certe storie e certi nomi divariati da la nostra lingua le quali queste chiose dichiarano e apertamente mostrano" (Here are the glosses to this book, which contains some stories and names that differ from our language: these glosses clarify and plainly explain them).[40] Transmitted by a total of nine codices, these glosses are a shortened version of Boccaccio's commentary. It is not clear whether these represent a redacted version created by Boccaccio or a redaction by some intervening scribe with access to the longer version of the commentary.[41] It is also unclear whether Adriano copied poem and glosses from two different antigraphs. What is clear, however, is that neither poem nor commentary mentions Boccaccio's authorship (only a fifteenth-century *ex libris* does, on fol. 1r). Also clear is that the same copyist prepared (for himself?) two different manuscripts of the same work. It is difficult to gauge if Adriano transcribed *Ai* before or after *Ph*. It is also difficult to hypothesize whether or not he attempted to produce a more complete copy of the work (one with Boccaccio's complete commentary). Adriano's transcriptions, however, seem to suggest that the *Teseida* could circulate both with and without a commentary at a relatively early stage of its transmission and—given Adriano's social proximity to Boccaccio and role in creating both manuscripts—that the distinction represents an editorial choice to engage with Boccaccio's text in multiple ways and not solely the outcome of chance encounters with copies that predate Boccaccio's commentary.

The material features of the *Teseida* manuscripts confirm its critical fortune among literate merchants. The vast majority of subscriptions and copyists' signatures further corroborate this, indicating a predominantly mercantile circulation of the poem.[42] These data comply with the verified popularity in fifteenth-century Florence of the "Boccaccio *minore*," highly appreciated by "an audience thirsty for aristocratic, cultivated, or entertaining readings."[43] They are also consistent with the literary fortune of chivalric poems and the strong presence of the Matter of Thebes in merchants' libraries.[44] The *Teseida* exemplifies the cultural interests of the mercantile class: their interest in embracing traditional medieval values of courtesy, honor, and liberality; their reliance on the proto-bourgeois ethics of prudence and profit; their search for an entertainment literature that valued action; their concern with education and literacy; and their openness to the new classicizing cultural tendencies. Even if the first epos in the Italian vernacular was, for Boccaccio, primarily an archeological and philological enterprise, a poem in *ottava rima* could likewise be received as a continuation of the tradition of *cantari* and oral performance.

Ferrara, 1435–1475

In a recent literary history of the *ottava rima*, Gianfranco Alfano has noted that after a strong start the *Teseida* declined in popularity over the second half of the fifteenth century and further in the sixteenth.[45] The only two editions of Boccaccio's works in *ottava rima*—including the *Teseida*—in the later sixteenth century were produced in Tuscany, suggesting local support for a Florentine classic rather than broad-based popularity.[46] Without disagreeing with Alfano's accurate analysis, we should note that the *Teseida*'s history in early Renaissance Ferrara—where the interest for the *ottava rima* peaked and the development of the genre climaxed—signals its continued prestige and influence on *ottava rima* romance and heroic literature.

Between 1435 and 1471, at least three of the extant codices of the *Teseida* were commissioned and produced at the Este court. Their material features indicate a higher status—and a different reception for Boccaccio's poem—than we have observed in the previous pages. The three manuscripts are now in the collections of the Biblioteca Ambrosiana in Milan (MS Cod. D, 524 inf.), the University of Chicago Library (MS 541), and Harvard University's Houghton Library in Cambridge, Massachusetts (MS Typ 227).[47] The *editio princeps* of the poem was also printed in Ferrara in 1475.[48] The four exemplars considered here—the three manuscripts and the incunable—constitute a literary and editorial microcosm, whose exponents (most of them little-known philologists, copyists, illuminators, and printers) represent an effective link between the literary works of the Tuscan Trecento and the artistic production of northern Italy's Renaissance. These books are witnesses to the *Teseida*'s circulation and transmission and show the peculiar outcome of Boccaccio's authorial zeal regarding hermeneutic control over the reading audience: these three manuscripts and the incunable, in fact, all transmit the poem with a commentary that is not Boccaccio's own.[49]

Milan, Biblioteca Ambrosiana, MS Cod. D, 524 inf.

The Ambrosiana manuscript of the *Teseida* (hereafter, *MA*) is a multitext codex.[50] It preserves Boccaccio's epic poem together with Ferrarese courtier Pietro Andrea de' Bassi's commentary to the poem, the latter's mythological romance in prose *Le fatiche de Hercule* (*The Labors of Hercules*) (alluded to as forthcoming in the commentary to the *Teseida*),[51] and Niccolò Malpigli's *canzone* "Spirto gentile da quel gremio sciolto" (Noble spirit, freed from the bosom) also with a commentary by Pietro Andrea de' Bassi.

From a material point of view, *MA* is a sumptuous parchment codex of large format (403 x 290 mm) in *littera textualis* (with humanisitc traits), enriched by illuminations and decorated initials. Commissioned by the munificent Niccolò III d'Este, Marquis of Ferrara, Modena, and Reggio, for the education of his son Leonello, its production involved notable artists at the Este court. The production history of *MA* can be followed through its completion in 1437, thanks to the documentation provided by Adriano Franceschini in his monumental archival research on literary and artistic production in Ferrara during the Renaissance.[52] The copyist Biagio Bosoni from Cremona and the illuminator Jacopino d'Arezzo are the *Blasius scriptor* and *Iacobus Aretinus*, who (in the genitive case) show up in the Estes' registers in the margins of a payment entry dated September 24, 1435.[53]

The manuscript is richly decorated (see pl. 5.3). On fol. 1v, a frame with a phytomorphic frieze (with blue, red, violet, and green fruits, and gilded globes) surrounds the text of Bassi's preface to the *Teseida* and forms intersections in the four corners of the folio. The frame is interspersed with the names (in red) of notable Estes. A large filigreed blue initial *P* corresponding to fourteen lines of text stands on a golden background with flowery decorations; above the frame is the script IESVS in red capitals; immediately below the frame, a *rubrica* with the invocation "Adsit principio uirgo beata meo" (May the blessed Virgin assist my beginning); on the *bas-de-page*, an effaced stemma. On fol. 5r, the reader is presented with a large blue initial *O* with

Plate 5.3. Milan, Biblioteca Ambrosiana, MS Cod. D, 524 inf., fol. 1v. Copyright Veneranda Biblioteca Ambrosiana.

floral decorations, on a gold background, indicating the incipit of book 1, with a gold and blue vertical bar on the inner side ending in a vegetal decoration on both ends (see pl. 5.4). The same type of initial marks the incipit of the following books.[54] Medium filigreed initials open the octaves immediately after a rubric.[55] On fol. 22r, a medium decorated initial marks the incipit of the first verse of the sonnet preceding book 2.[56]

Four vertical and two horizontal hard-point ruled lines frame the octaves. The initial of each octave is inscribed between the two vertical frame lines. The ruling also frames the commentary, where the distance between horizontal lines is halved.[57] The octaves are connected to the related commentary blocks through repetition of the extract being commented on (sometimes underlined in red), red alphabetic signs in the commentary (sometimes without corresponding referencing sign in the text), or other graphic devices (flowers, various geometric figures, and even rather intimidating daggers).

In his critical edition of the poem, Battaglia inaccurately surmised that the copyist of *MA* could be Bassi himself, who would have written "the unsuccessful compilation, trusting his own debatable poetic taste and unproven humanistic scholarship."[58] Battaglia was correct, however, about *MA*'s textual corruption. Like all of the five codices transmitting Bassi's commentary,[59] the text of *MA* contaminates manuscripts from both families α and β (i.e., from branches of the *Teseida*'s *stemma* likely unrelated to *Aut*): the result is a very unreliable text.

Bassi's *Teseida* and *Le fatiche de Hercule* were paired in a single manuscript for the education of Leonello d'Este. Leonello's intellectual formation, however, was not the only purpose behind the construction of the codex. Bassi's commentary inscribes the poem within the Estes' agenda of dynastic legitimation.[60] Whereas Boccaccio's preface gives particular relevance to the mysterious *Doppelgänger* of the *persona loquens* (be he Arcita or Palemone), Bassi's preface revolves around Theseus, in a mode of courtly interpretation that still transfigured classical antiquity in medieval and chivalric images and "disguised what was read in Latin and Greek books as well," Antonia Tissoni Benvenuti points out.[61] The magnanimous, generous, and rigorous Athenian "duke" looks like the literary *figura* of the Este duke.

The critical fortune of the *Teseida* in Ferrara is intimately connected with Bassi's cultural activity at the Este court.[62] Bassi's commentary is preserved in

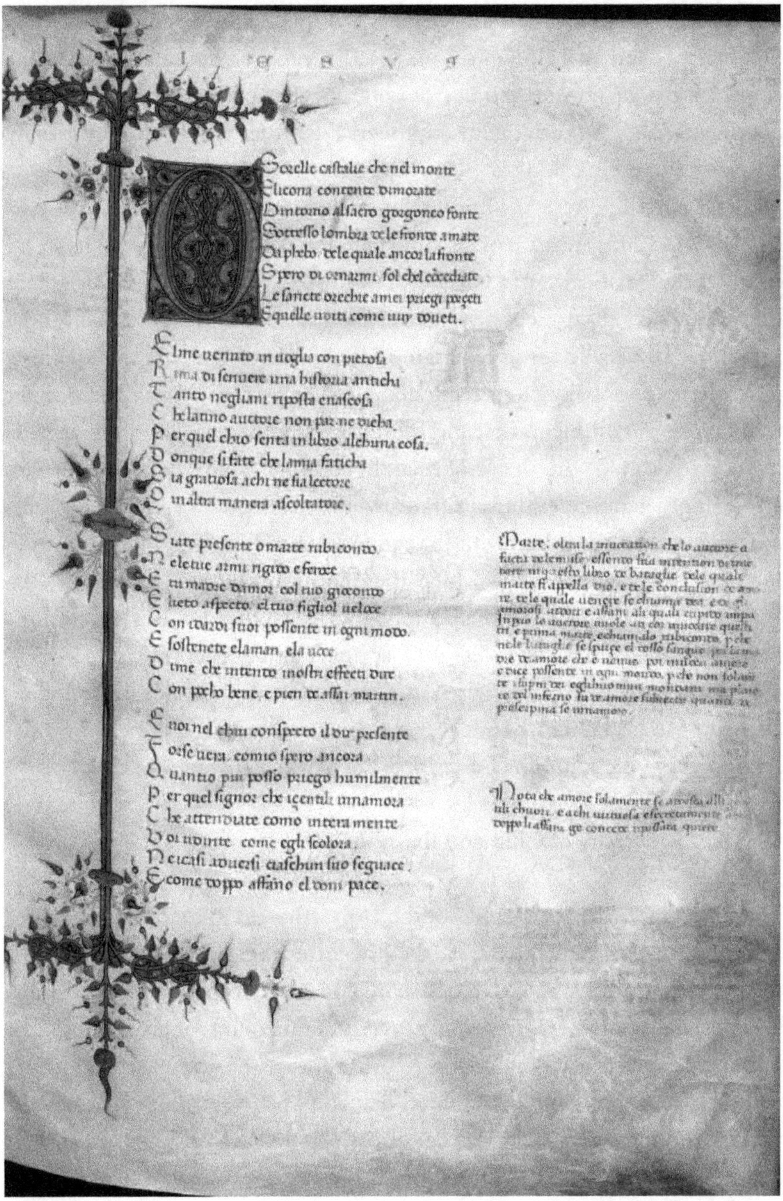

Sorelle castalie che nel monte
Elicona contente dimorate
Dintorno al sacro gorgoneo fonte
Sottesso lombra dele fronde amate
Da phebo dele quale ancor la fronte
Spero di ornarmi sol chel concediate
Le sancte orecchie a mei priegi porgeti
E quelle udita come uuy doueti.

Elme uenuto in uoglia con pietosa
Rima di scriuere una historia anticha
Tanto neglianni riposta e nascosa
Che latino auctore non par ne dicha
Per quel chio senta in libro alchuna cosa.
Donque si fate che la mia faticha
Sia gratiosa a chi ne fia lectore
In altra maniera ascoltatore.

Siate presente o marte rubicondo
Nele tue armi rigido e ferocce
E tu madre damor col tuo giocondo
Lieto aspecto. el tuo figliol ueloce
Con dardi suoi possente in ogni modo.
E sostenete elaman ela uoce
Dime che intendo mostri effecti dire
Con pecho bene e pien de assai martiri.

E uoi nel chui conspecto il dir presente
Forse uerra. como io spero ancora
Quantio piu posso priego humilmente
Per quel signor che igentil innamora
Che attendiate como intera mente
Voi udirite come egli scolora.
Deicasi aduersi ciaschun suo seguace.
E come doppo affano el doni pace.

Plate 5.4. Milan, Biblioteca Ambrosiana, MS Cod. D, 524 inf., fol. 5r. Copyright Veneranda Biblioteca Ambrosiana.

a total of five manuscripts and in the 1475 incunable.[63] *MA*, the Chicago manuscript, and the Houghton manuscript each present a version of the commentary, versions differing from one another with regard to both language and content. Each manuscript works, in other words, toward specific purposes and destinations.

MA partially preserves Boccaccio's preface, even if it displaces the *persona loquens*'s erotic pursuit of Fiammetta to the end of the poem. In its stead, Bassi writes a dedication to Niccolò III, which expands into a genealogy of the Estes. Every time a representative of the Este family is mentioned for the first time, a red rubric in the margin indicates his or her name. Humanists were often commissioned or requested by their patrons to write vernacular translations or commentaries, and they often complained about the degrading task of dealing with the vernacular. In contrast, Bassi's dedication exudes a seemingly genuine enthusiasm and willingness to be of service. A preface follows the dedication, with the proposition of intent and the beginning of the commentary proper, which then continues in the margins of the poem. The dedication and the prosopographic section imply a strong connection between *MA*, the Estes, and Ferrara. This connection is also noticeable at a linguistic level: *MA* presents characteristically northeastern Italian elements—especially in Bassi's commentary—whereas the Chicago manuscript and the Houghton manuscript are closer to a Tuscan *koiné*.[64]

Chicago, University of Chicago Library, MS 541

The watermarks situate MS 541 of the University of Chicago Library (hereafter, *Ch*) in the third quarter of the fifteenth century.[65] Once in the possession of notorious book connoisseur, thief, and forger Guglielmo Libri Carrucci della Sommaja, *Ch* is a paper codex of medium-large format (320 x 230 mm).[66] Even if its material support (paper as opposed to parchment) makes it a less prestigious book-object than *MA*, *Ch* still displays an honest—though unimpressive—set of decorative elements (see pl. 5.5). On fol. 3r, a large champ initial *S* (*Teseida* 1.1, "Sorelle castalie") colored blue and red with simple white lead braids is placed on a golden background. A similar initial also opens book 2, and smaller decorated initials mark the sonnet and first octave of the other books. The text proper is enclosed in a phytomorphic scroll frame colored in indigo, pink, purple, and gold ochre. In the outer

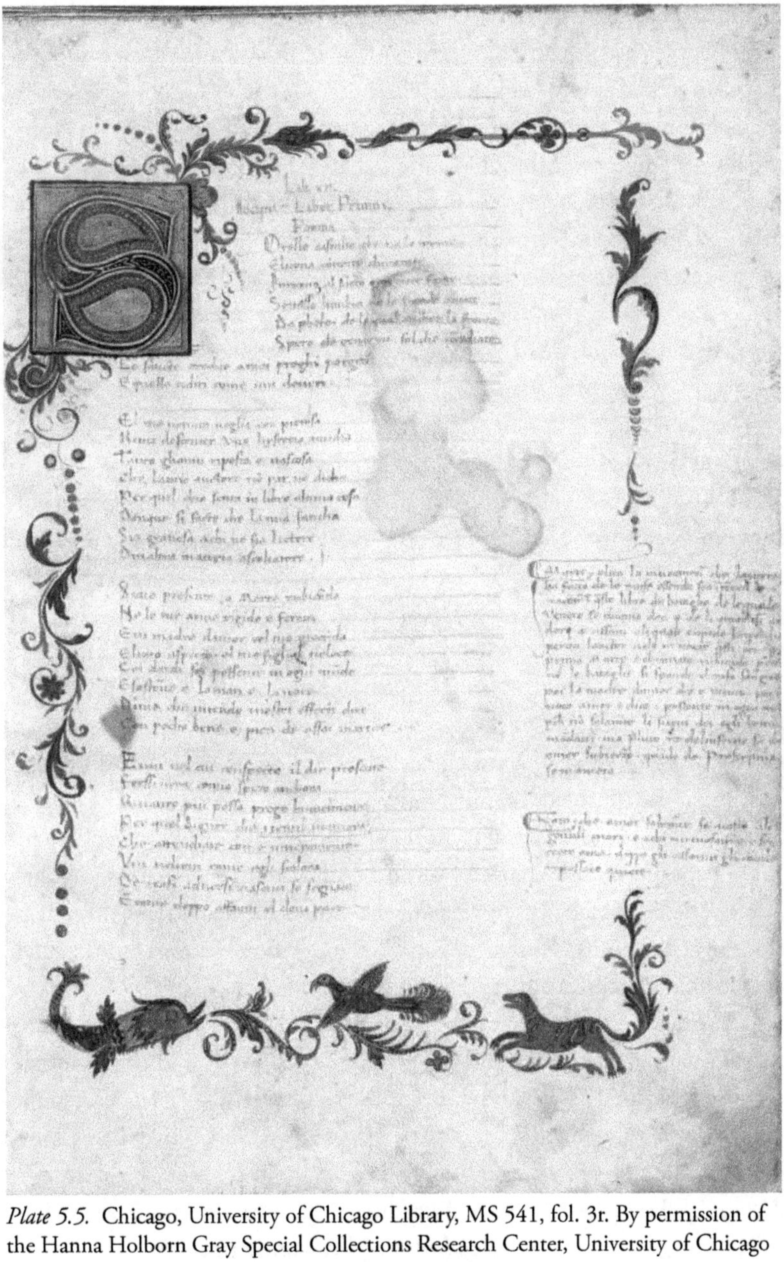

Plate 5.5. Chicago, University of Chicago Library, MS 541, fol. 3r. By permission of the Hanna Holborn Gray Special Collections Research Center, University of Chicago Library.

margin, the frame intersects Bassi's commentary. On the lower margin, the vines are elegantly intermingled with a dolphin (left) and a parrot (center) chased by a hound (right): the vines become the seawater blown out by the dolphin and the wind currents on which the parrot flies. On fol. 129v, the drawing of a playful monkey immediately follows the colophon: "Qui finisce il libro nominato *Teseida* chompilato e fatto per lo ecelente poeta misser Zovanne da Certaldo la chui gratiosa anima abbia ricevuta nele sue braccia Il beato Misser santo Michele Angelo e rapresentata ne la gloria di vita eterna dinanci al vero e eterno Ydio nostro Signore Yesu Xristo Amen" (Here ends the book titled *Teseida*, compiled by the excellent poet Giovanni Boccaccio, whose gracious soul may Saint Michael Archangel receive in his arms and present in the glory of eternal life before the true and eternal God our Lord Jesus Christ. Amen).

On fol. 1r, a large champ initial *C* colored in pink with floral swirls superimposed on a gold ochre background opens Boccaccio's preface to Fiammetta ("Chome a memoria"); on the *bas-de-page*, a hare wearing a purple coat. The smartly dressed hare on fol. 1—and the quire fol. 1 belongs to—were, however, a later integration to fill what was clearly perceived as a lacuna. In its current status, in fact, *Ch* is a composite manuscript. A main copyist transcribed the poem in a neat humanistic book hand—on color ruled lines—and copied Bassi's glosses in humanistic cursive, and in good Tuscan, in the (unruled) margins (fols. 3r–129v, all *quinterni*). The octaves are transcribed in one central column, four octaves on each façade of the folios. The sections of the octaves provided with a commentary are underlined in red, and red paragraph signs mark the glosses in the margins. In red are also the annotations "Nota bene" and "Comparation" (comparison), which are distinctive features of Bassi's commentary.

A second scribe—contemporary or slightly later than the first—added the colophon on fol. 129v and integrated the beginning and ending of the manuscript—fols. 1r–2v and 129r–133v, respectively—after one or more *quinterni* went missing (if indeed they went missing, rather than being missing from the antigraph or omitted by the first scribe). The alleged lacuna—preface to Fiammetta, general introductory sonnet, introductory sonnet to book 1—features in other codices. In this manuscript, the second scribe filled the gap with a binio in the front. He also added Bassi's dedication to Niccolò III—again marked by a large initial like the one opening Boccaccio's preface to Fiammetta—and the opening of its commentary (before that commentary transfers to the margins on fol. 3r) to the rear of the manuscript.

The second scribe—or the compiler who has commissioned the integration—surrounds the poem with a twofold form of paratext: in Gérard Genette's terminology of paratextual kinds, he restores the authorial peritext (Boccaccio's "preliminaries"); he also supplies a second-degree epitext (Bassi's dedication and the beginning of his commentary).[67] Inscribing the poem in the Renaissance Ferrarese context of its reception with the addition of the Este dedication, the compiler-scribe also integrates the full fiction of the poem by reinstating Boccaccio's fictional—or at least conventional—dedication to Fiammetta. The second copyist also transcribes Boccaccio's rubrics, which are limited to those at the beginning of each book in the quires copied by the first scribe. Its material features make *Ch* a less sophisticated manuscript than *MA* and the Houghton manuscript, which we will consider next. The manuscript handed down to us, however, is the result of a determined effort that we could cautiously label para-philological, aimed at restoring—or maybe creating *ex novo*—a more complete (if eclectic) version of Boccaccio's work. This restorative effort denotes a certain degree of attention toward the integrity of the poem's fiction, while also providing further material evidence of the split reception of text and authorial commentary.

Cambridge, Massachusetts, Houghton Library, MS Typ 227

The Houghton manuscript of the *Teseida* (hereafter, *CaM*) is a parchment codex of medium-large format (364 x 265 mm), produced in Ferrara for a Milanese destination.[68] The parchment, exemplarily polished goatskin, is enriched with decorated initials and illuminations (see pl. 5.6).

The rich decorations on fol. 1r deserve a detailed description. An illuminated frame borders the writing space. The frieze, distinctly Ferrarese, is phytomorphic and geometric, in cold and highly saturated colors.[69] The upper-left corner presents a large pink and green historiated initial *O* (corresponding to eight lines of text) with a braided rope and leafy ornaments in pen, for the incipit of *Teseida* 1.1 ("O sorelle castalie"). The historiated initial *O* is placed against gold foil (framed in black), and the initial's inner part features a blue background, threaded in white lead, and a portrait of Arcita and Palemone in arms with an anthropomorphic representation of the Sun on their

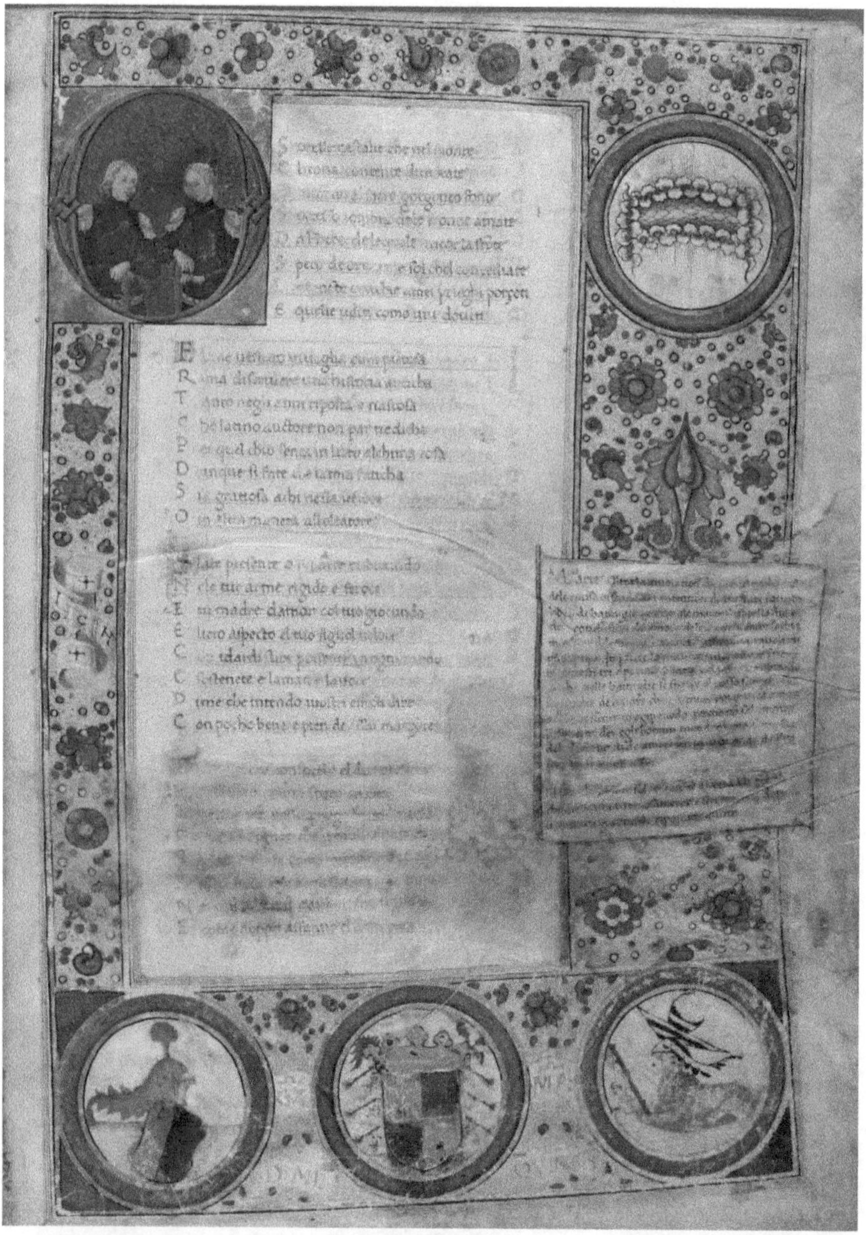

Plate 5.6. Cambridge, Massachusetts, Houghton Library, Typ 227, fol. 1r. Courtesy of the Houghton Library, Harvard University.

shoulder pads. Arcita and Palemone are identified by name in a white lead-threaded caption in Roman capitals. The decoration has been ascribed to an artist from the school of Guglielmo Giraldi, a Ferrarese illuminator in the circle of painter Cosmè Tura. Federica Toniolo recently attributed the portrait to Guglielmo Giraldi himself.[70]

In the outer margin is a scroll with seventeen significantly damaged lines of Bassi's commentary. In the inner margin, between two crosses, is a scroll with the inscription "ICH" (in capitals, trigraph for the *nomen sacrum* of Jesus Christ). In the *bas-de-page*, the acronym of Galeazzo Maria Sforza stands in gilded capitals: GZ MA D. MLI QUINTUS (*Galeazzo Maria Dux Mediolani Quintus*). The acronym is accompanied by the *imprese* of the Visconti-Sforza (without mottos): in the upper-right corner, a phytomorphic medallion, formed by laurel leaves, enclosing a radiant cloud; in the inner tondo, the galeated lion over a bipartite shield (possibly portraying the eagle and the *biscione*, "viper"); in the central tondo, a very damaged quadripartite shield with alternating *biscione* and eagle, framed by six burning embers with ropes and buckets; and in the outer tondo, the squatting galeated lion holding the ember with ropes and buckets in its paws.[71] The coat of arms and emblems were probably added in Milan after the manuscript was delivered.

The manuscript also presents twenty-one decorated initials, one for each introductory sonnet and the first octave of books 3–12 (see pl. 5.7). The initials—filigreed, leafy, in pink, blue, green, and red, superimposed on an outer background in gold foil, and surrounded by phytomorphic and geometric decoration (gold spheres)—extend vertically in a gold and green shaft and end in a decorative braid, limited at the top and bottom margins by two triangles with phytomorphic and geometric frieze. Initials for each octave are presented alternately in gold or blue with red filigree.

The text is in a humanistic book hand: slightly tending to verticality, stylistically essential, and formally rigorous. In the margins and in the same hand are Pietro Andrea de' Bassi's commentary and distinctive, infrequent annotations: "Nota bene" and "Comparation."[72] Also in red are the facial profiles used as attention marks for critical stanzas.

The codex consisted of sixteen or seventeen *quinterni*. The text is currently incomplete: eight folios are missing from the first and second fascicle.[73] The dedicatory preface, the general introductory sonnet, and the introductory sonnet to book 1 are also missing, possibly indicating an omission

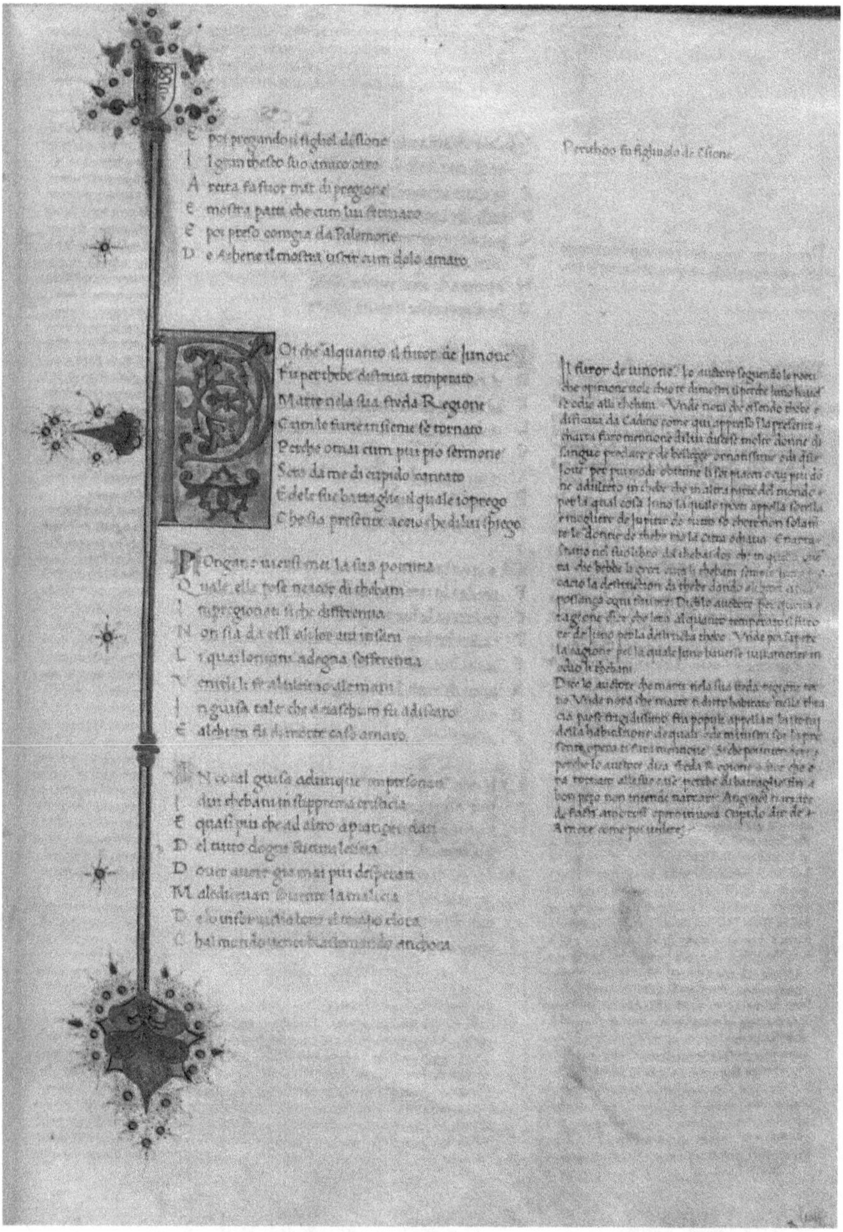

Plate 5.7. Cambridge, Massachusetts, Houghton Library, Typ 227, fol. 23r. Courtesy of the Houghton Library, Harvard University.

by the scribe, the loss (or intentional removal) of a bifolio, or a lacunose antigraph. On fol. 155v, the colophon reads: "Sit laus christo omnipotenti deo. | Finito libro referamus gratia [*sic*] christo | FINIS DEO AMEN | FINI" (Praise be to Christ the almighty God. The book is finished: let us thank Christ. The end. Amen to God. The end). From a textual point of view, *CaM* descends from *MA*.

Agostinelli's identification of *CaM* with the *Theseo* mentioned in the *Creditori e debitori* register of the Este family is now corroborated by the documentation provided by Franceschini.[74] According to entries on *carta* 49 of the *Creditori e debitori* register for February through June 1471 (Modena, Archivio di Stato, Camera Ducale Estense, Guardaroba 91), the chamberlain Carlo di San Giorgio, the scribe Nicolò de Passino (or de Passim), and the stationer Francesco Gigli were involved in making the book:[75] the number of *quinterni* mentioned in the register entry is consistent with the material conditions of *CaM*.[76] Carlo di San Giorgio was Borso's chamberlain and a major figure in the Ferrarese literary milieu during the dukedoms of Borso and Ercole. The result of this commission is an elegant humanistic book that shows all the material characteristics of a presentation copy: parchment support, illuminations, and the new *antiqua* script, following the latest humanistic models and trends.[77]

The scribe and illuminator who copied and decorated *CaM* also authored Houghton Library MS Typ 226, which presents similar codicological features to *CaM* and transmits Bassi's *Le fatiche de Hercule*.[78] The two codices were commissioned by Alberto d'Este and sent as a gift to Galeazzo Maria Sforza (whose murder in 1476 is our *terminus ante quem*), probably on the occasion of Ercole's controversial succession as duke of Ferrara.[79] Alberto, an eloquent and cultivated patron of the arts, was a crucial supporter for Ercole as he assumed control over Ferrara following Borso's death. Ercole graciously rewarded him with the Palazzo Schifanoia, which Borso had recently transformed into a luxurious residence consecrated to *otium*. Alberto was secretly in contact with Galeazzo Maria Sforza, although the latter had favored the advancement of Leonello's son.[80] The gift of the two manuscripts served a clear political agenda of dynastic legitimation and political *grandeur*.[81] The myth of Hercules had originally been retrieved under Niccolò III to provide a mythological reference for the newborn Ercole. Ercole would exploit this literary legacy for obvious onomastic reasons, but also to reaffirm a genealogic connection with Niccolò and reject the legacy of his own step-brothers, who had reigned before him.[82]

In its current state, however, *CaM* contains no dedication to Niccolò III, no preface, and no beginning of the commentary. This lacuna could be the accidental result of the lack of the first fascicle. But it is also possible that those paratextual elements were deemed a single textual unit and perceived as irrelevant (or received as politically inopportune) in a gift to a foreign power, and thus either omitted by the giver or removed by the recipient. As a result, there is no indication of the author of text or commentary. Notably, this omission reflects—if not necessarily reproduces—the condition of *Aut*, in which the distinction between author and commentator and the former's anonymity were nonetheless part of a different editorial strategy.

Alberto would not have made such a considerable investment in the production of a literary text that was not considered uniquely appropriate as a gift from the Estes. We might read this as a book-scale celebration of *otium*—the glorification of leisure reading—by the very owner of a palace of *otium*. On the other hand, given the wealth of the Este libraries, and the ready availability of respectable book-gift alternatives for a foreign ruler, we might also read this investment—and the accuracy with which this exemplar was realized—as a sign of the prestige that Boccaccio's poem had achieved within the canon of vernacular texts. The proliferation and circulation of the *Teseida*—here painstakingly reproduced in elaborately illustrated codices, while elsewhere hastily recorded on paper in a *mercantesca* script—seem to confirm the effectiveness of the doubled editorial guidelines that Boccaccio materially embedded in the poem's autograph.

Pietro Andrea de' Bassi's Commentary

The presence of Pietro Andrea de' Bassi's commentary in the elaborately illuminated Ferrarese codices (*MA* and *CaM*, especially) further confirms the success of Boccaccio's program. Significantly, the *mise-en-texte* and *mise-en-page* of Bassi's commentary in *MA*, *Ch*, and *CaM* resemble those in *Aut*. This does not mean a direct genealogic relationship between *Aut* and the three Ferrarese manuscripts (an antigraph/apograph relationship). But their material resemblance seemingly signals the kind of power of visual attraction often exerted by author's books within the manuscript tradition. And the similarity in their physiognomy certainly suggests their shared relationship to the extension of commentative practices from classical, biblical, and scholastic texts to vernacular literature: an innovation that Boccaccio himself had theorized and contributed to establish. We cannot assume for certain, in other words, that Bassi knew that a *Teseida* commented by Boccaccio existed. But we can recognize that Bassi was a reader of Boccaccio's message to the extent that he had absorbed the (Boccaccian) lesson that a commented version of a vernacular text was perfectly plausible and was worthy of being presented as literary classic at the highest levels.

In *MA*, Bassi's commentary proper is initially articulated into a fivefold *accessus ad auctorem* commenting on author (*nomen auctoris*), title (*titulus libri*), subject matter (*materia libri*), author's intention (*intentio auctoris*), and the part of philosophy to which the work belongs (*cui parti philosophiae supponitur*). Absent in *CaM* (whether omitted or missing), this section of the commentary was added or restored to *Ch* by a later scribe or compiler. Rita Copeland writes that the subtext of the *accessus ad auctorem* almost always provides an *accessus ad commentatorem*: "The *accessus*, with its rhetorical overtones, pre-empts authorial intentionality to lay the ground for exegetical intention."[83] It offers, in short, direct insight into the commentator's exegetical practices and priorities. In terms of literary criticism and exegesis, Bassi's hermeneutic priorities are very different from those of Boccaccio (fol. 2v):

> E per lo amore el quale a poesia portati, avendo vuy de la lectura del *Theseo* sommo piacere, ritrovandosi alchuni a li quali le historie poetice non sono cussì note, come a vuy, vi ha piaçuto commandare a mi Piero Andrea dei Bassi, vostro antiquo e fidele famiglio, dechiari lo obscuro texto del ditto *Theseo* facendo a quello giose, per le quale li lectori possano cavare sugo de la loro lectura; el quale texto per la obscurità de le fictione poetice è difficile ad intendere.[84]

(And because of Love, which leads you to poetry, you immensely enjoy the reading of the *Theseus*, and since there are people to whom these poetic stories are not so well known as they are to you, you wished to order me, Pietro Andrea de' Bassi, your longtime and loyal servant, to explain the obscure text of the said *Theseus*, adding glosses through which the readers can get the gist of the reading, since the text is difficult to understand due to the obscurity of poetic fictions.)

The obscurity to which Bassi refers here is not the same as Boccaccio's "chiuso parlare" (figurative speech). If Bassi probably read Boccaccio's self-commentary—at least in the abridged version that appears in both α and β branches of the first redaction of the *Teseida*—then he also systematically dismissed it. Bassi seems for the most part uninterested in the lexicological and rhetorical aspects of the *Teseida*, which were a central focus of Boccaccio's self-exegesis. Bassi also neglects Boccaccio's distinctive *allegoresis*. In spite of explicitly underscoring, on fol. 2v, the relevance of the poem's allegorical meaning—"la medulla, quale se cava de le fictione poetice" (the kernel that can be extracted from poetic fictions)—Bassi does not provide any gloss on the temples of Mars and Venus, whereas in Boccaccio's commentary, glosses on both temples constituted an entire nexus of interpretive directions, if not an implicit poetic manifesto on the nature of Love. Copeland has pointed out that as "conditions of understanding" change, medieval commentaries often reshape the text to meet the new conditions.[85] Boccaccio considers allegorical interpretation to be an apologetic proposition on the usefulness of poetry: poetry is the matrix of an edifying message hidden behind the veil of the letter. Bassi operates instead in a cultural milieu where such an apology is somewhat taken for granted and may be uncalled for, thanks to the rigorous efforts of Boccaccio's generation to justify poetic fiction (in the vernacular).[86] Boccaccio's commentary has, in other words, succeeded to the point of rendering itself superfluous.

In the passage cited above, Bassi's reference to the *Teseida*'s obscurity must be read in terms of the *recherché* and cultivated nature of Boccaccio's mythological references, as we also see in the words Bassi puts in Niccolò III's mouth as the closing remarks of *Le fatiche* (fol. 219v): "Certo grande multiplicità de historie poetice sono velate nel texto de questo libro, e piaceme molto, ma più me piaceria se al texto dove rechiede ge fossero a modo de giose le historie descripte" (There are certainly a number of poetic stories veiled under the text of this book, and I really like this. But I would like it more if there were stories written in the form of glosses, where necessary).[87] Rather than evoking Boccaccio's *allegoresis* as apology for poetry, the mythographic and narrative expansions in Bassi's commentary seem to suit the traditional interest in fiction at the Este court, where narrative texts in *ottava rima* would soon culminate in the works of Matteo Maria Boiardo and Ludovico Ariosto.

The marginalia of *MA* and *CaM* are the privileged location for Bassi's development of the *fabula*'s narrative and motivic subject matter. Introduced by fixed formulas such as "Nota che . . ." (Note that . . .) and "È da sapere che . . ." (It should be known that . . .), some of these digressions could be easily considered as autonomous mythological novellas. An extreme case is Bassi's deliberate decision to keep a nonauthorial *lectio* in a verse of the poem—even after having recognized its textual corruption—in order to retain the narrative gloss that he had attached to the admittedly wrong variant (fol. 9v):[88]

> Perché trovo in uno altro texto el verso qui di sotto notato, e' parmi star meglio; però nota che aveva questa glosa qui scripta, credendo di lucidare quello che nel texto diceva lo auctore. El quale come è usança de li poetanti non si curano de narrare una cosa fuor de la natura de quello che tratano per allegrare una pelegrina historia. Io adunque trovando el texto giacere come di sotto appare, annotai la historia sotto scripta. Ma vedando come dico uno altro texto, el quale me pare più confaciente a la mente de lo auctore . . . dico concludendo che el verso di fuori sta meglio. Non me è però discaro aver narrata la scripta historia perché altrove lo auctore la tocha. Sì che pur era necessario saperla.

> (As I find in a different text the line noted below, I believe that to be a better reading. But consider that I had written this gloss here, thinking it would elucidate what the author said in the text. Poets customarily are not afraid of narrating something off-topic in order to make a bizarre tale more entertaining. Finding the text as it reads below, therefore, I annotated the following story. But seeing another text, as I said, that seems to me more consistent with the author's meaning . . . I state, in conclusion, that the verse in the margin is more appropriate. But it does not displease me to have told this story, since the author touches on it elsewhere. It was thus still necessary to know it.)

This gloss suggests that Bassi ignored—or intentionally disregarded—Boccaccio's authorship with respect to the commentary, since Boccaccio's gloss obviously comments on the correct variant. The gloss also confirms that Bassi contaminated texts and commentaries indiscriminately from various sources without too many scruples of editorial consistency. Bassi was more focused on expanding extemporaneously on the poem (albeit via a nonauthorial textual variant) than on the textual integrity of his primary text. Ultimately, the gloss displays Bassi's chief literary codes and goals: narrative *varietas* and *delectatio*, both clearly emerging from the reference to the poets' custom of "allegrare" (brightening up) a story. Bassi's commentary is the hybrid work by a humanist who is also the narrator of his own fictions and sometimes sets up an antagonistic attitude toward Boccaccio in matters of narrative skills.

Bassi's digressive endeavors clearly show in the formulas introducing this kind of narrative excursus: "E benché non faça a proposito, perché mi pare fra l'altre degna de memoria non lasserò . . ." (And although it is not appropriate, since this fact is worth remembering among the others, I will not neglect . . .) (fol. 3v); "Non perché faccia al proposito, ma acciò che più compiutamente questa historia ti sia manifesta, nota che . . ." (Not because it is appropriate, but in order for this story to be more fully clear, note that . . .) (fol. 7r). These formulas show Bassi was well aware that many of these expansions are not strictly related to the poem's main narrative. The *mise-en-page* of Bassi's often aberrant digressions—surrounding the poem but also diverging from it and continuing over a different folio—materially objectifies the literary technique known as *entrelacement.* The narrative's variously interlaced stories and subplots develop along diverging and reconverging lines and tease the reader into the unfeasible task of consuming text and commentary simultaneously rather than sequentially—to use Roman Jakobson's well-known formulation. The spatial irradiation of narrative units in the *mise-en-page* of Bassi's commentary almost seems to anticipate the modes of Matteo Maria Boiardo's and Ludovico Ariosto's "rhizomatic" fiction.

As we observed in chapter 4, Boccaccio adopted a specific textual strategy of distinction and dissimulation of his authorial voice into several textual roles. As a result of this strategy, Boccaccio's glosses circulated anonymously and Bassi probably read Boccaccio's commentary—as his abovementioned explicit engagement with one of Boccaccio's glosses confirms—without recognizing the latter's authorship. In his *accessus*, Bassi clearly identifies the author of the poem as Boccaccio (fol. 3r): "lo auctore del presente libro fo Zohanne da Certaldo cognominato Bochazo" (the author of this book was Giovanni Boccaccio from Certaldo). He is also aware of Boccaccio's authorship of the *Teseida*'s introductory sonnets and book divisions (fol. 3r):

> vegneremo a la divisione, la quale il sapientissimo auctore ha elegantissimamente facta: çoè, diviso in .xij. libri ciaschuno con debito ordine per che nel principio de ciaschuno de li dicti .xij. libri lui ha ordinatamente premissi .xiiij. versi li quali sotto brevità sono continenti de tutto quello che lo auctore vole tractare nel dicto libro.
>
> ---
>
> (we will come to the division that the very knowledgeable author very elegantly made: that is, twelve books, each of them with an appropriate order, since at the beginning of the said twelve books he neatly started with fourteen lines that compendiously contain all that the author wants to treat in each book.)

He never identifies, however, the commentary as either authorial or authoritative. The same lack of knowledge may explain the discontinuous presence of Boccaccio's rubrics in the Ferrarese codices (with the partial exception of the section of *Ch* added by a later actor): where they are not neglected altogether, they are rarely transcribed verbatim.

Boccaccio's scholarship paradoxically returns as an indirect presence in Bassi's commentary. Bassi often finds his mythological sources in the *Genealogie deorum gentilium*, which he explicitly cites: for instance, on fol. 48r: "Lo auctore presente nel suo libro de le *Genologie* di questo Dionisio dice . . ." (In the *Genealogies*, the author of the present book says about Dionysus . . .). As Cristina Montagnani has remarked, however, Boccaccio's critical effort to provide different versions of a single myth as treated by different authors is mostly absent from Bassi's often confused mythography.[89]

And yet, Bassi often makes intriguing critical choices, even when complying with conventional rhetorical norms. He obliges the traditional *topos* of modesty when addressing his patron (fol. 86r, on omitting detailed explanation of the cult of Venus in *Teseida* 7.50): "Né circha la distinctione de quelli intendo afadigarme, perché aprovo de vuy excelso mio signore ne è integra peritia. E se non fusse, aveti ne la corte vostra molti a ço sì perfectamente istructi che meglio di me ve lo saperano lucidare" (I do not intend to labor further about this distinction, since I know your Excellence has full knowledge of it; and even if this were not the case, there are people in your court more prepared than I to clarify it for you). He does not hide his mild dissatisfaction with others' scholarship (fol. 21v): "Ma questa opinione non mi satisfa" (I find this opinion unsatisfactory). He expresses his reticence to address disturbing myths, such as that of Tereus (fol. 52v): "Seria contento che la materia presente non mi desse casone de narrare quelo ch'io intendo a declaratione de la presente historia. Né crediate, sereno mio signore, ch'io non cognoscha . . ." (I wish the present matter did not give me reason to narrate what I am about to as an explanation of this story. My serene lord, do not think that I ignore . . .). And he betrays a sense of irritation, if not defeatist discouragement, at the textual multiplying of different versions of a myth, such as the myth of Phrixus and Helle (fol. 10r): "E nota che li auctori l'à[n] tanto ampliata questa historia ch'el non se ne pò cognoscere la mera veritade e perché non fa ad proposito però no[n] ne parlarò più oltre" (And note that the authors have so amplified this story that one can no longer know the plain truth, and since it is not appropriate, I will not talk further about it).

A disinterested examination of Bassi's literary and editorial agenda—one that is not aimed at establishing the critical text of the *Teseida*—would likely treat Bassi more gently than Battaglia did while evaluating the poem's textual tradition. Bassi was neither a superb narrator nor an editor trained in modern (or even early modern) textual criticism. His literary analysis can seem shortsighted and his mythological accounts are often simple vernacular translations of Boccaccio's *Genealogie*. Nonetheless, Bassi's propensity for source cross-contamination, his narrative eclecticism, and his semantic complication and literary curiosity collectively demonstrate key influences of Boccaccio's literary production on subsequent generations of writers in the vernacular, constituting a significant link between late medieval Tuscan literature and the culture of the northern Italian Renaissance.

Colophon

On the nature of details in narrative, Roland Barthes writes: "What is noted is by definition notable. Even were a detail to appear irretrievably insignificant, resistant to all functionality, it would nonetheless end up with precisely the meaning of absurdity or uselessness: everything has a meaning, or nothing has."[90] Barthes's notion of detail could fruitfully include the various elements of discourse semiotics and the material *minutiae* of the text's "container." In manuscript works where authors are known to have played a significant scribal role, everything produces meaning. If we want our interpretation to be historically relevant, we must consider the bijective correspondences between textual unit and material unit, content and medium, visual-verbal message and physical support.

By outlining the material features of the autograph of the *Teseida*, this second case study has defined the literary relevance of Boccaccio's choice of a specific book form for his complex editorial project. On the one hand, the autograph displays a strict interweaving between its visual configuration and the content of the poem: the account of visual elements within the text, the visual apparatus of the codex, and the writing as verbal-visual technology all concur to set up this fascinating *Gesamtkunstwerk*. On the other hand, the autograph clearly indicates an attempt to condition the perception, reception, and transcription of the text it carries, by duplicitously portraying it as an *auctor*'s work but with all the appeal of a more leisurely, popular read.

As Guglielmo Cavallo pointed out, "in specific cases, the material characters denoting the vehicles of the text can indicate facts, modes, and phases of its history (and even of its own writing)."[91] Boccaccio's sophisticated literary and editorial strategy left its traces in the fourteenth- and fifteenth-century manuscript tradition of the poem and also in its translation into print. The critical reception of the *Teseida* in print was strictly associated with Bassi's philology, publisher Agostino Carnerio (or Carneri), the diffusion of typography in Ferrara, and the rise of Ferrarese Humanism.[92] Carnerio published both Bassi's "edition" of the *Teseida* (1475) and his mythological romance *Le fatiche d'Ercole* (1475).[93]

Malcolm Parkes observed, "The late medieval book differs more from its early medieval predecessors than it does from the printed book of our own day."[94] When we compare the Ferrarese codices of the poem (*MA*, *Ch*, and *CaM*) and their counterpart first printed in 1475, we notice a relationship of continuity rather than fracture.[95] From a material point of view, the *Teseida* in print confirms the similarity Parkes described between manuscripts and incunables. The incunable of the *Teseida* presents blank spaces (without guide letters) for decorated or rubricated initials to be added, corresponding to the first verse of all books and the introductory sonnets.[96] Also, like the autograph and the Ferrarese manuscripts, the incunable presents the poem in a single central column, four octaves on each side of the folio. Each book is headed by a majuscule Latin rubric in epigraphic capitals. The commentary occupies the upper, lower, and lateral margins (see pl. 5.8). Bassi's preface, which takes the place of Boccaccio's dedicatory preface to Fiammetta, occupies the entire writing space of the preliminaries.[97] The text of the *editio princeps* was based on *MA* (most probably on a copy of *MA*, too precious to be taken to the printing press). Battaglia's unflattering assessment of the editorial value of this manuscript—its scribe's "overall very suspicious critical surveillance"—could thus apply also to the textual unreliability we detect in the incunable.[98]

The colophon (fol. 155v) is a double elegiac couplet that indicates the date of printing and its publisher Agostino Carnerio:[99] "Hoc opus impressit theseida nomine dictum | Bernardo genitus bibliopola puer: | Augustinus ei nomen cum: dux bonus urbem | Herculeus princeps ferrariam regeret | M°. CCCC°. LXXIIIII°" (The young bookseller son of Bernardo printed this work titled *Teseida*—his name is Agostino—at the time when the good duke Ercole ruled over Ferrara. 1475). Carnerio's career as printer and publisher did not last long, even for the standards of the financially risky early phases of the printing industry. The catalogue of his production extends only from 1474 to 1479. If we examine this catalogue, however, we can discern key information about the reception of the *Teseida*. Boccaccio-Bassi's *Teseida* was published in close temporal proximity to a series of texts that are clearly humanistic in nature. In addition to two classics of canon law—Clemens V's *Constitutiones* and Boniface VIII's *Liber sextus*—and the more devotionally inspired vernacular translations of books 4 and 5 of the *Vitae sanctorum patrum*, we have Guarino Veronese's Latin grammar, Ognibene da Lonigo's Latin grammar, Horace's *Carmina*, Bassi's *Le fatiche d'Ercole*, the Pseudo-Hyginus's *Poeticon astronomicon*, and Ovid's *Metamorphoses.*[100]

Carnerio's catalogue seems to confirm and promote the success of Boccaccio's plan to be inscribed within the canon of cultivated authors. And, by association, the Ferrara court viewed the production and circulation of the incunables of the *Teseida* and of *Le fatiche d'Ercole*—with their panegyric of the Este family and their classicizing presentation—as an opportunity to

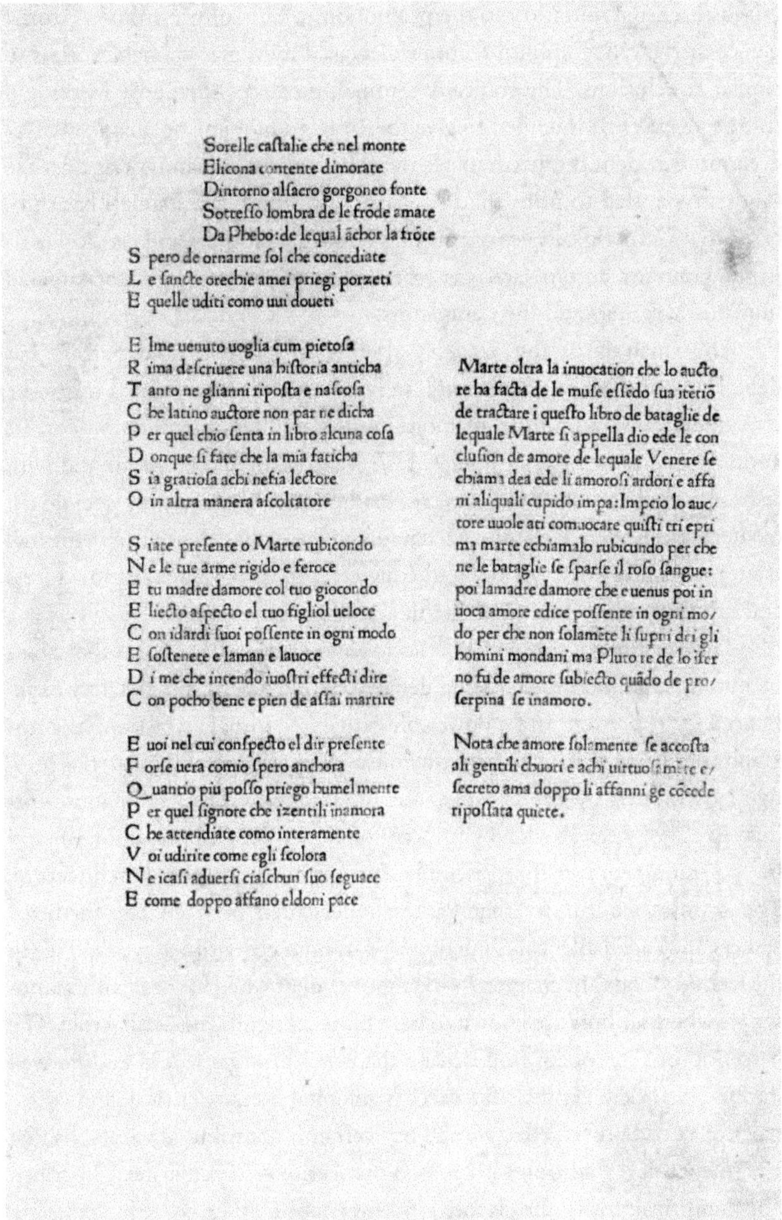

Soreſſe caſtalie che nel monte
Elicona contente dimorate
Dintorno alſacro gorgoneo fonte
Sotteſſo lombra de le frõde amate
Da Phebo: de lequal ãchor la frõte
S pero de ornarme ſol che concediate
L e ſancte orechie amei priegi porzeti
E quelle uditi como uui doueti

E lme uenuto uoglia cum pietoſa
R ima deſcriuere una hiſtoria anticha
T anto ne glianni ripoſta e naſcoſa
C he latino auctore non par ne dicha
P er quel chio ſenta in libro alcuna coſa
D onque ſi fate che la mia faticha
S ia gratioſa achi neſia lectore
O in altra manera aſcoltatore

S iate preſente o Marte rubicondo
N e le tue arme rigido e feroce
E tu madre damore col tuo giocondo
E liecto aſpecto el tuo figliol ueloce
C on idardi ſuoi poſſente in ogni modo
E ſoſtenete e laman e lauoce
D i me che intendo iuoſtri effecti dire
C on pocho bene e pien de aſſai martire

E uoi nel cui conſpecto el dir preſente
F orſe uera comio ſpero anchora
Q uantio piu poſſo priego humel mente
P er quel ſignore che izentili inamora
C he attendiate como interamente
V oi udirite come egli ſcolora
N e icaſi aduerſi ciaſchun ſuo ſeguace
E come doppo affano eldoni pace

Marte oltra la inuocation che lo aucto
re ha facta de le muſe eſſẽdo ſua ĩtẽtiõ
de tractare i queſto libro de bataglie de
lequale Marte ſi appella dio ede le con
cluſion de amore de lequale Venere ſe
chiama dea ede li amoroſi ardori e affa
ni aliquali cupido impa: Impcio lo auc/
tore uuole ati comuocare quiſti tri epti
ma marte echiamalo rubicundo per che
ne le bataglie ſe ſparſe il roſo ſangue:
poi lamadre damore che e uenus poi in
uoca amore edice poſſente in ogni mo/
do per che non ſolamẽte li ſupni dei gli
homini mondani ma Pluto re de lo ifer
no fu de amore ſubiecto quãdo de pro/
ſerpina ſe inamoro.

Nota che amore ſolamente ſe accoſta
ali gentili chuori e achi uirtuoſamẽte e/
ſecreto ama doppo li affanni ge cõcede
ripoſſata quiete.

Plate 5.8. Cambridge, Massachusetts, Houghton Library, Inc 5735 (28.2), fol. 6r. Courtesy of the Houghton Library, Harvard University.

attach the Este reputation to the promotion of humanistic culture. A brief glance at the typographical features displayed by these incunables leads to similar conclusions. The choice of a roman typeface—for those works and for the *Teseida*—is intended to give these texts a humanistic quality. This is even more evident if one compares the choice of the roman type against the Gothic type used to print the two classics of canon law: Daniels has indicated that Carnerio's choice of printing vernacular authors and classical texts in the same roman typeface was part of a marketing strategy that targeted humanistic readers and their emulators.[101]

This analysis of the *Teseida*'s afterlife in Florence and Ferrara has demonstrated that the poem could, in fact, be perceived as both a text to be commented on and a form of more immediate literary entertainment, its author being associated with *auctoritates* (Christian and classical) and with less cultivated forms of oral poetry. In the terms proposed by sociologist of literature Robert Escarpit, we could conclude that Boccaccio's editorial strategy—expressed so vividly and concretely in *Aut*—managed to address and capture both the cultured circuit and the popular circuit.[102]

The exact relationship of Boccaccio's autograph to the rest of the extant manuscript tradition is still being debated. Nonetheless, *Aut* certainly experienced great prestige and a power of textual and visual attraction, as autographs often did within the early manuscript tradition.[103] Its material prestige is witnessed by the homogenous physiognomy of those manuscripts that, like *Aut*, were provided with a commentary (albeit nonauthorial), and by the *editio princeps*: they resemble *Aut*'s textual and spatial architecture. The seamless continuity that Parkes underscored between late medieval codices and incunables can sometimes—but not necessarily, as we shall see in the section "Coda" in chapter 7—be more evident when we deal with manuscripts where authors are known to have played a significant scribal role. The perception of the poem imposed by the *editio princeps* would endure well into the twentieth century. Boccaccio's ancipital literary, critical, and editorial project had proven effective and had certainly contributed to establishing a hermeneutical tradition for his own pioneering vernacular text, in continuity and rivalry with the classics.

PART III

Materiality and Poetics in Petrarca's Sestinas

CHAPTER SIX

Materiality and Meter

Itaque nullum emendandi genus omitto.
—Pliny, *Epistulae* 7.17.7

NUGELLE

Despite his own ostentatiously dismissive attitude toward his lyric production in the vernacular, Francesco Petrarca dedicated more than thirty years (ca. 1342–74) to organizing his *nugelle vulgares* (vernacular trifles) (*Seniles* 13.11) and self-styled fragmented soul, "sparsa anime fragmenta" (scattered fragments of my soul) (*Secretum* 3.18), into a cohesive literary work and a coherent exemplary self-representation.[1] The 366 poems that Petrarca collected into his songbook detail an existential parable of Augustinian conversion from the poet-protagonist's sensual and unwavering desire for his beloved Laura to the final entrusting of his soul to the Virgin Mary. Collectively, these poems narrate the ethical redemption and poetic development of an *agens* (Petrarca the protagonist) presented as the persona of an *auctor* (Petrarca the poet), who historically—materially—transcribed them in his role as a *scriptor* (Petrarca the copyist). The hypostatic coincidence of literary composition and material execution of Petrarca's book-project provides the case study for this chapter and the next.

The *Rerum vulgarium fragmenta* (*Fragments in the Vernacular*), the title Petrarca gave to his work, portray a poetic subject divided between self-deception and the search for a better version of himself; between celebration of Laura (with her various metaphorical meanings) and condemnation of love for her as a contemptible deviation from love for God; between sensitivity to the fugacity of time and perception of eternity; between secular authors and sacred texts. The poems counterfeit a temporal progression through a series of internal oppositions between past and present and the dissemination of texts (the anniversary poems) that establish the fictitious chronology of his relationship with Laura. The *canzoniere* (as the *Fragmenta* are often referred to antonomastically) employs a two-part structural division to reify the account of this dilemmatic existence and the succeeding ideological renovation. In the first part, the poet clings to the ever-elusive mirage of concluding his erotic quest, reaching poetic glory, and achieving existential contentedness. In the second part, Laura's sudden death enhances his intellectual maturation, promotes his conversion, and locates within heavenly grace the only remedy against the temporal and transcendental consequences of temptation and the only source of existential serenity: the final word of the *Fragmenta* is "pace" (peace). Although the poet's moral palinode (in *canzone* 264) does not coincide textually with Laura's death (in sonnet 267), that death, for the poet, eventually takes on allegorical—Christological and Mariological—and liturgical features that expose his love for her as improper and help him realize the vanity of all earthly values.

The dialectic between the coherent textualization of the poet's persona and his fragmentary and ephemeral existence corresponds to one between the unity of the book-project and the variety of its style and metrical forms (317 sonnets, 29 *canzoni*, 9 sestinas, 7 *ballate*, 4 *madrigali*). The tormented elaboration of the *Rerum vulgarium fragmenta* (hereafter, *RVF*) emerges from Petrarca's frantic activity of composing, transcribing, correcting, collecting, rejecting, ordering, and reordering his poems. It is hard to know if the mention of a *libellus* (booklet) in a marginal note Petrarca left in 1330 on his copy of Horace's *Odes* refers to the original nucleus of the *RVF*, but we can track a first organized collection to as early as 1342.[2] The ultimate (if not definitive) result of this decades-long endeavor is collected in seventy-two partially autograph (and partially idiograph) folios that now form MS Vatican Latin 3195, preserved in the Vatican Library.[3] Between the initial conception of the book (an original matrix of twenty-five poems) and the last traces of Petrarca's scribal activity on the autograph stand several redactions of the *canzoniere*, a production history that has significantly affected its editorial tradition. Even if recent paleographic and codicological scholarship has partially discredited Ernest H. Wilkins's proposition that Petrarca made the *canzoniere* in "nine forms,"[4] the more than two hundred codices dating to the fourteenth and fifteenth century preserve at least four or five different "editions" of Petrarca's songbook (the so-called Chigi, Malatesta, Pre-Vatican, Queriniana, and Vatican forms).[5] Despite an affectation of repulsion for wide popularity—at least among the common people—and for recognition as a vernacular poet,[6] Petrarca himself was the intellectual originator of these versions and was directly responsible for their circulation among friends and admirers, thus indirectly facilitating the ensuing uncontrolled dissemination and dispersion of his poems in unauthorized (and often textually subpar) copies.

This chapter and the next explore Petrarca's material and textual treatment of the poetic genre of the sestina in the autograph of the *RVF*: the aforementioned MS Vat. Lat. 3195. When we ask questions about what is legible in the sestinas and what is visible of the sestinas—about what is verbal and conceptual and what is material and spatial—we recognize the sestinas' corpus as the core of the *canzoniere*'s poetics. Petrarca's material choices (which isolate the sestinas and give them visual prominence in the autograph), and the specific ways he elected to facilitate the interaction of *mise-en-page*, meter, rhetorical articulation, and subject matter, together define the sestinas as a coherent semantic unit. Petrarca's choices as intellectual originator and vigilant supervisor of—if not always actual copyist for—the *RVF* as a physical container thus direct the reader to attend to the sestinas as to the "spine" of the autograph, which Petrarca materially, and also thematically and rhetorically, singles out as the *canzoniere*'s privileged space for reflecting, recapitulating, reassessing, and reviewing (in metaliterary terms) the poetic and existential itinerary he portrays in the *canzoniere*. The first case study in part I of this book has described how the materiality of manuscript culture intersects the narrative of Dante Alighieri's *Vita nova*: it has shown how the very substance of the prosimetrum's enunciated consists of the material dynamics of its composition, circulation, and reception. The second case study has examined how, in the autograph of the *Teseida*, Giovanni Boccaccio made the most of the medium's materiality to simulate multiple simulacra of his role as enunciator: it has shown how Boccaccio employed his expertise in matters of making books to shape a plural authorial identity and condition the reception of his poem. By integrating an examination of Petrarca's material presentation of the sestinas into their literary analysis, this third case study will show how Petrarca intended poetry—the very act of his textual enunciation—as an indissoluble unity of scribal and discursive practices.

Meter and Materiality

The morphological description of the sestina—verse, strophic structure, rhyme scheme—is relatively straightforward. Its genealogy, in both textual and material terms, is instead more elusive. Petrarca's recognized predecessors—Arnaut Daniel and Dante—composed only one "sestina" each. And medieval metrical theorists, including Dante, treated the "sestina"—a term they never used—simply as a peculiarly structured *canzone* rather than an autonomous metrical kind. Both the first possible (but indecisive) testimony of the form and the first mention of the term involve Petrarca, but we shall see that Petrarca himself unequivocally groups sestinas and *canzoni* together in an explicit (if tachygraphical) testimony. Petrarca does serialize the sestinas and normalize the structure he derived from his predecessors. In the autograph of the *canzoniere*, what is more, the sestinas assume a distinct vertical layout that isolates them from the overall horizontality of the other metrical kinds. Building on Carlo Pulsoni's metrical history of the sestina in the Romance sphere and on H. Wayne Storey's analyses of its visual pattern and poetics in the *RVF*'s autograph, this section argues that Petrarca's "theorization" of the sestina as genre is performed materially, by means of an innovative syntactical relationship between space and text.

Meter

Often referred to as the lyrical sestina—to distinguish it from the narrative sestina or *sesta rima* (rhyme scheme: ABABCC)—the sestina consists of six 6-line strophes plus a 3-line *tornada* of all hendecasyllables. As Aurelio Roncaglia described the form, "within each strophe, words at the end of the lines are not subject to any rhyme scheme, but are repeated identically in all strophes, combining lexical insistence with the device of *rims dissolutz*. . . .

From strophe to strophe, only the order of presentation varies: it is different at every round, though it still complies with a rigorous law of permutation."[7] Roncaglia's mention of *rims dissolutz* (or *rimas dissolutas*; also *rims estramps* or *rimas estrampas*, literally, "rhymes with a limp") references a rhyme scheme of Old Occitan poetry, in which words do not rhyme within the individual stanza, but rather between stanzas.[8] Interstanzaic correspondences are regulated on the law of permutation of the sestina, which obeys the rules of what is known as *retrogradatio cruciata*. Both *retrogradatio* and *crucifixio* are techniques of Medieval Latin poetry: *retrogradatio* describes the "backward progression" of the rhyme-words; *crucifixio* relates to their mutual contiguity and chiastic arrangement. It was philologist and metricologist Giovanni Mari who recognized and named the combination of the two techniques as *retrogradatio cruciata*.[9] In the sestina, the same rhyme-words close the lines of each stanza, and their retrograde presentation throughout the poem is determined by the position those rhyme-words occupy in the previous stanza: 1–2–3–4–5–6 > 6–1–5–2–4–3 > 3–6–4–1–2–5, and so forth. The *tornada* includes all six rhyme-words in any order. A hypothetical seventh stanza would repeat the rhyme scheme of the first, restarting the cycle.[10]

Diachrony

If a morphological description of the sestina as form is relatively easy, its genealogy (its "invention," as Roncaglia terms it) is more elusive. Recent critical studies have advanced a challenge to a previously long-standing consensus around a genetic interpretation of the sestina.[11] Influential Renaissance critics such as Pietro Bembo, Lodovico Dolce, and Ludovico Castelvetro[12] agreed in recognizing the Occitan troubadour Arnaut Daniel as the "inventor" of the sestina with his *canso* 18 "Lo ferm voler qu'el cor m'intra" (The firm will that enters my heart).[13] Through an approach to metrical forms that is more teleological than historical, these early readers of the *RVF* outline a sort of metrical *translatio studii* from Provence to Tuscany. In this idealistic reconstruction of the form's development, Dante and Petrarca would receive Arnaut's *Ur-Sestina* and perfect it.

Modern commentators of Petrarca's *RVF* have often concurred in this genealogy. Dante's "sestina" (7 [CI, 44]) "Al poco giorno ed al gran cerchio d'ombra" (To the short day and the great circle of *shadow*)[14] would standardize the metrical signifier and achieve a rigorous "interpenetration" of metrical technique and inner disposition of the soul: Salvatore Battaglia argues that "the passion for the technique builds on the soul's passion. And little by little the latter is surpassed and transformed into the pain and obsession of the former."[15] According to this narrative, Petrarca would follow in Arnaut's and Dante's footsteps.[16] And he would work toward a more intimate connection between the sestina's form and its contents. With the intricate geometry of its metrics, in other words, Petrarca's sestina would be the only form able to express a specific set of semantic features.

This reconstruction makes a number of valid points. A dynamic of intertextual exchanges undoubtedly occurs between Arnaut, Dante, and Petrarca. And Petrarca explicitly authorized a line of inquiry that emphasizes his intellectual connections with Arnaut and Dante in *RVF* 70, the *canzone* "Lasso me, ch'i' non so in qual parte pieghi" (Alas, I do not know where to turn the hope). In what is generally referred to as the *canzone delle citazioni*, Petrarca followed the medieval Latin poetic tradition of the *versus cum auctoritate* and concluded each of the *canzone*'s five stanzas with an incipit from a poem by Arnaut (or someone he believed to be Arnaut), Guido Cavalcanti, Dante, Cino da Pistoia, and Petrarca himself.[17] If Dante, in the *Vita nova*, the *De vulgari eloquentia*, and the *Commedia*, had outlined an oriented literary history populated by poets-turned-characters and punctuated by citations and self-citations, in *canzone* 70 Petrarca compressed a chronological and teleological progression of poetic accomplishment—climaxing in his work—within the turn of fifty hendecasyllables: two can play at this game.

It may also be legitimate to see a progression from Arnaut's *trobar ric* (poetic writing characterized by technical virtuosity) to Dante's reconciliation of verse and theme into a superior unit. Dante viewed the metrical form not only as a way to create a technical challenge, but also as a chance to maximize the "message" of the poem.[18] At a technical level, Dante's version of Arnaut's "sestina" is characterized by the elimination of irregularities and the rejection of excessively captious techniques. Like the Occitan troubadour Pons Fabre d'Uzes before him,[19] Dante imposes on the stanzas a definite homoeometry: he assigns to the "sestina" a strophe of all hendecasyllables, whereas the first line of every stanza in Arnaut's "Lo ferm voler" is a feminine heptasyllable followed by masculine octosyllables. Dante's "sestina" is also characterized by regular interstrophic correspondences between rhymes and a "statutory absence of the *aequivocum*," as Gabriele Frasca has described the circumstance where no homophones are used as rhyme-words.[20] It is philologically correct to read Petrarca's sestinas as a dialogue with his two illustrious precursors: his appropriation of technical and lexical features from their corpora is in line with his distinctly "active" intertextual practices.[21] Moreover, Petrarca methodically expanded the corpus with nine sestinas (including one double sestina), thus paving the way to the codification of the sestina as a genre: Pulsoni underscored that Petrarca assumes "full consciousness of composing a text recognizable as typologically reproducible and therefore part of a homogenous series."[22] Finally, it seems reasonable to state that after Petrarca's standardization of the form, his grammaticalization,[23] we can observe its repetition and progressive involution in the virtuosic exhibitionism of quasi-centonian experiments preserved in Mannerist and Baroque anthologies.

Theorization

But the textual and material condition of the sestina is far more articulated and difficult to decipher. William Paden has pointed out that assuming intentionality regarding choice of genre is difficult work when evaluating the medieval literary context, in which genres and poems, poetics and poetry, often developed simultaneously.[24] Whereas Renaissance scholars of Petrarchan pedigree show interest in the sestina (and know its name), Petrarca himself seems to lack an unequivocable theoretical consciousness of, and a name for, the sestina as well-defined metrical form. In the outer margin of the final and chronologically late *canzone* (*RVF* 366) "Vergine bella, che, di sol vestita" (Beautiful Virgin who, clothed with the sun) on fol. 72v of MS Vat. Lat. 3195, a gloss in Petrarca's hand indicates that sestinas and *canzoni* are still typologically and numerically associated: "38. cum duabus que sunt in papiro" (thirty-eight, counting two that are on paper).[25] Upon transcribing *RVF* 366, the gloss shows, the "legislator" of the genre-sestina still considers the twenty-nine *canzoni* and nine sestinas of the *RVF* as one homogenous metrical series.[26]

Medieval literary critics before Petrarca also seem to lack critical awareness of the sestina's specificity. Guilhem Molinier's Old Occitan grammar *Leys d'Amors*, written between 1328 and 1337 and providing a description of the troubadours' corpus at the twilight of Old Occitan culture, offers little help, treating Arnaut's "sestina" as a *canso* with *rimas estrampas*: "la canso que fo Arnaud Daniel can dish: Lo ferms volers quel cor mintra" (the *canso* composed by Arnaut Daniel when he wrote: *Lo ferm voler qu'el cor m'intra*).[27] Medieval *trattatisti* (writers of treatises) on the art of metrics, such as Antonio da Tempo and Gidino da Sommacampagna, neither mention the sestina by name nor recognize it as a distinctive form.

Dante's *De vulgari eloquentia* generally offers invaluable information for the understanding of medieval poetic techniques. When it comes to sestinas, however, Dante's work supplies more questions than answers.[28] In the treatise, Dante refers twice to his own "sestina" "Al poco giorno." While discussing different typologies of stanzas (2.10.2), he associates the stanzas of "Al poco giorno"—with no division (*diesis* or *volta*) between the *fronte* (or two *piedi*) and the *sirma* (or two *volte*)—to those of Arnaut's *cansos*: "et huiusmodi stantia usus est fere in omnibus cantionibus suis Arnaldus Danielis, et nos eum secuti sumus cum diximus *Al poco giorno e al gran cerchio d'ombra*" (Stanzas of this kind were used by Arnaut Daniel in nearly all his *canzoni*, and I followed him when I wrote *Al poco giorno e al gran cerchio d'ombra*). The second mention of "Al poco giorno" also references Arnaut. In this case Dante deals, not less problematically, with the rhyme scheme of the "sestina" (2.13.2): "Unum est stantia sine rithimo, in qua nulla rithimorum habitudo actenditur: et huiusmodi stantiis usus est Arnaldus Danielis frequentissime, velut ibi: *Se·m fos Amor de ioi donar*; et nos dicimus *Al poco giorno*" (One of these is the unrhymed stanza, in which no organization according to rhyme occurs; Arnaut Daniel used this kind of stanza very frequently, as in his *Se·m fos Amor de ioi donar*, and I also used it in *Al poco giorno*). As indicated by Pier Vincenzo Mengaldo in the commentary *ad locos*, Dante refers here to the Occitan technique of the *coblas dissolutas* (or *estrampas*): stanzas without rhymes within the stanzas themselves. Dante's self-exegesis offers no grounds for considering "Al poco giorno" anything other than a *canzone* with a peculiar metrical configuration. Dante does acknowledge Arnaut's influence in the context of "Al poco giorno"—and Arnaut's "Lo ferm voler," albeit never mentioned explicitly, looks like the most plausible template for Dante's poem within Arnaut's corpus. Nevertheless, there is no evidence to suggest that Dante's "sestina" is, for its own author, a genre of its own that demands its own name.[29]

If from Dante's critical engagement with his own "sestina" we can conclude that he considered it only a particularly complex instantiation of *canzone* instead of a well-defined metrical kind, in his fourteenth-century commentator Benvenuto da Imola we see a possible critical reference to the sestina as metrical kind. Remarkably, the reference associates Arnaut and Dante with Petrarca. And the plot thickens. Benvenuto leaves an enigmatic note in his commentary to Dante's *Commedia*, as he discusses Arnaut's appearance in *Purgatorio* 26.115–18: "qui [*sc.* Arnaldus] invenit multa et pulcra dicta vulgaria; a quo Petrarcha fatebatur sponte se accepisse modum et stilum cantilenae de quatuor rhythmis, et non a Dante" (Arnaut composed many beautiful texts in the vernacular. Directly from him, and not from Dante, Petrarca would freely admit to have derived the mode and style of the song of four rhymes).[30] In anticipation of a reliable critical edition of Benvenuto's *Comentum super Dantis Aldigherii Comediam* for the Edizione Nazionale dei Commenti Danteschi to be published by the Centro Pio Rajna, it might be intriguing to consider here the possibility of a misreading (a metathesis) from *VI* (*sex*) to *IV* (*quattuor*) in the transmission of the commentary—or perhaps an incorrect deciphering of the sequence of Gothic minims—and thus to query this note as possibly referencing the sestina.[31]

If Benvenuto's report of Petrarca's self-affiliation with Arnaut may already sanction the sestina's specificity,[32] Petrarca's manuscript tradition records the term *sestina* for the first time. Pulsoni traced the first occurrence of the term *sestina* in a miscellaneous manuscript transmitting Petrarca's corpus.[33] Manuscript Laurenziano Strozzi 178 of the Biblioteca Medicea Laurenziana in Florence is a parchment codex, generally dated around the end of the fourteenth century. Folios 4r–137r preserve the "Chigi form" of Petrarca's *canzoniere* interspersed with other *disperse* (poems not included in the final version of the *RVF*). The manuscript is divided into two blocks: the first organizes the poems according to their meter, the second alphabetically, by the first letter of their incipit. Not only do the five sestinas of the "Chigi form" occupy their own section in the first block, but the heading *Sestine* also opens this section on fol. 21r. This testimony is even more relevant if we consider that, according to Gino Belloni, the typology of glosses in MS Strozzi 178 guarantees the "glossator's familiarity with Petrarchan matters."[34] For late medieval scholars and scribes, in short, the sestina's consolidation as a genre in and of itself is established in connection with, and with reference to, Petrarca's work. Before Petrarca serializes and consolidates it, in other words, it is difficult, and perhaps incorrect, to conceptualize and describe the sestina as autonomous genre.

Regularization

Petrarca's consolidation of the sestina operates in multiple directions: he replicates it, regulates it, and enhances it materially. Petrarca provides a conspicuous and homogenous corpus of poems. Raffaella Pelosini writes that Petrarca "took the sestina away from the experimentalism of his predecessors' single realizations."[35] What had been a *hapax* for Arnaut and Dante becomes for Petrarca a systematic genre.[36] The very number of Petrarca's sestinas (nine in all) indicates his leading role in the elevation of this form.

Petrarca also regulates the form of the sestina, appropriating Old Occitan versification through Dante's magisterium. Like Dante, he chooses homoeometry and opts for isosyllabic stanzas of all hendecasyllables. Like Dante, he generally avoids *aequivocatio* (or *aequivocum*: the use of homophones with different meanings).[37] Like Dante, he also avoids Arnaut's *rims derivativs*, the systematic rhyme alternation of terms with identical lexical morphemes but different grammatical morphemes (e.g., the alternation between masculine and feminine endings of the same noun or adjective). In Petrarca's sestinas, even when a rhyme-word is used in a metaphorical sense, its signifier does not change. Additionally, and in a noteworthy departure from both Arnaut and Dante, Petrarca progressively codifies the rhyme scheme of the *tornada*. The *tornadas* of Petrarca's last five sestinas present a fixed rhyme scheme that reprises that of the first stanza: (A) B (C) D (E) F, with letters in parentheses indicating internal rhyme-words.[38]

With his final sestina, a double sestina with six rhyme-words, twelve stanzas, and a *tornada*, Petrarca furthers the technique by providing a metrical reduplication of the form. If all sestinas ideally reconnect Petrarca's own corpus of sestinas to Guiraut Riquier's *cansos redondas* (the two "circular songs" where the permutation of the rhymes stops after completing all configurations), the *sestina doppia* defies the limits of the *redonda* by developing its generative potential and restarting the rhyme cycle, thus underscoring the incantatorial and obsessive force of the rhyme-words.[39] Petrarca's final sestina is simultaneously exception to and, therefore, confirmation of the successful solidification of the form.

Material Codification

The consolidation of the sestina as form—and its consequent elevation to reproducible genre—is achieved also (if not foremost) by means of its material presentation in the autograph of the *RVF*.[40] Whereas Petrarca's textual treatment of the sestina is for the most part a refunctionalization of features that he could derive from Dante and the troubadours, his *material* treatment is extremely innovative (see pl. 6.1).[41] Storey has observed that in the autograph of the *RVF*,

> the sestina is always copied in two independent columns, following a "vertical" reading track that contrasts the "horizontal" reading track of the other genres of the poetic collection. The reader, therefore, has to reach the bottom of the left column before moving to the right one. Since in the combinatory system of the texts of the *Fragmenta* Petrarca's preference is for the pairing sestina/sonnet . . ., what is immediately clear is the contrast perceived (while both transcribing and reading) between a vertical cursory proceeding of the pen or the eye (for the sestina) and a horizontal one (for the sonnet).[42]

The systematic columnar disposition of the sestina—where each verse starts a new line (vis-à-vis sonnets and *canzoni*) and the reader proceeds vertically down the left column toward the folio's *bas-de-page*—shows that concerning different metrical genres, Petrarca recognizes for each a different materiality of written signs.[43] Petrarca's material awareness seems to precede a critical and theoretical consciousness, and we see this awareness more clearly if we consider the material treatment of Arnaut's and Dante's "sestinas." The twenty Occitan *chansonniers* preserving Arnaut's "Lo ferm voler" almost universally lay out the text like the other *cansos*: transcribed horizontally, like prose, with the end of each verse indicated by a *punctus* or other diacritical sign.[44] The only extant exceptions are two codices (belonging to the so-called third tradition of Occitan *chansonniers*), dated between the end of the

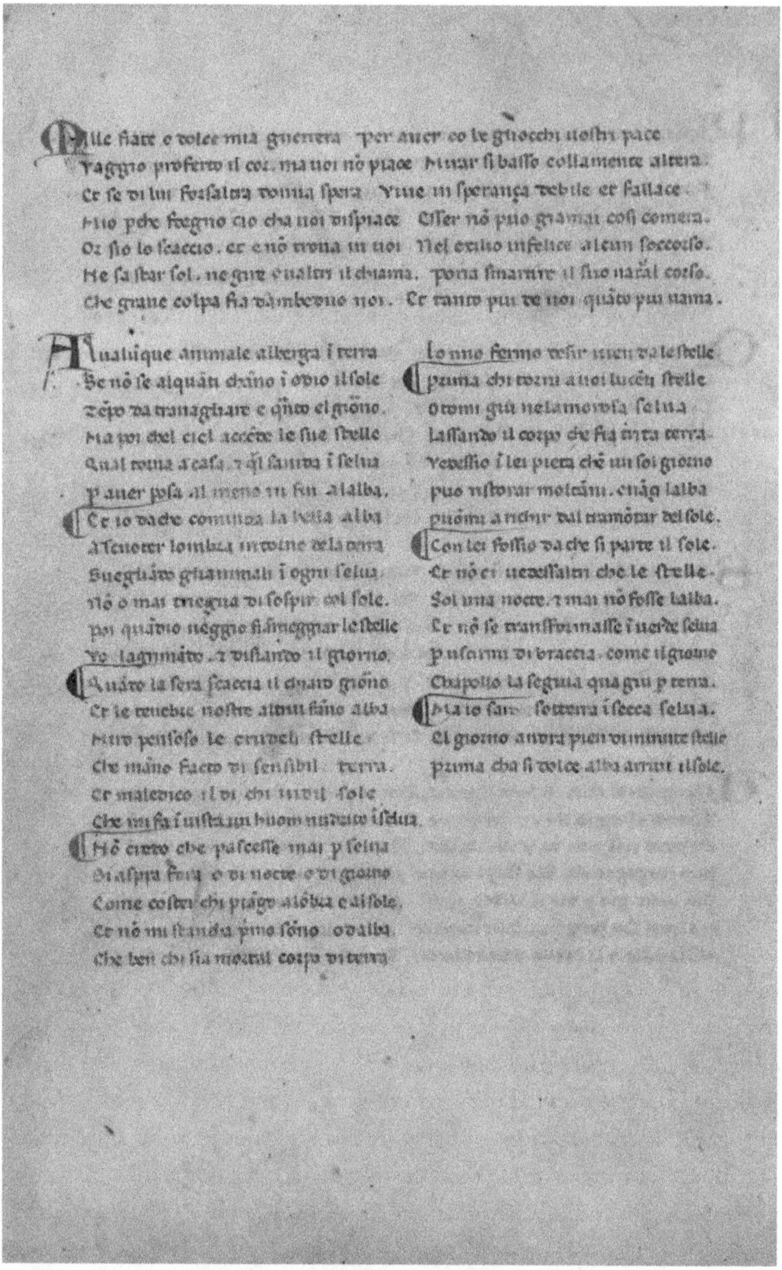

Plate 6.1. Vatican City, Biblioteca Apostolica Vaticana, MS Vat. Lat. 3195, fol. 3v. By permission of the Biblioteca Apostolica Vaticana.

thirteenth century and the beginning of the fourteenth:[45] Oxford, Bodleian Library, MS Douce 269 (denoted by the *siglum S* after Karl Bartsch's classification), compiled in the Veneto; and Florence, Biblioteca Medicea Laurenziana, MS Pluteo 41.43 (denoted by the *siglum U* after Bartsch), produced in central Tuscany.[46] These two codices do present Arnaut's "sestina" in a vertical layout, but the exception they provide is only relatively compelling: the same vertical verse disposition characterizes all poetic compositions included in these manuscripts. Furio Brugnolo suggests that this exceptional format may be because of the unusually oblong form of the manuscripts.[47] This seems especially persuasive for the aforementioned MS Douce 269, which William Pierce Shepard, preparing a diplomatic edition of the manuscript early in the twentieth century, described as a "small, elongated octavo."[48]

These exceptions notwithstanding, authoritative fourteenth-century manuscripts that preserve Dante's "Al poco giorno" present the "sestina" in the usual horizontal prose-like layout: for instance, Florence, Biblioteca Medicea Laurenziana, MS Martelli 12 (fols. 27v–28r); Florence, Biblioteca Nazionale Centrale, MS Magliabechi VI.143 (fol. 25rv [22rv]); and Vatican City, Biblioteca Apostolica Vaticana, MS Chigi L.VIII.305 (fol. 31rv).[49] Boccaccio's treatment of "Al poco giorno" provides additional confirmation. Indeed, Dante's "sestina" is always included (as *canzone*) in the Boccaccian corpus of Dante's fifteen *canzoni distese* as Boccaccio's autographs MS Toledo 104.6 (fol. 261rv), MS Riccardiano 1035 (fol. 182v), and MS Chigi L.V.176 (fol. 38r) preserve it. Moreover, for Dante's "sestina" the prose-like horizontal transcriptional layout, characteristic of the *canzone* genre in said codices, is always employed.[50] Boccaccio follows the horizontal transcriptional layout even for the visual rendition of Petrarca's sestinas in the "Chigi form" of the *RVF* (the *Liber fragmentorum*), preserved in the MS Chigi L.V.176 (fols. 43v–79r).[51] Beginning from the second stanza of the first sestina, however, each stanza of the five sestinas is preceded by alternating blue and red paragraph signs. If Boccaccio had derived this "transcriptional variant" from the layout of the antigraph from which he was copying, this could be evidence of the material emancipation of the sestina from the *canzone* at the time of transcription (ca. 1363–66).[52]

And yet, on fol. 48v, Boccaccio uses the same alternative textual style for both the *canzone* "Verdi panni, sanguigni, oscuri o persi" (Green garments, crimson, black, or purple) and the sestina "Giovene donna sotto un verde lauro" (A youthful lady under a green laurel). This transcriptional inconsistency could certainly reflect the poems' material presentations in the antigraph from which Boccaccio was copying. Boccaccio is generally respectful of the *mise-en-page* of the antigraphs—less so of their *lectiones*—and thus this variance could be a simple oversight. This inconsistency could also indicate, instead, a still ongoing process of emancipation of the sestina or the scribe's resistance to characterize two metrical forms—sestina and *canzone*—perceived as kindred by means of a different material presentation. We will come upon a comparable resistance, though more explicitly asserted, in the section "Coda" of chapter 7.

We have seen how Petrarca's consolidation of the sestina as form entails the simultaneous regularization of its metrical features and standardization of an innovative (if not fully unprecedented) material presentation. From what we can infer from his gloss explicitly grouping *canzoni* and sestinas together, in Petrarca's system of poetic kinds, the material specification of the sestina precedes its terminological and theoretical emancipation from the *canzone*. In this iteration of Petrarca's manuscript poetics, the columnar transcription of the sestina is the codicological correlative of the *retrogradatio cruciata*. In devising a unique material solution to enhance the specificity of a meter, Petrarca shows that material arrangement and poetic composition are mutually dependent. The former is intended to affect the reception of the latter by readers who are, first of all, viewers: words become what Willard Bohn suggestively describes as "building blocks in a visual edifice."[53] Petrarca's specific solution for the sestina is proof of the relationship of consubstantiality (if not of immanence) between literary word and scribal practice, between text as a linguistic sign and text as visual entity, between the verbal and the spatial. The following section will inscribe Petrarca's material treatment of the sestina within the poetic and material system of MS Vat. Lat. 3195 as it relates to a larger perspective on his manuscript poetics.

Manuscript Poetics

Manuscripts are the embodiment of Petrarca's literary and intellectual career. They represent for him an instrument to investigate the texts of classical antiquity and a textual laboratory of references and critical annotations. Building on Armando Petrucci's works on Petrarca's graphic reform, this section inscribes the material and textual treatment of the sestina—as presented in the *RVF*'s autograph—into Petrarca's all-absorbing experience of the codex as an instrument for poetic and philological research.[54] In Petrarca's literary production as a poet, the book must be examined as an aesthetic component distinct from, and in dialogue with, the texts it contains. In his research on visual poetics in early Italian literature, Storey has explained how authors, as scribes of their own work, used compositional principles such as the *mise-en-page* as a material counterpart to the poetic message. Petrarca is among the most innovative of those experimenters who "integrated scribal forms as part of their written poetics and codes of meaning."[55] Where Storey's investigations considered these scribal forms primarily as the visual and graphological conceptualization of meters and genres, this section considers their effect on the reader's perception of the sestina's distinctive metrical feature—the *retrogradatio cruciata*—and their role in establishing a corpus within the *canzoniere*.

Books and Scripts

Books represent a constant preoccupation for Petrarca, figuring as major characters in his epistolary and as objects of continual craving and searching. In a letter referring to his gift of Augustine's *Confessiones* to Augustinian friar and man of letters Luigi Marsili (*Seniles* 15.7), Petrarca describes this *pugillaris* (small-format book) as an ideal extension of his hand, a book that accompanied his trips throughout his whole life: "eundo et redeundo mecum senuit" (coming and going it has become old with me).[56] The beginnings of what we call Latin humanism can be found on the shelves of Petrarca's library, one that consisted of books avidly accumulated and heavily glossed (such as his copy of Cicero's *Tusculanae disputationes*), along with books that always eluded his network of meticulous book hunters, such as those he asked his relative Giovanni dell'Incisa to search for on his behalf (*Familiares* 3.18).[57] Petrarca figures prominently in the material connections between humanistic philology, the library of Cassiodorus, and Roman private and public collections.[58]

Books often represent for Petrarca the matter of controversies and criticism. Petrarca's dissatisfaction with contemporary manuscript culture, its scribes, and its scripts is well documented by remarks in his own works: for instance, in a letter to his brother Gherardo written in 1354 (*Familiares* 18.5) and in the chapter "De librorum copia" (Many Books) of the *De remediis utriusque fortunae* (1.43). In the former, he connects the textual unreliability of contemporary codices to the authors' lack of interest in the correct circulation and transmission of their own works; furthermore, he critiques the multiplication of roles in manuscript production, lamenting the lack of unity in artistic control. In the latter, he stresses deficiencies and failures—"doctrinae omnis ignarus, expers ingenii, artis egens" (no knowledge whatsoever, no mind, and no skill)—in the technical training and professionalization of contemporary scribes.[59]

His evaluation of the excessive calligraphy of the *litterae scholasticae* (the Gothic book hands used for university textbooks) is no more charitable. In a letter to Philippe de Cabassoles dated 1366 (*Seniles* 6.5), Petrarca spurns the unnecessary thickness of the written space, the frequency of abbreviations, and the lack of any harmony in the ratio between blanks and words on the page.[60] In a letter to Boccaccio also dated 1366 (*Familiares* 23.19), Petrarca praises the elegant and legible exemplar of his *Familiares* copied by a young scribe (generally identified as Giovanni Malpaghini) and condemns the affected, illegible script "qualis est scriptorum seu verius pictorum nostri temporis, longe oculos mulcens, prope autem afficiens ac fatigans, quasi ad aliud quam ad legendum sit inventa, et non, ut grammaticorum princeps ait, litera 'quasi legitera' dicta sit" (so typical of contemporary scribes or rather painters that from a distance appeals to the eyes but from up close confuses and wearies them—as though it were destined for something other than reading, and, to cite the prince of grammarians, as though the word *litera* does not derive from *legitera*).[61]

Annotations and Marginalia

Petrarca's annotations and figurative marginalia also show that books often represented for him an archive of personal records and intellectual reflections. On fol. 58v of his copy of Cassiodorus's *De anima* and Augustine's *De vera religione* (Paris, Bibliothèque nationale de France, MS latin 2201), for instance, a young Petrarca notes down a list of favorite books ("libri mei peculiares") in a cursive chancery minuscule.[62] The visual architecture of that folio provides material evidence of Petrarca's activity of mapping the conceptual library of his literary and philosophical culture, curating its virtual collection, and integrating its pagan and Christian acquisitions. Most notably, the flyleaves of the so-called Ambrosian Virgil also transmit the obituaries of Petrarca's own friends (fol. Ir) and the narrative chronology of one of the most relevant episodes in his life, at least for his poetics: his encounter with Laura and her death (fol. Iv).[63]

Books even more represented for Petrarca a material site of textual and intertextual investigation, where he expressed noteworthy literary and critical reflections.[64] In the margins of the Ambrosian Virgil, we observe an immense intertextual depository of Petrarca's poetic memory—what Vincenzo Fera describes as "a great connector of data"—where Petrarca organizes an archive of citations from and annotations on other books.[65] A paradigmatic example of this practice comes from Petrarca's marginal annotation to *Georgics* 2.385–86, where Virgil references peasant farmers and their "uncultivated" poetic performances: "coloni / versibus incomptis ludunt" (peasants play with unrefined verses). Servius's commentary (transmitted with Virgil's poem in the same Ambrosian manuscript) explains the passage by referencing the dual nature of ancient Latin poetry, both metrical (quantitative) and rhythmical (based on stressed accents). On fol. 31v, Petrarca partially transcribes Servius's explanation in the margin, in a sophisticated chalice-shaped gloss: "Rithmum solum vulgares componere solitos" (the common people used to compose only rhythmical poems). The passage reoccurs in Petrarca's corpus (*Familiares* 1.1.6), when he deals with the tripartite classification of his own opus into Latin prose, Latin poetry, and vernacular poetry: that is, when he seeks to validate his vernacular production as a form of humanistic recovery of classical antiquity. In sum, in Servius's commentary Petrarca finds "the legitimation to compose in the vernacular," and this legitimation is promptly appropriated in his own manuscripts for further reference and use.[66]

Autography

Books especially represented for Petrarca a site of artistic research and literary experimentation. The material features of his autographs and idiographs are, in fact, a fundamental aspect of Petrarca's poetry. It is from the remarkable corpus of autographs (written entirely in Petrarca's various scripts, preserving his own texts or those of other authors) and idiographs (transcribed under Petrarca's supervision) that Petrarca's "genuine religion of writing" most vividly emerges.[67]

Consistent with the criticisms he registers as a reader of others' manuscripts, Petrarca, in his own literary and editorial project, addresses both the aesthetics of the script and the correct circulation of his texts.[68] Petrarca bases his book hand on the formal equilibrium of the *littera textualis* (Gothic book hand) but attenuates the latter's extreme compression and angularity with the clarity, sobriety, and legibility of the Caroline minuscule that he read in Carolingian manuscripts.[69] Petrarca's book hand is the material counterpart to his literary classicism. His graphic ideal is a reduction of complexity that can be coupled with the linguistic model of *fiorentinità trascendentale* (transcendental Florentinity)—to use Gianfranco Contini's formula—for his vernacular compositions.[70] Petrarca also attempts to condition the correct reproduction and circulation of his texts by providing autograph and idiograph exemplars of his works to a small circle of men of letters and friends for transcription and divulgation.

Manuscript Vat. Lat. 3195, the last (though not definitive) version of the *RVF*, clearly reveals both of these priorities.[71] Partly in Petrarca's hand and partly transcribed under his direct supervision, MS Vat. Lat. 3195 is a paradigmatic example of what Petrucci describes as "author's book," the product of a multiphased process of textual and material composition and revision, whose authenticity and reliability were sanctioned by Petrarca's "total autography," his direct execution or determined supervision of the entire writing process.[72] Manuscript Vat. Lat. 3195 is a parchment manuscript, consisting of seventy-two folios, organized in eleven quires.[73] The codex is the result of the collaboration between Petrarca and a young scribe and man of letters, traditionally identified as Giovanni Malpaghini, who was a guest of Petrarca's in his Venetian house between 1364 and 1367 (and then briefly again in 1368).[74] With few exceptions, Malpaghini is responsible for the writing on fols. 1r–38v and 53r–62v, produced in the spring of 1367. The other folios, fols. 38v–49r and 62r–72v, are in Petrarca's hand. Petrarca's contributions to the writing were sporadic in the final years before his death in 1374. The text of the *RVF* occupies fols. 1–72, with the exception of 49v–52v, which are blanks and create a material division into two sections, often (if not entirely accurately) referred to as *rime in vita* and *rime in morte*.[75] The title of the work heads fol. 1r: *Francisci Petrarche laureate poete. Rerum vulgarium fragmenta*, in red except for the initial F in blue. The incipitarian letters of *RVF* 1 (fol. 1r, "Voi ch'ascoltate") and *RVF* 264 (fol. 53r, "I' vo pensando") are elegantly decorated in pink, scarlet, green, and violet, on a golden background, with geometric (golden globes) and foliate motifs. These two *litterae florissae* further underscore the material bipartition of the songbook. On fols. 1r–39v and 53r–62v, red and blue initials alternate in marking the incipits of the poems (with the red letter always being the first of the folio, even in the cases where the last poem of the previous folio had also begun with a red initial). Red and blue paraphs sign the stanzas following the first in all pluristrophic compositions, except for the sonnets. Majuscules also mark the first letter of each verse. Finally, brown Arabic numerals (in Petrarca's hand) appear in the right margin of the first line of the last thirty-one poems (fols. 66v through 71v). These numerals reorder the sequence of the poems after the late addition of two new bifolia (fols. 67–70). The renumbering of the sequence leads to the assumption that MS Vat. Lat. 3195 had slowly shifted from fair copy to service copy (a working draft).

In the previous section of this chapter, we described the *mise-en-page* of the sestina as characterized by a distinctly vertical orientation. This feature is all the more distinct when we consider the overall horizontal alignment of the other poetic genres (sonnets, *canzoni*, *ballate*, and *madrigali*). These are distributed in two columns, with two (or, less commonly, three) verses per line, separated by an intercolumniation (substituted by punctuation in the case of three verses per line). Lino Leonardi points out Petrarca's innovation in extending the sonnet's horizontal transcription in two columns to *canzone*, *ballata*, and *madrigale*—which Italian thirteenth- and fourteenth-century songbooks generally present written as prose—thus sanctioning the *RVF*'s horizontal structure.[76]

A reading of the codex proceeds first horizontally, from left to right, and then vertically. A single blank line separates poems from one another. Exceptions to this architecture do not affect the overall visual consistency of the codex. Petrarca's project seems to balance the specificity of different metrical forms with the necessity for the overall harmony and proportion of the manuscript: he is, Storey argues, "careful to harmonize all aspects of the literary product, in light of an ideal correspondence between the clarity and homogeneity of the content and the structuring capacities of the container."[77] The case of the *canzone* is emblematic: the extremely flexible and diversified argumentative and syntactical structure of the twenty-nine *canzoni* is counterbalanced by a highly systematic visual rendition.[78]

The optical tension between the layout of the sestina and that of the other metrical forms accomplishes various effects. First, it underscores the peculiar regressive rhyme scheme that is unique to the sestina. Leonardi argued that manuscripts transmitting medieval Latin poetry (both rhythmic and metrical) generally resort to a columnar disposition to put emphasis on the presence or combination of rhymes.[79] Here, the *retrogradatio cruciata* and the vertical sequence of the hendecasyllables create a tension between linear progression in the reading of the text and the need to reconsider the rhyme scheme in the previous stanzas so as to decipher the poem's peculiar rhyme scheme and check its regularity. The reader proceeds sequentially, but the rhyme scheme performs a regressive movement, enhances a repeated inversion of the usual direction of reading, and urges a recursive metrical rereading. The visual presentation of the sestina redirects the reader from a sequential temporality to a retrogressive perception of its acrobatic meter. Chapter 7 will further elaborate on the mutual interplay between this visually enhanced inversion of the usual direction of reading and the formal and thematic circularity of the sestina.

Second, the eccentric layout of the sestinas isolates them within the macrostructure of the *canzoniere*: Brugnolo notes that this layout functions to "ensure their immediate distinction from the other genres of the Canzoniere."[80] Concurrently, it connects the various sestinas in a cohesive corpus that entails an intermediate status between the microstructure of the single poem and the macrostructure of the whole text-book.[81] That layout institutes a material correlation between the sestinas, which corresponds to their formal and semantic coherence, in partial compliance with Ruth Phelps's notion of a "principle of association, which creates little groups and clusters of poems upon similar subjects."[82] The consistency of a highly codified graphic pattern, in other words, underscores a corresponding set of thematic common traits and enhances their interconnection within the autograph.

Roncaglia authoritatively maintained that the definition of the sestina rests exclusively on formal criteria, rather than thematic features.[83] In what we have described as Petrarca's manuscript poetics, however, the sestina should not be merely defined in terms of its formal structure, but rather in terms of the material and textual intersection of its codicological, metrical, rhetorical, and thematic elements. Before discussing the meaning of this interaction for the *canzoniere* as macrotext, which will be the primary focus of investigation in chapter 7, it is valuable to review the sestinas' many other expressions of coherence. The interpretation of the material presentation of the sestinas in Petrarca's autograph is in fact dependent on that of their discursive substance: the one presupposes and implicates the other.

The Sestinas as Corpus

The sestinas' recursive and highly consistent *mise-en-page* corresponds to a series of repeated basic meaning traits that unite the sestinas into a collection within the collection. Like other metrically homogenous clusters of poems in Petrarca's autograph (e.g., the four madrigals), the sestinas collectively form a coherent corpus of texts sharing semantic and formal similarities and mutually complementing each other's meaning. Their visual, thematic, and stylistic consistency establishes, in other words, an intricate system of correspondences that urge the readers to recall and relate the different texts of that homogenous corpus, a system that mediates between the single poem and the *RVF*'s overarching book structure. In the previous section, we have described Petrarca's material presentation of the sestina as an innovative aspect of his consolidation (if not foundation proper) of the form. Expanding on existing studies on the semantic connections between the sestinas, this section explains the recursiveness of those relations of meaning as the thematic, stylistic, and rhetorical counterpart to that codified material presentation. It shows how the highly distinguishable layout of the sestinas in the autograph corresponds to, and frames the condition for, a series of repeated features—both thematic and formal—that unify the sestinas into a cohesive and coherent structure within the *canzoniere*.

Corpus within the Corpus

The case for reading the sestinas as an organic subunit of poems isolated by layout, meter, and content is made compelling by Petrarca's treatment of another group of poems: the madrigals (*RVF* 52, 54, 106, 121). Until Petrarca, the madrigal was one of the least codified metrical forms of early Italian poetry.[84] He was, in fact, the first to advance an "author's madrigal."[85] Petrarca regularizes both the meter and the *mise-en-page* for the madrigal, opting for a couplet as closure in three out of four cases (*RVF* 52, 54, 106) and adopting a double transcriptional format: binary (two hendecasyllables per line, one in each column) and ternary (two hendecasyllables in the first line, and one hendecasyllable in the left column of the second line, followed by a blank in the right column).[86] Petrarca also somewhat normalizes their subject matter. The four madrigals present a homogenous atmosphere imbued with the pictorial and auditory effects of a pastoral and idyll. They are all depictions of Laura, who assumes various shapes within a rural scene: shepherdess, pilgrim, angel, and temptress. The madrigals also articulate a basic narrative: in Kenelm Foster's description, "the poet falls in love and then repents of his love (52, 54); tempted, he falls again (106), only to encounter, in the end, cold indifference (121)."[87]

With such clusters of poems, Petrarca reprises (and materially enhances) compositional micro-textual practices already present in the Old Occitan and Galician-Portuguese traditions. Similar mini-corpora within an author's corpus have been identified, for instance, in the cycle of six *pasturelas* in Guiraut Riquier's *libre* (where the interconnection is based on the immediate contiguity of the poems rather than layout) and in the series of *cantigas de loor* (songs of praise) within the *Cantigas de Santa María* attributed to Alfonso X of Castile.[88] Like these mini-corpora, Petrarca's sestinas collectively articulate an organic intermediate structure between the single composition and the songbook as a whole.

Cohesion: Focus on Meaning

Materially isolated by the visual presentation of the noncontiguous poems it contains, the corpus of the sestinas is also distinguished by coherence (the sestinas function as a semantic unity within the *canzoniere*) and cohesion (the sestinas cohere to each other through relations of meaning). Scholars have often pointed out the semantic cohesion between the sestinas, deriving from their homogenous lexicon and insistence on favored themes. Cesare Segre, for instance, described the sestinas as privileged textual space for the isotopies of

Laura. Drawing upon Algirdas J. Greimas's notion of isotopy as the repetition of semantic units, Segre unveiled how Petrarca disseminated Laura's name in the sestinas through her multiple *senhals*: pseudo-homographs and homophones (*laura*/*l'aura*); their derivatives and allotropes (*l'aurora*/*lauro*/*l'auro*/*l'oro*); and their metonymic (or synecdochical) transfigurations—*frondi* (leaves) for locks of hair and *rami* (branches) for arms imply Laura's physical traits.[89] Focusing on the principle of repetition and variation of rhyme-words and syntagmatic clauses to track formal and semantic connections among the nine sestinas and to identify the pattern of their *dispositio* within the *canzoniere*, Pelosini has compellingly shown how each sestina—within what she described as "sistema-sestine"—references and responds to the sestina immediately preceding, thus expanding on and explaining the metaphoric equivalence between Laura, her emblems, and her *senhals* (*laura*/*l'aura*/*l'aurora* and *l'auro*/*lauro*). The sestinas, additionally, have been indicated as the designated form for the explicit enunciation of Laura's full name. Of the three unequivocal occurrences of Laura's name in the *canzoniere*, two are in the sestinas (*RVF* 239, v. 8; *RVF* 332, v. 50; but see also *RVF* 291, v. 4).[90]

The presence of isotopies—like the isotopy of person referenced above—figures among the connective principles that endow a poetic collection with the organic structure of a *libro di poesia* (book of poems) in Enrico Testa's seminal monograph on twentieth-century *canzonieri*.[91] Other such organizing principles of cohesion include isotopies of time and space, *dispositivi* (textual devices of opening and closure, signals of internal partition within the collection), "poesie di poetica" (poems of poetics), and the progression of sense (which institutes a narrative). These are all features of semantic redundancy and syntactic respondence that make a poetry book a cohesive macrostructure. These features are also helpful for explaining how an internal subunit of a book of poems—in our case, the sestinas as a group—can achieve structural cohesion. In addition to the isotopies of Laura, and forming a close semantic relationship with them, the corpus of the sestinas is also characterized by isotopies of time and space: homogenous sequences of recurring (and interrelated) temporal and spatial circumstances. In the sestinas, the perception of these isotopies is intensified by the incidence of their lexical-semantic units as rhyme-words.

The corpus of the sestinas shows a preference for expressions related to the spatial representation of landscapes (including their "meteorological predicates"), particularly frequent in the rhyme-words: *RVF* 22, "selva" (wood); *RVF* 30, "neve" (snow), "riva" (shore); *RVF* 66, "nebbia" (cloud), "vènti" (winds), "pioggia" (rain), "fiumi" (rivers), "valli" (valleys), "ghiaccio" (ice); *RVF* 142, "frondi" (leaves), "poggi" (hills), "rami" (branches); *RVF* 214, "bosco" (wood); *RVF* 237, "boschi" (woods), "piaggia" (meadow); and *RVF* 239, "fiori" (flowers). Deeply allusive of the language of Dante's proto-sestina discussed above ("Al poco giorno ed al gran cerchio d'ombra"), this type of spatial isotopy complies with Petrarca's tendency to represent the relationship between nature and Laura (or nature and his poetic self) in terms of homology: Sara Sturm-Maddox points out that "the elusive lady . . . is known to the reader in part through her association with place."[92] The insistence on the representation of landscape and weather entails, in the end, a continued reference to Laura, be it the spring as an epiphany of her beauty or the winter as metaphor for the poet's discontent and restlessness concerning her. The assumption of the individual poet-persona within the natural environment provides the sestinas with their peculiar *Stimmung* of universality and inevitability.

The sestinas' rhyme-words also articulate a semantic network of expressions regarding the passing of time: *RVF* 22, "giorno" (day), "alba" (dawn); *RVF* 30, "anni" (years); *RVF* 237, "notte" (night), "sera" (evening); *RVF* 332, "notti" (nights). These temporal expressions can be associated to expressions related to notions of "cosmology": *RVF* 22, "terra" (earth), "stelle" (stars), "sole" (sun); *RVF* 142, "cielo" (heaven), "lume" (light); and *RVF* 237, "luna" (moon). The semantic clusters revolving around the notion of time and the cycle of day and night are part of the songbook's overarching sensitivity for, and aesthetic perception of, the inexorable passing of time. Gianfranco Folena remarked that Petrarca "senses his being in time, not before time (unlike Dante)."[93] The sestinas paradoxically stress both the eternal cyclicity of time and a sense of vanishing present. Their intense participation with temporality enhances a sense of fatality and anguish through which the poet's persistent, unsatisfied desire for Laura transpires.

If the sestinas are the privileged form for the official record of the "speciosum Lauree nomen" (the beautiful name of Laura) (*Familiares* 2.9), they also are the designated form for the sexualization of Laura's body. The sestinas provide the only two explicit mentions of the lyrical persona's longed-for physical intercourse with Laura (*RVF* 22, vv. 31–33):

Con lei foss'io da che si parte il sole,
et non ci vedess'altri che le stelle,
sol una nocte, et mai non fosse l'alba;

(Might I be with her from when the sun departs
and no other see us but the stars,
just one night, and let the dawn never come!)

The same unexpected expression of the desire to possess Laura in the flesh re-occurs with minimal variation, in sestina 237 (vv. 31–36). Petrarca retrieves the motif of a single, yet never-ending night of passion with Laura from Propertius's elegies (2.15, 40): "nocte una quivis vel deus esse potest" (with just one night any man can be a god).[94] But the privileged mode of expression for the poet's sensual eroticism and carnal desire is the intertextual appropriation of the genre's recognized precursors: Arnaut Daniel (specifically, "Lo ferm voler") and Dante (the "sestina" "Al poco giorno" in particular, but more generally his so-called *rime petrose* and "comic" production).[95] Arnaut's distinctive adjective *ferm* ("firm") describes the poet's voluptuous desire (*RVF* 22, v. 24), underscores his obtuse consistency in sinning (*RVF* 80, v. 1: "è fermato," "has decided"), and generally defines his distorted loyalty to the fetishized image of the beloved. Continuous allusions to Dante's *rime petrose* punctuate the sestinas. Even the ethereal and spiritual nature of Laura (as *aura*) assumes the adamantine consistency of stones and metals (*RVF* 30, vv. 24 and 37), with noticeable reference to the precious imagery of lapidaries that characterizes Dante's poems for his stony Lady Petra. The sustained use of intertextual references to Arnaut and Dante extends the semantic coherence of the sestinas as corpus to the formal plane, by providing them with an eminently distinguishable linguistic and stylistic register.

Cohesion: Focus on Form

Isotopies tendentially gather around the rhyme-words. Their obsessive repetition functions as a structural agent of cohesion and coreference between (and within) sestinas. We can further describe how cohesive relationships are formally established within the corpus by adopting—and adapting—the inventory of cohesive devices ("cohesive ties") that Michael A. K. Halliday and

Ruqaiya Hasan outlined in their classic study on textual cohesion: reference, substitution, ellipsis, conjunction, and lexical cohesion (which include reiteration and collocation).[96] The isotopies of Laura, for instance, only acquire sense when semic units are made to reference and substitute other semic units disseminated through the corpus of the sestinas (and the *canzoniere* as a whole): in order for *rami* ("branches") to be effectively decoded as arms, for instance, the reader must refer to the relationship between Laura and *lauro* ("laurel"). The lexical reiteration (identical repetitions, synonymy, antonymy, hyponymy, and metonymy) and collocation (coreferential words, words from the same semantic domain), which insist on temporal circumstances, provide the sestinas with their distinct sense of existential impasse.[97] The hallucinatory presence of Laura in the interstices of the sestinas' spatial representation draws on the continuous resurfacing of her *senhals* in the landscape's characterization.

A formal description of the sestinas' cohesion based on Halliday and Hasan's "cohesive ties" partially yields to results that parallel those of a more traditional rhetorical approach to the corpus. Scholars have underscored the rhetorical affinity between Petrarca's sestinas and various figures of repetition. János Riesz, for instance, described these figures as the sestinas' distinctive rhetorical features.[98] *Ornatus difficilis* is not exclusive to the sestinas. But its interaction with their meandering rhyme scheme often achieves effects of *oltranza stilistica* (taking style to its ultimate). The temporal and cosmological notations discussed just above, for instance, tend to irradiate backward from the verse clause and invest the whole body of the hendecasyllable with figures of repetition and emphasis, which underscore the apperception of time and inscribe the poet's desire and erotic fixation into the obsessive recursiveness and artificial eternity of a perennial present. Several figures are of particular use here. Prominent among these is a series of dittologies: we see "o di nocte o di giorno" (either by night or by day) (*RVF* 22, v. 20), here with correlative *polysyndeton* and antithesis; a similar opposition is repeated with minimal variation in *RVF* 237, v. 12, *RVF* 332, v. 38, *RVF* 22, v. 21 (as "a l'ombra e al sole," "in the shadow and in the sun"), and *RVF* 22, v. 22 (as "primo sonno od alba," "the first sleep or the dawn" with metaphor and antithesis). Another noteworthy figure is *geminatio*, seen in "molti et molt'anni" (many and many years) (*RVF* 30, v. 3), with a further delaying of time by means of the conjunction's *interiectio*, and in a further instance as "ognor di tempo in tempo" (from season to season) (*RVF* 142, v. 19). Petrarca also, in this strategy, turns to hyperbole, such as "dopo mill'anni (a thousand years from now) (*RVF* 30, v. 35).[99] Similar rhetorical strategies further characterize the treatment of the natural scenery (*RVF* 142, vv. 25–26):

> Selve, sassi, campagne, fiumi et poggi,
> quanto è creato, vince et cangia il tempo.
>
> (Woods, rocks, fields, rivers, and hill—
> all that is made—are vanquished and changed by time.)

The two lines present a strong prolepsis of the object that gives prominence to the subject (and rhyme-word) *tempo*. In the first hendecasyllable, the pentacolic expression of complementary terms can be read as a detailed *distributio* (division of a genus into its species) of the comprehensive and absolute "quanto è creato."[100] Covering both the mineral and the vegetal world, the first four names are grouped asyndetically, with an alternated disposition of the *homoeoteleuta* (identity of endings of adjacent words: *selvE* with *campagnE*, *sassI* with *fiumI*) and sustained alliteration of the sibilant in the first two elements (*Selve*, *SaSSi*). The fifth substantive instead is introduced syndetically (with a deliberate *variatio* not required by the prosody). The progression between the five epexegetical nouns and the ensuing comprehensive phrase creates a conceptual and syllabic climax. The quasi-synonymic dicolon "vince et cangia" is also characterized by a *hysteron-proteron* (the reversal of the natural and rational order of the terms), which aptly mimics the sestinas' *retrogradatio cruciata*.

If figures of repetition underscore the return of the sestinas' rhyme-words and, in the lines cited above, the *hysteron-proteron* conforms to the backward progression of their rhyme scheme, one specific rhetorical device figures so prominently in the sestinas—its action so intimately complies to their meter—that it functions as a major connecting force within the corpus. The use of *adynata* (rhetorical devices magnifying an event by comparison with something impossible) is unusually frequent in the sestinas vis-à-vis the *canzoniere* as a whole.[101] We have six instances of *adynaton* in the nine sestinas (*RVF* 22, vv. 37–39; *RVF* 30, vv. 7–10; *RVF* 66, vv. 22–24; *RVF* 237, vv. 16–18; *RVF* 239, vv. 10 and 36) against a comparatively unimpressive total of 8 in the other 357 poems of the songbook.[102] And it is no accident that Petrarca's sexual drive—so outspoken in the sestinas—relies heavily on the rhetorical strategies of hyperbole and *adynaton*. On the one hand, these *adynata* reiterate the fixity of love—and the poet's fixation on it—in spite of any external obstacle: the "sense of catastrophe" that they convey entails the inability to conceive of a plausible alternative.[103] On the other hand, these *adynata* literally portray an inversion of the natural cycles. Before the poet is able to find peace, daylight will switch from sun to moon and night will become day: *RVF* 22, vv. 38–39, "e 'l giorno andrà pien di minute stelle / prima ch'a sì dolce alba arrivi il sole" (and the day will be lit by the tiny stars, / before the sun arrives at so sweet a dawn); and *RVF* 237, vv. 16–18, "Ben fia, prima ch'i' posi, il mar senz'onde, / et la sua luce avrà 'l sol da la luna, / e i fior' d'april morranno in ogni piaggia" (Before I rest, the sea will be without waves, / and the sun will receive his light from the moon, / and the flowers of April will die in every meadow). The oceans will dry up, just like rivers will flow backward from the sea in Dante's "sestina" "Al poco giorno" (v. 31).

This reversal of natural events and cycles appropriately finds its metrical counterpart in the *retrogradatio cruciata*, in which a retrograde torsion counteracts linearity. The actual regression of the forms mirrors the cataclysmic inversion described in the *adynata*, and Petrarca's sestina eventually "nad[a] contra suberna" (swims against the tide), like Arnaut in his *canso* 10 "Ab gai so coinde ⟨e⟩ leri" (On a nice, joyful, and elegant melody) (v. 45). The last reference to Arnaut is far from coincidental. The two additional *adynata* with which Arnaut presents himself in that *canso* (v. 43: "amas l'aura," "hoard the air"; v. 44: "cas la leure ab lo boeu," "hunt the hare with the ox") are variously alluded to and fused together in *RVF* 239 (v. 36: "et col bue zoppo andrem cacciando l'aura," "we shall go with a lame ox hunting the breeze"; v. 37: "In rete accolgo l'aura," "In a net I catch the breeze"). Moreover, the last *adynaton* seems to imply a metaphor for poetic writing: the net easily implicates the notion of text as interwoven structure; "l'aura" hides a *senhal* for Petrarca's beloved woman; and *ret-* provides a paronomastic (and quite Petrarchan) echo of Laura's hypocorism in Old Occitan (*LauRETa*). This echo would constitute, in Saussurean terms, a paragrammatic artifice: the dissemination and pulverization of the lexical and graphemic constituents of a theme-word (*Laura*/*Lauret[t]a*) within (and throughout) the fibers of the text.[104]

The last *adynaton* paradoxically loses its character of impossibility when applied to the realm of literature. It assumes, in fact, the force of a *praeteritio*: it mentions what it claims to occult. On the one hand, it states the vanity of hoarding the breeze in a net, the ephemerality of any textualization of Laura, very fragile and precarious as cobwebs ("opra d'aragna," *RVF* 173, v. 6). On the other hand, it performs the very act (writing) that it otherwise questions as unfeasible. Literature seems (if only seems) to make everything possible (*RVF* 239, v. 28): "Nulla al mondo è che non possano i versi" (There is nothing in the world that cannot be done by verses). The *adynaton* ideally connects Petrarca to another Occitan precursor of the genre: Raimbaut d'Aurenga, whose *trobar ric* offers early examples of *coblas doblas* and *ternas*, chiastic rhyme schemes, and rhyme-words that also constitute the technical apparatus of Petrarca's sestinas. In the final *cobla* of his poem "Ar resplan la flors enversa" (Now the reversed flower shines), Raimbaut uses the rhyme-word *enverse* (*rim derivatif* of *enversa*) as the first-person singular of the verb *enversar* ("to put into verse"), semantically (if equivocally) associating the inversion/transfiguration of reality with compositions in verse.[105] As Roncaglia argued, "the principle of inversion is therefore declared the essential principle of poetry."[106] Raimbaut's "reversed flower" signifies the winter, thus providing a conceptual inversion of spring flowers made possible by the repetition and resemanticization of the same rhyme-word. Sestina 239 also employs—allusively—the rhyme-words "fiori" (flowers) and "versi" (versi): while catching the breeze (Laura) in a net, the *persona loquens*—like Raimbaut's—also catches flowers on ice (v. 37, "'n ghiaccio i fiori"). Markedly averse to any *aequivocatio*, Petrarca yearns for an inversion of reality in the unattainable forms of the *adynaton*, while also performing this inversion metrically by means of the *retrogradatio cruciata*. As we shall see more clearly in the next subsection and further examine in chapter 7, Petrarca's allusion to Raimbaut points toward a prominent feature, and additional agent of cohesion, in the corpus of the sestinas: their recurring metaliterary references.

Cohesion: Focus on Poetic Discourse

Testa's categories of macrotextual cohesion include semantic elements (isotopies), syntactic devices (signals of internal subdivisions), and metatextual cues (poems of poetics). In light of Petrarca's role in shaping forms and institutions of Italian and European poetry through the centuries, it is hardly surprising to trace many of these principles to the *RVF*. The label "poems of poetics" is especially suited for the sestinas based on the recurrence of metaliterary references. Chapter 7 will show how the sestinas work as such in relation to their contribution to the *canzoniere*, but here we observe how the recurrence of metaliterary references—a special kind of semantic isotopy—furthers the cohesion of the sestinas as a coherent subset of texts.

The number itself of rhyme-words relating to poetry indicates the affinity between sestinas and discourse on poetics. These "specialized" rhyme-words are concentrated mainly in the *sestina doppia* (*RVF* 332), but they surface in the whole corpus (if not always in verse clauses): "lauro" (laurel) in *RVF* 30 and *RVF* 142, v. 13; "vènti" (winds) in *RVF* 66 (in the metaphorical acceptation of "sighs" in v. 30); "nove" (new), a key term from Petrarca's Tuscan antecedents, in *RVF* 214; "note" (notes) and "versi" (verses) in *RVF* 239; "pianto" (weeping), "rime" (rhymes), and "stile" (style) in *RVF* 332. Other cues of metaliterary reflection include the use of a literarily/critically connoted terminology to refer to the poet's experience; the frequent association between poetry and the semantic cluster of *sospiri* (sighs), *pianto* (weeping), and *canto* (singing) (e.g., in *RVF* 22, v. 21; *RVF* 30, v. 7; and *RVF* 239, v. 35); the Orphic references to poetry's incantatorial powers (*RVF* 239, v. 29: "et li aspidi incantar sanno in lor [*sc.* dei versi] note," "they [*sc.* verses] know how to enchant asps with their notes"), echoed by the use of *versi* to indicate magic spells in *RVF* 214, v. 17); and the aforementioned emphasis on poetry's power to create alternative realities.

But it is in the figure of Laura, again, that we see the sestinas informed with highest degree of metaliterary reference. In this perspective, the Laura portrayed in the sestinas shares the kind of metaliterary aggregating function that Gianfranco Contini assigned to the female character in Dante's *rime petrose*: "Lady Pietra is simply the link that gathers the most virtuosically technical of Dante's lyrics, in which the lexical energy and the rarity of rhythms turn, content-wise, into the theme of the harsh lady, of difficult love."[107] In spite of Petrarca's statements on the truthfully autobiographic nature of his own *canzoniere*, readers as early as Boccaccio recognized the allegorical nature of Laura's character:

> Et quamvis in suis quampluribus vulgaribus poematibus, in quibus perlucide decantavit, se Laurettam quamdam ardentissime demonstrarit amasse, non obstat: nam, prout ipsemet et bene puto, Laurettam illam allegorice pro laurea corona quam postmodum est adeptus accipiendam existimo.[108]
>
> ---
>
> (And although in several of his beautifully composed vernacular poems he stated that he loved a certain Lauretta very passionately, this does not disprove my statement: in fact, as I personally and positively believe, I determine that this famous Lauretta must be interpreted allegorically as the poetic laurel, which he then obtained.)

The presence of Laura's name, the invention of a *sermo lauranus* ("Laurean speech")—to use Fredi Chiappelli's formula[109]—evoking her name through a sustained phonosymbolism, the semantic coincidence of Laura and Daphne in the mythologeme of Apollo's unrequited love for the nymph as an allegory for the poet's unfulfilled passion, the ensuing association of (and even poetic rivalry between) the *persona loquens* and the Olympian god, the relationship between the myth of an unattainable erotic satisfaction and the poetic expression of it, the frenetic pursuit of intellectual glory by means of a poetic coronation (in fact, a *laurea delphica*), the reciprocal assimilation between the elusive lady and the ever-perfectible literary expression, the progressive realization that any lauding of Laura's earthly persona may be improper (pseudo-etymological pun intended), and the substitution of the laurel with the wood of the Holy Cross (or the moralized interpretation of the living flesh turning to laurel as a symbol of algid chastity): these are the many *tesserae* of metapoetic discourse that make the literary self-awareness of Petrarca's sestinas rival (unsurprisingly) Dante's continual self-exegesis. Furthermore, the polysemic value of laurel as *senhal* for Laura and symbol for poetry suggests that the poet can only escape uncontrolled passion by sublimating his erotic craving and sensual desire into writing.

An Intermediate Structure

Dispersed throughout the *RVF*, the corpus of the sestinas, as it is presented in the autograph, is kept together by agents of cohesion comparable to the relations of formal and thematic equivalence that Santagata noticed, in the *RVF*, between contiguous poems, whose interconnectivity is obtained through the articulation over several texts of "a discourse that surpasses the limits (blank spaces) that should circumscribe it within a self-sufficient text, in order for this to be specified, enriched, or completed in those that surround it."[110] Whereas Santagata's model of thematic and formal interconnectivity stresses textual proximity between poems, this chapter has made the sestinas' highly recognizable transcriptional format the material prerequisite, in the autograph, for facilitating their semantic coherence and establishing them as corpus and intermediate structure between the single poems of the *canzoniere* and the *RVF* as an organic structure. The clear contrast between the vertical orientation of the sestinas and the overall horizontal presentation of the *canzoniere* makes the sestinas easy to search and identify. Temporal, spatial, and semantic isotopies can, moreover, be read as the textual correlative of the easily detectable and decisively codified visual pattern of the sestinas' *mise-en-page* in the autograph. Although the formal and thematic agents of cohesion discussed in the previous pages do not necessarily figure in all of the sestinas simultaneously, their dissemination creates a dense interrelationship among internal echoes, allusions, and references. In other words, the semantic coherence of the sestinas parallels, in the autograph, the material choice of a unique transcriptional format. Their formal cohesion, their status as privileged text for the epiphany of Laura's *senhals*, the density of their intertextual references to Arnaut's *trobar clus* and Dante's *rime petrose*, the insistence on the natural and cosmological elements as setting for the scene they portray, the magnified sense of erotic obsessiveness pursued through their *adynata*, and the frequency of metaliterary cues all contribute to the formation of a homogeneous subset of texts. Chapter 7 will more specifically explore how these mutually complementary features—material, metrical, thematic, rhetorical—interact within the sestinas and how (and why) this interaction makes them the designated poems of poetics (and *on* poetics) of the *canzoniere*.

CHAPTER SEVEN

Carmina Figurata

> Forms remember.
>
> —Hugh Kenner, *The Pound Era*, 369

The Corpus of the Sestinas

We have seen in chapter 6 that in Francesco Petrarca's autograph of the *Rerum vulgarium fragmenta* (*RVF*) the sestinas are characterized by the unique verticality of their *mise-en-page*, wherein each verse starts a new line, vis-à-vis the overall horizontal presentation of the other metrical genres. We have also seen that this vertical presentation enhances the peculiarity of the sestinas' rhyme scheme (the *retrogradatio cruciata*) and creates visually distinctive and interrelated textual niches. The various modes of the sestinas' thematic and rhetorical consistency further organize them into a coherent and cohesive corpus. Within the autograph of the *RVF* (MS Vat. Lat. 3195 of the Vatican Library), in other words, a series of material, textual, and literary components isolate the sestinas from the other compositions and connect them to form an intermediate structure between single *fragmentum* and *Fragmenta*.

The corpus of the nine sestinas is asymmetrically distributed in the autograph of the *canzoniere*, with eight sestinas in the first part and one sestina (the double sestina *RVF* 332) in the second:

RVF 22, fol. 3v: "A qualunque animale alberga in terra" (For whatever animals dwell on earth)

RVF 30, fol. 7v: "Giovene donna sotto un verde lauro" (A youthful lady under a green laurel)

RVF 66, fol. 14v: "L'aere gravato, et l'importuna nebbia" (The burdened air and the importunate cloud)

RVF 80, fol. 19r: "Chi è fermato di menar sua vita" (He who has decided to lead his life)

RVF 142, fol. 32rv: "A la dolce ombra de le belle frondi" (To the sweet shade of those beautiful leaves)

RVF 214, fol. 42v: "Anzi tre dì creata era alma in parte" (Three days before, a soul had been created in a place)

RVF 237, fol. 45v "Non à tanti animali il mar fra l'onde" (The sea has not so many creatures among its waves)

RVF 239, fol. 46r: "Là ver' l'aurora, che sì dolce l'aura" (At the time near dawn when so sweetly the breeze)

RVF 332, fols. 65v–66r: "Mia benigna fortuna e 'l viver lieto" (My kind fortune and glad life)

The coherence, cohesion, and coreference within this corpus have attracted scholarly attention. And the progression of sense outlined by the sestinas' sequence—also in relation to the *canzoniere*—has been the object of in-depth investigation.[1]

But the mechanisms and implications of the intersection between—and interdependence of—visual, metrical, rhetorical, and semantic elements in the poems of this corpus have never been fully investigated. This chapter claims that the retrogressive-crossing torsion of the sestinas' rhyme scheme (visually underscored by their *mise-en-page*), the vertiginous recursiveness and paradoxical fixity of their rhyme-words, and the retention of the narrative progression by the constraining immanence of their metrical form make the sestinas the specialized form for recapitulating, epitomizing, surveying, reassessing, and reflecting (in metaliterary terms) on the poetic and existential itinerary that Petrarca portrays in the *canzoniere*. The pages that follow partially expand on Furio Brugnolo's suggestion—which in turn drew on studies by Adolfo Jenni and Luigi Vanossi—that the sestinas constitute fundamental turning points and reflect major themes of the songbook "in a playful specularity that affects the formal organization of the text and allows us to speak, for each sestina and even more so for the series of the sestinas, of a sort of *mise-en-abyme* of the Canzoniere as a whole."[2] But this chapter will argue that we should see the sestinas not as "turning points" but instead as the privileged textual space for a "retrospective function" in (and on) Petrarca's songbook.[3]

When we further interrogate the rationale behind the concurrence of unique verticality, selected foundational themes, and various metaliterary cues in Petrarca's sestinas as they appear in the *RVF*'s autograph, we recognize, on the one hand, that the sestinas produce meaning (and affect reception) in the modes and forms of visual and concrete poems. And we better qualify, on the other hand, the function of the sestinas' dense metaliterary references as they relate to the *canzoniere*. This chapter conceptualizes the sestinas—in their presentation in the *RVF*'s autograph—as the material and poetological core of Petrarca's *canzoniere*. In the specific modes in which visual poems integrate textual and material elements through a highly rhetoricized language, the sestinas constitute the *RVF*'s poems of poetics, where the poetics of the *canzoniere* finds its most eloquent textual-material representation or is explicitly discussed in metaliterary terms.

If the columnar disposition of the hendecasyllables emphasizes rhyme-words and rhyme scheme through the exact coincidence of verse and line—and the *retrogradatio cruciata* performs for the reader the dilemmatic torments of a soul conflicted between ascesis and sensuality, between progression and retraction—the corpus of the sestinas interrupts the sequencing of events that informs the narrative of the *canzoniere* and creates niches of retrospection, reflection, and autoreferentiality. Petrarca translates the theoretical and speculative discourse on Love—such as we read in Guido Guinizzelli's, Guido Cavalcanti's, and Dante's manifesto *canzoni*—into the textual and material immanence of the sestina's own form.

In thus investigating the literary aspect of Petrarca's sestinas, this chapter may seem to engage in a more "traditional" reading of poetic texts, thus departing, or at least deviating, from the book's overarching program of exploring simultaneously the textuality and materiality of literary works. The analysis provided here, however, is premised on the same theoretical assumption that holds together the three case studies: in medieval works, not least because of authors' involvement in scribal production, the verbal and the conceptual interact dynamically with the visual and the spatial for the production of meaning. Rather than departing from the book's general contention, what follows here emanates from that contention and that interaction.

In chapter 6 we have observed how the visual presentation of the sestinas composes a semantic and material subunit within the autograph; here we explore the relationship between visual and verbal at the level of the poem. This chapter first outlines some operative definitions of visual poetry and poetry of poetics as they relate to the study of Petrarca's sestinas. It then highlights the congruence—in Hjelmslevian terms—between matter, form, and substance (of expression and content). And finally it underscores the recapitulative, reflexive, and autoreferential aspects of the sestinas while also indicating how this "evaluative" function assumes more explicit metatextual and metaliterary connotations in the double sestina. By reading the *RVF*'s sestinas as visual poems and emphasizing their function as the *canzoniere*'s poems of poetics, this chapter argues that Petrarca's act of poetic composition—and the actual writing of the sestinas—in fact epitomizes the congruence of conceptual and spatial: it is an intellectual act modeled on exact material forms and materially executed through specific book techniques.

Carmina Figurata: The Sestinas as Visual Poems

Visual poems are seen throughout the Western literary tradition: from the *technopaegnia* by Hellenistic poet Simmias of Rhodes to futurist and vorticist manifestos; from Optatianus Porphyrius's late antique *carmina cancellata* to Guillaume Apollinaire's *calligrammes*; from the collection of *carmina quadrata* by Carolingian poet Rabanus Maurus to postwar concretist poets' experimentations.[4] Giovanni Pozzi defined a visual poem as a twofold entity in which a linguistic message and an iconic formation hypostatically coexist and affect each other: "Language, though still producing its own congenial meanings, is used as medium to achieve meanings that are normally produced by the other order of representation."[5] The autograph of Petrarca's *canzoniere* presents a peculiar type of iconic formation. Both Petrarca and the copyist he supervised—whether or not the latter was Giovanni Malpaghini—sought sobriety, essentiality, and *ante litteram* minimalism. Pursuant to such graphic-editorial project, the *RVF*'s autograph shows no actual "illustrative" apparatus: the visual element of MS Vat. Lat. 3195 is largely composed of the script's aesthetics, the *mise-en-page* of the poems, the regulation of blanks and rulings, and the presentation of the verses on each line. The iconic formation in the sestina, correspondingly, is nonrepresentational. The sestinas, in the autograph, are not materially shaped to reflect their contents. In the sestinas, rather, poetic language and visual rendition by means of written signs cooperate to produce meaning and visually guide the reader through specific paths of textual decoding. In chapter 6 we have observed that, at a macrotextual level, the coordination of textual and visual elements in the sestinas facilitates their recognition as a subset of texts: as a corpus within the corpus. Here the relationship of the textual and the visual is explored at a microtextual level and is shown to reflect—and almost allegorize—recapitulate, reassess, and review (in metaliterary terms) the *RVF*'s poetry and poetics.

Upon analyzing *Le rêve* (*The Dream*), a large oil-on-canvas painted in 1910 by postimpressionist painter (and poet) Henri "Le Douanier" Rousseau, Roman Jakobson described the octastich attached to the painting as isomorphic to the painting's pictorial representation proper. According to Jakobson, the poem's rhetorical articulation mimics the figurative categories of the painting—including textual rhymes homologous to figurative ones.[6] Jakobson's indication of the isomorphy and homology between painting and poem can help us understand the dialectic between linguistic structure and material presentation of the sestinas in Petrarca's autograph of the *RVF*. The meaning of the sestinas does not depend solely on the linear sequence of signs that signify the narrative order of the events or describe the condition of the poetic subject; rather, the meaning of the sestinas also involves their material forms and visual-spatial syntax. The text fulfils its nonverbal potentials by means of its visual and spatial form.

The verticality of the sestinas' visual presentation in the autograph puts emphasis on its rhyme scheme. Additional interactions between metrical-prosodical elements and *mise-en-page* can also be observed. In Petrarca's prosody, as Gianfranco Contini pointed out, it is often the case that "the most substantial and aggressive word stands at the beginning of the verse, with all the potentiality of distending and taking respite."[7] In the sestinas, concurrently with these "aggressive" opening terms, we can also see that the constraint imposed by the limited numbers of rhyme-words concentrates the most semantically momentous lexemes in the verse clause. The hendecasyllable thus extends toward its own extremities, a phenomenon further emphasized by the very dichotomous urge of Petrarca's poetry described by Contini. Highlighted by figures of repetition and amplification, this centrifugal movement orients the verse's phrasing on a horizontal axis.

This orientation of the hendecasyllable toward its extremities—described by Gabriele Frasca as "bipolar balancing" of the meter[8]—is orthogonal to the vertical sequence of the hendecasyllables within the stanza. From a visual point of view, in the autograph, this orthogonality describes the characteristic quadrate shape of the stanzas of Petrarca's sestina. Similar to the late antique *carmina quadrata*, Petrarca's sestinas shape a grid (a *quadratum*) in which the reading from left to right and downward is counterbalanced by the opposite movement (retrogressive and upward) of the rhyme-words. The tension between the two directions of apperception (the horizontal and the vertical), the position of semantically and rhythmically substantial words at the opposite ends of the hendecasyllable—and also their "potentiality of distending," to use Contini's words—and the retrograde-crossing motion of the rhyme-words concur to delay, if not invalidate, a merely sequential reading (word by word, line by line). We still read through the sestina sequentially. But we can only appreciate its peculiar rhyme scheme if we "advance" regressively and recursively.

Petrarca's sestina defies Gotthold Ephraim Lessing's traditional *paragone* (comparison) between poetry and figurative arts as an irreducible opposition of time versus space and motion versus stasis. Because of the interstanzaic nature of its rhyme pattern—as opposed to the intrastanzaic rhymes of the other metrical genres in the *RVF*—and the strictly vertical arrangement of the rhyme-words, Petrarca's sestina in the autograph seems to presuppose a simultaneous approach to all its textual and material components. Drawing upon W. J. T. Mitchell's use of a "mathematical" model to differentiate word from image—one which evokes/invokes "the relationship between algebra and geometry, the one working by arbitrary phonetic signs read progressively, the other displaying equally arbitrary figures in space"[9]—we could describe the mutual interplay between visual code and highly formalized discourse in the sestinas as the relationship between a continuous function and its graphical representation (the "curve") on the Cartesian plane. The verbal predicts and shapes the visual. The visual displays, spatially represents, and materially reifies the verbal.

With remarkable intuition, Marianne Shapiro terms the sestina a "hieroglyph of time," but she ultimately focuses on "the temporal perception of what is being read" and insists "on the *metaphorical* quality of the space involved."[10] In other words, her definition of hieroglyph does not address the *literal* materiality of the sestinas in the *RVF*'s autograph, thus missing out on the pictorial potential of the image she uses. From a material perspective, instead, the interaction between the aesthetic of Petrarca's script, the visual presentation of the sestinas in the autograph, their content, and their literary modes of expression resemble the type of diagrammatic figuration envisioned by Jean-Gérard Lapacherie in his essay on "grammatextuality" to describe aspects of textuality in which the graphic features of script and page can produce alter-linguistic (nonphonic, nondiscursive) orders of representation. Hybrid products between the figurative and the abstract, diagrammatic grammatexts encode hierarchical relations and orientations of meaning into the visual presentation of the text.[11] The *mise-en-page* of Petrarca's sestina displays (and highlights) a particular metrical scheme. The shaping of this scheme, in its turn, also ignites a precise mechanism of perception by which the reader is continuously prompted back to the previous stanza. And it elicits from the reader—also through a differential consumption of the other layouts in the autograph—both a recognition and an interpretation of the sestina in its visual-verbal materiality.

Poems of Poetics

In chapter 6, we have cursorily observed that several categories of macrotextual cohesion identified in the twentieth-century book of poems by Enrico Testa can also be recognized as demonstrating the long-standing influence of Petrarca's *RVF* on Italian and European poetry. In Petrarca's *canzoniere*, semantic elements of cohesion—for instance, various types of semantic isotopies—give coherence to the songbook as an organic whole, while also associating groups of poems to form intermediate structures. In the case of the sestinas, this semantic cohesion is further underscored by their unique *mise-en-page*. We have also observed that a "technical" type of semantic isotopy in the sestinas involves the frequency of metaliterary references. Petrarca's texts are generally rich in references to writing poems, the tools and places for writing them, their circulation, intended audience, and dynamics of reception, but here in the sestinas the perception of metaliterary references is further intensified by their privileged position as verse clauses and recursiveness as rhyme-words—and that positioning similarly orients the sestinas' semantics. In addition to rhyme-words relating to poetry, the metaliterary implications of Laura's figure further underscore the affinity between sestinas and poetic discourse. This section further argues that the visual dimension of the sestina described earlier—enhancing retrogression and delaying a linear narrative of progression—and its semantic and rhetorical substance provoke a retroactive reflection on, and reconsideration of, the *RVF*'s narrative in its textual form; these visual, semantic, and rhetorical elements allegorize the obsessive return of erotic torments as well as, paradoxically, their inescapable fixity; and they lure the reader to a consumption of the sestina that resembles the labyrinthine sentimental experience of the *persona loquens*. It is precisely by the materiality of their textuality that the sestinas are suited for their function as the *RVF*'s poems of poetics, the ideological and poetological core of Petrarca's *canzoniere*, the privileged site for a coherent (if intermittent) discourse on poetics. On the one hand, the visual presentation of the sestina form isolates and shapes the analytical and recapitulative space of its own imaginative illusion. And on the other hand, the reading modality that the sestinas' layout enhances conveys, for the reader, the textual and material counterpart of the subject's anguished experience.

As Testa has noted regarding twentieth-century poetry books, in poems of poetics "the exercise of writing seems to slow down, in order to refer, more or less explicitly, to its scaffolding, its proceeding, and sometimes its ideological and psychological etymon."[12] As the *RVF*'s poems of poetics, the sestinas implicate the overall structure of the *canzoniere* and acquire sense through their uninterrupted relationship with the broader poetic context of the collection. They also explicate the *canzoniere*, in that they present the *can-*

zoniere's main themes in the perspective of an anguishing cyclicity that frustrates the perception of a narrative centered on the protagonist's ethical progression and disrupts the book's closure and, ultimately, its completion. In sum, they constitute the *canzoniere*'s peculiar mirror image: one that is—to use Testa's description of poems of poetics—"refracted and partial, anamorphic and paradoxical."[13] Materially isolated within the *RVF*'s autograph and visually enhanced as to their retrograde-crossing rhyme scheme, the sestinas paradoxically signify and counterpoint the poet's ever-delayed *conversio* and unfulfilled aspiration to spiritual peace. The circularity of their rhyme scheme, in other words, implies the obsessive return of the poet's obsessions and epitomizes (in sestina form) the unremitting psychomachy expressed in the poet's itinerary of repentance and salvific progress put forth a posteriori in the songbook's first sonnet and sealed in the last *canzone* to the Virgin.

Arrested Development

The verticality of the sestinas' layout, the retrogressive torsion of their rhyme scheme, and the orientation of the hendecasyllable toward its extremities create a friction between directions of reading (and re-reading). In other words, the sestina's tendency to duplication and repetition, its columnar *mise-en-page*, and the metrical artifice of the *retrogradatio cruciata* concur to increase the iconic potential of the poem: the sestina realizes the nonverbal aspect of its textuality and elicits the kind of simultaneous consumption of all its components that we more readily associate with visual forms. On the one hand, this mode of consumption delays the sequential reading of the poem. And on the other hand, this nonlinear mode of reading parallels the delayed ethical progression of the *persona loquens* and the nonlinear development of the songbook's narrative: it suspends its "plot."

If at a macrotextual level the material presentation of the sestinas creates visual niches in the songbook, then at a microtextual level the interaction between their textuality and materiality presents the major themes of the *canzoniere*—and the ethical condition of its protagonist—in terms of a tantalizing impasse, while also inscribing the reader's experience in this nonlinear mode of consumption. Teodolinda Barolini has pointed out that the sestina textualizes the illusion of stopping time: "If meter (and hence rhyme) is the poetic means of measuring time, then the sestina has discovered a meter that subverts itself, that—by producing circular stasis instead of linear movement—in effect refuses to do what meter must do."[14] A spatial dimension paradoxically ensues from, encircles, and substitutes the poem's temporal element. The sestina's dynamic itinerary of expectation and retrospection finds a temporary equilibrium: one might hazard to mention here those "effects of dynamic staticity" with which Marco Praloran described the orchestration of Petrarca's *canzoni.*[15] The narrative dimension of the *fabula*—and of the poet's conversion—gives way to the allegory and textual enaction of a troubled progression or, particularly in the *sestina doppia* (*RVF* 332), to an explicit meditation on the writing of poetry and, specifically, of the *canzoniere.* The continuous motion of the sestina's rhyme-words completes its cycle and eventually resolves into a quasi-stabilized *Gestalt*: we shall see below, in the section titled "*Tornada*: Closure and Conclusions," how this unresolved stability relates to the textual condition of the *RVF* as structure.

Circularity and Catalogue

We have seen how Petrarca's sestinas associate, in the *RVF*'s autograph, a unique material form to a set of metrical, discursive, and thematic features. The perceived suspension of linear temporality and the circularity of the form—wherein the same rhyme-words obsessively rotate throughout the stanzas—make the sestinas particularly apt for presenting fundamental aspects of Petrarca's eroticism in terms of unalleviated anguish and obsessive compulsion. "A qualunque animale alberga in terra" (For whatever animals dwell on earth)—the first sestina and first long poem of the *canzoniere* (*RVF* 22)—can be read, for instance, as a poignant catalogue of love's labors in the *RVF*: the relationship between vision and erotic desire; insomnia caused by the torments of love; the human condition of solitude, estrangement, and isolation within the created universe; and the sensual restlessness of the *persona loquens.*[16] The aimlessness of the poet's wandering at night is exacerbated by the consciousness of the peaceful state of the creation around him. The poem provides a paradigmatic example and a textual embodiment of erotic obsession and unrelenting desire expressed through the recursiveness of the rhyme-words and the regressive torsion upon itself of the *retrogradatio cruciata*, materially enhanced in the autograph by the rhyme-words' columnar presentation. The sestina sets the fixity of the poet's erotic obsessiveness against the image of passing time. The semantics of time, inexorably unchanging and yet untamable, is emphasized by the hammering insistence of temporal expressions that spread throughout lengthy, articulated periphrases: "ma poi che 'l ciel accende le sue stelle" (but when the sky lights up its stars), that is, at dusk (v. 4); or "Quando la sera scaccia il chiaro giorno, / et le tenebre nostre altrui fanno alba" (When the evening drives away the bright day, / and our darkness makes elsewhere a dawn), that is, at twilight (vv. 13–14).

The inexorable circularity with which sestina 22 displays, and anaphorically reprises, the themes hinted at in the first two "decades" of poems is further underlined by the *canzone* that immediately follows (*RVF* 23): "Nel dolce tempo de la prima etade" (In the sweet time of my first age). Described by Giovanna Rabitti as the new beginning of the *RVF*—and not by chance chosen by Petrarca to be included in his *canzone delle citazioni* (*RVF* 70)—*canzone* 23 retraces and presents the different stages of the protagonist's erotic biography in the eminently narrative terms of a sequence of metamorphoses that affect the poet (transformed into evergreen laurel, swan, living stone, fountain, voice, and deer).[17] Sestina 22 also thematizes metamorphosis, by referencing the Ovidian myth of Apollo and Daphne (*Metamorphoses* 1.450–567). As the paradoxical combination of change and persistence, it is only appropriate that this myth of metamorphosis and the double identification of Apollo with the poet and of Daphne with Laura occurs—for the first time with an explicit simile—in a poem consisting of structural and metrical permutations (vv. 34–36):[18]

> et non se transformasse in verde selva
> per uscirmi di braccia, come il giorno
> ch' Apollo la seguia qua giù per terra.
>
> ———
>
> (and let her not be transformed into a green wood
> to escape from my arms, as the day
> when Apollo pursued her down here on earth!)

But contrary to the vertiginous sequence of transformations that affects the poet in *canzone* 23, in sestina 22 metamorphosis involves Laura. In the simile cited above, sestina 22 institutes a parallel between the poetic persona's erotic experience and Apollo's violent and irresistible (if unfulfilled) passion for Daphne (who escapes rape by becoming a laurel tree). Like Daphne, Laura escapes the poet's assault through her metaphorical transformation into the evergreen laurel of poetry. And her finally acquired unchangeability confers the same everlasting quality onto the poet's sexual frustration. The categories of time that guarantee a peaceful night for the natural world are set against the perennial emblem of Laura's unreachable persona. Marco Santagata contended that "the elusiveness of the love object and the frustration of desire remain without the compensation of any sublimation."[19] In other words, the quest is denied any fulfillment. The poet-persona is denied any progression. And the sestina is determinedly condemned to repeat the same rhyme-words. Furthermore, as opposed to the consistent use of narrative past tenses in *canzone* 23, the only narrative tense of sestina 22—the imperfect indicative denoting durative or repeated action—is relegated to the world of myth (vv. 35–36): "come il giorno / ch' Apollo la seguia qua giù per terra" (as the day / when Apollo pursued her down here on earth!). In sestina 22, the rewriting of the myth and its inscription into the fibers of the poem are the only relics of a narrative sequence of events: only the fiction of the myth can overcome the sestina's distinct sense of atemporality. Laura's obstinate indifference brings about the poet's hallucinated subjunctive in the sixth stanza and consigns his vision of an endless night of love to the aggravated and hopeless dimension of the *adynaton* (v. 33): "sol una nocte, et mai non fosse l'alba" (just one night, and let the dawn never come!).

Reevocation and Assessment

If sestina 22 can be described as a catalogic outline of the major erotic motifs in the *RVF* (and in the corpus of the sestinas), the rhyme-words of sestina 30, "Giovene donna sotto un verde lauro" (A youthful lady under a green laurel), read like a catalogue of Laura's various *senhals* and isotopies that underscores their perturbing recursiveness: *lauro* (laurel), *neve* (snow), *anni* (years), *chiome* (locks), *occhi* (eyes), *riva* (shore).[20] Sestina 30, in other words, epitomizes the *canzoniere*'s central concern, insists on the oneiric contemplation of Laura by means of her *senhal*, and constitutes a real cardinal point in the presentation of the poet's relationship to her. Appropriately, the "pun" between *l'auro* (the gold of Laura's hair), *lauro* (laurel), and *Laura* appears here for the first time.

The poem evokes Laura's beauty in terms of harshness and cruel indifference, often recurring to the lexis of Dante's *rime petrose*: her vivid hardness assumes the form of a sculpted idol (v. 27: "l'idolo mio, scolpito in vivo lauro," "my idol carved in living laurel"): and this idol is both an Apollonian image to worship and an idolatrous deviation from the true God.[21] Domenico De Robertis indicated that Petrarca "puts forward that word, 'idol,' as a signification of an impassibility exalted vis-à-vis his own transmutability and finding its representation in the image of the sculpted simulacrum."[22] With a remarkable variation of perspective, sestina 30 inverts the dynamism between fixity and mutation that informed sestina 22: the ever-fleeing figure of Daphne is now a laurel tree. Laura has already assumed the rigid fixity of "a post-transformational condition,"[23] while the lover's obtuse perseverance manifests through the metamorphosis and decay of his body over the years. Consequently, the physical changes in the poet's appearance (v. 15: "o colle brune o colle bianche chiome," "either with dark or with white locks"), the contemplation of his future death (v. 18: "fin che l'ultimo dì chiuda quest'occhi," "until the last day closes these eyes"; v. 39: "che [*sc.* gli occhi] menan gli anni miei sì tosto a riva," "[the eyes] that lead my years so quickly to shore"), and the inscription of his existential experience into the cyclical alternation of the days and seasons (v. 30: "la notte e 'l giorno, al caldo ed a la neve," "night and day, in heat and in snow") cannot change the icy, reactionless immobility of the beloved. If the statue is the visual and material embodiment of the sestina's perennial present—while also indicating Laura's immanence and paradoxical unattainability—the sestina, in turn, dissolves the notion of structured temporality and relegates present, past, and future to the irrational atemporality of hyperbole, myth, and *adynaton* (vv. 7–12):

Allor saranno i miei pensieri a riva
che foglia verde non si trovi in lauro;
quando avrò queto il cor, asciutti gli occhi,
vedrem ghiacciare il foco, arder la neve;
non ò tanti capelli in queste chiome
quanti vorrei quel giorno attender anni.

(Then my thoughts will have come to shore
when green leaves are not to be found on a laurel;
when I have a quiet heart and dry eyes
we shall see the fire freeze, and burning snow;
I have not so many hairs in these locks
as I would be willing, in order to see that day, to wait years.)

If sestina 22 characterizes the association between Laura and the Daphnean laurel in terms of a dialectic of change and persistence, then sestina 30 reassigns Laura to the static and silent beauty of the emblem and the figurative.

As the first explicit anniversary poem of the songbook, sestina 30 provides a reevocation of desire's etiology and a provisional balance-taking of the poet's experience, set against the paradoxical background of time, actually evanescent though imperfectly perceived as eternal.[24] With an accurate translation into numbers of the poet's erotic vicissitudes—v. 28, "oggi à sett'anni" (today it is seven years)—the poem marks seven years from the protagonist's fateful falling in love with Laura.[25] Like sestina 30, "Anzi tre dì creata era alma in parte" (Three days before, a soul had been created in a place) is a kind of anniversary poem (*RVF* 214). Sestina 214 is also articulated as an evaluative assessment of the protagonist's love story.[26] Antonio Stäuble described it as "a sort of autobiography of the poet, or, better a chronological recall of his affair."[27] More specifically, the poem expands on the dichotomy between the time of falling in love and the desperate appeal for freedom from the agonies of love. The temporal datum that opens the poem marks in fact a peculiar type of anniversary (vv. 1–3):

Anzi tre dì creata era alma in parte
da por sua cura in cose altere et nove,
et dispregiar di quel ch'a molti è 'n pregio.

(Three days before, a soul had been created in a place
where it might put its care in things high and new
and despise what the many prize.)

The *persona loquens* is in the third age ("dì") of human life (*adulescentia*), according to Isidore's *Etymologiae* (11.2, 1–7).[28] This synecdochic, anguishing expression of time implies that each age of human life only lasts the brevity of a day. The poet was twenty-two years old when he fell in love with Laura in the spring of 1327: the chronological indication leads the reader to retrace the genesis of Petrarca's error and his subsequent erratic wandering in the wood of erotic life, one which is (v. 15) "usato di sviarne a mezzo il corso!" (accustomed to making us stray in the midst of our course!). Quite distinctly, sestina 214 institutes a continuity between the circularity of the metrical form and the figurative levels of the narrative. And the poet's mental experience of temporality is made intelligible through a spatial metaphor: the narrative of damnation and intended—if ever uncertain—redemption assumes the shape of a labyrinthine wood. The poet's awareness of his going astray, and the urge to overcome his error and errancy, transpire in fact from the semantic shift in the rhyme-word "bosco," which changes from denoting a *locus amoenus* to resembling, and alluding to, the Dantean "selva oscura" (dark wood) of moral perdition. The infernal connotation of this labyrinthic grove unfolds in the fourth and fifth stanzas (v. 23, "folto di spine," "thick with thorns"; v. 25, "Pien di lacci et di stecchi un duro corso," "Full of snares and thorns is the course"), exhibiting what Saverio Bellomo has described as a "more significant emulative tension" toward Dante and, indirectly, Arnaut Daniel.[29]

Petrarca's gesture of emulation toward Dante and Arnaut, however, reads as both an allusion to and a move away from a certain erotic lexicon (exemplified by the *fin'amor* rhyme-word *pregio*, "worth"). The protagonist's ambiguous conduct and irresolute attitude are manifest, in the third stanza, in the tetracolic oxymoron with which the sestina describes the prize that Laura represents (v. 13): "Caro, dolce, alto et faticoso pregio" (Dear, sweet, high, laborious prize), where the four adjectives are organized in pairs of antonyms. The fourth stanza opens with a strong adversative and a syntagm distinctly associated—beginning from the proemial sonnet itself—with the palinodial reconsideration of the poet's trajectory (v. 19): "Ma, lasso, or veggio" (But now, alas, I see). And with its nominal style and chiastic disposition, the dilemmatic closure of the *tornada* emphasizes a sense of paralysis and uncertainty over whether the poet-protagonist can escape the labyrinth of vice and sensual temptations (v. 39): "o l'alma sciolta, o ritenuta al bosco" (if my soul is free or captive in the wood).[30]

Coaction of Repetition

"L'aere gravato, et l'importuna nebbia" (The burdened air and the importunate cloud) (*RVF* 66) follows a compact sequence of six short poems (five sonnets and a *ballata*) enacting conflict between earthly love and heavenly love, *eros* and *caritas*; these six poems oscillate between the extremes of perdition and salvation and oppose the two forms of love through the irreconcilable forms of obsecration and benediction.[31] Whereas this sequence of poems explores the phenomenology of the protagonist's moral contradictions—he is unable to reject mundanity (love, poetry, glory) and yet strives to embrace salvation (contemplative life, the true God)—sestina 66 translates his chronic indecision into the arrested progression of the *retrogradatio cruciata*. The poet's conflicts are set against the claustrophobic depiction of a *locus* that has become, at this point, far from *amoenus*. The overpowering inclemency of the elements represented in the first stanza applies both to the poet's emotional state in the second stanza—vv. 7–8, "Et io nel cor via più freddo che ghiaccio / ò di gravi pensier' tal una nebbia" (And I have in my heart, much colder than ice, / heavy thoughts in such a cloud)—and to Laura's indifference in the fourth stanza.[32] The etymological wordplay on the closed valleys of Valchiusa (vv. 9–11: "queste valli, / serrate . . . / et circundate," "these valleys, / closed . . . / and surrounded") institutes a homology between orography, winter landscape, the poet's anguish, and the prison house of syntax and rhyme scheme, which entraps the anguished lover in a condition of existential (and ethical) cyclicity and metrical circularity. Mario Petrini maintains that the sestina is "the most appropriate form to express these meandering *twists* of hopeless passion."[33] Sestina 66 also establishes the isotopic equivalence between the rhyme-word *vènti* ("winds") and Laura by means of her homophone *l'aura* ("breeze"): her ethereal identity envelops the poet by insinuating memories and offering hypnotic suggestions. This entangling semantic pattern is further complicated to include poetic diction itself, since the expression *dolorosi vènti* ("sorrowing winds") (v. 30) here metaphorically indicates the aural nature of Petrarca's sighs, whose sound in scattered rhymes describes the poetry of the *canzoniere* from its very incipit (*RVF* 1, vv. 1–2: "Voi ch'ascoltate in rime sparse il suono / di quesi sospiri," "You who hear in scattered rhymes the sound of those sighs").

The sestina thus confirms its privileged position to express the coincidence between the persona of the beloved and the writing of poetry: *Laura/l'aura* is at once the beloved, the poetry that yearns for her, and its translation into words and sounds. In establishing these metonymic transitions, the sestina reinforces that coincidence and sanctions both its own nature as poem of poetics and the songbook's metaliterary foundation as "poetry of poetry."[34]

The affinity between sestina 66 and the *canzoniere*'s proemial sonnet also underlines the ideological function of the sestina as form and further explains the material emphasis put on its unique *mise-en-page*: where the sonnet interprets a posteriori the dilemmatic existential experience portrayed in the *canzoniere*, the sestina performs this experience as ongoing condition through the visually enhanced retrogression of its meter. If the third stanza of *RVF* 66 outlines the reassuring amenity of nature's reawakening, the fourth exhibits the poet's obsession on his unrequited desire (vv. 19–21):

> Ma, lasso, a me non val fiorir de valli,
> anzi piango al sereno et a la pioggia
> et a' gelati et a' soavi vènti.
>
> ———
>
> (But, alas! I am not helped by the flowering of the valleys;
> rather I weep in clear water and in rain,
> and in freezing and in warming winds.)

Isolated and highlighted by a deprecative interjection, the strong adversative conjunction opening the fourth stanza of sestina 66 in the verses cited above foretells that any linear development and moral progress is prevented. In sestina 22, a strong adversative at the incipit of the second stanza introduced an opposition between the poet's concupiscent fixation and the natural cycle of day and night (v. 7: "Et io," "And I"). Here in sestina 66, the counteractive force of the *epanorthosis* (vv. 19–20: "non . . ., / anzi . . .," "not . . ., / rather . . ."), the antitheses and chiastic disposition of the descriptors (*sereno* vs. *pioggia*, *gelati* vs. *soavi*), and the spelling out and exhaustion of the alternatives through an unrelenting *amplificatio* show that no change can apply to the poet. The very rivers of the poet's cherished valley ultimately become the objective correlative of his own moral stagnation (v. 11: "stagnanti fiumi," "stagnating rivers"). The immutability of his condition appears, in Luigi Blasucci's words, as a "record of a permanent state."[35] To put it differently, content, syntax, rhetoric, and meter echo the unresolved circularity of Petrarca's poetic discourse. Petrarca's temporality can only assume the emblematic character of a coaction of repetition.

In Werner von Koppenfels's articulation of the progression of sense outlined within the sestinas' corpus,[36] the moral correction of the *RVF*'s erotic narrative and the poet's Augustinian *mutatio animi* start with "Chi è fermato di menar sua vita" (He who has decided to lead his life) (*RVF* 80).[37] Johannes Bartuschat has also underscored sestina 80's discourse of moral conversion: "The almost narrative linearity of this sestina creates a deep contrast to the fundamentally circular character of the metrical genre. . . . it now becomes the form that mirrors the path to redemption."[38] Sestina 80 undoubtedly looks back to past experiences. And it unquestionably provides a critical assessment and an admission of inadequacy—v. 14, "errai" (I wandered)—in light of a new religious ethos (vv. 16–17): "poi piacque a lui che mi produsse in vita / chiamarme tanto indietro da li scogli" (then it pleased Him who gave me life / to call me back far enough from the rocks).

And yet, the hoped-for ethical progression and spiritual salvation can be barely glimpsed (v. 18: "almen da lunge," "at least from afar") through the discourse of a sustained allegory of life as navigation and the dubiously effective mode of the optative subjunctive (v. 31: "S'io esca vivo de' dubbiosi scogli," "So may I come out alive from these perilous rocks"), frustrated by the violence of habit and by unexhausted, consuming desire (vv. 35–36):

Se non ch'i' ardo come acceso legno,
sì m'è duro a lassar l'usata vita.

(Except that I burn like kindled wood,
it is so hard for me to leave my accustomed life.)

The poet's attempt to embrace a life renewed by Christian *caritas* is indeed painful, and the outcome uncertain. A variation on the classical and, indeed, Petrarchan *topos* of life as traveling by sail (with all of the attendant perils), sestina 80 can only articulate a textual space in which, Rosanna Bettarini argued, "the circularity and undulating recurrence inherent to the sestina 'genre' instrumentally includes in itself the alternation of hope and shipwreck."[39] Furthermore, the *persona loquens* is objectified in the metaphor of the body as ship, metonymically degraded into the arid wood of which ships are made (v. 12: "dentro al legno," "within the ship"), ensnared in the claustrophobic condition that is the moral blindness of the sinful flesh (v. 13: "Chiuso gran tempo in questo cieco legno," "Shut up a long time in this blind ship," with an eloquent hypallage of the adjective), and textually prevented from progressing because he is metrically pushed back by the regressive torsion of the rhyme-words, which visually climb back—and drag the reader with them—up the vertical column of the verse clauses.

Sestina 80 materializes both a narrative pause and an ethical deadlock, wherein the "lyrical I" oscillates between the consciousness of a disgraced (and ever-alluring) life and the aspiration for a spiritual elevation. Expanding on the dysphoric intimations already transpiring in sestina 66, sestina 80 exposes the negative consequences of an obsession that brings about an errant state of the soul, an incapacity to conceive of one's life without the beloved, and a perilous obliviousness to the true, Christian source of all good. Within this theme of human ephemerality, we see subsumed an additional motif: the bitter awareness that human life might be too brief to complete the whole itinerary of salvation (v. 27): "è gran viaggio in così poca vita" (there is still a long journey for so short a life). The sestina functions, even in metaliterary terms, as a penitential text. Arnaut's "ferm voler" (alluded to in v. 1) is reread—and rejected—as obstinacy in leading a sinful life.[40] The sestina is also a poetic and ideological confutation of Petrarca's own Stilnovist suggestions: in spite of any and all attempts at self-deception, the sensual love for the phenomenic beauty of a creature, however chaste, is a deviation from—and not an intermediary for—the love for the creator. The *tornada* takes the actual form of a prayer to succeed in righting a still-unrectified sinful course (v. 39: "drizza a buon porto l'affannata vela," "direct to a good port my weary sail") and links sestina 80 to the explicitly religious outcome and assorted repentance of sonnet 81 ("Io son sì stanco sotto 'l fascio antico," "I am so weary under the ancient bundle").

The Third Dimension of the Sestina

We have seen how the sestina produces meaning through both the linear dimension of its linguistic signs and the visual order of its material presentation. The friction between the sequential decryption of the script and the visual reception of the sestina's layout as it is shaped by that script parallels a similar relationship between the linear temporality of the narrative—the protagonist's development, the songbook's plot—and the retrospection onto the *canzoniere*'s story and discourse. Furthermore, this dual order of representation (verbal and visual) enhances the dichotomic nature of the *RVF*'s thematic, rhetorical, and structural substance: its lacerating pull between *eros* and *caritas*; its existential and ethical conflict between perdition and salvation, between relapse and contrition; and also the linguistic and stylistic manifestations of these opposing poles. This conflictual structure of Petrarca's sestinas can be described, in Louis Althusser and Étienne Balibar's terms, as "a cause immanent in its effects."[41] And cause and effects are here both textual and material.

But this dual, bidimensional order does not exhaust the material condition of the sestinas in Petrarca's autograph. As Christine Putzo has pointed out in her study of Middle High German narratives, existing beside the linear and planar extensions of a text—that is, the sequence of its signs and its arrangement on the page—is "the actual spatial (three-dimensional) extension of its expansion through the body of the book."[42] When we consider the material treatment of Petrarca's sestinas in the *RVF*'s autograph, we recognize that, in at least two cases, the sestinas assume semiotic value in the properly spatial, three-dimensional terms outlined by Putzo. In chapter 6, we have seen how Petrarca generally opts to pair a sestina with a sonnet per folio façade.[43] Exceptions to this tendency are represented by sestina 142, which begins on the recto of fol. 32 after sonnets 140 and 141 and continues on the verso, followed by sonnets 143–145; and the *sestina doppia*—which will be the specific object of our inquiry in the section below titled "*Ars Poetica*"—transcribed on fols. 65v–66r. An intermediate hybrid condition also affects sestinas 237 and 239, whose symmetrical transcription on fols. 45v and 46r overrides both the aesthetic of the single folio façade and the dialectic between recto and verso, thus eliciting from the reader a material consumption that transgresses the measure of the single folio.

"What's past is prologue"

The sestinas' recapitulative qualities and reassessment features find both an exemplary execution and a momentous variation in sestina 142, "A la dolce ombra de le belle frondi" (To the sweet shade of those beautiful leaves). Its median position within the corpus, fifth of nine sestinas, marks for the protagonist—within the narrative of the songbook—the maturation of a commitment to redeem himself, but it also confirms his obstinate erotic pulsion toward Laura. Sestina 142 emblematizes both the poet's existential laceration (or, rather, the condition of his split consciousness) and his anxiety for spiritual renewal. In his hypothetical reconstruction of the *canzoniere*'s "Correggio form," or "pre-Chigi form"—one that would have antedated the *RVF*'s autograph by about a decade—Ernest H. Wilkins placed sestina 142 at the very end of the first part of the *canzoniere*, where he posited it would have been situated in that form.[44] This alleged privileged position of partial, provisional closure was also emphasized by Guglielmo Gorni, who maintained that sestina 142, at some point, "seemed to the author the *only* possible solution."[45] But it is not necessary to speculate on the exact sequence of poems in a book—be it bipartite or not—that does not, in fact, materially exist.[46] The relevance of sestina 142 within the economy of Petrarca's collection, rather, emerges from the modes in which its *inventio* and *elocutio* interact with its *mise-en-page*—its material transcription, its *actio*—and exist in the space of the autograph.

Sestina 142 bends its own form—traditionally profane and sensual par excellence—to express a new poetics of conversion. The poet's rethinking of his poetic and existential past is underscored, in this sestina, by the dense intratextual connections to previous poems in the songbook.[47] And the polarization of the rhyme-words around the two antithetical semantic clusters of the heavenly spheres—"lume" (light), "cielo" (heaven)—and the earthly world—"frondi" (leaves), "rami" (branches), "poggi" (hills)—predicts the end of the songbook's erotic component and the conversion from the olden *rami* as emblem for Laura to "altri rami" (other branches), traditionally interpreted as a religious metaphor for the Christian cross. But if sestina 142 explicitly thematizes the palinode of profane *eros* in favor of spiritual *caritas*, at the same time the circularity of the sestina as form—further underlined here, as we shall see, by the return of its rhyme-words in the *tornada* to their initial formation—implicitly invalidates a linear narrative discourse and, therefore, the protagonist's claims and aspirations to a narrative of redemption. Furthermore, the sestina's actual *mise-en-page*—its transgression of the single folio-façade "norm" and its three-dimensional expansion into the book-object—and the material act of turning the folio that its reading requires reveal the poet's negligence of his own propositions and mimetically enacts for the reader the frustration of the protagonist's incomplete conversion. As the protagonist vacillates between sinful disposition and redemptive inclination, the reading of a sestina that is on two sides of a folio makes the reader flip back and forth to trace and revisit the poem's rhyme scheme. Sestina 142, in short, manifests the synergy and friction between codicological structure and linguistic code.

Natascia Tonelli points out that in sestina 142, Petrarca replaces narrative with "an allegorical recount of his own love destiny triggered by heavenly influence."[48] Whereas the sestina's first stanza describes how the influence of Venus prompted the poet's love for Laura and how the latter preserved him from an excess of sensual love, the ensuing stanzas mark his progressive distancing from the caducity and contingency of earthly love (however pure) and lead him to embrace a higher standard of moral perfection and true faith. The poet's inner dilaceration and contradictory quest manifest in the erratic movement of the *persona loquens* through the *coblas*: v. 2, "corsi fuggendo" (I ran, fleeing); v. 15, "son gito" (I have gone); v. 22, "tornai sempre devoto" (I have come back always devoted); v. 29, "fuggir disposi" (I have made ready to flee); and v. 32, "passai" (I traversed). The "soave et chiaro lume" (mild and clear light) of Laura's eyes (v. 21) mitigates Venus's "dispietato lume" (pitiless light) (v. 2): that is, the planet's influx and the impious eroticism it conveys. It is a true illumination from heaven, however, that urges the poet to "veder lume" (see the light) (v. 30). Through the enlightened acknowledgment of mortal life's ephemerality, he can now direct himself to yet "altro lume" (another light) (v. 37): the light of celestial grace.

The opposition between the poet's redemptive proposition and the harsh and passionate desire described in the first three sestinas of the *RVF* is confirmed by the double series of antithetical deictics in the sixth stanza (vv. 31–36):

Tanto mi piacque prima il dolce lume
ch'i' passai con diletto assai gran poggi
per poter appressar gli amati rami:
ora la vita breve e 'l loco e 'l tempo
mostranmi altro sentier di gire al cielo
et di far frutto, non pur fior' et frondi.

(So pleasing to me at first was the sweet light
that joyfully I traversed great hills
in order to approach the beloved branches.
Now the shortness of life and the place and the season
show me another pathway to go to Heaven
and bear fruit, not merely flowers and leaves.)

The opposition between temporal adverbs (*prima*, "at first," vs. *ora*, "now") parallels the one between the past tenses of the narrative sections (vv. 31–33) and the present tenses of the commentative ones (vv. 34–36).

At the level of its *elocutio*, analogously, sestina 142 condenses a series of rhetorical strategies that underscore its structural relevance for epitomizing and rethinking the subject matter in the *RVF*. Specifically, the *tornada* is articulated as both *recapitulatio* and *correctio*. The hammering *polyptoton* of the adjective *altro* ("another")—its sixfold repetition declined in different genre and number—performs the self-denunciation of a sinful life with a tone that evokes the liturgical formularity of a *mea culpa* (vv. 37–39):

Altr'amor, altre frondi et altro lume,
altro salir al ciel per altri poggi
cerco, ché n'è ben tempo, et altri rami.

(Another love, other leaves, and another light,
another climbing to Heavens by other hills
I seek (for it is indeed time), and other branches.)

If the *polyptoton* sanctions here the sincere pursuit of an Augustinian *mutatio animi*, the *ornatus difficilis* also indicates the onerousness of the protagonist's conversion: the proliferation of lemmas (*enumeratio*), the *variationes* of constructs, the postponement of the subject, and the hyperbaton of "altri rami" concur to lengthen the time of contrition. But the rhythm's overwhelming progression toward the strong and (in a sestina) rather unusual enjambment between the two final hendecasyllables counterbalances the *retrogradatio* of the rhyme scheme and exhibits the honest intention of the *persona loquens*. These rhetorical strategies are not exclusive to the sestina. But here their frequency and their mutual implication with content and medium are remarkable. At a metrical level, as noted by Carlo Pulsoni, the poetics of conversion further affects the rhyme scheme of the *tornada*, such that from this point on in the *canzoniere* the final *cobla* will mirror the sequence of the first stanza: a formal *rappel à l'ordre* in response to a spiritual conversion.[49]

And yet, this additional metrical formalization, this profession of ethical conversion, and this intimation of an epilogue as crucial prelude to a new spiritual phase are all immediately undermined by the uninterrupted sequence of sixty-three short poems—all sonnets with the sole exception of *ballata* 149—that follow the sestina and re-present the initial dialectic of contradictions between the protagonist's youthful sinful inclination and his mature self-critical awareness, continuously destabilized by senile obstinacy: Paola Vecchi Galli has pointed out with reference to this compact subsection of short poems, "Francesco [*sc.* the *RVF*'s poet protagonist] has not made a single step forward since the beginning of the story."[50] The protagonist's intended redemption and renewed ethical conscience yields before his sensual and erotic compulsion. What we could metaphorically describe as the subject's attempt to turn the page is frustrated and exposed as delusional and deceptive through the reader's act of materially turning the page. Turning the page discloses to the reader the protagonist's unaccomplished conversion. And it mimes for the reader the frustration of an imperfect repentance. If sestina 142 reiterates the protagonist's will of redemption, its peculiar spatial reification in the autograph mirrors instead his irreducible ethical conflict and engages with the bipartite autograph in a synecdochical relationship of *pars pro toto*. The protagonist's course of action in the imaginative space of the *canzoniere*'s narration finds its counterpart in the reader's tangible interaction with the material space of the autograph as book-object.

À Livre Ouvert

In the autograph of the *RVF*, sestina 237 ("Non à tanti animali il mar fra l'onde," "The sea has not so many creatures among its waves") and sestina 239 ("Là ver' l'aurora, che sì dolce l'aura," "At the time near dawn when so sweetly the breeze") are transcribed symmetrically: the former (copied under sonnet 236) occupies fol. 45v; and the latter (copied under sonnet 238) occupies fol. 46r. As pointed out by Brugnolo,[51] this symmetrical *mise-en-page* conforms to a material aesthetics that centers on the visual unity provided by the two folio façades of the book (verso-recto) opened before the reader: an aesthetics *à livre ouvert* ("with the book open"), to use Léon Gilissen's formulation.[52] The visual and textual correlation of these two folios side by side corresponds to a dialectical relationship of thematic correspondence and opposition between the two sestinas: both sestinas reevoke the protagonist's youthful errancy in the Arnaldian modes of *adynata*, but the protagonist's striving to put an end to his erotic agony in sestina 237 gives in to new delusions of poetically appeasing Laura in sestina 239. The symmetrical presentation of the sestinas, in other words, is further visual argument for the dilemmatic quality of the lover's existence and poetry. And this material and textual correlation prefigures the intrinsic reduplication of the sestina form in the *sestina doppia* (*RVF* 332) (see pls. 7.1 and 7.2).[53]

Sestina 237, "Non à tanti animali il mar fra l'onde" (The sea has not so many creatures among its waves), expands on the dual relationship of affinity and distinction between natural setting and the poet's soul.[54] The alternating rhythm of day and night highlights (if only by opposition) the uninterrupted continuity of the poet's restless condition. The first stanza is articulated as a compound simile between the multifarious natural elements and the poet's innumerable love thoughts (vv. 1–6): "Non à tanti animali . . . / quant'à 'l mio cor pensier' ciascuna sera" (The sea has not so many creatures . . . / as I have cares in my heart every evening). The simile, however, can only be phrased apophatically as one of negative equivalence—"denied equivalence," in Claudia Berra's classification of Petrarchan similes[55]—and the fourfold comparison only gives a pale idea of the poet's agony. The second stanza provides an additional negative simile, emphasized by a hyperbolic expression that anticipates the ensuing *adynata* (vv. 10–11): "tanti affanni uom mai

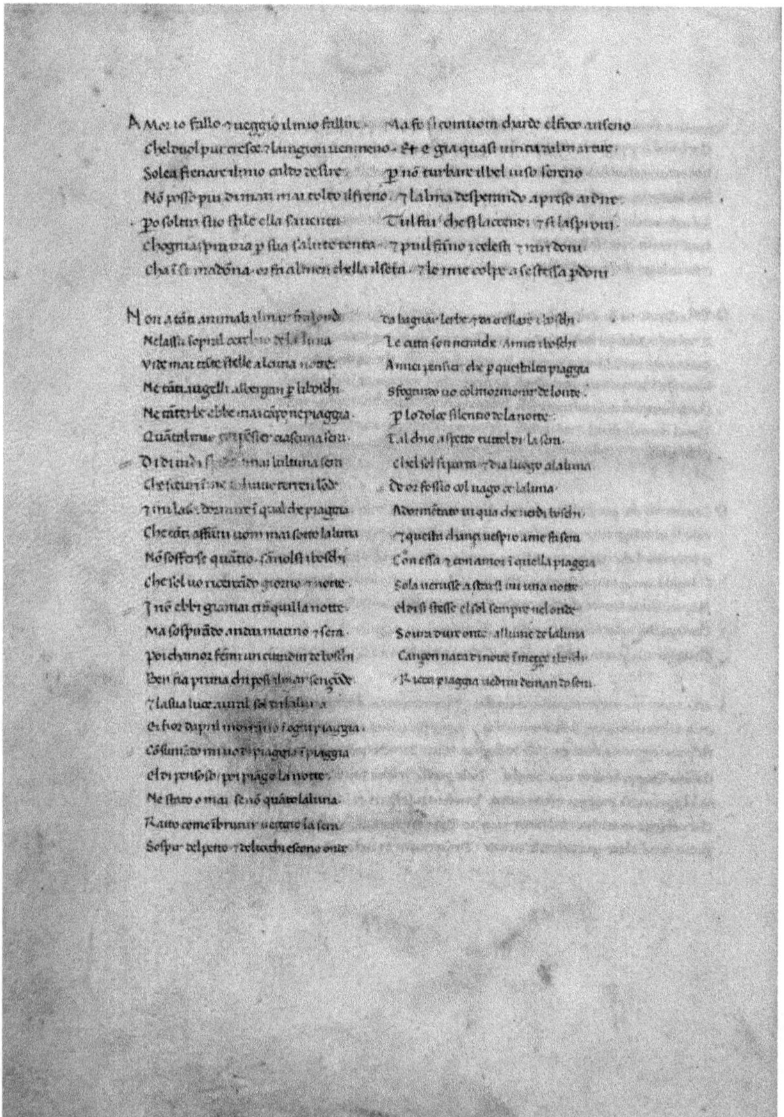

Plate 7.1. Vatican City, Biblioteca Apostolica Vaticana, MS Vat. Lat. 3195, fol. 45v. By permission of the Biblioteca Apostolica Vaticana.

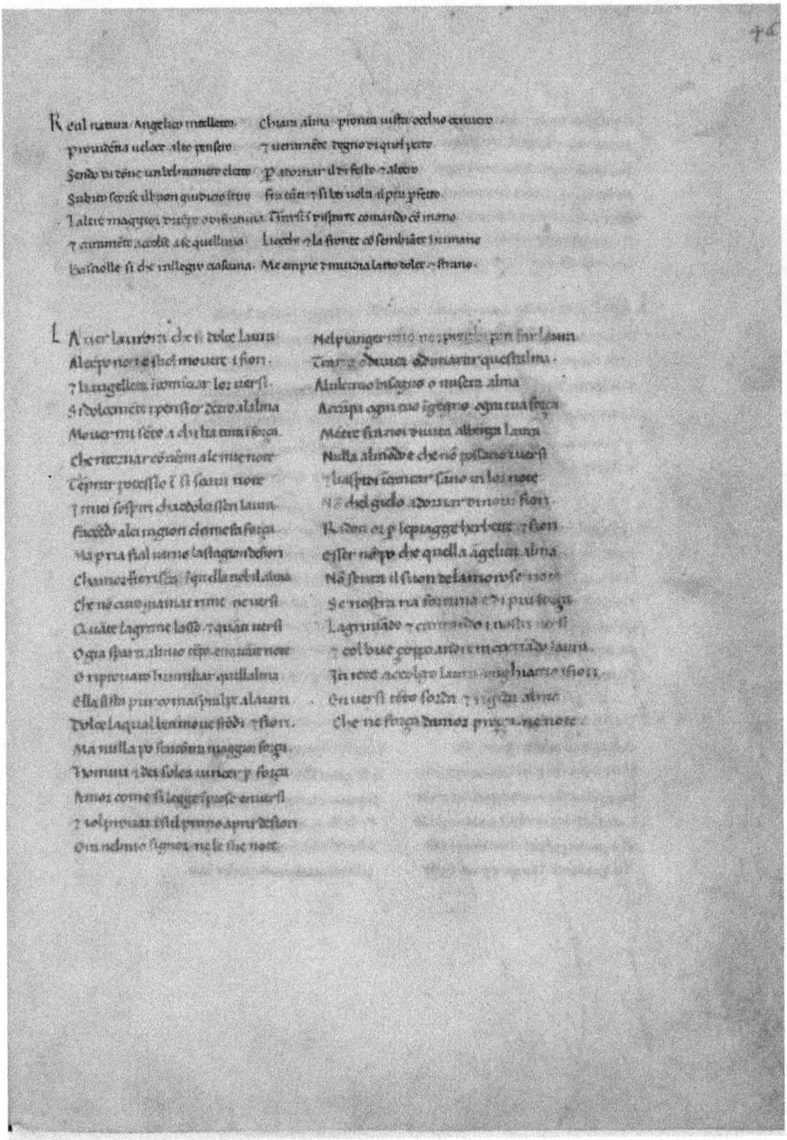

Plate 7.2. Vatican City, Biblioteca Apostolica Vaticana, MS Vat. Lat. 3195, fol. 46r. By permission of the Biblioteca Apostolica Vaticana.

sotto la luna / non sofferse quant'io" (so many troubles no man under the moon / ever suffered as I do). In the second stanza, the unceasing progression of time—v. 7, "Di dì in dì" (From day to day); v. 12, "giorno et notte" (day and night)—is counterbalanced by the immutability of the poet's woeful condition. In the congruence between metrical mechanism and psychological coaction, the inexorable circularity of the sestina reflects the poet's paradoxical condition: his inability to find peace (v. 21: "né stato ò mai, se non quanto la luna," "nor have I any steadfastness except as does the moon") and his failure to move on. The anguishing restlessness of the paralyzed "lyrical I" affects even the syntactic structure of the phrasing. The sestina insists repeatedly on the use of the gerund: v. 12, "vo ricercando" (I go searching); v. 14, "sospirando andai" (I . . . have gone sighing); vv. 19–20, "Consumando mi vo di piaggia in piaggia / el dì pensoso, poi piango la notte" (I go consuming myself from meadow to meadow / full of cares all day; then I weep at night), with a strong *variatio* between the periphrastic gerundial syntagm and the verbal form with predicative adjective; and v. 27, "sfogando vo" (I go venting). According to Maurizio Vitale, "with its insistent repetition, this syntagm confers . . . a melodic motion of prolonged intensity; even more, it vividly stresses the meaning of the verb in the gerund in the expression of protracted, progressive action."[56] Here in sestina 237, more specifically, the gerundial syntagm brings about a sense of incompletion, suggests a dimension of waiting and anticipation, and foresees the desire to leave earthly life that will feature more prominently in the double sestina (*RVF* 332).

A series of excruciating *adynata* that invert the natural order, hyperbolic metaphors (v. 23: "de li occhi escono onde," "from my eyes waves / come forth"), and oxymoronic expressions (v. 13: "cittadin de' boschi," "citizen of the woods") anticipate the change of tone in the sixth stanza, where for the second time the optative subjunctive evokes (and invokes) an eternal, unattainable night of passion with Laura.[57] On the one hand, the text reproposes the carnal desire of sestina 22 with analogous references to troubadour poetry and Dante's *rime petrose*.[58] On the other hand, Laura's unusual absence from what Frasca has described as this "theater of desire" stresses the self-deceiving aspects of profane love.[59] The cultivated reference to the myth of Endymion visited by Diana during his perpetual sleep endows the poet's desire for Laura with oneiric tones, fixes it against the atemporality of the myth, and perpetuates its irrational illusiveness through the incantatorial circularity of the sestina's form (vv. 35–36):

> sola venisse a starsi ivi una notte;
> e 'l dì si stesse e 'l sol sempre ne l'onde.
>
> ([would that Laura] might come alone to stay there one night,
> and that the day might stay, and the sun, forever under the waves!)

The crepuscular phenomenology of the lover's insomnia and its association with the act of narrating his vicissitudes—often through metaphors of crying and sighing—evoke such texts as *RVF* 50 (vv. 71–73: "Canzon, se l'esser meco / dal matino a la sera / t'à fatto di mia schiera," "Song, if being with me from morning to night has made you of my party"), *RVF* 216 (vv. 1–4: "Tutto 'l dì piango; et poi la notte, quando / prendon riposo i miseri mortali, / trovomi in pianto, et raddoppiarsi i mali: / così spendo 'l mio tempo lagrimando," "All day I weep; and then at night, when miserable mortals take rest, I find that I am in tears and that my pains are doubled; thus I spend my time weeping"), and *RVF* 223 (vv. 10–11: "Il sonno è 'n bando, et del riposo è nulla; / ma sospiri et lamenti infin a l'alba," "Sleep is banished and there is no rest, but sighs and laments till dawn"). But the metaliterary coincidence between relentless nocturnal anguish and the writing of one specific poetic composition has its apogee in this sestina, when in the *tornada* sestina 237 addresses itself as a nocturnal text (v. 38): "canzon nata di notte in mezzo i boschi" (O song born at night amid the woods).

Set against a spring dawn, sestina 239, "Là ver' l'aurora, che sì dolce l'aura" (At the time near dawn when so sweetly the breeze), represents the diurnal counterpart of sestina 237.[60] It also marks the acme of intertextual references to Arnaut, with the abovementioned *adynata*—hoarding air, hunting the hare with an ox—and the presence of the Arnaldian rhyme-word *alma* (soul, *arma* in Arnaut). An additional allusion to Arnaut, via Dante, is the peculiar mode in which the poet expresses simultaneous acts of crying and singing (vv. 35–36): "lagrimando et cantando i nostri versi / et col bue zoppo andrem cacciando l'aura" (weeping and singing our verses / we shall go with a lame ox hunting the breeze), which replicates the lexicon and, at least partially, the syntax of Arnaut Daniel *agens*'s self-disclosure in Occitan in *Purgatorio* 26.142 ("*Ieu sui Arnaut, que plor e vau cantan*," "*I am Arnaut, who weep and go singing*"). The Arnaldian references contribute to displaying the sestina's systematic metatextual discourse, which in turn anticipates the diffused metaliterary implications of the *sestina doppia* (*RVF* 332). Sestina 239 presents two explicitly poetry-oriented rhyme-words: "versi" (verses) and "note" (notes). Various metaliterary signifiers also punctuate its stanzas: v. 1, "dolce" (sweet), with *figura etymologica* at vv. 4 and 8, and with antithesis at vv. 16–17; v. 3, "incominciar" (begin); v. 7, "Temprar" (tune); v. 12, "rime" (rhymes); v. 20, "come si legge in prose e 'n versi" (as one reads in prose and in verses), with an additional reference to Guido Guinizzelli's description of Arnaut in *Purgatorio* 26.118; v. 26, "ingegno" (wit); v. 29, "incantar" (to enchant); v. 30, "adornar" (adorning); and the list could continue.[61]

Francesco Zambon has observed that the quasi-synonymic terms *versi* and *note* describe the sestina in which they feature, "thus including it *en abyme* in some of its very rhyme-words (as do *stile* and *rime* in "Mia benigna fortuna" [*sc.* the double sestina, *RVF* 332])."[62] The exceptional presence of Laura's name as rhyme-word (v. 7) resonates in the various acceptations of the isotopy of her persona, deepens the metatextual depth of the poem, and confirms the indissoluble link between her name, her character, and the writing of poetry. Expanding on the Occitan *topos* of the *temps novel* (the spring), the sestina institutes a parallel between *l'aura* (the breeze and, metonymically, the spring), which inspires birds to sing, and the poet's amorous thoughts of Laura, which inspire his song (vv. 1–6):

Là ver' l'aurora, che sì dolce l'aura
al tempo novo suol movere i fiori,
et li augelletti incominciar lor versi,
sì dolcemente i pensier' dentro a l'alma
mover mi sento a chi li à tutti in forza,
che ritornar convenmi a le mie note.

(At the time near dawn when so sweetly the breeze
in the springtime is wont to move the flowers
and the little birds begin their verses,

so sweetly I feel my thoughts within my soul
stirred by him who has them all in his power,
that I must return to my notes.)

When we transcribe the first line of the sestina diplomatically from fol. 46r of Petrarca's autograph, the triple iteration of /laura/ visually performs a ritual invocation—an epiclesis of sorts—of her name: "LA|uer laurora che si dolce laura."[63] The profuse alliteration of the liquid sound /l/ and the assonance in *ictus* of the central vowel /a/ disseminate Laura's *senhal* (and her *phantasma*) through the prosodic structure of the hendecasyllable with a calculated, hallucinated phonosymbolism that verges on *lambdacismus*.[64]

With a significant intratextual reference to the *canzoniere*'s proemial, programmatic (a posteriori), and palinodial sonnet (*RVF* 1), the poet depicts himself in the act of scattering his rhymes and, therefore, of composing the very *Fragmenta* of which this sestina constitutes one *fragmentum* (vv. 13–15):

Quante lagrime, lasso, et quanti versi
ò già sparti al mio tempo, e 'n quante note
ò riprovato humilïar quell'alma!

———

(How many tears, alas, and how many verses
have I already scattered in my time! And in how many notes
have I attempted to humble that soul!)

In addition to evoking the hendiadyc complementarity (v. 35) between *lagrimare* ("to weep") and *cantare* ("to sing") with which the songbook also opens—*RVF* 1, v. 5: "piango et ragiono" (I weep and speak)—sestina 239 revisits the theme of Laura's indifference and conjugates it with a metaliterary contemplation of poetry's potential (vv. 28–30):

Nulla al mondo è che non possano i versi:
et li aspidi incantar sanno in lor note,
nonché 'l gielo adornar di novi fiori.

———

(There is nothing in the world that cannot be done by verses;
they know how to enchant asps with their notes,
not to speak of adorning the frost with new flowers.)

The Orphic references to the enchanting powers of music conjure up the notion of literature's ability to create worlds conceptually alternative to reality. Zambon, after Aurelio Roncaglia, has argued that the use of *versi* as a rhyme-word alludes to Raimbaut's abovementioned "Er resplan la flors enversa," where "the transformation or 'inversion' of negative into positive is achieved precisely through the formal principle of the composition, which reuses the same rhyme-word for each *cobla*, thus inverting its value systematically."[65] The power of poetic *logos* is hyperbolically unlimited (vv. 28–30). And yet, Laura's soul is "sorda" (deaf) to verse (v. 38), and her refusal of the poet's love is unremitting. The opposition between real and virtual, past and future, desire and moral conscience reignites a yearning for the first term of these antitheses. The explicit enunciation of Laura's name (v. 8) marks the last resurgence of a desperate passion that foresees both her postmortem celebration in the second part of the *canzoniere* and the poet's wish to end his own poetry in the double sestina.

Ars Poetica

The *RVF*'s final sestina "Mia benigna fortuna e 'l viver lieto" (My kind fortune and glad life), the sole sestina in the second part of the *canzoniere* (*RVF* 332), furthers the textual and material innovation of pairing two sestinas illustrated above: distributed over two folio façades (fols. 65v–66r) like *RVF* 142, sestina 332 is a double sestina with six rhyme-words, twelve 6-line stanzas, and a *tornada*[66] If Petrarca's sestinas can be generally considered the privileged site for a discourse on poetry and poetics, the double sestina more pointedly resembles a compendious *ars poetica*. It presents poetry as its own subject matter by providing a sample of *inventio* regarding those materials of which the *RVF*'s poetry consists. It revolves around the technical vocabulary of poetry and poetics—in a dense intertextual dialogue with classical literature and contemporary vernacular poetry—and thematizes the rhetorical relationship between the contents of poetry and the categories of style.[67] In sum, the double sestina functions as a reflection on the ineffability of the intellectual and emotional status of the *persona loquens*, while also exploring the technical potentials of poetic diction through a redefined idea of discourse (in verse) on poetics.

We have observed how rhyme-words orient the semantics of the sestinas with the force of their recursiveness and privileged position as verse clauses. In the *sestina doppia*, two of the rhyme-words—*rime* ("rhymes") and *stile* ("style")—directly relate to the lexicon of poetic diction. A third rhyme-word, *pianto* ("weeping"), is also rich in metaliterary innuendos: *pianto* evokes the late antique and medieval genre of the *planctus* (Occitan, *planh*), a codified dirge or funeral lamentation; and the semantic constellation of *pianto*, particularly dense in the corpus of the sestinas, works as a constant metatextual reference for the elegiac components of Petrarca's poetry, programmatically exposed in the incipitarian sonnet of the *canzoniere* (*RVF* 1, v. 5: "Del vario stile in ch'io piango et ragiono," "for the varied style in which I weep and speak"). Roncaglia recognized the archetypal conciliation of invariants and variation as specific to Petrarca's sestinas.[68] A transphrastic analysis of these rhyme-words will show how this conciliation, in the *sestina doppia*, becomes a sophisticated consideration of the variety and complexity of the subject matter of love poetry and its corresponding style in Petrarca's *canzoniere*.

Medieval critical terminology retains, in Zygmunt Barański's words, a "denotatively volatile" character.[69] Whereas a certain degree of consistency in the use of literary-critical terminology is noticeable in Petrarca's corpus (in both Latin and the vernacular), its exact meaning in terms of poetic diction remains highly suggestive but vague. Petrarca's terminology implies the interplay and mutual definition of aesthetic opposites. It often conflates stylistic categories with content. And it associates different rhetorical traditions (*trobar clus* and *trobar leu* with *asperitas* and *suavitas*). The understanding of Petrarca's terminology requires, in other words, a contrastive analysis of the various terms in their synchronic and diachronic use. It brings up the intertextual dynamics between Petrarca's technical lexicon and the poetics terminology used by his Latin and Romance interlocutors. And it imposes a continuous comparison with the aporias that Dante's poetological language also brings about. Although such systematic study goes well beyond the scope of this chapter, here we can outline some operative points with specific reference to *RVF* 332.[70]

Varietas

The theme that most prominently emerges from the various declinations of the rhyme-words and their relationship to the other matrices of verse meaning is the dichotomous nature of the poet's literary, erotic, and existential experience: a paralyzing tension between mutually exclusive alternatives. The ultimate repercussion occasioned by this dilemmatic predisposition for the *RVF* is the macrostructural division, both thematic and material, into two sections, often (if somewhat inaccurately) referred to as poems *in vita* and poems *in morte* of Laura. But every verse of the *RVF* virtually hinges on this dichotomous inclination, on a pull between thematic and linguistic opposites emphasized by the binary proceeding of Petrarca's poetic diction: damnation and redemption, *eros* and *caritas*, persistence and conversion, secular and heavenly, corporeal and spiritual.

We have noted the distinctive use of rhetorical devices, such as anadiplosis, hendiadys, dittology of synonymous and complementary terms, and antithesis: if these devices represent a typical stylistic cipher of Petrarca's diction, the sestinas foster their proliferation. The double sestina, furthermore, expands on the stylistic dichotomy epigrammatically expressed in *canzone* 125—v. 16, "parlo in rime aspre, et di dolcezza ignude" (I speak in harsh rhymes naked of sweetness)[71]—and develops it into a poetic analysis of the varied style, language, and thematic disposition that lyric poetry embodies in Petrarca's work: sweet and graceful versus harsh and hoarse; *dulcedo* and *lenitas* versus *asperitas* and *raucitas* (and even *subtilitas*, according to *RVF* 247, vv. 5–7, with possible philosophical implications). The metaliterary component of sestina 332 increases its theoretical depth if we assume, after Marco Grimaldi's persuasive survey, that the very notion of lyric in the Middle Ages is based on the dual value, moral and rhetorical, of *varietas*: in Petrarca's *canzoniere*, the variety of style (and meters and tones) is the textual equivalent of the protagonist's moral fluctuation and parallels the fragmentation of his soul.[72]

The notions of varied style, sweetness, and harshness affect all orders of linguistic signification. They first and foremost describe the varying musicality of Petrarca's style. They underline his attention to the phonetic values of poetic diction and confirm the reality—the essentiality, according to Franco Suitner[73]—of the *RVF*'s orality and aurality. This is amply corroborated by Petrarca's own notes in the already mentioned *codice degli abbozzi* (MS Vat. Lat. 3196), which Rosanna Bettarini has described as fragments "of a secret Rhetoric, of a private *De vulgari eloquentia*, itself scattered, intended for a phonic phenomenology of poetic facts."[74] At a phonetic level, *dulcedo* involves the search for euphony, harmony, and *eurhythmia*: it is mostly achieved through the *iunctura* (combination) of assonant or alliterating words (especially adjective and noun), with a special privilege for palatal vowels.[75] *Dulcedo* also implies an exercise in selection: the sweet lexicon seeks clarity, avoids crude loans (Latinisms, Gallicisms, but also Italian regionalisms), and rejects obscurity; the sweet syntax is plain and smooth, with a distinct preference for coordination over subordination. The risk of monotony and excessive uniformity is avoided (or dissimulated) by strategically inserting rare words, with which Petrarca also counterbalances the *canzoniere*'s notorious tendency to default to generic semantics; by complicating the syntax with sudden hypotactic spins (often organized in binary oppositions); and by attentively and sparingly using *rimas caras*, rhymes that are difficult because of the rarity of the endings involved and the number of sounds affected. Dante's *De vulgari eloquentia* (2.7) provides a plausible (if militant) gateway to understanding the stylistic domain of harshness as a quality of sound in the *RVF*. Dante associates the aural features of asperity to initial aspiration, certain consonant sequences (double consonants, liquid followed by occlusive), oxytones, monosyllables, and polysyllables with more than three syllables. Asperity often accompanies the intense speculative effort of *subtilitas* (subtlety).

The traits of varied style, sweetness, and harshness, however, affect the thematic and temporal orders of signification also—or, rather, are justified by the nature of the poetic persona as this is irreducibly split between hope and anguish, past and present, desire and contrition. The double sestina elaborates and dramatizes the conflict between the inescapable love for love (and glory) and the self's striving for a better alternative. The paralysis of will with which *canzone* 264—"I' vo pensando, et nel penser m'assale" (I go thinking and in thought pity for myself assails me)—opens the second part of the *RVF*, and the moral inconclusiveness that the *Secretum* stages through the *dramatis personae* of *Franciscus* (Petrarca) and *Augustinus* (Augustine), are now reoriented toward categories of style and resemanticized in terms of contemplation of life and death.

Dulcedo and *Asperitas*

Varietas requires the controlled combination of the opposite registers of *dulcedo* and *asperitas* to achieve a homogenous poetic diction in which extremes are continuously balanced and their conflict is tentatively resolved. This subsection and the next focus on the rhyme-words *stile* and *rime* and on the various connotations and sign orientations that their modifiers assign to them: v. 3, "dolce stile" (sweet style); v. 12, "ogni stile" (every style); v. 13, "amoroso stile" (amorous style); v. 20, "agro stile" (bitter style); v. 28, "vo . . . cangiando stile" (I go changing . . . my style); v. 35, "sì vario stile" (so varied a style); v. 39, "doppia lo stile" (redoubles his style); v. 48, "debile stile" (weak style); v. 49, "sì pietoso stile" (so sorrowful a style); v. 56, "doloroso stile" (grieving style); v. 64, "mutato stile" (changed style); v. 71, "antiquo stile" (ancient style); v. 74, "aspro stile" (harsh style); and then v. 4, "in versi e 'n rime" (in verses and rhymes); v. 11, "non vanno in rime" (cannot go into rhymes); v. 15, "u' son giunte le rime" (where are the rhymes); v. 24, "basse rime" (low rhymes); v. 25, "mie rime" (my rhymes); v. 32, "roche rime" (hoarse rhymes); v. 40, "lacrimose rime" (tearful rhymes); v. 47, "tessea in rime" (I wove . . . into rhymes); v. 51, "senza rime" (without rhymes); v. 60, "canto et piango in rime" (I sing and bewail in rhymes); v. 61, "stanche rime" (weary rhymes); v. 68, "ch'ascoltate d'Amore o dite in rime" (who listen about Love write in rhymes); v. 74, "angosciose rime" (anguished rhymes). More specifically, what follows is an analysis of the semantic and poetological itinerary that marks the contextual, sequential, and contrastive use of these rhyme-words in the double sestina.

The first stanza connects love poetry and the stylistic category of *dulcedo* (vv. 3–4):

> e i soavi sospiri e 'l dolce stile
> che solea resonare in versi e 'n rime.

> (and gentle sighs and a sweet style
> that used to resound in verses and rhymes.)

The sweet style, which used to coincide with the writing of poems "in versi e 'n rime," is now presented as an irretrievable poetic mode. Through the alliteration of the sibilant, the imperfect "solea" is intimately connected to "stile," "soavi sospiri," and the infinitive "resonare." The imperfect implies repetition and continuousness in the past. It may also allude to the similar shift in poetics—from *dulcedo* and *suavitas* to *asperitas* and *subtilitas*—that we read in Dante's "Le dolci rime d'amor ch'io *solea*" (The sweet love-poetry I was accustomed to seek out) (4 [LXXXII]; emphasis mine):[76] coexisting in Dante's *canzone* are the sweetly absorbed tone of his "dolci rime d'amor" (sweet love-poetry) of the past, and his "soave stile," vv. 1 and 10, respectively; and the sharpness and distinct speculative intensity of the "rima aspr'e sottile" (harsh and subtle rhymes) of this *canzone*'s doctrinal poetry (v. 14).

In the double sestina, poetic practice implicitly becomes the content of literary writing itself. Used fifty-one times in the *RVF* (but in fact 312 times if we also consider its cognates), the epithet *dolce* critically connotes stylistic sonority and sweetness.[77] In this context, it also implies, intertextually, a compendious historico-critical affiliation to the Tuscan literary tradition. On the other hand, the Latinism *resonare* seemingly echoes the beginning of Virgil's first *Bucolic* (v. 5): "formosam resonare doces Amaryllida silvas" (you teach the woods to resonate the name of beautiful Amaryllis). The pursuit of a sweet style would ideally conjugate here classical tradition and *uso moderno.*

But *dulcedo* does not appear to be a viable stylistic typology to express the poet's current emotional status. The second stanza exposes the futility of "ogni stile" (every style). The usual correspondence between style and sighs does not inspire new rhymes (vv. 11–12):

> I miei gravi sospir' non vanno in rime,
> e 'l mio duro martir vince ogni stile.
>
> ---
>
> (my heavy sighs cannot go into rhymes,
> and my harsh torment surpasses every style.)

The only outcome for poetry is a self-reflexive evaluation of poetry itself.

The third stanza more subtly implies the negation of poetic writing and calls into question the very plausibility of the sestina as a form. Poetic writing is associated here with the *ubi sunt* theme: questioning the transient character of all that is not divine.[78] Where for the classical tradition poetry exorcises human ephemerality and evanescence—it is, in Horace's words (*Odes* 3.30,

1) a "monumentum aere perennius" (monument more lasting than bronze)—here the third stanza questions the validity of both poetry in general and this poem in particular. The anguished question "u' son giunte le rime" hides an amphibology: Where have the rhymes gone? but also, Where do the rhymes rhyme (where are they metrically linked)? This verse, in other words, probes both the plausibility of poetry and the peculiar nature of these *rimas*: *dissolutas* (disjointed, not rhyming within the stanza) and, consequently, not immediately *giunte* (interconnected).[79] Such explicit skepticism toward the ground of possibility for poetry compromises poetic writing at the moment of its own conception. Most rare in Petrarca's corpus, the apocopated form of the interrogative *u'* suggests that ineffability extends to the articulation of sound itself and reduces it to a quasi-aphasic (or, perhaps, apophatic) expression through a dark guttural sound.[80]

The fourth stanza (v. 20) depicts the poet's style as *agro* (bitter) and further underlines the various declinations of the erotic subject matter of the *RVF*. The mutual exclusiveness between *homo vetus* (old man) and *homo novus* (renewed man), the duality between "primo giovenile errore" (first youthful error) and "quel ch'i' sono" (what I am now) of the *RVF*'s incipitarian sonnet (vv. 3–4), correlate with two opposite registers of poetic diction—sweetness and harshness—reconcilable only through the rigorous exercise of *varietas*. The double sestina goes so far as to insinuate that the gravity of this pathetic experience is no longer an acceptable subject matter for poetic writing (v. 24): it cannot constitute the "alto soggetto" (high subject) of the poet's "basse rime" (low rhymes), which formerly served as consolation and relief even when expressed in the stylistic modes of *asperitas* (harshness). The *sestina doppia* ostensibly (if not irretrievably) reevaluates the admissibility of poetry itself, when poetry is deprived of one of its major sources of inspiration: the hope, however vague and delusional, for earthly love. The double sestina questions, in sum, the conceivability of a songbook *in morte*. It was hope that had previously allowed for a fluctuation between *asperitas* and *lenitas*. To the reader's surprise, the poet's nostalgia even makes sweetness and harshness overlap in his memory (vv. 19–20):

> Già mi fu col desir sì dolce il pianto,
> che condia di dolcezza ogni agro stile.

(Formerly, so sweet with desire was weeping
that it seasoned with sweetness every bitter style.)

The rhetorical principle of the *conveniens* or *aptum*—the necessary poetic and ontological correspondence between subject matter and style—is the topic of metaliterary analysis in the fifth, sixth, and seventh stanzas. Stylistic *varietas* (v. 28: "io vo col penser cangiando stile," "I go changing with my cares my style") is the direct emanation of the poet's sentimental situation after Laura's death. The variable style of the fifth stanza anticipates the "sì vario stile" (so varied a style) of the sixth (v. 35), with a clear echo that once again reverberates from the double sestina back to the *canzoniere*'s opening sonnet. Stylistic mutations affect the analysis and expression of the poetic persona's sorrowful (*tristo*) status, which has replaced what was once glad (*lieto*). As Claudia Berra has pointed out, *RVF* 332 voices *asperitas* by articulating the insisted-upon use of the Stilnovistic lexicon of sorrow and anguish through a specific set of phonetic-rhythmic characteristics: an unusual frequency of monosyllables; the use of oxytones or apocopated words in caesura; the dissemination of double consonants and consonant sequences conventionally perceived as harsh (occlusive followed by the vibrant /r/); and, above all, the diffused presence of the /r/ sound.[81] The double sestina, in other words, both thematizes and performs *asperitas*.

Reduplication

Frasca indicates that "the sixth stanza, which should ideally close the sestina's theme before the doubling impulse, revisits the 'stylistic' effects of the death of the beloved, giving way to the reduplication of the style by the verification of its change."[82] When we move from the poem proper to its relationship to the macrostructural and thematic level, the shift from sweet style to sour verses (v. 32: "roche rime," "hoarse rhymes") also seems to correspond to the *canzoniere*'s partition into the two sections—its *bifrontismo* (bifront structure), as Roberto Antonelli termed it.[83] In chapter 6, we have noted the rhetorical affinity between the sestina as form and various figures of repetition.[84] In the seventh stanza of the double sestina, the presence of many such figures—*geminatio*, *reduplicatio*, *polyptoton*, *figura etymologica*, *anaphora*, *epiphora, paronomasia*—is systemic, structural, and thematic. Figures of repetition, in other words, inform the poem's content and articulate the orchestration of its discourse (vv. 37–42):

> Nesun visse già mai più di me lieto,
> nesun vive più tristo et giorni et notti;
> et doppiando 'l dolor, doppia lo stile
> che trae del cor sì lacrimose rime.
> Vissi di speme, or vivo pur di pianto,
> né contra Morte spero altro che Morte.

> (No one ever lived more glad than I,
> no one lives more sorrowful both day and night
> or, sorrow doubling, redoubles his style
> that draws from his heart such tearful rhymes.
> I lived on hope, now I live only on weeping,
> nor against Death do I hope for anything but death.)

In the stanza cited here, the *polyptoton* of the verb *doppiare*—in line with that "incitement to dichotomy" that Contini isolated as a distinctive trait of the sestinas' diction[85]—invests the overall syntactic structure of the period and the prosodic alignment of the stanza, punctuated by figures of repetition and variation (also informed by a general *parallelismus membrorum*). These figures include the various series of antitheses (*lieto*/*tristo*, *giorni*/*notti*, *vivo*/*Morte*); the *figura etymologica* ("speme . . . spero"); the anaphora of "nesun," combining the intensity and uniqueness of the poet's existential experience with his claim of poetic self-awareness; the dicolon of complementary/antithetical terms ("et giorni et notti"); the quadruple *polyptoton* of *vivere*, emphasizing that self-awareness through a switch from past tense to present, from third person to first person; and, conversely, the *conduplicatio* of *Morte*, which increases the pregnancy of its meaning along the verse. The immediate *anadiplosis* of *Morte*—which closes v. 42 and opens v. 43—states that the only defense against spiritual death is Death itself. Its signifier moves back from its position as rhyme-word, and is disseminated thrice within a single verse (vv. 43–44):

Morte m'à morto, et sola pò far Morte
ch' i' torni a riveder quel viso lieto.

(Death has killed me, and only Death
has the power to make me see again that glad face.)

In a self-referential spin, death has become the only content that the poet's verses can express (v. 33): "non sanno trattare altro che morte" (cannot treat anything but death). The philosophical implications of the verb *trattare* (to treat) seems to imply the same stylistic *subtilitas* of Dante's *canzone* (11, [LXXXIII] 30) "Poscia ch'Amor del tutto m'ha lasciato" (Since Love has completely abandoned me): vv. 68–69, "con rima più sottile / tratterò il ver di lei, ma non so cui" (with more subtle rhymes, I will set down the truth concerning it—though for whom I do not know).[86] The rhetorical strategies of repetition model the duplication of this *sestina doppia*, whose seventh stanza reignites the permutation of the forms. They also articulate the bipartite structure (narrative, stylistic, conceptual, and material) of the *RVF* into poems gravitating around (if not altogether centered on) the poet's relationships to Laura's *vita* and *morte*.

In the ninth stanza (v. 49), the doubled (and, perhaps, infinitely amplifiable) sestina proposes a style that is "pietoso" (sorrowful)—arguably better translated with its active meaning of "inducing to piety." The outcome of such "pietoso" style is ultimately the writing of this very *sestina doppia*, here (v. 51) defined in terms of poetry "senza rime" (without rhymes). This definition underlines the continuity between metrical feature and stylistic principle. This implicit reference to the sestina's versification technique is embedded into the overarching mythical episode of Eurydice and Orpheus (vv. 49–52):[87]

Or avess'io un sì pietoso stile
che Laura mia potesse tôrre a Morte,
come Euridice Orpheo sua senza rime,
ch'i' viverei anchor più che mai lieto!

(Would I had so sorrowful a style
that I could win my Laura back from Death

as Orpheus won his Eurydice without rhymes,
for then I would live more glad than ever!)

Orpheus's metrics and prosody (quantitative, not accentual) involve no rhyme scheme and are, quite literally, without rhymes.[88] As the optative subjunctive of the *adynaton* corresponds to the unattainable dimension of the myth, so do the poet's own *coblas dissolutas* represent the vernacular counterpart of the unrhymed meters of classical poetry. In the *sestina doppia*, the myth of Orpheus and Eurydice takes over that of Apollo and Daphne: it becomes, as suggested by Luca Marcozzi, the "central mythopoetic core of the *canzoniere*."[89] Orpheus becomes, in other words, a new *Doppelgänger* for the poet. Worth noting here is that Petrarca does not align with the tradition of those medieval exegetes who read Orpheus as a typological *figura Christi* (because Orpheus, like Christ, also defeated death): Nicola Gardini has remarked that "the myth of Orpheus in Petrarca's *canzoniere* comes directly from the classical source, not contaminated by allegorizing readings of subsequent ages."[90] To put it differently, Orpheus's victory over death through poetry is illusory: he, like the *persona loquens* of Petrarca's *canzoniere*, is eventually destined to lose his beloved. The Apollonian myth of Daphne already signified the ephemerality of love, poetry, and poetic glory. In the emblem of the ever-escaping nymph, the myth also pointed toward the unattainability of any definitive poetic expression. Sestina 332 also assigns to Orpheus a high degree of metaliterary connotation. The myth of Orpheus's unsuccessful *katabasis* further emphasizes the consciousness of the fugacity of time and the evanescence of poetry. What emerges from the severe *hyperbaton* separating substantive and possessive adjective (v. 51, "Euridice . . . sua") is the tragic awareness of the inescapable lability of any human achievement.

In the eleventh stanza, the sestina encompasses the various opposite poles—the weeping and the speaking, the sorrow and the hopes—toward which Petrarca's poetry is directed and for which he hoped to gain the readers' piety and obtain their forgiveness in the very proemial sonnet (*RVF* 1, vv. 5–6): "del vario stile in ch'io piango et ragiono, / fra le vane speranze e 'l van dolore" (for the varied style in which I weep and speak between vain hopes and vain sorrow). Here in the double sestina, stylistic mutation (v. 64: "mutato stile," "changed style") now leans toward *asperitas* as the obvious counterpart of a thematic mutation. And in the twelfth stanza, the mutation of style involves Death herself, when the poet—echoing, again, the very first verse of the *RVF*—addresses an audience of lovers, readers, and writers and asks them to pray Death to let him die (vv. 67–72):

> O voi che sospirate a miglior' notti,
> ch'ascoltate d'Amore o dite in rime,
> pregate non mi sia più sorda Morte,
> porto de le miserie et fin del pianto;
> muti una volta quel suo antiquo stile,
> ch'ogni uom rattrista, et me pò far sì lieto.

> (O you who sigh for better nights,
> who listen about Love or write in rhymes,
> pray that Death be no longer deaf to me,
> the port of misery and the end of weeping;
> let her for once change her ancient style
> that makes everyone sorrowful but can make me so glad.)

The poet is exhausted by the split consciousness of his fragmented self, and he is moved by his own exhaustion. By unveiling the inefficacy of any attempt by Orpheus (and therefore, antonomastically, by poetry) to eventually regain Eurydice, he also relinquishes the fiction of his own erotic discourse. Death is the only desirable linear development and outcome that can prevent from the frustrating cyclicity of the sestina's form. De Robertis noted that "the *canzoniere* is established by and under Laura's death: which paradoxically means by and under the death of the topic and of the motive itself for poetry."[91] If Laura and poetic laurel coincide, her disappearance then makes death the ultimate poetic motif.

If from sestina 142 the *tornada* reconfigures the rhyme structure of the first stanza—with the alternation of the rhyme-words in desinential and internal positions: (A) B (C) D (E) F—here the reoccurrence of the initial rhyme scheme intimates the dreaded possibility of further iterations and reconfigurations of the form (vv. 73–75):

Far mi pò lieto in una o 'n poche notti:
e 'n aspro stile e 'n angosciose rime
prego che 'l pianto mio finisca Morte.

(She can make me glad in one or a few nights,
and in harsh style and anguished rhymes
I pray that my weeping may be ended by Death.)

The supplication to Death to end the poet's *planh*, which, in fact, constitutes the theme of the sestina itself, is also a request for closure—and an explicit—for this poem, the ultimate embodiment of an "aspro stile" (harsh style) that produces "angosciose rime" (anguishing rhymes).

As Marco Ariani maintains, Petrarca's vernacular classicism is based on technical mastery and self-awareness.[92] Here, metapoetic and metatextual reflections operate on multiple levels: they affect the *sestina doppia* itself, the songbook, and their poetic diction at large. On the one hand, they ground the microstructural level of the poem (subject matter, style, genre, prosody, and meter of *RVF* 332): their eminently self-referential nature dramatizes the potentialities of the poem's own writing and reproducibility. And on the other hand, they reflect the macrostructural level of the songbook (the narrative and bipartite structure of *RVF*): they reflect, in other words, material features of the book-text of the *RVF.*

Tornada: Closure and Conclusions

Barbara Herrnstein Smith argues that closure is the readers' appreciation of conclusiveness, finality, and integrity based on their experience of the poem as a structural whole: closure occurs when formal changes at the end of the poem disrupt the formal expectations the poem had established.[93] And Giorgio Agamben suggests that the sole purpose of textual devices such as *tornadas* and envoys is to affirm the end of the poem, "as if the end needed these institutions, as if for poetry the end implied a catastrophe and loss of identity so irreparable as to demand the deployment of very special metrical and semantic means."[94] When it comes to the sestinas in Petrarca's autograph of the *RVF* (with the exception of the double sestina), a visual and metrical pattern is first established through six 6-line stanzas, then disrupted by the 3-line *tornada*. This violation brings about the ultimate revelation and recognition of the poem's structure by means of the formal changes it presents. By combining this disruptive device with structural features (such as the poem's address to itself as a text in *RVF* 237) or thematic references to existential and poetic conclusiveness (the last word of *RVF* 332 being "Morte"), the *tornada* announces that the poem is complete and/or materially ready for circulation. Without this sanction of closure, the possibility of repeating the first stanza's rhyme scheme or (as also shown by the *sestina doppia*) restarting the cycle of permutations is theoretically unlimited: despite the textual cohesiveness of Petrarca's sestina and the algebraic exactness of the relationship among its rhyme-words, the device that actually qualifies as a rigorous boundary for the sestina is, in the end, the *tornada*.[95]

The *tornadas* underscore one of the textual elements that emerges most urgently from the sestinas' convergence of prosody, meter, and material arrangement: a tension between holistic closure and defiance of it, between structural cohesiveness and, conversely, resistance to completion. On the one hand, there are the rigorously interweaving rhyme structure, the tight interconnection of textual elements, and the formal conclusion imposed by the visually distinct *tornada*. But on the other hand, beginning with sestina 142, the return of the rhyme pattern to its initial configuration at the end of its first rhymical cycle—the first six stanzas—implies the potential reopening of the sestina, the actual reduplication of the form of the *sestina doppia*, and the virtual continuous reiteration and amplification of the poem's form.[96] If the material features and the metrical structure of Petrarca's sestinas are responsible for a tension between aperture and closure, centripetal and centrifugal forces, the end of a cycle and its continuous reinvention, the *sestina doppia* epitomizes this tension. On the one hand, the double sestina illustrates that the rhyme scheme is capable of endless reiteration, and that it cannot be reduced to a closed system. On the other hand, its eminently self-referential and metatextual nature dramatizes the potentialities of its own writing and reproducibility.

When we consider this immanent tension between openness and closure as the sestinas' potential mode of articulation—which finds its entelechy in the *sestina doppia*—we realize that this tension reflects the longing for a final closure to the book of the *RVF*, frustrated by the continuous activity of its revision and reordering. Using Petrarca's Latin from *Familiares* 11.3, Picone observed that the "fragments" collected in the *canzoniere* retell a *fabula inexpleta* ("unfinished tale"), centered on its own development rather than its conclusion. Consequently, Dante's metaphor of the book as all-encompassing semiotic vehicle in the final canto of the *Commedia* (*Paradiso* 33.85–90) is substituted by Petrarca's eponymous *fragmenta* and their various *ersatz*-terms disseminated throughout the *canzoniere*: "The book is replaced by the parts that compose it (such as rhymes), or by the instruments or materials that were used to produce it (such as pens)."[97] When we observe the materiality of the *RVF*'s autograph, we see that the frustrated aspiration to finality observed by Picone has a direct material counterpart in the manuscript's instability and its shift, over the course of its transcription, from fair copy to service copy, with the insertion over time of ten new bifolia (fols. 41–48, 49–52, 63–66, and 67–70) and the project of recombination involving the last thirty-one poems of the songbook (on fols. 66v–72v).[98] The renumeration of these poems with brown Arabic numerals in the margins sanctions a new postponement of the book's closure, as elusive and inaccessible as Daphne's and Eurydice's ever-fleeing figures.

But more generally, it is the very technique of permutation and recombination of the sestinas' rhyme-words that functions as a microtextual correlative of the *canzoniere* as a macrotext in progress. Storey argues that "each composition's revision reinterprets the larger genre structure of the song book itself."[99] In other words, the technique of permutation of the sestina reflects Petrarca's practices of substitution, *rasura* ("erasure"), and revision, which continuously refunctionalize the whole arrangement and systemic organization of the *RVF*. The metrical concurrence of *retrogradatio* and *crucifixio* brings about a continuous regressive reconfiguration that elicits the simultaneous consumption of the text in all its parts. At the microtextual level of the sestina, the linear reading from left to right and downward needs to be compensated by the retrogressive and upward pursuing of the rhyme-words. Analogously, at a macrotextual level, any new intervention throughout the sequence of the compositions or within a single poem demands the overall reconsideration of the *canzoniere* as system and of its occult geometries. Petrarca's work, Aldo Scaglione pointed out, is "never definitive, unless in a relative sense."[100] With its ambivalent nature as a further-amplifiable (and ever-perfectible) text and nonmodifiable cohesive structure where everything is tightly intertwined, the sestinas reproduce *en abyme* the systemic characteristics of Petrarca's songbook. By reflecting both the *canzoniere*'s indissoluble organic structure and the continuous permutation and revision of its parts, the sestinas also underscore the unremitting practice of *labor limae*—both literal and figurative—which (with compelling evidence) distinguishes Petrarca's literary and editorial project.

Coda

In his in-depth study of the interactions between meter and syntax in the sestina as the form developed and evolved from its troubadour antecedents to the Renaissance Petrarchists' exercises and beyond, Frasca has explained that the sestina operates as the "most special *canzone*, the locus assigned to the counterpoint and, in a way, the summary of the forces engaged on the field of love's dynamics."[101] When we more specifically direct our attention to the sestina in the *RVF*'s autograph, we further recognize that the particular presentational style of the sestina—which counterbalances progression with retrogression, sequentiality with simultaneity—makes this genre particularly suitable for expressing the ideology and poetics of Petrarca's conflictual *eros*: it makes the sestinas the *canzoniere*'s "poems of poetics." And in the double sestina, this ever-precarious and illusory balance of conflictual forces explicitly occasions Petrarca's lucid self-scrutiny regarding the essence and form of his poetry and songbook.

The interaction between the material codification of the sestina's textual signifier, its metrical orchestration, and the reflexive (and often antinarrative) features of its content all concur to lend this poetic form a character of retrospection that assumes the spatial form of a metatextual refraction. The narrative content in textual form of the sestina and its material expression—its writing—provide the reader with guidelines, if not constraints proper, for its consumption and interpretation. Petrarca's artistic and editorial program associates the scribe's activity with the poet's by fostering an ideal coincidence between literary expression and writing, text and book, poem and leaf.[102] Corrado Bologna remarked that we see in Petrarca "an osmosis of creative thinking, organizational design, metamorphic rethinking, and pagination technique."[103] Petrarca's artistic and intellectual project, in other words, implies a bijective relationship between the material domain and the textual codomain, wherein each element of the former is paired with exactly one element in the latter. Writing about Petrarca's autographs—and MS Vat. Lat. 3195 in particular as Petrarca's intended best possible "reading book"—Petrucci indicated that "the perfect textuality, directly emanating from the author and warranted by his autograph, was (and always remained) the guarantee of absolute legibility for the reader."[104] Although the autograph's "perfect textuality" and "absolute legibility" proved crucial for determining an authoritative text, during the proto-diffusion and early circulation of the *canzoniere* the complexity of the autograph's textual and material strategies did not prove easy to reproduce serially.[105] Only the autograph itself and a few manuscripts from the late fourteenth and early fifteenth centuries preserve Petrarca's sophisticated system of *mise-en-texte* and *mise-en-page*. In studying a corpus of twenty-nine manuscripts of the *canzoniere* antedating the dissemination of the new humanistic book form in *littera antiqua* in the fifteenth century, Cursi found a full adherence to Petrarca's textual solutions in only eleven codices.[106]

A remarkable example of material nonconformity to Petrarca's editorial program is MS Riccardiano 1088, a paper codex of seventy folios, dated between the end of the fourteenth century and the beginning of the fifteenth, and conserved in Florence in the Biblioteca Riccardiana.[107] Manuscript Riccardiano 1088 is a multitext codex, which preserves a vernacular version of Aesop's fables, an anthology of Tuscan poets (from Dante and Guido Cavalcanti to such lesser-known poets as Pietro Faitinelli and Lancillotto Anguissola), and a redaction of Petrarca's *canzoniere* (in the "Malatesta form").[108] It is written by one main hand, with minor additions by two other scribes and various annotations in modern hands. The copyist starts transcribing the poems of Petrarca's *canzoniere* in two columns, the odd verses on the left and the even verses on the right, with the significant exception of the sestinas, which are copied in a single column on fols. 17r, 20rv, and 25v. After fol. 26v, a sudden change of pen, ink, and layout occurs. Halfway through his transcription, the copyist places the often cited, dramatic testimony of his scribal resolutions. From now on, he tells the readers on fol. 27r, he will discontinue the practice of following different layouts for different metrical genres, distancing himself from Petrarca's conventions as he knew them from the antigraph before him and as we know them from the autograph of the

RVF. Instead, the copyist will uniformly transcribe poems of any type in the same format, one verse per line, proceeding vertically:

> Non mi piace di più seguire di scrivere nel modo che ò tenuto da quinci adietro cioè di passare da l'uno colonello a l'altro, ançi intendo di seguire giù per lo cholonello tanto che si compia la chançone o sonetto che sia.[109]
>
> (I don't wish to continue writing the same way I have done so far, that is, switching from one column to the other. Instead, I plan on writing down one column until either the *canzone* or sonnet is complete.)

An urge for standardization and simplicity here replaces a more "respectful" approach to the *mise-en-page* of the exemplar and Petrarca's authorial (and authoritative) editorial decisions.[110] The attitude of the copyist of MS Riccardiano 1088 seems to provide a material confirmation of Remigio Sabbadini's criterion for detecting trivializations in textual traditions: *poeta variat, librarii iterant*.[111] The poet varies and opts for specific solutions, whereas copyists repeat and tend to uniformity.

The passage from manuscript to print further witnessed the progressive detachment between Petrarca's material resolutions and the finished editorial artifact. With the advent of print, the author is effectively excluded from the process of mechanical reproduction, kept out of the printing works where the separation between text form and book form is progressively institutionalized. Practical and financial reasons gradually impose standardized serial reproductions over the individual choices dictated by writers' artistic purposes. The early printings of Petrarca's *canzoniere* in the fifteenth and sixteenth centuries reflect this tendency, in compliance with the streamlining of various textual styles into the one we now know. In the case of Petrarca's *RVF*, three early editions profoundly influenced the text's subsequent print history: the *editio princeps* ([Venice]: Vindelinus de Spira, 1470); the Valdezoco edition (Padua, 1472); and the Aldine (Venice, 1501), curated by Pietro Bembo.[112] Presumably prepared by Cristoforo Berardi of Pesaro, as the cryptic reference in the colophon—"Christophori et feruens pariter cyllenia cura" (by Christophorus's zealous Cyllenian care)—seems to suggest, Vindelinus's elegant edition in roman type reflects the "Malatesta form" of Petrarca's *canzoniere* rather than the last version transmitted in MS Vat. Lat. 3195. Paduan jurist and printer Bartolomeo de Valdezoco and Prussian printer Martinus de Septem Arboribus published the first edition of the *canzoniere* (and the *Triumphi*) to work directly from Petrarca's autograph—"ex originali | libro extracta" (derived from the original), as the colophon reads—which at the time was preserved in Tommasina Savonarola and Daniele Santasofia's family library in Padua. Flawed by a number of transcriptional errors, the Valdezoco edition preserves Petrarca's punctuation system but dismisses the meter-specific textual styles of the autograph. The copy text that Bembo later prepared for Aldo Manuzio's publishing house (now MS Vat. Lat. 3197), contrary to the exaggerated claims of the Aldine's colophon—"tolto con | sommissima diligenza dallo scritto di mano me | desima del Poeta" (transcribed with utmost care from the very Poet's autograph)—was not derived from Petrarca's autograph and was only collated against it at an advanced stage of Bembo's transcription. The Venetian editions prepared by Alessandro Vellutello (de Sabbio, 1525, then reprinted twenty-six times before the end of the sixteenth century) further established an actual separation between Petrarca's *canzoniere* and the products of the printing press: Vellutello codified the practice of encapsulating the text with a commentary, in a notable departure from Petrarca's "minimalist" editorial project; and more importantly, this heavy-handed editor-commentator reorganized the poetic sequence to establish a (nonauthorial) chronological order and a narrative coherence in the allegedly scattered *scartafacci* (loose leaves) on Petrarca's desk.[113]

The conscious dismissal of Petrarca's editorial strategies by the "imprudent copyist" of MS Riccardiano 1088 had, by Vellutello's time, effectively become common practice.[114] The diversified visual and scribal techniques that Petrarca had cultivated until the very last days of his life were thus irretrievably lost within the first few decades of editorial intervention in his work after his death.

Afterword

In Praise of Materiality

> A method that fits the small work but not the great has obviously started at the wrong end.
>
> —Edgar Wind, *Pagan Mysteries in the Renaissance*, 238

An Ostentatious Materiality

The present book set out to investigate medieval Italian literature in its indissoluble nexus of materiality and textuality. Its theoretical and procedural premises are grounded, on the one hand, in the unique singularity of each text-book in manuscript culture, and on the other hand, in the essential and unavoidable reality that to produce, transmit, consume, and interpret literary works necessarily involves a material medium. The overarching contention of *Manuscript Poetics* is that an adequate understanding of medieval literary works demands a coordinated analysis of both their material and their textual features: how a book is made defines how a literary text is composed—and even conceived—and defines the practices through which it is read and interpreted.

This is not a wholly new and unique line of inquiry—not least in the field of medieval Italian studies—as has been documented in the book's notes throughout. But this book's approach has afforded the opportunity to apply the premises and contention succinctly indicated in the previous paragraph to a broad and heterogeneous selection of literary texts and books. This project has brought an interdisciplinary set of tools to works by the three major authors of the Italian Middle Ages; in attempting to cross over manuscript studies, history of the book, medieval and humanistic philology, and literary theory, its ambition has been to articulate a more systematic appreciation of how the corelationship of materiality and textuality produces meaning. The ostentatious materiality of medieval literature, to put it differently, provides more than a substrate that displays and transmits texts; rather, it is an integral component of what (and how) those texts mean, and it calls attention to specific aspects of their meaning. The textuality of medieval literature—oral, written, printed—in turn, subsists in a sensuous and utterly objectual form: authors, scribes, patrons, and readers, in their corporeal presence, interact with that objectual form; the materiality of their bodies further mediates the sensible and multisensorial experience of mediums (and of their technologies) as well as the intellectual understanding of how literature is incorporated into those mediums. In medieval literature, certainly—and easily also in the literature of prior and subsequent periods—literary works exist only in the material interactions that command their production, tradition, and consumption.[1] Literary works, in other words, entail actions on the matter that forms and formalizes them at the level of both production (in the author's handling of the writing toolkit) and reception (in the reader's contact with the physicality of the book-object).

The conspicuous number of extant autographs in vernacular from the fourteenth century—and the editorial and aesthetic planning they entailed—could indicate the need to further reassess the poststructuralist notion of author as depersonalized function. Despite the anonymity, pseudonymity, partial onymity, and obscure identity that often characterized medieval authorship and its collaborative and choral textuality, authors regain a corporeal immanence in the context of a reasserted relationship between their embodied personae and the material texts they produced. Authors thus resist the progressive abstraction and dematerialization to which they and their works have often been reduced in the various theoretical obituaries written for them in the twentieth century and beyond. And they resist the grammaticalization of their literary selves into structural "positions" and a hyperformalization of their works that disproportionally privileges forms, codes, and genres.[2] In

Dante Alighieri's *Vita nova*—if only within the textual domain of its fictionalized representation—we have observed how Dante represents himself as an embodied author who passionately chronicles the composition, performance, circulation, and commission of his poems, and how he authoritatively details the material and textual features of his works. In the autograph of the *Teseida*, Giovanni Boccaccio authorizes his vernacular epos by encoding in it the authorial figures of *auctor*, commentator, and scribe, and also by devising material differentiations—such as in layout and script—for their respective manifestations and activities. In the autograph of Francesco Petrarca's *Rerum vulgarium fragmenta*, the corporeal presence of the author is directly engaged in the unity of aesthetic control over the material and textual components of the *canzoniere*: in Petrarca's poetics, composing is tantamount to transcribing.

The actual participation of various writer figures in the production of their works is coextensive with and reflected in the high degree of literary self-awareness and meta-referentiality that we have observed in the literary texts examined here: in the *Vita nova*, the story in the book—the story of the author's poetic apprenticeship—is also the story *of* the book; in the *Teseida*, the commentator refers to and authorizes his authorial *Doppelgänger* using the third person; and in Petrarca's sestinas, we read a metadiscourse on poetic diction and on the poetry of the *canzoniere* itself. Underscoring these works' self-referentiality and their authors' self-awareness is not intended to constrain medieval literary texts to an insulated, closed system in which literature only writes (about) itself and the text's self-citation represents its own sense and ultimate coronation. Rather, the attention paid to the various types of metatextuality originates in the material presence of the authors' personalities in their works. This reaffirmed union of materiality and metatextuality finds its figurative counterpart in the repertoire of pictorial self-representations with which illuminators and scribes profusely documented their work and its instruments in the margins and historiated letters of illuminated manuscripts.[3]

The three parts of this book can be consulted as independent case studies on Dante's *Vita nova*, Boccaccio's *Teseida*, and Petrarca's sestinas in the *Rerum vulgarium fragmenta*. But the book's structure has been devised to illustrate and celebrate more generally—from the perspective of both authorship and readership—how the technology of the codex shapes all kinds of devices and conventions we would ordinarily classify as literary, such as expository order and discursive articulation of the plot, textual mediation of authorial voice, and meter. From the opening proposal to investigate literary works using the frame and terminology of Émile Benveniste's discourse model, the three resulting case studies have outlined patterns and exemplified instances where authors reveal a conscious awareness of the material forms and scribal practices available to them and capitalize on this awareness to layer meanings, to attempt to guarantee authoritative versions of their texts, to authorize and canonize their works, and to shape the experience of reading them. In the various instances of manuscript poetics examined in this book, the work's narrative and expository order (the substance and form of its utterance), the roles and functions of its various enunciative personae (the textual manifestations of the enunciator), and the very act of literary composition (the writing of poems, the act of enunciating) are modeled on, visualized through, and epitomized by exact book forms.

Part I of *Manuscript Poetics* illustrated that the narrative and poetics of Dante's *Vita nova* are predicated on the tangibility of the book *qua* material form. The reception and transcription of the *Vita nova* elaborated—albeit in diverging and unpredictable ways—on the interpretive suggestions and aspirations that Dante indicated for the prosimetrum at the most material level: the specific book form to contain and transmit the prosimetrum's textual cohesion, the reciprocal organization of poems and prose texts on the page, the text's subdivision into discrete sections, and even the work's title proper. Part II captured Boccaccio's staged impersonation, in the autograph of the *Teseida*, of various writer roles that matched his exploration of different literary genres and intellectual activities. Boccaccio's playful command of various textual styles to characterize the *auctor*'s poetry and the commentator's marginal and interlinear glosses contributed to the often diverging material treatment (and destiny) of these two authorial instances and ultimately shaped the poem's transmission and interpretation. Part III found in Petrarca's autograph/idiograph of the *Rerum vulgarium fragmenta* the most complete and final—albeit unfinished—realization of a manuscript poetics in which matter, form, and substance (of expression and content) sublimely coincide. Petrarca chose specific material forms for specific textual forms. In the *Rerum vulgarium fragmenta*'s autograph, the text of the sestinas is born of and bound with its materiality: the corpus of the sestinas maximizes its verbal-iconic signification potential—and its function as designated ideological spine of the *canzoniere*—through its spatial isolation in the autograph and the visual enhancement of the poems' retrogressive meter.

Codex to Kindle

We have herein underscored how the materiality of mediums affects all elements of the literary system. The materiality of mediums also affects our situation—as agents conducting humanistic research—in relation to the objects of our investigations. This book has advocated for and practiced a literary criticism that centers on the book-objects of manuscripts and early printed editions. Documents in their "original" material form have an inherent value for research that goes beyond nostalgia for their aura, bibliophilism, and familiarity with or affection for them: they are indispensable for recapturing otherwise irretrievable aspects of the past and more thoroughly appreciating the literary objects we seek to understand.

Autoptic descriptions relying on the specialized terminology of manuscript studies—and on quantifiable data—follow necessarily from the recognition that materiality and meaning are inextricably entwined. Directly examining codices is crucial for ascertaining specific aspects of their formation. For instance, analyzing a book's fasciculation—the structural organization of its quires—can shed light on the fabric of the book and point toward the cultural project behind its creation. We have observed how different commissioners, compilers, and scribes variously integrated Dante's *Vita nova* into their manuscripts based on different interpretations of Dante's prosimetrum and in turn shaped and constrained the range of interpretations for subsequent readers. And we have mentioned how, in the autograph of the *Rerum vulgarium fragmenta*, Petrarca used fascicles as separate codicological units in a way that allowed him to edit or erase poems and add on new ones without undermining the songbook's presentational harmony and literary coherence. The autograph's fasciculation, to put it differently, can be summoned as material witness to Petrarca's constantly evolving poetics.

The autoptic examination and updated description of primary sources, furthermore, can bring forth what was previously ignored, forgotten, or left out. We have seen how material evidence of continuity between oral *cantari* and epic poetry resurfaced in a heretofore overlooked codex of Boccaccio's

Teseida. A material approach to textuality can expose the various and often lesser-known actors involved in the making and consuming of books. The elusive Bartolomeo di Tomaso—who left his somewhat humorous possession note on the exemplar of Boccaccio's *Teseida* we examined in chapter 5—may remain relatively unknown, but his unrefined *mercantesca* script evokes the cultural environment of Florence's newly literate mercantile society. And the various scribes and illuminators mentioned in the archival sources of the duchy of Ferrara regain their individual artistic personalities when they are linked—if only tentatively—to the Ferrarese manuscripts of the *Teseida*. Through the autoptic examination of manuscripts, then, we can glimpse the collaborative scenarios and aesthetic relationality of medieval and early modern literature.

Even the most scholarly and reliable critical editions necessarily standardize historically specific textual styles and sacrifice unique material presentations in the legitimate interest of delivering a text that is more legible for the modern reader.[4] It is disheartening to consider the implications of superimposing a standardized layout onto the sophisticated interplay of medium and poem that we have seen in the specific case of the sestinas in Petrarca's songbook. But when we further consider instances of nonlinear and nontextual elements, such as glosses, neumes, or images, then the superimposition of a standardized design seems even more detrimental to an adequate appreciation of medieval works.

But the documents that were used in researching this project came in various other material forms: physical facsimiles, digital reproductions, diplomatic editions, critical editions, and digital editions. A trans- and multimedial approach to medieval materiality and textuality brings about a deeper awareness of medium-specificity, exhibits the individual features of different inscription technologies and material supports, and challenges the assumption of their neutrality and transparency. Marshall McLuhan underlined how media catalyze scholarly attention when they are made obsolete and replaced by new media.[5] The notion of a manuscript poetics, after all, makes sense only in retrospect: Lisa Gitelman has argued in her media history of documents and paper that "far from being a simple precursor, manuscript stands as a back formation of printing."[6] Manuscript, in other words, acquires a marked character (and a name) only with the advent of print. Before printing, writing exists only as handwriting. And in the first two centuries of printing with movable type in Europe, David McKitterick has shown in his reexamination of the relationship between manuscript and print in the early modern period, there seems to be no bibliographical nor bibliothecographical distinction between manuscript and print: they are described and catalogued—and even stacked—in the same way.[7]

The questions *Manuscript Poetics* asks join others scholars have raised regarding how changes in book technology affect the reception and understanding of verbal and visual information. In a fundamental treatise on codicology, Alphonse Dain recognized the opportunity to investigate what the transition from scroll to codex meant for the book.[8] We can eventually hope to see an equally needed comprehensive study of what the transition from analogue to digital texts means for the book.[9] Such a study could also shed light on the consequences of this transmigration for medieval philology and the literary criticism of medieval and early modern texts.[10]

On the one hand, the digital does not represent an a priori advancement over the analogue. Digital facsimiles of medieval manuscripts cannot deliver the same depth of information regarding the original materials they reproduce. And digital surrogates rarely convey the same experience of nostalgia that even material facsimiles can sometimes evoke. On the other hand, when medieval manuscripts and early printed books migrate to—and are made easily available in—networked environments, they can facilitate new and enhanced modes of inquiry and also augmented editorial and curatorial practices.[11]

This project unfolded over several years and across two continents. Throughout the research process, digital facsimiles made it possible to isolate portions of text and emphasize the contours of unclear scripts. Image enlargement, layering techniques, altered color levels, and the use of filters—even with relatively inexpensive raster graphics editors such as Adobe Photoshop—made it less arduous to decipher heavily damaged or obscured portions of text.[12] Digital facsimiles enabled virtual but straightforward side-by-side comparisons of digital images with critical text and also comparisons between manuscripts otherwise irremediably separated by library walls and geographical distance.[13] They allowed me to continuously "shuffle" and display fragile materials without compromising the latter's integrity.

All the necessary caveats about social and economic inequality marking resource distribution notwithstanding, the digital remediation of medieval manuscripts and early printed editions can expand access to a significant degree.[14] It can promote shared expertise and real-time feedback. It can make what is unique ubiquitous.

Excusationes Non Petitae

The materiality of mediums alike affects scholars who perform humanistic research and the objects of their research. Michel Foucault underscored in a seminal essay on the genealogical method that knowing subjects and objects of knowledge exist in a relationship of codependency.[15] Historical investigations cannot be undertaken independently from the epistemic situatedness—and the positionality—of the researcher conducting those investigations. Exposing this situatedness with its inherent limitations does not undermine the outcomes of those inquiries: rather, it inscribes in them the premises for further investigations.

The ambitious goals of integrating multiple fields of scholarship, of abstracting from the material and textual particularities of the three case studies a more general methodology and procedure, and of inscribing the unique specificities of individual book-objects within a broader theoretical frame inevitably set up their own complications and lacunae: more codices could have been examined; more attention could have been paid to the crucial transition from manuscript to print; different theoretical models—especially from the fields of visual studies and material culture studies—could have been considered. And an updated investigation into the material, metatextual, metaphorical, and metaphysical coherence of the figure and idea of the book in Dante's *Commedia* remains a desideratum that the present book has only begun to address.

A critical discourse on the materiality and textuality of the *Vita nova*, the *Teseida*, and the *Rerum vulgarium fragmenta*—perhaps any discourse on each of these works—faces the same risks Mario Lavagetto attached to studying the narrative frame of Boccaccio's *Decameron*: the immense secondary literature inevitably brings about unconscious and good-faith plagiarisms; students and scholars alike risk producing only the repetition of that which has already been written and contributing no more than "a systematic—if, unfortunately, self-unaware—suppression of quotation marks."[16] The Three

Crowns of Italian literature command a heterogeneous and intimidating bibliography. As researchers, we elaborate on the data and hypotheses that previous scholars collected, advanced, and generously shared with us, striving to fill in details and add meaning. Optimistically, this book will achieve the type of literary criticism James Wood describes in his memoir *The Nearest Thing to Life*: one that may not always be especially analytical or innovative but is rather "a kind of passionate redescription."[17] And potentially readers will see some value in the way existing scholarship is referenced and scrutinized through the lens of material textuality. A material approach to medieval textuality, in other words, can help us revisit both the primary sources and the interpretive work on them that has accrued and evolved over the centuries.

Understanding material features in symbolic terms is always speculative and rarely conclusive, and the findings of a particular investigation are often hardly applicable to a broader corpus of texts. A statement such as Armando Petrucci's, on Petrarca's effort to mold in his obituary gloss for Laura a script aesthetically expressive of that gloss's content, is as illuminating and brilliantly formulated as it is difficult to emulate and extend.[18] Similarly, when we consider Boccaccio's encyclopedic command of multiple textual styles, literary genres, and artistic practices, or Petrarca's sublimely coherent integration of materiality and textuality as foundation for his literary production, it remains unclear how far these should be characterized as unique and isolated solutions and how far they might emerge as illustrations of wider patterns of medieval poetry and poetics applicable beyond the unique personalities of these artists and the autograph testimonies of their authorial practices.

A certain sense of undigested heterogeneity lurks behind the scope of addressing three works—produced over the course of a century by three influential authors—pertaining to three different literary genres and summoned here to exemplify three aspects of literary communication. The differing state of these works' manuscript tradition—and especially the absence of Dante's autographs—further complicates the comparative project. Readers will have noticed the interpretive shift from studying the textual representation of materiality (for the *Vita nova*) to working on materiality and textuality as they inhere in autograph registrations (of the *Teseida* and the *Rerum vulgarium fragmenta*). This afterword offers no palliative for this loss of a parallel in structure. But that inevitable shift has allowed for a more expansive investigation of the multiple domains—from the perspectives of both authorship and readership—in which the relationships between materiality and textuality impact medieval poetics.

In an essay that concluded with a warning against the delusions of all crypto-positivistic conclusions, Maria Corti described literature as an "unruly subject matter."[19] Literature is contumacious and unbending not only in its prerogatives of mobile and ever-elusive social event—as argued by Corti—but also in the quantifiable and allegedly indisputable facts of its materiality. With all our measuring, counting, describing, attributing, situating, charting, deciphering, decoding, deconstructing, reconstructing, and critiquing, we may attain only a precarious and ephemeral understanding of literary phenomena. *Manuscript Poetics* has attempted to recognize this unruliness in its most material repercussions and to celebrate—and further complicate—literature's inexhaustible and fruitful recalcitrance to being tamed.

NOTES

INTRODUCTION

1. Kahn, "Lecture," 271.

2. The bibliography on writing materials in classical antiquity is, of course, extensive. For a general introduction to the topic, see, among others, including for additional bibliography, Kenyon, *Books*; Turner, *Greek Manuscripts*; Reynolds and Wilson, *Scribes and Scholars*, "Antiquity," 1–43; and Bülow-Jacobsen, "Writing Materials." On *ostraca*, see Maltomini, "Greek *Ostraca*," and Caputo and Lougovaya, *Using Ostraca*. On *ostraca* and school exercises, see Cribiore, *Writing*.

3. On the Sappho *ostracon* (Florence, Biblioteca Medicea Laurenziana, PSI XIII 1300) and its discovery, see, among others, Norsa, "Dai Papiri"; Malnati, "Revisione"; Cribiore, *Writing*, 231–32; Ferrari, "Due note"; Pintaudi, "Ermeneutica"; Canfora, *Il papiro*, 135–38; and Coppola, "Scritti," 86–89. For the text of Sappho's poem (including references to its indirect transmission), see Lobel and Page, eds., *Poetarum Lesbiorum Fragmenta*, 4–5 (Fragment 2), and Voigt, ed., *Sappho et Alcaeus*, 33–36 (Fragment 2); for an English translation, see Campbell, ed. and trans., *Sappho and Alcaeus*, 56–59.

4. As we shall see in chapter 6, MS Vat. Lat. 3195 of Petrarca's *canzoniere* (housed in the Biblioteca Apostolica Vaticana) is partially autograph (in Petrarca's hand) and partially idiograph (transcribed by a professional copyist under Petrarca's supervision). Sonnet 25 is on fol. 5v. On the acrostic structure of sonnet 25, see Brugnolo, "Libro d'autore," 105–6. On the autograph, see chapter 6, "*Nugelle*" and note 3

5. For material approaches to literature, see, among others, Levenston, *The Stuff*; Eliot, Nash, and Willison, *Literary Cultures*; and Allen, Griffin, and O'Connell, *Readings*. For recent studies in medieval Italian literature inspired by the material turn in literary history and criticism, see, below, note 9.

6. On writing/reading interfaces, see, among others, Mak, *How the Page*; Emerson, *Reading*; and Bornstein and Tinckle, *The Iconic Page*.

7. See Goodman, *Languages*, 112–15. Goodman dismisses the material features of literary works: "Let us suppose that there are various handwritten copies and many editions of a given literary work. Differences between them in style and size of script or type, in color of ink, in kind of paper, in number and layout of pages, in condition, etc., do not matter. All that matters is what may be called *sameness of spelling*: exact correspondence as sequences of letters, spaces, and punctuation marks" (115).

8. For a definition of *mise-en-page* (layout, page design), see Muzerelle, *Vocabulaire*, 109: "Disposition générale des différents éléments figurant sur une page" (General disposition of the various elements appearing on a page). For a definition of *mise-en-texte*, see Maniaci, *Terminologia*, 159 (*s.v.* "Presentazione del testo"): "Insieme delle operazioni relative all'organizzazione della pagina e alla sua utilizzazione (scrittura, decorazione, collegamento tra il testo e la glossa)," "All the procedures concerning the organization and use of the page (writing, decoration, connection between text and gloss)." The *mise-en-page* of a text includes features such as indentation, justification, ruling, columns, and spaces between paragraphs; the *mise-en-texte* includes elements such as abbreviations, punctuation, textual segmentations. For a comprehensive examination of *mise-en-page* and *mise-en-texte* in antiquity and the Middle Ages, see Martin and Vezin, *Mise en page*. See also Chang, Grafton, and Most, *Impagination*.

9. See Daniels, *Boccaccio*; Eisner, *Boccaccio*; Todorović, *Dante*; Banella, *La "Vita nuova"*; and Arduini, *Dante's "Convivio."* And see also Holmes, *Assembling*; Steinberg, *Accounting*; and Barolini and Storey, *Petrarch*.

10. See Benveniste, "L'appareil"; Greimas and Courtés, *Semiotics*, "Enunciation (*énonciation*)," 103–5, "Enunciator/Enunciatee (*énonciateur/énonciataire*), 105, and "Utterance (*énoncé*)," 362–64; and Ducrot and Todorov, *Encyclopedic Dictionary*, "Enunciation," 323–31.

11. See Barbi, *La nuova filologia*, x–xi.

12. As indicated above, note 4, MS Vat. Lat. 3195 of the Biblioteca Apostolica Vaticana—which preserves the *Rerum vulgarium fragmenta*—is partially autograph (in Petrarca's hand) and partially idiograph (transcribed by a professional copyist under Petrarca's supervision).

13. See Merleau-Ponty, *Phenomenology*, 181–84.

14. See Chartier, "Laborers," 53. See also Cavallo and Chartier, *A History*, "Introduction," 1–36 (esp. 1–5).

15. But cf., among others, Irvine, "Medieval Textuality"; the essays in the 2006 special topic issue of *PMLA* (121, no. 1) on *The History of the Book and the*

Idea of Literature (esp. Price, "Introduction"; McDonald, "Ideas"; and Lerer, "Epilogue"); and the essays in the 2018 special topic issue of *Comparative Literature* (70, no. 3) on *The Material Turn in Comparative Literature* (esp. Brillenburg Wurth, "The Material Turn"; and Baetens, "Visual-Verbal Materiality").

16. See Ginzburg, "Our Words," esp. 107–11; and Ginzburg, "Storia dell'arte," esp. 276–77. On emic and etic categories (and on the insider/outsider debate), see, including for additional references, Headland, Pike, and Harris, *Emics and Etics*.

17. Shillingsburg, *Resisting Texts*, 101. All emphases in quoted material in this book are original unless otherwise indicated.

18. Derrida, *Of Grammatology*, 14.

19. For a critical approach to the notion of materiality (and matter), see, among others, Wolfreys, "Materialism/Materiality"; Miller, "Materiality"; Brown, "Materiality"; Björkvall and Karlsson, "The Materiality"; and Mitchell, "Materiality." On materiality in the context of book studies and literary criticism, see, at least, Gumbrecht and Pfeiffer, *Materialities*; Greetham, *Textual Transgressions*, "Interweave 13: Materiality/Book as Meaning," 438–54, and "Book as Meaning/Meaning in the Book," 456–66; Ayers, "Materialism"; Rockenberger, "Materiality"; and Treharne and Willan, *Text Technologies*, "Conceptual Framework," 1–31. On the connections between literary criticism and studies in book and print culture, see, among others, Howsam, *Old Books*. On the relationships between literacy, writing, materiality, and technology, see Haas, *Writing Technology*, "The Technology Question," 3–23.

20. See Kittler, *Gramophone*, xxxix: "Media determine our situation which—in spite or because of it—deserves a description."

21. In a hendiadys, two coordinated terms are used to express a single concept: thus "materiality and textuality" would here mean "material textuality." In a hypostatic union, two or more natures subsist nonhierarchically in one entity: materiality and textuality would then be different modes and manifestations of a unique substance. On the distinction between artworks' immanence (their material presence) and transcendence (the experiences they produce), see Genette, *The Work*. On the tangibility of cultural phenomena (before and beyond the reconstruction of their meaning), see Gumbrecht, *Production*.

22. See, at least, McKenzie, "Typography," and McKenzie, "Bibliography"; McGann, *The Textual Condition*, esp. 3–98; Storey, *Transcription*; Petrucci, "Dal manoscritto antico"; and Petrucci, "La scrittura," esp. 62–65. On McKenzie's and McGann's textual theories, see Greetham, *Theories*, "Society and Culture in the Text," 367–432.

23. McKenzie, "Typography," 200.

24. McGann, *The Textual Condition*, 77.

25. See how McLuhan described his *The Gutenberg Galaxy* in relation to Harold Innis's work in what was originally published as introduction to the 1964 edition of Innis, *The Bias of Communication* ("Media," 90): "I am pleased to think of my own book *The Gutenberg Galaxy* (University of Toronto Press, 1962) as a footnote to the observations of Innis on the subject of the psychic and social consequences, first of writing and then of printing."

26. Petrucci, "Dal manoscritto antico," 112: "il tasso di partecipazione diretta, cioè propriamente grafica, dell'autore all'opera di registrazione scritta di un suo testo in una qualsiasi fase della sua elaborazione, dal materiale preparatorio alla prima traccia, agli abbozzi, fino alla stesura finale."

27. On autographs in ancient Rome, see, among others, including for additional bibliography, Cavallo, "Testo," 307–18; and Dorandi, *Nell'officina*, "Tra autografia e dettato," 47–64.

28. See Chiesa and Pinelli, *Gli autografi medievali*; Petrucci, "Autografi"; and Long, *Autografia*.

29. See Bartoli Langeli, "Francesco d'Assisi."

30. See chapter 1, "Metanarrative Models and Method."

31. The substance of the next few paragraphs is based on Petrucci, "Alle origini"; Petrucci, "Minute"; Petrucci, "Reading"; Petrucci, *Breve storia*; Petrucci, "La scrittura," esp. 61–76; Petrucci, "Storia e Geografia," 127–94; Ornato, *Apologia*, esp. 7–18; Robins, "The Study"; and Busby and Kleinhenz, "Medieval French." See also Attridge, *The Experience*, "The Twelfth and Thirteenth Centuries: Performing Genres," 177–205 (esp. 194–201).

32. Petrucci, "Minute," esp. 152–58, showed that notary practices of authentication also influenced the perception of autography, authorship, and authenticity, with particular reference to the trust ascribed to the written word, the attention to the precise transcription of a statement, and the correctness of quotations. A notary act required the direct participation of a notary (in fact, the author of an autograph), was supposed to be unique, implied a progressive articulation into different phases of writing, and would explicitly show any sign of corrective intervention. We will find references to and analogies with these writing practices in the three authors studied in this book. And it is worth pointing out that men of letters in the thirteenth and fourteenth centuries were often affiliated with chanceries or grew up in notaries' families. On the relationship between notarial culture, the secularization of intellectual life, and literary production in Italy from the twelfth to the fourteenth centuries, see, among others, including for additional bibliography, Witt, *The Two Latin Cultures*, chaps. 9–12.

33. The thirteenth century also saw the gradual affirmation of the book-object as private property and commodity as well as the parallel proliferation of autographs and "traces" (brief occasional texts adventitiously inscribed on the fly-leaves of manuscripts). On the notion of *traccia* (trace), see Petrucci, "Spazi," and Stussi, "Tracce."

34. On the *pecia* system, see, among others, Destrez, *La Pecia*; Fink-Errera, "La produzione"; Pollard, "The *pecia* system"; and Ornato, *Apologia*, "I testi giuridici commentati e il sistema della *pecia*," 102–27.

35. See Panofsky, *Gothic Architecture*, 30–35.

36. See, at least, Petrucci, "Reading," 179–94.

37. See, among others, Petrucci, *Breve storia*, 162–86, and Ornato, *Apologia*, "Il libro umanistico fra tradizione e innovazione," 128–42.

38. The bibliography on orality, literacy, and literature in the Middle Ages is extensive. See, among others, Bäuml, "Varieties"; Ong, "Orality"; Bäuml, "Medieval Texts"; Saenger, "Silent Reading"; Zumthor, *La lettera*; Doane and Pasternack, *Vox Intexta*; Zumthor, "Una cultura"; and Duggan, "Modalità."

39. See Gasparri, "Authenticité."

40. On *dictare* and *scribere*, see, among others, Saenger, "Silent Reading."

41. See Carruthers, *The Book*, 4–7; but cf. Torrell, *The Person*, 28–29 and n42 for the reading *illegibilis* (vs. *inintelligibilis*).

42. See Halliwell, ed. and trans., *Poetics*, 28–29, for the passage in Aristotle's *Poetics* alluded to here.

Chapter 1

1. Avalle, *Latino "circa romançum,"* ix–xv: "registr[o] intermedi[o]" (but cf. Marazzini, *La lingua italiana*, 151–52). The text is on fol. 3r of MS LXXXIX of the Biblioteca Capitolare in Verona. A third line, an expression of gratitude to God in proper Latin, is by a different hand; see Petrucci and Romeo, "L'*Orazionale* visigotico."

2. I cite the interpretive transcription from Tagliavini, *Le origini*, 524–27 (translation mine). See also Monteverdi, *Saggi neolatini*, 39–58.

3. See Schiapparelli, "Note paleografiche," 113.

4. See De Bartholomaeis, ed., *Rime giullaresche*, 3.

5. For an account of the "discovery," see De Bartholomaeis, "Ciò che sia," and Rajna, "Un indovinello."

6. De Robertis, *Il libro*, 5: "il primo libro." Appropriately, De Robertis underscores the nature of the *Vita nova* qua book from the very title of his essay.

7. The secondary literature on the date of composition of the *Vita nova* is extensive; see, among others, including for additional bibliography, Carrai, *Il primo libro*, 21–34; Casadei, "Puntualizzare"; Carrai, "Puntualizzazioni"; Casadei, "Dalla *Vita nova*"; Barolini, "The Case"; Ciavorella, "Sulla composizione"; Bertolucci Pizzorusso, "La *Vita nova*"; Inglese, *L'intelletto*, 60–67; and Rea, *Dante: Guida*, 14–17.

8. Santagata, *Dal sonetto*, 136: "un libro subdolo." Carrai, *Dante elegiaco*, 15, also writes on the *Vita nova*'s "inclassificabilità" (unclassifiable nature).

9. On the *Vita nova* as prosimetrum, see, among others, Dronke, *Verse with Prose*, 107–14; Petrocchi, "Il prosimetrum"; Picone, "Il *prosimetrum*"; and Battaglia Ricci, "Tendenze prosimetriche," 57–65. I use the term "prosimetrum" in the loose acceptation generally adopted in Dante studies. The most comprehensive study of late antique and medieval prosimetra (Pabst, *Prosimetrum*) is often, if vaguely, referenced in scholarly articles on Dante's *Vita nova* (and *Convivio*). Pabst's chryselephantine catalogue, however, explicitly excludes the *Vita nova*: his definition of "prosimetrum," in fact, programmatically leaves out all citational works (including self-citational works) and, more generally, all texts characterized by a metaleptic transgression from framing to framed discourse (see Pabst, *Prosimetrum*, esp. 1:12). I use "poetic autobiography" in the sense proposed by Gilson, *Dante the Philosopher*, 91: "As a poetic autobiography, the *Vita Nuova* may permit itself foreshortenings or extensions of perspective according to the poet's taste." See also Auerbach, *Dante: Poet*, 61: "Thus the *Vita nuova* is useless as a source of information about Dante's actual biography; the events that occur in it, the meetings, journeys, and conversations cannot have taken place as they are set forth and no biographical data can be derived from them."

10. Botterill, ". . . però che la divisione," 61.

11. More specifically, five *canzoni* (of which one is monostrophic and one consists of two stanzas), one *ballata*, and twenty-five sonnets (of which three are *rinterzati*). On the variety of lyric genres in the *Vita nova*, see Picone, "Traditional Genres," 151–54 (later expanded and reelaborated in Picone, "Songbook").

12. On the two time frames for the composition of the poetry and the prose, see, at least, Shaw, *Essays*, "The Date," 1–52; Apollonio, *Dante*, 1:330–35; and Leporatti, "Ipotesi."

13. For a historical and theoretical introduction to the topic, see, at least, Garin, "La nuova scienza"; Curtius, *European Literature*, "The Book as Symbol," 302–47 (326–32 on Dante); Spitz, *Die Metaphorik*, 41–46; Büttner, "*Mens divina*"; Josipovici, *The World*, "The World as a Book," 25–51; Blumenberg, *Die Lesbarkeit*, esp. 9–85; Gellrich, *The Idea*, 29–93 and 139–66; Jager, *The Book*,

esp. 74–77; and Blumenberg, *Paradigms*, 70–72 and 75–76. For more specifically on Dante's treatment of the topic, see, at least, Spitzer, *Studi*, "Osservazioni sulla *Vita Nuova* di Dante," 103–7; Singleton, *An Essay*, "The Book of Memory," 24–54; Battistini, "L'universo"; Landoni, *La grammatica*, 71–85; and Fenzi, "Il libro."

14. Ahern attributes Dante's expertise on what we would now call the codicological aspects of the book and the material dimension of its production and circulation to his still-elusive stint in Bologna. See Ahern, "The Reader," 28, but cf. Petrucci, "Storia e geografia," 160.

15. But cf. Kelemen, "Carattere," 47: "Da qui [*sc.* dalla relazione tra Dante autore e testo] gli viene lo zelo ardente, ossia la premura, quasi maniaca, di corredare di commenti le sue opere. Come se non avesse fiducia nella forza delle parole e si sentisse ostacolato dal carattere finito e chiuso del *signifiant*, egli raddoppia (e potenzialmente rende infinito) il sistema significativo" (Hence [*sc.* from Dante's relationship, as an author, to the text] he derives his ardent zeal, or rather, his almost maniacal urge, to provide his work with commentaries. As though he did not trust the words' force and felt hindered by the finite and closed character of the *signifiant*, he doubles [and renders potentially infinite] the signifying system). These three chapters in this book on Dante argue, rather, that what concerns Dante is the excess of the signified over the signifier and the impossibility of conditioning the reception of his work once it has been "published."

16. Ong, "The Writer's Audience," 16.

17. Studies on the metaliterary aspects of Dante's work (not strictly limited to the *Vita nova*) include De Robertis, *Il libro*, "Nascita della coscienza letteraria italiana," 177–238 (a critical inventory of the *libello*'s metaliterary lexicon); Iannucci, "Autoesegesi dantesca"; Abramé Battesti, "Les fonctions"; D'Andrea, "Dante interprete"; Barolini, *Dante's Poets*; Noferi, "Rilettura (I)"; Noferi, "Rilettura (II)"; Barolini, *The Undivine Comedy* (esp. chaps. 3, 4, 6, and 7); Barański, "Tres enim"; Barański, "'nfiata labbia"; Tavoni, "Il nome"; Bologna, *Il ritorno*; Mula, "Modus loquendi"; Marchesi, *Dante*; Wehle, *Poesia*; and Cachey, "Title, Genre." Picone investigated the metaliterary aspects of the *Vita nova* in a number of fundamental essays, to which I refer throughout this chapter and the next. These essays can be read in the Vitanovan sections of Picone, *Percorsi*, esp. 219–65, and Picone, *Studi danteschi*, esp. 23–145.

18. See, for instance, Giunta, *Codici*, 317–41 (esp. 337–41), and Giunta, "Su Dante lirico," 28–29.

19. On the general issue of Dante's self-exegesis, see, among others, Jenaro-MacLennan, "Autocomentarismo"; Sarolli, *Prolegomena*, "Autoesegesi dantesca e

tradizione esegetica medievale," 1–39; Perrus, "Dante critique"; Roush, *Hermes' Lyre,* 25–51; Barański, "Dante Alighieri"; Barański, "Dante *poeta* e *lector*"; Kelemen, "Carattere"; and Brilli, "Dante's Self-Commentary."

20. Ascoli, *Dante,* 197.

21. See Bellomo, "La *Commedia,*" 83–84.

22. I cite from the Dartmouth Dante Project: http://dante.dartmouth.edu (translation mine).

23. Bellomo, "L'Epistola," 16: "Il poeta rappresenta sé stesso nell'atto di scrivere attraverso un viaggio che è metafora della scrittura."

24. Reynolds, trans., *La Vita Nuova,* 11; Mazzotta, "The Language," 3; Sanguineti, "Per una lettura," 5: "non è racconto lungo, ma ragionamento storico intorno a un'idea di poesia"; Menocal, *Writing,* 13–14; Wehle, *Poesia,* 16: "un'opera di poesia, ma è al contempo poesia sulla poesia—poesia e metapoetica in uno"; Todorović, *Dante,* 3.

25. Barański, "Lascio cotale trattato," 3.

26. On the *divisio textus,* see Minnis, *Medieval Theory,* 145–59. On Occitan *razos* (and *vidas*), see Poe, "The *Vidas* and *Razos,*" and Burwinckle, "The *chansonniers,*" esp. 249–54. On Dante's models for exegetical prose, see Rajna, "Lo schema"; Crescini, "Le *Razos*"; De Robertis, *Il libro,* 207–23, and Sarteschi, "Uno scaffale" (on the influence of Brunetto's *Rettorica*); and Mazzaro, *The Figure,* "The Prose of the *Vita Nuova,*" 71–94. On the *divisioni* as form, see D'Andrea, "La struttura"; Botterill, ". . . però che la divisione"; Gorni, "Divisioni"; and Cherchi, "The *divisioni.*" On the relationship between self-exegesis and authority, see Levers, "The Image"; Picone, "La teoria"; Pacioni, "L'*auctoritas* poetica"; and Ascoli, *Dante,* 175–201.

27. The critical bibliography on each of these topics is extensive. For a brief survey of the various models that have been proposed, see Paolazzi, *La "Vita nuova,"* "Novità e fortuna di un prosimetro," 1–18. Studies specifically focused on the various models include Nasti, "La memoria," and Nasti, *Favole d'amore,* "La disciplina d'amore," 43–85 (Song of Songs); Stillinger, *The Song,* 57–72 (Psalms); Martinez, "Mourning Beatrice," and Allegretti, "Dante geremiade" (Lamentations); Nolan, "The *Vita Nuova*" (Ezekiel and Revelation); Picone, "Il *prosimetrum,*" 185–89, Picone, "L'Ovidio," esp. 196–99, Picone, "Per Ovidio," 298–306, and Picone, "Dante e il canone," 154–55 (*Remedia amoris*); and D'Andrea, "La struttura," 26–31, Lombardo, *Boezio in Dante,* 537–49, and Todorović, *Dante,* 18–66 (*Consolatio philosophiae,* with or without reference to its transmission in glossed manuscripts). On medieval *accessus ad auctores,* see Quain, "The Medieval Accessus"; on their influence on the *Vita nova,* see Todorović, *Dante,* 76–92. On the influence of *vidas* and *razos,* in addition to the ar-

ticles cited in note 26, above, see Poe, "The Poetics," esp. 86–93; Picone, "La *Vita Nuova* fra autobiografia e tipologia," esp. 71–73; and, including for additional bibliography, Todorović, *Dante,* 102–34. On Guittone's "book" as a model for the prosimetrum, see Leporatti, "Il libro," and Kay, "Redefining"; the manuscript preserving Guittone's metrical letters together with his letters in prose is one of the three early *canzonieri* of Italian poetry: MS Redi 9 (fols. 1r–38r) of the Biblioteca Medicea Laurenziana in Florence (generally indicated by the *siglum L*).

28. Stimulating (if asystematic) observations have, however, been made on the relationship between literary theory and narrative. See, for instance, Giovannuzzi, "Beatrice," 62: "L'enunciazione teorica [*sc.* sulla poesia], salvo rari casi, non occupa una zona ritagliata ai margini, si discioglie in immagini ed alimenta dall'interno la trama narrativa, fino ad essere indistinguibile rispetto ad essa" (The theoretical statement on poetry, except in rare cases, does not occupy areas set apart in the margins: it dissolves in images and nourishes the narrative plot from the inside, to the point of being indistinguishable from it); or Barański, "Dante Alighieri," 574: "Such explanations [*sc.* internal allusions providing critical aids to interpretation] tend to be closely integrated with the development of the action and with Dante's stylistic presentation of this. Literature and reflection on literature are tightly fused, so that it is rare to find examples of explicit and independent commentary in the poem." Barolini, *Dante's Poets,* and Barolini, *The Undivine Comedy,* have provided suggestions on the interplay between narrative, formal solutions, and metatextual discourse. *Dante's Poets* conjugates the study of the metaliterary aspects of Dante's work with the textual analysis of Dante's representation of his fellow poets: Barolini's interpretation, however, focuses more on notions of literary history than on the metanarrative aspects of Dante's works. More valuable methodological hints on the subsumption of metaliterary statements within the fibers of the enunciated have come from Barolini, *The Undivine Comedy*: e.g., in studying the relationship between figures of fraud and the necessarily mystifying language of fiction (see the chapter titled "Ulysses, Geryon, and the Aeronautics of Narrative Transition," 48–73); in investigating the mimetic nature of figurative arts in the terrace of pride as metatextual discourse on, and self-legitimation of, the artifactuality of the *Commedia* and the artistry of its author-scribe (chapter "Re-presenting What God Presented: The Arachnean Art of the Terrace of Pride," 122–42); and in instituting parallels between fiction, claims to truth, and otherworldly journey (chapter "Nonfalse Errors and the True Dreams of the Evangelist," 143–65).

29. Partial exceptions include Storey, "Di libello," esp. 281–90; Storey, "Following Instructions"; Barański, "Lascio cotale trattato," esp. 16–23; and

Todorović, *Dante*, 135–62. For recent studies on the materiality of the prosimetrum's manuscript tradition, see, among others, Eisner, *Boccaccio*; Todorović, *Dante*; and Banella, *La "Vita nuova."*

30. To my knowledge, the term *Meta-ization* was first employed by Hempfer, "Die potentielle Autoreflexivität," 130.

31. See, at least, Wolf, *Ästhetische Illusion*; Wolf, "Metareference"; Nünning, "Mimesis"; Nünning, "On Metanarrative"; Fludernik, "Metanarrative and Metafictional"; and Neumann and Nünning, "Metanarration and Metafiction."

32. The relatively few theoretical works on metanarrative and metafiction mostly focus on the antimimetic features of modern and postmodern works and generally lack a diachronic perspective. In my doctoral dissertation (Aresu, "The Author as Scribe," chap. 1,"Dante's *Vita Nova*: A Metaphorology of the Book," 41–90), I used theoretical models inspired by postmodern notions of metafictionality: e.g., Scholes, "Metafiction"; Alter, *Partial Magic*; Hutcheon, *Narcissistic Narrative*; Waugh, *Metafiction*; and Dällenbach, *The Mirror*. Those models, however, mostly focus on anti-illusionist and antimimetic functions of postmodern fiction.

33. Fludernik, "Metanarrative and Metafictional," 29.

34. On Dante's various forms of addressing the audience in his early poetry, see Auerbach, *Dante: Poet*, 36–38. This dialogic mode will feature distinctively in the narrator's addresses to his narratees in the *Commedia*; see, among others, Gmelin, "Die Anrede"; Auerbach, "Dante's Addresses"; Spitzer, "The Addresses"; Petronio, "Appunti"; Russo, "appello"; Ledda, *La guerra*, "Creare il lettore, creare l'autore: Dante poeta negli appelli al lettore," 117–58; and De Ventura, "Gli appelli."

35. See Nünning, "On Metanarrative." In her discussion of Nünning's model, Fludernik, "Metanarrative and Metafictional," more specifically locates metanarration on the level of discourse and situates the objects of metanarrative comments "*in* the story (commentary on the *histoire*), on the discourse level (commentary on the act of narrating), on the paratextual level (comment on the frame, title of a novel), and on the intertextual or intermedial level (comment on the novel, on aesthetics, on the novel and society, on poets and writers, etc.)" (16).

36. Nünning, "On Metanarrative," 22.

37. On Dante's dual nature of poet and character, the obvious reference is to Contini, *Varianti*, "Dante come personaggio-poeta della *Commedia*," 335–61 (at 341): "il soggetto del fare poetico" and "il soggetto dell'attività morale, del fare pratico." Bonaventure of Bagnorea's fourfold classification of writing figures (scribe, compiler, commentator, author)—which can be read in Fleming, ed.,

Opera Omnia, 1:14–15—has often been referenced to explain compositional aspects and functions of Dante's *Vita nova*; see, at least, Minnis, "*Amor*"; Stillinger, *The Song*, 1–22 and 45–72; Levers, "The Image"; Picone, "*Vita Nuova* fra autobiografia," 66; Picone, "La teoria"; and Todorović, *Dante*, esp. 8–9. Singleton, *An Essay*, "The Book of Memory," 24–54, describes Dante in terms of author, scribe, and commentator: although Singleton makes several references to other works by Bonaventure, he does not mention the latter's fourfold classification. See also chapter 4, "Authorship and Authority" and note 127, where Bonaventure's classification will be adopted to explain certain aspects of Boccaccio's multiple authorial identities. Picone, "Dante come autore/narratore," applies the narratological distinctions of empirical author, implied author, and narrator to the *Commedia*, and, more briefly (12–14), the *Vita nova*. Genette's model is applied to the *Commedia* by Ledda, *La guerra*, "'Dire grandissime cose': Protasi, invocazioni, indicibilità," 13–55, esp. 13–17. With regard to the *Commedia*, Santagata, *L'io e il mondo*, 364–66, recently proposed the notion of "arcipersonaggio" (archcharacter), articulated in author, narrator, and character. In its transition from one work to another, the *arcipersonaggio* progressively acquires new literary and autobiographical traits. For a cogent narratological approach to the *Commedia*, see Mezzadroli, "Enigmi." On authorship and authority in Dante, see also the recent Steinberg, "The Author."

38. See Genette, *Narrative Discourse*, "Person," 243–52, esp. 248.

39. Booth, *The Rhetoric*, 155.

40. Hugh's *Didascalicon* is cited from Migne, ed., *Didascalicon de studio legendi*, in *PL* 176:772A. The English translation is from Taylor, trans., *The "Didascalicon" of Hugh of St. Victor*, 92. On Hugh's reading and hermeneutical strategies in the *Didascalicon*, see, among others, Illich, *In the Vineyard*. On Dante's use of *sentenzia*, see Niccoli, "sentenza (sentenzia)." A crucial term in the proem and for the prosimetrum, *sentenzia* has been variously glossed in the commentaries *ad locum*: e.g., Contini, ed., *Letteratura*, 305–6, "interpretazione generale" (general interpretation) and "vero significato metafisico" (true metaphysical meaning); Gorni, ed., *Vita Nova*, 4, "definizione autentica e compendiosa" (compendious, authentic definition); Rossi, ed., *Vita Nova*, 6, "sostanza, parte essenziale" (substance, essential part); Carrai, ed., *Vita nova*, 41, "in sunto quanto meno il contenuto" (at least a summary of the content); and Pirovano, ed., *Vita nuova*, 78, "'la parte essenziale,' che per lui ha significato" ("the essential part," which is meaningful for him).

41. For the sake of clarity, I prefer to use here "hypodiegetic" instead of Genette's more widespread "metadiegetic" to refer to the second-degree narrative (story within the story). See Genette, *Narrative Discourse*, 231–34.

42. Kruger, *Dreaming*, 134 (and the whole of chap. 6, "Dreams and Fiction," 123–49). On dreams in the *Vita nova*, see Baldelli, "Visione"; Cervigni, *Dante's Poetry*, "Visionary Structure and Significance in the *Vita Nuova*," 39–70; Cappozzo, "Libri"; Steinberg, "Dante's First Dream"; and Livorni, "Dream."

43. Frisardi translates the Latin sentence in the footnote to p. 12: "My son, it is time for our false images [or simulations] to be put aside." The orthographic variation in the Latin between text and translation is because of the different editions used in this chapter (ed. Carrai) and as the base for Frisardi's translation (ed. Gorni).

44. See Salsano, "riguardare" (where, however, *VN* 5.10 [xii 3] is not listed), but cf. Allegretti, ed., *La canzone*, 25.

45. The citational nature of the prosimetrum has been underscored by Singleton, *An Essay*, "The Book of Memory," 25–54, and further investigated by Noferi, "Rilettura (I)," esp. 66–73. On the *Vita nova*'s self-citational practice, see also Stella, "La *Vita nuova*."

46. Gorni, ed., *Vita Nova*: 275: "quasi una 'vita nova' nella *Vita Nova*."

47. Nünning, "On Metanarrative," 23. On the notion of editor, see, among others, Villa, "Due schede," and Banella, *La "Vita nuova,"* 219–26.

48. See Genette, *Narrative Discourse*, 235, and Genette, *Métalepse*.

49. Fludernik, "Metanarrative and Metafictional," 22. On time structuring and tenses in *VN* 31 (xlii), see, among others, Harrison, *The Body*, "The Narrative Breakthrough," 129–43, and Levers, "The Image."

50. Genette, *Narrative Discourse*, 256.

51. Pirovano, "*Vita nuova*: A Novel Book," 157, reads these metatextual references as Dante's own indication of the prosimetrum's tripartite structure, in compliance with the symmetrical distribution of the poems (see ibid., 149–51 and n1 for previous bibliography): 10 + I + 4 + II + 4 + III + 10 (where Roman numerals indicate the three major *canzoni* and the Arabic numerals the number of shorter poems separating the *canzoni*, as previously noted, among others, by Singleton, *An Essay*, 79, and, for previous bibliography, 150). The dialectic between analepsis and prolepsis also affects the articulation of Dante's prose, resulting in the cohesion of its syntax and in its *legato* style (in the well-known terms formulated by Terracini, "Analisi").

52. Barolini, "Cominciandomi dal principio," 128. Barolini's essay proffers various examples (but not this one) of Dante's proleptic anticipations of the storyline.

53. Fludernik, "Metanarrative and Metafictional," 27. On Fludernik's subcategory of metacompositional, see note 63, below.

54. On the notion of ineffability in the *Vita nova*, see, at least, Colombo, *Dai mistici*, "'Ineffabile' e 'ineffabilitade' nella scrittura dantesca: la *Vita Nuova*, il *Convivio*, la *Commedia*," 31–51, esp. 31–36; and Fichera, "Ineffabilità."

55. See, at least, Antonelli, "La morte"; Gorni, "Beatrice agli Inferi," 146–51; Matucci, "Le 'tre ragioni'"; and Tavoni, "Converrebbe me."

56. Pirovano, ed., *Vita nuova*, 229 note *ad locum*: "Da questo punto centrale Dante invita il lettore a ripercorrere nuovamente la *Vita nuova*, rivestendo di nuova luce gli eventi raccontati, e lo fa suggerendo una chiave di interpretazione ontologica del numero dominante nel libello."

57. See Wehle, *Poesia*, "Del punto di vista," 9–16 (on the relationship between *fabula* and intertextuality); "Amare vuol dire poetare," 59–69 (on the reciprocity of love and love poetry); "Un libro di canzoni," 17–34 (on the selection and order of poems as a teleological inventory of *topoi*); "L'ascesa a un'altezza epica della parola," 71–120 (on female figures and typologies of poetic diction), and 109–16 (on the allegorical meaning of the microanthology in *VN* 30.1 [xli 1]).

58. On the dialectic and metaphysics of space in the *Vita nova*, see Shapiro, "Spatial Relationships."

59. Nünning, "On Metanarrative," 26.

60. I read the citation (referred to the *Commedia*) in Sollers, "Dante et la traversée," 15: "texte en train de s'écrire."

61. Nünning, "On Metanarrative," 27.

62. Dällenbach, *The Mirror*, 16.

63. Nünning, "On Metanarrative," 26. Fludernik, "Metanarrative and Metafictional," 23 and 26, adds the subcategories of metadiscursive ("metanarrative statements referring to the *ordering* of discursive elements in the text"), metanarrational ("metanarrative statements addressing the narratorial process and its participants"), and metacompositional, relating to "the *fictio* (rather than the *fictum*) status of the narrative discourse."

64. Martelli, "Proposte," 280: "'sbandate' sensuali."

65. For other cases of exclusion, see chapter 2, "Selection Mechanisms and Organizational Syntax" and "History and Chronicle of the *Libello*."

66. For the sake of clarity, I have opted for Frisardi's prose version of the sonnet from "Appendix A" of his translation; see Frisardi, trans., *Vita Nova*, 70–71. Frisardi's verse translation reads "[not] so far above my head" and "nimbly." The exact meaning of the two adverbs is debated. Scholars agree, however, that these expressions are intended both to define a stylistic ideal that pursues clarity and decorum and to underscore the poet's inadequacy before the task of praising Beatrice appropriately. See Crespo, "Il proemio," 6–7, and Paolazzi, *La maniera*, 117.

67. Emphasis and translation mine.

68. On Dante's theory of *cominciamento*, see Gorni, *Il nodo*, "La teoria del 'cominciamento,'" 143–86.

69. Allo-, proprio-, and general metanarration are Fludernik's translations into English of Nünning's *Fremdmetanarration*, *Eigenmetanarration*, and *Allgemeinmetanarration*. See Fludernik, "Metanarrative and Metafiction," 24.

70. See note 34, above.

71. The translation of the passage from *VN* 10.14 (xix 3), omitted by Frisardi, is mine. On the related topic of spatial metaphors denoting a narrative, see Barolini, *The Undivine Comedy*, 272–73n1.

72. On the spatial and nonspatial acceptations of *sotto* and *sopra* as well as their compounds, see the *GDLI*, *s.vv.* "sotto" (19:580–87); "sottoscritto" (19:607); "sottoscrivere" (19:607–8); "sopra" (19:425–30); and "soprascritto" (19:457).

73. Nünning, "On Metanarrative," 31.

74. On the notion of *novitas*, see Eberwein-Dabcovich, "Das Wort novus"; Tateo, "La *nuova matera*"; and, including for further bibliographical references, Ledda, *La guerra*, "Novità, incredibilità, meraviglia," 57–101. See also, Contini, *Varianti*, "Un'interpretazione di Dante," 399.

75. On the debated notion of medieval autobiography, see, at least, Zumthor, "Autobiography."

76. See Tonelli, "I tempi."

77. Goldknopf, "The Confessional Increment."

78. Chatman, *Story and Discourse*, 248.

79. Translation mine. Frisardi simply—and perhaps less precisely—interprets and translates "for him." On this form of commission poetry, see Giunta, *Versi*, 140–50.

80. On the notion of *ordo artificialis* (as opposed to *ordo naturalis*), see Lausberg, *Handbook*, 214 (§ 452). Leporatti, "Io spero," associates Dante's palinodic narrative to the argumentative strategy in Augustine's *Retractationes*.

81. See Picone, "Strutture poetiche," 124–27. As Santagata, *Amate e amanti*, 107, pointed out, "il canzoniere 'in morte' esiste solo in virtù del romanzo" (the songbook *in morte* exists only by virtue of the romance).

82. On the digression on poetry and poetics (*VN* 16 [xxv]), see, among others, Vallone, "*Vita Nuova* XXV"; Tateo, *Questioni*, "'Aprire per prosa,'" 51–75; Barański, "The Roots"; and Marchesi, *Dante*, 67–70 and 110–15. On the metalinguistic discourse of *VN* 16 (xxv) within the context of Dante's linguistic thought, see also Tavoni, "*Vita nuova* XXV 3," and Manni, *La lingua*, 31–32.

83. This is especially the case for various commentaries *ad locum*.

84. See, for instance, Leo, "Zum *rifacimento*."

85. See Candido, "Per una rilettura," esp. 31–39. On the *mise-en-abyme* in Dante's *Commedia*, see Ginzburg, "Dante's Blind Spot," and Ginzburg, "*Mise-en-abyme*."

86. See Dällenbach, *The Mirror*, 94–106. Dällenbach maps his description of the *mise-en-abyme* onto Jakobson's model of verbal communication and distinguishes a *mise-en-abyme* of the utterance, a *mise-en-abyme* of the enunciation, and a *mise-en-abyme* of the code. On Dällenbach's notion of *mise-en-abyme*, see Dickmann, *The Little Crystalline*, 11–30. On the rhetorical and theoretical implications of the *mise-en-abyme*, see also Ricardou, "The Story"; Verrier, "Le récit"; and Berta, *Oltre la Mise en Abyme*. On metalepsis and *mise-en-abyme*, see Cohn, "Metalepsis."

87. See Limentani, "Effetti," and Infurna, "Intertestualità."

88. See, at least, Ahern, "Dante's Last Word," 10; Dronke, "The Conclusion," 30; Güntert, "Canto XXXIII," 510; Tavoni, "La visione," 84–88; Rossini, *Dante*, 55–80; and Orsbon, "The Universe." See also the appendix to part I in this book.

89. On the veil of Veronica in the *Vita nova*, see Vettori, "Veronica," and Eisner, *Dante's New Life*, "The Veronica (*Tipped-in*)," 192–215. On Dante's interaction with the pilgrims as a reminder of his quest for Beatrice, see Picone, *"Vita Nuova" e tradizione*, "*Peregrinus amoris*: la metafora finale," 129–72.

90. On *imagine* (and imagination) in the *Vita nova*, see Borsa, "Immagine." The term *imagine* is used to indicate the poet's recollection of Beatrice in the early *canzone* (*Rime* 10 [LXVII, 20]) "E' m'incresce di me sì duramente" (I pity myself so intensely), in which the metaphor of the book of memory is also used for the first time: vv. 43–44, "L'imagine di questa donna siede / sù nella mente ancora" (The image of that lady still reigns up in the mind); v. 59, "nel libro della mente che vien meno" (written in the book of the mind that is passing away); and v. 66, "e se 'l libro non erra" (and if that book does not err). The term *mente* also occurs in vv. 20 and 87. The *canzone* is cited according to De Robertis's *editio minor* of Dante's lyric poems (ed., *Rime*, 131–41 [2005]); in the bibliographical indication *Rime* 10 (LXVII, 20), the first Arabic numeral references the collocation in De Robertis's edition, the Roman numeral and the Arabic numeral in parentheses reference, respectively, collocations in Barbi, ed., *Rime*, and Contini, ed., *Rime*. The English translation is by Foster and Boyde, eds. and trans., *Dante's Lyric Poetry*, 1:54–59 (no. 32). On "E' m'incresce di me sì duramente" (in addition to Contini's and Barolini's introductions to the *canzone* in their respective editions), see, at least, Barbi, "Per chi e quando"; Pazzaglia, "*E' m'incresce*"; Cristaldi, "Dante lettore," 67–76; Fenzi, "*E' m'increscе*," esp. 160–66; Barolini, "A Cavalcantian

Vita Nuova"; Marrani, "*E' m'incresce*"; and Barolini, *Dante's Lyric Poetry*, 175–76. See also chapter 3, "*Novus Libellus*."

91. See Auerbach, *Scenes*, "Figura," and Franklin-Brown, *Reading*, 38–48 and 333n18. See also Cerquiglini, "Histoire, image."

92. Pirovano, ed., *Vita nuova*, 279: "Se essi troveranno a Roma la tanto desiderata reliquia del volto di Cristo, Dante ha trovato nella propria poesia la reliquia di Beatrice, che aveva inutilmente cercato di riprodurre nel disegno (xxxiv) e che gli era sembrato di intravedere sul viso della donna pietosa e gentile (xxxvi)." The corresponding paragraphs in Carrai's edition are 23 and 25.

93. On the hagiographic features of the *Vita nova* as *legenda Sanctae Beatricis* and, in Hollander's words (*Studies*, 18), of Dante as *scriba Beatricis*, see, among others, Marigo, *Mistica e scienza*, esp. 37–40; Schiaffini, "La *Vita nuova*"; Branca, "Poetica del rinnovamento"; and Pazzaglia, "La *Vita Nuova*"; but cf. Picone, "La *Vita Nuova* fra autobiografia," and Picone, *Percorsi*, 225–31. On the evangelical elements in the *libello*, see Bàrberi Squarotti, "Introduzione," 24–30; Bàrberi Squarotti, "Artificio," 45–62; and Cristaldi, *La "Vita Nuova,"* esp. 171–78. On Beatrice as *figura Christi*, see Singleton, *An Essay*, "The Death of Beatrice," 6–24; Singleton, *Journey*, "Advent of Beatrice," 72–85; and Rea, *Dante: Guida*, 80–82. On Beatrice's numerology (and angelology), see, including for previous bibliography, Gorni, *Lettera*, "Il numero di Beatrice," 73–85; Vecce, "Beatrice"; Vecce, "Ella era," esp. 176–78; and Rea, *Dante: Guida*, 73–79. On the literary premises of Dante's use of the angel imagery, see, at least, Roncaglia, "Precedenti."

94. Auerbach, *Mimesis*, 183.

95. As Lewis noted (*English Literature*, 327), "the difference between the *Vita Nuova* and Petrarch's *Rime* is that Petrarch has abandoned the prose links."

Chapter 2

1. Dällenbach, *The Mirror*, 91.

2. Hayles, *Writing Machines*, 25.

3. See Fenzi, "Il libro," 30: "quel *mia* ('mia memoria') è pregnante, perché con il valore normale del possessivo trasmette anche quello del corrispondente genitivo oggettivo: in bocca a Dante, qui, all'inizio della *Vita nova*, la *mia memoria* è 'la memoria che io ho di me stesso'" (that *mia* ("mia memoria") is weighty, because to the standard meaning of the possessive it adds the meaning of the corresponding objective genitive: the way Dante voices it here, in the beginning of the *Vita nova*, the phrase *mia memoria* means "the memory I carry of myself").

4. But cf. De Robertis, *Il libro*, 27: "non mi sembra che Dante potesse pretendere dal lettore, anche dal lettore medioevale abituato alle impaginazioni dei manoscritti, un costante riferimento all'immagine iniziale e un così rigoroso impegno di deduzione" (I do not think that Dante could expect from the reader, even a medieval reader used to manuscript layouts, a constant reference to the initial image and such a rigorous deductive effort).

5. Farnetti, "Dante e il libro," 47–48: "il libro-*incipit* . . . è già un libro ulteriore, un libro che ne presume un altro e che si origina esso stesso da una prescrizione." See also Cristaldi, "Dante lettore," 63.

6. Barański, "Lascio cotale trattato," 12.

7. See, among others, Weinrich, *Metafora*, 31–48; Carruthers, *The Book*, 18–37; and Draaisma, *Metaphors*, 24–48.

8. With positivist precision, Zingarelli ("Il libro," 99) singled out a letter produced at the court of Frederick II as a plausible source for the metaphor of the book of memory. The letter was probably composed by distinguished poet and jurist Pier delle Vigne on behalf of Frederick II and addressed to King Henry III of England (Frederick's brother-in-law). The person who drafted the letter on Frederick's behalf recounts reading (*perlegere*) about his own marriage with the late Isabella (Henry's sister) in the *memorie liber* (book of memory). Brugnoli ("Un libello") rejected any metaphorical interpretation of Pier delle Vigne's *memorie liber* (the reference possibly indicating an actual, materially existing, family book). Additionally, Brugnoli proposed another source (Augustine, *De civitate Dei*, 18.35.3) but immediately rejected it, because it would have instituted a blasphemous parallel between *Vita nova* and the New Testament. Barański ("Lascio cotale trattato," 16–23) retrieved Brugnoli's hesitant intuition and plausibly argued for "the *libello*'s fundamental dependence on scripture" (18). Fenzi ("Il libro," 19–20) extended the list of possible sources to include Augustine (*Retractationes*), Pelagius, Rupert of Deutz, Geroch of Reichersberg, Peter of Blois, and Pope Innocent IV. On the notion of memory implied in the phrase, see Corti, "Il libro della memoria"; Maierù, "memoria" (esp. the subsection on "Il libro della memoria"); Weinrich, *La memoria*; and Malato, "La memoria." In the prosimetrum, memory also plays a role in the composition of nonverbal text: the sketching of an angel on boards in *VN* 23.1 (xxxiv 1) is also marked by Dante's memories of Beatrice ("ricordandomi di lei," "reminiscing about her"). See note 105, below.

9. See note 8, above, and Brugnoli, "Un libello," 56–58. Emblematically, Brugnoli rejected Zingarelli's abovementioned reference to Pier delle Vigne precisely on the basis of its indicating a material artifact: a family book. On how a family book (*libro di famiglia*) would have been understood and used in medieval

Tuscany (if not necessarily at the court of Frederick II), see Mordenti, "Per la definizione," 15: "un testo memoriale diaristico, plurale e plurigenerazionale, in cui la famiglia rappresenta tutti gli elementi del sistema comunicativo instaurato dal libro, costituisce cioè sia l'argomento (o contenuto) prevalente del messaggio testuale, sia il mittente che il destinatario della scrittura, sia infine il contesto e il canale della trasmissione," "a memorial journal, plural and transgenerational, in which the family represents all the elements of the communicative system the book institutes: it establishes the main topic (or content) of the textual message, the sender and the receiver of the writing, and, finally, the context and the channel of transmission." Rather than weakening the validity of Zingarelli's hypothesis, however, Brugnoli's corrective consideration of its historical (and material) specificity might strengthen it. It is intriguing to imagine a book of Dante's memory that might include authorial and nonauthorial texts, fragments and images, calculations and dates. Remarkably, in the first indirect testimony on the material existence of the *Vita nova*, the prosimetrum is bound together with other folios to form a family book: see chapter 3, "Material Discourse."

10. See Singleton, *An Essay*, "The Book of Memory," 25–54. On Singleton's reading of Dante's *Buchmetaphorik*, see Candido, "Il libro della scrittura." For a prudent approach to Singleton's reading, see Fenzi, "Il libro," esp. 17–18.

11. Tenor (the meaning of an image) and vehicle (the image used to convey that meaning) are the two parts of a metaphor in Richards's metaphor theory (*The Philosophy*, "Metaphor," 89–112).

12. All citations of Dante's *Commedia* are from Petrocchi, ed., *La Commedia*. The English translations are from Durling and Martinez, eds. and trans., *The Divine Comedy*.

13. Santagata, *Dal sonetto*, 140n104: "una raccolta di rime, ordinate in modo non dissimile da quello del libro . . . un organismo preesistente, già selezionato ed ordinato."

14. Tassinari, "Metalingua," 81: ". . . Dante avesse realmente un *libro*—il fatto che Dante fosse uno scrittore ci autorizza a pensarlo—(libro, o fogli sparsi, o volumi ammucchiati, non ha importanza) nel quale egli avesse annotato non solo gli avvenimenti puri e semplici, ma anche le composizioni poetiche che egli ci produrrà nel corso della *V.N.*"

15. Battaglia Ricci, "Comporre," 27: "una reale solidarietà fisica e simbolica."

16. On *dictare* and *scribere*, see, among others, Saenger, "Silent Reading."

17. Ginsberg, *Dante's Aesthetics*, 26.

18. A caveat against systematically implementing this "codicological model of the mind" can be derived from Evans's warning against the dangers of methodi-

cally applying geometrical and algebraic models to the psychology of cognitive processes (Evans, "The Geometry," 49): "no-one ever pretended that these [*sc.* geometric] schemata represented, in any sense, the way the brain functioned. But they do offer a unique commentary on the ratiocination; thought processes and modes of intellectual perception of the Middle Ages."

19. See Guglielminetti, *Memoria*, 44.

20. In the *libello*, *parole* is used ninety-three times (of which three times in the singular, *parola*). The conjugated forms of the corresponding verb *parlare* occur eighty-nine times. For the technical use of *parole* and *parlare* and their synonymic or complementary variants in the *Vita nova*, see De Robertis, *Il libro*, "Nascita della coscienza letteraria italiana," 177–238 (esp. 183–87). For a full survey of the term in Dante's *corpus*, see Consoli, "parola."

21. De Robertis, *Il libro*, 183: "*parlare, dire, parole* . . . significano soprattutto parlare in versi, poetare, poesia." The corresponding paragraph in Carrai's edition is 16.8. In the note *ad locum* in his edition of the *libello*, De Robertis's glossing of *parole* is less focused on the form of their expression: "le parole scritte (e che si leggono) in quella parte del libro della memoria, e che Dante intende ricopiare in questa sua operetta, sono i ricordi," "the words written (and readable) in that part of the book of memory, the ones which Dante intends to copy in this little work of his, are his memories." For Gorni, Carrai, and Rossi (with various degrees of confidence), the *parole* of the proem are poems, but Pirovano conciliatorily intends them as "ricordi" (memories) and "tracce di vita che si susseguono in forma continuata" (life traces following one another continuously) that are transcribed as prose but also exist as verse in the poet's mind (see the notes *ad locum* of their respective commented editions). Singleton's hard-line distinction among the mutually exclusive roles of Dante's writing personae also results in a separation (not entirely persuasive) between prose words as a metaphor for real things and words as actual text, in prose and verse, written in the book of memory (see Singleton, *An Essay*, 34–35). Barański ("Lascio cotale trattato," 22) considers the limitation of *parole* to just poems "reductive, not to say illogical," since the narrative sections of the prose texts describe events that are part of Dante's memory. And yet, the prose sections might simply constitute the *sentenzia* of poems not included in the *libello*, whether or not Dante actually composed these poems (like other poems he chose not to include, and indeed may never have written).

22. On the rather understudied practice of rubrication, see Clemens and Graham, *Introduction*, 24–25. On the *Vita nova*'s *rubrica*, see Shaw, *Essays*, "*Incipit Vita nova*," 53–76; Spitzer, *Studi*, "Osservazioni sulla *Vita Nuova* di Dante," 103–7; Livorni, "Il proemio"; Casadei, "Incipit"; and Malato, "L'incipit." For additional observations on rubrics (even if not specifically on those of the *Vita*

nova), see Clarke, "Boccaccio"; Daniels, "Where Does the *Decameron* Begin?"; and Clarke, "*Sotto la quale rubrica*." For a paratextual approach to Dante's *Vita nova*, see Pich, "On the Threshold," esp. 99–107.

23. Clarke, "Boccaccio," 84.

24. See Mattalia, ed., *La vita nuova*, and De Robertis, ed., *Vita Nuova*, in their respective notes *ad locum*. For the text of the epistle to Can Grande, see Villa, ed., *Epistole*, 1494–521 (at 1503).

25. Pacioni, "L'*auctoritas* poetica," 60: "mappa interna al 'libello.'"

26. Carruthers, *The Book*, 33. On memory as mental writing in Dante, see also Gardner, "Imagination," esp. 280–82.

27. See Casadei, "Incipit." On Augustinian models of conversion and palinode in Dante's *Vita nova*, see, at least, Took, "Dante and the *Confessions*," esp. 360–65, and Leporatti, "Io spero."

28. Ginsberg, *Dante's Aesthetics*, 38.

29. In the context of Dante's infatuation for the *donna gentile*, it is worth noting, Beatrice's epiphany in her "vestimenta sanguigne" (crimson clothes) (*VN* 28.1 [xxxix 1]) brings Dante to shame and to tears (*VN* 28.4 [xxxix 4]): his eye area turns to "uno colore porporeo, lo quale suole apparire per alcuno martirio che altri riceva" (a reddish color . . ., the sort of thing which appears because of some martyring agony one is going through).

30. On Dante's chromatic symbolism, see Perrone, "I colori," esp. 1033–36 (on the *Vita nova*). For further examples of Dante's attention to the chromatic details implicated in the act of writing, see the appendix to part I.

31. In his translation, Frisardi keeps the Latin in the body text and translates it in the footnote. Following Gorni's critical edition, he omits the closing *Amen*.

32. Bertolucci Pizzorusso, "Libri," 140: "il libro acquista la virtù miracolosa di una santa reliquia, che applicata al corpo dolente del suo autore, lo risana (miracolo 209)."

33. Dante also uses *libello* to refer to the *Vita nova* in the *Convivio* (2.2.2). Cristaldi underlines that such denomination is—in the *Vita nova*—exclusive and without qualifications (other than deictics), which implies that "è anzitutto al libro in sé che Dante mira" (it is first of all the book in itself that Dante contemplates) (*La "Vita nuova,"* 5).

34. See Storey, "Di libello," and Storey, "Following Instructions" (but cf. Mazzetti, "Dare forma," 163n1).

35. On these codicological units, see Robinson, "The 'Booklet,'" and Hannah, "Booklets." See also Rizzo, *Il lessico*, "Codice e libro a stampa," 3–12; Avalle, "I canzonieri"; and Fiorilla, "Il '*libellus*.'"

36. Storey, "Following Instructions," 120.

37. The technical-editorial use of the term *libello* as self-contained material form does not exclude possible intertextual references to the tradition of Latin erotic poetry collections, to which the term *libelli* is often applied, or even to specific texts: e.g., the incipit of Ovid's *Remedia amoris* (1.1), as indicated by Gorni in his commentary to *VN* 1.1 (i): "Legerat huius Amor titulum nomenque libelli" (Love had read the subject and title of this little book) (translation mine). See also Billanovich, *Petrarca*, "L'Orazio Morgan e gli studi del giovane Petrarca," 49–52. On Ovid's presence in the *Vita nova*, see chapter 1, "Metatextuality and the *Vita nova*: The Critical Debate" and note 27.

38. It is worth noting that the copyists of the *Commedia*—though, of course, this generally applies to most works composed and circulated as independent parts—recognized the correlation instituted within the text between material unit and literary unit and tended to begin the transcription of a new canticle on a new quire: in a survey of 201 complete manuscripts of the *Commedia* conducted by Boschi Rotiroti (*Codicologia*, 43–44), a codicological caesura separates *Purgatorio* from *Paradiso* in ninety-seven exemplars. See also Pomaro, "Codicologia," (esp. "Tavola A: Quadro sinottico dei manoscritti esaminati"), and Battaglia Ricci, "Comporre," 24–26.

39. Ahern, "Binding the Book," 804. See also Ahern, "Dante's Last Word"; Ahern, "What Did the First Copies"; and Mazzotta, "Cosmology," esp. 9–13.

40. See Gröber, "Die Liedersammlungen." See also Avalle, *I manoscritti*, "La tradizione manoscritta della lirica occitanica," 61–106 (esp. 61–72), but cf. Roncaglia, "Rétrospectives"; Paden, "Roll versus Codex"; and Paden, "Lyrics on Rolls." On Gröber's hypothesis, see, among others, Zinelli, "Gustav Gröber."

41. Avalle, *I manoscritti*, 4: "naufragio generale."

42. For a general introduction to the topic, see Brugnolo, "Il libro." On the formation of courtly songbooks, see, at least, Beltran, "Copisti e canzonieri," esp. 115–26. On Old French love songbooks, including for additional bibliographical references, see, among others, Formisano, "Prospettive."

43. See Chaytor, *From Script*, "Publications and Circulation," 115–37 (at 121).

44. The *cantigas* are transmitted by the so-called Vindel Parchment (New York, The Morgan Library & Museum, MS M.979). Jacopone's *laude* are transmitted by a *rotulus* now preserved in the Biblioteca Estense e Universitaria in Modena (Archivio Viti-Molza). The parchment folio transmitting the *planh* is housed in Cividale del Friuli, Archivio Capitolare, 1484. On the Vindel Parchment, see Ferreira, *O som*, and, for a palaeographic and codicological description, see Arbor Aldea and Ciaralli, "Il *Pergamiño*." On Jacopone's *rotulus*, see Bertoni,

"Poesie di Jacopone." On the *planh*, see Grattoni, "Un *planh* inedito." On the existence of *rotuli* in Italy through the fourteenth century, see Frasso, "Un rotolo."

45. The text is transmitted by MS Escorial e. III. 23 of the Real Biblioteca del Monasterio de El Escorial in Madrid (fol. 74rv).

46. Capelli ("Nuove indagini," 84–100) believes the exemplar did not provide enough space for execution of the illustration and must have been intended as a model.

47. See Storey, *Transcription*, 171–92, and Capelli, ed., *Del carnale amore.*

48. See, among others, Picone, "Guittone," but cf. Giunta, *Codici*, "Poesie che commentano poesie nel Medioevo: Il caso di Guittone d'Arezzo," 317–41.

49. See Leonardi, ed., *Canzoniere*, xxvi and n15.

50. On Monte's book see, including for previous bibliography, Storey, "Di libello," 272–79; Arduini, "Per una corona"; and Arduini, "*Dolente me.*"

51. I cite Giacomino's *canzone* from Brunetti, ed., "Giacomino Pugliese," 607. See Brunetti, "Il libro," 66–69, and Brunetti, *Il frammento*, 192–96.

52. Brugnolo ("Il libro," 10) suggests that, in Giacomino's case, we would be dealing with a metaphor. On indirect testimonies regarding Giacomino's and Monte's books, see Avalle, "I canzonieri," 369.

53. See Gorni, "Una silloge d'autore" (at 28: "novena dello sbigottito"). See also Marrani, "Macrosequenze d'autore," 255–61.

54. Rajna, "Lo schema," but cf. Santangelo, *Dante*, "Le biografie provenzali," 5–28. See also Meliga, "Le raccolte d'autore," 89, and Poe, "*L'autre escrit.*"

55. The current shelf mark of Occitan chansonnier *C* is Paris, Bibliothèque nationale de France, f.f. 856. Bertolucci Pizzorusso ("Il canzoniere," 112) sees in these rubrics the legacy of a metrical-rhetorical commentary (or even autocommentary) in the original collection.

56. Bertolucci Pizzorusso, "Libri," 129: "un fattore materiale ed eminentemente visivo, lo 'spazio' del libro, che ne rende possibile e fruibile la relativa segnalazione."

57. Harrison, *The Body*, 152, and Barolini, "Forging," 122, respectively.

58. Emphasis mine. Carrai appropriately glosses the phrase "maggiori paragrafi" with "paragrafi contrassegnati da un numero più alto" (paragraphs marked by a higher numeral) and, therefore, "relativi a un'età più matura" (relative to a more mature age). See Carrai, ed., *Vita nova*, 45n *ad locum*, but cf. Gorni, ed., *Vita Nova*, 14n *ad locum*, and Pirovano, ed., *Vita nuova*, 86n *ad locum*.

59. Contini, "Preliminari," 175: "*Dante war ein grosser Mystifikator.*"

60. On *ordinatio*, see Parkes, "The Influence," and Rouse and Rouse, *Authentic Witnesses*, "*Statim invenire*: School, Preachers, and New Attitudes to the

Page," 191–219, and "The Development of Research Tools in the Thirteenth Century," 221–55.

61. De Robertis detailed this research in various articles published in *Studi danteschi*, and those articles formed the basis for *I documenti*, Vol. 1 (in two *tomi*) of his *editio maior* of Dante's *Rime* (2002). In addition to *I documenti*, see also De Robertis, *Il canzoniere escorialense*, 22–43, and De Robertis, "Sulla tradizione." The thirteen poems are the following: "O voi che per la via d'Amor passate," "Con l'altre donne mia vista gabbate," "Ciò che m'incontra ne la mente more," "Negli occhi porta la mia donna Amore," "Tanto gentile e tanto onesta pare," "Vede perfettamente onne salute," "Venite a 'ntender li sospiri miei," "Era venuta ne la mente mia," "Videro li occhi miei quanta pietate," "Color d'amore e di pietà sembianti," "Lasso!, per forza di molti sospiri," "Deh peregrini, che pensosi andate," and "Oltre la spera che più larga gira." On the organic and inorganic textual tradition of the poems of the *Vita nova*, see also Folena, "La tradizione," 8–14, and Ciociola, "Dante," 144–57.

62. Gragnolati, "Authorship and Performance," 129. On the more general issue of Dante's refunctionalization of autobiographical statements, see Gragnolati and Lombardi, "Autobiografia."

63. See Mainini, "Schermi."

64. On the *sonetto rinterzato*, see Beltrami, *La metrica*, 113–15 and 283–84.

65. Barolini (ed., *Dante's Lyric Poetry*, 71) traces back the sonnet's metrical form to a "Guittonian pedigree."

66. Barolini, ed., *Dante's Lyric Poetry*, 71.

67. Foster and Boyde, eds. and trans., *Dante's Lyric Poetry*, 1:40.

68. Gorni, *Lettera*, 45: "Il nome di Beatrice, a un certo punto della *Vita Nuova*, si converte in quello d'Amore, per grazia e volontà dello stesso 'Segnore de la nobiltade.'"

69. See Rea, *Dante: Guida*, 94. For the text and translation of Cavalcanti's *Rime*, see note 123, below.

70. Tanturli proposed that the *Vita nova*'s love poetics and its characterization of Cavalcanti could have triggered the ideological and personal rupture between the two poets and, consequently, might have occasioned Cavalcanti's doctrinal *canzone* "Donna me prega," thus inverting the vulgate chronology that places "Donna me prega" before the *Vita nova*. Malato and Fenzi aligned with Tanturli's hypothesis, and Grimaldi deemed it "ormai opinione comune" (generally accepted by now) in his recent commented edition of Dante's *Rime*. A possibilist approach to Tanturli's chronology based on a balanced discussion of the intertextual relationships between Dante's and Guido's manifesto *canzoni* can be

read in Pasero, "Dante in Cavalcanti." Barolini has asked whether, in the absence of strong supporting data, scholars have too readily assumed this hypothesis as fact. See Tanturli, "Guido Cavalcanti"; Malato, *Dante e Guido*, 11–73; Barolini, "Dante and Cavalcanti," 60–63; Fenzi, *La canzone*, "Conflitto di idee e implicazioni polemiche fra Dante e Cavalcanti," 9–70; and Grimaldi, ed., *Rime*, 529. For a confutation of Tanturli's hypothesis, see also Marti, ". . . L'una appresso"; Marti, "Da 'Donna me prega'"; Inglese, ". . . illa Guidonis"; and Sarteschi, "*Donna me prega.*"

71. De Robertis, ed., *Vita Nuova*, 169: "Il sonetto non sembra sopportare il peso di responsabilità che la prosa gli attribuisce."

72. On the *interpretatio nominis* and the poetological implications of the names of Dante's beloved, see Gorni, *Lettera*, "Il nome di Beatrice," 19–44; Sarteschi, "Da Beatrice"; Bologna, "Beatrice," esp. 115–23; Landoni, "Beatrice"; and Saviotti, "L'énigme," 116–17.

73. On mono-stanzaic *canzoni*, see Camboni, "Canzoni monostrofiche." Camboni limits to nine the corpus of twelve *canzoni* listed in Gorni and Malinverni, *Repertorio metrico*.

74. See, for instance, De Robertis, ed., *Vita Nuova*, 188, and Gorni, ed., *Vita Nova*, 266. Sarteschi (*Il percorso*, 72–74) underlined the connections between "Sì lungiamente" and the sonnets of the *gabbo* (mockery) (*VN* 7–8 [xiv–xv]).

75. Grimaldi, ed., *Rime*, 488: "Non sappiamo ovviamente se Dante abbia scelto di collocare in questa sezione della *Vita nuova* un testo più arcaico per dimostrare l'impossibilità del ritorno a una fase già superata della propria esperienza poetica o se effettivamente, a quest'epoca, continuasse a muoversi su vari registri espressivi."

76. Barolini, ed., *Dante's Lyric Poetry*, 287.

77. I refer to Pirovano's tripartite subdivision (after Singleton's); see Pirovano, "*Vita nuova,*" esp. 158, and chapter 1, "Mode of Mediation" and note 51.

78. Leporatti ("Ipotesi") hypothesizes that the composition of "Donne ch'avete intelletto d'amore" may in fact concur with the writing of the *libello.*

79. On the incipitarian vocative as formal typology and *topos* (with reference to Occitan and Frederician poetry), see Scarpati, "Tipologie."

80. See De Robertis, "Il canzoniere escorialense," 29.

81. Shalom Vagata, "Appunti," 378: "La lezione della tradizione organica rivela una stretta aderenza della poesia all'impianto narrativo, esplicitato e giustificato dalla prosa, ed esibisce una maggiore coerenza semantica e stilistico-linguistica."

82. See De Robertis, "Il canzoniere escorialense," 40–42, and Shalom Vagata, "Appunti," 394–96.

83. Contini, "Esercizio," 168: "un'incarnazione di cose celesti."

84. See chapter 3, "Giovanni Boccaccio's Transcriptions."

85. Botterill, ". . . però che la divisione," 74. Only seven poems out of thirty-one are not divided. These are "Con l'altre donne mia vista gabbate," "Tanto gentile e tanto onesta pare," "Sì lungiamente m'à tenuto Amore," "Videro li occhi miei quanta pietate," "Color d'amore e di pietà sembianti," "Lasso!, per forza di molti sospiri," and "Deh peregrini, che pensosi andate."

86. D'Andrea, "La struttura," 39–40: "la creazione da parte dello scrittore-protagonista di un'immagine complessa ed elusiva di se stesso, in continuo progresso."

87. See chapter 6, "*Nugelle*" and note 1.

88. Franklin-Brown, *Reading*, 62.

89. Kleiner, "Finding the Center," 88. See also Botterill, ". . . però che la divisione," 72: "The shift from an appendicular to a premonitory role has definite consequences for the *divisioni*, since, as a matter of the concrete experience of reading, they become less easy to ignore when they precede their poems."

90. According to Storey ("Following Instructions," 123), this indication reinforces "the 'loneliness' of the poem at the completion of its reading since there will be no commentary to follow. Dante has now designed the scribal apparatus to reflect the theme and tone of the lonely sorrow caused by Beatrice's absence."

91. Iser, *The Act*, 65.

92. Frisardi appropriately cites the relevant lines of his own translation of the sonnet.

93. See Storey, "Following Instructions," esp. 122.

94. Zumthor conceptualized *mouvance* as the propagation of divergent manuscript versions of a given text: for an icastic definition of the concept, see Zumthor, "Médiéviste," 319 ("Le texte est 'mouvance': fragment de soi, et jamais le même, mutabilité fondamentale que camoufle à peine un masque d'organicité" (The text is *mouvance*: fragment of itself, and never the same, fundamental mutability that a mask of organicity barely camouflages) (translation mine); for a fuller treatment of the concept, see Zumthor, *Toward a Medieval Poetics*, 40–55.

95. The correctness of the *Vita nova*'s textual tradition is all the more notable when compared with the manuscript tradition of Dante's *Convivio*, instead a minefield of noneliminable textual *cruces*. The number of unquestionable archetype errors of the *Vita nova* oscillates between three (Barbi, ed., *La Vita Nuova*,

ccxlix) and two (Gorni, ed., *Vita Nova*, 342). In her edition of the *Convivio*, Brambilla Ageno indicates about 20 lacunae and 1,000 archetype errors. Gorni ("Appunti," 251) proposes that the copyist of the *Convivio*'s archetype was likely transcribing from an original that was extremely damaged or at a draft stage.

96. In the *Vita nova*, Dante uses the term *ragione* in its exegetical meaning (Old Occitan *razo*) seven times: 24.4 (xxxv 4), twice; 25.3 (xxxvi 3); 26.5 (xxxvii 5); 28.6 (xxxix 6); 28.7 (xxxix 7); 29.8 (xl 8). In *VN* 7.13 (xiv 13) the phrase "ragionata cagione" (commentary on what occasioned the poem) is used with an analogous meaning.

97. See Leporatti, "Io spero," 260: "Era difficile da parte dell'autore controllare e persino sapere, al di fuori della cerchia più ristretta degli amici poeti e degli abituali corrispondenti, su quali basi il lettore avrebbe conosciuto e valutato la sua poesia. Le liriche circolavano per lo più per piccole sillogi all'interno in genere di più vaste antologie compilate a discrezione del lettore, secondo i suoi gusti e interessi, le sue possibilità di aggiornamento, la sua sensibilità e intelligenza poetica, il suo rigore, diremmo oggi, filologico" (Outside his selected circle of friends and usual correspondents, it was difficult for the author to control and even know on what bases a reader would have comprehended and evaluated his poetry. Lyrical poems would mainly circulate in small compilations generally within larger anthologies compiled by the reader according to his tastes and interests, his access to updates, his poetic cognizance and intelligence, and what we would now call his philological accuracy).

98. Steinberg, *Accounting*, 9. Vallone (*La prosa*, 27) identified a possible "motivo-occasione" (reason-occasion) for the composition of the *Vita nova* in Dante's attempt to "salvare le rime dal frammentismo delle tenzoni o dalle occasioni o dall'anonimato e ricucirle nella prosa del libello" (rescue the poems from the fragmentation of the *tenzoni*—or the occasional nature or the anonymity—and sew them up in the *libello*'s prose).

99. See Zaccarello, ed., *Le trecento novelle*, 260–63. Dante also features in *novelle* 8 and 121.

100. See Dain, *Les manuscrits*, 140–41 (at 140: "l'éclectisme des manuscrits"). To my knowledge, the phrase *editio variorum* was first employed by Dain. The practice of compiling *variorum* editions is often hinted at in the context of horizontal contamination; see, among others, Reynolds and Wilson, *Scribes and Scholars*, 214–16 (for classical literatures); Segre, "Appunti" (for an analysis of various types of contamination in prose texts); Brambilla Ageno, *L'edizione critica*, "Appendice II: La contaminazione," 173–83; and Avalle, *I manoscritti*, 37–38 (for Occitan literature). The existence of *editiones* primarily designated for collecting variants has often been conjectured through the comparative study of the

manuscript tradition's *varia lectio* (the extant variants). No such collection of variants has been materially transmitted, but cf. Avalle, *I manoscritti*, 38–43, and Avalle, *La doppia verità*, "Una 'editio variorum' delle canzoni di Peire Vidal," 15–34, on the material juxtaposition of alternative variants in Occitan chansonnier *D* (Modena, Biblioteca Estense e Universitaria, α.R.4.4). There is no comprehensive study that deals with the concept and practice of compiling *editiones variorum* in a transhistorical and transgeographical perspective. For a brief definition of the concept, see also Stussi, *Nuovo avviamento*, 144; Stark-Gendrano, "Variorum Edition"; and Baldick, *The Oxford Dictionary of Literary Terms*, 375 (*sub voce*).

101. Fulfilling Gorni's unrealized intention, Pirovano appropriately opts for a parallel typographic layout of the two *cominciamenti* in his edition of the prosimetrum. See Pirovano, ed., *Vita nuova*, 255–57, and Gorni, ed., *Vita Nova*, 340.

102. On the exceptionality of an anniversary poem *in morte*, see Carrai, *Dante elegiaco*, 68, and Santagata, *L'io e il mondo*, 136. On the groundbreaking connections that Dante developed between death of the beloved, assimilation and overcoming of the notion of *fin'amor*, reminiscence as foundation of lyric poetry, and narrative structure of the *Vita nova*, see Antonelli, "La morte." See also Bertolucci Pizzorusso, "La mort."

103. See Giunta, "Su Dante lirico," 19. Giunta continues by referencing the comparable case in which the less famous poet Meo Abbracciavacca sent two very similar sonnets to Guittone d'Arezzo (each accompanied by a prose letter).

104. See De Robertis, "Il canzoniere escorialense," 36–40.

105. On the chronological order of composition of the two *cominciamenti*, see, also for previous bibliography, Moleta, "Oggi fa l'anno," esp. 96–104. For a fine analysis of the different temporalities implied in the two *cominciamenti*, see Pich, "L'immagine," esp. 345–55.

106. The compositional context of the bicephalous sonnet also points toward Dante's attention to the materiality of media beyond writing. On the one hand, the act of drawing is given specificity through the polyptoton of *disegnare* ("to draw"), the use of a technical term ("tavolette," "boards"), and the insistence on Dante's absorbed, close-to-ecstatic inspiration: "egli erano stati già alquanto anzi che io me ne accorgesse" (they had already been there for a while before I realized it). On the other hand, the affinity of drawing with literary composition (*dire parole*, *scrivere*) is implied by the indication of memory ("ricordandomi di lei," "reminiscing about her") as the source of mimetic representation (as stated in the *libello*'s proem) and by the lexical overlapping (*figura*) between the visual and the verbal. As Pich observes ("L'immagine," 349), "L'*agens* non completa il disegno scaturito dalla solitudine e dal ricordo, e asseconda invece un'ispirazione po-

etica guidata dall'anniversario e dalla decisione di spiegare agli uomini la ragione di quel suo stare assorto, isolato dalla percezione del mondo esterno. Questo non vuol dire che il disegno abbia un ruolo secondario, perché l'angelo abbozzato si configura come l'annuncio del sonetto, una sorta di sua prefigurazione *e contrario*" (The *agens* does not complete the drawing originating in loneliness and reminiscence; instead, he consents to a poetic inspiration guided by the anniversary and the decision of explaining to the men the reason for his being absorbed, isolated from the perception of the external world. This does not imply the drawing's secondary role, because the sketch of the angel configures the sonnet's announcement, a sort of *e contrario* prefiguration). See also Ciccuto, "Era venuta"; Cervigni, "[. . .] Ricordandomi"; Mazzetti, "Dare forma," esp. 163–65; Frosini, "Dante disegnatore"; and Camilletti, *The Portrait*, "Painting Angels."

107. Noferi, "Rilettura (I)," 66: "il racconto di un evento già accaduto e insieme chiamato a prodursi, senza il quale il racconto non potrebbe iniziare e che pure si attua solo nel racconto: evento della costituzione del soggetto e del senso."

108. Holmes, *Assemblying*, 124.

109. Pirovano, ed., *Vita nuova*, 283n *ad locum*.

110. Santagata, *L'io e il mondo*, 121: "una preziosa testimonianza del fatto che Dante, all'occasione, faceva circolare piccoli florilegi delle sue rime."

111. Santagata (*L'io e il mondo*, 121) thinks of an oversight by Dante. On the *planh* in medieval Italian lyric, see, among others, Russell, "Studio."

112. The current shelf mark of this manuscript is MS O 63 sup. The three sonnets are on fols. 38r, 34rv, and 39v–40r.

113. See Allegretti, "Dante geremiade," 176–78, and Barbi, ed., *La Vita Nuova*, lx–lxi. The five manuscripts are Florence, Biblioteca Medicea Laurenziana, Plut. 40.49 (fols. 61r–62r); Florence, Biblioteca Riccardiana, 1093 (fols. 47v–48r); Florence, Biblioteca Riccardiana, 1094 (fols. 147v–148r); Florence, Biblioteca Nazionale Centrale, Pal. Panciatichi 24 (fols. 23v–24r); and Paris, Bibliothèque nationale de France, 557 (fols. 25r–26r).

114. Pirovano, ed., *Vita nuova*, 283: "la sequenza a climax fa anche pensare—ora che la storia sta per finire e che presto l'io *agens* si riunificherà con l'io *auctor* (vd. xlii 2)—a progressive e successive tappe che hanno portato alla nascita di un libro di poesie come è appunto la *Vita nuova*." *VN* xlii 2 in Pirovano's edition corresponds to *VN* 31.2 in Carrai's.

115. On erotic visions with an invite to interpretation, see Meneghetti, "Beatrice," 239–42 and 244–45 (on "A ciascun'alma presa"). On the rhetorical and epistolographic aspects of the sonnet, see Pellegrini, "Intorno al primo sonetto," and Larson, "*A ciascun'alma*."

116. For the sake of clarity, I have opted for Frisardi's prose version of the sonnet from "Appendix A" of his translation; see Frisardi, trans., *Vita Nova,* 59–60. Frisardi's verse translation reads as follows: "To all besotted souls, my counterparts, / to whom these verses come with a petition / to write me what you think of my rendition: / greetings in Love, the lord of open hearts."

117. On *cospetto*, see *GDLI*, 3:890 (*s.v.* "Cospètto"), and *ThLL*, 4:489–93 (*s.v.* "cōnspectus"). In this context I prefer a more literal—and materially oriented—interpretation of the term *cospetto* than the one provided in the *TLIO*, *s.v.* "cospetto" (1.4), where compiler Milena Piermaria lists Dante's text under the term's figurative acceptation: "Fig. Vista intellettuale, pensiero preveggente, immaginazione. Locuz. prep. *Nel cospetto di*: davanti agli occhi (della mente). Fras. *Essere nel cospetto*: essere presente, vivo nella mente, nel pensiero" (Figurative: intellectual vision, predictive thinking, imagination. Prepositional phrase: *nel cospetto di*, in the mind's eye. Phraseology: *essere nel cospetto*, to be present, vivid in the mind, in one's thought). See also *ThLL*, 4:1339–78 (*s.v.* "cum") and, more briefly, Lewis and Short, *A Latin Dictionary*, *s.v.* "cum" (III.B): in verbal compounds (and their derivations)—in addition to the being/bringing together of several objects—the Latin preverb *con-* (< *cum*) can also designate the intensity, completion, and perfection of the action implied in the simple word.

118. See Todorović, *Dante*, 140–47.

119. The manuscripts and the early print tradition have preserved two additional responsive sonnets: Dante da Maiano's "Di ciò che stato sè dimandatore," and "Naturalmente chere ogni amadore," attributed to either Cino da Pistoia or Terino da Castelfiorentino. For the (richly annotated) text of the three responsive sonnets and an updated bibliography, see Grimaldi, ed., *Rime*, 336–50. On the disputed attribution of "Naturalmente chere ogni amadore," see the recent essays by Pinto, "*Naturalmente chere*," and Rigo, "Il sonetto conteso."

120. Steinberg, "Dante's First Dream," 112.

121. For a study of readers' roles and on the concepts of ideal reader, implied reader, fictive reader, abstract reader, virtual reader, and so on, see Wilson, "Readers."

122. This initial interpretive fallacy is confirmed, at a social level, by the failed attempt of the indiscreet to ascertain the identity of Dante's beloved (*VN* 2.4 [iv 2]): "e molti pieni d'invidia già si procacciavano di sapere di me quello ch'io volea del tutto celare ad altrui" (And many spitefully curious sorts of people hunted for ways to find out the very thing about me that I wanted to keep hidden from others).

123. All citations of Cavalcanti's poems are from Rea and Inglese, eds., *Rime* (here at 83). The English translation is by Mortimer, trans., *Complete Poems*, 23.

124. Brugnolo and Benedetti, "La dedica," 30–37 (at 31: "nel corso dell'opera e quasi di sfuggita e non in posizione accusata e liminare").

125. Pacioni, "L'*auctoritas* poetica," 42: "quella che viene chiamata impropriamente 'dedica' è più che altro una tangenza lasciata nominalmente non esplicitata che entra in rapporto 'con' Dante senza allocuzione diretta."

126. On the subtle nuances of the apparently identical periphrases indicating Cavalcanti, see Pipa, "Personaggi," 101.

127. See Cappello, "La *Vita nuova*," 55: "antifrastico e quasi parodico"; but cf. Marti, "Acque agitate," 167: "non è credibile, non è possibile che le profferte di amicizia e di esaltante stima di Dante per Guido siano false e ipocrite, o dette con spirito antifrastico" (it is unbelievable, it is impossible, that Dante's proffers of friendship and exalting esteem are false and hypocritical, or made with antiphrastic spirit). The tormented relationship between Dante and Cavalcanti has generated an extensive bibliography. With specific regard to the *Vita nova* (and in addition to the works referred to in note 70, above), see, at least, Contini, "Cavalcanti in Dante"; De Robertis, *Il libro*, "Cavalcanti ovvero la non-beatrice," 71–85; De Robertis, "Amore e Guido"; Barolini, *Dante's Poets*, "Fathers and Sons: Guinizzelli and Cavalcanti," 123–53; De Robertis, "Identità"; Malato, *Dante e Guido*, 11–73; Pasero, "Dante in Cavalcanti"; Bologna, "Beatrice"; Leonardi, "Cavalcanti, Dante," esp. 331–37; Durling, "Guido Cavalcanti"; Martinez, "Cavalcanti"; Gragnolati, "Trasformazioni"; Ghetti, *L'ombra*, 105–48; Pirovano, ed., *Vita nuova*, "Introduzione," esp. 33–35; Rea, "La *Vita nuova* e le *Rime*"; Borsa, "Identità sociale"; and Rea, *Dante: Guida*, "Il 'primo de li miei amici,'" 83–95.

128. See Rea, "La *Vita nuova* e le *Rime*," 358–61 and n18 for previous bibliography. Rea ("Avete fatto") recognizes the same polemical strategy in Occitan poetry and in the *tenzone* between Bonagiunta Orbicciani and Guido Guinizzelli.

129. On the Latin of the prosimetrum, see Singleton, "The Use of Latin."

130. See Rea, "La *Vita nuova* e le *Rime*," 362–69.

131. Rea and Inglese, eds., *Rime*, 114–15, and Mortimer, trans., *Complete Poems*, 41. On *Rime* 18, see Troiano, "Strumenti scrittori."

132. On the relative chronology of "Donne ch'avete intelletto d'amore" and "Donna me prega," see the critical literature listed in note 70, above.

133. Bäuml, "Varieties and Consequences," 253. See also Ong, "The Writer's Audience"; Wilson, "Readers"; and Nelles, "Historical and Implied."

134. Sarteschi, "Dante e il lettore," 135: "*lector*, in epoca medievale, significa sia lettore che commentatore." See also Barański, "Dante *poeta* e *lector*."

135. See Giunta, *Versi*, 71–166 (esp. 96–150).

136. See Wehle, *Poesia*, 105.

137. On the woman addressee in the *Vita nova* and on Beatrice as her most extreme development (with particular reference to the *Commedia*), see Lombardi, *Imagining*, "Addressees and Readers in Lyric Poetry," 38–77, and "*Bea(ta lec)trix*," 117–53.

138. Discussing the "didactic purpose" of the commentative sections, Amtower (*Engaging Words*, 92) highlights how "there seems to be a curious disjunction between the poet's expressed desire to gloss the text for us and at the same time withhold meaning."

139. As in the case of "A ciascun'alma," I have opted for Frisardi's prose version of the *canzone*; see Frisardi, trans., *Vita Nova*, 71. Frisardi's verse translation reads as follows: "And to avoid a waste of time don't go / where everyone you meet is coarse and dumb; / try, if you're able, only being seen / by men and women versed in what you mean / whose guidance will be swift, not burdensome."

140. Lombardi, "L''invenzione,'" 24: "la tensione tra il desiderio di divulgazione e quello di mantenere il controllo sui propri testi." Ahern provides a sociological characterization of the audience addressed in "Donne ch'avete intelletto d'amore": "Dante's opening line combines, then, the vernacular female world of courtly love and the male Latin world of philosophical dispute. It is an invitation to combine two different styles of reading: the leisurely textual immersion *per diletto* of upper-class women (like Francesca [*sc.* in *Inferno* 5]) in prose romances or love poems and the efficient reading of university-educated males trained for intellectual contests and to retrieve information for gain. . . . Dante here engages his entire audience, female and male, as if it were female" (Ahern, "The Reader," 30–31).

141. Pacioni, "L'*auctoritas* poetica," 58: "Nel vuoto lasciato dai destinatari, ora personaggi, si fa spazio l'ambizione di rivolgersi ad un pubblico come insieme dei lettori possibili."

142. Ascoli, *Dante*, 42–43.

143. See *TLIO*, *s.v.* "chiosatore" (1.1): "Estens. Chi interpreta gli eventi." The entry's compiler, Sara Sarti, cites *VN* 19.2 (xxviii 2).

144. Even though Hollander confessed to find the "hypothesis attractive" as late as 1992 ("Dante and Cino," 222n23), the once popular opinion that friend, fellow poet, and jurist Cino da Pistoia could be hiding behind the elusive figure of the "altro chiosatore" is now generally discredited as a mere autoschediasm originated from Cino's consolatory poem to Dante upon Beatrice's death ("Avegna ched el m'aggia più per tempo") as well as from Dante's sixfold self-description as Cino's friend ("amicus eius [*sc.* Cyni Pistoriensis]") in the *De vulgari eloquentia* (1.10.2, 1.17.3, 1.18.4, 2.2.8, 2.5.4, and 2.6.6). In addition to

Hollander's article and the commentaries *ad locum* in the editions of the *Vita nova* listed in "On Editions and Citations" at the beginning of this book, see, at least, Gorni, "Beatrice agli Inferi," 147 and n6 (but cf. the commentary *ad locum* in Gorni, ed., *Vita Nova*).

145. Allen, *The Ethical Poetic*, 217.

146. Putzo, "The Implied Book," 384.

147. On the reader's participation in the prosimetrum's itinerary of erotic and poetic conversion, see Amtower, *Engaging Words*, 90–105.

148. Petronio, "Appunti," 107: "la destinazione intenzionale di un'opera, cioè quella che il suo autore si propone, e la destinazione o diffusione effettiva di essa, quella che essa effettivamente consegue."

Chapter 3

1. For a thorough description of the document (with images), the complete edition of the text, the account of its rediscovery, and additional bibliographical references, see Azzetta, "Note," 63–68. The document was first mentioned by Zaccagnini ("Un nuovissimo documento") in 1918 but soon thereafter vanished without a trace, or even a shelf mark.

2. Azzetta, "Note," 65: "quem [*sc.* Petrum] . . . tractate, apensate, maliciose, furtive et malo modo accepisse eidem unum librum qui vocatur *Vita nova*, scriptum in cartis pecudinis, et quasdam alias rationes diversas ligatas cum ipso in duabus assidibus de ligno, valoris et extimationis in summa liber predictus et rationes quindecim librarum bononinorum."

3. See Zaccagnini, "Un nuovissimo documento," 3.

4. See Azzetta, "Note," 67.

5. Irvine, "Medieval Textuality," 181.

6. As Dante scholars often point out, we do not even have a surviving instance of the poet's signature. The search for an autograph of the *Commedia* haunted even sober philologists, such as Branca (*Ponte Santa Trinita*, 197–99). Florentine humanist Leonardo Bruni (see Viti, ed., *Opere letterarie*, 548) left a precious record of Dante's handwriting—he could still read it in some chancery documents—and described it as "magra et lunga et molto corretta" (thin, elongated, and quite correct): a chancery minuscule?

7. In my doctoral dissertation ("The Author as Scribe," 44–45 and n9)—"che di necessità qui si registra"—I referred to the catalogue in Roddewig, *Dante Alighieri*, of 844 manuscripts. In the five years that separate the writing of this

chapter from completion of the dissertation, that number has increased. Roddewig's list must now also be updated with the recent discovery of certain codices held in private collections; see, for instance, Tonello, "Concerning Three Manuscripts." The extraordinary number of extant codices of the *Commedia* shows the full range of codicological forms available to copyists and patrons in the first half of the fourteenth century: according to Petrucci ("Storia e geografia," 168), the *Commedia* is "l'unico grande testo volgare che nel corso del trecento sia stato riprodotto e diffuso secondo tutta la gamma dei modelli graficolibrari correnti" (the only important vernacular text that, during the fourteenth century, was reproduced and circulated in all contemporary graphic and book models).

8. For an example of interpretive strategies along these lines (applied to the *Commedia*), see Ahern, "What Did," and Savino, "L'autografo virtuale." Savino, however, extends his analysis so far as to outline a hypothetical description of Dante's autograph of the *Commedia.* On the materiality of Dante's text, see also the recent Eisner, "The Materiality."

9. For an example of the former, see Savino, "L'autografo virtuale"; for the latter line of investigation, see Storey, "Following Instructions."

10. See the appendix to part I and note 6.

11. Writing about the commissioners of the *Commedia,* Miglio ("Dante Alighieri," 629) refers to "il desiderio di ostensione, più ancora che di acculturazione, della nuova committenza borghese" (the new bourgeois commissioners' desire for ostentation, rather than acculturation). The mercantile and notary audience that determined the success of the *Commedia* as a "bestseller" would commission luxurious exemplars to enrich their private libraries, without giving up the codicological features (e.g., the layout and the chancery minuscule script) to which they were more accustomed.

12. See Petrucci, "Storia e geografia," 160: Dante's misconception about the *Commedia* is "una delle spie della profonda incomprensione che Dante aveva nei riguardi dell'organizzazione e dell'articolazione della cultura libraria del suo tempo, con i cui nuovi centri e soggetti produttori, egli, intellettuale non professionale, bandito dalla sua città d'origine e girovago in un'area geografica relativamente limitata, non riuscì mai ad avere reali e durevoli rapporti" (one of the signs of Dante's deep incomprehension of the organization and articulation of contemporary book culture, with whose new production centers and subjects a nonprofessional intellectual like him, banned from his native city and wandering through a relatively limited geographic area, could never establish actual longlasting relationships).

13. These manuscripts also occupy a high position in three of the four branches (*k*, *b*, *s*, *x*) of the two families (α and β) of Barbi's *stemma codicum* for the *Vita nova*. See Barbi, ed., *La Vita Nuova* (the two nonnumerated, folded bifolios with the *stemma* conclude chap. 4 of the introduction: "Classificazione dei testi," cxix–cclii).

14. Banella wrote the most recent comprehensive study of the *Vita nova*'s manuscript tradition. I defer to her detailed description of the codices and of Boccaccio's role in shaping the *libello*'s textual tradition: see Banella, *La "Vita nuova,"* "Le trascrizioni del Boccaccio," 3–71, and "La tradizione parallela," 72–106. On the *Vita nova*'s early circulation, see also Todorović, "Who Read."

15. The critical literature on the intersections between ideology and codicology in medieval lyric anthologies is extensive. See, among others, Avalle, "I canzonieri"; Bertolucci Pizzorusso, "Libri"; Brugnolo, "Il libro"; Petrucci, "Reading"; Bologna, *Tradizione*, "Il tema di fondo: tradizione e innovazione nella forma-canzoniere," 3–156, and "Dai canzonieri al *Canzoniere*: un corto-circuito letterario," 1:157–273; Brugnolo, "Libro d'autore"; Borriero, "Sull'*antologia*"; Signorini, "Spunti"; Holmes, *Assembling*, "Assembling the Book and Its Author: A Historical Overview," 1–24; Storey, "Cultural Crisis"; Leonardi, "Creazione e fortuna"; Galvez, *Songbook*, "The Medieval Songbook as Emergent Genre," 1–16; and Marrani, "Miscellaneous Manuscripts."

16. See Tavoni, *Qualche idea*, "Il *De vulgari eloquentia* a Bologna," 96–103.

17. On the codicological acceptation of format, see chapter 4, "MS Acquisti e doni 325 (*Aut*)" and note 19. For a codicological description of *M*, see Barbi, *La Vita Nuova*, xxii–xxv; Bertelli, *I manoscritti*, 120–22; and Pirovano, "Per una nuova edizione," 297–301. See also Castellani, "Sul codice." A digital reproduction is available at http://vitanova.unipv.it/immagini/images.php?test=VNM.

18. On *M*'s association of the *Vita nova* (and excerpts of its poems) with dream books (in this case the *Somniale Danielis* and a vernacular version of it), see Cappozzo, "Un volgarizzamento," in which this material association is presented as having "un fine esegetico" (an exegetical purpose) (79).

19. See Bertelli, "Nota." The current shelf mark of chansonnier *P* is Florence, Biblioteca Medicea Laurenziana, MS Pluteo 41.42.

20. See Avalle, *I manoscritti*, 98–100, and Santangelo, *Dante*, "Il canzoniere provenzale adoperato da Dante," 61–86.

21. See Todorović, *Dante*, 114. On verse citations within the *vidas*, see Menichetti, "Le citazioni."

22. See Castellani, "Sul codice Laurenziano"; Trovato, *Il testo*, 80; and Bertelli, "Nota," esp. 371–72, but cf. Banella, *La "Vita nuova,"* 76.

23. The only letter larger in module is, on fol. 35r, the prosimetrum's first initial (*I*), corresponding to nine lines of text.

24. Paragraph signs (within the text) also mark Latin quotations with certain regularity. The alleged coincidence in paragraph divisions between *M* and Boccaccio's transcriptions led Gorni ("Paragrafi," 119–24) to infer the archaicity of this subdivision and hypothesize its provenance from the archetype or even the autograph of the *libello*. For additional bibliography on the text of the *libello*, see "On Editions and Citations" at the beginning of this book.

25. See Gorni, *Vita Nova*, 295, and Banella, *La "Vita nuova,"* "Prosimetro o canzoniere con prose," 87–93.

26. Semidiplomatically: "Incipit uita noua." For the transcription of Medieval Latin and Italian texts, I follow the guidelines put forth in Tognetti, *Criteri*, and Smith, "Conseils."

27. See De Robertis, ed., *Vita Nuova* (*ad locum*), and, also for a list of the manuscripts with this feature, De Robertis, "Poetica del (ri)cominciamento," 104n4. Spitzer ("Osservazioni," 104) reads this notation as a naïve demetaphorization of the metaphor.

28. Semidiplomatically: "Incipit illibro della nuoua uita di date." Manuscript Strozziano owes its name to its former owner: Carlo di Tommaso Strozzi. It is currently preserved in the Florentine Biblioteca Nazionale Centrale (shelf mark: Magliabechi VI.143). For a codicological description, see Barbi, ed., *La Vita Nuova*, xxx–xxxii, and Pirovano, "Per una nuova edizione," 291–95. A digital reproduction is available at http://vitanova.unipv.it/immagini/images.php?test=VNS.

29. Semidiplomatically: "Dante allaghieri." The indication of the title *Vita nuova* is unostentatiously provided in black ink on the outer margin. For a codicological description of *K*, see Barbi, *La Vita Nuova*, xvii–xix; Borriero, "Quantum illos"; Borriero, ed., *Canzonieri italiani*, 176; Pirovano, "Per una nuova edizione," 276–78; and Pirovano, "Il manoscritto chigiano," esp. 160–67. On the manuscript's paleography, see Signorini, "Il Codice Chigiano." A digital facsimile is available at https://digi.vatlib.it/view/MSS_Chig.L.VIII.305. For a diplomatic edition, see Molteni and Monaci, eds., *Il canzoniere chigiano*. Importantly, *K* is often referred to as *Ch*.

30. For the most part, quaternions. The fasciculation of *K* shows an accurate planning for the section with the major *Stilnovisti* (fascicles i–vi), while the other sections of the codex indicate a copy in progress; see Borriero, "Quantum illos," esp. 283–86, and Borriero, "Nuovi accertamenti."

31. Vandelli, "Il più antico," 47. For an *expertise* on scribe A's graphic characteristics, see Signorini, "Il Codice Chigiano," esp. 225–30.

32. Borriero, ed., *Canzonieri italiani*, 176: "gran disordine." Borriero uses this unflattering phrase to reference (and refute) Panvini's suggestion that *K* lacks any organizational principle. See Panvini, "Studio," esp. 42–54.

33. Borriero, "Sull'*antologia*," 219: "una sorta di *climax* insieme discendente e ciclica."

34. Pirovano, "Il ms. Chig.," 161: "il codice del Dolce stil novo secondo la prospettiva dantesca." See also Borriero, "Quantum illos," 285: "L'*ordo* che ci trasmette Ch appare, nelle sue linee essenziali, la traduzione libraria del *canone* dantesco, in prima istanza quello del *De vulgari eloquentia* dove Dante è alla ricerca di una propria *tradizione* poetica nonché della definizione di possibili sviluppi" (The *ordo* transmitted by Ch appears, in its essential traits, as the translation into book of Dante's *canon*, first and foremost the one in the *De vulgari eloquentia*, where Dante is seeking for his own poetic *tradition* as well as the definition of possible developments).

35. Large and medium initials correspond to seven and three lines of text, respectively. Large initials open the sections on Guinizzelli (fol. 1r), Cavalcanti (fol. 3r), Dante (fol. 29r), and Cino (39r).

36. Pirovano, "Per una nuova edizione," 278: "la mano A manifesta una tendenza generale a evidenziare all'attenzione del lettore i componimenti poetici con segni affini a quelli utilizzati nelle altre sezioni liriche del Canzoniere chigiano."

37. Chartier and Stallybrass, "What Is a Book?," 200.

38. See Eisner, *Boccaccio*.

39. For a general overview of Boccaccio's writings on Dante, see, among others, Delcorno, "Gli scritti danteschi," and Fumagalli, "Boccaccio e Dante." See also chapter 4, "Autography."

40. See note 13, above. The *b* branch of the α family includes twenty-four manuscripts and seven fragments. For the list of fragmentary and complete codices, see Pirovano, "Per una nuova edizione," 289–91; for an extensive analysis, see Banella, *La "Vita nuova,"* "I codici *descripti*," 107–217.

41. For the dates of composition, see Cursi, *La scrittura*, 129–34, and Cursi, "Cronologia e stratigrafia." For a material and textual description of the codices, see Bertelli and Cursi, "Boccaccio copista"; Cursi and Fiorilla, "Giovanni Boccaccio"; Pirovano, "Per una nuova edizione"; Pirovano, "Boccaccio editore"; Bettarini Bruni, Breschi, and Tanturli, "Giovanni Boccaccio," 60–70; Tanturli, "Le copie"; Bertelli, "La prima silloge"; Bertelli, "La seconda silloge"; Bertelli, "Codicologia," 4–6 (K^2) and 20–23 (*To*); and Banella, *La "Vita nuova,"* "Le trascrizioni del Boccaccio," 3–71. A digital facsimile is available at https://digi.vatlib.it/view

/MSS_Chig.L.V.176. For a facsimile reproduction of K^2, see, including for its ample introduction (7–72), De Robertis, ed., *Il Codice Chigiano*.

42. We do not have the antigraphs Boccaccio copied from, but editors generally agree that K^2 derives from *To* (with an unspecifiable number of *codices interpositi*), with the exception of Gorni, who thinks that the two manuscripts are collateral. See Gorni, "Restituzione formale," 166–68, and Gorni, "Per il testo."

43. For a detailed analysis of Boccaccio's editorial decisions as a copyist of the *Vita nova*, see Banella, *La "Vita nuova,"* 3–71. On Boccaccio as writer of his own prosimetra, see Battaglia Ricci, "Tendenze prosimetriche," esp. 66–82, and Carrai, "Boccaccio e la tradizione."

44. *To* is "predated" by the Dantean materials in the so-called *Zibaldone Laurenziano* (Florence, Biblioteca Medicea Laurenziana, MS Pluteo 29.8): see, including for additional references, Zamponi, Pantarotto, and Tomiello, "Stratigrafia"; and Petoletti, "Gli Zibaldoni," 291–300 and 305–13. For a facsimile of the *Zibaldone Laurenziano*, see Biagi, ed., *Lo Zibaldone Boccaccesco*.

45. The glossing of *canzoni distese* as polystrophic *canzoni* is in De Robertis, ed., *Rime* (2002), 1/1:xix. On the so-called *silloge del Boccaccio*, see Tanturli, "Come si forma," but cf. Barolini, "Critical Philology." On the three redactions of the *Trattatello*, see, at least, Ricci, "Le tre redazioni." For a general introduction to the *Trattatello*, see, including for additional bibliography, S. Gilson, *Dante*, 25–32 (on the first redaction) and 40–41 (on the second redaction); Filosa, "To Praise Dante"; and Berté and Fiorilla, "Il *Trattatello*." For the text of the three redactions, see Ricci, ed., *Trattatello*, 437–96 (first redaction) and 497–538 (second redaction, texts A and B).

46. De Robertis, ed., *Il Codice Chigiano*, 21.

47. Battaglia Ricci, "Tendenze prosimetriche," 87: "un'ideale biblioteca volgare autografa di Boccaccio."

48. K^2 is a composite miscellaneous manuscript that binds together codicological units that were not originally joined. De Robertis (ed., *Il Codice Chigiano*, 17–27) conclusively demonstrated that the position currently occupied by the quire dedicated to Cavalcanti (fols. 29r–32v) was originally reserved for Boccaccio's transcription of the *Commedia* (now MS Chigiano L.VI.213 of the Vatican Library). Prior to De Robertis's demonstration, Vandelli ("Giovanni Boccaccio editore," 64) had hypothesized an original pairing of these two manuscripts. It is unclear if Boccaccio himself split the original codex into two. De Robertis (ed., *Il Codice Chigiano*, 28 and 39–40) proposed that the division might be linked to the compilation of the so-called *Raccolta aragonese*, an anthology of Tuscan poetry

curated by Angelo Poliziano on behalf of Lorenzo de' Medici around 1476–77. See also Bologna, *Tradizione*, 206. On the *carmen* "Ytalie iam certus honos," see Trovato et al., "La tradizione e il testo" (the text, edited by Fiorentini, is at 106–11, from which I cite). The referenced gift copy of the *Commedia* is either MS Vat. Lat. 3199 (*Vat*), preserved in the Biblioteca Apostolica Vaticana, or a closely related manuscript.

49. See Cursi, "Boccaccio," esp. 19–20 and 31.

50. See Bertelli, "La prima silloge," 267.

51. Semidiplomatically: "Incipit uita noua clarissimi uiri dantis aligerij florentini."

52. Pirovano, "Per una nuova edizione," 284: "un punto sormontato da una virgola con svolazzo verso destra." The initials marking the beginning of the poems and the ensuing prose sections are followed by majuscules in brown ink with yellow traits. For a detailed description of the four orders of initials, see Banella, *La "Vita nuova,"* 22–64.

53. A similar set of letters and diacritical signs is also used for the prosimetrum's only *ballata*.

54. In the second redaction of the *Trattatello* (also known as the first compendium or compendium A), the choice of the vernacular for the *rubrica* is consistent with the vernacular title for the prosimetrum (*Vita nuova*), the omission of the title of the Latin political treatise *Monarchia*, and the omitted mention of the Latin epistles in the section on Dante's works. The third redaction (or second compendium or compendium B), of which no autograph exists, is transmitted by twenty-nine manuscripts; see, also for further bibliography, Fiorilla, ed., *Trattatello*, "Nota," 19–27 (esp. 19).

55. Minor differences in paragraph division (e.g., the ascription to the main text of parts of the *divisione* of the *ballata*, as opposed to their marginalization in *To*) and paragraphemic signs (e.g., paragraph signs dividing the sonnets' sirmas into two tercets) are less relevant to this chapter's discourse.

56. See Gorni, ed., *Vita Nova*, 225.

57. I borrow the efficacious formula *proemio al mezzo* from Conte, "Proems." Boccaccio certainly knew the text of *Epistle* 11 (addressed to the Italian cardinals gathered in conclave in Carpentras and composed between April and July 1314), since he transcribed it on fols. 62v–63r of the so-called *Zibaldone Laurenziano* (see note 44, above).

58. See Wilkins, *The Making*, 145–94, and Santagata, *I frammenti*, 253–67. On the bipartite structure of the *Vita nova*, see Antonelli, "La morte," but cf. Pirovano, "*Vita nuova*: A Novel Book," 157–58, for whom—after Singleton—the *Vita nova* presents a tripartite structure.

59. See, for instance, Ascoli, *Dante*, 178: "Intense self-consciousness in these areas [*sc.* Dante's own poetic evolution and relation to his vernacular predecessors] only makes the absence of meta-critical reflection on the project of the book as a whole—and especially on its unique brand of auto-commentary—all the more noticeable."

60. For a detailed description of the earliest scribes' material treatment of the textual components associated with Beatrice's death, see Storey, "Following Instructions," esp. 124–26.

61. Ricci, ed., *Trattatello* (I. red.), 481 (§ 175). The English translation is by Bollettino, trans., *Life of Dante*, 46. Significantly, the second redaction of the *Trattatello* (Ricci, ed., *Trattatello* [II red., A], 525, § 115) omits the first redaction's specific reference to the material organization of poems and prose: "Compose questo glorioso poeta più opere ne' suoi giorni, tra le quali si crede la prima un libretto volgare, che egli intitola *Vita nuova*: nel quale egli e in prosa e in sonetti e in canzoni gli accidenti dimostra dell'amore, il quale portò a Beatrice" (This glorious poet composed several works in his time: the first among these is believed to be a little book in the vernacular, which he titles *Vita nuova*: in which he demonstrates in prose, sonnets, and *canzoni* the accidents of the love he showed for Beatrice) (translation mine). On Boccaccio's bibliological lexicon with regard to Dante's work, see Storey, "A Note."

62. I cite from Barbi, ed., *La Vita Nuova*, xiv–xv (n1).

63. Banella, "La ricezione," 392: "Boccaccio nella funzione di editore si assume . . . alcune funzioni proprie dell'autore."

64. With self-conscious anachronism, I use the notion of finality of intention in the problematic terms articulated by Tanselle (*A Rationale*, 76): "If we grant that authors have intentions and therefore that the intentions of past authors are historical facts, we require no further justification for the attempt to recover those intentions and to reconstruct texts reflecting them, whatever our chances of success may be." See also Tanselle, "The Editorial Problem." On the formularity of the phrase *persone degne di fede*, see Todorović, "Boccaccio's Editing," 163–64. On the dependability of the phrase (and Boccaccio's own reliability as Dante scholar), see Storey, "A Note," esp. 115–16.

65. Barbi, ed., *La Vita Nuova*, xiv–xv (n1).

66. See Brambilla Ageno, ed., *Convivio*, 2:6–7: "E se nella presente opera, la quale è Convivio nominata e vo' che sia, più virilmente si trattasse che nella Vita Nova, non intendo però a quella in parte alcuna derogare, ma maggiormente giovare per questa quella; veggendo sì come ragionevolemente quella fervida e passionata, questa temperata e virile essere conviene. Ché altro si conviene e dire e operare ad una etade che ad altra; per che certi costumi sono idonei e laudabili ad

una etade che sono sconci e biasimevoli ad altra, sì come di sotto, nel quarto trattato di questo libro, sarà propia ragione mostrata. E io in quella dinanzi, all'entrata della mia gioventute parlai, e in questa dipoi, quella già trapassata" (And if the present work, which is called, as I would have it, the *Convivio*, treats its material in a more virile manner than did the *Vita nova*, I do not mean in any way to diminish the value of that work, but to enhance the earlier work through this one, since it was fitting for that work to have been fervid and passionate while this is temperate and virile. It is appropriate to speak and work in different modes at different ages, since some modes are suitable and praiseworthy at one age that are harmful and blameworthy at another, the specific reason for which will be shown below, in the fourth treatise of this book. In that earlier work I was speaking at the outset of my youth, and in this later one, after it already had been left behind). The English translation is from Frisardi, trans., *Convivio*, 7; see also the entry "derogare" compiled by Francesca Faleri in the *TLIO* (*s.v.*). On Boccaccio's knowledge of Dante's *Convivio*, see, including for previous bibliography, Arduini, *Dante's "Convivio,"* "Boccaccio and the Rediscovery of the *Convivio* in Laurentian Florence," 49–69 (esp. 53–58).

67. See Todorović, "Boccaccio's Editing," 158: "Boccaccio wrote and understood his work as Dante's biography the same way he read Dante's *libello* as an autobiographical account, a sort of self-written *vita auctoris/vida*." See also Armstrong, "Boccaccio and Dante," 124: "This [*sc. To*'s *Trattatello* or *Life of Dante*] is followed by Dante's own *Vita nova* (fols. 29r–46v), an alternative version of the 'Life,' now autobiographical and written in the first person." On Boccaccio's narratives of Dante's life, see Storey, "Boccaccio narra." On the relationship between the *Vita nova* and the *Trattatello* (and on the presence of the former in the latter), see Carrai, "La *Vita nova* nel *Trattatello*."

68. See, for instance, Gorni, "Ancora sui *paragrafi*," 548, and Banella, *La "Vita nuova,"* 15 and 284n98.

69. What the aesthetic and visual uniformity enhances is not necessarily the prosimetrum's narrativity. Even if the purpose served by initials and paragraphemic elements must be accounted for on a case-by-case basis, it might be useful to mention Battaglia Ricci's observations (*Boccaccio*, 122–28) on the material presentation of the autograph of the *Decameron* (Berlin, Staatsbibliothek Preußischer Kulturbesitz, MS Hamilton 90): what modern readers consider the quintessential work of fiction there assumes the codicological form of a scholastic treatise. The codex is modeled on the university desk book (medium-large format, Gothic book hand, text in two columns, ample margins for annotations) and its hierarchical system of majuscules and paragraph signs is intended to draw

attention to the argumentative prefaces rather than the novellas. See also Malagnini, "Mondo commentato."

70. See Bruni, *Boccaccio*, 19–33. The second redaction of the *Trattatello* provides a more concise account of Dante's life and omits various anecdotes, but it explains the origin of two poetic compositions by referencing two additional women Dante loved. A quintessentially literary perspective also shapes Boccaccio's Latin biography of Petrarca, which presents Laura as a strictly poetological figure in spite of and against Petrarca's statements; see chapter 6, "Cohesion: Focus on Poetic Discourse."

71. Billanovich, "La leggenda dantesca," 102: "Il tema corale del *Trattatello* è l'esaltazione dell'aspra difesa con cui Dante ha mantenuto una fedeltà eroica alla vocazione di dotto e di poeta contro gli impedimenti di una vita disagiata."

72. The broadly accepted title of *Trattatello* comes from Boccaccio's own unfinished *Esposizioni sopra la Comedia* ("Accessus," § 36), written ten years after K^2 and twenty years after *To*. See Padoan, ed., *Esposizioni*, 1:8: "scrissi in sua laude un trattatello" (I have already written a brief treatise in praise of him). The English translation is from Papio, trans., *Boccaccio's Expositions*, 44.

73. That Boccaccio modeled the *Trattatello* on ancient biographies of poets to promote Dante and vernacular literature is discussed in Larner, "Traditions," and Berté and Fiorilla, "Il *Trattatello*," 56–62. On the *Trattatello*'s "classicism," see also Kirkham, "The Parallel Lives," and S. Gilson, *Dante*, 27–31. The structural influence of ancient biography does not exclude the novellistic elements in the *Trattatello* (especially when we consider the novellas with men of letters as characters in the *Decameron*); see Bellomo, "Tra biografia e novellistica." The second redaction of the *Trattatello*, however, suppresses several anecdotal elements; see Bartuschat, *Le "Vies,"* 71–74.

74. In K^2, the incipitarian *rubricae* of the *Trattatello* and "Donna me prega" describe Dante and Cavalcanti as "di Firenze" (fols. 1r and 29r, respectively); Boccaccio's rare signature at the bottom of the *carmen* "Ytalie iam certus honos" identifies him as "Florentinus" (fol. 34r); the *rubrica* that opens Dante's fifteen *canzoni* describes Dante as "di Firenze" (fol. 34v); and the *rubrica* of the *Fragmentorum liber* describes Petrarca as "de Florentia" (fol. 43v). K^2 also elides *To*'s ambivalence toward the *Vita nova*, omitting *To*'s reference to Dante's regrets about his juvenile work.

75. See Bologna, *Tradizione*, 166–70, where a significant parallel is drawn (167) with the "*metamorfosi strutturale*" (*structural metamorphosis*) that philologically trained scribes realized in the Occitan chansonniers from the Veneto. I use here the term "adscript" in opposition to both "subscript" and "superscript."

76. Storey, "Following Instructions," 124.

77. See, including for previous bibliography, Banella, "La ricezione," and Banella, *La "Vita nuova,"* "I codici *descripti*," 107–217.

78. The *editio princeps* reproduces the poems as they are presented in book 1 of the anthology *Sonetti e canzoni di diversi antichi autori toscani in dieci libri raccolte*, often referred to as *Giuntina di rime antiche* (Florence: Giunta, 1527). The prose text is based instead on a *descriptus* of *To* (a manuscript derived from *To*) that omitted the *divisioni*: Barbi identified this manuscript as MS Pluteo 40.42 of the Biblioteca Medicea Laurenziana in Florence. On the Sermantelli edition, see Barbi, ed., *La Vita Nuova*, lxxviii–lxxxiii, and, more recently, Todorović, "Un'operetta."

79. See, respectively, Noakes, *Timely Reading*, 83–84; Houston, *Building a Monument*, 44; Eisner, *Boccaccio*, 57; and Banella, *La "Vita nuova,"* 105 ("i testi in oggetto sono classici della letteratura, non solo da leggere, ma anche da studiare").

80. Vandelli, "Giovanni Boccaccio editore," 66: "i *molti* sono il pubblico de' lettori, presso i quali il novello editore vuole preventivamente giustificare la novità."

81. The current shelf marks of the manuscripts preserving these transcriptions are, respectively, Milan, Biblioteca Ambrosiana, MS A 204 inf.; Florence, Biblioteca Medicea Laurenziana, MS Pluteo 54.32; and Florence, Biblioteca Medicea Laurenziana, MS Pluteo 38.6; see chapter 4, "Autography"; on the peculiar case of Boccaccio's *Thebaid*, see ibid., "*Teseida* and *Thebaid*."

82. Ricci, ed., *Trattatello* (I. red.), 457–58 (§ 84), and Bollettino, trans., *Life of Dante*, 23.

83. An alternative, suggestive reading of the last word could be "fi[nxi]t" (created). On the portrait and its discovery, see Bertelli and Cursi, "Novità"; Cursi, *La scrittura*, 105–6; Bertelli and Cursi, "Homero poeta"; Bertelli and Cursi, "Ancora sul ritratto"; Bertelli, "L'immagine"; and Martinelli Tempesta and Petoletti, "Il ritratto." For a different opinion on the identity of the subject of this portrait (in this case, a self-portrait), see Signorini, "Boccaccio as Homer," and Battaglia Ricci, "L'Omero di Boccaccio." On Boccaccio's Homer as "double de Dante" (Dante's double), see Bartuschat, *Le "Vies,"* 74–77. On the Homer-Dante connections within and beyond Boccaccio, see, among others, including for additional references, Eisner, *Dante's New Life*, "The New Homer (*Ultraviolet Colophon*)," 109–26.

84. See Bergin and Fish, eds. and trans., *The New Science*, 271 (§ 786).

85. The Latin text of the *Ecloge* is cited from Albanese, ed., *Ecloge*, 1640, to which I also refer for additional linguistic observations and bibliographical refer-

ences. I cite the English translation from Wicksteed and Gardner, *Dante and Giovanni,* 153 (where *Eclogues* 1 and 2 correspond to *Ecloge* 2 and 4 in Albanese's edition). For an elegant translation in iambic pentameters, see Wicksteed and Gardner, trans., *Eclogues,* 373: "In letters black, upon receptive white, / I saw the modulations milked for me / From the Pierian bosom."

86. On the imagery of the Muses' milk in Dante, see Bologna, "Dante e il latte."

87. De Robertis, *Il libro,* 179 (and notes 1–2): "storia . . . interna."

88. Pazzaglia, "E' m'incresce," 664: "primo tentativo di una storia totale di un'esperienza." Barolini appropriately gave the *canzone* the oxymoronic label of "Cavalcantian *Vita nuova*" in her eponymous article. For the text of the *canzone,* its English translation, and additional critical bibliography, see chapter 1, note 90.

89. *Mente* and *memoria* were both thought to stem from the Latin *memini* (to remember): e.g., in Hugh of Pisa's *Derivationes.* For the entry *memini* in Hugh's *Derivationes,* see Cecchini et. al., eds., *Derivationes,* 2:749–52.

90. Carruthers, *The Book,* 29.

91. The theoretical, nonnarrative *Convivio* and *De vulgari eloquentia* conceptualize a written vernacular and a culture in the vernacular whose material correlative, as Petrucci conclusively argued ("Storia e geografia," 160), is the university desk book used to textualize contemporary official culture in Latin; see also Gargan, "Per la biblioteca," esp. 5–7. On the various orders of signification—material, metanarrative, metaphorical, metaphysical—in references to books, writing, and literature in the *Commedia,* see the appendix to part I.

92. See Picone, "Il prosimetrum," 183–85.

93. Barański, "Lascio cotale trattato," 23–26 (at 25).

94. This interpretation of the Latin verse by second-century grammarian Terentianus Maurus (*De litteris, de syllabis, de metris libri tres,* 1286: "Pro captu lectoris, habent sua fata libelli") is, of course, debated: citations also have their own destiny. I cite Terentianus Maurus from Keil, ed., *De litteris* (at 363).

Chapter 3 Appendix

The "beautiful metaphor of the quire and the volume" that titles this appendix is a citation from Benvenuto da Imola's Latin commentary to *Paradiso* 33.85–87 (see note 19, below).

1. For a historical and theoretical introduction to the *Commedia*'s book metaphorics, see references in chapter 1, note 13.

2. Steinberg, *Accounting*, 9. See also Contini, "Dante come personaggio-poeta," 355, who describes canto 26 of *Purgatorio* as an "anfizionia di rimatori" (amphictyony of poets).

3. On Dante's self-citational practice, see Barolini, *Dante's Poets*, "Autocitation and Autobiography," 3–84.

4. Dragonetti, *Dante pèlerin*, 249: "elle 'sonne bien.'" See also Bologna, *Il ritorno*, "'Antiquam exquirite matrem,'" 66–76. On Geryon's metanarrative and metapoetic significance (in addition to Barolini's book chapter mentioned in chapter 1, note 28), see, including for additional bibliography, Cachey, "Dante's Journey"; Ginzburg, "Dante's Blind Spot"; and Ferrante, "Il paradosso." On allegorical modes of metanarration (with regard to *Inferno* 28), see also Aresu, "Intertestualità," esp. 87–91.

5. Wlassics, "Le postille," 125: "tecnica postillante."

6. On the *Commedia* as "libro da banco universitario" (university desk or lectern book), see Petrucci, "Alle origini," 141, and Petrucci, "Reading," 189–90; on *Paradiso* 10.22–23, see also Battaglia Ricci, "Comporre," 28–29. An example of the *Commedia* with features of this book form is MS Egerton 943 of the British Library in London (denoted by the *siglum Eg* after Petrocchi's edition), copied on parchment in *littera textualis* in northern Italy in the first half of the fourteenth century, accompanied by the so-called Anonymous Theologian's Latin glosses, enriched by three large historiated initials at the beginning of each canticle (fols. 3r, 63r, 129r), by decorated foliate initials with friezes extending along the margins, by colored paragraph signs, and by a total of 261 illuminated vignettes (in colors and gold, throughout) attributed to the Master of the Paduan Antiphonaries. See Petrocchi, ed., *La Commedia*, 1:64–65; Brieger, Meiss, and Singleton, *Illuminated Manuscripts*, 1:262–69; Roddewig, *Dante Alighieri*, 163–64 (no. 392); Boschi Rotiroti, *Codicologia trecentesca*, 131 (no. 177); Romanini, "Manoscritti e postillati," 51; and Medica, "Maestro degli Antifonari." Only a limited number of *Commedia* exemplars conform to this university desk book form/mode. Although eight of the nine oldest codices of the *Commedia* are in *littera textualis*, the effective diffusion of the poem has followed a route different than that suggested by the metatextual indications embedded in the poem. MS Egerton 943, in fact, represents an exception, if considered within the so-called *antica vulgata*, the corpus of twenty-seven manuscripts preceding—according to Petrocchi—Boccaccio's editorial activity on Dante's text systematically collated by Petrocchi for his critical edition of the *Commedia*. Among the relatively homogeneous manuscripts of this group, the most diffuse book form is the "deluxe register-book," recursive features of which include the use of parchment, the distribution of the text in two columns, a decorative apparatus of average execution, and chancery minuscule. One might mention here the editorial production of Fran-

cesco di Ser Nardo da Barberino and the "Danti del Cento," a group of codices of the *Commedia* in deluxe register-book form dating from around the middle of the fourteenth century, legendarily linked to a scribe who allegedly provided the dowry for his daughters by producing and selling a hundred copies of the poem. See, among others, Petrocchi, ed., *La Commedia*, 1:289–313; Savino, "L'autografo virtuale"; and Boschi Rotiroti, *Codicologia trecentesca*, 75–98.

7. According to Durling's suggestive interpretation and translation, Dante would thus represent himself in the act of ruling the folios as he prepares to write (*Purgatorio* 26.64): "ditemi, acciò ch'ancor carte ne verghi" (tell me, that I may rule paper for it still). See also Singleton's translation (ed. and trans., *The Divine Comedy*, Vol. 2/1, *Purgatorio: Italian Text and Translation*, 283): "tell me—so that I may yet trace it on paper"; and his commentary *ad locum* (ibid., Vol. 2/2, *Purgatorio: Commentary*, 633), "Literally: 'that I may yet rule pages about it.' The verb *vergare* refers to the drawing of lines to guide the writing in manuscripts; here, of course, it signifies the writing itself, the report the wayfarer will make of his journey through the afterlife. This turn of phrase anticipates the fact that the verses are now to turn precisely on the subject of writing poetry." But cf. the second acceptation in the entry "vergare" compiled by Marco Maggiore for the *TLIO*: "Tracciare righi *di testo* su un supporto scrittorio, scrivere. Estens. Mettere per scritto" (To trace lines *of text* on a writing support, to write. Extens. To put in writing) (emphasis mine).

8. In *Paradiso* 23.62, it is the *Commedia* itself that leaps over: "convien saltar lo sacrato poema" (the consecrated poem must leap over).

9. Fenzi, "Il libro," 17: "l'elenco o registrazione dei beati . . . che da sempre è presente nella mente divina, e dunque, in senso lato, non è cosa diversa dalla mente divina medesima considerata nella sua infinita prescienza."

10. For a fascinating variation on the color brown as referencing the materiality of the support for writing, see *Inferno* 25.64–66, where the mutual transmutations of a thief and a snake are assimilated to the chromatic variations of a paper sheet that burns: "come procede innanzi da l'ardore / per lo papiro suso, un color bruno / che non è nero ancora e 'l bianco more" (as, when paper burns, a dark color moves up it preceding the flame; it is not yet black, but the white is dying).

11. On the verb *rilevare*, see, including for additional bibliography, the commentary *ad locum* in Chiavacci Leonardi, ed., *Commedia*, Vol. 3, *Paradiso*, 511.

12. On this complex passage and its various allegorical interpretations, see, at least, Malato, "emme."

13. Orbson, "The Universe," 101. See also Hollander, *Allegory*, "God's Visible Speech," 297–300, where the divine script of *Paradiso* 18, the marble reliefs of *Purgatorio* 10, and the epigraph on the gate of hell in *Inferno* 3 are presented as reified examples of visible speech; but cf. Pertile, "*Paradiso* XVIII," esp. 38–39.

14. In the third-oldest dated manuscript of the *Commedia*, MS 1080 of the Biblioteca dell'Archivio Storico Civico e Trivulziana in Milan (dated 1337), Dante is portrayed inside the historiated initials opening *Inferno* (fol. 1r) and *Purgatorio* (fol. 36r).

15. The text of Alanus's "Rhythmus" is cited from Migne, ed., *PL* 210:579a (translation mine).

16. See chapter 2, "*Libello*" and note 31.

17. Singleton, *Dante's "Commedia,"* viii. Basing his arguments on a thorough investigation of scriptural and patristic sources, Singleton outlined a trajectory from the book of Dante's memory in the proem of the *Vita nova* to the *volume* in *Paradiso* 33 and underscored the relationship between God's books and Dante's books; see Singleton, *An Essay*, "The Book of Memory," 25–54, and Singleton, *Dante's "Commedia,"* "Symbolism," 18–44 (esp. 25–28). As indicated by Candido ("Il libro," 67–68 and n69), Singleton's scholarship on the topic takes its cues from Curtius's 1926 essay "Das Buch als Symbol" (subsequently reworked into "The Book as Symbol," in *European Literature*, 302–47). Subsequent scholarship has qualified Singleton's considerations without undermining their hermeneutical capacity; see, for instance, Fenzi, "Il libro," esp. 15–20.

18. Battistini, "L'universo," 67: "Il libro, simbolo adattissimo di un creato concepito come perenne e inesauribile epifania, assurge allora a veicolo di un sistema semiotico onnicomprensivo con cui certificare, insieme con l'unità del creato, il nesso indissolubile tra ordine naturale e ordine morale."

19. Benvenuto da Imola's gloss to *Paradiso* 33.85 reads: "*s'interna*, idest, interlocatur" (*s'interna*: that is, one enters the other). Francesco da Buti's gloss is probably inspired by the meaning of *internarsi* in *Paradiso* 28.119–20, where Dante listens to the ternary angelic choir of Dominations, Powers, and Virtues sing Hosanna "con tre melode, che suonano in tree / ordini di letizia onde s'interna" (with three melodies, sounding in three orders of gladness that make it triple): Francesco glosses "*s'interna*; cioè si fa di tre la detta gerarcia" (*s'interna*: that is, the said hierarchy is composed out of three); and Benvenuto himself glosses "*onde s'interna*, idest, ex quibus constituitur ipse ternarius" (*onde s'interna*: that is, of which the group itself is constituted as a ternary). In his commentary to *Paradiso* 33.85, Cristoforo Landino follows Francesco da Buti: "Et *vidi* nella profondità della divinità, la quale *s'interna, i.* fa trinità, di tre persone, padre et figliuolo et spirito sancto (And *vidi* in the depth of the divinity, which *s'interna*, i.e., is made a trinity of three persons, father and son and the holy ghost). I cite Benvenuto da Imola, Francesco da Buti, and Cristoforo Landino from the Dartmouth Dante Project: http://dante.dartmouth.edu (translations mine). On *in-*

ternare/*internarsi*, see the two unsigned entries in the *Enciclopedia Dantesca*, 3:483 (*s.v.* "internarsi"); the two entries by Luca Morlino in the *TLIO* (*s.v.* "internare"); and Ahern, "Binding," 807n17.

20. Rossini (*Dante*, 55–88) argues that the dialectic between three and four that pervades the tercet also anticipates the geometrical problem of squaring the circle mentioned further into the canto (*Paradiso* 33.133–35). See also Mazzotta, "Cosmology," 11–12: "In the light of this language [*sc.* the terminological distinction between *volume*-scroll and *libro*-codex] from the history of manuscripts, it can be inferred that Dante figures the cosmos as the paradoxical simultaneous combination of scroll and codex, of a circle and a square, which the geometer—as he will say in one of his last tercets—in vain seeks to trace ("Qual è 'l geomètra che tutto s'affige / per misurar lo cerchio, e non ritrova, / pensando, quel principio ond'elli indige") (*Par.* 33.133–35)."

21. The book metaphor is, indeed, one of Blumenberg's absolute metaphors. See Blumenberg, *Paradigms*, 1–5, 70–72, and 75–76. Blumenberg (*Paradigms*, 3) defines absolute metaphors as "*foundational elements* of philosophical language, 'translations' that resist being converted back into authenticity and logicality" and then continues (*Paradigms*, 4): "Evidence of absolute metaphors would force us to reconsider the relationship between logos and the imagination. The realm of the imagination could no longer be regarded solely as the substrate for transformations into conceptuality—on the assumption that each element could be processed and converted in turn, so to speak, until the supply of images was used up—but as a catalytic sphere from which the universe of concepts continually renews itself, without thereby converting and exhausting this founding reserve." As indicated in chapter 1, note 13, Blumenberg dedicated an extensive study to book metaphorics; see Blumenberg, *Die Lesbarkeit*, esp. 9–85.

22. Mandelstam, "Conversation," 400.

23. On the acceptation of *internarsi* as "enclose" and "contain," see, including for bibliographical references, the first "internarsi" entry in the *Enciclopedia Dantesca*, 3:483.

Chapter 4

The title of this chapter references Hans Christian Andersen's 1840 collection of prose poems *Billedbog uden Billeder* (*A Picture-Book without Pictures*): contrary to Andersen's collection of prose sketches, Boccaccio's autograph was intended to contain actual illustrations, but the illustrative program was only partially executed.

1. The debate on the origin of the octave (popular or Boccaccian) is heated. See, among others, Limentani, "Struttura"; Roncaglia, "Per una storia"; Picone, "Boccaccio e la codificazione"; Gorni, "Un'ipotesi"; Balduino, "Pater semper incertus"; Balduino, "Le misteriose origini"; and Bartoli, "Considerazioni."

2. Hollander, *Boccaccio's Two Venuses*, 64.

3. For a history of the *Teseida*'s critical misfortune in the nineteenth century, see Anderson, *Before the Knight's Tale*, 1–37. See also subsection "Critical Fortune" (and the relative notes) in this chapter.

4. See Vandelli, "Un autografo." The "discovery" of Boccaccio's autograph is discussed in Cursi, *La scrittura*, 1–14.

5. For the shelf marks of these exemplars, see chapter 5, "Materiality and Reception."

6. Eco, *Lector*, 54: "*un testo è un prodotto la cui sorte interpretativa deve far parte del proprio meccanismo generativo*; generare un testo significa attuare una strategia di cui fan parte le previsioni delle mosse altrui."

7. See, respectively, Agostinelli, "A Catalogue"; Malagnini, "Il libro d'autore," Malagnini, "Sul programma illustrativo," and Malagnini, "Due manoscritti"; Daniels, *Boccaccio*, "Authorship, Publication, and the Importance of Materiality," 12–40, and "*Teseida*," 41–75; and Mazzetti, "Tra testo e paratesto," Mazzetti, "Dare forma," and Mazzetti, "Boccaccio e l'invenzione." Agostinelli's descriptive catalogue of a corpus of sixty-three manuscripts (and twenty-three "irreperibili," "untraceable") is an invaluable, strictly codicological, effort intended first and foremost as *recensio* of the poem's manuscript tradition and as preliminary research for the establishment of its critical text. Malagnini's articles show the nature of Boccaccio's autograph as a visual (and not merely textual) artifact. Daniels's monograph focuses on the historical readership of the *Teseida* by charting the material aspects of the manuscripts and early printings of the poem within the cultural context of their producers and readers. Mazzetti's essays examine the functions of visual and illustrative components in Boccaccio's autographs.

8. On the *forma tractatus*, see, at least, Minnis, *Medieval Theory*, 145–59.

9. On Petrucci's notion of "rapporto di scrittura" (writing relationship), see the "Introduction" to this book and note 22 there.

10. See Mazza, "L'inventario"; Auzzas, "I codici autografi"; Signorini, "Considerazioni"; Cursi, *La scrittura*; Cursi and Fiorilla, "Giovanni Boccaccio"; De Robertis, "Boccaccio copista"; De Robertis, "L'inventario"; and Armstrong, Daniels, and Milner, *The Cambridge Companion to Boccaccio*, "List of Manuscripts," xvii–xxiii. For recent codicological descriptions of these manuscripts, see De Robertis et al., *Boccaccio*, 336–80. For a general introduction to Boccaccio's writing practices, see Arduini, "Boccaccio."

11. Branca, "Parole," 7: "gusto enciclopedico, . . . genio dello sperimentale e del composito." On Boccaccio's attention to all "fatti grafici" (graphic facts), see also Casamassima, "Dentro lo scrittoio": Casamassima's notion of "fatti grafici" includes "non soltanto il sistema dei segni e la loro sequenza (forme, legature, abbreviazioni, etc.), le diverse tipologie grafiche, i fatti di stile, ma l'intero complesso fenomeno della realizzazione del testo; quindi anche i fatti grafematici, l'interpunzione, l'impaginazione, la struttura stessa del codice, etc." (not only the system of signs and their sequence [forms, ligatures, abbreviations, etc.], the various graphic typologies, and the facts of style, but also the whole complex phenomenon of the making of the text; therefore also the graphematic facts, the punctuation, the *mise-en-page*, the very structure of the codex, etc.) (ibid., 253).

12. See Cursi, *La scrittura*, 15–41.

13. See de la Mare, *Handwriting*, 17–29, and Cursi, *La scrittura*, 129–34. On Boccaccio's scripts, see also Ricci, "Evoluzione," and De Robertis, "Il posto."

14. The shelf marks of these exemplars are the following: Florence, Biblioteca Medicea Laurenziana, MS Pluteo 29.8 (*Zibaldone Laurenziano*); Milan, Biblioteca Ambrosiana, MS A 204 inf. (Thomas Aquinas's commentary to Robert Grosseteste's Latin translation of Aristotle's *Nicomachean Ethics*); Florence, Biblioteca Medicea Laurenziana, MS Pluteo 38.6, fols. 43, 100, 111, and 169 (Statius's *Thebaid*); Florence, Biblioteca Medicea Laurenziana, MS Pluteo 38.17 (Terence's comedies); and Florence, Biblioteca Medicea Laurenziana, MS Pluteo 33.31, fols. 39r–45v (*Carmina Priapea*); see Zamponi, "Nell'officina." On Aquinas's commentary, see Petoletti, "L'*Ethica Nicomachea*." On the Statius, see, at least, Vandelli, "Un autografo," 73–76; Anderson, "Boccaccio's Glosses"; Anderson, "Which Are"; and Cursi, "La *Tebaide*." On the Terence, see Finazzi and Marchiaro, "Il codice," and Finazzi, "Le postille."

15. Cursi, *La scrittura*, 98: "per la realizzazione di progetti librari così eterogenei, il Boccaccio aveva fatto ricorso a varie soluzioni grafiche, codicologiche e di organizzazione del testo nella pagina."

16. See Breschi, "Boccaccio editore," and Tanturli, "Le copie." See also chapter 3, "Giovanni Boccaccio's Transcriptions."

17. On Boccaccio's drawings, see, among others, Morello, "Disegni"; Volpe, "Boccaccio illustratore"; Kirkham, "A Visual Legacy"; and Pasut, "Boccaccio disegnatore."

18. See Tanturli and Zamponi, "Biografia," 64. Scholars' opinions vary regarding date of composition and place of completion: for Billanovich (*Restauri*, 28), it is 1341 and Florence; for Battaglia (ed., *Teseida*, cviii) and Roncaglia (ed., *Teseida*, 495), it is 1339–40 and Naples; for Muscetta (*Giovanni Boccaccio*, 79), the poem was written in Naples between 1339 and 1340, and then edited and commented in Florence a few years later; for Branca (*Giovanni Boccaccio*, 49–50),

the poem was composed in Naples before Boccaccio's return to Florence in 1340 and then reworked in Tuscany; for Bruni (*Boccaccio*, 189) and Battaglia Ricci (*Boccaccio*, 96), the Dantean reference in *Teseida* 12.84 places the completion of the poem in Florence. In an article on Boccaccio's knowledge of Dante's *De vulgari eloquentia*, Pistolesi recently consolidated the hypothesis of a Neapolitan completion of the *Teseida*; see Pistolesi, "Il *De vulgari eloquentia*," 163–71 and 194–99. On the relationship between the *Teseida* and the Neapolitan court, see Librandi, "Corte."

19. See Petrucci, "Reading," 179–94. I translate the French *taille* (Italian *taglia*) as "format." The notion of *taille*, formalized by Bozzolo and Ornato ("Les dimensions," 217–18), classifies codices into four categories based on the sum of height and length (the semiperimeter): small (<320 mm); medium-small (between 321 mm and 490 mm); medium-large (between 491 mm and 670 mm); and large (>670 mm). This system of classification has been further used in Italian codicology by Maniaci (*Terminologia*, 144) and Boschi Rotiroti (*Codicologia*, 28–32).

20. Although I refer to Bertelli and Malagnini for recent systematic descriptions of *Aut*, I intend to delineate here a set of codicological features that make clear the literary-textual implications of *Aut*'s materiality. See Malagnini, "Il libro d'autore," and Bertelli, "Codicologia," 14–17 (with essential bibliography) and 24–34. An extensive description is also in Vandelli, "Un autografo." For more concise descriptions, see Branca, *Tradizione*, 66, and Branca, *Mostra di manoscritti*, 31–32. A digital facsimile is available online at http://www.autografi.net/dl/resource/2794.

21. The large initials correspond to eight lines of text, the medium initials to three, and the small initials to one. See Malagnini, "Il libro d'autore," 31–37 and 56–57. Some irregularities can be seen/detected in the alternation of blue and red.

22. Malagnini, "Il libro d'autore," 38–52 (at 38–39: "la messa in rilievo di alcune fasi della narrazione").

23. See Menichetti, *Metrica*, 160–61.

24. Bertelli, "Codicologia," 30–31: "una straordinaria capacità di visualizzazione della pagina, in cui tutti gli elementi (testo, paratesto, scrittura e decorazione) sono disposti in maniera tale da creare un sostanziale equilibrio, una ricercata armonia tra le parti, frutto chiaramente di un bagaglio tecnico ed artistico assai pronunciato."

25. See Ciardi Dupré Dal Poggetto, "Boccaccio 'visualizzato' dal Boccaccio," 204–5. On Boccaccio's eclecticism between the visual and the verbal, see Mazzetti, "Boccaccio disegnatore."

26. The blank spaces are on fols. 5r, 8v, 11r, 15r, 17rv, 19rv, 21v, 25r, 26v, 27v, 28v, 29r, 30r, 32v, 35v, 36v, 39r, 40r, 41v, 44v, 49r, 51r, 53rv, 54v, 59rv, 62r, 71v, 73r, 76v, 78r, 81r, 84r, 87r, 99r, 100v, 103r, 104v, 107r, 109r, 110v, 111r, 113r, 115r, 117r, 120v, 124r, 125r, 126v, 127v, 129r, 130r, 132v, and 139rv.

27. The current shelf mark of this codex is Naples, Biblioteca Oratoriana del Monumento Nazionale dei Gerolamini, MS C.F.2.8 [Pil. X.36]. See Coleman, "The Oratoriana *Teseida*."

28. Agostinelli and Coleman, eds., *Teseida*, lxxxiii.

29. See Malagnini, "Il libro d'autore," 12–13: "l'immagine chiude visualmente un'azione indicata nella o nelle ottave che la precedono" (the image visually closes an action described in the preceding octave or octaves). See also Malagnini, "Due manoscritti," 176–93 (esp. 192). On the different illustrative programs of *Aut* and the Neapolitan codex, see Gabriele, "Le illustrazioni."

30. Daniels, *Boccaccio*, 42–47.

31. In the preface to the *Teseida*, the poem—in compliance with the modesty *topos*—is also described as "picciolo libretto" (small book), but small only in expressing the author's littleness compared to Fiammetta's greatness. On the modesty *topos* in Boccaccio, see, among others, Quaglio, "Picciolo libretto," and Natali, "Progetti." For additional examples of book terminology in Boccaccio's work, see, among others, Geri, *Ferrea voluptas*, 124–27, and Daniels, "Rethinking," esp. 429–45.

32. Delcorno, ed., *Elegia*, 186. The English translation is from Causa-Steindler and Mauch, trans., *The Elegy*, 156.

33. On the origins of the poet's apostrophe to his own book, see, among others, Citroni, "Le raccomandazioni."

34. Vandelli, "Un autografo," 18.

35. Similarly, in the *Filocolo*, Fiammetta is character, dedicatee, and commissioner.

36. In book 1 of the *Filocolo*, the author presents himself as *componitore* (composer); see Salinari and Sapegno, eds., *Il Filocolo*, 770.

37. See *TLIO*, *s.v.* "compilare," where the entry compiler Fabio Romanini lists the following definitions: "1. Accumulare e riunire dati in un unico testo; comporre un'opera servendosi di materiali già esistenti. 1.1. Scrivere (un doc. ufficiale). 2. Dare forma a un'entità mediante l'accumulazione di elementi. 2.1. Avvolgere un materiale filante," "1. Collect and unite data into a single text; compose a work with preexisting materials. 1.1. Write (an official document). 2. Give shape to an entity by means of accumulation of elements. 2.1. Spool a spinning fabric." On *compilatio*, see, at least, Minnis, "Late-Medieval Discussions," and Hathaway, "Compilatio."

38. See Anderson, "Boccaccio's Glosses," 52–54.

39. On Bonaventure's classification, see the section on "Authorship and Authority" in this chapter.

40. See the subsection titled "Authorial Figures" in this chapter. Kirkham, *Fabulous Vernacular*, 89, noted: "The elusive *Teseida* poet is really a plurality."

41. Another (fictionalized) reference to the rewriting of preexisting materials is made in the gloss to *Teseida* 1.2, 2–4, where the verses on the "hystoria antica, / tanto negli anni riposta et nascosa / che latino autor non par ne dica / per quel ch'io senta, in libro alcuna cosa" (an ancient tale, set aside and left long undisclosed over the years, so that no Latin author appears to have recounted it in any book, as far as I know) are glossed with "non è stata di greco translatata in latino" (It has not been translated from Greek into Latin). In this instance, however, the terminology used is that of writing (*scrivere*), rather than compiling.

42. Translation mine. McCoy (trans., *The Book of Theseus*, 330) intends "come seppi" as a parenthetical element (instead of a modal clause), assigns the action to the Muses (instead of the *persona loquens* indicated by the verb's first-person singular), and translates: "as you know."

43. Noakes, *Timely Reading*, 91.

44. See Parkes, "The Influence," and Rouse and Rouse, *Authentic Witnesses*, 191–255.

45. On Boccaccio's rubrics, see Branca, "Il tipo boccacciano." For additional references on rubrics and rubrication, see chapter 2, note 22.

46. Parkes, "The Influence," 35.

47. See, among others, Carruthers, *The Book*, 234–73, and Minnis, *Medieval Theory*, 118–59.

48. Malagnini, "Il libro d'autore," 28: "è come se Boccaccio avesse progettato il codice e la sua macrostruttura e poi, nella confezione, avesse celata proprio la sua stessa struttura."

49. Mazzetti, "Boccaccio e l'invenzione," 141. See also Malagnini, "Il libro d'autore."

50. In this paragraph and the next I am indebted to the analysis of Dante's *Purgatorio*, cantos 10–12, in Barkan, *Mute Poetry*, 27–73.

51. Stillers ("L'*Amorosa visione*," 340) similarly interprets the dreaming youngster observing figurative panels in Boccaccio's *Amorosa visione* as an allegory of the reader.

52. Bartuschat, "Appunti," 83: "il poema viene implicitamente paragonato ad un'opera figurativa per il suo carattere monumentale, ossia per la sua capacità di trasmettere alle future generazioni la memoria degli eroi."

53. Carruthers, *The Book*, 314.

54. See Malagnini, "Sul programma illustrativo."

55. Boccaccio's interest in figurative art characterizes various aspects of his work. The bibliography on this topic is extensive. In addition to Branca, *Boccaccio visualizzato*, see, among others, Ciardi Dupré Dal Poggetto, "Boccaccio 'visualizzato' dal Boccaccio"; Ciccuto, "Immagini"; Gilbert, "La devozione"; Ciccuto, "La figura"; Ciardi Dupré Dal Poggetto, "Il rapporto"; and Mazzetti, "Boccaccio disegnatore."

56. On the relationship between the *Teseida* and Dante's *De vulgari eloquentia*, see, at least, Pistolesi "Il *De vulgari eloquentia*," 163–71 and 194–99. For the text and translation of Dante's *De vulgari eloquentia*, see chapter 6, note 28.

57. Translation mine. In McCoy's more literal translation (trans., *The Book of Theseus*, 328), "in the vernacular of Latium."

58. See chapter 3, "Giovanni Boccaccio's Transcriptions."

59. Eisner, *Boccaccio*, 9.

60. See Petrucci, "Reading," 183–87; Boschi Rotiroti, *Codicologia*; and Cursi, *La scrittura*, 83–97.

61. Such attention to the codex as a whole is highly indicative and can be compared to the care that the young Petrarca and his father, Petracco di Parenzo, devoted to imposing material continuity between different works in constructing the so-called Ambrosian Virgil (Milan, Biblioteca Ambrosiana, MS A 79 inf.), where the incipit and explicit of each of Virgil's texts never coincide with the end of a quire. This aspect is of particular interest when we compare it to the codicological choices of the older Petrarca for the *Rerum vulgarium fragmenta* and his innovative strategy of beginning and closing each bifolio with the incipit and explicit of a poem, interpreting each folio as a visual and semantic unit. See Billanovich, *Petrarca*, 11–12; Petoletti, "Petrus Parentis Florentinus"; Brugnolo, "Libro d'autore," 124–26; and Storey and Capelli, "Modalità," 177.

62. Schnapp, "A Commentary," 825.

63. On the *Thebaid* as source for the *Teseida*, see Crescini, "Appendice." On the reception of Statius's *Thebaid* in the Middle Ages, see, at least, de Angelis, "I commenti"; Munk Olsen, "La réception"; Battles, *The Medieval Tradition*, 1–17; and Edwards, "Medieval Statius." On the relationship between Boccaccio and the Matter of Thebes (including Statius's *Thebaid*), see Anderson, "Mythography or Historiography?," and Punzi, *Oedipodae confusa domus*, 147–74. On the role played by Dante's characterization of Statius for Boccaccio's reading of the *Thebaid*, see Martinez, "Before the *Teseida*." On the concurrence of the Matter of Troy and the Matter of Thebes in the *Teseida*, see Battles, *The Medieval Tradition*, 61–83.

64. See Mackail, *The Springs*, 26. See also Hollander, "The Validity," 179–80n36; and Anderson, "Boccaccio's Glosses."

65. Schnapp, "A Commentary," 824.

66. See Munk Olsen, "La réception," 245–46, and Munk Olsen, *I classici*, 118–22.

67. The most recent total is 253; see Anderson, *The Manuscripts*, 2:xxxii. For a description of Statius's manuscripts, see Munk Olsen, *Catalogue*, 521–67; Munk Olsen, *Addenda*, 128–31; and volume 2 of Anderson, *The Manuscripts*. On the manuscript tradition of the *Thebaid*, see Reeve, "Statius," 394–96.

68. For the Latin text of the epistle (with translation into Italian), see Auzzas, ed., *Epistole*, 526–41 (at 536; English translation mine) and 767–73 (notes). On the *Zibaldone Laurenziano*, see, among others, Cazalé Berard, "Boccaccio's Working Notebooks," and Petoletti, "Gli Zibaldoni." The current shelf mark of the *Zibaldone Laurenziano* is Florence, Biblioteca Medicea Laurenziana, MS Pluteo 29.8.

69. See Billanovich, *Restauri*, 69–78. Billanovich's hypothesis has been recently reprised and consolidated by Antonazzo and Santagata; see Antonazzo, "Ecdotica" (with the *status quaestionis* and extensive bibliography), and Santagata, *Boccaccio indiscreto*, 16–22. See also Munk Olsen, *I classici*, 16–17.

70. On the conventional statement that commentaries are indispensable for understanding texts, see Villa, *La "lectura Terentii,"* 10; Alessio, "Edizioni medievali," 35–36; and de Angelis, "Testo," 7–10.

71. See Cursi, "La *Tebaide*."

72. One of these manuscripts, without Lactantius Placidus's commentary, has been tentatively identified by Punzi ("I libri") with Vatican City, Biblioteca Apostolica Vaticana, MS Barberiniano Lat. 74, even though this codex carries no evidence of Boccaccio's hand.

73. See Anderson, *Before the Knight's Tale*, 251–53, and Anderson, "Boccaccio's Glosses." See also de Angelis, "I commenti," 94–118.

74. Petrucci "Reading," 204.

75. Punzi, *Oedipodae confusa domus*, 158: "viene invece recuperato a livello del commento come sfondo di riferimento su cui innestare le proprie invenzioni poetiche."

76. Edwards, "Medieval Statius," 507.

77. See Rafti, "Riflessioni," 284: "un Boccaccio scriba influenzato dal modello relativamente alla sfera grafico-estetica e quindi teso a riprodurne fedelmente, o almeno nell'intenzione di fondo, l'assetto e l'aspetto" (a Boccaccio-as-scribe influenced by the graphical-aesthetic dimension of the model and, there-

fore, dedicated to faithfully reproducing its structure and appearance, at least in terms of an overall intention).

78. See Anderson, "Boccaccio's Glosses." On the date of Boccaccio's restorative intervention, see Cursi, "La *Tebaide*." On MS Laurenziano Pluteo 36.8, see also Berté, "Un codice," 22–28.

79. See Anderson, *Before the Knight's Tale*, 144. The second portion of the title was, however, written by a different hand.

80. See Vandelli, "Un autografo," 72–73. Vandelli ("Un autografo," 72–76) also mentions the similarity between the one executed miniature of *Aut* (fol. 1r, the author presenting the poem to his beloved) and an illumination with the same subject in a manuscript of the *Thebaid* from the Fondo Santa Croce of the Biblioteca Medicea Laurenziana in Florence (MS Pluteo 18 sin. 4, fol. 1v). For an alternative hypothesis on possible models for this miniature, cf. Malagnini, "Il libro d'autore," 25.

81. See Limentani, "Tendenze," but cf. Hollander, "The Validity." On Lactantius Placidus's commentary to Statius, see Clogan, "The Manuscripts"; Sweeney, *Prolegomena*; and Brugnoli, *Identikit*.

82. See Anderson, *Before the Knight's Tale*, 59: "the poem's allusive style and its scholarly apparatus propose . . . a vernacular experience of poetry in the classical tradition."

83. See Branca, *Il cantare*, 51–87 and 88–93, with a cutthroat *coup de grace* (at 91): "questo modo pedestre di sentire le tradizioni, che si schiacciano a vicenda, dà quel continuo senso di pesantezza, d'imprecisione, di chiarezza artistica non raggiunta, d'incertezza di stile, in continuo compromesso; difetti che caratterizzano i due poemetti" (this pedestrian mode of feeling the traditions [*sc.* the popular and the erudite], which crush each other, brings about that constant sense of heaviness, imprecision, unachieved artistic clarity, and insecurity of a continuously compromising style: shortcomings that characterize the two poems [*sc. Teseida* and *Filostrato*]).

84. See Limentani, ed., *Teseida*, 233 and 241–42. Limentani acknowledged, however, the exceptionality of Boccaccio's autodidactic acquisition of classical culture; see Limentani, ed., *Teseida*, 231–44 (esp. 242); Limentani, "Tendenze," 533; and Limentani, "Boccaccio 'traduttore,'" 241. On Boccaccio's classicizing efforts, see Velli, "L'apoteosi." On Boccaccio's sources for the *Teseida*, see, among others, Savj-Lopez, "Sulle fonti," and Di Sabatino, "Spigolature." On Boccaccio's anachronism in the *Teseida*, see McGregor, *The Image*, esp. 12–14. On the chivalric elements in the poem, see, among others, Branca, "La morte." For a brief report on twentieth-century readers' negative evaluation of the poem's fusion

of classical and medieval features, see McGregor, "Boccaccio's Athenian Theater," 4–5.

85. See Boitani, "Style," 185–88, and Boitani, "An Essay," 18 (for the citation). Boitani ("Style," 188) also commended the poem's vigorous characterization and recognized the *Teseida* as an influential new type of narrative poetry ("a mine of *topoi,* images, erudite information, and a mixture of styles and themes").

86. Wetherbee, "History," 177.

87. Respectively, Battaglia, ed., *Teseida,* cxlix: "violenza alle norme della versificazione tradizionale"; Limentani, "Struttura," 38: "vere e proprie zeppe"; and Soldani, "Osservazioni," 172: "una certa mancanza di compiuta consapevolezza del mezzo espressivo." See also Soldani, "L'ottava." For a more gratifying assessment of Boccaccio's versification technique, see Menichetti, "La prosodia." Menichetti, however, also acknowledges "la modesta qualità letteraria del poema, l'effetto sfocato che produce, le sue riconosciute debolezze strutturali, le sue diseguaglianze stilistiche, le sue carenze espressive, la sua metrica molle, senza nerbo . . ." (the modest literary quality of the poem, the blurred effect it produces, its recognized structural weaknesses, its stylistic discontinuities, its expressive shortcomings, its weak, nerveless metrics) (351). For additional observations on the versification of the *Teseida,* see Castellani, *Grammatica storica,* 1:519–20, and Bordin, "Boccaccio versificatore."

88. See Bruni, *Boccaccio,* 141–59 and 188–201 (at 190: "doppia ispirazione"). This double inspiration would be aimed at pursuing *variatio* and affirming that the irascible and concupiscible appetites are mutually incompatible. For strikingly differing readings of the mutual relationship between these two appetites, see Hollander, "The Validity," and Ginsberg, "Boccaccio's Characters."

89. Battaglia Ricci (*Boccaccio,* 76–99) points to the at least partially parallel modes and times of composition of the three major Neapolitan works (*Filostrato, Filocolo,* and *Teseida*), the rewriting of similar themes within different genres, the exploration of various figures of self-representation, and the variations on the playful interaction between characters, narrators, and authorial figures, which seem to "felicemente anticipare singolari procedimenti messi in atto nella composizione del *Decameron*" (successfully reveal in advance peculiar strategies enacted in the composition of the *Decameron*) (79) and mirror the intertextual relationships among the novellas. See also Battaglia Ricci, "Comporre il testo."

90. Vandelli, "Un autografo," 64–65: "non senza lambiccature e stiracchiature in buon numero" and "singolarissime."

91. Limentani, "Tendenze," 542: "una confusa ed assurda analisi allegorica."

92. Hollander, "The Validity," 164.

93. Malagnini, "Sul programma illustrativo," 528: "le glosse, come la tradizione manoscritta testimonia, . . . non sono strettamente necessarie all'opera."

94. See Kristeller, "The Scholar."

95. Zumthor, "La glose créatrice," 14: "toute poésie médiévale apparaît comme continuation, d'une part; commentaire, de l'autre."

96. On self-exegesis in Italian literature, see, at least, Peron, *L'autocommento*; Berisso, Morando, and Zublena, *L'autocommento*; and Carrai, "Il commento."

97. Segre, "Per una definizione," 3: "il commento si inserisce tra emittente e ricevente come decrittatore del messaggio" and "distanza epistemica."

98. See Eco, *The Limits*, 50–51.

99. Battaglia, ed., *Teseida*, xiii: "commento dispiegato, organico, che si rifà al contenuto della poesia, integrando, allargando, parafrasando; esso si dispone lungo i quattro margini della pagina, attorno al testo poetico, ma con regolare e bella simmetria."

100. See Powitz, "Textus," 81–84.

101. On this acceptation of *figura*, see chapter 1, "Nonnarrative Self-Reflexivity" and note 91.

102. See Maniaci, "La serva padrona"; Holtz, "Glosse"; Sautel, "Essai"; and Derolez, *The Palaeography*, 34–39 and 46.

103. See Vandelli, "Un autografo," 45–46, and de la Mare, *The Handwriting*, 22.

104. See Faleri, "Riflessioni," 140–141 and 162, and Vandelli, "Un autografo," 70n1 (but cf. Battaglia, ed., *Teseida*, xiv and cix).

105. See chapter 1, "Textual Levels" and note 40.

106. Hollander, "The Validity," 168.

107. Schnapp, "Un commento," 196.

108. On Boccaccio's scholarship in the *Genealogie*, see, among others, including for additional references, Kriesel, *Boccaccio's Corpus*, "The Allegory of the Corpus: *Genealogie deorum gentilium* and Scholarly Works," 25–58, and Lummus, *The City*, "Giovanni Boccaccio, Poet for the City," 156–216 (esp. 170–216).

109. Zaccaria, ed., *Genealogie*, 7-8/2, 1430–37.

110. Ibid., 1538.

111. Ibid., 1418–23.

112. The classic study on Venus's twofold nature is by Hollander, *Boccaccio's Two Venuses*, esp. 53–65, but cf. Freccero, "From Amazon to Court Lady."

113. Boccaccio will transcribe Cavalcanti's "Donna me prega" with Dino del Garbo's commentary and include them—as mentioned in chapter 3, "Gio-

vanni Boccaccio's Transcriptions"—in MS Chigi L.V.176 of the Biblioteca Apostolica Vaticana. On Dino del Garbo's commentary, see Fenzi, *La canzone.*

114. See Zaccaria, ed., *Genealogie*, 1538: "Quod a me persepe factum intelligenti satis apparet, cum non nunquam non tantum ad novos autores diverterim, sed ad glosulas etiam autoris nomine carentes recursum habuerim. Et id circo queruli, sic oportunitate volente, non solum inauditis veteribus, sed et novis etiam autoribus acquiescant" (A discerning reader will readily see how often this has happened, for I have not only appealed on occasion to modern authors, but have had recourse to anonymous notes. Wherefore let these cavillers bow to expediency and accept the authority of both the unfamiliar Ancients and the moderns); English translation from Osgood, trans., *Boccaccio on Poetry*, 117–18, with minor adjustment to the punctuation.

115. Kirkham, "Chiuso parlare," 341. See also Kirkham, *Fabulous Vernacular*, 89: "Unhappy in love, he [*sc.* the *Teseida* poet] resembles either Arcita or Palemone; that is for Fiammetta, who is the target reader, to decide."

116. McCoy, trans., *The Book of Theseus*, 336.

117. See Edwards, "Medieval Statius," 507: "The work framed by this interpretive machinery not only contains an erotic narrative but also itself serves as an erotic object."

118. Smarr, *Boccaccio*, 82.

119. Agostinelli and Coleman, eds., *Teseida*, 4.

120. See Schnapp, "A Commentary," 818.

121. Hollander, "The Validity," 164.

122. Ibid., 168.

123. Carruthers, *The Book*, 271.

124. The reference here, of course, is to Barthes, "The Death," 148: "The birth of the reader must be at the cost of the death of the Author."

125. Carruthers continues, "Authorial intention in itself is given no more weight than that of any subsequent reader who uses the work in his own meditative composition" (*The Book*, 237).

126. See Carrai, *Boccaccio e i volgarizzamenti*, esp. 18–19. On the reception environment of the *Teseida*, see Everson, *The Italian Romance Epic*, "Books, Readers, and Reception," 127–60.

127. Bonaventure articulates this classification in the prologue of his commentary to the first book of Peter Lombard's *Sententiarum libri quattuor* (*The Four Books of Sentences*); see Fleming, ed., *Opera Omnia*, 1:14–15 (translation mine): "Ad intelligentiam dictorum notandum, quod quadruplex est modum faciendi librum. Aliquis enim scribit aliena, nihil addendo vel mutando; et iste mere dicitur *scriptor*. Aliquis scribit aliena, addendo, sed non de suo; et iste *compilator* dicitur.

Aliquis scribit et aliena et sua, sed aliena tamquam principalia et sua tamquam annexa ad evidentiam; et iste dicitur *commentator*, non auctor. Aliquis scribit et sua et aliena, sed sua tanquam principalia, aliena tamquam annexa ad confimationem; et talis debet dici *auctor*" (To understand this point [*sc.* who the actual author of the *Sententiarum libri quattuor* is], it should be noted that there are four ways to make a book. Some write the words of others, without adding or changing anything: these are simply *scribes*. Some write the words of others, adding on, but nothing of their own: these are *compilers*. Some write the words of others as well as their own, but the former are the main text and the latter elucidate the meaning: these are *commentators*, not *authors*. Some write their own words and those of others', but their own words are the main text, and those of others are added to confirm: these must be called *authors*). For William of Alton's similar classification of authorial figures, see de Angelis, "Testo," 6. On Boccaccio and Bonaventure, see also Daniels, "Boccaccio's Narrators," esp. 38–41.

128. See Segre, "La prosa del Duecento," 30: "la distinzione tra volgarizzamento e opera originale è assai elastica: se Bono tratta come cosa sua la materia del *De miseria*, rifacendone la cornice, eliminando e aggiungendo capitoli, riassumendo e ampliando, e guardandosi dal riconoscere il suo debito verso Lotario e le altre sue fonti, d'altra parte i racconti del *Novellino* (spesso, per quanto ci consta, abilmente rielaborati), son talora dedotti quasi alla lettera da raccolte affini" (The distinction between vernacular translation and original work is very equivocal. If Bono treats the subject matter of the *De miseria* as his own, rewriting the frame, eliminating and adding whole chapters, summarizing and expanding, without recognizing his debt toward Lothar and other sources, then the short stories of the *Novellino*—often, we believe, skillfully reworked—are sometimes almost literally extracted from similar collections).

129. Although relative to a much earlier date than the *Teseida* and, therefore, symptomatic of a more archaic situation, the example of the eleventh-century Oxonian witness of the *Chanson de Roland* (Oxford, Bodleian Library, MS Digby 23, fols. 1r–72r) is still revealing. On fol. 72r, Turoldus, most probably only a copyist, ambiguously seals the poem with his name: "Ci falt la geste que Turoldus declinet" (Here ends the tale that Turoldus recounts). Turoldus appropriates the work and equivocally declares himself its author-composer. See Riquer, *Les chansons*, 105–16.

130. See Cursi, *La scrittura*, 70–72. Kirkham ("Iohannes") sees an artistic project in Boccaccio's erasure of his own signature in his autographs. See also Kirkham, *Fabulous Vernacular*, "Signed Pieces," 76–134.

131. Agostinelli and Coleman, eds. *Teseida*, xli.

132. See Coleman, "The Oratoriana *Teseida*," 122.

133. See Malagnini, "Due manoscritti," 196.

134. See de Angelis, "Testo," 15. On medieval titles, see the two *Hefte* of Lehman, *Büchertitel*.

135. Ascoli, *Dante*, 7. See also Minnis, *Medieval Theory*, 10: "In a literary context, the term *auctor* denoted someone who was at once a writer and an authority, someone not merely to be read but also to be respected and believed."

136. On the analogously exceptional case of Dante, see, among others, Ascoli, *Dante*.

137. Alfano, "In forma di libro," 29: "la produzione angioina di Boccaccio mostra che egli tentò di stabilire una sorta di equivalenza tra esistenza del libro e identificazione di una funzione d'autore."

138. On Boccaccio as a modern author *in statu nascendi* in the *Teseida*, see Stillinger, *The Song*, 1–22 (esp. 3–7).

139. See Spitzer, "Note," and Zumthor, *Parler*, 58.

140. Marginal gloss to *Teseida* 12.86 (translation mine).

141. In v. 8, Agostinelli and Coleman italicized the ultima (final syllable) in "cota*li*" to indicate that it should be prosodically expunged from a hypermetric verse; see Agostinelli and Coleman, eds., *Teseida*, xxvii.

142. Translation mine. In McCoy's less literal translation (trans., *The Book of Theseus*, 95): "I am that man."

143. Vandelli, "Un autografo," 47: "come se si trattasse di parole da mettere in mostra il meno possibile e, sto per dire, di confidenza segreta."

144. Cursi, *La scrittura*, 61–63.

145. Ibid., 63: "riflessioni di carattere strettamente personale, nelle quali l'autore abbozza un dialogo tutto interiore con il suo testo."

146. Stillinger, *The Song*, 6.

147. See, at least, Surdich, *La cornice*, "Il *Filostrato*: Ipotesi per la datazione e per l'interpretazione," 77–117; Bruni, *Boccaccio*, 151–52 and 169–73; Daniels, "Boccaccio's narrators"; and Santagata, *Boccaccio indiscreto*, "Il silenzio su Fiammetta," 99–125.

148. See, most recently, Daniels, *Boccaccio*, 53.

149. See Agostinelli, "A Catalogue."

150. On the anonymous commentary in MS Par. Ital. 582, see Maggiore, "Lo *Scripto*," and Maggiore, ed., *Scripto sopra Theseu Re* (critical edition and extensive commentary). On Bassi's commentary to the *Teseida*, see chapter 5, "Pietro Andrea de' Bassi's Commentary."

151. See Carruthers, *The Book*, 264: "It is commentary and imitation which make a text an *auctor*—not the activities of its writers but of its readers."

152. See Copeland, *Rhetoric*, 64: "Even though medieval commentary works around the text, alongside the text, as addenda to the text, it can take on a primary productive character: it continually refashions the text for changing conditions of understanding. . . . In interlinear, marginal and narrative commentary, the text can be the subject of re-creative exposition from lexical and tropic detail to comprehensive architectonics, from judgment of authorial intention to directives for reader-response (the realm of affectivity or persuasion)."

Chapter 5

1. See Battaglia Ricci, "Edizioni d'autore," 134.

2. See Daniels, *Boccaccio*, 70.

3. For the incunable, I consulted the copy housed in Cambridge, Massachusetts, Houghton Library (Inc 5735 [28.2]). Seventeen extant exemplars of the incunable are preserved in sixteen institutions across Europe and the United States (*GW* 4499, *IGI* 1810, *ISTC* ib00761000).

4. McGann, *The Textual Condition*, 10.

5. See Zaccaria, "Le fasi redazionali."

6. Padoan, Zampieri, and Lippi, "Trasmissione manoscritta," 3: "non ad un 'originale' da cui sia discesa meccanicamente tutta la tradizione manoscritta, e neppure soltanto a più 'originali' a ciascuno dei quali risalga meccanicamente la tradizione manoscritta delle varie redazioni, bensì ad un ventaglio di autografi alcuni dei quali si collocano all'interno dello stemma di una medesima redazione."

7. See Battaglia, ed., *Teseida*.

8. See ibid., "Rapporti," lxxix–xcix.

9. See Roncaglia, ed., *Teseida*, and Limentani, ed., *Teseida*.

10. See Contini, "Il *Teseida*"; Coleman, "The Knight's Tale," 99–124; Coleman, "The Oratoriana *Teseida*"; and Coleman, "*Teseida*." Remarks on Coleman's reconstruction are in Clarke, *Chaucer*, 51, and Daniels, *Boccaccio*, 41–42. A sober critique of Coleman, "*Teseida*," is in Cappi, "Riflessioni" (esp. 323–24). Interesting observations on Battaglia's *stemma* are also in Dempster, "Salvatore Battaglia's Edition."

11. See Agostinelli and Coleman, eds., *Teseida*, xxxv: "The three families have significantly different texts [of the commentary]: an *alpha* version (258 *Aut* glosses, 74 of which are unique to the *alpha* family), a *beta* version (215 *Aut* glosses, 35 of which are unique to the *beta* family), and a *gamma* version (140 *Aut* glosses, 18 of which are unique to P^2, the *gamma* copy)."

12. See Agostinelli and Coleman, eds., *Teseida*. On this edition, see Delcorno, "Una nuova proposta."

13. Editorial choices are discussed in the rich introduction (Agostinelli and Coleman, eds., *Teseida*, xi–xxxii) and seven appendices (ibid., xxxiii–cxxviii, with plates).

14. See Mazzetti, "Tra testo e paratesto," 117–26, Mazzetti, "Il segno," 252–53, and Mazzetti, "Nuovi Studi," but cf. Brunetti, "La *lectura*," 86, where the hypothesis that *Aut* is the archetype is considered "onerosa" (onerous).

15. Iser, "The Reading Process," 285.

16. See Faye, *Supplement*, 484; Branca, "Un terzo elenco," 5; Zacour and Hirsch, *Catalogue*, 94; Coleman, "Giovanni Boccaccio, *Il Teseida*"; Agostinelli, "A Catalogue," 52–53; and Coleman, *Watermarks*, 113–17. For a detailed codicological and paleographic description, see Cursi and Aresu, "Un codice."

17. See Coleman, *Watermarks*, 113–17.

18. See Petrucci, "Reading," 180–89.

19. See, among others, Orlandelli, "Osservazioni"; Miglio, "L'altra metà"; Miglio, "Criteri"; Petrucci, "Fatti protomercanteschi"; Petrucci, "Le mani"; and Ceccherini, "La genesi."

20. Daniels, *Boccaccio*, 43.

21. The first number indicates the current foliation of the manuscript; the number in square brackets indicates the original foliation in the scribe's hand as it appears in the upper-right corner of the folios' recto.

22. Mazzetti, "Tra testo e paratesto," 126: "ciò che risultava troppo oneroso in termini di spesa (la pergamena, le illustrazioni o le iniziali decorate) o in termini di tempo (la trascrizione del lungo auto commento) per la classe sociale che maggiormente lo ricevette, la classe mercantile."

23. Clarke, *Chaucer*, 52.

24. See Cursi, *Le forme*, 151.

25. In semidiplomatic transcription: "Questo Libro e di Bartolomeo | di Tomaso choluj chessello amore | fossi ispiento lo ritrovorne | solo p(er) amore di suora [*rasura*] | e di suora china e della piacente | suora isabetta tuta piena | damore."

26. Knight, "Textual Variants," 46.

27. I cite Cursi's transcription (with minor adjustments) from Cursi and Aresu, "Un codice," 150 (translation mine).

28. De Robertis, "Introduzione," xxxvii.

29. See De Robertis, "Problemi."

30. These are MS Càmpori App. 37 γ.0.5.44 of the Biblioteca Estense in Modena and MS Palatino 95 of the Biblioteca Medicea Laurenziana in Florence.

See Mantovani, ed., *La Guerra*. See also Mantovani, "Una prospettiva." The text of the second *cantare* (based on the Florentine manuscript) had previously been published in Ugolini, *I cantari*, 197–209.

31. These are Florence, Biblioteca Nazionale Centrale, MS Magliabechi VIII.1272, and Florence, Biblioteca Medicea Laurenziana, MSS Gaddi 183 and Tempi 2.

32. On Pucci and his complicated relationship with Boccaccio, see, among others, Ferreri, "Una risposta"; Quaglio, "Antonio Pucci"; Bettarini Bruni, "Un quesito"; Robins, "Antonio Pucci"; and Banella, "The Fortunes." See also the essays collected in Bendinelli Predelli, *Firenze*.

33. Branca, "Copisti": "tradizione di memoria."

34. See Barbiellini Amidei, "I cantari," and Bendinelli Predelli, "The Textualization."

35. For the formulaic aspects of the *cantare* as genre, see Cabani, *Le forme*.

36. Referencing works such as *Guerra di Troia*, *Istoria di Alessandro Magno*, *Cantari di Febus-el-Forte*, and *Piramo e Tisbe*, Mantovani ("Una prospettiva," 140) writes of "'officina' mercantesca" (*mercantesca* workshop) and "esperienze diaframmatiche, mediane, di letteratura mercantesca" (diaphragmatic, median experiences of *mercantesca* literature).

37. See Brunetti, "La *lectura*," 80–81; Adriano de' Rossi's hand has been authoritatively confirmed by Cursi in Cursi and Aresu, "Un codice," 147–48. On Adriano de' Rossi, see also Levi, "Adriano de' Rossi"; and Brunetti, "Rossi, Adriano de'."

38. Levi, "Adriano de' Rossi," 237.

39. See Petrucci, "Reading," 180–89. On *Ai*, see (including for additional references), Agostinelli, "A Catalogue," 6–7; Coleman, *Watermarks*, 39–41; Brunetti, "Adriano de' Rossi"; and Brunetti, "La *lectura*," 74–79.

40. The text of the glosses to book 1 can be read in Levi, "Adriano de' Rossi," 255–65. On the commentary transmitted by *Ai*, see Spettoli, "Le chiose."

41. Agostinelli and Coleman (eds., *Teseida*, xxxv) have discussed the difficulty of determining the authority of these abbreviated glosses.

42. See Agostinelli, "A Catalogue," 73 (Appendix 2: Copyists) and 75–77 (Appendix 5: Colophons).

43. Bec, "Le letture," 184: "un pubblico avido di letture aristocratiche, dotte o divertenti."

44. See Bec, "Sur la lecture"; Bec, "Le letture"; and Bec, "I mercanti."

45. See Alfano, "Una forma," 34: "è da osservare come—nell'età di Gutenberg—il vero successo abbia arriso al Boccaccio prosatore, e ovviamente *in primis* all'autore del *Decameron*. Pur essendo Boccaccio il responsabile del trasferimento

della nostra forma metrica [*sc.* l'ottava] dal mondo orale della poesia canterina alla dignità della pagina manoscritta, gli incunaboli e le edizioni di primo Cinquecento raggiunsero un risultato piuttosto scarso rispetto alla diffusione massiccia che l'ottava rima conosceva nello stesso periodo come forma del racconto misto di fatti d'arme e d'amore; i dati evidenziano inoltre un autentico tracollo nei restanti cinquant'anni del XVI secolo, quando apparvero soltanto due edizioni di opere boccacciane, ed entrambe a Firenze: segno di affezione per una gloria locale" (It must be observed how, in Gutenberg's age, real success smiled upon Boccaccio the prose writer, and obviously the author of the *Decameron* above all. Even if Boccaccio was responsible for transferring our meter [*sc.* the *ottava rima*] from the oral dimension of *cantari* to the dignity of manuscripts, incunabula and early sixteenth-century editions attained a rather mediocre result compared to the massive diffusion that *ottava rima* gained in the same age as a form of mixed tales of arms and love. Moreover, these data underscore a real collapse in the second half of the sixteenth century, with only two editions of Boccaccio's works, both in Florence: an indication of affection for a local glory).

46. Some scholars would see as significant that almost half of the extant manuscripts of the *Teseida* are currently housed in Florentine libraries. The current location of extant copies is one of the seven assumptions Lowe employs in identifying the localization—the place of production—of manuscripts (Lowe, "Introduction," xii–xiv, at xii): when a manuscript has been preserved for generations in an ancient center of manuscript production and is traditionally connected with it, "the presumption is that it originated in that centre, provided, of course, there is no palaeographical evidence to the contrary." But cf. Masai, "Le collectaire," and Petrucci, *La descrizione*, 65–69 (esp. 67), for cautionary remarks and qualifications. In the absence of paleographical counterarguments, the current location may contribute to ascertaining the transmission history of a manuscript.

47. Petoletti ("I codici," 93) has suggested that a fourth manuscript of the *Teseida* (Milan, Biblioteca Ambrosiana, MS I, 57 inf.) may also be of Ferrarese origin.

48. See the section titled "Colophon" in this chapter.

49. An exhaustive description of the manuscript and the incunable can be found in Agostinelli, "A Catalogue," 9–11; Mariani Canova, "I codici"; and Daniels, *Boccaccio*, 41–75.

50. A digital facsimile of the manuscript is available at http://213.21.172.25/0b02da82801d63b5.

51. See, for instance, fol. 15r: "come se narrerà ne le *Fatiche* del ditto Hercule" (as it will be told in the *Fatiche* of the said Hercules); or fol. 88v: "dove le

sue fatiche narrarò per me serà a pieno chiarito" (where I shall narrate his labors it will be fully elucidated by me). The *Fatiche* also refer back to Bassi's commentary to the *Teseida* (for instance, on fol. 218r, just before the author's conclusions: "Questa historia haveti ne le giose del vostro *Theseo* per mi facte," "You find this story in the glosses I wrote to your *Theseus*").

52. See Franceschini, *Artisti*, 1/1:174 (no. 404 q, fol. 183 dated 12/20/1435): "Mandato Illustris domini nostri Nicolai Marchionis Estensis, vos factores generales ipsius domini dari et solvi faciatis Ser Blasio de Cremona librario florenos decem auri, quos habere debet pro resto et complemento solutionis laboris sui impensi ad scribendum prelibato domino librum Thesei et Laborum Herculis, cum glossis. Et expediatur cito, quia ire vult ad patriam" (By commission of our illustrious lord Marquis Niccolò d'Este, you, *fattori generali* of said lord, proceed to pay Ser Biagio da Cremona ten gold Florins to finish writing, for our beloved lord, the book of *Theseus* and *The Labors of Hercules*, with glosses); 177 (no. 412 b, fol. 8 dated 02/05/1436): "Mandato Illustris domini Marchionis Estensis etc., vos factores generales ipsius domini dari et solvi faciatis Iacopino de Arretio miniatori ducatos octo auri pro sua mercede miniandi Theseum et quosdam alios libros prefato domino" (By commission of our illustrious lord Marquis Este etc., you, *fattori generali* of said lord, proceed to pay illuminator Iacopino d'Arezzo eight gold Florins for his illumination of the *Theseus* and some other books for said lord); 179 (no. 412 p, fol. 72 dated 11/13/1436): "Nicolaus Marchio Estensis etc. Carissimi nostri. Maistro Iacomo de Arezo nostro aminiadore ce ha adminiato uno nostro officiolo et uno Theseo. Et per parte de pagamento have ad questi di passati da quella nostra camera ducati diece. Volemo che ge faci dare al presente altri ducati vintiduo d'oro, et de tale pagamento facie fare quelle scripture te parano necessarie" (Marquis Niccolò d'Este etc. Our dearest, our illuminator Master Iacopino d'Arezzo has illuminated for us one of our *offizioli* and a *Theseus*. As part of his pay he has received so far ten Florins from our chamber. We want you to have him receive another twenty-two Florins now and to have him complete those writings you deem necessary); and 184 (no. 421 e, fol. 129 dated 06/23/1437): "Maistro Iacomino amiatore de havere . . . Uno Teseo cum trii principii, a libre IIII l'uno . . . L. XII. Principi XII de altri libri, a soldi VIII l'uno . . . L. IIII. XVI. Lettere ingropade LV, a soldi II l'una, dinari VI . . . L. VI. XVII. 6" (Master Iacomino the illuminator must receive . . . for a *Theseus* with three principal initials, at four pounds each, twelve pounds; for the twelve initials of the other Books, at eight *soldi* each, four pounds and sixteen *soldi*; for fifty-five filigreed letters, at two *soldi* and six *dinari* each, six pounds seventeen *soldi* and six *marchesani*). See also Azzetta, "Il *Teseida*," and Petoletti, "I codici," 91–93.

53. See Franceschini, *Artisti*, 1/1:173 (no. 404 m, c. 141): "*A margine*: Blasii scriptoris et Iacobi Aretini." On Biagio Bosoni, see Bertoni, "Un copista." On Jacopino, see Bollati, "Jacopino d'Arezzo."

54. On fols. 22v, 35r, 46r, 57v, 71r, 80r, 98v, 115r, 126r, 140v, and 152r.

55. This practice is discontinued after fol. 9v. Large and medium initials correspond to eight and four lines of text, respectively.

56. On fols. 34v, 45v, 57r, 70v, 79v, 98r, 115r, 125v, 140r, 152r, and 163r (for the two closing sonnets). The first sonnet is omitted.

57. The codex has catchwords in the bottom right corner of the last folio of each quire.

58. Battaglia, ed., *Teseida*, xxxiv: "la infelice compilazione, affidandosi troppo al suo discutibile gusto poetico e alla sua presunta dottrina umanistica."

59. See note 63, below.

60. On the intersection of dynastic politics and letters in the courts of the Po, see Tissoni Benvenuti, "Le armi," and Santagata, *Pastorale modenese*.

61. Tissoni Benvenuti, "L'antico," 396: "di sé travestiva anche quanto veniva letto nei libri latini e greci."

62. Very little is known of Pietro Andrea de' Bassi. Orlandi proposed the last quarter of the fourteenth century for his date of birth, while Bertoni placed his death around the mid-fifteenth century. Montagnani has written the most recent and comprehensive studies on Bassi. The only texts she was able to ascribe to him with confidence are those preserved in *MA*: his commentary to the *Teseida*, the commentary to Malpigli's *canzone* (dedicated to Niccolò III), and the still unedited *Le fatiche de Hercule*. For an anthological translation of *Le fatiche de Hercule* (based on the Houghton Library manuscript), see Thompson, ed. and trans., *The Labors*. On Bassi, see Levi, "Adriano de' Rossi," 241–43; Orlandi, "Intorno alla vita"; Bertoni, *La biblioteca*; Bertoni "Pietro Andrea Basso"; Montagnani, "Il commento"; Montagnani, "La tradizione"; Montagnani, "L'eclissi"; and Branca, *Tradizione delle opere di Giovanni Boccaccio 2*, 536–38. See also Tissoni Benvenuti, "Il commento," 213–18; Tissoni Benvenuti, "Guarino," 66–70; and Maggiore, "Lo *Scripto*," esp. 93–98. On *Le fatiche de Hercule*, see Matarrese, "Il 'materno eloquio'"; Tissoni Benvenuti, "L'antico," 391–94; Quondam, *Cavallo e cavaliere*, 166–69; and Looney, "The Reception," 167–69. On Niccolò Malpigli, see Quaquarelli, "Malpigli, Niccolò."

63. Besides the exemplars examined in this chapter (from the Biblioteca Ambrosiana, the University of Chicago Library, and the Houghton Library), see also Vatican City, Biblioteca Apostolica Vaticana, MS Vat. Lat. 10656, a paper codex in cursive script produced in Italy in the second half of the fifteenth century (digital reproduction available at https://digi.vatlib.it/view/MSS_Vat.lat

.10656); and Vatican City, Biblioteca Apostolica Vaticana, MS Urbinate Lat. 691, a paper codex in humanistic script produced in Italy and dated (on fol. 202v) April 30, 1462 by its scribe "Nicolaus Ser Marci" (digital reproduction available at https://digi.vatlib.it/view/MSS_Urb.lat.691). These two exemplars are excluded from the present case study—geographically centered on Ferrara—because I was not able to ascertain more accurately their localization (place of production).

64. At an orthographic and phonetic level, *MA* employs *z* instead of *c* to indicate the voiceless palatal affricate (e.g., fol. 2v: *zo* for *ciò*), and again *z* instead of *g* to indicate the voiced palato-alveolar affricate (e.g., fol. 1v: *inzegno* for *ingegno*). Moreover, whereas *CaM* shows a certain tendency to keep double consonants, the incunable is characterized by a typically northeastern Italian halving of consonants and improper doubling because of hypercorrection. At a lexical level, *CaM* tends to retain cultivated variants, as in *glossa* (instead of *giosa* in *MA*). At a morphological level, we will cite only *MA*'s preference for the northern Italian use of *mi* as nominative, instead of *io* (regularly used in the more Tuscan language of *CaM*). For additional linguistic details, see Montagnani, "Il commento." On Bassi's language, see also Matarrese, "Il 'materno eloquio.'"

65. See Ricci and Wilson, *Census*, 1:590 (no. 541); Agostinelli, "A Catalogue," 11–12; and Marcon, "I codici," 261–62.

66. The manuscript is listed in the auction catalogue (pt. 1, p. 40) of the 1859 sale of Libri's collection in London. On Libri, see the recent Norman, *Scientist*.

67. See Genette, *Paratexts*.

68. A digital facsimile of the manuscript is available at https://iiif.lib.harvard.edu/manifests/view/drs:454918865$1i.

69. On illuminators in Ferrara, see Campori, "I miniatori"; Bertoni, "Notizie"; Bertoni, *La biblioteca*, 35–52; Canova, "La committenza"; Hermann, *La miniatura*; and Toniolo, *La miniatura*. The tables in the volumes edited by Mottola Molfino and Natale and by Toniolo are an invaluable iconographic resource to track the illumination of MS Typ 227 to the artistic environment of the time of Borso and Ercole.

70. See Toniolo's catalogue entry in Hamburger et al., *Beyond Words*, 244. On Guglielmo Giraldi, see Alexander, *The Painted Page*, 77–78, 109, 131–33, 216–18; Canova, *Guglielmo Giraldi*; Toniolo, "Giraldi (Ziraldi), Guglielmo"; Toniolo, "Giraldi, Guglielmo"; and Canova, "Guglielmo Giraldi."

71. See Pellegrin, *La bibliothèque*, 61–64. See also Gelli, *Divise-motti*.

72. Various pencil notes by a modern hand can be read on the front pastedown and the flyleaves. Numeration of the folios and indication of the first folio of every fascicle are also by a modern hand.

73. The manuscript consists of fols. I + 151 + I'. The collation is I^{10-2} (wants 4 and 7), II^{10-6} (wants 3–8), III–XV^{10}, XIV^{10-1} (wants 10). The flyleaves are datable to the eighteenth century. The sections affected by the lacuna are book 1, 25–32; 49–56; 97–138; and book 2, 1–4.

74. See Agostinelli, "A Catalogue," 9–11. Agostinelli's description initially proposes a hypothetical identification of date ("1471?"), place ("Ferrara?"), and scribe ("Niccolo dei Passini?"), but then switches to a more assertive tone. The catalogue description mentions the *Creditori e debitori* register somewhat incidentally, despite providing specific dates. It is not clear if Agostinelli is citing from the primary source or from a secondary source. The relevant passages from the register had previously appeared in Bertoni, *La Biblioteca*, 39–41. The title of the poem varies. *Aut* refers to its own text as *Theseyda di nozze d'Emilia* (in the second of the closing sonnets) and as *Theseyda delle nozze d'Emilia* (in the final rubric of book 12). The rubrics refer to the text as *Theseyda* (variously spelled). The titles in the manuscript tradition range from *Il (libro di) Teseo* to *Il Teseida d'amore*. The titles as they appear in the manuscripts are reported in Agostinelli, "A Catalogue." See also Vandelli, "Un autografo," 18n2.

75. See Franceschini, *Artisti*, 1/1:791 (no. 1228 i, c. 49): "Maistro Francesco dai Ziglii cartolaro de havere adi XXI de febraro lire tre de marchesani per tri quinterni de carte de capreto rassadi et acunci, dati insina adi 19 de questo, de comissione de Carlo da San Zorzo, a Messer Nicolò de Passino per scrivere uno libro chiamato Theseo, de forma grande, delo Illustro Messer Alberto da Est . . . E adi XX de marzo lire dodexe, soldi otto de marchesani per li appresso scripti quinterni de capreto dati de comissione de Carlo da San Zorzo ali infrascripti scripturi per continuare de scrivere li infrascripti libri che loro hano nele mano principiati, videlicet . . . Quinterni 4 de forma grande dati a Messer Nicolò de Passim per uno libro chiamato Theseo, che lui scrive per lo prefacto Messer Alberto da Est, a soldi 21 il quinterno" (On February 21 Master Francesco Gigli the stationer is due three *marchesani* for three *quinterni* of dehaired and tanned goatskin requested by Carlo di San Giorgio and given on the past 19 to *Messer* Nicolò de Passino for the writing of a book titled *Theseus*, of large format, for the illustrious Sir Alberto d'Este . . . And on March 20 [he is due] 12 *marchesani* and eight *soldi* for the goatskin *quinterni* described below, given for the continuation of the writing of the books cited below on which they are currently working, i.e., . . . four *quinterni* of large format given to Mr. Nicolò de Passim for a book titled *Theseus*, which he is writing for said Sir Alberto d'Este, for 21 *soldi* per *quinterno*).

76. See also Franceschini, *Artisti*, 1/1:792 (no. 1228 o, c. 112): "Carlo da San Zorzo, uno de li camarlengi de la corte del Nostro Illustrissimo Signore, de havere adi VI de zugno lire vinte quatro, soldi sedexe de marchesani per tanti lui ha spesi de li soi proprii in li infrascripti quinterni de carte de capreto per fare

compire de scrivere li appresso scripti libri se fano scrivere per lo Illustro Messer Alberto da Est, li qualli libri suno stati principiati più e più mesi fano, videlicet: . . . Quinterni 12 de la sopradicta forma per fare compire de scrivere uno libro che se chiama il Theseo a soldi 22 il quinterno" (On June 6, Carlo di San Giorgio, a chamberlain at the court of our illustrious lord, is due twenty-four *lire* and sixteen *soldi de marchesani*, which he spent out of his pocket for the goatskin parchment *quinterni* to finish writing for illustrious *Messer* Alberto Este those books started several months ago, i.e., . . . twelve *quinterni* of the abovementioned form to complete a book titled *Theseus*, at twenty-two soldi the *quinterno*).

77. On humanistic books, see Petrucci, "Alle origini," 141–42: "libro umanistico."

78. See Toniolo's brief description in Hamburger et al., *Beyond Words*, 244. See also Bertoni, *La biblioteca*, 35–52, and Wieck, *Late Medieval*, 72–73. A digital facsimile of the manuscript is available at https://iiif.lib.harvard.edu/manifests/view/drs:454917305$1i.

79. We have a fair amount of information about the library of the Sforzas and Viscontis; see Pellegrin, *La bibliothèque*; Albertini Ottolenghi, "La biblioteca"; Cerrini, "Libri"; Fumagalli, "Appunti"; and Zaggia, "Appunti." The manuscript does not appear, however, in the library inventories, possibly because, as Tissoni Benvenuti has suggested ("Il commento," 198), "questi manoscritti, appunto perché in qualche modo più personali—commissionati o donati—potevano risultare inaccessibili ai catalogatori della biblioteca centrale dato che rimanevano a lungo nelle stanze private" (these manuscripts, precisely because they are somewhat more personal—commissioned or donated—could be inaccessible to the central library's cataloguers, since they stayed in private rooms for a long time).

80. See Gundersheimer, *Ferrara*, 148, 166, 187, 257, 290, 295, 297–300; Covini, "Alberto d'Este"; Tuhoi, *Herculean Ferrara*; and Chiappini, *Gli Estensi*.

81. According to Coleman ("Boccaccio's 1475 *Teseida*," 70), the two manuscripts were "chosen to serve as ambassadors to the Duke of Milan." Sforza's fascination with soldiery was probably a key factor in the choice of the *Teseida*.

82. See Tissoni Benvenuti, "Il mito di Ercole," and Matarrese, "Il mito di Ercole."

83. Copeland, *Rhetoric*, 72.

84. Unless otherwise indicated, all citations of Bassi's commentary are from *MA*, with few adjustments to punctuation and orthography (translations mine).

85. Copeland, *Rhetoric*, 64.

86. See Montagnani, "Il commento," 16: "appare ormai del tutto superata la necessità di giustificare per via allegorica un mondo classico altrimenti avvertito come pericoloso, mentre prevale il gusto della libera narrazione, del fantastico,

che tanto peso avrà nella cultura ferrarese a venire" (the necessity to give an allegorical justification to a classical world otherwise perceived as dangerous is completely overcome: the enthusiasm for free narration and fantasy prevails, which will be so relevant in the Ferrarese culture to come).

87. All citations of *Le fatiche de Hercule* are from *MA*.

88. On this extreme case, see Montagnani, "Il commento," 11–13.

89. See Montagnani, "Il commento," 17: "i nomi degli scrittori che Boccaccio cita quali fonti per taluni miti, o scompaiono, o lasciano il posto al vaghissimo 'alchuni,' come d'altro canto vengono eliminate le differenti versioni di una stessa vicenda, a volte addirittura fuse in un solo racconto, con i ben prevedibili danni per la connessione logica degli avvenimenti" (the names that Boccaccio quotes as sources for some myths either disappear or are replaced by the extremely vague formula "alchuni" [*sc.* some]; on the other hand, different versions of the same facts are eliminated, or at times even merged into a single tale, with the easily predictable damages to the logical connection of the events).

90. Barthes, "Introduction," 89.

91. Cavallo, "Un'aggiunta," 377: "i caratteri materiali connotanti i vettori del testo possono indicare in determinati casi fatti, modi, fasi della sua storia (e talora della sua stessa *scrittura*)."

92. On printing in Ferrara, see Antonelli, *Ricerche* (on Carnerio, 16–22, 30–33, and 37–39) Balsamo, "Commercio librario"; Chiappini, "Fermenti umanistici"; and Nuovo, *Il commercio librario* (on Carnerio, 18–21, 36–38, and esp. 43–51).

93. See Pietro Andrea de' Bassi, *Le fatiche d'Ercole*, Ferrara: Augustinus Carnerius, 1475 (*GW* 3721, *IGI* 1419, *ISTC* ib00280000). The copy preserved in Rome, Biblioteca universitaria Alessandrina, Inc. 495 is available online through the website of the Biblioteca europea di educazione e cultura: http://digitale.beic.it/primo_library/libweb/action/dlDisplay.do?vid=BEIC&docId=39bei_digitool1537881.

94. Parkes, "The Influence," 66.

95. A digital facsimile of the incunable is available through Gallica, the digital library of the Bibliothèque nationale de France: http://gallica.bnf.fr/ark:/12148/bpt6k70419x.r=teseide.langEN.

96. On the incunable, see Daniels, *Boccaccio*, 57–66 and 180–85, and Coleman, "Boccaccio's 1475 *Teseida*."

97. Boccaccio's preface might have actually been destined for fol. 5rv, which is blank in the Houghton Library copy but preserves the preface in other exemplars, according to the *Incunabula Short Title Catalogue*. The dedication is sometimes found attached in error to Carnerio's edition of Bassi's *Le fatiche d'Er-*

cole (1475). This is the case of the copy of *Le fatiche* that I consulted (Rome, Biblioteca universitaria Alessandrina, Inc. 495). Pagination, foliation, signature, and register are absent. Each fascicle has a catchword, printed vertically at the center of the lower margin.

98. Battaglia, ed., *Teseida*, xxxiv: "assai sospetta sorveglianza critica."

99. For Carnerio's biography, see Veneziani, "Carnerio, Agostino."

100. See Daniels, *Boccaccio*, 57–75.

101. See ibid., 60: "By using a roman font for vernacular as well as Latin works (and including the *Teseida*), it may have been Carnerio's intention to emphasize their classical elements and make them more appealing to readers with learned or humanistic pretentions." Coleman ("Boccaccio's 1475 *Teseida*") has specifically commented on the Carnerio edition of the *Teseida* as a tool for the Este court as it sought to promote Ferrara as center of the arts.

102. Escarpit, *Sociology*, 57–74.

103. See Battaglia Ricci, "Edizioni d'autore," 134. On the stemmatic relationship between *Aut* and the rest of the extant manuscript tradition, see the section titled "Textual Tradition: An Overview" (and the relative notes) in this chapter.

Chapter 6

Sections of chapters 6 and 7 appeared—in different iterations—in Aresu, "Modalità," and Aresu, "Visual Discourse." I thank the editorial boards of *Textual Cultures* and *Mediaevalia* for permission to reuse.

1. See Rizzo, ed., *Res Seniles*, 72, and Mann, ed. and trans., *My Secret Book*, 254 (Latin text) and 255 (English translation).

2. The note (to *Odes* 2, 9.10–12) is on fol. 16r of MS M.404 of the Pierpont Morgan Library in New York City. The intriguing hypothesis of the note's relationship to the *RVF* is in Billanovich, *Petrarca*, "L'Orazio Morgan e gli studi del giovane Petrarca," 49–52, but cf. Fiorilla, "Il 'libellus'" for a different assessment and additional bibliography. On the first phases of the collection, see Santagata, *I frammenti*, 133–37.

3. For a facsimile of the codex, see Belloni et al., eds., *Rerum vulgarium fragmenta*. Modigliani, ed., *Il Canzoniere*, is a diplomatic edition; Vattasso, ed., *L'originale*, is a phototypic edition. For a codicological description, see Zamponi, "Il libro." A digital facsimile of the codex is available through the Vatican Library online repository: https://digi.vatlib.it/view/MSS_Vat.lat.3195. See also Storey, Walsh, and Magni, *Petrarchive*, a rich-text digital edition of Petrarca's *canzoniere*:

transcriptions, multilayered commentary, and English translation; https://dcl.ils.indiana.edu/petrarchive/.

4. See Wilkins, *The Making*, in many respects preceded by Phelps, *The Earlier and Later Forms*. For a critical approach to Wilkins's notion of the nine forms of Petrarca's *canzoniere*, see Del Puppo and Storey, "Wilkins"; Barolini, "Petrarch at the Crossroads"; Warkentin, "Infaticabile maestro"; and Pulsoni, "Il metodo."

5. Wilkins, *The Making*, and Santagata, *I frammenti*, should be complemented by Frasso, "Pallide sinopie"; Feo, "In vetustissimis cedulis"; Pancheri, "Ramificazioni"; Pulsoni, "Il metodo," esp. 262–70; and Salvatore, "Sondaggi." See also Santagata, ed., *Canzoniere*, "Le redazioni," ccv–ccix.

6. Petrarca's repulsion is well documented by remarks in his works. See, for instance, the letter addressed to Boccaccio (*Familiares* 21.15), in which he denigrates the crowd of *ineptissimi laudatores* ("tasteless admirers") of Dante's works and pities those whose works—including his own—are disfigured "in tabernis et in foro" (in taverns and in the square) and "in triviis" (at the street corners); or see the verse letter to Barbato da Sulmona (*Epystole* 1.70–72), in which he dismisses popular plaudit: "Durum, sed et ipse per urbes / Iam populo plaudente legor, nec Musa regressum / Secreti iam callis habet vetitumque latere est" (It is a harsh fate, but I am also read by an applauding crowd in the cities; my Muse finds no private retreat, and she is forbidden to hide) (translation mine). For the text of the *Familiares*, see note 57, below. For the text of the *Epystole*, see Schönberger and Schönberger, eds. and trans., *Epistulae metricae* (at 32). On Petrarca's conflictual attitude toward the "publication" of his work (and toward his readers), see, among others, Root, "Publication," esp. 420–27, and Geri, Ferrea voluptas, "La diffusione dei testi e il rapporto con i lettori," 315–40 (esp. 315–19).

7. Roncaglia, "L'invenzione," 5–6: "Le parole che terminano i versi non soggiacciono, entro la singola strofa, a vincolo di rima, ma si ripetono identiche in ogni strofa, combinando all'insistenza lessicale il dispositivo dei *rims dissolutz*. . . . Da una strofa all'altra varia soltanto l'ordine di successione, che risulta a ciascuna ripresa diverso, governato però da una legge di permutazione rigorosa." On the sestina as a form and on the historical development of that form, see, among others, Mari, "La sestina"; Davidson, "The Origin"; Battaglia, *Le rime "petrose"*; Riesz, *Die Sestine*; Di Girolamo, "Forma e significato"; Canettieri, *La sestina*; Frasca, *La furia*; Billy, "La sextine à la lumière"; Canettieri, *Il gioco*; Billy, "La sextine réinventée"; Pulsoni, "Petrarca e la codificazione"; and D'Agostino, *Il pensiero*. A semifacetious approach is in Fo, Vecce, and Vela, *Coblas*.

8. For a general introduction to Old Occitan metrics and metrical terminology, see Di Girolamo, *Elementi*, and Chambers, *An Introduction*. For an inven-

tory of troubadour texts in *coblas dissolutas*, see Frank, *Répertoire métrique* (nos. 864, 875, 879, 881, 882, 883, 884); and Bampa, "Primi appunti."

9. See Mari, "La sestina" (see 961n18 for the term *retrogradatio cruciata*). The term *retrogradatio* was first documented in Martianus Capella's *De nuptiis Mercuri et Philologiae* (fifth century CE); see Mari, "Ritmo latino," 86, and Roncaglia, "L'invenzione," 19n80.

10. More recently, Billy proposed the notion of "permutation antipodique" (antipodal permutation) to replace Mari's successful formula. See Billy, *L'architecture lyrique*, 200–201: "l'ordre de reprise procède en effet de la recherche des termes les plus éloignés—donc aux antipodes—dans l'ordre de départ, dans les limites des choix successivement possibles" (the order of repetition effectively proceeds from the search for the furthest terms—those at the antipodes—from the starting point, within the limits of the subsequently possible choice).

11. See Pulsoni, "Petrarca e la codificazione."

12. Respectively in *Prose della volgar lingua*, 1.9; *I quattro libri delle Osservationi*, 4, "Delle sestine"; *Opere varie critiche*, "Se sia male scritto il verso del Petrarca *Sì ch'alla morte in un punto s'arriva*." See Marti, ed., *Prose della volgar lingua*, 67–70; Guidotti, ed., *I quattro libri*, 527–31; and Muratori, ed., *Opere varie critiche*, 133–34.

13. All citations of Arnaut's poems are from Perugi, ed., *Canzoni* (translations mine).

14. The first Arabic numeral references the collocation in De Robertis's *editio minor* (2005), from which I cite. The Roman numeral and the Arabic numeral in square brackets reference, respectively, Barbi's and Contini's classifications. See De Robertis, ed., *Rime*, 103–10 (2005); Barbi, ed., *Rime*; and Contini, ed., *Rime*. The English translation is from Foster and Boyde, eds. and trans., *Dante's Lyric Poetry*, 1:162–65 (no. 78). The bibliography on "Al poco giorno" is extensive. In addition to the aforementioned Battaglia, *Le rime "petrose,"* Riesz, *Die Sestine*, 62–68, and Frasca, *La furia*, 123–57, see, at least, Picchio Simonelli, "La sestina dantesca"; Pulega, "Modelli trobadorici"; Cudini, "Il Dante della sestina"; Durling and Martinez, *Time and the Crystal*, 109–37; Picone, "All'ombra"; Billy, "L'art et ses leurres"; Allegretti, "Il maestro"; Formisano, "*Al poco giorno*"; and Brugnolo, "Sotto il vestito, niente?" See also the recent collection by the Grupo Tenzone in Vilella, *Al poco giorno* (essays by Pasquini, Arqués, Fenzi, Pinto, Scrimieri, and Varela-Portas De Orduña).

15. Battaglia, *Le rime "petrose,"* 67: "compenetrazione"; and "alla passione dell'animo si assomma la passione della tecnica. E poco per volta la prima è superata nella pena e nell'assillo dell'altra."

16. Paden ("Petrarch as a Poet," 36) describes Petrarca's use of Occitan genres and meters in terms of continuity, extrapolation, and reversal, and concludes that "seen as a poet of Provence, he [*sc.* Petrarca] marks a culmination of the history of troubadour poetry."

17. The attribution to Arnaut of the Occitan verse closing the first stanza of *canzone* 70—v. 10, "Drez et rayson es qu'ieu ciant e·m demori" (It is right and just that I sing and be joyful)—is disputed. "Raso e dreyt"—as the *canso* alternatively begins in the extant manuscripts—is transmitted anonymously by Occitan chansonnier *K* (Paris, Bibliothèque nationale de France, f.f. 12473), produced in the Veneto in the thirteenth century; it is attributed to Guilhem de Saint Gregori in Occitan chansonnier *C* (Paris, Bibliothèque nationale de France, f.f. 856), produced in Provence in the fourteenth century. On the vexed issue of attribution, see, among others, Appel, "Petrarka"; Zingarelli, "Petrarca e i trovatori"; Perugi, "A proposito"; and Perugi, "Arnaut." Well-established in medieval Latin poetry, the *versus cum auctoritate* appear in two poems in the Romance sphere besides Petrarca; see Frank, "La chanson."

18. Fubini, *Metrica*, 332, has persuasively claimed that "Dante ha inteso la sestina come esasperazione della coscienza dell'artista" (Dante understood the sestina as intensification of artistic consciousness).

19. See Chambers, *An Introduction*, 123; Frasca, *La furia*, 118–22; and Bec, "La sextine." Among the troubadours, Bertolome Zorzi and Guilhem de Saint Gregori also composed *contrafacta* of Arnaut's poem; see Frasca, *La furia*, 103–22. On Occitan contrafacture, see Chambers, "Imitation."

20. Frasca, *La furia*, 153: "statutaria assenza dell'*aequivocum*."

21. On Petrarca's *imitatio*, see, at least, Velli, "La memoria poetica," and McLaughlin, *Literary Imitation*, 22–48. The bibliography on Petrarca's relationship with Occitan poetry is extensive. See, among others, Scarano, "Fonti"; Appel, "Petrarka"; Zingarelli, "Petrarca e i trovatori"; Casella, "Dai trovatori"; Manfredi, *La poesia*; Gáldi, "Les Origines"; Fontana, "La filologia"; Perugi, "Petrarca"; Perugi, *Trovatori*; Pulsoni, *La tecnica*; Paden, "Petrarch"; and Ravera, *Petrarca.* On Petrarca and Arnaut, see, at least, Santagata, "Petrarca e Arnaut" (republished as *Per moderne carte*, "Arnaut Daniel," 157–211); Perugi, "A proposito"; and, including for additional references, Ravera, *Petrarca*, "Arnaut Daniel," 25–38.

22. Pulsoni, "Petrarca e la codificazione," 56: "piena coscienza di comporre un testo individuabile come tipologicamente riproducibile e quindi facente parte d'un insieme omogeneo."

23. See Gorni, *Metrica*, 58.

24. See Paden, "The System," 22: "The concept of genre grew up simultaneously with the poems themselves, starting at ground zero with the earliest

troubadours," and "Many poems we categorize in this or that genre cannot have been so intended, since the concepts of the genres did not exist yet when the poems were written." On Occitan genres, see also Gonfroy, "Les genres," and Canettieri, "Appunti."

25. I transcribe from the facsimile of the autograph (translation mine). See Belloni et al., eds., *Rerum vulgarium fragmenta.* See also *RVF* 237, v. 38, where the poem is addressed as *canzone*. For the transcription of Medieval Latin and Italian texts, I follow the guidelines developed in Tognetti, *Criteri*, and (occasionally) Smith, "Conseils."

26. Petrarca acts as "legislatore" of Italian meters, according to Santagata, ed., *Canzoniere*, xli.

27. Gatien-Arnoult, ed., *Las Flors*, 3:330 (minor adjustments in punctuation) (translation mine).

28. Dante's *De vulgari eloquentia* is cited from Mengaldo, ed., *De vulgari eloquentia* (with minor adjustments in punctuation); English translation from Botterill, ed., *De vulgari eloquentia.*

29. On Dante's references to Arnaut in the *De vulgari eloquentia* (often only incidentally touched upon within the analysis of Arnaut's presence in *Purgatorio* 26), see, among others, Santangelo, *Dante*, "L'esaltazione di Arnaldo Daniello," 207–40; Bowra, "Dante," esp. 466–68; Melli, "Dante"; Toja, ed., *Canzoni*, 65–106; Folena, Vulgares eloquentes, iii–xii; Battaglia, *La rime "petrose,"* 67–100; Bondanella, "Arnaut"; Perugi, "Arnaut"; Barolini, *Dante's Poets*, 96–100 and 176–79; Beltrami, "Arnaut"; Asperti, "Dante"; and Kay, *Dante's Lyric*, 155–204.

30. I cite Benvenuto's commentary from the Dartmouth Dante Project: http://dante.dartmouth.edu.

31. See Canello, *La vita*, 56–57, but cf. Mari, "La sestina," esp. 980–84; Neri, "La canzone"; and Camporesi, "La sestina." On Petrarca's presence in medieval scholarship on Dante, see Rossi, "Presenze" (456 and n43 on Benvenuto's reference).

32. Benvenuto's anecdote would fittingly appear next to Petrarca's celebration of Arnaut as *maître-à-penser* (*contra Dantem*, reduced to a mere erotic poet in company of Beatrice) in the *Triumphus Cupidinis* (4.40–42): "fra tutti il primo Arnaldo Daniello, / gran maestro d'amor, ch'a la sua terra / ancor fa onor col suo dir strano e bello" (First of them all was Arnaut Daniel, / Master in love; and he his native land / Honors with the strange beauty of his verse). I cite the *Trionfi* from Neri, ed., *Trionfi*, 503; English translation from Wilkins, ed., *The Triumphs*, 29.

33. See Pulsoni, *La tecnica*, 82–83, and Pulsoni, "Da Petrarca," 202.

34. See Belloni, *Laura*, 16: "vicinanza del postillatore ai fatti petrarcheschi." The five sestinas are "A qualunque animale alberga in terra"; "Giovene donna sotto un verde lauro"; "L'aere gravato, et l'importuna nebbia"; "Chi è fermato di menar sua vita"; and "A la dolce ombra de le belle frondi" (*RVF* 22, 30, 66, 80, and 142 of Santagata's edition, respectively).

35. Pelosini, "Il sistema-sestine," 665: "ha . . . sottratto la sestina allo sperimentalismo degli *unica* dei suoi predecessori."

36. Dante's so-called *sestina doppia* "Amor, tu vedi ben che questa donna" (Love, you see well that this *lady*) (8 [CII, 45]), classified as "sestina rinterzata o doppia" by Contini (ed., *Rime*, 158) after Francesco Saverio Quadrio, is a peculiar type of *canzone* organized on five (not six) rhyme-words, governed by *retrogradatio* (but not *crucifixio*), and presenting rhymic correspondences within the stanzas. On Dante's "Amor, tu vedi ben," see, at least, Jeanroy, "La 'sestina doppia'"; Guérin, "Proposte"; and, including for additional bibliographical references, the collection of essays by the Grupo Tenzone in Pinto, *Amor, tu vedi ben* (essays by Pasquini, Borsa, Fenzi, Scrimieri Martín, and Varela-Portas De Orduña).

37. The few (if substantial) exceptions are *RVF* 30, v. 14 ("riva" : "s'arriva"); *RVF* 214, v. 38 ("corso" : "(è) corso"); and *RVF* 332, v. 55 ("pianto" : "(ò) pianto").

38. On the *tornadas* of Petrarca's sestinas, see Pulsoni, "Sulla morfologia," and Pulsoni, *La tecnica*, 83–92.

39. On the *canso redonda*, see Billy, "La *canso redonda*."

40. Pulsoni, *La tecnica*, 83–84, observes: "solo grazie alla perfetta riproducibilità di una forma si possono avere testi riconducibili ad un insieme omogeneo" (only through the perfect reproducibility of a form can there be texts ascribable to a homogenous set).

41. The sestinas appear on the following folios of Petrarca's autograph: 3v (*RVF* 22), 7v (*RVF* 30), 14v (*RVF* 66), 19r (*RVF* 80), 32rv (*RVF* 142), 42v (*RVF* 214), 45v (*RVF* 237), 46r (*RVF* 239), 65v–66r (*RVF* 332, the *sestina doppia*).

42. Storey, "All'interno della poetica," 155: "la sestina è sempre copiata su due colonne indipendenti, secondo un percorso di lettura 'in verticale' che contrasta con quello 'in orizzontale' degli altri generi della raccolta poetica: il lettore deve pertanto arrivare in fondo alla colonna di sinistra prima di passare a quella di destra. Dal momento che nel sistema combinatorio dei testi dei *Fragmenta* la preferenza petrarchesca sembra cadere sull'abbinamento sestina/sonetto . . . , emerge immediatamente il contrasto percepito tanto in fase di trascrizione, quanto in fase di lettura, tra un andamento cursorio della penna o dell'occhio verticale (per la sestina) o orizzontale (per il sonetto)."

43. See Brugnolo, "Libro d'autore," 120.

44. For a list of the manuscripts, see D'Agostino, *Il pensiero,* 93; Eusebi, "Lettura," 128–36; and Perugi, ed., *Canzoni,* 329–30.

45. On the "terza tradizione," see Avalle, *I manoscritti,* 98–103.

46. See Bartsch, *Grundriss.* For a diplomatic transcription of "Lo ferm voler" according to *S* and *U,* see D'Agostino, *Il pensiero,* 191–92 and 193–94, respectively; in the list of manuscripts (*Il pensiero,* 223), the *siglum U* is erroneously explained as Paris, Bibliothèque nationale de France, MS 15211 (cf. Grützmacher, "Die provenzalische," 381). For a diplomatic edition of *S,* see Shepard, ed., *The Oxford Provençal Chansonnier.*

47. See Brugnolo, "Libro d'autore," 110 and n21. See also Brugnolo, "Come scrivere," 34.

48. Shepard, ed., *The Oxford Provençal Chansonnier,* vii.

49. See http://vitanova.unipv.it. The double indication of the folio for MS Magliabechi VI.143 refers to the modern and ancient foliations (the latter in square brackets).

50. See Grimaldi, "Boccaccio editore," and Pacioni, "*Visual Poetics.*"

51. The sestinas are on fols. 45v ("A qualunque animale alberga in terra"), 48v–49r ("Giovene donna sotto un verde lauro"), 54v ("L'aere gravato, et l'importuna nebbia"), 57v–58r ("Chi è fermato di menar sua via"), and 68v ("A la dolce ombra delle belle frondi"). On Boccaccio's transcription of Petrarca's *Liber fragmentorum* in MS Chigi L.V.176, see Bettarini Bruni, Breschi, and Tanturli, "Giovanni Boccaccio," 70–95; Bettarini Bruni, "Il Petrarca chigiano"; and Eisner, *Boccaccio,* "The Making of Petrarch's Vernacular *Book of Fragments* (*Fragmentorum liber*)," 74–94.

52. The antigraph was not, however, one of Petrarca's autographs; see Bettarini Bruni, Breschi, and Tanturli, "Giovanni Boccaccio," 70–71.

53. Bohn, *Reading,* 13.

54. Any serious study of Petrarca's writing must not forget to make preliminary mention of Armando Petrucci's fundamental contribution to the field; especially Petrucci, *La scrittura;* Petrucci, "Libro e scrittura"; Petrucci, "Dalla minuta"; Petrucci, "Minute," esp. 161–68; Petrucci, "Reading and Writing," esp. 192–95; and Petrucci, "La scrittura," esp. 71–73.

55. Storey, *Transcription,* xxi. Storey's studies have such probative force that the reader cannot help but feel their conclusions should long have been obvious. In addition to Storey, *Transcription,* esp. 201–426, see also Storey, "All'interno della poetica"; Storey, "Cultural Crisis"; Storey, "Petrarch's 'Original'"; and Storey, "The Formation."

56. Rizzo, ed., *Res seniles*, 268 (translation mine).

57. The current shelf mark of this codex is Rome, Biblioteca Nazionale, MS Vitt. Em. 1632. Once commonly accepted, the attribution of the transcription to Malpaghini is now disputed. See Signorini, "Sul codice," but cf. Rizzo, "Un nuovo codice," and Rizzo, "Il copista." All references to the *Familiares* are to Rossi, ed., *Le familiari*.

58. The narrative of these material connections was reconstructed over several decades, from the late nineteenth century through the first half of the twentieth, by Nolhac, Sabbadini, and Billanovich; see Nolhac, *Pétrarque*; Sabbadini, *Le scoperte*, 23–27; and Billanovich, *Petrarca*. On Petrarca and books, see also Geri, Ferrea voluptas, "Lettura e scrittura, scrittore e lettore," 273–314 (esp. 291–310); Mann, "*Petrarca philobiblon*"; and Rico, "La biblioteca."

59. For the *Familiares*, see note 57, above. No critical edition exists for the Latin text of *De remediis utriusque fortunae*. The *editio princeps* is generally identified as the (rather unreliable) edition printed by Heinrich Eggestein in Strassburg ca. 1473–75 (the chapter "De librorum copia" on fols. 37r–38v). For the Latin text (with critical apparatus) of the section "De librorum copia," see Contini, ed., "De librorum copia" (at 77), republished in Contini, *Frammenti*, "Dal *De remediis utriusque fortunae*," 1:141–50. For an annotated English translation (from which I cite), see Rawski, trans., *Petrarch's Remedies*, "43. Many Books," 1:138–42 (at 140). For the complete Latin text—based on the early prints—of the *De remediis* with a French translation, see Carraud, ed. and trans., *Les remèdes*; on Carraud's edition of the Latin text is based Dotti, ed. and trans., *I rimedi* (Latin–Italian parallel text).

60. See Petrucci, "Libro e scrittura," 5–6 and 12–14. See also Geri, Ferrea voluptas, "Inquietudine esistenziale e inquietudine 'filologica,'" 249–72 (esp. 249–62).

61. The English translation is from Bernardo, trans., *Letters*, 3:301. Somewhat antihistorically, Lowe, "Handwriting," 223, aligns with Petrarca's opinion: "The Gothic script is difficult to read. It has the serious faults of ambiguity, artificiality, and overloading. . . . It is as if the written page was to be looked at and not read. Instead of legibility its objective seems to be a certain effect of art and beauty, which it accomplishes by loving care bestowed upon each stroke and by the unerring consistency of its style." Cf. Petrucci's description of *littera textualis* ("Libro e scrittura," 6) as "mirabile esempio di equilibrio formale e di alto livello di realizzazione estetica" (admirable example of formal equilibrium and high level of aesthetic achievement). On Malpaghini, see note 57, above, and note 74, below.

62. See Delisle, *Notice*; Ullman, "Petrarch's Favorite Books"; Fera, "I *Libri peculiares*"; and Signorini, *Sulle tracce*, 89–94 (providing the interpretive edition and analysis of the list, with ample bibliography).

63. For a photographic reproduction with interpretive edition, translation, commentary, and updated bibliography, see Signorini, *Sulle tracce*, 140–43. On the Ambrosian Virgil, see Baglio et al., eds., *Le postille*. The current shelf mark of this manuscript is Milan, Biblioteca Ambrosiana, MS A 79 inf.

64. See Petoletti, "Francesco Petrarca."

65. Fera, "La filologia," 380: "un grande punto di raccordo di dati."

66. Feo, "Petrarca, Francesco," 276: "la legittimazione a poetare in volgare." See also Feo, "Petrarca ovvero l'avanguardia."

67. Petrucci, "Minute," 161. For a catalogue of Petrarca's autograph and annotated manuscripts, see Petrucci, *La scrittura*, 115–29. On Petrarca's figurative marginalia, see Fiorilla, Marginalia *figurati*.

68. See Petrucci, *La scrittura*, and de la Mare, *The Handwriting*, 1–16.

69. On Petrarca's book hand, see Signorini, "La scrittura libraria," which provides a critical and bibliographical discussion of "semi-Gothic" as a formerly accepted but now discounted label. See also Petrucci, *Breve storia*, 162–66; Cencetti, *Lineamenti*, 264; and Supino Martini, "Per la storia."

70. See Contini, "Preliminari," 175. On the language of the *RVF*, see Vitale, *La lingua*; on its orthography, see Petrucci, "La lettera."

71. Bartoli Langeli ("Scrivere," 248) assigns the finality of the autograph to an "accidente del fato" (accident of fate) rather than a "scelta dell'uomo" (Petrarca's choice).

72. See Petrucci, "Reading and Writing," 194: "The author's book represented the culmination of a long process of textual elaboration over all of which the author himself exercised strict control by means of writing the various stages entirely in his own hand, from the first draft on paper to the last page of the definitive codex; this last, indeed, often turned into an archive-codex for an open work, receiving corrections, additions, and reconsiderations." See also Petrucci, "Minute," esp. 161–68, and Petrucci, "Dalla minuta."

73. This brief description narrowly addresses material features that are pertinent to this chapter's argument. For a complete description and analysis of Vat. Lat. 3195, see Zamponi, "Il libro."

74. On the identity of Giovanni Malpaghini, see Berté, "Giovanni Malpaghini," and Signorini, "Malpaghini." For a fictional characterization, see Santagata, *Il copista*.

75. Two initial additional folios (1a and 1b) transmit the incipits of the poems in a contemporary or perhaps slightly later hand.

76. See Leonardi, "Le origini," 284: "l'uniformazione della canzone alla scrittura a coppie del sonetto di fatto sancisce la struttura orizzontale del *Canzoniere*" (the *canzone*'s layout with verses paired horizontally, modeled on the sonnet's, effectively sanctions the horizontal structure of the *Canzoniere*).

77. Storey, "All'interno della poetica," 131: "attento ad armonizzare tutti gli aspetti del prodotto letterario, nell'ottica di una corrispondenza ideale tra chiarezza ed omogenità di contenuto e possibilità strutturanti del contenitore."

78. On the richness and complexity of Petrarca's *canzone*, see Praloran, *La canzone*.

79. See Leonardi, "Le origini," 287–88: "la disposizione in colonna è applicata ovunque si voglia mettere in risalto la presenza o la combinazione di una o più rime" (the columnar disposition is used anywhere the presence or combination of one or more rhymes needs to be emphasized).

80. Brugnolo, "Libro d'autore," 120: "garantire la distinzione immediata rispetto agli altri generi metrici del Canzoniere."

81. Pelosini, "Il sistema-sestine." On the dialectics between micro- and macropoetics in the *RVF* see Genot, "Strutture"; Santagata, *Dal sonetto*, "Connessioni intertestuali nel *Canzoniere* del Petrarca," 9–55; and Gorni, *Metrica*, 113–34. See also Segre, "Sistema"; Corti, "Testi o macrotesto?"; Longhi, "Il tutto"; Cappello, *La dimensione*, esp. 183–232; and Scaffai, *Il poeta*, esp. 15–131. For the notion of *RVF* as a lyric sequence, see Martinelli, "L'ordinamento"; Rico, "*Rime sparse*"; Barolini, "The Making"; Rico, "Prólogos"; Greene, *Post-Petrarchism*, 22–62; and Holmes, *Assemblying*, "Petrarch's *Canzoniere*," 180–90.

82. Phelps, *The Earlier and Later Forms*, 172.

83. See Roncaglia, "L'invenzione," 5: "la *sestina* si definisce non su basi tematiche—come, poniamo, l'*alba* o la *pastorella*—ma esclusivamente come struttura formale" (the *sestina* is not defined thematically—like, for instance, the *alba* or the *pasturela*—but, rather, exclusively as formal structure).

84. See Beltrami, *La metrica*, 281–83. See also Capovilla, "Materiali"; Capovilla, "I madrigali"; and Gorni, *Metrica*, 85–93.

85. See Ariani, *Petrarca*, 280–81.

86. See Storey, "All'interno della poetica," 159–60.

87. Foster, *Petrarch*, 110.

88. See Bertolucci Pizzorusso, "Libri," 125–46, and Bossy, "Cyclical Composition." On Guiraut's mini-corpus of *pasturelas*, see Bossy, "Twin Flocks," and Bertolucci Pizzorusso, "Guiraut Riquier."

89. Segre, "Le isotopie," esp. 78–79. Segre cites the definition of "isotopy" from Greimas and Courtés, *Sémiotique*, 197–98 (English translation: *Semiotics*, 164): "la récurrence de catégories sémiques, que celles-ci soient thématiques (ou abstraites) ou figuratives" (the recurrence of semic categories, be they thematic (or abstract) or figurative). See also Contini, "Préhistoire"; Segre, "I sonetti"; Canettieri, "L'aura"; and Lannutti, "Il paradiso," esp. 1002–19.

90. See, for instance, Pelosini, "Il sistema-sestine," 710: "Il genere-sestina, genere che più di ogni altro evidenzia la pregnanza della singola parola, con la ripetizione 'allucinatoria' delle sei parole-rima, è scelto da Petrarca a dare voce alla parola per eccellenza, *Laura*, collocandolo all'interno di quel sistema coerente di isotopie intorno alle quali ruota l'intero Libro" (The sestina-genre, one which more than any other emphasizes the pregnancy of the single word, with its hallucinatory repetition of the six rhyme-words, is chosen by Petrarca to voice the word par excellence, *Laura*, thus placing it within that coherent system of isotopies around which the whole Book orbits). See also *RVF* 5 (with its wordplay on *Laura*/*Laureta*) and *RVF* 225, v. 4 (with the Latin trisyllabic form *Laurëa*). On the pervasiveness of Laura's name in the *RVF*, see Chiappelli, "L'esegesi."

91. See Testa, *Il libro*.

92. Sturm-Maddox, *Petrarch's Laurels*, 63. On the relationship between Laura and landscape descriptions, see Bertone, *Lo sguardo*, 95–147, and Stierle, "Paesaggi."

93. Folena, "L'orologio," 277: "sente di essere nel tempo, non in presenza del tempo come Dante." On temporality in the *RVF*, see also Bosco, *Francesco Petrarca*, "Il senso della labilità," 54–67 (esp. 64–67); Taddeo, "Il tempo"; and Soldani, "Voce."

94. On the presence of Propertius in the *RVF*, see Tonelli, "Petrarca," and Caputo, "Petrarca."

95. See, among others, Santagata, "Presenze"; Possiedi, "Petrarca petroso"; De Robertis, "Petrarca petroso"; Ceserani, "Petrarca"; and Bologna, "PetrArca petroso." For a comprehensive inventory of Dantisms in Petrarca, see Trovato, *Dante in Petrarca*. On the exuberant eroticism of Arnaut's and Dante's "sestinas," see, among others, Jernigan, "The Song of Nail and Uncle"; Kleinhenz, "Texts," esp. 89–91; Durling and Martinez, *Time and the Crystal*, esp. 126–27; and Brugnolo, "Sotto il vestito, niente?"

96. See Halliday and Hasan, *Cohesion*.

97. A meticulously varied use of descriptors wards off the stylistic defect of repetitiousness, a true polemical target of Petrarca's poetics, as we learn from *Familiares* 8.5: "identitas . . . tedii mater" (sameness . . . mother of boredom).

98. See Riesz, *Die Sestine*, 219: "Sämtliche Figuren der Wiederholung sind demnach kennzeichnende rhetorische Elemente der Sestine: die Geminatio und die Reduplikation, das Polyptoton und die Figura etymologica, Anapher und Epipher, Annomination und Wortspiel" (All figures of repetition are therefore distinctive rhetorical elements of the sestina: *geminatio* and *reduplicatio*, *polyptoton* and *figura etymologica*, *anaphora* and *epiphora*, *annominatio* and wordplay).

99. Examples could multiply ad nauseam and often combine a number of rhetorical strategies within a short syntagm. For a glossary of rhetorical terms used in this chapter and the next, see Lausberg, *Handbook*.

100. The organization of the terms also features a *synathroesmus*.

101. See Fucilla, "Petrarchism"; Camporesi, "Il tema"; Maier-Troxler, "*In rete*"; Spaggiari, "Cacciare"; Shapiro, "The Adynaton"; and Ravera, *Petrarca*, "*Adynata*," 88–101. On the *adynaton* in the troubadours, see Cherchi, "Gli adynata." Helpful observations are also in Curtius, *European Literature*, 94–98.

102. In percentage terms, the 2.5 percent of the poems contains the 43 percent of the *adynata*. Scholars disagree, however, on the actual number of *adynata*, depending on how broadly they understand the term. See Vitale, *La lingua*, 412–13.

103. Shapiro, "The Adynaton," 234.

104. In Greimas's terms (*Semiotics*, 165), this artifice would be an example of transposition of "the concept of isotopy, developed and restricted up until now to the content plane, to the expression plane"; but cf. Segre, "Le isotopie," 66–69, where the concept of "isotopia dell'espressione" (isotopy of expression) is subject to limitations. On the language of *Laureta*, see Chiappelli, "L'esegesi," 65–67 and n21. On Saussure's paragrams, see, among others, Lepschy, *La linguistica*, 37–55.

105. For the text of Raimbaut's poem, see Pattison, ed., *The Life*, 199–203, and Folena, ed., *Caras rimas*, 26–27.

106. Roncaglia, "L'invenzione," 30: "il principio dell'inversione è insomma dichiarato come principio essenziale della poesia." See also Brusegan, "Le secret," and Zambon, "Il bue zoppo," esp. 129–32.

107. Contini, ed., *Rime*, 148: "la donna Pietra è semplicemente il legame che unisce le liriche più tecnicistiche di Dante, nelle quali l'energia lessicale e la rarità dei ritmi si trasformano, a norma di 'contenuto,' nel tema della donna aspra, dell'amore difficile." See also Sarteschi, "Da Beatrice," and Saviotti, "L'énigme."

108. Villani, ed., *Vita*, 86 (translation mine). For an example of Petrarca's statements on the nonsimulated (and nonmetaphorical) nature of his love for Laura, see his letter to Giacomo Colonna (*Familiares* 2.9), written in 1336: "Quid ergo ais? . . . re autem vera in animo meo Lauream nichil esse, nisi illam forte poeticam, ad quam aspirare me longum et indefessum studium testatur; . . . Sed, crede michi, nemo sine magno labore diu simulat; laborare autem gratis, ut insanus videaris, insania summa est" (What in the world do you say? . . . that indeed there was no Laura on my mind except perhaps the poetic one for which I have aspired as is attested by my long and untiring studies. . . . But believe me no

one can pretend at great length without great toil, and to toil for nothing so that others consider you mad is the greatest of madnesses); English translation from Bernardo, trans., *Letters*, 1:102.

109. See Chiappelli, "L'esegesi."

110. Santagata, *Dal sonetto*, 17: "un discorso che travalica i limiti (spazi bianchi) che dovrebbero circoscriverlo in un testo autosufficiente per specificarsi, arricchirsi o completarsi in quelli che lo contornano."

Chapter 7

1. For instance, Koppenfels ("Dantes 'Al poco giorno'") has divided the corpus into three subgroups of three sestinas each, based on their thematic dominant: a first group (*RVF* 22, 30, 66) of strictly erotic inspiration (in line with the precursors of the genre); a second group (*RVF* 80, 142, 214) dedicated to the unresolved conflict between sacred and profane love; and a third group that rewrites the themes of the first under the tragic presentiment of death (*RVF* 237, 239, 332). And Pelosini has indicated how each sestina builds on the previous sestina explicating and amplifying its Laurean references. On the progression of sense as a condition for macrotextual functionality, "per cui ogni testo non può stare che al punto in cui si trova" (whereby each text [*sc.* in a macrotext] can only be exactly where it is), see Corti, "Testi o macrotesto?" (at 186).

2. Brugnolo, "Libro d'autore," 120: "in un gioco di specularità che investe anche l'organizzazione formale del testo, e che ci può far parlare, per ogni singola lirica e più ancora per il loro insieme, di una sorta di *mise en abîme* dell'intero Canzoniere." See also Jenni, *La sestina*, and Vanossi, "Identità."

3. Similar reservations are expressed by Durling, "*Rerum vulgarium fragmenta*: From Manuscript to Print," 62n16, for whom "it is the great groups of important canzoni . . . that have a clearly punctuating function and allow fuller development of the major themes of the collection."

4. For a comprehensive historical excursus, see, among others, Ernst, *Carmen figuratum* (through the end of the Middle Ages), and Dencker, *Optische Poesie* (through the twentieth century). See also Pozzi, *La parola*, and Higgins, *Pattern Poetry*. On the visual aesthetics and semantics of graphic signs, see Assunto, "Scrittura come figura." On the relationships between poetry's sound, generic conventions, and syntax, and the visual shape of the printed poem, see also Hollander, *Vision*, "The Poem in the Eye," esp. 245–87.

5. Pozzi, *La parola*, 27: "La lingua, pur producendo significati a lei congeniali, viene usata come medium per ottenere significati prodotti normalmente

dall'altro ordine di rappresentazione." See also the definition by Ernst, "The Figured Poem," 9, of *carmen figuratum* as "a lyrical text (up to modern times generally also a versified text) constructed in such a way that the words—sometimes with the help of purely pictorial means—form a graphic figure which in relation to the verbal utterance has both a mimetic and symbolic function."

6. Jakobson, "On the Verbal Art," esp. 11–17. The painting is now housed in New York City's Museum of Modern Art (MoMA).

7. Contini, "Preliminari," 190: "la parola più corposa e aggressiva sta all'inizio, con tutte le possibilità di distendersi e ripararsi."

8. Frasca, *La furia*, 244: "bilanciamento bipolare."

9. Mitchell, *Iconology*, 44.

10. Shapiro, *Hieroglyph*, 3 (emphasis mine). And see Wittgenstein's definition of hieroglyphic script (*Tractatus*, 47; proposition 4.016) as one that "depicts the facts that it describes."

11. See Lapacherie, "De la grammatextualité"; see also Harpold, *Exfoliations*, "Revenge of the Word: Grammatexts on the Screen," 81–109 (88–92 on Lapacherie); and Baetens, "Visual-Verbal Materiality," 363–64.

12. Testa, *Il libro*, 96: "l'esercizio della scrittura sembra rallentare per riferirsi, in maniera più o meno esplicita, alle sue impalcature, al suo procedere e, talvolta, al suo etimo ideologico e psicologico."

13. See Testa, *Il libro*, 12: "rifratta e parziale, anamorfica e paradossale."

14. Barolini, "The Making," 14.

15. Praloran, *La canzone*, 22: "effetti di staticità dinamica." Barolini, "The Making," 16, describes Petrarca's use of the sestina as pursuing "the paradox of mobile stasis/static movement."

16. See Figurelli, "Nota," 214–15; Fubini, *Metrica*, 305–8; Picchio Simonelli, "La sestina," 140–43; Shapiro, "The Petrarchan *Selva*"; Shapiro, *Hieroglyph*, 99–108; Parzen, "A Peculiar Reading"; Frasca, *La furia*, 173–206; De Nichilo, "Petrarca"; Carrai, "La sestina"; Kuon, "Sol una nocte," 75–79; and Tonelli, *Leggere*, 146–48.

17. Rabitti, "*Nel dolce tempo*: Sintesi o nuovo cominciamento?" On the *canzone delle citazioni*, see chapter 6, "Diachrony" and note 17.

18. The myth is variously cited, alluded to, and paraphrased in approximately fifty poems of the *canzoniere*. For a list of these occurrences, see Marcozzi, *La biblioteca*, 248n277. For a first approach to Petrarca's treatment of the myth, see Dotti, "Petrarca"; Cottino-Jones, "The Myth"; Hainsworth, "The Myth"; Sturm-Maddox, *Petrarch's Metamorphoses*; Mann, "Pétrarque"; and Rossellini, *Nel "trapassar del segno,"* 143–77.

19. Santagata, *Per moderne carte*, 279: "l'inafferrabilità dell'oggetto d'amore e la frustrazione del desiderio si accampano senza il compenso di alcuna sublimazione."

20. See Calcaterra, "Giovene donna"; Durling, "Petrarch's 'Giovene donna'"; Cottino-Jones, "The Myth," 166–69; Freccero, "The Fig Tree"; Frasca, *La furia*, 263–72; and Kuon, "Sol una nocte," 90–93.

21. See Durling, "Petrarch's 'Giovene donna,'" 13–15, and Freccero, "The Fig Tree," 38–40.

22. De Robertis, "Petrarca petroso," 35: "accampa quella parola, 'idolo,' come significazione d'un'impassibilità esaltata a confronto della propria trasmutabilità, e che trova la sua raffigurazione nell'immagine del simulacro scolpito."

23. Cottino-Jones, "The Myth," 166.

24. On the anniversary poems, see, among others, Dutschke, "The Anniversary," and Carrai, "Petrarca."

25. The specific date we will retrieve from the pounding verse-filling indication of *RVF* 211, vv. 12–13: "Mille trecento ventisette, a punto / su l'ora prima, il dì sesto d'aprile" (One thousand three hundred twenty-seven, exactly at the first / hour of the sixth day of April).

26. See Riesz, *Die Sestine*, 81–83; Shapiro, *Hieroglyph*, 119–30; Frasca, *La furia*, 292–99; Bellomo, "La sestina"; and Stäuble, "Dal labirinto," esp. 270–72. See also Shapiro, "The Petrarchan *Selva*."

27. Stäuble, "Dal labirinto," 470: "una specie di autobiografia del poeta, o piuttosto rievocazione cronologica della sua vicenda amorosa."

28. I read the reference to Isidore (*Etymologiae* 11.2, 1–7) in Bettarini, ed., *Canzoniere*, 2:1002. Petrarca was dismissive of Isidore's framework in *Secretum* 3.12; see Mann, ed. and trans., *My Secret Book*, 211.

29. Bellomo, "La sestina," 346: "maggiore tensione emulativa."

30. Sestina 214 also confirms the highly cohesive quality of the sestinas as corpus. In addition to the retrospective feature that we have characterized as inherent to the sestinas and that is underscored by the visual enhancement of the sestinas' rhyme pattern, sestina 214 has a recapitulative and self-citational quality within the corpus of the sestinas. It reprises, revisits, and shares structural and thematic elements of the previous sestinas: the overall structure of a continued metaphor (*RVF* 80); the poet's invocation to God to ransom him from a sinful life (*RVF* 142); the representation of the poet as a feral dweller of the woods (*RVF* 22, and then again *RVF* 237); and the quality of a peculiar anniversary poem (*RVF* 30).

31. See Shapiro, *Hieroglyph*, 108–15; Blasucci, "La sestina"; Frasca, *La furia*, 272–78; Picone, "Petrarca," 173–78; and Praloran, *Metro*, 82–84.

32. See Picone, "Petrarca," 175: "ad ogni referente metereologico e geografico della prima stanza viene dunque attribuita una significazione psicologica o esistenziale nella seconda" (each meteorological and geographical referent of the first stanza is given a psychological or existential signification in the second).

33. Petrini, *La risurrezione*, 121: "il metro più congruo per rendere questi *avvolgimenti* meandrici della passione senza speranza."

34. Antonelli, "*Rerum vulgarium fragmenta*," 412: "*poesia della poesia*."

35. Blasucci, "La sestina," 57: "registrazione di uno stato permanente."

36. See note 1, above.

37. See Shapiro, *Hieroglyph*, 210–13; Frasca, *La furia*, 278–84; Perrus, "La sextine"; and Bartuschat, "Il ritratto," 209–12.

38. Bartuschat, "Il ritratto," 211: "la linearità quasi narrativa di questa sestina crea un profondo contrasto con il carattere fondamentalmente circolare del genere metrico. . . . essa diventa ora la forma che rispecchia il cammino della redenzione."

39. Bettarini, ed., *Canzoniere*, 1:404: "la circolarità e ricorrenza ondulare inerente al 'genere' sestina include strumentalmente in sé l'alternarsi di speranza e di naufragio." On the *topos* of life as traveling by sail, see, at least, Blumenberg, *Shipwreck*.

40. For Frasca (*La furia*, 279), Arnaut's "ferm voler," alluded to in *RVF* 80, becomes "sinonimo dell'ottusa volontà di peccare" (synonymous with the obtuse will to sin).

41. Althusser and Balibar, *Reading Capital*, 189.

42. Putzo, "The Implied Book," 391.

43. On fol. 3v, sestina 22 follows sonnet 21; on fol. 7v, sestina 30 precedes sonnet 31; on fol. 14v, sestina 66 precedes sonnet 67; on fol. 19r, sestina 80 precedes sonnet 81; on fol. 42v, sestina 214 precedes sonnet 215; on fol. 45v, sestina 237 follows sonnet 236; and on fol. 46r, sestina 239 follows sonnet 238.

44. On the "Correggio form," see Wilkins, *The Making*, 93–106. On *RVF* 142, see Riesz, *Die Sestine*, 79–81; Gorni, "Metamorfosi"; Shapiro, *Hieroglyph*, 115–19; Vanossi, "Identità"; Frasca, *La furia*, 284–92; Santagata, *I frammenti*, 238–41; Gorni, *Metrica*, 171–82; Pasquini, "La sestina"; Prandi, "Ritorno a Laura," 339–46; and Tonelli, *Leggere*, 148–50.

45. Gorni, "Metamorfosi," 4: "a un certo punto, essa parve all'autore la *sola* soluzione possibile."

46. On the allegedly bipartite structure of the "Correggio form," see, at least, Santagata, *I frammenti*, 148.

47. On the sestina's intratextual references to previous poems in the songbook, see Riesz, *Die Sestine*, 80, and Gorni, "Metamorfosi."

48. Tonelli, *Leggere*, 148: "un racconto allegorico del proprio destino amoroso indotto dagli influssi celesti."

49. See Pulsoni, "Sulla morfologia," and Pulsoni, *La tecnica*, 83–92.

50. Vecchi Galli, eds., *Canzoniere*, 688: "Francesco non è avanzato di un passo rispetto all'inizio della storia."

51. See Brugnolo, "Libro," 121–22.

52. See Gilissen, *Prolégomènes*, 113–14 and esp. 139.

53. On "Mia benigna fortuna" (*RVF* 332), see the section "*Ars Poetica*" in this chapter.

54. See Frasca, *La furia*, 299–306; Picone, "La forza," 513–16; and Albonico, "La sestina 237."

55. See Berra, *La similitudine*, 87–93: "uguaglianza negata."

56. Vitale, *La lingua*, 361–62: "Nel suo insistito ripetersi il sintagma conferisce . . . un movimento melodico di prolungata intensità, ma ancor piú accentua vivamente il significato del verbo al gerundio nella espressione dell'azione protratta, progressiva." See also Colella, "La perifrasi," 85.

57. A stimulating interpretation of this *adynaton* as manifesting the poet's sepulchral hope that Laura will visit his grave (rather than expressing his carnal desire for her) is in Albonico, "La sestina 237," 505–8.

58. See Santagata, *I frammenti*, 101–2.

59. Frasca, *La furia*, 302: "teatro del desiderio."

60. See Riesz, *Die Sestine*, 84–86; Maier-Troxler, "*In rete*"; Frasca, *La furia*, 306–11; Picone, "La forza," 516–18; and Zambon, "Il bue."

61. On the metaliterary implications of *incominciare*, see Gorni, "La teoria."

62. Zambon, "Il bue," 127: "includendola così *en abyme* proprio in alcune delle sue parole-rima (come *stile* e *rime* in *Mia benigna fortuna*)."

63. I transcribe from the facsimile (Belloni et al., eds., *Rerum vulgarium fragmenta*). The diacritic indicates a possible word-division device. On punctuation in the *RVF*'s autograph, see Capovilla, "Un sistema," and Rafti, "Alle origini."

64. On *lambdacismus* as a form of *homoeoprophoron* ("the frequent repetition of the same consonant, chiefly the initial consonant, in a sequence of several words"), see Lausberg, *Handbook*, 432–33 (§ 975.2).

65. Zambon, "Il bue," 131: "La trasformazione o 'inversione' del negativo in positivo si realizza proprio grazie al principio formale del componimento, che riprendendo ad ogni *cobla* le stesse parole-rima ne rovescia sistematicamente il valore."

66. See Shapiro, *Hieroglyph*, 130–40; Berra, "La sestina"; Frasca, *La furia*, 207–58; Caputo, "Et doppiando," 725–26; Aresu, "Modalità"; and Hannesson, "Making Sense."

67. See Sapegno, "Francesco Petrarca," 298: "il Petrarca giunge ad una sorta di linguaggio che può definirsi tecnico" (Petrarca arrives at a type of language that we could call technical).

68. See Roncaglia, "L'invenzione," 15.

69. Barański, "Tres enim," 55n45.

70. On Petrarca's technical use of *dulcedo* and its cognates, see Suitner, "La fisionomia"; Suitner, "Le rime," esp. 270–78; Vitale, *La lingua*, 3–26; Ariani, *Petrarca*, 311–35; Noferi, *Frammenti*, 197–227; and McLaughlin, "Petrarch," 23–33. On the notion of *dulcedo*, see also Corti, "Il linguaggio," esp. 188–93, for its presence in Cino da Pistoia; Heinimann, "Dulcis," for its use in Medieval Latin, Old Occitan, and Old French; Marti, *Storia*, 1:183–223, for its role in the Stilnovisti's poetics; Bruni, "Semantica," esp. 1–9, for its relationship to the semantics of *subtilitas*; Villa, *La "lectura Terentii,"* 39–42 and 191–216, for *dulcedo* in the exegetical tradition for the works of Terence; Villa, "Il lessico," for its function in the rhetorical and didactic tradition; Zamarra, "Dolce," for a survey of the related terminology in thirteenth- to sixteenth-century Italian poetry; Barański, "'nfiata labbia," for its relevance to the system of genres in medieval literature and Dante; Paolazzi, *La maniera*, for its scriptural and Horatian foundations; Mengaldo, *Linguistica*, 79; Barański, "Tres enim," 26–28 and esp. 56n50–51; and Picone, "Dante e la tradizione," 1–2. Useful indications on Dante's use of *dulcedo, asperitas, lenitas*, and their cognates can be found in the entries *asperitas, aspro, dolce, dolcezza, lenitas, soave* in Bosco, *Enciclopedia Dantesca* (*sub vocibus*). The scholarship on the topic is less extensive than one may predict and tends toward circular argument.

71. A similar presentation of this dichotomy is in *RVF* 71, v. 8; 187, v. 7; 206, vv. 30–31; 247, vv. 5–7; 293, vv. 7–8; and 304, v. 13.

72. See Grimaldi, "Petrarca."

73. See Suitner, "La fisionomia," 142: "la dimensione dell'oralità è ancora essenziale" (the oral dimension is still essential).

74. Bettarini, "Il libro," 168: "d'una Retorica segreta, d'un *De vulgari* privato e anch'esso sparso, vòlto alla fenomenologia fonica dei fatti poetici." Upon rearranging the quatrains of sonnet 155, for instance, Petrarca makes reference to issues of euphony in the left margin of fol. 3v: "At(tende) q(uia) hos 4. u(er)sus ue(n)it i(n) ani(mum) mutare ut q(ui) p(r)imj su(n)t e(ss)ent ultimj . (et) e (con-vers)o .s(ed) dimisi p(ro)p(ter) sonu(m) [. . .]" (watch out: I thought of changing these four lines, in order for the first to go last and vice versa, but I held back because of the sound [. . .]). Paolino, the editor of MS Vat. Lat. 3196, pertinently adds the continuation of the note (now trimmed off) as it was copied on MS Casanatense 924; Petrarca refrained from changing the order of the quatrains be-

cause of the sound: "pri(n)cipij (et) finis .(et) quia sona(n)tiora era(n)t . . . in medio. rauciora in principio (et) fine q(uod) est contra rhetorica(m)," "of the beginning and the end and because the more resounding lines were in the middle and the more raucous in the beginning and the end (against the norms of rhetoric)." See Paolino, ed., *Il Codice*, 203. MS Casanatense 924 is housed in the Biblioteca Casanatense in Rome.

75. See Picchio Simonelli, "Strutture." For a reading focused on the aural aspects of the *RVF*'s varied style, see Orelli, *Il suono*.

76. The Arabic numeral and the Roman numeral refer, respectively, to De Robertis's edition (ed., *Rime*, 52–78 [2005]) and Barbi's edition: Contini's edition includes only the poems of the *extravagante* tradition and consequently omits "Le dolci rime d'amor" (included in the *Convivio*). For the English translation, see Foster and Boyde, eds. and trans., *Dante's Lyric Poetry*, 1:128–39 (no. 69).

77. See Vitale, *La lingua*, 480–81; and Zamarra, "Dolce," 85.

78. On the *ubi sunt* theme, see, among others, Liborio, "Contributi" (esp. 179–81).

79. The same syntagm, but not the amphibology, occurs in *RVF* 309, v. 9: "Non son al sommo anchor giunte le rime" (Poetry has not yet reached the summit).

80. The apocopated interrogative *u'* (from the Latin *ubi*, medieval Italian *uve*) also occurs in the following *loci* of Petrarca's corpus: *RVF* 208 (v. 7); *Triumphus mortis*, 1.82 (twice in the same verse, an *ubi sunt* in both cases); and *Rime disperse* 70 (v. 13), 97 (v. 2), 110 (v. 2), 152 (v. 7), 177 (v. 13). The references to the *Rime disperse* are from Solerti, ed., *Rime disperse* (pp. 158, 173, 181, 217, and 234, respectively). But on Solerti's edition, see Barber, ed. and trans., *Rime disperse*, xlviii: "It [*sc.* Solerti's edition] remains the text of reference, though it contains serious defects in the areas of authenticity and textual accuracy."

81. See Berra, "La sestina," 228–31. For a thorough examination of Petrarca's hendecasyllable, see, among others, Praloran, "Figure."

82. Frasca, *La furia*, 208: "la sesta stanza che idealmente dovrebbe chiudere la tematica della sestina prima dello slancio duplicatore, ripercorre gli effetti 'stilistici' della morte della donna amata, preparando nella constatazione del mutamento dello stile il suo raddoppiamento."

83. See Antonelli, "Bifrontismo."

84. See chapter 6, "Cohesion: Focus on Form."

85. Contini, "Preliminari," 186: "incitamento alla dicotomia." See also Frasca, *La furia*, 228: "su questo verbo [*sc.* doppiare] (costruito entrambe le volte intransitivamente) ruota inevitabilmente il senso tutto della sperimentazione pe-

trarchesca; il *dolor*, infatti, raddoppia, perché al dolore di vivere *tristo* (dopo la morte di Laura) si aggiunge quello di sapere di aver vissuto, mentre ch'ella viveva, più d'ogni altro *lieto*," "the overall sense of Petrarca's poetic experimentation revolves around this verb (used intransitively twice); in fact, the *dolor* (grief) is doubled, as the grief of living in sadness after Laura's death is now joined to the notion of having lived more happily than anyone else when she was alive."

86. On the text of Dante's *Rime*, see chapter 6, note 14. The English translation is from Foster and Boyde, ed. and trans., *Dante's Lyric Poetry*, 1:139–47 (no. 70).

87. Orphic traits are recurrent in the sestinas (and in the *RVF*). On Petrarca's rewriting of the Virgilian and Ovidian myth of Orpheus, see Gardini, "Un esempio"; Rossellini, *Nel "trapassar del segno,"* 53–102; Brunori, "Il mito"; Migraine-George, "Specular Desires"; and Marcozzi, *La biblioteca*, 219–31. The myth is treated in passing in Mazzotta, *The Worlds*, 129–46. See also Barański, "Piangendo e cantando," esp. 637–39.

88. The question whether "senza rime" indicates classical (unrhymed) poetry is highly debated. For a brief survey of the debate (including for additional bibliographical references), see, among others, Berra, "La sestina," 227; Frasca, *La furia*, 223; Santagata, ed., *Canzoniere*, 1288; Bettarini, ed., *Canzoniere*, 1474; and Marcozzi, *La biblioteca*, 231.

89. Marcozzi, *La biblioteca*, 225: "nucleo mitopoietico centrale del canzoniere."

90. Gardini, "Un esempio," 144: "il mito d'Orfeo nel canzoniere petrarchesco arriva dunque direttamente dalla fonte classica, intatto dalle contaminazioni allegorizzanti delle letture d'epoca successiva." On the Christian allegorization of the myth of Orpheus, see Friedman, *Orpheus*, 38–85.

91. De Robertis, "Contiguità," 65–66: "il canzoniere si costituisce a partire e in forza della morte di Laura: che vuol dire, paradossalmente, della morte dell'oggetto e della ragione stessa della poesia." See also Berra, "La sestina," 221–22.

92. See Ariani, *Petrarca*, 281: "la poetica che ne motiva il complicato funzionamento formale è quella di un'implacabile analisi del mezzo e dello strumentario a disposizione, operato dall'ultimo supremo artefice di una tradizione riassunta e commutata" (the poetics that motivates its complex formal functioning is that of a relentless analysis of the medium and instruments available, conducted by the last supreme craftsman of a tradition he epitomized and transformed).

93. Herrnstein Smith, *Poetic Closure*, 1–36.

94. Agamben, "The End," 112.

95. Canettieri (*Il gioco*, 62) notes the "eccezionale coesione estetica" (exceptional aesthetic cohesiveness) of the sestina as form.

96. Shapiro, *Hieroglyph*, 134, observes that "one of Petrarch's major innovations was to show how the same poem could be reinvented endlessly."

97. Picone, "Petrarch and the Unfinished Book," 50 and 55. See also Geri, Ferrea voluptas, "Interruzione e ripresa della scrittura," 341–69 (esp. 357–69).

98. On the dialectic between openness and closure with specific reference to the renumbering of the last thirty-one poems in the autograph, see, among others, Soldani, "Un'ipotesi"; Tonelli, "Vat. Lat. 3195: un libro concluso?"; and Sarteschi, "*Rerum vulgarium fragmenta*: Un libro sempre aperto?"

99. Storey, *Transcription*, 354.

100. Scaglione, "La struttura del *Canzoniere*," 138: "la sua opera non è mai definitiva, se non in modo relativo." See also Picone, "Petrarch and the Unfinished Book."

101. Frasca, *La furia*, 173: "specialissima canzone, luogo deputato al contrappunto e, in un certo senso, al riepilogo delle forze in campo della dinamica amorosa."

102. See Petrucci, *La scrittura*, 71–88.

103. Bologna, *Tradizione*, 300: "questa volontà testuale-libraria è talmente coerente e forte, in Petrarca, da sollecitarlo a ideare una forma nuova di *libro d'autore*, non solo idealmente, ma *materialmente scritto* da lui, in una osmosi di pensiero creativo, disegno organizzativo, ripensamento metamorfico, tecnica d'impaginazione, che rendono perfettamente organici, solidali e persino speculari l'uno all'altro la *mente* che pensa, la *mano* che scrive, il *testo* che dà forma all'idea, la *pagina* che quell'idea rispecchia" (this text-book determination is so coherent and strong in Petrarca as to urge him to devise a new form of *author's book*, not only ideally but also *materially written* by him, in an osmosis of creative thinking, organizational design, metamorphic rethinking, and pagination technique, which render organic, united, and even mutually symmetrical the *mind* thinking, the *hand* writing, the *text* giving shape to the idea, and the *page* mirroring that idea).

104. Petrucci, "Reading," 194.

105. See Signorini, "Fortuna."

106. See Cursi, "Per la prima circolazione," esp. 236–40. See also Storey, "Il codice"; Savoca, *Il Canzoniere*, 97–129; Cursi, "Sulla tradizione"; and Cursi, "Nuove acquisizioni."

107. For a description of this codex, see De Robertis, ed., *Rime* (2002), 1/1:354–56.

108. See Wilkins, *The Making*, 170–83 and 242–46; Santagata, *I frammenti*, 267–82; and Pulsoni, "Il metodo," 263–66.

109. The folio with the scribe's note has been reproduced in various studies. See, most recently, Petrucci, *Letteratura italiana*, table 61.

110. See Storey, *Transcription*, 226–27; Storey, "Cultural Crisis," 875; and Storey, "Petrarch's 'Original,'" 34–35.

111. Sabbadini's epigrammatic "rule" can be found in the critical apparatus to *Georgica* 4.173 of his edition of Virgil's *opera*; see Sabbadini, ed., *Bucolica et Georgica.*

112. On Petrarca's incunables, see Dionisotti, "Fortuna del Petrarca." On the *editio princeps* (*GW* M31675, *IGI* 7517, *ISTC* ip00371000), see, among others, Sandal, "La prima edizione"; Trovato, *Con ogni diligenza*, 103 and 121–22; and Richardson, *Print Culture*, xi–xii. On the Valdezoco edition (*GW* M31636, *IGI* 7519, *ISTC* ip00373000), see the anastatic edition curated by Belloni, ed., *Rerum vulgarium fragmenta* (with ample introduction and bibliographical references). On the Aldine edition, see, among others, Pillinini, "Traguardi linguistici"; Frasso, "Appunti"; Giarin, "Petrarca e Bembo"; and Pulsoni, "Le fonti."

113. On Vellutello's edition, see, at least, including for additional references, Belloni, *Laura*, "Alessandro Vellutello," 58–96.

114. Cursi, "Per la prima circolazione," 241: "incauto copista."

Afterword

1. On the human body as "living medium" for the experience of material images and artifacts, see Belting, "Image," 304: "The what of an image (the issue of what the image serves as an image or to what it relates as an image) is steered by the how in which it transmits its message. . . . No visible images reach us unmediated."

2. See Guiette's notion of *poésie formelle* ("formal poetry") as interpretive paradigm for medieval poetry (*D'une póesie*, 33–34): "Le thème n'est qu'un prétexte, c'est l'œuvre formelle, elle-même, qui est le sujet" (The theme is nothing more than a pretext; the subject is the formal work itself). For a critique of Guiette's *poésie formelle*, see Giunta, *Versi*, esp. 20–26.

3. On these self-referential images and the history of their development, see, among others, including for additional bibliography, Alexander, *Medieval Illuminators*, "The Medieval Illuminator: Sources of Information," 4–34 (esp. 15–34).

4. The tension between medieval scribal practices and modern editorial solutions has been examined, for instance, by Storey with reference to Minetti's critical edition of Monte Andrea's poems; see Storey, *Transcription*, "Transferring Vi-

sual Ambiguity: Semantic-Visual Orientations of a Medieval Text," 71–109, and Minetti, ed., *Le rime*. The case of Michelangelo's poems, whose unstructured (or prestructured) textual condition was manipulated and homogenized into a Petrarchan *canzoniere* in the 1623 *editio princeps*, has been surveyed by Barkan, "La voce."

5. See McLuhan, "The Relation."

6. Gitelman, *Paper Knowledge*, 7.

7. See McKitterick, *Print*, "The Printed Word and the Modern Bibliographer," 1–21 (esp. 11–17).

8. See Dain, *Les manuscrits*, 116.

9. But see, among others, Shillingsburg, *From Gutenberg*.

10. See, among others, Treharne, "Fleshing Out the Text."

11. See, among others, including for additional references, Pierazzo, *Digital Scholarly Editing*, and the essays collected in Pierazzo and Driscoll, *Digital Scholarly Editing*. See also Kirschenbaum and Werner, "Digital Scholarship." On digital remediation and reliability, see Kichuk, "Loose, Falling Characters."

12. See, among others, including for additional bibliography, Ainsworth and Meredith, "e-Science"; Havens, "Adobe"; and Ciula, "Digital palaeography."

13. Limitations to library access and travel restrictions imposed by the global pandemic made the evading of these physical barriers between manuscripts all the more urgent.

14. On the advantages of digital and ubiquitous libraries and archives, their dark side (economic and social inequities and inequalities marking access), and the issues they pose (e.g., technological obsolescence, software deterioration, bit rot), see, among others, Burdick et al., *Digital_Humanities*, "Emerging Methods and Genres," 29–60 (esp. 45–47 and 58–60), and "The Social Life of the Digital Humanities," 75–98 (esp. 95–96); and Fiormonte, Numerico, and Tomasi, *The Digital Humanist*, esp. 67–89, 156–59, and 184–91.

15. See Foucault, "Nietzsche."

16. Lavagetto, *Oltre le usate leggi*, 57: "una sistematica—ma purtroppo inconsapevole—soppressione di virgolette." In the endnotes (61n2), Lavagetto refers to Barthes and Nadeau, *Sur la littérature*, 23: "L'écrivain . . . combine des citations dont il enlève les guillemets" (The writer . . . puts together citations from which he suppresses the quotation marks).

17. Wood, *The Nearest Thing*, 83.

18. See Petrucci, *La scrittura*, 44: "è evidente in lui lo sforzo di adoperare—anzi, meglio, di plasmare—una scrittura esteticamente espressiva del contenuto; ora, infatti, il Petrarca rende la sua 'scriptura notularis' ancor più minuta, sottile e sinuosa del solito, e tocca uno dei più alti livelli della sua calligrafia" (we clearly

see his [*sc.* Petrarca's] effort to use—or, better, to mold—a script aesthetically expressive of the content; in fact, Petrarca now renders his *scriptura notularis* [gloss script] even more minute, more sinuous, and thinner than usual and he reaches one of the highest levels of his calligraphy). On the obituary gloss to Laura, see chapter 6, "Annotations and Marginalia."

19. Corti, "Il binomio," 130: "materia indocile."

BIBLIOGRAPHY

Abramé Battesti, Isabelle. "Les fonctions du méta-discours poétique chez Dante, de la *Vita nuova* au *Convivio*." In *Dire la création: La culture italienne entre poétique et poïétique*, edited by Dominique Budor, 69–76. Lille: Presses Universitaires de Lille, 1994.

Agamben, Giorgio. "The End of the Poem." In *The End of the Poem: Studies in Poetics*, 109–15. Stanford, CA: Stanford University Press, 1999.

Agostinelli, Edvige. "A Catalogue of the Manuscripts of *Il Teseida*." *Studi sul Boccaccio* 15 (1985–1986): 1–83.

Agostinelli, Edvige, and William E. Coleman, eds. *Teseida: Delle nozze d'Emilia*. By Giovanni Boccaccio. Florence: SISMEL—Edizioni del Galluzzo, 2015.

Ahern, John. "Binding the Book: Hermeneutics and Manuscript Production in *Paradiso* 33." *PMLA* 97, no. 5 (1982): 800–809.

———. "Dante's Last Word: The *Comedy* as a *liber coelestis*." *Dante Studies* 102 (1984): 1–14.

———. "The New Life of the Book: The Implied Reader of the *Vita Nuova*." *Dante Studies* 110 (1992): 1–16.

———. "The Reader on the Piazza: Verbal Duels in Dante's *Vita Nuova*." *Texas Studies in Literature and Language* 32, no. 1 (1990): 18–39.

———. "Singing the Book: Orality in the Reception of Dante's *Comedy*." In *Dante: Contemporary Perspectives*, edited by Amilcare Iannucci, 214–39. Toronto: University of Toronto Press, 1997.

———. "What Did the First Copies of the *Comedy* Look Like?" In *Dante for the New Millennium*, edited by Teodolinda Barolini and H. Wayne Storey, 1–15. New York: Fordham University Press, 2003.

Ainsworth, Peter F., and Michael Meredith. "e-Science for Medievalists: Options, Challenges, Solutions and Opportunities." *DHQ: Digital Humanities Quarterly* 3, no. 4 (2009). http://www.digitalhumanities.org/dhq/vol/3/4/000071/000071.html.

Albanese, Gabriella, ed. *Ecloge*. By Dante Alighieri. In *Convivio, Monarchia, Epistole, Egloghe*, Vol. 2 of *Opere*, edited by Gianfranco Fioravanti, Claudio Giunta, Diego Quaglioni, Claudia Villa, and Gabriella Albanese, 1593–1783. Milan: Mondadori, 2014.

Albonico, Simone. "La sestina 237." *Lectura Petrarce* 29 (2009): 491–515.

Alessio, Gian Carlo. "Edizioni medievali." In *La ricezione del testo*, Vol. 3 of *Lo spazio letterario del Medioevo: 1. Il Medioevo latino*, edited by Guglielmo Cavallo, Claudio Leonardi, and Enrico Menestò, 29–58. Rome: Salerno, 1995.

Alexander, Jonathan J. G. *Medieval Illuminators and Their Methods of Work*. New Haven, CT: Yale University Press, 1992.

———. *The Painted Page: Italian Renaissance Book Illumination, 1450–1550*. Munich: Prestel, 1994.

Alfano, Giancarlo. "In forma di libro: Boccaccio e la politica degli autori." In *Boccaccio angioino: Materiali per la storia culturale di Napoli nel Trecento*, edited by Giancarlo Alfano, Teresa d'Urso, and Alessandra Perriccioli Saggese, 15–29. Brussels: Peter Lang, 2012.

———. "Una forma per tutti gli usi: L'ottava rima." In *Dalla Controriforma alla Restaurazione*, Vol. 2 of *Atlante della letteratura italiana*, edited by Sergio Luzzatto, Gabriele Pedullà, and Erminia Irace, 31–57. Turin: Einaudi, 2012.

Alfano, Giancarlo, Teresa d'Urso, and Alessandra Perriccioli Saggese, eds. *Boccaccio angioino: Materiali per la storia culturale di Napoli nel Trecento*. Brussels: Peter Lang, 2012.

Allegretti, Paola. "Dante geremiade: Un modello per la *Vita nova*." In *Adespoti, prosimetri e filigrane: Ricerche di filologia dantesca*, 165–78. Ravenna: Longo, 2013.

———. "Il maestro de 'lo bello stilo che m'ha fatto onore' (*Inf.* I 87), ovvero la matrice figurativa della sestina da Arnaut Daniel a Virgilio." *Studi danteschi* 68 (2002): 11–56.

———, ed. *La canzone "montanina."* By Dante Alighieri. Verbania: Tararà, 2001.

Allen, Graham, Carrie Griffin, and Mary O'Connell, eds. *Readings on Audience and Textual Materiality*. London: Pickering & Chatto, 2011.

Allen, Judson Boyce. *The Ethical Poetic of the Later Middle Ages: A Decorum of Convenient Distinction*. Toronto: University of Toronto Press, 1982.

Alter, Robert. *Partial Magic: The Novel as a Self-Conscious Genre*. Berkeley: University of California Press, 1975.

Amtower, Laurel. *Engaging Words: The Culture of Reading in the Later Middle Ages*. New York: Palgrave, 2000.

Anderson, David. *Before the "Knight's Tale": Imitation of Classical Epic in Boccaccio's "Teseida."* Philadelphia: University of Pennsylvania Press, 1988.

———. "Boccaccio's Glosses on Statius." *Studi sul Boccaccio* 22 (1994): 3–134.
———. "Mythography or Historiography? The Interpretation of Theban Myths in Late Medieval Literature." *Florilegium* 8 (1986): 113–39.
———, ed. *Sixty Bokes Olde and Newe.* Catalogue of the Exhibition: Manuscripts and Early Printed Books from Libraries in and near Philadelphia Illustrating Chaucer's Sources, His Works and Their Influence. Knoxville, TN: New Chaucer Society, 1986.
———. "Which Are Boccaccio's Own Glosses?" In Picone and Bérard, eds., *Gli Zibaldoni di Boccaccio*, 327–31.
Antonazzo, Antonino. "Ecdotica e interpretazione in un dictamen del giovane Boccaccio (*Epist.* IV)." *Studi medievali e umanistici* 12 (2014): 197–216.
Antonelli, Giuseppe. *Ricerche bibliografiche sulle edizioni ferraresi del secolo XV.* Ferrara: Gaetano Bresciani, 1830.
Antonelli, Roberto. "Bifrontismo, pentimento e forma-canzoniere." In *La palinodia*, Atti del XIX Convengo Interuniversitario, Bressanone, 1991, edited by Gianfelice Peron, 35–49. Padua: Esedra, 1998.
———. "La morte di Beatrice e la struttura della storia." In *Beatrice nell'opera di Dante e nella memoria europea 1290–1990*, Atti del Convegno internazionale, 10–14 dicembre 1990, edited by Maria Picchio Simonelli, 35–56. Fiesole (Florence): Cadmo, 1994.
———. "*Rerum vulgarium fragmenta* di F. Petrarca." In *Le opere*, Vol. 4:1 of *Letteratura italiana*, edited by Alberto Asor Rosa, 379–471. Turin: Einaudi, 1983.
Apollonio, Mario. *Dante: Storia della "Commedia."* Milan: Vallardi, 1951.
Appel, Carl. "Petrarka und Arnaut Daniel." *Archiv fur das Studium der neueren Sprachen und Literaturen* 147 (1924): 212–35.
Arbor Aldea, Mariña, and Antonio Ciaralli, "Il Pergamiño Vindel: Stato codicologico e paleografico." In *The Vindel Parchment and Martin Codax/El Pergamiño Vindel e Martin Codax: The Golden Age of Medieval Galician Poetry/O esplendor da poesía galega medieval*, edited by Alexandre Rodríguez Guerra and Xosé Bieito Arias Freixedo, 137–66. Amsterdam: John Benjamins, 2018.
Arduini, Beatrice. "Boccaccio and His Desk." In Armstrong, Daniels, and Milner, eds., *The Cambridge Companion to Boccaccio*, 20–35.
———. *Dante's "Convivio": The Creation of a Cultural Icon.* Florence: Cesati, 2020.
———. "*Dolente me: Son morto ed ag[g]io vita!* The Sonnet *Corona* of *Disaventura* by Monte Andrea da Firenze." In *Interpretation and Visual Poetics in Medieval and Early Modern Texts: Essays in Honor of H. Wayne Storey*, edited by

Beatrice Arduini, Isabella Magni, and Jelena Todorović, 175–188. Leiden: Brill, 2021.

———. “Per una corona di sonetti di Monte Andrea da Firenze.” *Acme* 56, no. 3 (2003): 167–93.

Aresu, Francesco Marco. “The Author as Scribe: Materiality and Textuality in the *Trecento*.” PhD diss., Harvard University, 2015.

———. “Intertestualità dantesche: Un’allusione a Ennio?” *Romanic Review* 112, no. 1 (2021): 85–96.

———. “Modalità iconica e istanza metatestuale nella sestina petrarchesca *Mia benigna fortuna el uiuer lieto* (*Rvf* CCCXXXII).” *Textual Cultures* 5, no. 2 (2010): 11–25.

———. “Visual Discourse in Petrarch’s Sestinas.” *Mediaevalia* 39 (2018): 185–215.

Ariani, Marco. *Petrarca*. Rome: Salerno, 1999.

Armstrong, Guyda. “Boccaccio and Dante.” In Armstrong, Daniels, and Milner, eds., *The Cambridge Companion to Boccaccio*, 121–38.

Armstrong, Guyda, Rhiannon Daniels, and Stephen J. Milner, eds. *The Cambridge Companion to Boccaccio*. Cambridge: Cambridge University Press, 2015.

Ascoli, Albert Russell. *Dante and the Making of a Modern Author*. Cambridge: Cambridge University Press, 2008.

Asperti, Stefano. “Dante, i trovatori, la poesia.” In *Le culture di Dante: Studi in onore di Robert Hollander*, Atti del quarto Seminario dantesco internazionale, University of Notre Dame, 25–27 settembre 2003, edited by Michelangelo Picone, Theodore J. Cachey, and Margherita Mesirca, 61–92. Florence: Cesati, 2004.

Assunto, Rosario. “Scrittura come figura, figura come segno.” *Rassegna dell’istruzione artistica* 2, no. 2 (1967): 5–18 (I); 2, no. 4 (1967): 5–15 (II).

Attridge, Derek. *The Experience of Poetry: From Homer’s Listeners to Shakespeare’s Readers*. Oxford: Oxford University Press, 2019.

Auerbach, Erich. *Dante: Poet of the Secular World*. New York: New York Review of Books, 2007.

———. “Dante’s Addresses to the Reader.” *Romance Philology* 7, no. 4 (1954): 268–78.

———. “Figura.” In *Scenes from the Drama of European Literature*, 11–76 (text) and 229–37 (notes). Minneapolis: University of Minnesota Press, 1984.

———. *Mimesis: The Representation of Reality in Western Literature*. Princeton, NJ: Princeton University Press, 2003.

Auzzas, Ginetta. "I codici autografi: Elenco e bibliografia." *Studi sul Boccaccio* 7 (1973): 1–20.

———, ed. *Epistole e lettere*. By Giovanni Boccaccio. In *Tutte le opere di Giovanni Boccaccio*, edited by Vittore Branca, 5/1:493–743 (text) and 745–846 (notes). Milan: Mondadori, 1992.

Avalle, D'Arco Silvio. "I canzonieri: Definizione di genere e problemi di edizione." In *La critica del testo: Problemi di metodo ed esperienze di lavoro*, Atti del Convegno di Lecce, 22–26 ottobre, 1984, 363–82. Rome: Salerno, 1985.

———. *La doppia verità: Fenomenologia ecdotica e lingua letteraria del Medioevo romanzo*. Tavarnuzze (Florence): SISMEL—Edizioni del Galluzzo, 2002.

———, ed. *Latino "circa romançum" e "rustica romana lingua": Testi del VII, VIII, IX secolo*. Padua: Antenore, 1970.

———. *I manoscritti della letteratura in lingua d'oc*. Turin: Einaudi, 1993.

Ayers, David. "Materialism and the Book." *Poetics Today* 24, no. 4 (2003): 759–80.

Azzetta, Luca. "'Fece molte canzoni per lo suo amore et come pare a uno suo librecto cui ei pose nome la vita nova': Note sui primi lettori della *Vita nova*." *Studj romanzi*, n.s., 14 (2018): 57–91.

———. "Il *Teseida* di Boccaccio con il commento del ferrarese Pier Andrea de' Bassi (Milano, Biblioteca Ambrosiana, D 524 inf.)." In *Francesco Petrarca: Manoscritti e libri a stampa della Biblioteca Ambrosiana*, edited by Marco Ballarini, Giuseppe Frasso, and Carla Maria Monti, 88–89. Milan: Scheiwiller, 2004.

Azzetta, Luca, and Andrea Mazzucchi, eds. *Boccaccio editore e interprete di Dante*, Atti del convegno internazionale di Roma, 28–30 ottobre 2013. Rome: Salerno, 2014.

Baetens, Jan. "Visual-Verbal Materiality." *Comparative Literature* 70, no. 3 (2018): 357–68.

Baglio, Marco, Antonietta Nebuloni Testa, and Marco Petoletti, eds. *Le postille del Virgilio Ambrosiano*. By Francesco Petrarca. Padua: Antenore, 2006.

Baldelli, Ignazio. "Visione, immaginazione e fantasia nella *Vita Nuova*." In *I sogni nel Medioevo*, Seminario internazionale (Roma, 2–4 ottobre 1983), edited by Tullio Gregory, 1–10. Rome: Edizioni dell'Ateneo, 1985.

Baldick, Chris. *The Oxford Dictionary of Literary Terms*. Oxford: Oxford University Press, 2015.

Balduino, Armando. "Le misteriose origini dell'ottava rima." In *I cantari: Struttura e tradizione*, Atti del Convegno Internazionale di Montréal, 19–20 marzo 1981, edited by Michelangelo Picone and Maria Bendinelli Predelli, 25–47. Florence: Olschki, 1984.

———. "*Pater semper incertus*: Ancora sulle origini dell'ottava rima." *Metrica* 3 (1982): 107–58.

Balsamo, Luigi. "Commercio librario attraverso Ferrara fra 1476 e 1481." *La Bibliofilia* 85, no. 3 (1983): 277–98.

Bampa, Alessandro. "Primi appunti sulle *coblas dissolutas* dei trovatori." *Medioevi: Rivista di letterature e culture medievali* 1 (2015): 15–43.

Banella, Laura. "The Fortunes of an 'Authorial' Edition: Boccaccio's *Vita nuova* in Antonio Pucci and il Saviozzo." In *Boccaccio 1313–2013*, edited by Francesco Ciabattoni, Elsa Filosa, and Kristina Olson, 237–47. Ravenna: Longo, 2015.

———. "La ricezione dell'edizione della *Vita nuova* a opera del Boccaccio: Primi appunti." In Azzetta and Mazzucchi, eds., *Boccaccio editore e interprete di Dante*, 391–401.

———. *La "Vita nuova" del Boccaccio: Fortuna e tradizione.* Padua: Antenore, 2017.

Barański, Zygmunt. "Dante Alighieri: Experimentation and (self-)exegesis." In *The Cambridge History of Literary Criticism*, edited by Alastair Minnis and Ian Johnson, 2:561–82. Cambridge: Cambridge University Press, 2005.

———. "Dante *poeta* e *lector*: 'Poesia' e 'riflessione tecnica' (con divagazioni sulla *Vita nova*)." *Critica del testo* 14, no. 1 (2011): 81–110.

———. "'Lascio cotale trattato ad altro chiosatore': Form, Literature, and Exegesis in Dante's *Vita nova*." In *Dantean Dialogues: Engaging with the Legacy of Amilcare Iannucci*, edited by Maggie Kilgour and Elena Lombardi, 1–40. Toronto: University of Toronto Press, 2013.

———. "''nfiata labbia' e 'dolce stil novo': A Note on Dante, Ethics, and the Technical Vocabulary of Literature." In *Sotto il segno di Dante: Scritti in onore di Francesco Mazzoni*, edited by Leonella Coglievina and Domenico De Robertis, 17–35. Florence: Le Lettere, 1998.

———. "'Piangendo e cantando' con Orfeo (e con Dante): Strutture emotive e strutture poetiche in *Rvf* 281–90." In Picone, ed., *Il Canzoniere*, 617–40.

———. "The Roots of Dante's Pluringualism: 'Hybridity' and Language in the *Vita nova*." In *Dante's Pluringualism: Authority, Knowledge, Subjectivity*, edited by Sara Fortuna, Manuele Gragnolati, and Jürgen Trabant, 98–121. London: Legenda, 2010.

———. "'Tres enim sunt manerie dicendi . . .': Some Observations on Medieval Literature, 'Genre,' and Dante." *The Italianist* 15, Supplement no. 2 (1995): 9–60.

Barber, Joseph A., ed. and trans. *Rime disperse*. By Francesco Petrarca. London: Routledge, 2019.

Bàrberi Squarotti, Giovanni. "Artificio ed escatologia della *Vita nuova*." In *L'artificio dell'eternità: Studi danteschi*, 35–105. Verona: Fiorini, 1972.

——— "Introduzione alla *Vita nuova*." In *L'artificio dell'eternità: Studi danteschi*, 9–34. Verona: Fiorini, 1972.

Barbi, Michele. *La nuova filologia e l'edizione dei nostri scrittori da Dante al Manzoni*. Florence: Sansoni, 1938.

———, ed. *Rime*. By Dante Alighieri. In *Le Opere di Dante*, edited by Michele Barbi, Ernesto Giacomo Parodi, Flaminio Pellegrini, Ermenegildo Pistelli, Pio Rajna, Enrico Rostagno, and Giuseppe Vandelli, 55–144. Florence: Bemporad, 1921.

———, ed. *La Vita Nuova*. By Dante Alighieri. Florence: Bemporad, 1932.

———, ed. *Vita Nuova*. By Dante Alighieri. In *Le Opere di Dante*, edited by Michele Barbi, Ernesto Giacomo Parodi, Flaminio Pellegrini, Ermenegildo Pistelli, Pio Rajna, Enrico Rostagno, and Giuseppe Vandelli, 1–53. Florence: Bemporad, 1921.

———, ed. *La Vita Nuova*. By Dante Alighieri. Florence: Società Dantesca Italiana, 1907.

Barbiellini Amidei, Beatrice. "I cantari tra oralità e scrittura." In *Il cantare italiano fra folklore e letteratura*, Atti del Convegno internazionale di Zurigo, Landesmuseum, 23–25 giugno 2005, edited by Michelangelo Picone and Luisa Rubini, 19–28. Florence: Olschki, 2007.

Barkan, Leonard. *Mute Poetry, Speaking Pictures*. Princeton, NJ: Princeton University Press, 2013.

———. "La voce di Michelangelo." In *Dalla Controriforma alla Restaurazione*, Vol. 2 of *Atlante della letteratura italiana*, edited by Sergio Luzzatto, Gabriele Pedullà, and Erminia Irace, 374–79. Turin: Einaudi, 2012.

Barolini, Teodolinda. "The Case of the Lost Original Ending of Dante's *Vita Nuova*: More Notes toward a Critical Philology." *Medioevo letterario d'Italia* 11 (2014): 37–43.

———. "A Cavalcantian *Vita nuova*: Dante's Canzoni *Lo doloroso amor che mi conduce* and *E' m'incresce di me sì duramente*." In *Dantean Dialogues: Engaging with the Legacy of Amilcare Iannucci*, edited by Maggie Kilgour and Elena Lombardi, 41–65. Toronto: University of Toronto Press, 2013.

———. "'Cominciandomi dal principio infino a la fine' (*V.N.*, XXIII, 15): Forging Anti-Narrative in the *Vita Nuova*." In Moleta, ed., La gloriosa donna de la mente, 119–40.

———. "Critical Philology and Dante's *Rime*." *Philology* 1 (2015): 91–114.

———. "Dante and Cavalcanti (On Making Distinctions in Matters of Love): *Inferno* v in Its Lyric Context." *Dante Studies* 116 (1998): 31–63.

———, ed. *Dante's Lyric Poetry: Poems of Youth and of the "Vita Nuova" (1283–1292)*. By Dante Alighieri. Translation by Richard Lansing. Toronto: University of Toronto Press, 2014.

———. *Dante's Poets: Textuality and Truth in the "Comedy."* Princeton, NJ: Princeton University Press, 1984.

———. "The Making of a Lyric Sequence: Time and Narrative in Petrarch's *Rerum vulgarium fragmenta*." *Modern Language Notes* 104, no. 1 (1989): 1–38.

———, ed. *Medieval Constructions in Gender and Identity: Essays in Honor of Joan M. Ferrante*. Tempe: Arizona Center for Medieval and Renaissance Studies, 2005.

———. "Petrarch at the Crossroads of Hermenutics and Philology: Editorial Lapses, Narrative Impositions, and Wilkins' Doctrine of the Nine Forms of the *Rerum vulgarium fragmenta*." In *Petrarch and the Textual Origins of Interpretation*, edited by Teodolinda Barolini and H. Wayne Storey, 21–44. Leiden: Brill, 2007.

———. *The Undivine Comedy: Detheologizing Dante*. Princeton, NJ: Princeton University Press, 1992.

Barolini, Teodolinda, and H. Wayne Storey, eds. *Petrarch and the Textual Origins of Interpretation*. Leiden: Brill, 2007.

Barthes, Roland. "The Death of the Author." In *Image–Music–Text*, 142–48. London: Fontana Press, 1977.

———. "Introduction to the Structural Analysis of Narratives." In *Image–Music–Text*, 79–124.

Barthes, Roland, and Maurice Nadeau. *Sur la littérature*. Grenoble: Presses universitaires de Grenoble, 1980.

Bartoli, Lorenzo. "Considerazioni attorno ad una questione metricologica: Il Boccaccio e le origini dell'ottava rima." *Quaderns d'Italià* 4–5 (1999–2000): 91–99.

Bartoli Langeli, Attilio. "Francesco d'Assisi." In *Le origini e il Trecento*, Vol. 1 of *Autografi dei letterati italiani*, edited by Giuseppina Brunetti, Maurizio Fiorilla, and Marco Petoletti, 171–80. Rome: Salerno, 2013.

———. "Scrivere, riscrivere, trascrivere: La genesi del *Canzoniere*." In *Dalle origini al Rinascimento*, Vol. 1 of *Atlante della letteratura italiana*, edited by Sergio Luzzatto, Gabriele Pedullà, and Amedeo De Vincentiis, 241–51. Turin: Einaudi, 2010.

Bartsch, Karl. *Grundriss zur Geschichte der provenzalischen Literatur*. Elberfeld: Friderichs, 1872.

Bartuschat, Johannes. "Appunti sull'ecfrasi in Boccaccio." *Italianistica: Rivista di letteratura italiana* 38, no. 2 (2009): 71–90.

———. "Il ritratto di Laura (*Rvf* 76–80)." In Picone, ed., *Il Canzoniere*, 207–23.

———. *Les "Vies" de Dante, Pétrarque et Boccace en Italie (XIVe–XVe siècles): Contribution à l'histoire du genre biographique*. Ravenna: Longo, 2007.

Battaglia, Salvatore. *Le rime "petrose" e la sestina: Arnaldo Daniello, Dante, Petrarca*. Naples: Liguori, 1964.

———, ed. *Teseida*. By Giovanni Boccaccio. Florence: Sansoni, 1938.

Battaglia Ricci, Lucia. *Boccaccio*. Rome: Salerno, 2000.

———. "Comporre il testo: Elaborazione e tradizione." In *Intorno al testo: Tipologie del corredo esegetico e soluzioni editoriali*, Atti del convegno di Urbino, 1–3 ottobre 2001, 21–40. Rome: Salerno, 2003.

———. "Edizioni d'autore, copie di lavoro, interventi di autoesegesi: testimonianze trecentesche." In *"Di mano propria": Gli autografi dei letterati italiani*, Atti del convegno internazionale di Forlí, 24–27 novembre 2008, edited by Guido Baldassarri, Matteo Motolese, Paolo Procaccioli, and Emilio Russo, 123–57. Rome: Salerno, 2010.

———. "L'Omero di Boccaccio." In *Boccaccio: Gli antichi e i moderni*, edited by Anna Maria Cabrini and Alfonso D'Agostino, 7–45. Milan: Ledizioni, 2018.

———. "Tendenze prosimetriche nella letteratura del Trecento." In *Il prosimetro nella letteratura italiana*, Atti del Seminario (Trento, dicembre 1997), edited by Andrea Comboni and Alessandra Di Ricco, 57–96. Trent: Università degli Studi di Trento, Dipartimento di Scienze Filologiche e Storiche, 2002.

Battistini, Andrea. "L'universo che si squaderna: Cosmo e simbologia del libro." *Letture classensi* 15 (1985): 61–78.

Battles, Dominique. *The Medieval Tradition of Thebes: History and Narrative in the OF "Roman de Thèbes," Boccaccio, Chaucer, and Lydgate*. New York: Routledge, 2004.

Bäuml, Franz H. "Medieval Texts and the Two Theories of Oral-Formulaic Composition: A Proposal for a Third Theory." *New Literary History* 16, no. 1 (1984): 31–49.

———. "Varieties and Consequences of Medieval Literacy and Illiteracy." *Speculum* 55, no. 2 (1980): 237–65.

Bec, Christian. "I mercanti scrittori." In *Produzione e consumo*, Vol. 2 of *Letteratura italiana*, edited by Alberto Asor Rosa, 269–97. Turin: Einaudi, 1983.

———. "Le letture dei borghesi fiorentini nel Quattrocento." In *Cultura e società a Firenze nell'età della Rinascenza*, 144–84. Rome: Salerno, 1981.

———. "Sur la lecture de Boccace à Florence au Quattrocento." *Studi sul Boccaccio* 9 (1975–1976): 247–60.

Bec, Pierre. "La sextine de Pons Fabre d'Uzès: Essai d'interprétation." In *Miscellanea Mediaevalia: Mélanges offerts à Philippe Ménard*, edited by Jean-Claude Faucon, Alain Labbé, and Danielle Quéruel, 1:91–100. Paris: Champion, 1998.

Bellomo, Saverio. "La *Commedia* attraverso gli occhi dei primi lettori." In *Leggere Dante*, Atti del seminario tenutosi a Pisa nell'a.a. 2001–2002, edited by Lucia Battaglia Ricci, 73–84. Ravenna: Longo, 2003.

———. "L'Epistola a Cangrande, dantesca per intero: 'a rischio di procurarci un dispiacere.'" *L'Alighieri* 45 (2015): 5–19.

———. "Problemi di ecdotica: In margine a nuove edizioni critiche di opere dantesche." In *Generi, architetture e forme testuali*, Atti del VII Convegno SILFI, Società Internazionale di Linguistica e Filologia Italiana, Roma, 1–5 ottobre 2002, edited by Paolo D'Achille, 503–10. Florence: Cesati, 2004.

———. "La sestina CCXIV (*Anzi tre dì creata era alma in parte*)." *Lectura Petrarce* 27 (2007): 333–46.

———. "Tra biografia e novellistica: Le novelle su Dante e il *Trattatello* di Boccaccio." In *Favole parabole istorie: Le forme della scrittura novellistica dal Medioevo al Rinascimento*, Atti del Convegno di Pisa (26–28 ottobre 1998), edited by Gabriella Albanese, Lucia Battaglia Ricci, and Rossella Bessi, 151–62. Rome: Salerno, 2000.

Belloni, Gino. *Laura tra Petrarca e Bembo: Studi sul commento umanistico-rinascimentale al "Canzoniere."* Padua: Antenore, 1992.

———, ed. *"Rerum vulgarium fragmenta": Anastatica dell'edizione Valdezoco, Padova 1472*. By Francesco Petrarca. Venice: Marsilio, 2001.

Belloni, Gino, Furio Brugnolo, H. Wayne Storey, and Stefano Zamponi, eds. *Rerum vulgarium fragmenta. Codice Vat. lat. 3195, edizione facsimilare* and *Commentario all'edizione in fac-simile*. By Francesco Petrarca. Padua: Antenore, 2003–2004.

Belting, Hans. "Image, Medium, Body: A New Approach to Iconology." *Critical Inquiry* 31, no. 2 (2005): 302–19.

Beltrami, Pietro G. "Arnaut e la 'bella scola' dei trovatori di Dante." In *Le culture di Dante: Studi in onore di Robert Hollander*, Atti del quarto Seminario dantesco internazionale, University of Notre Dame, 25–27 settembre 2003, edited by Michelangelo Picone, Theodore J. Cachey, and Margherita Mesirca, 29–59. Florence: Cesati, 2004.

———. *La metrica italiana*. Bologna: il Mulino, 1991.

Beltran, Vicenç. "Copisti e canzonieri: I canzonieri di corte." *Cultura neolatina* 63, nos. 1–2 (2003): 115–63.

Bendinelli Predelli, Maria, ed. *Firenze alla vigilia del Rinascimento: Antonio Pucci e i suoi contemporanei*, Atti del convegno di Montreal, 22–23 ottobre 2004, McGill University. Florence: Cadmo, 2006.

———. "The Textualization of Early Italian *Cantari*." In *Textual Cultures of Medieval Italy*, edited by William Robins, 145–64. Toronto: University of Toronto Press, 2011.

Benveniste, Émile. "L'appareil formel de l'énonciation." In *Problèmes de linguistique générale*, 2:79–88. Paris: Gallimard, 1974.

Bergin, Thomas G., and Max H. Fisch, eds. and trans. *The New Science*. By Giambattista Vico. Ithaca, NY: Cornell University Press, 1948.

Berisso, Marco, Simona Morando, and Paolo Zublena, eds. *L'autocommento*, Atti della giornata di studi (Genova, 16 maggio 2002). Alessandria: Edizioni dell'Orso, 2004.

Bernardo, Aldo S., trans. *Letters on Familiar Matters (Rerum familiarium libri)*. By Francesco Petrarca. New York: Italica Press, 2005.

Berra, Claudia. "La sestina doppia CCCXXXII." *Lectura Petrarce* 11 (1991): 219–35.

———. *La similitudine nei "Rerum vulgarium fragmenta."* Lucca: Pacini Fazzi, 1992.

Berta, Luca. *Oltre la mise en abyme: Teoria della metatestualità in letteratura e filosofia*. Milan: Franco Angeli, 2006.

Berté, Monica. "Un codice della *Tebaide* fra Boccaccio, Petrarca e Francesco Nelli." *Studi sul Boccaccio* 45 (2017): 1–28.

———. "Giovanni Malpaghini copista di Petrarca?" *Cultura neolatina* 75, nos. 1–2 (2015): 205–16.

Berté, Monica, and Massimo Fiorilla. "Il *Trattatello in laude di Dante*." In Azzetta and Mazzucchi, eds., *Boccaccio editore e interprete di Dante*, 41–72.

Bertelli, Sandro. "Codicologia d'autore: Il manoscritto in volgare secondo Giovanni Boccaccio." In *Dentro l'officina di Giovanni Boccaccio: Studi sugli autografi in volgare e su Boccaccio dantista*, edited by Sandro Bertelli and Davide Cappi, 1–80. Vatican City: Biblioteca Apostolica Vaticana, 2014.

———. "L'immagine di Omero nel Dante toledano." In *Boccaccio letterato*, Atti del convegno internazionale di studi (Firenze–Certaldo, 10–12 ottobre 2013), edited by Michelangiola Marchiaro and Stefano Zamponi, 171–76. Florence: Accademia della Crusca, 2015.

———. "Nota sul canzoniere provenzale P e sul Martelli 12." *Medioevo e Rinascimento* 18/n.s. 16 (2004): 369–75.

———. "La prima silloge dantesca: l'autografo Toledano." In De Robertis et al., eds., *Boccaccio autore e copista*, 266–68.

———. "La seconda silloge dantesca: Gli autografi Chigiani." In De Robertis et al., eds., *Boccaccio autore e copista*, 270–72.

Bertelli, Sandro, and Marco Cursi. "Ancora sul ritratto di Omero nel ms. Toledano." *Rivista di studi danteschi* 14, no. 1 (2014): 170–80.

———. "Boccaccio copista di Dante." In Azzetta and Mazzucchi, eds., *Boccaccio editore e interprete di Dante*, 73–111.

———. "Homero poeta sovrano." In *Dentro l'officina di Giovanni Boccaccio: Studi sugli autografi in volgare e su Boccaccio dantista*, edited by Sandro Bertelli and Davide Cappi, 131–36. Vatican City: Biblioteca Apostolica Vaticana, 2014.

———. "Novità sull'autografo Toledano di Giovanni Boccaccio: Una data e un disegno sconosciuti." *Critica del testo* 15, no. 1 (2012): 187–95.

Bertolucci Pizzorusso, Valeria. "Il canzoniere di un trovatore: Il 'libro' di Guiraut Riquier." *Medioevo romanzo* 5 (1978): 216–59.

———. "Guiraut Riquier e il 'genere' della pastorella." In *Studi trobadorici*, 139–50. Ospedaletto (Pisa): Pacini, 2009.

———. "Libri e canzonieri d'autore nel medioevo: Prospettive di ricerca." In *Morfologie del testo medievale*, 125–46. Bologna: il Mulino, 1989.

———. "La mort de la dame dans les genres lyriques autres que le *planh*." In *Studi trobadorici*, 119–25. Ospedaletto (Pisa): Pacini, 2009.

———. "La *Vita Nova* nella cronologia dantesca: Nuove considerazioni." *Studi mediolatini e volgari* 56 (2010): 5–25.

Bertone, Giorgio. *Lo sguardo escluso: L'idea di paesaggio nella letteratura occidentale*. Novara: Interlinea, 1999.

Bertoni, Giulio. *La biblioteca estense e la coltura ferrarese ai tempi del duca Ercole I (1471–1505)*. Turin: Loescher, 1903.

———. "Un copista del Marchese Leonello d'Este (Biagio Bosoni da Cremona)." *Giornale storico della letteratura italiana* 72 (1918): 96–106.

———. "Notizie sugli amanuensi estensi nel Quattrocento." *Archivum Romanicum* 2 (1918): 29–57.

———. "Pietro Andrea Basso." *Giornale storico della letteratura italiana* 78 (1921): 142–46.

———. "Poesie di Jacopone in un rotolo." *Archivum Romanicum* 22 (1938): 118–19.

Bettarini, Rosanna, ed. *Canzoniere/"Rerum vulgarium fragmenta."* By Francesco Petrarca. Turin: Einaudi, 2005.

———. "Il libro sommerso degli scartafacci." In *Lacrime e inchiostro nel Canzoniere di Petrarca*, 161–76. Bologna: CLUEB, 1998.

Bettarini Bruni, Anna. "Il Petrarca chigiano." In De Robertis et al., eds., *Boccaccio autore e copista*, 261–65.

———. "Un quesito d'amore tra Pucci e Boccaccio." *Studi di filologia italiana* 38 (1980): 33–54.

Bettarini Bruni, Anna, Giancarlo Breschi, and Giuliano Tanturli. "Giovanni Boccaccio e la tradizione dei testi volgari." In *Boccaccio letterato*, Atti del convegno internazionale di studi (Firenze–Certaldo, 10–12 ottobre 2013), edited by Michelangiola Marchiaro and Stefano Zamponi, 9–104. Florence: Accademia della Crusca, 2015.

Biagi, Guido, ed. *Lo Zibaldone Boccaccesco Mediceo Laurenziano Plut. XXIX.8*. Florence: Olschki, 1915.

Billanovich, Giuseppe. "La leggenda dantesca del Boccaccio dalla lettera di Ilaro al *Trattatello in laude di Dante*." *Studi danteschi* 28 (1949): 45–144.

———. *Petrarca e il primo umanesimo*. Padua: Antenore, 1996.

———. *Restauri boccacceschi*. Rome: Edizioni di Storia e Letteratura, 1947.

Billy, Dominique. *L'architecture lyrique médiévale: Analyse métrique et modélisation des structures interstrophiques dans la poésie lyrique des troubadours et des trouvères*. Montpellier: Section française de l'association internationale d'études occitanes, 1989.

———. "L'art et ses leurres: À propos du commiato d'*Al poco giorno*." *Antico-Moderno* 2 (1996): 41–54.

———. "La *canso redonda* ou les déconvenues d'un genre." *Medioevo Romanzo* 11 (1986): 369–78.

———. "La sextine à la lumière de sa préhistoire: Genèse d'une forme, genèse d'un genre." *Medioevo Romanzo* 18, no. 2 (1993): 207–39; no. 3 (1993): 371–402.

———. "La sextine réinventée suivi d'un essai de métrique génétique." *Stilistica e metrica italiana* 4 (2004): 3–32.

Björkvall, Anders, and Anna Marlin Karlsson. "The Materiality of Discourse and the Semiotics of Materials: A Social Perspective on the Meaning Potentials of Written Texts and Furniture." *Semiotica* 187 (2011): 141–65.

Blasucci, Luigi. "La sestina LXVI." *Lectura Petrarce* 2 (1982): 41–60.

Blumenberg, Hans. *Die Lesbarkeit der Welt*. Frankfurt a. M.: Suhrkamp, 1981.

———. *Paradigms for a Metaphorology*. Ithaca, NY: Cornell University Press, 2010.

———. *Shipwreck with Spectator: Paradigm of a Metaphor for Existence*. Cambridge, MA: MIT Press, 1997.

Bohn, Willard. *Reading Visual Poetry*. Madison, NJ: Fairleigh Dickinson University Press, 2011.

Boitani, Piero. "An Essay on Boccaccio's *Teseida*." In *Chaucer and Boccaccio*, 1–60. Oxford: Society for the Study of Mediaeval Languages and Literature, 1977.

———. "Style, Iconography and Narrative: The Lesson of the *Teseida*." In *Chaucer and the Italian Trecento*, edited by Piero Boitani, 185–99. Cambridge: Cambridge University Press, 1985.

Bollati, Milvia. "Jacopino d'Arezzo." In *Dizionario biografico dei miniatori italiani: Secoli IX–XVI*, edited by Milvia Bollati and Miklós Boskovits, 346. Milan: Sylvestre Bonnard, 2004.

Bollati, Milvia, and Miklós Boskovits, eds. *Dizionario biografico dei miniatori italiani: Secoli IX–XVI*. Milan: Sylvestre Bonnard, 2004.

Bollettino, Vincenzo Zin, trans. *The Life of Dante (Trattatello in laude di Dante)*. By Giovanni Boccaccio. New York: Garland, 1990.

Bologna, Corrado. "Beatrice e il suo *ánghelos* Cavalcanti fra *Vita Nova* e *Commedia*." In *"Per correr miglior acque . . .": Bilanci e prospettive degli studi danteschi alle soglie del nuovo millennio*, Atti del Convegno internazionale di Verona–Ravenna, 25–29 ottobre 1999, 1:115–42. Rome: Salerno, 2001.

———. "Dante e il latte delle Muse." In *Dalle origini al Rinascimento*, Vol. 1 of *Atlante della letteratura italiana*, edited by Sergio Luzzatto, Gabriele Pedullà, and Amedeo De Vincentiis, 145–55. Turin: Einaudi, 2010.

———. "PetrArca petroso." *Critica del testo* 6, no. 1 (2003): 367–420.

———. *Il ritorno di Beatrice: Simmetrie dantesche fra "Vita nova," "petrose" e "Commedia."* Rome: Salerno, 1998.

———. *Tradizione e fortuna dei classici italiani: 1. Dalle origini al Tasso*. Turin: Einaudi, 1993.

Bondanella, Peter. "Arnaut Daniel and Dante's *Rime Petrose*: A Re-Examination." *Studies in Philology* 68, no. 4 (1971): 416–34.

Booth, Wayne C. *The Rhetoric of Fiction*. Chicago: University of Chicago Press, 1983.

Bordin, Michele. "Boccaccio versificatore: La morfologia ritmica dell'endecasillabo." *Studi sul Boccaccio* 31 (2003): 137–201.

Bornstein, George, and Theresa Lynn Tinkle. *The Iconic Page in Manuscript, Print, and Digital Culture*. Ann Arbor: University of Michigan Press, 1998.

Borriero, Giovanni, ed. *Canzonieri italiani. 1. Biblioteca Apostolica Vaticana: Ch (Chig. L. VIII. 305)*, Vol. 3/1 of *"Intavulare": Tavole di canzonieri romanzi*. Vatican City: Biblioteca Apostolica Vaticana, 2006.

———. "Nuovi accertamenti sulla struttura fascicolare del canzoniere Vaticano Chigiano L. VIII. 305." *Critica del testo* 1, no. 2 (1998): 723–50.

———. "'Quantum illos proximius imitemur, tantum rectius poetemur': Note sul Chigiano L. VIII. 305 e sulle 'antologie d'autore.'" *AnticoModerno* 3 (1997): 259–86.

———. "Sull'*antologia* lirica del Due e Trecento in volgare italiano: Appunti (minimi) di metodo." *Critica del testo* 2, no. 1 (1999): 195–219.

Borsa, Paolo. "Identità sociale e generi letterari: Nascita e morte del sodalizio stilnovista." *Reti Medievali Rivista* 18, no. 1 (2017): 271–303.

———. "Immagine e immaginazione: Una lettura della *Vita nova* di Dante." *Letteratura & Arte* 16 (2008): 139–57.

Boschi Rotiroti, Marisa. *Codicologia trecentesca della "Commedia": Entro e oltre l'antica vulgata.* Rome: Viella, 2004.

Bosco, Umberto, ed. *Enciclopedia Dantesca.* Rome: Istituto della Enciclopedia Italiana, 1970–1978.

———. *Francesco Petrarca.* Bari: Laterza, 1965.

Bossy, Michel-André. "Cyclical Composition in Guiraut Riquier's Book of Poems." *Speculum* 66 (1991): 277–93.

———. "Twin Flocks: Guiraut Riquier's *Pastorelas* and His Book of Songs." *Tenso* 9, no. 2 (1994): 149–76.

Botterill, Steven, ed. *De vulgari eloquentia.* By Dante Alighieri. Cambridge: Cambridge University Press, 1996.

———. "'. . . però che la divisione non si fa se non per aprire la sentenzia de la cosa divisa' (*V.N.*, XIV, 13): The *Vita Nuova* as Commentary." In Moleta, ed., La gloriosa donna de la mente, 61–76.

Bowra, Maurice. "Dante and Arnaut Daniel." *Speculum* 27, no. 4 (1952): 459–74.

Bozzolo, Carla, and Ezio Ornato. "Les dimensions des feuillets dans les manuscrits français du Moyen Âge." In *Pour une histoire du livre manuscrit au Moyen Âge: Trois essais de codicologie quantitative*, 217–351. Paris: C.N.R.S., 1980.

Brambilla Ageno, Franca, ed. *Convivio.* By Dante Alighieri. Florence: Le Lettere, 1995.

———. *L'edizione critica dei testi volgari.* Padua: Antenore, 1984.

Branca, Daniela. "La morte di Tristano e la morte di Arcita." *Studi sul Boccaccio* 4 (1967): 255–64.

Branca, Vittore, ed. *Boccaccio visualizzato: Narrare per parole e per immagini fra Medioevo e Rinascimento.* Turin: Einaudi, 1999.

———. *Il cantare trecentesco e il Boccaccio del "Filostrato" e del "Teseida."* Florence: Sansoni, 1936.

———. "Copisti per passione, tradizione caratterizzante, tradizione di memoria." In *Studi e problemi di critica testuale*, Atti del Convegno di studi di filologia italiana nel centenario della Commissione per i testi di lingua (7–9 aprile 1960), 69–83. Bologna: Commissione per i testi di lingua, 1961.

———. *Giovanni Boccaccio: Profilo biografico*. Florence: Sansoni, 1997.

———. "Parole di apertura." In Picone and Bérard, eds., *Gli Zibaldoni di Boccaccio*, 5–10.

———. "Poetica del rinnovamento e tradizione agiografica nella *Vita nuova*." In *Studi in onore di Italo Siciliano*, 1:123–48. Florence: Olschki, 1966.

———. *Ponte Santa Trinita: Per amore di libertà, per amore di verità*. Venice: Marsilio, 1987.

———. "Un terzo elenco di codici." *Studi sul Boccaccio* 4 (1968): 1–8.

———. "Il tipo boccacciano di rubriche-sommari e il suo riflettersi nella tradizione del *Filostrato*." In *Book Production and Letters in the Western European Renaissance: Essays in Honour of Conor Fahy*, edited by Anna Laura Lepschy, John Took, and Dennis E. Rhodes, 17–31. London: Modern Humanities Research Association, 1986.

———. *Tradizione delle opere di Giovanni Boccaccio: 1. Un primo elenco di codici e tre studi*. Rome: Edizioni di Storia e Letteratura, 1958.

———. *Tradizione delle opere di Giovanni Boccaccio: 2. Un secondo elenco di manoscritti e studi sul testo del "Decameron" con due appendici*. Rome: Edizioni di Storia e Letteratura, 1991.

Breschi, Giancarlo. "Boccaccio editore della *Commedia*." In De Robertis et al., eds., *Boccaccio autore e copista*, 247–53.

Brieger, Peter, Millard Meiss, and Charles S. Singleton. *Illuminated Manuscripts of the "Divine Comedy."* Princeton, NJ: Princeton University Press, 1969.

Brillenburg Wurth, Kiene. "The Material Turn in Comparative Literature: An Introduction." *Comparative Literature* 70, no. 3 (2018): 247–63.

Brilli, Elisa. "Dante's Self-Commentary and the Call for Interpretation." *Glossator* 12 (2022): 115–32.

Brown, Bill. "Materiality." In *Critical Terms for Media Studies*, edited by W. J. T. Mitchell and Mark B. N. Hansen, 49–63. Chicago: University of Chicago Press, 2010.

Brugnoli, Giorgio. *Identikit di Lattanzio Placido: Studi sulla scoliastica staziana*. Pisa: ETS, 1988.

———. "Un libello della memoria asemplato per rubriche." *La parola del testo* 1 (1997): 55–65.

Brugnolo, Furio. "Come scrivere (e leggere) versi: La poetica grafico-visiva di Francesco Petrarca." In *Petrarca e l'Umanesimo*, Atti del Convegno di Studi.

Treviso, 1–3 aprile 2004, edited by Giuliano Simionato, 29–58. Treviso: Ateneo di Treviso, 2006.

———. "Libro d'autore e forma-canzoniere: Implicazioni grafico-visive nell'originale dei *Rerum vulgarium fragmenta*." In *Commentario all'edizione in facsimile*, Vol. 2 of *Rerum vulgarium fragmenta. Codice Vat. lat. 3195, edizione facsimilare*, edited by Gino Belloni, Furio Brugnolo, H. Wayne Storey, and Stefano Zamponi, 105–29. Padua: Antenore, 2003–2004; updated version of "Libro d'autore e forma-canzoniere: Implicazioni petrarchesche." *Lectura Petrarce* 11 (1991): 259–90.

———. "Il libro di poesia nel Trecento." In *Il libro di poesia dal copista al tipografo*, edited by Marco Santagata and Amedeo Quondam, 9–23. Ferrara: Panini, 1989.

———. "Sotto il vestito, niente? Divagazioni esegetiche su un verso della sestina di Dante." *Quaderni veneti* 2 (2013): 83–94.

Brugnolo, Furio, and Roberto Benedetti. "La dedica tra Medioevo e primo Rinascimento: Testo e immagine." In *I margini del libro: Indagine teorica e storica sui testi di dedica*, Atti del Convegno Internazionale di Studi, Basilea, 21–23 novembre 2002, edited by Maria Antonietta Terzoli, 13–58. Padua: Antenore, 2004.

Brunetti, Giuseppina. "Adriano de' Rossi." In *Le origini e il Trecento*, Vol. 1 of *Autografi dei letterati italiani*, edited by Giuseppina Brunetti, Maurizio Fiorilla, and Marco Petoletti, 149–56. Rome: Salerno, 2013.

———. *Il frammento inedito "Resplendiente stella de albur" di Giacomino Pugliese e la poesia italiana delle origini.* Tübingen: Niemeyer, 2001.

———, ed. "Giacomino Pugliese." In *Poeti della corte di Federico II*, Vol. 2 of *I poeti della Scuola siciliana*, edited by Costanzo di Girolamo, 557–642. Milan: Mondadori, 2008.

———. "La *lectura* di Boccaccio: Il *Teseida* fra autografo e ricezione." In *Boccaccio in versi*, Atti del Convegno di Parma, 13–14 marzo 2014, edited by Pantalea Mazzitello, Giulia Raboni, Paolo Rinoldi, and Carlo Varotti, 71–87. Florence: Cesati, 2016.

———. "Il libro di Giacomino e i canzonieri individuali: Diffusione delle forme e tradizione della Scuola poetica siciliana." In *Dai Siciliani ai Siculo-toscani: Lingua, metro e stile per la definizione del canone*, Atti del Convegno (Lecce, 21–23 aprile 1998), edited by Rosario Coluccia and Riccardo Gualdo, 61–92. Galatina (Lecce): Congedo, 1999.

———. "Rossi, Adriano de'." In *Dizionario biografico degli italiani*, 88:576–78. Rome: Istituto della Enciclopedia Italiana, 2017.

Bruni, Francesco. *Boccaccio: L'invenzione della letteratura mezzana*. Bologna: il Mulino, 1990.

———. "Semantica della sottigliezza: Note sulla distribuzione della cultura nel Basso Medioevo." *Studi medievali* (s. III) 19, no. 1 (1978): 1–36.

Brunori, Federica. "Il mito ovidiano di Orfeo e Euridice nel *Canzoniere* di Petrarca." *Romance Quarterly* 44, no. 4 (1997): 233–44.

Brusegan, Rosanna. "Le secret de la *flors enversa*." *Revue des Langues Romanes* 96 (1992): 119–43.

Bülow-Jacobsen, Adam. "Writing Materials in the Ancient World." In *The Oxford Handbook of Papyrology*, edited by Roger S. Bagnall, 3–29. Oxford: Oxford University Press, 2011.

Burdick, Anne, Johanna Drucker, Peter Lunenfeld, Todd Presner, and Jeffrey Schnapp. *Digital_Humanities*. Cambridge, MA: MIT Press, 2012.

Burgwinkle, William E. "The *chansonniers* as Books." In *The Troubadours: An Introduction*, edited by Simon Gaunt and Sarah Kay, 246–62. Cambridge: Cambridge University Press, 1999.

Busby, Keith, and Christopher Kleinhenz. "Medieval French and Italian literature: Towards a Manuscript History." In *The Medieval Manuscript Book: Cultural Approaches*, edited by Michael Robert Johnston and Michael Van Dussen, 215–42. Cambridge: Cambridge University Press, 2015.

Büttner, Frank Olaf. "*Mens divina liber grandis est*: Zu einigen Darstellungen des Lesens in spätmittelalterlichen Handschriften." *Philobiblon* 16 (1972): 92–126.

Cabani, Maria Cristina. *Le forme del cantare epico-cavalleresco*. Lucca: Pacini Fazzi, 1988.

Cachey, Theodor J. "Dante's Journey between Fiction and Truth: Geryon Revisited." In *Dante: Da Firenze all'aldilà*, Atti del terzo Seminario dantesco internazionale (Firenze, 9–11 giugno 2000), edited by Michelangelo Picone, 75–92. Florence: Cesati, 2001.

———. "Title, Genre, Metaliterary Aspects." In *The Cambridge Companion to Dante's "Commedia*," edited by Zygmunt G. Barański and Simon Gilson, 79–94. Cambridge: Cambridge University Press, 2019.

Calcaterra, Carlo. "'Giovene donna sotto un verde lauro': La raffigurazione umanistica dell'amore e del lauro nei *Rerum vulgarium fragmenta*." *Aevum* 5, nos. 2–3 (1931): 379–96.

Camboni, Maria Clotilde. "Canzoni monostrofiche." *Nuova Rivista di Letteratura Italiana* 4, no. 1 (2002): 9–49.

Camilletti, Fabio A. *The Portrait of Beatrice: Dante, D. G. Rossetti, and the Imaginary Lady*. Notre Dame, IN: University of Notre Dame Press, 2019.

Campbell, David A., ed. and trans. *Sappho and Alcaeus,* Vol. 1 of *Greek Lyric.* Cambridge, MA: Harvard University Press, 1982.

Camporesi, Piero. "La sestina del Petrarca e l'interpretazione di un passo di Benvenuto da Imola." *Giornale italiano di filologia* 4, no. 2 (1951): 148–50.

———. "Il tema dell'*Adynaton* nel *Canzoniere* del Petrarca." *Studi Urbinati* 26, no. 1 (1952): 3–6.

Campori, Giuseppe. "I miniatori degli Estensi." *Atti e Memorie delle RR. Deputazioni di Storia Patria per le Provincie modenesi e parmensi* 6 (1872): 245–73.

Candido, Igor. "Il libro della Scrittura, il libro della Natura, il libro della Memoria: L'esegesi dantesca di C. S. Singleton fra tradizione giudaico-cristiana e trascendentalismo emersoniano." *Modern Language Notes* 122, no. 1 (2007): 46–79.

———. "Per una rilettura della *Vita Nova*: La prima *visio in somniis.*" *Lettere italiane* 71 (2019): 21–50.

Canello, Ugo Angelo. *La vita e le opere del trovatore Arnaldo Daniello.* Halle: Niemeyer, 1883.

Canettieri, Paolo. "Appunti per la classificazione dei generi trobadorici." *Cognitive Philology* 4 (2011). https://rosa.uniroma1.it/rosa03/cognitive_philology/article/view/9349/9231.

———. "L'aura dei sospiri." *Critica del testo* 6, no. 1 (2003): 541–58.

———. *Il gioco delle forme nella lirica dei trovatori.* Rome: Bagatto, 1996.

———. *La sestina e il dado: Sull'arte ludica del* trobar. Rome: Colet, 1993.

Canfora, Luciano. *Il papiro di Dongo.* Milan: Adelphi, 2005.

Canova, Maria Giordana. "I codici dell'area padana orientale: Tra Bologna, Ferrara e Mantova." In *Boccaccio visualizzato: Narrare per parole e per immagini,* edited by Vittore Branca, 2:273–76. Turin: Einaudi, 1999.

———. "La committenza dei codici miniati alla corte estense al tempo di Leonello e di Borso." In *Saggi,* Vol. 1 of *Le muse e il principe: Arte di corte nel Rinascimento padano,* edited by Alessandra Mottola Molfino and Mauro Natale, 87–117. Modena: Panini, 1991.

———. "Guglielmo Giraldi e la grande miniatura per la Chiesa e per i Principi." In *La miniatura a Ferrara dal tempo di Cosmè Tura all'eredità di Ercole de' Roberti,* Catalogo della mostra, Ferrara, Palazzo Schifanoia 1 marzo–31 maggio 1998, edited by Federica Toniolo, 185–223. Modena: Panini, 1998.

———. *Guglielmo Giraldi miniatore estense.* Modena: Panini, 1995.

Capelli, Roberta, ed. *Del carnale amore: La corona di sonetti del codice Escorialense.* By Guittone d'Arezzo. Rome: Carocci, 2007.

———. "Nuove indagini sulla raccolta di rime italiane del ms. Escorial e.III.23." *Medioevo letterario d'Italia* 1 (2004): 73–113.

Capovilla, Guido. "I madrigali (LII, LIV, CVI, CXXI)." *Lectura Petrarce* 3 (1983): 5–40.

———. "Materiali per la morfologia e la storia del madrigale 'antico': Dal ms. Vaticano Rossi 215 al Novecento." *Metrica* 3 (1982): 159–252.

———. "Un sistema di indicatori metrici nell'originale del *Canzoniere* petrarchesco." In *Il libro di poesia dal copista al tipografo*, edited by Marco Santagata and Amedeo Quondam, 103–9. Ferrara: Panini, 1989.

Cappello, Giovanni. *La dimensione macrotestuale: Dante, Boccaccio, Petrarca.* Ravenna: Longo, 1998.

———. "La *Vita Nuova* tra Guinizzelli e Cavalcanti." *Versants* 13 (1988): 47–66.

Cappi, Davide. "Riflessioni su un catalogo: *Boccaccio autore e copista.*" *Studi sul Boccaccio* 42 (2014): 311–52.

Cappozzo, Valerio. "Libri dei sogni e letteratura: L'espediente narrativo di Dante Alighieri." In *Studi di letteratura italiana: In memoria di Achille Tartaro*, edited by Giulia Natali and Pasquale Stoppelli, 99–119. Rome: Bulzoni, 2009.

———. "Un volgarizzamento trecentesco del *Somniale Danielis* nel cod. Laurenziano Martelli 12." *Medioevo letterario d'Italia* 11 (2014): 77–90.

Caputo, Clementina, and Julia Lougovaya, eds. *Using Ostraca in the Ancient World: New Discoveries and Methodologies*. Berlin: De Gruyter, 2020.

Caputo, Rino. "'Et doppiando 'l dolor, doppia lo stile' (*Rvf* 331–40)." In Picone, ed., *Il Canzoniere*, 725–31.

———. "Petrarca e Properzio 'che d'amor cantaro fervidamente.'" In *A confronto con Properzio (da Petrarca a Pound)*, Atti del convegno internazionale, Assisi, 17–19 maggio 1996, edited by Giuseppe Catanzaro and Francesco Santucci, 113–23. Assisi: Accademia Properziana del Subasio, 1999.

Carrai, Stefano. *Boccaccio e i volgarizzamenti*. Padua: Antenore, 2016.

———. "Boccaccio e la tradizione del prosimetro: Un'ipotesi per la forma della *Comedia delle ninfe fiorentine*." *Rassegna europea di letteratura italiana* 29–30 (2007): 61–68.

———. "Il commento d'autore." In *Intorno al testo: Tipologie del corredo esegetico e soluzioni editoriali*, Atti del Convegno di Urbino, 1–3 ottobre 2001, 223–41. Rome: Salerno, 2003.

———. *Dante elegiaco: Una chiave di lettura per la "Vita nova."* Florence: Olschki, 2006.

———. *Il primo libro di Dante: Un'idea della "Vita nova."* Pisa: Edizioni della Normale, 2020.

———. "Puntualizzazioni sulla datazione della *Vita nova*." *L'Alighieri* 52 (2018): 109–15.

———. "Quale lingua per la *Vita nova*? La restituzione formale di un testo paradigmatico." *Filologia italiana* 4 (2007): 39–49.

———, ed. *Vita nova*. By Dante Alighieri. Milan: Rizzoli, 2009.

———. "La *Vita nova* nel *Trattatello in laude di Dante*." *Letture classensi* 42 (2013): 105–17.

Carraud, Christophe, ed. and trans. *Les Remèdes aux deux fortunes*. By Francesco Petrarca. Grenoble: Jérôme Millon, 2002.

Carruthers, Mary J. *The Book of Memory: A Study of Memory in Medieval Culture*. Cambridge: Cambridge University Press, 2008.

Casadei, Alberto. "Dalla *Vita nova* al *Convivio*." *Dante: Rivista internazionale di studi su Dante Alighieri* 12 (2015): 29–40.

———. "Incipit vita nova." *Nuova Rivista di Letteratura Italiana* 13, nos. 1–2 (2010): 11–18.

———. "Puntualizzare le puntualizzazioni: Ancora sui rapporti *Vita nova–Convivio*." *L'Alighieri* 54 (2019): 117–20.

Casamassima, Emanuele. "Dentro lo scrittoio del Boccaccio: I codici della tradizione." In *"Il Decameron": Pratiche testuali e interpretative*, edited by Aldo Rossi, 253–60. Bologna: Cappelli, 1982.

Casella, Mario. "Dai trovatori al Petrarca." *Annali della cattedra petrarchesca* 6 (1935–1936): 151–74.

Castellani, Arrigo. *Grammatica storica della lingua italiana*. Bologna: il Mulino, 2000.

———. "Sul codice Laurenziano Martelliano 12." In *Sotto il segno di Dante: Scritti in onore di Francesco Mazzoni*, edited by Leonella Coglievina and Domenico De Robertis, 85–97. Florence: Le Lettere, 1998.

Causa-Steindler, Mariangela, and Thomas Mauch, trans. *The Elegy of Lady Fiammetta*. By Giovanni Boccaccio. Chicago: University of Chicago Press, 1990.

Cavallo, Guglielmo. "Un'aggiunta al 'decalogo' di Giorgio Pasquali." *Rivista di filologia e di istruzione classica* 112 (1984): 374–77.

———. "Testo, libro, lettura." In *La circolazione del testo*, Vol. 2 of *Lo spazio letterario di Roma antica*, edited by Guglielmo Cavallo, Paolo Fedeli, and Andrea Giardina, 307–41. Rome: Salerno, 1989.

Cavallo, Guglielmo, and Roger Chartier, eds. *A History of Reading in the West*. Amherst: University of Massachusetts Press, 2003.

Cazalé Berard, Claude. "Boccaccio's Working Notebooks (*Zibaldone Laurenziano, Miscellanea Laurenziana, Zibaldone Magliabechiano*)." In *Boccaccio: A Critical Guide to the Complete Works*, edited by Victoria Kirkham, Michael Sherberg, and Janet Levarie Smarr, 307–18. Chicago: University of Chicago Press, 2013.

Ceccherini, Irene. "La genesi della scrittura mercantesca." In *Régionalisme et internationalisme: Problèmes de Paléographie et de codicologie du Moyen Âge*, Actes du XVe Colloque du Comité International de Paléographie latine (Vienne, 13–17 septembre 2005), edited by Otto Kresten and Franz Lackner, 123–37. Vienna: Verlag der Österreichischen Akademie der Wissenschaften, 2008.

Cecchini, Enzo, Guido Arbizzoni, Settimio Lanciotti, Giorgio Nonni, Maria Grazia Sassi, and Alba Tontini, eds. *Derivationes*. By Hugh of Pisa. Tavarnuzze (Florence): SISMEL—Edizioni del Galluzzo, 2004.

Cencetti, Giorgio. *Lineamenti di storia della scrittura latina*. Bologna: Pàtron, 1954.

Cerquiglini, Jacqueline. "Histoire, image: Accord et discord du sens à la fin du Moyen Âge." *Littérature* 74 (1989): 110–26.

Cerrini, Simonetta. "Libri dei Visconti-Sforza: Schede per una nuova edizione degli inventari." *Studi petrarcheschi*, n.s., 8 (1991): 239–81.

Cervigni, Dino S. *Dante's Poetry of Dreams*. Florence: Olschki, 1986.

———. "[. . .] ricordandomi di lei, disegnava uno angelo sopra certe tavolette (*VN* 34.1): Realtà disegno allegoria nella *Vita nuova*." *Letture classensi* 35–36 (2007): 19–34.

———. "Segni paragrafali, maiuscole e grafia nella *Vita Nuova*: Dal libello manoscritto al libro a stampa." *Rivista di letteratura italiana* 13, nos. 1–2 (1995): 283–362.

Cervigni, Dino S., and Edward Vasta. "From Manuscript to Print: The Case of Dante's *Vita nuova*." In *Dante Now: Current Trends in Dante Studies*, edited by Theodor J. Cachey, 83–114. Notre Dame, IN: University of Notre Dame Press, 1995.

Ceserani, Remo. "'Petrarca': Il nome come auto-reinvenzione poetica." *Quaderni petrarcheschi* 4 (1987): 121–37.

Chambers, Frank M. "Imitation of Form in the Old Provençal Lyric." *Romance Philology* 6, nos. 2–3 (1952–1953): 104–20.

———. *An Introduction to Old Provençal Versification*. Philadelphia: American Philosophical Society, 1985.

Chang, Ku-ming (Kevin), Anthony Grafton, and Glenn W. Most, eds. *Impagination—Layout and Materiality of Writing and Publication: Interdisciplinary Approaches from East and West*. Berlin: De Gruyter, 2021.

Chartier, Roger. "Laborers and Voyagers: From the Text to the Reader." *Diacritics* 22, no. 2 (1992): 49–61.

Chartier, Roger, and Peter Stallybrass. "What Is a book?" In *The Cambridge Companion to Textual Scholarship*, edited by Neil Fraistat and Julia Flanders, 188–204. Cambridge: Cambridge University Press, 2013.

Chatman, Seymour. *Story and Discourse: Narrative Structure in Fiction and Film.* Ithaca, NY: Cornell University Press, 1978.

Chaytor, Henry John. *From Script to Print: An Introduction to Medieval Literature.* Cambridge: Cambridge University Press, 1945.

Cherchi, Paolo. "The *divisioni* in Dante's *Vita nuova.*" *Le tre corone: Rivista internazionale di studi su Dante, Petrarca, Boccaccio* 5 (2018): 73–88.

———. "Gli 'adynata' dei trovatori." *Modern Philology* 68, no. 3 (1971): 223–41.

Chiappelli, Fredi. "L'esegesi petrarchesca e l'elezione del *sermo lauranus* per il linguaggio dei *Rerum vulgarium fragmenta.*" *Studi petrarcheschi*, n.s., 4 (1987): 47–85.

Chiappini, Alessandra. "Fermenti umanistici e stampa in una biblioteca ferrarese del secolo XV." *La Bibliofilia* 85, no. 3 (1983): 299–320.

Chiappini, Luciano. *Gli Estensi: Mille anni di storia.* Ferrara: Corbo, 2001.

Chiesa, Paolo, and Lucia Pinelli, eds. *Gli autografi medievali: Problemi paleografici e filologici*, Atti del convegno di studio (Erice, 25 settembre–2 ottobre 1990). Spoleto: Centro italiano di studi sull'alto medioevo, 1994.

Chiòrboli, Ezio, ed. *Le "Rime sparse."* By Francesco Petrarca. Milan: Trevisini, 1924.

Ciardi Dupré Dal Poggetto, Maria Grazia. "Boccaccio 'visualizzato' dal Boccaccio, I: *Corpus* dei disegni e cod. Parigino It. 482." *Studi sul Boccaccio* 22 (1994): 197–225.

———. "Il rapporto testo e immagini all'origine della formazione artistica e letteraria di Giovanni Boccaccio." In *Medioevo: Immagini e racconto*, Atti del Convegno internazionale di studi (Parma, 27–30 settembre 2000), edited by Adriano Carlo Quintavalle, 456–73. Milan: Electa, 2003.

Ciavorella, Giuseppe. "Sulla composizione della *Vita nova.*" *La parola del testo* 16, nos. 1–2 (2012): 19–65.

Ciccuto, Marcello. "'Era venuta ne la mente mia' (*V.N.*, XXXIV, 7): La visione nel libello e l'immagine in Dante." In Moleta, ed., La gloriosa donna de la mente, 181–93.

———. "L'esegesi del testo: Lettera e figura." In *Intorno al testo: Tipologie del corredo esegetico e soluzioni editoriali*, Atti del convegno di Urbino, 1–3 ottobre 2001, 243–62. Rome: Salerno, 2003.

———. "Immagini per i testi di Boccaccio: Percorsi e affinità dagli Zibaldoni al *Decameron.*" In Picone and Bérard, eds., *Gli Zibaldoni di Boccaccio*, 141–60.

Ciociola, Claudio. "Dante." In *La tradizione dei testi*, Vol. 10 of *Storia della letteratura italiana*, edited by Enrico Malato and Claudio Ciociola, 137–99. Rome: Salerno, 2001.

Citroni, Mario. "Le raccomandazioni del poeta: Apostrofe al libro e contatto col destinario." *Maia: Rivista di letterature classiche* 38 (1986): 111–46.

Ciula, Arianna. "Digital Palaeography: What Is Digital about It?" *DSH: Digital Scholarship in the Humanities* 32, no. 2, suppl. (2017): 89–105. https://doi.org/10.1093/llc/fqx042.

Clarke, Kenneth P. "Boccaccio and the Poetics of the Paratext: Rubricating the Vernacular." *Le tre corone: Rivista internazionale di studi su Dante, Petrarca, Boccaccio* 6 (2019): 69–106.

———. *Chaucer and Italian Textuality*. Oxford: Oxford University Press, 2011.

———. "*Sotto la quale rubrica*: Pre-reading the *Comedìa*." *Dante Studies* 133 (2015): 147–76.

Clemens, Raymond, and Timothy Graham. *Introduction to Manuscript Studies*. Ithaca, NY: Cornell University Press, 2007.

Clogan, Paul M. "The Manuscripts of Lactantius Placidus' Commentary on the *Thebaid*." *Scriptorium* 22, no. 1 (1968): 87–91.

Cohn, Dorrit. "Metalepsis and Mise en Abyme." *Narrative* 20, no. 1 (2012): 105–14.

Colella, Gianluca. "La perifrasi '*andare/venire* + gerundio' nella poesia delle origini." *La lingua italiana: Storia, strutture, testi* 2 (2006): 71–90.

Coleman, William E. "Boccaccio's 1475 *Teseida*: Este Partisan and John Rylands Library Ghost." *Heliotropia* 14 (2017): 67–77.

———. "Giovanni Boccaccio, *Il Teseida*." In *Sixty Bokes Olde and Newe*, Catalogue of the Exhibition: Manuscripts and Early Printed Books from Libraries in and Near Philadelphia Illustrating Chaucer's Sources, His Works and Their Influence, edited by David Anderson, 53–57. Knoxville, TN: New Chaucer Society, 1986.

———. "The Knight's Tale." In *Sources and Analogues of the "Canterbury Tales,"* edited by Robert M. Correale and Mary Hamel, 2:87–247. Cambridge: DS Brewer, 2005.

———. "The Oratoriana *Teseida*: Witness of a Lost 'Beta' Autograph." *Studi sul Boccaccio* 40 (2012): 105–85.

———. "*Teseida delle nozze d'Emilia*." In De Robertis et al., eds., *Boccaccio autore e copista*, 89–99.

———. *Watermarks in the Manuscripts of Boccaccio's "Il Teseida": A Catalogue, Codicological Study and Album*. Florence: Olschki, 1997.

Colombo, Manuela. *Dai mistici a Dante: Il linguaggio dell'ineffabilità*. Florence: La Nuova Italia, 1987.

———, ed. *Vita Nuova*. By Dante Alighieri. Milan: Feltrinelli, 2008.

Concordanze del "Canzoniere" di Francesco Petrarca. Edited by the Ufficio lessicografico dell'Opera del Vocabolario. Florence: Accademia della Crusca, 1971.

Consoli, Domenico. "parola." In *Enciclopedia Dantesca*, edited by Umberto Bosco, 4:318–20. Rome: Istituto della Enciclopedia Italiana, 1973.

Conte, Gian Biagio. "Proems in the Middle." In *The Poetry of Pathos: Studies in Virgilian Epic*, 219–31. Oxford: Oxford University Press, 2007.

Contini, Gianfranco. "Dante come personaggio-poeta della *Commedia*." In *Varianti e altra linguistica*, 335–61.

———, ed. "De librorum copia." By Francesco Petrarca. In *Mostra di codici petrarcheschi laurenziani*, 73–81. Florence: Olschki, 1974.

———. "Esercizio d'interpretazione sopra un sonetto di Dante." In *Varianti e altra linguistica*, 161–68.

———, ed. *Letteratura italiana delle origini.* Florence: Sansoni, 1946.

———. "Préhistoire de l'*aura* de Pétrarque." In *Varianti e altra linguistica*, 193–99.

———. "Preliminari sulla lingua del Petrarca." In *Varianti e altra linguistica*, 169–92.

———, ed. *Rime*. By Dante Alighieri. Turin: Einaudi, 1946.

———. "Il *Teseida* di Salvatore Battaglia, il *Filostrato* e il *Ninfale Fiesolano* nell'edizione di Vincenzo Pernicone." *Giornale storico della letteratura italiana* 112 (1938): 86–96.

———. *Varianti e altra linguistica: Una raccolta di saggi (1938–1968).* Turin: Einaudi, 1970.

Copeland, Rita. *Rhetoric, Hermeneutics, and Translation in the Middle Ages: Academic Traditions and Vernacular Texts.* Cambridge: Cambridge University Press, 1991.

Coppola, Goffredo. *Scritti papirologici e filologici.* Bari: Dedalo, 2006.

Corradino, Alessandra. "Rilievi grafici sui volgari autografi di Giovanni Boccaccio." *Studi di grammatica italiana* 16 (1996): 5–74.

Corti, Maria. "Il binomio intertestualità e fonti: Funzioni della storia nel sistema letterario." In *La scrittura e la storia: Problemi di storiografia letteraria*, edited by Alberto Asor Rosa, 115–30. Scandicci (Florence): La Nuova Italia, 1995.

———. "'Il libro della memoria' e i libri dello scrittore." In *Scritti su Cavalcanti e Dante: La felicità mentale, Percorsi dell'invenzione e altri saggi: Nuove prospettive per Cavalcanti e Dante*, 179–99. Turin: Einaudi, 2003.

———. "Il linguaggio poetico di Cino da Pistoia." *Cultura neolatina* 12, no. 3 (1952): 185–223.

———. "Testi o macrotesto? I racconti di Marcovaldo." *Strumenti critici* 27 (1975): 182–97.

Cottino-Jones, Marga. "The Myth of Apollo and Daphne in Petrarch's *Canzoniere*: The Dynamics of Literary Function and Transformation." In *Francis Petrarch, Six Centuries Later: A Symposium*, edited by Aldo Scaglione, 152–76. Chapel Hill, NC: Department of Romance Languages and Literatures, University of North Carolina/Chicago: The Newberry Library, 1975.

Covini, Nadia. "Alberto d'Este." In *Dizionario biografico degli italiani*, 43:297–300. Rome: Istituto della Enciclopedia Italiana, 1993.

Crescini, Vincenzo. "Appendice al cap. IX: Appunti sulle fonti della *Teseide*." In *Contributo agli studi su Boccaccio*, 220–47. Turin: Loescher, 1887.

———. "Le *Razos* provenzali e le prose della *Vita Nuova*." *Giornale storico della letteratura italiana* 32 (1898): 463–64.

Crespo, Roberto. "Il proemio di *Donne ch'avete intelletto d'amore*." *Studi di filologia e di letteratura italiana offerti a Carlo Dionisotti*, 3–13. Milan: Ricciardi, 1973.

Cribiore, Raffaela. *Writing, Teachers, and Students in Graeco-Roman Egypt*. Atlanta: Scholars Press, 1996.

Cristaldi, Sergio. "Dante lettore e scriba della memoria." In *Dante in lettura*, edited by Giuseppe De Matteis, 63–131. Ravenna: Longo, 2005.

———. *La "Vita Nuova" e la restituzione del narrare*. Messina: Rubbettino, 1994.

Cudini, Piero. "Il Dante della sestina." *Belfagor* 37, no. 2 (1982): 184–98.

Cursi, Marco. "Boccaccio between Dante and Petrarch: Manuscripts, Marginalia, Drawings." *Heliotropia* 14 (2017): 11–46.

———. "Cronologia e stratigrafia nelle sillogi dantesche di Giovanni Boccaccio." In *Dentro l'officina di Giovanni Boccaccio: Studi sugli autografi in volgare e su Boccaccio dantista*, edited by Sandro Bertelli and Davide Cappi, 81–130. Vatican City: Biblioteca Apostolica Vaticana, 2014.

———. *Il "Decameron": Scritture, scriventi, lettori: Storia di un testo*. Rome: Viella, 2007.

———. *Le forme del libro: Dalla tavoletta cerata all'e-book*. Bologna: il Mulino, 2016.

———. "Per la prima circolazione dei *Rerum vulgarium fragmenta*: I manoscritti *antiquiores*." In *Storia della scrittura e altre storie*, edited by Daniele Bianconi, 225–61. Rome: Accademia Nazionale dei Lincei, 2014.

———. *La scrittura e i libri di Giovanni Boccaccio*. Rome: Viella, 2013.

———. "La *Tebaide* restaurata del Boccaccio." In De Robertis et al., eds., *Boccaccio autore e copista*, 337–39.

Cursi, Marco, and Francesco Marco Aresu. "Un codice del *Teseida* conservato a Philadelphia e una nuova testimonianza dei cantari della *Guerra di Troia*." *Medioevo letterario d'Italia* 15 (2018): 141–53.

Cursi, Marco, and Maurizio Fiorilla. "Giovanni Boccaccio." In *Le origini e il Trecento*, Vol. 1 of *Autografi dei letterati italiani*, edited by Giuseppina Brunetti, Maurizio Fiorilla, and Marco Petoletti, 43–103. Rome: Salerno, 2013.

Cursi, Marco, and Carlo Pulsoni. "Nuove acquisizioni sulla tradizione antica dei *Rerum vulgarium fragmenta*." *Medioevo e Rinascimento*, n.s., 24 (2010): 215–76.

———. "Sulla tradizione antica dei *Rerum vulgarium fragmenta*: Un gemello del Laurenziano LXI 10 (Paris, Bibliothèque Nationale, It. 551)." *Studi di filologia italiana* 67 (2009): 91–114.

Curtius, Ernst Robert. "Das Buch als Symbol in der Divina Commedia." In *Festschrift zum sechzigsten Geburtstag von Paul Clemen*, edited by Wilhelm Worringer, Heribert Reiners, and Leopold Seligmann, 44–54. Bonn: F. Cohen, 1926.

———. *European Literature and the Latin Middle Ages*. New York: Harper & Row, 1963.

D'Agostino, Alfonso. *Il pensiero dominante: La sestina lirica da Arnaut Daniel a Dante Alighieri*. Milan: CUEM, 2009.

Dain, Alphonse. *Les manuscrits*. Paris: Diderot, 1997.

Dällenbach, Lucien. *The Mirror in the Text*. Chicago: University of Chicago Press, 1989.

D'Andrea, Antonio. "Dante interprete di se stesso: Le varianti ermeneutiche della *Vita Nuova* e il *Convivio*." In *Strutture inquiete: Premesse teoriche e verifiche storico-letterarie*, 53–83. Florence: Olschki, 1993.

———. "La struttura della *Vita Nuova*: Le divisioni delle rime." *Yearbook of Italian Studies* 4 (1980): 13–40.

Daniels, Rhiannon. *Boccaccio and the Book: Production and Reading in Italy, 1340–1520*. London: Legenda, 2009.

———. "Boccaccio's Narrators and Audiences." In Armstrong, Daniels, and Milner, eds., *The Cambridge Companion to Boccaccio*, 36–51.

———. "Rethinking the Critical History of the *Decameron*: Boccaccio's Epistle XXII to Mainardo Cavalcanti." *Modern Language Review* 106, no. 2 (2011): 423–47.

———. "Where Does the *Decameron* Begin? Editorial Practice and Tables of Rubrics." *Modern Language Review* 114, no. 1 (2019): 52–78.

Davidson, F. J. A. "The Origin of the Sestina." *Modern Language Notes* 25, no. 1 (1910): 18–20.

de Angelis, Violetta. "I commenti medievali alla *Tebaide* di Stazio: Anselmo di Laon, Goffredo Babione, Ilario d'Orléans." In *Medieval and Renaissance Scholarship*, Proceedings of the Second European Science Foundation Workshop on the Classical Tradition in the Middle Ages and the Renaissance (London, The Warburg Institute, 27–28 November 1992), edited by Nicholas Mann and Birger Munk Olsen, 75–136. Leiden: Brill, 1997.

———. "Testo, glossa, commento nel XII secolo." In *Il commento e i suoi dintorni*, edited by Bianca Maria Da Rif, 1–26. Milan: Guerini, 2002.

De Bartholomaeis, Vincenzo. "Ciò che sia veramente l'antichissima 'cantilena' *Boves se pareba*." *Giornale storico della letteratura italiana* 90 (1927): 197–204.

———, ed. *Rime giullaresche e popolari d'Italia*. Bologna: Zanichelli, 1926.

Degl'Innocenti, Luca. *"Al suon di questa cetra": Ricerche sulla poesia orale del Rinascimento*. Florence: Società Editrice Fiorentina, 2016.

de la Mare, Albinia Catherine. *The Handwriting of Italian Humanists*. Oxford: Oxford University Press, for Association Internationale de Bibliophilie, 1973.

Del Puppo, Dario, and H. Wayne Storey. "Wilkins nella formazione del canzoniere di Petrarca." *Italica* 80 (2003): 295–312.

Delcorno, Carlo, ed. *Elegia di Madonna Fiammetta*. By Giovanni Boccaccio. In *Tutte le opere di Giovanni Boccaccio*, edited by Vittore Branca, 5/2:1–24 (introduction), 25–189 (text), 191–412 (notes). Milan: Mondadori, 1994.

———. "Una nuova proposta per il *Teseida*." *Studi sul Boccaccio* 44 (2016): 389–98.

———. "Gli scritti danteschi del Boccaccio." In *Dante e Boccaccio: Lectura Dantis Scaligera, 2004–2005, in memoria di Vittore Branca*, edited by Ennio Sandal, 109–37. Padua: Antenore, 2007.

Delisle, Léopold. *Notice sur un livre annoté par Pétrarque (ms. latin 2201 de la Bibliothèque Nationale)*. Paris: Imprimerie Nationale, 1896.

Dempster, Germaine. "Salvatore Battaglia's Edition of the *Teseida*." *Modern Philology* 38, no. 2 (1940): 205–14.

Dencker, Klaus Peter. *Optische Poesie: Von den prähistorischen Schriftzeichen bis zu den digitalen Experimenten der Gegenwart*. Berlin: De Gruyter, 2011.

De Nichilo, Mauro. "Petrarca, Salutati, Landino: *RVF* 22 e 132." *Italianistica: Rivista di letteratura italiana* 33, no. 2 (2004): 143–61.

De Robertis, Domenico. "Amore e Guido ed io (relazioni poetiche e associazioni di testi)." *Studi di filologia italiana* 36 (1978): 39–65.

———. *Il canzoniere escorialense e la tradizione "veneziana" delle rime dello stil novo.* Supplement 27 of *Giornale storico della letteratura italiana.* Turin: Loescher, 1954.

———, ed. *Il Codice Chigiano L. V. 176 autografo di Giovanni Boccaccio.* Edizione fototipica. Florence: Alinari, 1974.

———. "Contiguità e selezione nella costruzione del canzoniere petrarchesco." *Studi di filologia italiana* 43 (1985): 45–66.

———. "Identità di Beatrice." In *Omaggio a Beatrice (1290–1990)*, edited by Rudy Abardo, 11–21. Florence: Le Lettere, 1997.

———. "'*Incipit vita nova*' (*V.N.*, 1): Poetica del (ri)cominciamento." In Moleta, ed., La gloriosa donna de la mente, 11–19.

———. "Introduzione." In *Cantari novellistici dal Tre al Cinquecento*, edited by Elisabetta Benucci, Roberta Manetti, and Franco Zabagli, 1:ix–xxxviii. Rome: Salerno, 2002.

———. *Il libro della "Vita nuova."* Florence: Sansoni, 1970.

———. "Petrarca petroso." *Revue des Études Italiennes* 29 (1983): 13–37.

———. "Problemi di metodo nell'edizione dei cantari." In *Studi e problemi di critica testuale*, Atti del Convegno di studi di filologia italiana nel centenario della Commissione per i testi di lingua (7–9 aprile 1960), 119–38. Bologna: Commissione per i testi di lingua, 1961.

———, ed. *Rime.* By Dante Alighieri. Florence: SISMEL—Edizioni del Galluzzo, 2005.

———, ed. *Rime.* By Dante Alighieri. Florence: Le Lettere, 2002.

———. "Sulla tradizione estravagante delle rime della *Vita Nuova.*" *Studi danteschi* 44 (1967): 5–84.

———, ed. *Vita Nuova.* By Dante Alighieri. In *Opere minori*, edited by Domenico De Robertis and Gianfranco Contini, 1/1:3–247. Milan: Ricciardi, 1984.

De Robertis, Teresa. "L'inventario della 'parva libraria' di Santo Spirito e la biblioteca del Boccaccio." In De Robertis et al., eds., *Boccaccio autore e copista*, 403–9.

———. "Il posto di Boccaccio nella storia della scrittura." In *Boccaccio letterato*, Atti del convegno internazionale di studi (Firenze–Certaldo, 10–12 ottobre 2013), edited by Michelangiola Marchiaro and Stefano Zamponi, 145–70. Florence: Accademia della Crusca, 2015.

De Robertis, Teresa, Carla Maria Monti, Marco Petoletti, Giuliano Tanturli, and Stefano Zamponi, eds. *Boccaccio autore e copista*, Catalogo della mostra (Firenze, Biblioteca Medicea Laurenziana, 11 ottobre 2013–11 gennaio 2014). Florence: Mandragora, 2013.

Derolez, Albert. *The Palaeography of Gothic Manuscript Books: From the Twelfth to the Early Sixteenth Century*. Cambridge: Cambridge University Press, 2003.

Derrida, Jacques. *Of Grammatology*. Baltimore: Johns Hopkins University Press, 1976.

Destrez, Jean. *La Pecia dans les manuscrits universitaires du XIIIe et du XIVe siècle*. Paris, Éditions Jacques Vautrain, 1935.

De Ventura, Paolo. "Gli appelli all'uditore e il dialogo con il lettore nella *Commedia*." *Dante: Rivista internazionale di studi su Dante Alighieri* 1 (2004): 81–99.

Dickmann, Iddo. *The Little Crystalline Seed: The Ontological Significance of* Mise en Abyme *in Post-Heideggerian Thought*. Albany: SUNY Press, 2019.

Di Girolamo, Costanzo. *Elementi di versificazione provenzale*. Naples: Liguori, 1979.

———. "Forma e significato della parola rima nella sestina." In *Teoria e prassi della versificazione*, 155–67. Bologna: il Mulino, 1976.

Dionisotti, Carlo. "Fortuna del Petrarca nel Quattrocento." *Italia medioevale e umanistica* 17 (1974): 61–113.

Di Sabatino, Luca. "Spigolature sulle fonti del *Teseida*." In *Boccaccio in versi*, Atti del Convegno di Parma, 13–14 marzo 2014, edited by Pantalea Mazzitello, Giulia Raboni, Paolo Rinoldi, and Carlo Varotti, 89–100. Florence: Cesati, 2016.

Doane, Alger N., and Carol Braun Pasternack, eds. *Vox Intexta: Orality and Textuality in the Middle Ages*. Madison: University of Wisconsin Press, 1991.

Dorandi, Tiziano. *Nell'officina dei classici: Come lavoravano gli autori antichi*. Rome: Carocci, 2007.

Dotti, Ugo, ed. *Canzoniere*. By Francesco Petrarca. Rome: Donzelli, 2004.

———, ed. and trans. *I rimedi per l'una e l'altra sorte*. By Francesco Petrarca. Turin: Nino Aragno, 2013.

———. "Petrarca: Il mito dafneo." *Convivium* 37 (1969): 9–23.

Draaisma, Douwe. *Metaphors of Memory: A History of Ideas about the Mind*. Cambridge: Cambridge University Press, 2000.

Dragonetti, Roger. *Dante pèlerin de la Sainte Face*. Gent/Gand: Romanica Gandensia, 1968.

Dronke, Peter. "The Conclusion of Dante's *Commedia*." *Italian Studies* 49 (1994): 21–39.

———. *Verse with Prose from Petronius to Dante: The Art and Scope of the Mixed Form*. Cambridge, MA: Harvard University Press, 1994.

Ducrot, Oswald, and Tzvetan Todorov. *Encyclopedic Dictionary of the Sciences of Language*. Baltimore: Johns Hopkins University Press, 1979.

Duggan, Joseph J. "Modalità della cultura orale." In *La produzione del testo*, Vol. 1/1 of *Lo spazio letterario del Medioevo: 2. Il Medioevo volgare*, edited by Piero Boitani, Mario Mancini, and Alberto Vàrvaro, 147–77. Rome: Salerno, 1999.

Durling, Robert M. "Guido Cavalcanti in the *Vita nova*." In *Guido Cavalcanti tra i suoi lettori*, Proceedings of the International Symposium for the Seventh Centennial of His Death, New York, November 10–11, 2000, edited by Maria Luisa Ardizzone, 177–85. Fiesole (Florence): Cadmo, 2003.

———. "Petrarch's 'Giovene donna sotto un verde lauro.'" *Modern Language Notes* 86, no. 1 (1971): 1–20.

———, ed. and trans. *Petrarch's Lyric Poems: The "Rime sparse" and Other Lyrics*. By Francesco Petrarca. Cambridge, MA: Harvard University Press, 1976.

———. "*Rerum vulgarium fragmenta*: From Manuscript to Print." *Humanist Studies & the Digital Age* 1 (2011): 50–65.

Durling, Robert M., and Roland L. Martinez, eds. and trans. *The Divine Comedy*. By Dante Alighieri. Oxford: Oxford University Press, 1996–2011.

———. *Time and the Crystal: Studies in Dante's "Rime Petrose."* Berkeley: University of California Press, 1990.

Dutschke, Dennis. "The Anniversary Poems in Petrarch's *Canzoniere*." *Italica* 58, no. 2 (1981): 83–101.

Eberwein-Dabcovich, Elena. "Das Wort novus in der altprovenzalischen Dichtung und in Dantes *Vita Nova*." *Romanistisches Jahrbuch* 2, no. 1 (1949): 171–95.

Eco, Umberto. *Lector in fabula: La cooperazione interpretativa nei testi narrativi*. Milan: Bompiani, 1979.

———. *The Limits of Interpretation*. Bloomington: Indiana University Press, 1990.

Edwards, Robert R. "Medieval Statius: Belatedness and Authority." In *Brill's Companion to Statius*, edited by William J. Dominik, Carole E. Newlands, and Kyle Gervais, 497–511. Leiden: Brill, 2015.

Eisner, Martin. *Boccaccio and the Invention of Italian Literature: Dante, Petrarch, Cavalcanti and the Authority of the Vernacular*. Cambridge: Cambridge University Press, 2013.

———. *Dante's New Life of the Book: A Philology of World Literature*. Oxford: Oxford University Press, 2021.

———. "The Materiality of the Text and Manuscript Culture." In *The Oxford Handbook of Dante*, edited by Manuele Gragnolati, Elena Lombardi, and Francesca Southerden, 49–62. Oxford: Oxford University Press, 2021.

Eliot, Simon, Andrew Nash, and I. R. Willison, eds. *Literary Cultures and the Material Book*. London: British Library, 2007.

Emerson, Lori. *Reading Writing Interfaces: From the Digital to the Bookbound.* Minneapolis: University of Minnesota Press, 2014.

Ernst, Ulrich. *Carmen figuratum: Geschichte des Figurengedichts von den antiken Ursprüngen bis zum Ausgang des Mittelalters.* Cologne: Böhlau, 1991.

———. "The Figured Poem: Towards a Definition of Genre." *Visible Language* 20, no. 1 (1986): 8–27.

Escarpit, Robert. *Sociology of Literature.* London: Cass, 1971.

Eusebi, Mario. "Lettura sinottica (con una congettura) della tradizione della sestina di Arnaut Daniel." *Cultura neolatina* 42 (1982): 181–99.

Evans, Michael W. "The Geometry of the Mind." *Architectural Association Quarterly* 12, no. 4 (1980): 32–55.

Everson, Jane E. *The Italian Romance Epic in the Age of Humanism: The Matter of Italy and the World of Rome.* Oxford: Oxford University Press, 2001.

Faleri, Francesca. "Riflessioni sulla lingua di Giovanni Boccaccio (a partire dalle opere volgari in copia autografa)." In *Dentro l'officina di Giovanni Boccaccio: Studi sugli autografi in volgare e su Boccaccio dantista,* edited by Sandro Bertelli and Davide Cappi, 137–62. Vatican City: Biblioteca Apostolica Vaticana, 2014.

Farnetti, Monica. "Dante e il libro della memoria." In *Il manoscritto ritrovato: Storia letteraria di una finzione,* 47–63. Florence: Società Editrice Fiorentina, 2005.

Faye, Christopher Urdahl, William Henry Bond, and Seymour de Ricci. *Supplement to the Census of Medieval and Renaissance Manuscripts in the United States and Canada.* New York: The Bibliographical Society of America, 1962.

Fenzi, Enrico. *La canzone d'amore di Guido Cavalcanti e i suoi antichi commenti.* Genoa: il melangolo, 1999.

———. "*E' m'incresce di me sì duramente.*" In *Le Rime di Dante,* edited by Claudia Berra and Paolo Borsa, 135–75. Milan: Cisalpino, 2010.

———. "Fascinazione verbale e forza discorsiva nella canzone dantesca 'Amor, tu vedi ben.'" In *Amor tu vedi ben che questa donna* (La Biblioteca de *Tenzone* [colección de la revista *Tenzone*] 11), edited by Raffaele Pinto, 41–68. Madrid: CEMA, 2018.

———. "Il libro della memoria." In *Dante in lettura,* edited by Giuseppe De Matteis, 15–38. Ravenna: Longo, 2005.

Feo, Michele Arcangelo. "'In vetustissimis cedulis': Il testo del postscriptum della senile XIII 11 γ e la 'forma Malatesta' dei *Rerum vulgarium fragmenta.*" *Quaderni Petrarcheschi* 11 (2001): 119–48.

———. "Petrarca, Francesco." In *La tradizione dei testi*, Vol. 10 of *Storia della letteratura italiana*, edited by Enrico Malato and Claudio Ciociola, 271–329. Rome: Salerno, 2001.

———. "Petrarca ovvero l'avanguardia del Trecento." *Quaderni petrarcheschi* 1 (1983): 1–22.

Fera, Vincenzo. "La filologia del Petrarca e i fondamenti della filologia umanistica." *Quaderni petrarcheschi* 9–10 (1992–1993): 367–91.

———. "I *Libri peculiares*." In *Petrarca, l'umanesimo e la civiltà europea*, Atti del Convegno internazionale (Firenze, 5–10 dicembre 2004), edited by Donatella Coppini and Michele Arcangelo Feo (= *Quaderni petrarcheschi* 17–18 [2007–2008]), 2:1077–100. Florence: Le Lettere, 2012.

Ferrante, Gennaro. "Il paradosso di Gerione." *Rivista di studi danteschi* 20, no. 1 (2020): 113–33.

Ferrari, Franco. "Due note al testo del fr. 2 di Saffo." *Analecta Papyrologica* 12 (2000): 37–44.

Ferreira, Manuel Pedro. *O som de Martin Codax: Sobre a dimensão musical da lírica galego-portuguesa (séculos XII–XIV)/The Sound of Martin Codax: On the Musical Dimension of the Galician-Portuguese Lyric (XII–XIV Centuries)*. Lisbon: Imprensa Nacional—Casa da Moeda, 1986.

Ferreri, Rosario. "Una risposta di Antonio Pucci al Boccaccio." *Romance Notes* 12, no. 1 (1970): 189–91.

Fichera, Eduardo. "Ineffabilità e crisi poetica nella *Vita Nuova*." *Italian Quarterly* 163–164 (2005): 5–22.

Figurelli, Fernando. "Note su dieci rime del Petrarca (nn. 14, 18, 22–24, 28, 29, 35, 37 e 39 del *Canzoniere*)." *Studi petrarcheschi* 6 (1956): 201–21.

Filosa, Elsa. "To Praise Dante, to Please Petrarch (*Trattatello in laude di Dante*)." In *Boccaccio: A Critical Guide to the Complete Works*, edited by Victoria Kirkham, Michael Sherberg, and Janet Levarie Smarr, 213–20. Chicago: University of Chicago Press, 2013.

Finazzi, Silvia. "Le postille di Boccaccio a Terenzio." *Italia medioevale e umanistica* 54 (2013): 81–133.

Finazzi, Silvia, and Michaelangiola Marchiaro. "Il codice di Terenzio di mano del Boccaccio e da lui firmato." In De Robertis et al., eds., *Boccaccio autore e copista*, 339–41.

Fink-Errera, Guy. "La produzione dei libri di testo nelle università medievali." In *Libri e lettori nel Medioevo: Guida storica e critica*, edited by Guglielmo Cavallo, 131–65. Bari: Laterza, 1977.

Fiorilla, Maurizio. "Il '*libellus*' in una nota del Petrarca in margine all'Orazio Morgan." *Studi medievali e umanistici* 4 (2006): 311–21.

———. Marginalia *figurati nei codici di Petrarca*. Florence: Olschki, 2005.

———, ed. *Trattatello in laude di Dante*. By Giovanni Boccaccio. In *Le vite di Dante dal XIV al XVI secolo: Iconografia dantesca*, edited by Monica Berté, Maurizio Fiorilla, Sonia Chiodo, and Isabella Valente, 11–154, in *Opere di dubbia attribuzione e altri documenti danteschi*, Vol. 7/4 of *Le opere*, by Dante Alighieri. Rome: Salerno, 2017.

Fiormonte, Domenico, Teresa Numerico, and Francesca Tomasi. *The Digital Humanist: A Critical Inquiry*. Brooklyn, NY: punctum books, 2015.

Fleming, David, ed. *Opera Omnia*. By Bonaventure of Bagnorea. Quaracchi: Typographia Collegii S. Bonaventurae, 1882–1902.

Fludernik, Monika. "Metanarrative and Metafictional Commentary: From Metadiscursivity to Metanarration and Metafiction." *Poetica* 35, nos. 1–2 (2003): 1–39.

Fo, Alessandro, Carlo Vecce, and Claudio Vela. *Coblas: Il mistero delle sei stanze*. Milan: Scheiwiller, 1987.

Folena, Gianfranco, ed. *Caras rimas: Liriche di Raimbaut d'Aurenga e Arnaut Daniel*. Padua: Liviana, 1967.

———. "L'orologio del Petrarca." In Textus testis*: Lingua e cultura poetica delle origini*, 266–89. Turin: Bollati Boringhieri, 2002.

———. "La tradizione delle opere di Dante Alighieri." In *Atti del congresso internazionale di studi danteschi*, A cura della Società Dantesca Italiana e dell'Associazione Internazionale per gli Studi di Lingua e Letteratura Italiana e sotto il patrocinio dei comuni di Firenze, Verona e Ravenna (20–27 aprile 1965), 1–78. Florence: Sansoni, 1965.

———. *Volgarizzare e tradurre*. Turin: Einaudi, 1991.

———, ed. Vulgares eloquentes*: Vite e poesie dei trovatori di Dante*. Padua: Liviana, 1961.

Fontana, Alessio. "La filologia romanza e il problema del rapporto Petrarca-trovatori (premesse per una ripresa del problema secondo nuove prospettive)." In *Petrarca 1304–1374: Beiträge zu Werk und Wirkung*, edited by Fritz Schalk, 51–70. Frankfurt a. M.: Klostermann, 1975.

Formisano, Luciano. "*Al poco giorno ed al gran cerchio d'ombra*." In *Le Quindici Canzoni (Lette da diversi)*, by Dante Alighieri, 1:212–239. Lecce: Pensa MultiMedia, 2009.

———. "Prospettive di ricerca sui canzonieri d'autore nella lirica d'oïl." In *La filologia romanza e i codici*, Atti del convegno, Messina, Università degli

Studi, Facoltà di Lettere e filosofia, 19–22 dicembre, edited by Saverio Guida and Fortunata Latella, 1:131–52. Messina: Sicania, 1993.

Foster, Kenelm. *Petrarch: Poet and Humanist.* Edinburgh: Edinburgh University Press, 1984.

Foster, Kenelm, and Patrick Boyde, eds. and trans. *Dante's Lyric Poetry.* By Dante Alighieri. Oxford: Clarendon, 1967.

Foucault, Michel. "Nietzsche, Genealogy, History." In *Language, Counter-Memory, Practice: Selected Essays and Interviews*, 139–64. Ithaca, NY: Cornell University Press, 1977.

Franceschini, Adriano. *Artisti a Ferrara in età umanistica e rinascimentale (I–II).* Ferrara: Corbo, 1993–1995.

Frank, István. "La chanson 'Lasso me' de Pétrarque et ses prédécesseurs." *Annales du Midi: Revue archéologique, historique et philologique de la France méridionale* 66 (1954): 259–68.

———. *Répertoire métrique de la poésie des troubadours.* Paris: Champion, 1953–1957.

Franklin-Brown, Mary. *Reading the World: Encyclopedic Writing in the Scholastic Age.* Chicago: University of Chicago Press, 2012.

Frasca, Gabriele. *La furia della sintassi: La sestina in Italia.* Naples: Bibliopolis, 1992.

Frasso, Giuseppe. "Appunti sul Petrarca aldino del 1501." In *Vestigia: Studi in onore di Giuseppe Billanovich*, edited by Rino Avesani, Mirella Ferrari, Tino Foffano, Giuseppe Frasso, and Agostino Sottili, 1:315–35. Rome: Edizioni di Storia e Letteratura, 1984.

———. "Pallide sinopie: Ricerche e proposte sulle forme pre-Chigi e Chigi del *Canzoniere.*" *Studi di filologia italiana* 55 (1997): 23–64.

———. "Un rotolo dei *Rerum vulgarium fragmenta.*" *Studi petrarcheschi* 16 (2003): 131–48.

Freccero, Carla. "From Amazon to Court Lady: Generic Hybridization in Boccaccio's *Teseida.*" *Comparative Literature Studies* 32, no. 2 (1995): 226–43.

Freccero, John. "The Fig Tree and the Laurel: Petrarch's Poetics." *Diacritics* 5, no. 1 (1975): 34–40.

Friedman, John B. *Orpheus in the Middle Ages.* Cambridge, MA: Harvard University Press, 1970.

Frisardi, Andrew, trans. *Convivio.* By Dante Alighieri. Cambridge: Cambridge University Press, 2018.

———, trans. *Vita Nova.* By Dante Alighieri. Evanston, IL: Northwestern University Press, 2012.

Frosini, Giovanna. "Dante disegnatore." In *"In principio fuit textus": Studi di linguistica e filologia offerti a Rosario Coluccia in occasione della nomina a professore emerito*, edited by Vito Luigi Castrignanò, Francesca De Blasi, and Marco Maggiore, 83–92. Florence: Cesati, 2018.

Fubini, Mario. *Metrica e poesia: Lezioni sulle forme metriche italiane*. Milan: Feltrinelli, 1962.

Fucilla, Joseph G. "Petrarchism and the Modern Vogue of the Figure ἀδύνατον." *Zeitschrift für romanische Philologie* 56 (1936): 671–81.

Fumagalli, Edoardo. "Appunti sulla biblioteca dei Visconti e degli Sforza nel castello di Pavia." *Studi petrarcheschi*, n.s., 7 (1990): 93–211.

———. "Boccaccio e Dante." In De Robertis et al., eds., *Boccaccio autore e copista*, 25–31.

Gabriele, Linda. "Le illustrazioni del *Teseida* dei Gerolamini di Napoli." In *Boccaccio angioino: Materiali per la storia culturale di Napoli nel Trecento*, edited by Giancarlo Alfano, Teresa d'Urso, and Alessandra Perricciolі Saggese, 357–67. Brussels: Peter Lang, 2012.

Gáldi, Ladislas. "Les origines provençales de la métrique des *canzoni* de Pétrarque." In *Actes du Xe Congrès International de Linguistique et Philologie Romanes, Strasbourg, 23–28 avril 1962*, edited by Georges Straka, 2:783–90. Paris: Klincksieck, 1965.

Galvez, Marisa. *Songbook: How Lyrics Became Poetry in Medieval Europe*. Chicago: University of Chicago Press, 2012.

Gardini, Nicola. "Un Esempio Di Imitazione Virgiliana Nel Canzoniere Petrarchesco: Il Mito Di Orfeo." *Modern Language Notes* 110, no. 1 (1995): 132–44.

Gardner, Edmund G. "Imagination and Memory in the Psychology of Dante." In *A Miscellany of Studies in Romance Languages & Literatures Presented to Leon E. Kastner*, edited by Mary Williams and James A. de Rothschild, 275–82. Cambridge: Heffer, 1932.

Gargan, Luciano. "Per la biblioteca di Dante." In *Dante, la sua biblioteca e lo studio di Bologna*, 3–36. Padua: Antenore, 2014.

Garin, Eugenio. "La nuova scienza e il simbolo del 'libro.'" In *La cultura filosofica del Rinascimento italiano*, 451–65. Florence: Sansoni, 1961.

Gasparri, Françoise. "Authenticité des autographes." In *Gli autografi medievali: Problemi paleografici e filologici*, Atti del convegno di studio della Fondazione Ezio Franceschini (Erice, 25 settembre–2 ottobre 1990), edited by Paolo Chiesa and Lucia Pinelli, 3–22. Spoleto: Centro italiano di studi sull'alto medioevo, 1994.

Gatien-Arnoult, Adolphe Félix, ed. *Las Flors del Gay Saber, estier dichas las Leys d'Amors*. By Guillam Molinier. Toulouse: Paya, 1841–1843.

GDLI = *Grande Dizionario della Lingua Italiana*. Edited by Salvatore Battaglia and Giorgio Bàrberi Squarotti. Turin: UTET, 1961–2002.

Gelli, Jacopo. *Divise-motti e imprese di famiglie e personaggi italiani*. Milan: Hoepli, 1928.

Gellrich, Jesse M. *The Idea of the Book in the Middle Ages: Language Theory, Mythology, and Fiction*. Ithaca, NY: Cornell University Press, 1985.

Genette, Gérard. *Métalepse: De la figure à la fiction*. Paris: Seuil, 2004.

———. *Narrative Discourse: An Essay in Method*. Ithaca, NY: Cornell University Press, 1980.

———. *Paratexts: Thresholds of Interpretation*. Cambridge: Cambridge University Press, 1997.

———. *The Work of Art: Immanence and Transcendence*. Ithaca, NY: Cornell University Press, 1997.

Genot, Gérard. "Strutture narrative della poesia lirica." *Paragone* 18 (1967): 35–52.

Geri, Lorenzo. "*Ferrea voluptas*": *Il tema della scrittura nell'opera di Francesco Petrarca*. Rome: Edizioni Nuova Cultura, 2007.

Ghetti, Noemi. *L'ombra di Cavalcanti e Dante*. Rome: L'Asino d'oro, 2010.

Giarin, Sandra. "Petrarca e Bembo: L'edizione aldina del *Canzoniere*." *Studi di filologia italiana* 62 (2004): 161–93.

Gilbert, Creighton. "La devozione di Giovanni Boccaccio per gli artisti e per l'arte." In *Boccaccio visualizzato: Narrare per parole e per immagini*, edited by Vittore Branca, 1:145–54. Turin: Einaudi, 1999.

Gilissen, Léon. *Prolégomènes à la codicologie: Recherches sur la construction des cahiers et la mise en page des manuscrits médiévaux*. Gand: Story-Scientia, 1977.

Gilson, Etienne. *Dante the Philosopher*. London: Sheed & Ward, 1948.

Gilson, Simon A. *Dante and Renaissance Florence*. Cambridge: Cambridge University Press, 2005.

Ginsberg, Warren. "Boccaccio's Characters and the Rhetorical 'Disputatio in utramque partem.'" In *The Cast of Character: The Representation of Personality in Ancient and Medieval Literature*, 98–133. Toronto: University of Toronto Press, 1983.

———. "Boccaccio's Early Romances: The *Filostrato* and the *Teseida*." In *Boccaccio and the European Literary Tradition*, edited by Piero Boitani and Emilia Di Rocco, 31–44. Rome: Edizioni di Storia e Letteratura, 2014.

———. *Dante's Aesthetics of Being*. Ann Arbor: University of Michigan Press, 1999.

Ginzburg, Carlo. "Dante's Blind Spot (*Inferno* XVI–XVII)." In *Dante's Plurilingualism: Authority, Knowledge, Subjectivity*, edited by Sara Fortuna, Manuele Gragnolati, and Jürgen Trabant, 150–63. Cambridge: Legenda, 2010.

———. "*Mise en abyme*: A Reframing." In *Tributes to David Freedberg: Image and Insight*, edited by Claudia Swan, 465–79. Turnhout: Brepols, 2019.

———. "Our Words, and Theirs: A Reflection on the Historian's Craft, Today." *Cromohs: Cyber Review of Modern Historiography* 18 (2014): 97–114.

———. "Storia dell'arte, da vicino e da lontano." *Mitteilungen des Kunsthistorischen Institutes in Florenz* 61, no. 3 (2019): 275–85.

Giovannuzzi, Stefano. "Beatrice, o della poesia." *Paragone. Letteratura*, n.s., xliv, 520–522 (1993): 56–78.

Gitelman, Lisa. *Paper Knowledge: Toward a Media History of Documents*. Durham, NC: Duke University Press, 2014.

Giunta, Claudio. *Codici: Saggi sulla poesia del Medioevo*. Bologna: il Mulino, 2005.

———. "Su Dante lirico." *Nuova Rivista di Letteratura Italiana* 13, nos. 1–2 (2010): 17–29.

———. *Versi a un destinatario: Saggio sulla poesia italiana del Medioevo*. Bologna: il Mulino, 2002.

Gmelin, Hermann. "Die Anrede an den Leser in Dantes Göttlicher Komödie." *Deutsches Dante-Jahrbuch* 29–30 (1951): 130–40.

Goldknopf, David. "The Confessional Increment: A New Look at the I-Narrator." *Journal of Aesthetics and Art Criticism* 28 (1969): 13–21.

Gonfroy, Gérard. "Les genres lyriques occitans et les traités de poetique: De la classification médiévale à la typologie modern." In *Actes du XVIIIe Congrès international de linguistique et philologie romanes, Université de Trèves (Trier), 1986*, edited by Dieter Kremer, 6:121–35. Tübingen: Niemeyer, 1988–1992.

Goodman, Nelson. *Languages of Art: An Approach to a Theory of Symbols*. Indianapolis: Hackett, 1976.

Gorni, Guglielmo. "Ancora sui 'paragrafi' della *Vita Nova*." *Rivista di Letteratura Italiana* 13, no. 3 (1995): 537–62.

———. "Appunti sulla tradizione del *Convivio*: A proposito dell'archetipo e dell'originale dell'opera." In *Dante prima della "Commedia,"* 239–51. Florence: Cadmo, 2001.

———. "Beatrice agli Inferi." In *Omaggio a Beatrice (1290–1990)*, edited by Rudy Abardo, 143–58. Florence: Le Lettere, 1997.

———. "Il 'copyright' della *Vita Nuova*." *Rivista di Letteratura Italiana* 12, no. 2–3 (1994): 481–90.

———. "'Divisioni' e formule introduttive delle poesie nella *Vita Nova*." *Studi testuali* 4 (1996): 57–66.

———. "Un'ipotesi sull'origine dell'ottava rima." *Metrica* 1 (1978): 79–94.

———. *Lettera nome numero: L'ordine delle cose in Dante*. Bologna: il Mulino, 1990.

———. "Metamorfosi e redenzione in Petrarca: Il senso della forma Correggio del Canzoniere." *Lettere italiane* 30, no. 1 (1978): 3–13.

———. *Metrica e analisi letteraria*. Bologna: il Mulino, 1993.

———. *Il nodo della lingua e il verbo d'amore: Studi su Dante e altri duecentisti*. Florence: Olschki, 1981.

———. "'Paragrafi' e titolo della *Vita Nova*." In *Dante prima della "Commedia*," 111–32. Florence: Cadmo, 2001.

———. "Per il testo della *Vita nuova*." *Studi di filologia italiana* 51 (1993): 5–38.

———. "Per la *Vita Nova*." *Studi di filologia italiana* 58 (2000): 29–48.

———. "Restituzione formale dei testi volgari a tradizione plurima." In *Dante prima della* Commedia, 149–76. Florence: Cadmo, 2001.

———. "Una silloge d'autore nelle rime del Cavalcanti." *Critica del testo* 4, no. 1 (2001): 23–39.

———, ed. *Vita Nova*. By Dante Alighieri. Turin: Einaudi, 1996.

Gorni, Guglielmo, and Massimo Malinverni. *Repertorio metrico della canzone italiana dalle origini al Cinquecento*. Florence: Cesati, 2008.

Gragnolati, Manuele. "Authorship and Performance in Dante's *Vita nova*." In *Aspects of the Performative in Medieval Culture*, edited by Manuele Gragnolati and Almut Suerbaum, 125–41. Berlin: De Gruyter, 2010.

———. "Trasformazioni e assenze: La *performance* della *Vita nova* e le figure di Dante e Cavalcanti." *L'Alighieri* 35 (2010): 5–23.

Gragnolati, Manuele, and Elena Lombardi. "Autobiografia d'autore." *Dante Studies* 136 (2018): 143–60.

Grattoni, Maurizio. "Un *planh* inedito in morte di Giovanni di Cucagna nell'Archivio Capitolare di Cividale." *La Panarie* 56 (1982): 90–98.

Gray, Donald J., ed. *Alice's Adventures in Wonderland*. By Lewis Carroll. In *Alice in Wonderland*, 1–97. New York: Norton, 2013.

Greene, Roland. *Post-Petrarchism: Origins and Innovations of the Western Lyric Sequence*. Princeton, NJ: Princeton University Press, 1991.

Greetham, David. *Textual Transgression: Essays toward the Construction of a Biobibliography*. New York: Garland, 1998.

———. *Theories of the Text*. Oxford: Oxford University Press, 1999.

Greimas, Algirdas J., and Joseph Courtés. *Semiotics and Language: An Analytical Dictionary*. Bloomington: Indiana University Press, 1982.

Grimaldi, Marco. "Boccaccio editore delle canzoni di Dante." In Azzetta and Mazzucchi, eds., *Boccaccio editore e interprete di Dante*, 137–57.

———, ed. *Rime* (*Le rime della "Vita nuova" e altre rime del tempo della "Vita nuova*). By Dante Alighieri. In *Vita Nuova—Le Rime della Vita nuova e altre Rime del tempo della Vita nuova*, Tome 1 of *Vita nuova—Rime*, Vol. 1 of *Le Opere di Dante*, edited by Marco Grimaldi and Donato Pirovano, 291–800. Rome: Salerno, 2015.

———. "Petrarca, il 'vario stile' e l'idea di lirica." *Carte romanze* 2, no. 1 (2014): 151–210.

Gröber, Gustav. "Die Liedersammlungen der Troubadours." *Romanische Studien* 2 (1877): 337–670.

Grützmacher, Wilhelm. "Die provenzalische Liederhandschrift Plut. XLI cod. 43 der Laurenziana Bibliothek in Florenz." *Archiv für das Studium der neueren Sprachen und Literaturen* 35 (1864): 363–463.

Guérin, Philippe. "Proposte per una lettura della canzone dantesca *Amor, tu vedi ben che questa donna*." *Per leggere* 20 (2011): 5–20.

Guglielminetti, Marziano. *Memoria e scrittura: L'autobiografia da Dante a Cellini*. Turin: Einaudi, 1977.

Guidotti, Paola, ed. *I quattro libri delle Osservationi*. By Lodovico Dolce. Pescara: Libreria dell'Università, 2004.

Guiette, Robert. *D'une poésie formelle en France au Moyen Age*. Paris: Nizet, 1972.

Gumbrecht, Hans Ulrich. *Production of Presence: What Meaning Cannot Convey*. Stanford, CA: Stanford University Press, 2003.

Gumbrecht, Hans Ulrich, and K. Ludwig Pfeiffer, eds. *Materialities of Communication*. Stanford, CA: Stanford University Press, 1994.

Gundersheimer, Werner L. *Ferrara: The Style of a Renaissance Despotism*. Princeton, NJ: Princeton University Press, 1973.

Güntert, Georges. "Canto XXXIII." In *Lectura Dantis Turicensis: Paradiso*, edited by Georges Güntert and Michelangelo Picone, 505–18. Florence: Cesati, 2002.

Haas, Christina. *Writing Technology: Studies on the Materiality of Literacy*. New York: Routledge, 1996.

Hainsworth, Peter R. J. "The Myth of Daphne in the *Rerum vulgarium fragmenta*." *Italian Studies* 34 (1979): 28–44.

Halliday, Michael A. K., and Ruqaiya Hasan. *Cohesion in English*. London: Longman, 1976.

Halliwell, Stephen, ed. and trans. *Poetics*. By Aristotle. In *Aristotle, "Poetics"—Longinus, "On the Sublime"—Demetrius, "On Style,"* edited, translated, and revised by Stephen Halliwell, W. H. Fyfe, Donald Russell, Doreen C. Innes, and W. Rhys Roberts, 3–141. Cambridge, MA: Harvard University Press, 1995.

Hamburger, Jeffrey F., William P. Stoneman, Anne-Marie Eze, Lisa Fagin Davis, and Nancy Netzer, eds. *Beyond Words: Illuminated Manuscripts in Boston Collections*. Chestnut Hill, MA: McMullen Museum of Art (Boston College), 2016.

Handerson, Harald. *The Manuscripts of Statius*. Arlington, VA, 2009.

Hanna, Ralph III. "Booklets in Medieval Manuscripts: Further Considerations." *Studies in Bibliography* 39 (1986): 100–111.

Hannesson, Kristján. "Making Sense of Form: The Semantic Implications of Structure in Petrarch's Double Sestina." *Modern Language Notes* 135, no. 1 (2020): 34–54.

Harpold, Terry. *Ex-foliations: Reading Machines and the Upgrade Path*. Minneapolis: University of Minnesota Press, 2009.

Hathaway, Neil. "Compilatio: From Plagiarism to Compiling." *Viator* 20 (1989): 19–44.

Havens, Hilary. "Adobe Photoshop and Eighteenth-Century Manuscripts: A New Approach to Digital Paleography." *DHQ: Digital Humanities Quarterly* 8, no. 4 (2014). http://www.digitalhumanities.org/dhq/vol/8/4/000187/000187.html.

Hayles, N. Katherine. *Writing Machines*. Cambridge, MA: MIT Press, 2002.

Headland, Thomas N., Kenneth L. Pike, and Marvin Harris, eds. *Emics and Etics: The Insider/Outsider Debate*. Newbury Park, CA: Sage Publications, 1990.

Heinimann, Siegfried. "Dulcis: Ein Beitrag zur lateinisch-romanischen Stilgeschichte des Mittelalters." In *Studia Philologica: Homenaje ofrecido a Dámaso Alonso por sus amigos y discípulos con ocasión de su 60° aniversario*, 2:215–32. Madrid: Editorial Gredos, 1960–1963.

Hempfer, Klaus W. "Die potentielle Autoreflexivität des narrativen Diskurses und Ariosts *Orlando Furioso*." In *Erzählforschung: Ein Symposion*, edited by Eberhardt Lämmert, 130–56. Stuttgart: Metzler, 1982.

Hermann, Hermann J. *La miniatura estense*. Modena: Panini, 1994.

Herrnstein Smith, Barbara. *Poetic Closure: A Study of How Poems End*. Chicago: University of Chicago Press, 1968.

Higgins, Dick. *Pattern Poetry: Guide to an Unknown Literature*. Albany: SUNY Press, 1987.

Hollander, John. *Vision and Resonance: Two Senses of Poetic Form*. New York: Oxford University Press, 1985.

Hollander, Robert. *Allegory in Dante's "Commedia."* Princeton, NJ: Princeton University Press, 1969.

———. *Boccaccio's Two Venuses*. New York: Columbia University Press, 1977.

———. "Dante and Cino da Pistoia." *Dante Studies* 110 (1992): 201–31.

———. *Studies in Dante*. Ravenna: Longo, 1980.

———. "The Validity of Boccaccio's Self-Exegesis in His *Teseida*." *Medievalia et Humanistica*, n.s., 8 (1977): 163–83.

Holmes, Olivia. *Assembling the Lyric Self: Authorship from Troubadour Song to Italian Poetry Book*. Minneapolis: University of Minnesota Press, 2000.

Holtz, Louis. "Glosse e commenti." In *La ricezione del testo*, Vol. 3 of *Lo spazio letterario del Medioevo: 1. Il Medioevo latino*, edited by Guglielmo Cavallo, Claudio Leonardi, and Enrico Menestò, 59–111. Rome: Salerno, 1995.

Houston, Jason M. *Building a Monument to Dante: Boccaccio as Dantista*. Toronto: University of Toronto Press, 2010.

———. "'Maraviglierannosi molti': Boccaccio's *Editio* of the *Vita Nova*." *Dante Studies* 126 (2008): 89–107.

Howsam, Leslie. *Old Books & New Histories: An Orientation to Studies in Book and Print Culture*. Toronto: University of Toronto Press, 2006.

Hutcheon, Linda. *Narcissistic Narrative: The Metafictional Paradox*. Waterloo: Wilfrid Laurier University Press, 1980.

Iannucci, Amilcare. "Autoesegesi dantesca: La tecnica dell' 'episodio parallelo.'" In *Forma ed evento nella "Divina Commedia,"* 84–114. Rome: Bulzoni, 1984.

Illich, Ivan. *In the Vineyard of the Text: A Commentary to Hugh's "Didascalicon."* Chicago: University of Chicago Press, 1993.

Infurna, Marco. "Intertestualità e *mise en abyme*." In *La produzione del testo*, Vol. 1/1 of *Lo spazio letterario del Medioevo: 2. Il Medioevo volgare*, edited by Piero Boitani, Mario Mancini, and Alberto Vàrvaro, 423–57. Rome: Salerno, 1999.

Inglese, Giorgio. *L'intelletto e l'amore: Studi sulla letteratura italiana del Due e Trecento*. Scandicci (Florence): La Nuova Italia, 2000.

———. "'. . . illa Guidonis de Florentia *Donna me prega*' (Tra Cavalcanti e Dante)." *Cultura neolatina* 55, nos. 3–4 (1995): 179–210.

Irvine, Martin. "Medieval Textuality and the Archaeology of Textual Culture." In *Speaking Two Languages: Traditional Disciplines and Contemporary Theory in Medieval Studies*, edited by Allen J. Frantzen, 181–210. Albany: SUNY Press, 1991.

Iser, Wolfgang. *The Act of Reading: A Theory of Aesthetic Response*. Baltimore: Johns Hopkins University Press, 1978.

Jager, Eric. *The Book of the Heart*. Chicago: University of Chicago Press, 2000.

Jakobson, Roman. "On the Verbal Art of William Blake and Other Poet-Painters." *Linguistic Inquiry* 1, no. 1 (1970): 3–23.

Jeanroy, Alfred. "La 'sestina doppia' de Dante et les origines de la sextine." *Romania* 42 (1913): 481–89.

Jenaro-MacLennan, Luis. "Autocomentarismo en Dante y comentarismo latino." *Vox Romanica* 19 (1960): 82–123.

Jenni, Adolfo. *La sestina lirica*. Bern: Lang, 1945.

Jernigan, Charles. "The Song of Nail and Uncle: Arnaut Daniel's Sestina 'Lo ferm voler q'el cor m'intra.'" *Studies in Philology* 71, no. 2 (1974): 127–51.

Josipovici, Gabriel. *The World and the Book: A Study of Modern Fiction*. London: Macmillan, 1979.

Kahn, Louis. "Lecture at Pratt Institute (1973)." In *Essential Texts*, 266–80. New York: Norton, 2003.

Kay, Tristan. *Dante's Lyric Redemption: Eros, Salvation, Vernacular Tradition*. Oxford: Oxford University Press, 2016.

———. "Redefining the 'matera amorosa': Dante's *Vita nova* and Guittone's (anti-)courtly 'canzoniere.'" *The Italianist* 29, no. 3 (2009): 369–99.

Keil, Heinrich, ed. *De litteris, de syllabis, de metris libri tres*. By Terentianus Maurus. In *Scriptores artis metricae*, Vol. 6/2 of *Grammatici latini*, 313–413. Leipzig: Teubner, 1857.

Kelemen, János. "Carattere e funzione degli autocommenti di Dante." *Tenzone* 12 (2011): 43–64.

Kenner, Hugh. *The Pound Era*. Berkeley: University of California Press, 1971.

Kenyon, Frederic G. *Books and Readers in Ancient Greece and Rome*. Oxford: Clarendon, 1951.

Kichuk, Diana. "Loose, Falling Characters and Sentences: The Persistence of the OCR Problem in Digital Repository E-Books." *portal: Libraries and the Academy* 15, no. 1 (2015): 59–91.

Kirkham, Victoria. "'Chiuso parlare' in Boccaccio's *Teseida*." In *Dante, Petrarch, Boccaccio: Studies in the Italian Trecento in Honor of Charles S. Singleton*, edited by Aldo S. Bernardo and Anthony L. Pellegrini, 305–51. Binghamton: Center for Medieval and Early Renaissance Studies, SUNY at Binghamton, 1983.

———. *Fabulous Vernacular: Boccaccio's "Filocolo" and the Art of Medieval Fiction*. Ann Arbor: University of Michigan Press, 2001.

———. "Iohannes de Certaldo: La firma dell'autore." In Picone and Bérard, eds., *Gli Zibaldoni di Boccaccio*, 455–68.

———. "The Parallel Lives of Dante and Virgil." *Dante Studies* 110 (1992): 233–53.

———. "A Visual Legacy (Boccaccio as Artist)." In *Boccaccio: A Critical Guide to the Complete Works*, edited by Victoria Kirkham, Michael Sherberg, and Janet Levarie Smarr, 321–40. Chicago: University of Chicago Press, 2013.

Kirkham, Victoria, Michael Sherberg, and Janet Levarie Smarr, eds. *Boccaccio: A Critical Guide to the Complete Works*. Chicago: University of Chicago Press, 2013.

Kirschenbaum, Matthew, and Sarah Werner. "Digital Scholarship and Digital Studies: The State of the Discipline." *Book History* 17 (2014): 406–58.

Kittler, Friedrich A. *Gramophone, Film, Typewriter*. Stanford, CA: Stanford University Press, 1999.

Kleiner, John. "Finding the Center: Revelation and Reticence in the *Vita Nuova*." *Texas Studies in Literature and Language* 32, no. 1 (1990): 85–100.

Kleinhenz, Christopher. "Texts, Naked and Thinly Veiled: Erotic Elements in Medieval Italian Literature." In *Sex in the Middle Ages: A Book of Essays*, edited by Joyce E. Salisbury, 83–109. New York: Garland, 1991.

Knight, Stephen. "Textual Variants: Textual Variance." *Southern Review* 16 (1983): 44–54.

Koppenfels, Werner von. "Dantes 'Al poco giorno' und Petrarcas 'Giovene Donna': Ein Intepretationsvergleich zweier Sestinen." *Deutsches Dante-Jahrbuch* 44–45, no. 1 (1967): 150–89.

Kriesel, James C. *Boccaccio's Corpus: Allegory, Ethics, and Vernacularity*. Notre Dame, IN: University of Notre Dame Press, 2019.

Kristeller, Paul. "The Scholar and His Public in the Late Middle Ages and the Renaissance." In *Mediaeval Aspects of Renaissance Learning*, 1–26. Durham, NC: Duke University Press, 1974.

Kruger, Steven F. *Dreaming in the Middle Ages*. Cambridge: Cambridge University Press, 1992.

Kuon, Peter. "'Sol una nocte' ed altre 'delire imprese': Petrarca narratore in *Rvf* 21–30." In Picone, ed., *Il Canzoniere*, 73–96.

Landoni, Elena. "Beatrice e il *verbum*: La poesia della lode e la *via beatitudinis*." *Italianistica* 42, no. 3 (2013): 109–19.

———. *La grammatica come storia della poesia: Un nuovo disegno storiografico per la letteratura italiana delle origini attraverso grammatica, retorica e semantica*. Rome: Bulzoni, 1997.

Lannutti, Maria Sofia. "Il paradiso perduto: Sull'origine e il significato dell'aura nel Canzoniere di Petrarca." In Cara scientia mia, musica: *Studi per Maria*

Caraci Vela, edited by Angela Romagnoli, Daniele Sabaino, Rodobaldo Tibaldi, and Pietro Zappalà, 991–1026. Pisa: ETS, 2018.

Larner, John. "Traditions of Literary Biography in Boccaccio's *Life of Dante*." *Bulletin of the John Rylands Library* 72 (1990): 107–17.

Larson, Pär. "*A ciascun'alma presa*, vv. 1–4." *Studi mediolatini e volgari* 46 (2000): 85–119.

Lausberg, Heinrich. *Handbook of Literary Rhetoric: A Foundation for Literary Study*. Leiden: Brill, 1998.

Lavagetto, Mario. *Oltre le usate leggi: Una lettura del "Decameron."* Turin: Einaudi, 2019.

Ledda, Giuseppe. *La guerra della lingua: Ineffabilità, retorica e narrativa nella "Commedia" di Dante*. Ravenna: Longo, 2002.

Lehman, Paul. *Mittelalteriche Büchertitel. Erstes Heft*. Sitzungsberichte der Bayerischen Akademie der Wissenschaften, Philosophisch-historische Klasse, Jahrgang 1948, Heft 4. Munich: Verlag der Bayerischen Akademie der Wissenschaften, 1949.

———. *Mittelalteriche Büchertitel. Zweites Heft*. Sitzungsberichte der Bayerischen Akademie der Wissenschaften. Philosophisch-historische Klasse. Jahrgang 1953, Heft 3. Munich: Verlag der Bayerischen Akademie der Wissenschaften, 1953.

Leo, Ulrich. "Zum *rifacimento* der *Vita nuova*." *Romanische Forschungen* 74, nos. 3–4 (1962): 281–317.

Leonardi, Lino, ed. *Canzoniere: I sonetti d'amore del codice laurenziano*. By Guittone d'Arezzo. Turin: Einaudi, 1994.

———. "Cavalcanti, Dante e il nuovo stile." In *Dante: Da Firenze all'aldilà*, Atti del terzo Seminario dantesco internazionale (Firenze, 9–11 giugno 2000), edited by Michelangelo Picone, 331–54. Florence: Cesati, 2001.

———. "Creazione e fortuna di un genere: La filologia dei canzoniere dopo Avalle." In *"Liber," "fragmenta," "libellus" prima e dopo Petrarca: In ricordo di d'Arco Silvio Avalle*, Seminario internazionale di studi, Bergamo, 23–25 ottobre 2003, edited by Francesco Lo Monaco, Luca Carlo Rossi, and Niccolò Scaffai, 3–21. Florence: SISMEL—Edizioni del Galluzzo, 2006.

———. "Le origini della poesia verticale." In *Translatar i trasferir: La transmissió dels textos i el saber (1200–1500)*, Actes del primer Colloqui internacional del Grup Narpan "Cultura i literature a la baixa edat mitjana" (Barcelona, 22 i 23 de novembre de 2007), edited by Anna Alberni, Lola Badia, and Lluís Cabré, 267–315. Santa Coloma de Queralt: Obrador Edèndum, Publicacions URV, 2010.

———, ed. *Studi critici*. Vol. 4 of *I canzonieri della lirica italiana delle origini*. Florence: SISMEL—Edizioni del Galluzzo, 2007.

Leporatti, Roberto. "'Io spero di dicer di lei quello che non fue detto d'alcuna' (*V.N.*, XLII, 2): La *Vita nuova* come *retractatio* della poesia giovanile di Dante in funzione della *Commedia*." In Moleta, ed., La gloriosa donna de la mente, 249–91.

———. "Ipotesi sulla *Vita nuova* (con una postilla sul *Convivio*)." *Studi italiani* 4, no. 1 (1992): 5–36.

———. "Il 'libro' di Guittone e la *Vita Nova*." *Nuova Rivista di Letteratura Italiana* 4, no. 1 (2001): 41–150.

Lepschy, Giulio C. *La linguistica del Novecento*. Bologna: il Mulino, 1992.

Lerer, Seth. "Epilogue: Falling Asleep over the History of the Book." *PMLA* 121, no. 1 (2006): 229–34.

Levenston, Edward A. *The Stuff of Literature: Physical Aspects of Texts and Their Relation to Literary Meaning*. New York: SUNY Press, 1992.

Levers, Toby. "The Image of Authorship in the Final Chapter of the *Vita Nuova*." *Italian Studies* 57 (2002): 5–19.

Levi, Ezio. "Adriano de' Rossi." *Giornale storico della letteratura italiana* 55 (1910): 201–65.

Lewis, Clive Staples. *English Literature in the Sixteenth Century, excluding Drama*. Oxford: Clarendon, 1954.

Liborio, Mariantonia. "Contributi alla storia dell'*Ubi sunt*." *Cultura neolatina* 20 (1960): 141–209.

Librandi, Rita. "Corte e cavalleria della Napoli angioina nel *Teseida* del Boccaccio." *Medioevo romanzo* 4 (1977): 53–72.

Limentani, Alberto. "Alcuni ritocchi al testo del *Teseida*." *Cultura neolatina* 19 (1959): 91–100.

———. "Boccaccio 'traduttore' di Stazio." *La Rassegna della letteratura italiana* 64 (1960): 231–42.

———. "Effetti di specularità nella narrativa medievale." *Romanistische Zeitschrift für Literaturgeschichte* 4 (1980): 307–21.

———. "Struttura e storia dell'ottava rima." *Lettere italiane* 13, no. 1 (1961): 20–77.

———. "Tendenze della prosa del Boccaccio ai margini del *Teseida*." *Giornale storico della letteratura italiana* 135 (1958): 524–51.

———, ed. *Teseida delle nozze d'Emilia*. By Giovanni Boccaccio. In *Tutte le opere di Giovanni Boccaccio (I–X)*, edited by Vittore Branca, 2:229–664 (text) and 873–899 (notes). Milan: Mondadori, 1964.

Livorni, Ernesto. "Dream and Vision in Dante's *Vita Nova.*" In *"Accessus ad Auctores": Studies in Honor of Christopher Kleinhenz*, edited by Fabian Alfies and Andrea Dini, 93–114. Tempe: Arizona Center for Medieval and Renaissance Studies, 2011.

———. "Il proemio de *La Vita Nuova*: Impostazione del discorso dantesco." *L'Alighieri* 29 (1988): 3–10.

Lobel, Edgar, and Denys Page, eds. *Poetarum Lesbiorum Fragmenta.* Oxford: Clarendon, 1963.

Lombardi, Elena. *Imagining the Woman Reader in the Age of Dante.* Oxford: Oxford University Press, 2018.

———. "L''invenzione' del lettore in Dante." In *C'è un lettore in questo testo? Rappresentazioni della lettura nella letteratura italiana*, edited by Giovanna Rizzarelli and Cristina Savettieri, 23–41. Bologna: il Mulino, 2016.

Lombardo, Luca. *Boezio in Dante: La "Consolatio philosophiae" nello scrittoio del poeta.* Venice: Edizioni Ca' Foscari, 2013.

Long, Micol. *Autografia ed epistolografia fra XI e XIII secolo: Per un'analisi delle testimonianze sulla "scrittura di propria mano."* Milan: Ledizioni, 2014.

Longhi, Silvia. "Il tutto e le parti nel sistema di un canzoniere (Giovanni Della Casa)." *Strumenti critici* 13 (1979): 265–300.

Looney, Dennis. "The Reception of Herodotus in the Ferrarese Quattrocento." *Annali Online di Ferrara (Lettere)* 1 (2012): 167–83. http://annali.unife.it/lettere/article/view/280.

Lowe, Elias Avery. "Handwriting." In *The Legacy of the Middle Ages*, edited by Charles George Crump and Ernest Fraser Jacob, 197–226. Oxford: Clarendon, 1926.

———. "Introduction." In *Italy: Perugia—Verona*, Vol. 4 of *Codices Latini Antiquiores: A Palaeographical Guide to Latin Manuscripts Prior to the Ninth Century*, v–xxviii. Oxford: Clarendon, 1947.

Lummus, David. *The City of Poetry: Imagining the Civic Role of the Poet in Fourteenth-Century Italy.* Cambridge: Cambridge University Press, 2020.

Mackail, John William. *The Springs of Helicon: A Study in the Progress of English Poetry from Chaucer to Milton.* London: Longmans, Green, 1909.

Maggiore, Marco, ed. *Scripto sopra Theseu Re: Il commento salentino al "Teseida" di Boccaccio (Ugento/Nardò, ante 1487).* Berlin: De Gruyter, 2016.

———. "Lo *Scripto sopra Theseu Re*: Un commento al *Teseida* di provenienza salentina (II metà del XV secolo)." *Medioevo letterario d'Italia* 7 (2010): 87–122.

Maier-Troxler, Katharina. "*In rete accolgo l'aura, e 'n ghiaccio i fiori*: Zur Adynata-Häufung in Petrarcas Sestine *Là ver' l'aurora* (Canzoniere, CCXXXIX)." *Romanische Forschungen* 93, no. 3–4 (1981): 372–82.

Maierù, Alfonso. "memoria." In *Enciclopedia Dantesca*, edited by Umberto Bosco, 3:888–92. Rome: Istituto della Enciclopedia Italiana, 1971.

Mainini, Lorenzo. "Schermi e specchi: Intorno a *Vita nova* 2, 6–9 e ad altre visioni dantesche." *Critica del testo* 14, no. 2 (2011): 147–78.

Mak, Bonnie. *How the Page Matters*. Toronto: University of Toronto Press, 2011.

Malagnini, Francesca. "Due manoscritti: La questione delle illustrazioni." *Studi sul Boccaccio* 44 (2016): 171–206.

———. "Il libro d'autore dal progetto alla realizzazione: Il *Teseida delle nozze d'Emilia* (con un'appendice sugli autografi di Boccaccio)." *Studi sul Boccaccio* 34 (2006): 3–102.

———. "Mondo commentato e mondo narrato nel *Decameron*." *Studi sul Boccaccio* 30 (2002): 3–124.

———. "Sul programma illustrativo del *Teseida*." *Giornale storico della letteratura italiana* 184 (2007): 523–76.

Malato, Enrico. *Dante e Guido Cavalcanti: Il dissidio per la "Vita nuova" e il "disdegno" di Guido*. Rome: Salerno, 1997.

———. "emme." In *Enciclopedia Dantesca*, edited by Umberto Bosco, 5:665–66. Rome: Istituto della Enciclopedia Italiana, 1970.

———. "L'incipit della *Vita nuova*." *Rivista di studi danteschi* 10, no. 1 (2010): 95–105.

———. "La memoria di Dante." *Filologia e critica* 40, nos. 2–3 (2015): 238–56.

———. *Per una nuova edizione commentata delle opere di Dante*. Rome: Salerno, 2004.

Malnati, Aristide. "Revisione dell'ostrakon fiorentino di Saffo." *Analecta Papyrologica* 5 (1993): 21–22.

Maltomini, Francesca. "Greek Ostraka: An Overview." *Manuscript Cultures* 5 (2017): 33–41.

Mandelstam, Osip. "Conversation about Dante." In *The Complete Critical Prose and Letters*, 397–451. Ann Arbor, MI: Ardis, 1979.

Manfredi, Umberto. *La poesia provenzale e la cultura del Petrarca*. Palermo: Unione Tipografico-Editrice Siciliana, 1947.

Maniaci, Marilena. "'La serva padrona': Interazioni fra testo e glossa sulla pagina del manoscritto." In *Talking to the Text: Marginalia from Papyri to Print*, Proceedings of a Conference held at Erice, 26 September–3 October 1998, as the 12th Course of International School for the Study of Written Records, edited by Vincenzo Fera, Giacomo Ferraù, and Silvia Rizzo, 1:3–35. Messina: Centro Interdipartimentale di Studi Umanistici, 2002.

———. *Terminologia del libro manoscritto*. Rome: Istituto Centrale per la Patologia del Libro–Editrice Bibliografica, 1996.

Mann, Nicholas, ed. and trans. *My Secret Book*. By Francesco Petrarca. Cambridge, MA: Harvard University Press, 2016.

———. "*Petrarca philobiblon*: The Author and His Books." In *Literary Cultures and the Material Book*, edited by Simon Eliot, Andrew Nash, and Ian Willison, 159–73. London: British Library, 2007.

———. "Pétrarque et les métamorphoses de Daphné." *Bulletin de l'Association Guillaume Budé* 53 (1994): 382–403.

Manni, Paola. *La lingua di Boccaccio*. Bologna: il Mulino, 2016.

———. *La lingua di Dante*. Bologna: il Mulino, 2013.

Mantovani, Dario, ed. *La "Guerra di Troia" in ottava rima*. Milan: Ledizioni, 2013.

———. "Una prospettiva inedita per un cantare antico: Le fonti scritte della *Guerra di Troia* in ottava rima." *Critica del testo* 16, no. 1 (2013): 113–42.

Marazzini, Claudio. *La lingua italiana: Profilo storico*. Bologna: il Mulino, 2002.

Marchesi, Simone. *Dante and Augustine: Linguistics, Poetics, Hermeneutics*. Toronto: University of Toronto Press, 2011.

Marcon, Susy. "I codici illustrati nell'area veneta." In *Boccaccio visualizzato: Narrare per parole e per immagini*, edited by Vittore Branca, 2:233–38 (essay) and 2:239–71 (manuscript catalogue). Turin: Einaudi, 1999.

Marcozzi, Luca. *La biblioteca di Febo: Mitologia e allegoria in Petrarca*. Florence: Cesati, 2002.

Mari, Giovanni. "Ritmo latino e terminologia ritmica medievale: Appunti per servire alla storia della poetica nostra." *Studj di filologia romanza* 8 (1901): 35–88.

———. "La sestina d'Arnaldo, la terzina di Dante." *Rendiconti dell'Istituto Lombardo di scienze e lettere* 32, no. 15 (1889): 953–85.

Marigo, Aristide. *Mistica e scienza nella "Vita nuova" di Dante: L'unità di pensiero e le fonti mistiche, filosofiche e bibliche*. Padua: Fratelli Drucker, 1914.

Marrani, Giuseppe. "E' m'incresce di me sì duramente." In *Le Quindici Canzoni (Lette da diversi)*, 2:65–86. By Dante Alighieri. Lecce: Pensa MultiMedia, 2012.

———. "Macrosequenze d'autore (o presunte tali) alla verifica della tradizione: Dante, Cavalcanti, Cino da Pistoia." In *La tradizione della lirica nel Medioevo romanzo: Problemi di filologia formale*, Atti del Convegno internazionale,

Firenze–Siena, 12–14 novembre 2009, edited by Lino Leonardi, 241–66. Florence: Edizioni del Galluzzo, 2011.

———. "Miscellaneous Manuscripts: The Case of Italian Medieval Lyric Tradition." *Per leggere* 29 (2015): 144–50.

Martelli, Mario. "Proposte per le *Rime* di Dante." *Studi danteschi* 69 (2004): 247–88.

Marti, Mario. "Acque agitate per *Donna me prega*." *Giornale storico della letteratura italiana* 177 (2000): 161–67.

———. "Da 'Donna me prega' a 'Donne ch'avete': Non viceversa." In *Da Dante a Croce: Proposte consensi dissensi*, 7–15. Galatina (Lecce): Congedo, 2005.

———, ed. *Prose della volgar lingua*. By Pietro Bembo. Padua: Liviana, 1955.

———. *Storia dello Stil nuovo*. Lecce: Milella, 1973.

———. "'. . . L'una appresso de l'altra maraviglia' (Dante, *Vita Nuova* XXXIV)." *Giornale storico della letteratura italiana* 168 (1991): 481–503.

Martin, Henri-Jean, and Jean Vezin, eds. *Mise en page et mise en texte du livre manuscrit*. Paris: Éditions du Cercle de la Librairie–Promodis, 1990.

Martinelli, Bortolo. "L'ordinamento morale del *Canzoniere* del Petrarca." *Studi petrarcheschi* 8 (1976): 93–167.

Martinelli Tempesta, Stefano, and Marco Petoletti. "Il ritratto di Omero e la firma greca di Boccaccio." *Italia medioevale e umanistica* 54 (2013): 399–409.

Martinez, Roland L. "Before the *Teseida*: Statius and Dante in Boccaccio's Epic." *Studi sul Boccaccio* 20 (1991–1992): 205–19.

———. "Cavalcanti 'Man of Sorrows' and Dante." In *Guido Cavalcanti tra i suoi lettori*, Proceedings of the International Symposium for the Seventh Centennial of His Death, New York, November 10–11, 2000, edited by Maria Luisa Ardizzone, 187–212. Fiesole (Florence): Cadmo, 2003.

———. "Mourning Beatrice: The Rhetoric of Threnody in the *Vita nuova*." *MLN* 113, no. 1 (1998): 1–29.

Masai, François. "Le collectaire et le missel de G. Natalis, abbé de Saint-Laurent de Liège." *Scriptorium* 3, no. 1 (1949): 136.

Matarrese, Tina. "Il materno eloquio del ferrarese Pier Andrea de' Bassi." In *Omaggio a Gianfranco Folena*, 1:793–812. Padua: Programma, 1993.

———. "Il mito di Ercole a Ferrara nel Quattrocento tra letteratura e arti figurative." In *L'ideale classico a Ferrara e in Italia nel Rinascimento*, edited by Patrizia Castelli, 191–203. Florence: Olschki, 1998.

Mattalia, Daniele, ed. *La vita nuova*. By Dante Alighieri. Turin: Paravia, 1936.

Matucci, Andrea. "Le 'tre ragioni' del silenzio: La *Vita Nuova* come vangelo laico." *Verbum—Analecta Neolatina* 3, no. 1 (2001): 41–50.

Mazza, Antonio. "L'inventario della 'parva libraria' di Santo Spirito e la biblioteca del Boccaccio." *Italia medioevale e umanistica* 9 (1966): 1–74.

Mazzaro, Jerome. *The Figure of Dante: An Essay on the "Vita Nuova."* Princeton, NJ: Princeton University Press, 1981.

Mazzetti, Martina. "Boccaccio disegnatore: Per un'idea di 'arte mobile.'" *Letteratura & Arte* 10 (2012): 9–37.

———. "Boccaccio e l'invenzione del libro illustrabile: Dal *Teseida* al *Decameron*." *Per leggere* 21 (2011): 135–61.

———. "Dare forma alla poesia: Semantica del libro tra Dante e Boccaccio (passando per Guittone)." *Italianistica: Rivista di letteratura italiana* 42, no. 2 (2013): 147–67.

———. "Nuovi studi sul *Teseida delle nozze d'Emilia* tra filologia d'autore e storia della tradizione." 2017. Courtesy of the Author.

———. "Il segno di Boccaccio: Sopravvivenze autoriali nella tradizione del *Teseida*." *Heliotropia* 14 (2017): 245–63.

———. "Tra testo e paratesto: Il *Teseida* di fronte alla sua tradizione." In *Intorno a Boccaccio/Boccaccio e dintorni*, Atti del Seminario internazionale di studi (Certaldo Alta, Casa di Giovanni Boccaccio, 25 giugno 2014), edited by Giovanna Frosini and Stefano Zamponi, 115–26. Florence: Firenze University Press, 2015.

Mazzitello, Pantalea, Giulia Raboni, Paolo Rinoldi, and Carlo Varotti, eds. *Boccaccio in versi.* Atti del Convegno di Parma, 13–14 marzo 2014. Florence: Cesati, 2016.

Mazzotta, Giuseppe. "Cosmology and the Kiss of Creation (*Paradiso* 27–29)." *Dante Studies* 123 (2005): 1–21.

———. "The Language of Poetry in the *Vita Nuova*." *Rivista di studi italiani* 1, no. 1 (1983): 3–14.

———. *The Worlds of Petrarch.* Durham, NC: Duke University Press, 1993.

McCoy, Bernadette Marie, trans. *The Book of Theseus: Teseida delle nozze d'Emilia.* By Giovanni Boccaccio. Sea Cliff, NY: Medieval Text Association/Teesdale Publishing Associates, 1974.

McDonald, Peter. "Ideas of the Book and Histories of Literature: After Theory?" *PMLA* 121, no. 1 (2006): 214–28.

McGann, Jerome J. *The Textual Condition.* Princeton, NJ: Princeton University Press, 1991.

McGregor, James H. "Boccaccio's Athenian Theater: Form and Function of an Ancient Monument in *Teseida*." *Modern Language Notes* 99, no. 1 (1984): 1–42.

———. *The Image of Antiquity in Boccaccio's "Filocolo," "Filostrato," and "Teseida."* New York: Peter Lang, 1991.

McKenzie, Donald Francis. "Bibliography and the Sociology of Texts." In *Bibliography and the Sociology of Texts*, 8–76. Cambridge: Cambridge University Press, 1999.

———. "Typography and Meaning: The Case of William Congreve." In *Making Meaning: "Printers of the Mind" and Other Essays*, 198–236. Amherst: University of Massachusetts Press, 2002.

McKitterick, David. *Print, Manuscript and the Search for Order, 1450–1830*. Cambridge: Cambridge University Press, 2003.

McLaughlin, Martin. *Literary Imitation in the Italian Renaissance: The Theory and Practice of Literary Imitation in Italy from Dante to Bembo*. Oxford: Clarendon, 1995.

———. "Petrarch and Cicero: Adulation and Critical Distance." In *Brill's Companion to the Reception of Cicero*, edited by William H. F. Altman, 19–38. Leiden: Brill, 2015.

McLuhan, Marshall. "Media and Cultural Change." In *Essential McLuhan*, edited by Eric McLuhan and Frank Zingrone, 89–96. London: Routledge, 1997.

———. "The Relation of Environment to Anti-Environment." In *Media Research: Technology, Art, Communication*, 110–125. Amsterdam: G & B Arts, 1997.

Medica, Massimo. "Maestro degli Antifonari di Padova." In *Dizionario biografico dei miniatori italiani: Secoli IX–XVI*, edited by Milvia Bollati and Miklós Boskovits, 447–48. Milan: Sylvestre Bonnard, 2004.

Meliga, Walter. "Le raccolte d'autore nella tradizione trobadorica." In *"Liber," "fragmenta," "libellus" prima e dopo Petrarca: In ricordo di d'Arco Silvio Avalle*, Seminario internazionale di studi, Bergamo, 23–25 ottobre 2003, edited by Francesco Lo Monaco, Luca Carlo Rossi, and Niccolò Scaffai, 81–91. Florence: SISMEL—Edizioni del Galluzzo, 2006.

Melli, Elio. "Dante e Arnaut Daniel." *Filologia romanza* 6 (1959): 423–48.

Mengaldo, Pier Vincenzo, ed. *De vulgari eloquentia*. By Dante Alighieri. Padua: Antenore, 1968.

———. *Linguistica e retorica di Dante*. Pisa: Nistri-Lischi, 1978.

Meneghetti, Maria Luisa. "Beatrice al chiaro di luna: La prassi poetica delle visioni con invito all'interpretazione dai Provenzali allo Stilnovo." In *Symposium in honorem prof. M. de Riquer*, 239–55. Barcelona: Cuaderns Crema, 1986.

Menichetti, Aldo. *Metrica italiana: Fondamenti metrici, prosodia, rima*. Padua: Antenore, 1993.

———. "La prosodia del *Teseida*." In *Studi in onore di Pier Vincenzo Mengaldo per i suoi settant'anni*, 1:347–72. Florence: SISMEL—Edizioni del Galluzzo, 2007.

Menichetti, Caterina. "Le citazioni liriche nelle biografie provenzali (per un'analisi stilistico-letteraria di *vidas* e *razos*)." *Medioevo romanzo* 36 (2012): 128–60.

Menocal, María Rosa. *Writing in Dante's Cult of Truth from Borges to Boccaccio.* Durham, NC: Duke University Press, 1991.

Merleau-Ponty, Maurice. *Phenomenology of Perception.* London: Routledge, 1981.

Mestica, Giovanni, ed. *Le Rime di Francesco Petrarca, restituite nell'ordine e nella lezione del testo originario sugli autografi col sussidio di altri codici e di stampe e corredate di varianti e note.* By Francesco Petrarca. Florence: Barbèra, 1896.

Mezzadroli, Giuseppina. "Enigmi del racconto e strategia comunicativa nei riassunti autotestuali della *Commedia* dantesca." *Lettere Italiane* 41, no. 4 (1989): 481–531.

Miglio, Luisa. 1995. "L'altra metà della scrittura: Scrivere il volgare (alle origini delle corsive mercantili)." *Scrittura e Civiltà* 10 (1986): 83–114.

———. "Criteri di datazione per le corsive librarie italiane dei secoli XIII–XIV: Ovvero riflessioni, osservazioni, suggerimenti sulla lettera mercantesca." *Scrittura e Civiltà* 18 (1994): 143–57.

———. "Dante Alighieri: Manoscritti miniati." In *Enciclopedia dell'arte medievale,* 5:627–35. Rome: Istituto della Enciclopedia Italiana, 1995.

Migne, Jacques Paul, ed. *Didascalicon de studio legendi.* By Hugh of Saint Victor. In *Patrologia Latina* [*PL*], 176:737–812.

———, ed. "Rhythmus." By Alanus de Insulis. In *Patrologia Latina* [*PL*], 210:579–80.

Migraine-George, Thérèse. "Specular Desires: Orpheus and Pygmalion as Aesthetic Paradigms in Petrarch's *Rime sparse.*" *Comparative Literature Studies* 36, no. 3 (1999): 226–46.

Miller, Daniel. "Materiality: An Introduction." In *Materiality,* edited by Daniel Miller, 1–50. Durham, NC: Duke University Press, 2005.

Miller, John C., ed. *Marginalia.* By Edgar Allan Poe. Charlottesville: University Press of Virginia, 1981.

Minetti, Francesco Filippo, ed. *Le rime di Monte Andrea da Fiorenza.* By Monte Andrea. Florence: Accademia della Crusca, 1979.

Minnis, Alaistir J. "*Amor* and *Auctoritas* in the Self-Commentary of Dante and Francesco da Barberino." *Poetica* 32 (1990): 25–42.

———. "Late-Medieval Discussions of *Compilatio* and the Role of the *Compilator.*" *Beiträge zur Geschichte der deutschen Sprache und Literatur* 101, no. 3 (1979): 385–421.

———. *Medieval Theory of Authorship: Scholastic Literary Attitudes in the Later Middle Ages.* Philadelphia: University of Pennsylvania Press, 1988.

Mitchell, Christine. "Materiality: Tracking a Term, Tackling a Turn." In *Kritische Perspektiven: "Turns," Trends und Theorien,* edited by Michael Gubo, Martin Kypta, and Florian Öchsner, 281–300. Berlin: Lit, 2011.

Mitchell, W. J. Thomas. *Iconology: Image, Text, Ideology*. Chicago: University of Chicago Press, 1986.

Modigliani, Ettore, ed. *Il Canzoniere di Francesco Petrarca riprodotto letteralmente dal Cod. Vat. Lat. 3195 con tre fotoincisioni*. By Francesco Petrarca. Rome: Società filologica romana, 1904.

Moleta, Vincent, ed. La gloriosa donna de la mente*: A Commentary on the* "*Vita Nuova*." Florence: Olschki, 1994.

———. "'Oggi fa l'anno che nel ciel salisti': Una rilettura della *Vita Nuova* XXVII–XXXIV." *Giornale storico della letteratura italiana* 161 (1984): 78–104.

Molteni, Enrico, and Ernesto Monaci, eds. *Il canzoniere chigiano L.VIII.305*. Bologna: Tipografia Fava e Garagnani, 1877.

Montagnani, Cristina. *"Andando con lor dame in aventura": Percorsi estensi*. Galatina (Lecce): Congedo, 2004.

———. "Il commento al *Teseida* di Pier Andrea de' Bassi." In "*Andando con lor dame in aventura*," 1–25.

———. "L'eclissi del codice lirico: Una canzone di Niccolò Malpigli nel commento di Pier Andrea de' Bassi." In *"Andando con lor dame in aventura,"* 51–64.

———. "La tradizione quattrocentesca di Ovidio nel commento al *Teseida* di Pier Andrea de' Bassi." In "*Andando con lor dame in aventura*," 27–49.

Monteverdi, Angelo. *Saggi neolatini*. Rome: Edizioni di Storia e Letteratura, 1945.

Mordenti, Raul. "Per la definizione dei libri di famiglia." In *Geografia e Storia*, Vol. 2 of *I libri di famiglia in Italia*, edited by Angelo Cicchetti and Raul Mordenti, 9–37. Rome: Edizioni di Storia e Letteratura, 2001.

Morello, Giovanni. "Disegni marginali nei manoscritti di Giovanni Boccaccio." In Picone and Bérard, eds., *Gli Zibaldoni di Boccaccio*, 161–77.

Mortimer, Anthony, trans. *Complete Poems*. By Guido Cavalcanti. Richmond, UK: Alma Classics, 2010.

Mostra di manoscritti, documenti e edizioni. VI centenario della morte di Giovanni Boccaccio: Firenze, Biblioteca medicea laurenziana, 22 maggio–31 agosto 1975: I. Manoscritti e documenti. Certaldo: Comitato promotore [Tipografia Giuntina], 1975.

Mula, Patrick. "'Modus loquendi': Conscience critique et technicité poétique. Les modalités de la communication dans la *Vita Nuova* de Dante." *Medioevo letterario d'Italia* 6 (2009): 61–88.

Munk Olsen, Birger. *Addenda et corrigenda—Tables*, Vol. 3/2 of *L'étude des auteurs classiques latins aux XIe et XIIe siècles*. Paris: C.N.R.S., 1989.

———. *Catalogue des manuscrits classiques latins copiés du XIe et XIIe siècle: Livius–Vitruvius. Florilèges. Essais de plume*, Vol. 2 of *L'étude des auteurs classiques latins aux XIe et XIIe siècles*. Paris: C.N.R.S., 1985.

———. *I classici nel canone scolastico altomedievale*. Spoleto: Centro italiano di studi sull'alto medioevo, 1991.

———. "La popularité des textes classiques entre le IXe et le XIIe siècle." *Revue d'Histoire des Textes* 14–15 (1984–1985): 169–81.

———. "La réception de Stace au moyen âge (du IXe au XIIe siècle)." In *Nova de veteribus: Mittel- und neulateinische Studien für Paul Gerhard Schmidt*, edited by Andreas Bihrer and Elisabeth Stein, 230–46. Munich: K. G. Saur Verlag, 2004.

Muratori, Lodovico Antonio, ed. *Opere varie critiche*. By Lodovico Castelvetro. Bern [Milan]: Foppens, 1727 (anastatic reprint in Vol. 11 of *Poetiken des Cinquecento*. Munich: Fink, 1969).

Muscetta, Carlo. "Giovanni Boccaccio." In *Il Trecento: Dalla crisi dell'età comunale all'umanesimo*, Vol. 2/2 of *La letteratura italiana: Storia e testi*, edited by Carlo Muscetta and Achille Tartaro, 1–366. Bari: Laterza, 1972.

Muzerelle, Denis. *Vocabulaire codicologique: Répertoire méthodique des termes français relatifs aux manuscrits*. Paris: Éditions CEMI, 1985.

Nasti, Paola. *Favole d'amore e "saver profondo": La tradizione salomonica in Dante*. Ravenna: Longo, 2007.

———. "La memoria del *Canticum* e la *Vita Nuova*: Una nota preliminare." *The Italianist* 18, no. 1 (1998): 14–27.

Natali, Giulia. "Progetti narrativi e tradizione lirica in Boccaccio." *Rassegna della letteratura italiana* 90 (1986): 382–96.

Nelles, William. "Historical and Implied Authors and Readers." *Comparative Literature* 45, no. 1 (1993): 22–46.

Neri, Ferdinando. "La canzone di quattro rime." *Atti della R. Accademia delle scienze di Torino* 49, no. 1 (1913–1914): 305–9.

———, ed. *Trionfi*. By Francesco Petrarca. In *Rime–Trionfi e poesie latine*, edited by Ferdinando Neri, Guido Martellotti, Enrico Bianchi, and Natalino Sapegno, 481–559. Milan: Ricciardi, 1951.

Neumann, Birgit, and Ansgar Nünning. "Metanarration and Metafiction." In *Handbook of Narratology*, edited by Peter Hühn, Jan Christoph Meister, John Pier, and Wolf Schmid, 1:344–52. Berlin: De Gruyter, 2014.

Niccoli, Alessandro. "sentenza (sentenzia)." In *Enciclopedia Dantesca*, edited by Umberto Bosco, 5:169–71. Rome: Istituto della Enciclopedia Italiana, 1976.

Noakes, Susan. *Timely Reading: Between Exegesis and Interpretation*. Ithaca, NY: Cornell University Press, 1988.

Noferi, Adelia. *Frammenti per i Fragmenta di Petrarca*. Rome: Bulzoni, 2001.

———. "Rilettura della *Vita nuova* (I)." *Paradigma* 4 (1982): 63–83.

———. "Rilettura della *Vita nuova* (II)." *Paradigma* 5 (1983): 15–34.

Nolan, Barbara. "The *Vita Nuova*: Dante's Book of Revelation." *Dante Studies* 88 (1970): 51–77.

Nolhac, Pierre de. *Pétrarque et l'humanisme*. Paris: H. Champion, 1907.

Norman, Jeremy M. *Scientist, Scholar, and Scoundrel: A Bibliographical Investigation of the Life and Exploits of Count Guglielmo Libri, Mathematician, Journalist, Patriot, Historian of Science, Paleographer, Book Collector, Bibliographer, Antiquarian Bookseller, Forger and Book Thief.* New York: The Grolier Club, 2013.

Norsa, Medea. "Dai Papiri della Società Italiana: I. Elezione del Κεφαλαιωτής di una corporazione del V secolo d.C.; II. Versi di Saffo in un ostrakon del sec. II a.C." *Annali della R. Scuola Normale Superiore di Pisa: Lettere, Storia e Filosofia*, s. II, 6, nos. 1–2 (1937): 1–15.

Nünning, Ansgar. "Mimesis des Erzählens: Prolegomena zu einer Wirkungsästhetik, Typologie und Funktionsgeschichte des Akts des Erzählens und der Metanarration." In *Erzählen und Erzähltheorie im 20. Jahrhundert: Narratologische Studien aus Anlass des 65. Geburtstags von Wilhelm Füger*, edited by Jörg Helbig, 13–47. Heidelberg: Winter, 2001.

———. "On Metanarrative: Towards a Definition, a Typology and an Outline of the Functions of Metanarrative Commentary." In *The Dynamics of Narrative Form: Studies in Anglo-American Narratology*, edited by John Pier, 11–57. Berlin: De Gruyter, 2004.

Nuovo, Angela. *Il commercio librario a Ferrara tra XV e XVI secolo: La bottega di Domenico Sivieri*. Florence: Olschki, 1998.

Ong, Walter J. "Orality, Literacy, and Medieval Textualization." *New Literary History* 16, no. 1 (1984): 1–12.

———. "The Writer's Audience Is Always a Fiction." *PMLA* 90, no. 1 (1975): 9–21.

Orelli, Giorgio. *Il suono dei sospiri: Sul Petrarca volgare*. Turin: Einaudi, 1990.

Orlandelli, Gianfranco. "Osservazioni sulla scrittura mercantesca nei secoli XIV e XV." In *Studi in onore di Riccardo Filangieri*, 1:445–60. Naples: L'Arte Tipografica, 1959.

Orlandi, Giorgio. "Intorno alla vita e alle opere di Pietro Andrea de' Bassi." *Giornale storico della letteratura italiana* 83 (1924): 285–320.

Ornato, Ezio. *Apologia dell'apogeo*. Rome: Viella, 2000.

Orsbon, David A. "The Universe as Book: Dante's *Commedia* as an Image of the Divine Mind." *Dante Studies* 132 (2014): 87–112.

Osgood, Charles G., trans. *Boccaccio on Poetry*. By Giovanni Boccaccio. New York: The Liberal Arts Press, 1956.

Ottolenghi Albertini, Maria Grazia. "La biblioteca dei Visconti e degli Sforza: Gli inventari del 1488 e del 1490." *Studi petrarcheschi*, n.s., 8 (1991): 1–238.

Pabst, Bernhard. *Prosimetrum: Tradition und Wandel einer Literaturform zwischen Spätantike und Spätmittelalter*. Cologne: Böhlau, 1994.

Pacioni, Marco. "L'*auctoritas* poetica e il personaggio Cavalcanti nella *Vita Nova*." In *Auctor/Actor: Lo scrittore personaggio nella letteratura italiana*, edited by Gilda Corabi and Barbara Gizzi, 41–61. Rome: Bulzoni, 2006.

———. "*Visual Poetics* e *mise en page* nei *Rerum vulgarium fragmenta*." *Letteratura italiana antica* 5 (2004): 367–83.

Paden, William D. "Lyrics on Roll." In *"Li premerains vers": Essays in Honor of Keith Busby*, edited by Catherine M. Jones and Logan E. Whalen, 315–40. Leiden: Brill, 2011.

———. "Petrarch as a Poet of Provence." *Annali d'Italianistica* 22 (2004): 19–44.

———. "Roll versus Codex: The Testimony of Roll Cartularies." *Rivista di studi testuali* 6–7 (2004–2005): 153–90.

———. "The System of Genres in Troubadour Lyric." In *Medieval Lyric: Genres in Historical Context*, edited by William D. Paden, 1–67. Urbana: University of Illinois Press, 2000.

Padoan, Giorgio, ed. *Esposizioni sopra la Comedia di Dante*. By Giovanni Boccaccio. Milan: Mondadori, 1994.

Padoan, Giorgio, Adriana Zampieri, and Emilio Lippi. "Trasmissione manoscritta e varianti d'autore: Apparenti anomalie in opere del Boccaccio." *Studi sul Boccaccio* 11 (1979): 1–29.

Pancheri, Alessandro. "Ramificazioni 'malatestiane': 1. Due discendenti del Laurenziano XLI 17." *Studi di filologia italiana* 66 (2008): 35–73.

Panofsky, Erwin. *Gothic Architecture and Scholasticism: An Inquiry into the Analogy of the Arts, Philosophy, and Religion in the Middle Ages*. New York: Meridian Books, 1957.

Panvini, Bruno. "Studio sui manoscritti dell'antica lirica italiana." *Studi di filologia italiana* 11 (1953): 5–136.

Paolazzi, Carlo. *La maniera mutata: Il* dolce stil novo *tra Scrittura e* Ars poetica. Milan: Vita e Pensiero, 1998.

———. *La "Vita nuova": Legenda sacra e historia poetica*. Milan: Vita e Pensiero, 1994.

Paolino, Laura, ed. *Il Codice degli abbozzi: Edizione e storia del manoscritto Vaticano latino 3196*. By Francesco Petrarca. Milan: Ricciardi, 2000.

Papio, Michael, trans. *Boccaccio's Expositions on Dante's "Comedy."* By Giovanni Boccaccio. Toronto: University of Toronto Press, 2009.

Parkes, Malcolm B. "The Influence of the Concepts of Ordinatio and Compilatio on the Development of the Book." In *Scribes, Scripts and Readers: Studies in the Communication, Presentation and Dissemination of Medieval Texts*, 35–70. London: Hambledon, 1991.

Parzen, Jeremy. "A Peculiar Reading of the Hendecasyllable: Petrarch's Sestina 22." *Lettere Italiane* 47, no. 2 (1995): 248–62.

Pasero, Nicolò. "Dante in Cavalcanti: Ancora sui rapporti fra *Vita nuova* e *Donna me prega*." *Medioevo romanzo* 22 (1998): 388–414.

Pasquini, Emilio. "La sestina CXLII (*A la dolce ombra*)." *Lectura Petrarce* 24 (2004): 337–46.

Pasut, Francesca. "Boccaccio disegnatore." In De Robertis et al., eds., *Boccaccio autore e copista*, 51–59.

Pattison, Walter Thomas, ed. *The Life and Works of the Troubadour Raimbaut d'Orange*. By Raimbaut d'Aurenga. Minneapolis: University of Minnesota Press, 1952.

Pazzaglia, Mario. "*E' m'incresce di me sì duramente*." In *Enciclopedia Dantesca*, edited by Umberto Bosco, 2:663–64. Rome: Istituto della Enciclopedia Italiana, 1970.

———. "La *Vita Nuova* fra agiografia e letteratura." *Letture classensi* 6 (1977): 189–210.

Pellegrin, Elisabeth. *La bibliothèque des Visconti et des Sforza, ducs de Milan, au XVe siècle*. Paris: C.N.R.S., 1955.

Pellegrini, Silvio. "Intorno al primo sonetto della *Vita nova*." In *Varietà romanze*, 406–11. Bari: Adriatica, 1977.

Pelosini, Raffaella. "Il sistema-sestine nel *Canzoniere* (e altre isotopie di Laura)." *Critica del testo* 1, no. 2 (1998): 665–721.

Peron, Gianfelice, ed. *L'autocommento*. Atti del 18. Convegno interuniversitario, Bressanone, 1990. Padua: Esedra, 1994.

Perrone, Carlachiara. "I colori nell'opera di Dante: La ricerca in Italia." In *"Per correr miglior acque . . .": Bilanci e prospettive degli studi danteschi alle soglie del nuovo millennio*, Atti del Convegno internazionale di Verona–Ravenna, 25–29 ottobre 1999, 2:1025–54. Rome: Salerno, 2001.

Perrus, Claude. "La sextine LXXX du *Canzoniere*." *Chroniques italiennes* 61, no. 1 (2000): 5–15.

Perrus, Claudette. "Dante critique de Dante." In *Les commentaires et la naissance de la critique littéraire: France/Italie (XIVe–XVIe siècles)*, Actes du Colloque international sur le Commentaire, Paris, mai 1988, edited by Gisèle Mathieu-Castellani and Michel Plaisance, 83–89. Paris: Aux Amateurs des Livres, 1990.

Pertile, Lino. "*Paradiso* XVIII tra autobiografia e scrittura sacra." *Dante Studies* 109 (1991): 25–49.

Perugi, Maurizio. "A proposito di alcuni scritti recenti su Petrarca e Arnaut Daniel." *Studi medievali*, ser. III, 32 (1991): 369–84.

———. "Arnaut Daniel in Dante." *Studi danteschi* 51 (1978): 59–152.

———, ed. *Canzoni*. By Arnaut Daniel. Florence: SISMEL—Edizioni del Galluzzo, 2015.

———. "Petrarca provenzale." *Quaderni petrarcheschi* 7 (1990): 109–81.

———. *Trovatori a Valchiusa: Un frammento della cultura provenzale del Petrarca*. Padua: Antenore, 1998.

Petoletti, Marco. "I codici di Giovanni Boccaccio." In *Tra i fondi dell'Ambrosiana: Manoscritti italiani antichi e moderni*, Atti del convegno: Milano, 15–18 maggio 2007, edited by Marco Ballarini, Gennaro Barbarisi, Claudia Berra, and Giuseppe Frasso, 1:83–102. Milan: Cisalpino, 2008.

———. "L'*Ethica Nicomachea* di Aristotile con il commento di San Tommaso autografo di Boccaccio." In De Robertis et al., eds., *Boccaccio autore e copista*, 348–50.

———. "Francesco Petrarca e i margini dei suoi libri." In *"Di mano propria": Gli autografi dei letterati italiani*, Atti del convegno internazionale di Forlí, 24–27 novembre 2008, edited by Guido Baldassarri, 93–121. Rome: Salerno, 2010.

———. "Gli Zibaldoni di Giovanni Boccaccio." In De Robertis et al., eds., *Boccaccio autore e copista*, 291–99.

———. "'Petrus Parentis Florentinus, qui hoc modo volume hoc instituit': Il codice." In *Le postille del Virgilio Ambrosiano*, edited by Marco Baglio, Antonietta Nebuloni Testa, and Marco Petoletti, 1:6–29. Padua: Antenore, 2006.

Petrini, Mario. *La risurrezione della carne: Saggi sul "Canzoniere."* Milan: Mursia, 1993.

Petrocchi, Giorgio, ed. *La Commedia secondo l'antica vulgata*. By Dante Alighieri. Florence: Le Lettere, 1966–1967.

———. "Il prosimetrum nella *Vita Nuova*." In *La selva del protonotaro: Nuovi studi danteschi*, 17–31. Naples: Morano, 1988.

Petronio, Giuseppe. "Appunti per uno studio su Dante e il pubblico." *Beiträge zur Romanischen Philologie* 4, no. 2 (1965): 98–108.

Petrucci, Armando. "Alle origini del libro moderno: Libri da banco, libri da bisaccia, libretti da mano." In *Libri, scrittura e pubblico nel Rinascimento: Guida storica e critica*, edited by Armando Petrucci, 137–56. Bari: Laterza, 1979.

———. "Autografi." *Quaderni di storia* 63 (2006): 111–25.

———. *Breve storia della scrittura latina*. Rome: Bagatto, 1992.

———. "Dalla minuta al manoscritto d'autore." In *La produzione del testo*, Vol. 1 of *Lo spazio letterario del Medioevo: 1. Il Medioevo latino*, edited by Guglielmo Cavallo, Claudio Leonardi, and Enrico Menestò, 353–72. Rome: Salerno, 1992.

———. *La descrizione del manoscritto: Storia, problemi, modelli*. Rome: Carocci, 2001.

———. "Fatti protomercanteschi." *Scrittura e Civiltà* 25 (2001): 167–76.

———. "Libro e scrittura in Francesco Petrarca." In *Libro, scrittura e pubblico nel Rinascimento: Guida storica e critica*, edited by Armando Petrucci, 3–20. Bari: Laterza, 1979.

———. "Minute, Autograph, Author's Book." In *Writers and Readers in Medieval Italy: Studies in the History of Written Culture*, 145–68. New Haven, CT: Yale University Press, 1995.

———. "Reading and Writing *Volgare* in Medieval Italy." In *Writers and Readers in Medieval Italy: Studies in the History of Written Culture*, 169–253. New Haven, CT: Yale University Press, 1995.

———. "La scrittura del testo." In *Letteratura italiana: Una storia attraverso la scrittura*, 63–92. Rome: Carocci, 2017.

———. *La scrittura di Francesco Petrarca*. Vatican City: Biblioteca Apostolica Vaticana, 1967.

———. "Spazi di scrittura e scritte avventizie nel libro altomedievale." In *Ideologie e pratiche del reimpiego nell'alto Medioevo*, Atti della XLVI settimana di studio del Centro italiano per lo studio dell'Alto Medioevo (Spoleto, 16–21 aprile 1998), 2:981–1005. Spoleto: Centro italiano di studi sull'alto medioevo, 1999.

———. "Storia e geografia delle culture scritte (dal secolo XI al secolo XVIII)." In *Letteratura italiana: Una storia attraverso la scrittura*, 127–246. Rome: Carocci, 2017.

Petrucci, Armando, and Carlo Romeo. "L'*Orazionale* visigotico di Verona: Aggiunte avventizie, indovinello grafico, tagli maffeiani." *Scrittura e Civiltà* 22 (1998): 13–30.

Petrucci, Livio. "La lettera dell'originale dei *Rerum vulgarium fragmenta*." *Per leggere* 5 (2003): 67–134.

Phelps, Ruth Shepard. *The Earlier and Later Forms of Petrarch's "Canzoniere."* Chicago: University of Chicago Press, 1925.

Picchio Simonelli, Maria. "La sestina dantesca fra Arnaut Daniel e il Petrarca." *Dante Studies* 91 (1973): 131–44.

———. "Strutture foniche nei *Rerum vulgarium fragmenta*." In *Francis Petrarch, Six Centuries Later: A Symposium*, edited by Aldo Scaglione, 66–104. Chapel Hill, NC: Department of Romance Languages and Literatures/Chicago: The Newberry Library, 1975.

Pich, Federica. "L'immagine *donna de la mente* dalle Rime alla *Vita Nova*." In *Le Rime di Dante*, edited by Claudia Berra and Paolo Borsa, 345–76. Milan: Cisalpino, 2010.

———. "On the Threshold of Poems: A Paratextual Approach to the Narrative/Lyric Opposition in Italian Renaissance Poetry." In *Self-Commentary in Early Modern European Literature, 1400–1700*, edited by Francesco Venturi, 99–134. Leiden: Brill, 2019.

Picone, Michelangelo. "All'ombra della fanciulla in fiore: Lettura semantica della sestina dantesca." *Letture classensi* 24 (1995): 91–108.

———. "Boccaccio e la codificazione dell'ottava." In *Boccaccio: Secoli di vita*, Atti del Congresso Internazionale: Boccaccio 1975, Università di California, Los Angeles, 17–19 ottobre 1975, edited by Marga Cottino-Jones and Edward F. Tuttle, 53–65. Ravenna: Longo, 1977.

———, ed. *Il Canzoniere: Lettura micro e macrotestuale*. Ravenna: Longo, 2007.

———. "Dante come autore/narratore della *Commedia*." *Nuova Rivista di Letteratura Italiana* 2, no. 1 (1999): 9–26.

———. "Dante e il canone degli *auctores*." In *Studi danteschi*, 150–64.

———. "La forza di Amore e il potere della poesia (*Rvf* 230–40)." In Picone, ed., *Il Canzoniere*, 501–18.

———. "L'Ovidio di Dante." In *Studi danteschi*, 193–222.

———. *Percorsi della lirica duecentesca: Dai Siciliani alla* "*Vita Nova*." Fiesole (Florence): Cadmo, 2003.

———. "'Per Ovidio parla Amore . . .': Dante *auctor* della *Vita Nova*." In *Studi danteschi*, 295–306.

———. "Petrarca fra patimento amoroso e pentimento religioso (*Rvf* 61–69)." In Picone, ed., *Il Canzoniere*, 161–82.

———. "Petrarch and the Unfinished Book." *Annali d'Italianistica* 22 (2004): 45–60.

———. "Il *prosimetrum* della *Vita Nova*." *Arzanà* 7 (2001): 177–94.

———. "Songbook and Lyric Genres in the *Vita Nuova*." *The Italianist* 15, Supplement no. 2 (1995): 158–70.

———. *Studi danteschi*. Ravenna: Longo, 2017.

———. "Strutture poetiche e strutture prosastiche nella *Vita Nuova*." *Modern Language Notes* 92, no. 1 (1977): 117–29.

———. "La teoria dell'*Auctoritas* nella *Vita nova*." *Tenzone* 6 (2005): 173–91.

———. "Theories of Love and the Lyric Tradition from Dante's *Vita Nuova* to Petrarch's *Canzoniere*." *Romance Notes* 39, no. 1 (1998): 83–93.

———. "Traditional Genres and Poetic Innovation in Thirteenth-Century Italian Lyric Poetry." In *Medieval Lyric: Genres in Historical Context*, edited by William D. Paden, 146–57. Urbana: University of Illinois Press, 2000.

———. "*Vita Nuova" e tradizione romanza*. Padua: Liviana, 1979.

———. "La *Vita Nuova* fra autobiografia e tipologia." In *Dante e le forme dell'allegoresi*, edited by Michelangelo Picone, 59–70. Ravenna: Longo, 1987.

Picone, Michelangelo, and Claude Cazalé Bérard, eds. *Gli Zibaldoni di Boccaccio: Memoria, scrittura, riscrittura*. Atti del seminario internazionale di Firenze–Certaldo (26–28 aprile 1996). Florence: Cesati, 1998.

Pierazzo, Elena. *Digital Scholarly Editing: Theories, Models and Methods*. London: Routledge, 2016.

Pierazzo, Elena, and Matthew James Driscoll, eds. *Digital Scholarly Editing: Theories and Practices*. Cambridge: Open Book Publishers, 2016.

Pillinini, Stefano. "Traguardi linguistici nel Petrarca bembino del 1501." *Studi di filologia italiana* 39 (1981): 57–76.

Pintaudi, Rosario. "Ermeneutica *per epistulas*: L'ostrakon fiorentino di Saffo (*PSI* XIII 1300)." *Analecta Papyrologica* 12 (2000): 45–62.

Pinto, Raffaele, ed. *Amor, tu vedi ben che questa donna* (La Biblioteca de Tenzone 11). Madrid: CEMA, 2018.

———. "*Naturalmente chere ogne amadore* e il dialogo fra Cino, Dante e Guido." In *Cino da Pistoia nella storia della poesia italiana*, edited by Rossend Arqués Corominas and Silvia Tranfaglia, 61–74. Florence: Cesati, 2016.

Pipa, Arshi. "Personaggi della *Vita Nuova*: Dante, Cavalcanti e la famiglia Portinari." *Italica* 62, no. 2 (1985): 99–115.

Pirovano, Donato. "Boccaccio editore della *Vita nuova*." In Azzetta and Mazzucchi, eds., *Boccaccio editore e interprete di Dante*, 113–35.

———. "Per una nuova edizione della *Vita nuova*." *Rivista di studi danteschi* 12 (2012): 248–325.

———. "*Vita nuova*: A Novel Book." *Studj romanzi*, n.s., 14 (2018): 149–63.

———, ed. *Vita nuova*. By Dante Alighieri. In *Vita Nuova–Le Rime della Vita nuova e altre Rime del tempo della Vita nuova*, Tome 1 of *Vita nuova–Rime*, Vol. 1 of *Le Opere di Dante*, edited by Marco Gramaldi and Donato Pirovano, 1–289. Rome: Salerno, 2015.

Pistolesi, Elena. "Il *De vulgari eloquentia* di Giovanni Boccaccio." *Giornale storico della letteratura italiana* 191, no. 2 (2014): 161–99.

Poe, Edgar Allan. *Marginalia*. Edited by John C. Miller. Charlottesville: University Press of Virginia, 1981.

Poe, Elizabeth Wilson. "*L'Autr'escrit* of Uc de Saint Circ: The *Razos* for Bertran de Born." *Romance Philology* 44, no. 2 (1990): 123–36.

———. "The Poetics of Copying: The Scribe as Artist in the *Chansonniers* and Dante's *Vita Nuova*." In *From Poetry to Prose in Old Provençal: The Emergence of the* Vidas, *the* Razos, *and the* Razos de Trobar, 83–95. Birmingham: Summa Publication, 1984.

———. "The *Vidas* and *Razos*." In *A Handbook of the Troubadours*, edited by F. R. P. Akehurst and Judith M. Davis, 185–97. Berkeley: University of California Press, 1995.

Pollard, Graham. "The *pecia* System in the Medieval Universities." In *Medieval Scribes, Manuscripts and Libraries: Essays presented to N. R. Ker*, edited by Michael B. Parks and Andrew G. Watson, 145–61. London: Scolar, 1978.

Pomaro, Gabriella. "Codicologia dantesca: 1. L'Officina di Vat." *Studi danteschi* 58 (1986): 343–74.

Possiedi, Paolo. "Petrarca petroso." *Forum italicum* 8 (1974): 523–45.

Powitz, Gerhardt. "Textus cum commento." *Codices Manuscripti: Zeitschrift für Handschriftenkunde* 5, no. 3 (1979): 80–89.

Pozzi, Giovanni. *La parola dipinta*. Milan: Adelphi, 1981.

Praloran, Marco. *La canzone di Petrarca: Orchestrazione formale e percorsi argomentativi*. Padua: Antenore, 2013.

———. "Figure ritmiche dell'endecasillabo." In *La metrica dei "Fragmenta,"* edited by Marco Praloran 125–89. Padua: Antenore, 2003.

———. *Metro e ritmo nella poesia italiana: Guida anomala ai fondamenti della versificazione*. Florence: Edizioni del Galluzzo, 2011.

Prandi, Stefano. "Ritorno a Laura (*Rvf* 141–50)." In Picone, ed., *Il Canzoniere*, 335–60.

Price, Leah. "Introduction: Reading Matter." *PMLA* 121, no. 1 (2006): 9–16.

Pulega, Andrea. "Modelli trobadorici della sestina dantesca: Esercizi di lettura." *Acme* 31, no. 2 (1978): 261–328.

Pulsoni, Carlo. "Da Petrarca all'Europa: Appunti sulla fortuna della sestina lirica." *Atti e memorie dell'Accademia galileiana di Scienze, Lettere ed Arti* 123 (2010–2011): 201–17.

———. "Le fonti dell'edizione aldina di Petrarca (1501)." In Cantares de amigos: *Estudoes en homenaxe a Mercedes Brea*, edited by Esther Corral Díaz, Elvira Fidalgo Francisco, and Pilar Lorenzo Gradín, 733–37. Santiago de Compostela: Universidade de Santiago de Compostela, Servizo de Publicacións e Intercambio Científico, 2016.

———. "Il metodo di lavoro di Wilkins e la tradizione manoscritta dei *Rerum vulgarium fragmenta*." *Giornale italiano di filologia* 61 (2009): 257–69.

———. "Petrarca ultimo trovatore." In *Toulouse à la croisée des cultures*, Actes du Ve Congrès International de l'Association Internationale d'Études Occitanes, Toulouse, 19–24 août 1996, 1:69–74. Pau: Association Internationale d'Études Occitanes, 1998.

———. "Petrarca e la codificazione del genere sestina." *AnticoModerno* 2 (1996): 55–65.

———. *La tecnica compositiva dei "Rerum vulgarium fragmenta": Riuso metrico e lettura autoriale.* Rome: Bagatto 1998.

———. "Sulla morfologia dei congedi della sestina." *Aevum* 69, no. 3 (1995): 505–20.

Punzi, Arianna. "Boccaccio lettore di Stazio." In *Testimoni del vero: Su alcuni libri in biblioteche d'autore*, edited by Emilio Russo, 131–45. Rome: Bulzoni, 2000.

———. "I libri del Boccaccio e un nuovo codice di Santo Spirito: Il Barberiniano lat. 74." In "Per le biblioteche del Boccaccio e del Salutati," by Arianna Punzi and Antonio Manfredi, 193–203. *Italia medioevale e umanistica* 37 (1994): 193–214.

———. *Oedipodae confusa domus: La materia tebana nel Medioevo latino e romanzo.* Rome: Bagatto, 1995.

Putzo, Christine. "The Implied Book and the Narrative Text: On a Blind Spot in Narratological Theory—from a Media Studies Perspective." *Journal of Literary Theory* 6, no. 2 (2012): 383–415.

Quaglio, Antonio Enzo. "Antonio Pucci: Primo lettore-copista-interprete di Giovanni Boccaccio." *Filologia e critica* 1 (1976): 15–79.

———. "Picciolo libretto." *Lingua nostra* 20 (1959): 35–36.

Quain, Edwin A. "The Medieval Accessus ad Auctores." *Traditio* 3 (1945): 215–64.

Quaquarelli, Leonardo. "Malpigli, Niccolò." In *Dizionario biografico degli italiani*, 68:278–80. Rome: Istituto della Enciclopedia Italiana, 2007.

Quondam, Amedeo. *Cavallo e cavaliere: L'armatura come seconda pelle del gentiluomo moderno.* Rome: Donzelli, 2003.

Rabitti, Giovanna. "*Nel dolce tempo*: Sintesi o nuovo cominciamento?" *Italianistica: Rivista di letteratura italiana* 33, no. 2 (2004): 95–108.

Rafti, Patrizia. "Alle origini dell'interpunzione petrarchesca." *Scrittura e Civiltà* 19 (1995): 159–81.

———. "Riflessioni sull'*usus distinguendi* del Boccaccio negli *Zibaldoni*." In Picone and Bérard, eds., *Gli Zibaldoni di Boccaccio*, 283–306.

Rajna, Pio. "Un indovinello volgare scritto alla fine del secolo VIII o al principio del IX." *Speculum* 3, no. 3 (1928): 291–313.

———. "Lo schema della *Vita Nuova*." *Biblioteca delle Scuole Italiane* 2 (1890): 161–64.

Ravera, Giulia. *Petrarca e la lirica trobadorica: Topoi e generi della tradizione nel Canzoniere*. Milan: Ledizioni, 2017.

Rawski, Conrad H., trans. *Petrarch's Remedies for Fortune Fair and Foul: A Modern English Translation of "De remediis utriusque fortune," with a Commentary*. By Francesco Petrarca. Bloomington: Indiana University Press, 1991.

Rea, Roberto. "'Avete fatto como la lumera' (sulla tenzone fra Bonagiunta e Guinizzelli)." *Critica del testo* 6, no. 3 (2003): 933–58.

———. *Dante: Guida alla "Vita nuova."* Rome: Carocci, 2021.

———. "La *Vita nova*: Questioni di ecdotica." *Critica del testo* 14, no. 1 (2011): 233–77.

———. "La *Vita nuova* e le *Rime*: *Unus philosophus alter poeta*: Un'ipotesi per Cavalcanti e Dante." In *Dante fra il settecentocinquantenario della nascita (2015) e il settecentenario della morte (2021)*, Atti delle celebrazioni in Senato, del Forum e del Convegno internazionale di Roma: maggio–ottobre 2015, edited by Enrico Malato and Andrea Mazzucchi, 2:351–81. Rome: Salerno, 2016.

Rea, Roberto, and Giorgio Inglese, eds. *Rime*. By Guido Cavalcanti. Rome: Carocci, 2011.

Reeve, Michael D. "Statius." In *Texts and Transmission: A Survey of the Latin Classics*, edited by Leighton D. Reynolds and Nigel G. Wilson, 394–99. Oxford: Clarendon, 1983.

Reynolds, Barbara, trans. *La Vita Nuova*. By Dante Alighieri. New York: Viking Penguin, 1969.

Reynolds, Leighton Durham, and Nigel Guy Wilson. *Scribes and Scholars: A Guide to the Transmission of Greek and Latin Literature*. Oxford: Clarendon, 1991.

Ricardou, Jean. "The Story within the Story." *James Joyce Quarterly* 18, no. 3 (1981): 323–38.

Ricci, Pier Giorgio. "Evoluzione nella scrittura del Boccaccio e datazione degli autografi." In *Studi sulla vita e le opere del Boccaccio*, 286–96. Milan: Ricciardi, 1985.

———, ed. *Trattatello in laude di Dante*. By Giovanni Boccaccio. In *Tutte le opere di Giovanni Boccaccio*, edited by Vittore Branca, 3:425–538. Milan: Mondadori, 1998.

———. "Le tre redazioni del *Trattatello in laude di Dante*." *Studi sul Boccaccio* 8 (1974): 197–214.

Richards, Ivor Armstrong. *The Philosophy of Rhetoric*. New York: Oxford University Press, 1965.

Richardson, Brian. *Print Culture in Renaissance Italy: The Editor and the Vernacular Text, 1470–1600*. Cambridge: Cambridge University Press, 1994.

Rico, Francisco. "La biblioteca di Petrarca." In *Dalle origini al Rinascimento*, Vol. 1 of *Atlante della letteratura italiana*, edited by Sergio Luzzatto, Gabriele Pedullà, and Amedeo De Vincentiis, 229–34. Turin: Einaudi, 2010.

———. "Prólogos al *Canzoniere* (*Rerum vulgarium fragmenta*, I–III)." *Annali della Scuola Normale Superiore di Pisa. Classe di Lettere e Filosofia*, ser. III, 18, no. 3 (1988): 1071–104.

———. "*Rime sparse*, *Rerum vulgarium fragmenta*: Para el título y el primer soneto del *Canzoniere*." *Medioevo romanzo* 3 (1976): 101–38.

Riesz, János. *Die Sestine: Ihre Stellung in der literarischen Kritik und ihre Geschichte als lyrisches Genus*. Munich: Fink, 1971.

Rigo, Paolo. "Il sonetto conteso: La storia di *Naturalmente chere ogne amadore* tra testo, contesto e finzione." *Cuadernos de Filología Italiana* 24 (2017): 115–30.

Riquer i Morera, Martí de. *Les chansons de geste françaises*. Paris: Librairie Nizet, 1957.

Rizzo, Silvia. "Il copista di un codice petrarchesco delle *Tusculanae*: Filologia vs paleografia." In *Paleography, Manuscript Illumination and Humanism in Renaissance Italy: Studies in Memory of A. C. de la Mare*, edited by Robert Black, Jill Kraye, and Laura Nuvoloni, 335–43. London: The Warburg Institute, 2016.

———. *Il lessico filologico degli umanisti*. Rome: Edizioni di Storia e Letteratura, 1973.

———. "Un nuovo codice delle *Tusculanae* dalla biblioteca del Petrarca." *Ciceroniana*, n.s., 9 (1996): 75–104.

———, ed. *Res seniles. Libri XIII–XVII*. By Francesco Petrarca. Florence: Le Lettere, 2017.

Robathan, Dorothy M. "Boccaccio's Accuracy as a Scribe." *Speculum* 13, no. 4 (1938): 458–60.

Robins, William. "Antonio Pucci, Guardiano degli Atti della Mercanzia." *Studi e problemi di critica testuale* 61 (2000): 29–70.

———. "The Study of Medieval Italian Textual Cultures." In *Textual Cultures of Medieval Italy*, edited by William Robins, 11–50. Toronto: University of Toronto Press, 2011.

Robinson, Pamela R. "The 'Booklet': A Self-Contained Unit in Composite Manuscripts." *Codicologica* 3 (1980): 46–69.

Rockenberger, Annika. "Materiality and Meaning in Literary Studies." *Schriften zur Kultur- und Mediensemiotik* 2 (2016): 39–60.

Roddewig, Marcella. *Dante Alighieri, "Die göttliche Komödie": Vergleichende Bestandsaufnahme der Commedia-Handschriften.* Stuttgart: Hiersemann, 1984.

Romanini, Fabio. "Manoscritti e postillati dell'"antica vulgata."" In *Nuove prospettive sulla tradizione della "Commedia": Una guida filologico-linguistica al poema dantesco,* edited by Paolo Trovato, 49–60. Florence: Cesati, 2007.

Roncaglia, Aurelio. "L'invenzione della sestina." *Metrica* 2 (1981): 3–41.

———. "Per una storia dell'ottava rima." *Cultura neolatina* 25 (1965): 5–14.

———. "Precedenti e significato dello 'Stil Novo' dantesco." In *Dante e Bologna nel tempo di Dante,* 13–34. Bologna: Commissione per i testi di lingua, 1967.

———. "Rétrospectives et perspectives dans l'étude des chansonniers d'oc." *Lyrique romane médiévale: La tradition des chansonniers,* Actes du Colloque de Liège, 1989, edited by Madeleine Tyssens, 19–41. Liège: Faculté de Philosophie et Lettres de l'Université de Liège, 1991.

———, ed. *Teseida: Delle nozze d'Emilia.* By Giovanni Boccaccio. Bari: Laterza, 1941.

Root, Robert K. "Publication before Printing." *PMLA* 28, no. 3 (1913): 417–31.

Rossellini, Ingrid. *Nel "trapassar del segno": Idoli della mente ed echi della vita nei "Rerum vulgarium fragmenta."* Florence: Olschki, 1995.

Rossi, Luca Carlo. "Presenze di Petrarca in commenti danteschi fra Tre e Quattrocento." *Aevum* 70, no. 3 (1996): 441–76.

———, ed. *Vita Nova.* By Dante Alighieri. Milan: Mondadori, 1999.

Rossi, Vittorio, ed. *Le familiari.* By Francesco Petrarca. Florence: Sansoni, 1933–1942.

Rossini, Antonio. *Dante, il nodo e il volume: Una* lectura *di "Paradiso" 33.* Pisa: Fabrizio Serra, 2011.

Rouse, Mary A., and Richard H. Rouse. *Authentic Witnesses: Approaches to Medieval Texts and Manuscripts.* Notre Dame, IN: University of Notre Dame Press, 1991.

Roush, Sherry. *Hermes' Lyre: Italian Poetic Self-Commentary from Dante to Tommaso Campanella.* Toronto: University of Toronto Press, 2002.

Russell, Rinaldina. "Studio dei generi medievali italiani: Il compianto per la morte dell'amata." *Italica* 54, no. 4 (1977): 449–67.

Russo, Vittorio. "appello al lettore." In *Enciclopedia Dantesca,* edited by Umberto Bosco, 1:324–26. Rome: Istituto della Enciclopedia Italiana, 1970.

Sabbadini, Remigio, ed. *Bucolica et Georgica.* By Publius Virgilius Maro. Vol. 1 of *Opera.* Rome: Regia Officina Polygraphica, 1930.

———. *Le scoperte dei codici latini e greci ne' secoli XIV e XV.* Florence: Sansoni, 1905–1914.

Saenger, Paul. "Silent Reading: Its Impact on Late Medieval Script and Society." *Viator* 13 (1982): 367–414.

Salinari, Carlo, and Natalino Sapegno, eds. *Il Filocolo*. By Giovanni Boccaccio. In *Decameron–Filocolo–Ameto–Fiammetta*, edited by Enrico Bianchi, Carlo Salinari, and Natalino Sapegno, 767–899. Milan: Ricciardi, 1952.

Salsano, Fernando. "riguardare." In *Enciclopedia Dantesca*, edited by Umberto Bosco, 4:927–28. Rome: Istituto della Enciclopedia Italiana, 1973.

Salvatore, Tommaso. "Sondaggi sulla tradizione manoscritta della 'forma Chigi' (con incursioni pre-chigiane)." *Studi petrarcheschi* 27 (2014): 47–105.

Sandal, Ennio. "La prima edizione delle opere volgari del Petrarca." In *Illustrazione libraria, filologia ed esegesi petrarchesta tra Quattrocento e Cinquecento: Antonio Grifo e l'incunabolo Queriniano G V 15*, edited by Giuseppe Frasso, Giordana Mariani Canova, and Ennio Sandal, 1–17. Padua: Antenore, 1990.

Sanguineti, Edoardo. "Per una lettura della *Vita nuova*." In *Dante reazionario*, 3–33. Rome: Editori Riuniti, 1992.

Santagata, Marco. *Amate e amanti: Figure della lirica amorosa fra Dante e Petrarca*. Bologna: il Mulino, 1999.

———. *Boccaccio indiscreto: Il mito di Fiammetta*. Bologna: il Mulino, 2019.

———, ed. *Canzoniere*. By Francesco Petrarca. Milan: Mondadori, 1996.

———. *Il copista*. Palermo: Sellerio, 2000.

———. *Dal sonetto al canzoniere: Ricerche sulla preistoria e la costituzione di un genere*. Padua: Liviana, 1979.

———. *I frammenti dell'anima: Storia e racconto nel Canzoniere di Petrarca*. Bologna: il Mulino, 1992.

———. *L'io e il mondo: Un'interpretazione di Dante*. Bologna: il Mulino, 2011.

———. *Pastorale modenese: Boiardo, i poeti e la lotta politica*. Bologna: il Mulino, 2016.

———. *Per moderne carte: La biblioteca volgare di Petrarca*. Bologna: il Mulino, 1990.

———. "Petrarca e Arnaut Daniel (con appunti sulla cronologia di alcune rime petrarchesche)." *Rivista di letteratura italiana* 5 (1987): 40–89.

———. "Presenze di Dante 'comico' nel *Canzoniere* del Petrarca." *Giornale storico della letteratura italiana* 146 (1969): 163–211.

Santangelo, Salvatore. *Dante e i trovatori provenzali*. Catania: Giannotta, 1921.

Sapegno, Natalino. "Francesco Petrarca." In *Il Trecento*, Vol. 2 of *Storia della Letteratura Italiana*, edited by Emilio Cecchi and Natalino Sapegno, 187–313. Milan: Garzanti, 1965.

Sarolli, Gian Roberto. *Prolegomena alla "Divina Commedia."* Florence: Olschki, 1971.

Sarteschi, Selene. "Da Beatrice alla Petra: Il nome come *senhal* e metafora dell'arte poetica." *Rassegna europea di letteratura italiana* 12, no. 2 (1998): 37–60.

———. "Dante e il lettore." In *Dante in lettura*, edited by Giuseppe De Matteis, 133–54. Ravenna: Longo, 2005.

———. "*Donna me prega–Vita Nuova*: La direzione di una polemica." *Rassegna europea di letteratura italiana* 15, no. 1 (2000): 9–35.

———. *Il percorso del poeta cristiano: Riflessioni su Dante*. Ravenna: Longo, 2006.

———. "*Rerum vulgarium fragmenta*: Un libro sempre aperto?" *La Rassegna della letteratura italiana* 112, no. 1 (2008): 64–92.

———. "Uno scaffale della biblioteca volgare di Dante: Dalla *Rettorica* di Brunetto Latini alla *Vita Nuova*." In *Leggere Dante*, Atti del seminario tenutosi a Pisa nell'a.a. 2001–2002, edited by Lucia Battaglia Ricci, 171–90. Ravenna: Longo, 2003.

Sautel, Jacques-Hubert. "Essai de terminologie de la mise en page des manuscrits à commentaire." *Gazette du livre médiéval* 35 (1999): 17–31.

Savino, Giancarlo. "L'autografo virtuale della *Commedia*." In *"Per correr miglior acque . . .": Bilanci e prospettive degli studi danteschi alle soglie del nuovo millennio*, Atti del Convegno internazionale di Verona–Ravenna, 25–29 ottobre 1999, 2:1099–110. Rome: Salerno, 2001.

Saviotti, Federico. "L'énigme du *senhal*." *Medioevi: Rivista di letterature e culture medievali* 1 (2015): 102–21.

Savj-Lopez, Paolo. "Sulle fonti della *Teseide*." *Giornale storico della letteratura italiana* 36 (1900): 57–78.

Savoca, Giuseppe. *Il Canzoniere di Petrarca tra codicologia ed ecdotica*. Florence: Olschki, 2008.

Scaglione, Aldo. "La struttura del *Canzoniere* e il metodo di composizione del Petrarca." *Lettere italiane* 27, no. 2 (1975): 129–40.

Scaffai, Niccolò. *Il poeta e il suo libro: Retorica e storia del libro di poesia nel Novecento*. Milan: Mondadori, 2005.

Scarano, Nicola. "Fonti provenzali e italiane della lirica petrarchesca." *Studj di filologia romanza* 8 (1899): 250–360.

Scarpati, Oriana. "Tipologie dell'esordio nei poeti della scuola siciliana tra riprese e mutamenti." *Bollettino–Centro di studi filologici e linguistici siciliani* 22 (2010): 27–41.

Schiaffini, Alfredo. "La *Vita nuova* come *legenda Sanctae Beatricis*." In *Tradizione e poesia nella prosa d'arte italiana dalla latinità medievale a Giovanni Boccaccio*, 83–106. Genoa: Emilano degli Orfini, 1934.

Schiapparelli, Luigi. "Note paleografiche: Sulla data e provenienza del cod. LXXXIX della Biblioteca Capitolare di Verona (l'Orazionale Mozarabico)." *Archivio Storico Italiano* 82, no. 1 (1924): 106–17.

Schnapp, Jeffrey T. "A Commentary on Commentary in Boccaccio." *The South Atlantic Quarterly* 91, no. 4 (1992): 813–34.

Scholes, Robert. "Metafiction." *The Iowa Review* 1, no. 4 (1970): 100–15.

Schönberger, Otto, and Eva Schönberger, eds. and trans. *Epistulae metricae/Briefe in Versen*. By Francesco Petrarca. Würzburg: Königshausen & Neumann, 2004.

Segre, Cesare. "Appunti sul problema delle contaminazioni nei testi in prosa." In *Studi e problemi di critica testuale*, Atti del Convegno di studi di filologia italiana nel centenario della Commissione per i testi di lingua (7–9 aprile 1960), 63–67. Bologna: Commissione per i testi di lingua, 1961.

———. "Le isotopie di Laura." In *Notizie dalla crisi*, 66–80.

———. *Notizie dalla crisi: Dove va la critica letteraria?* Turin: Einaudi, 1993.

———. "Per una definizione del commento ai testi." In *Il commento ai testi*, edited by Ottavio Besomi and Carlo Caruso, 3–14. Basel: Birkhäuser Verlag, 1992.

———. "La prosa del Duecento." In *Lingua, stile e società: Studi sulla storia della prosa italiana*, 13–47. Milan: Feltrinelli, 1963.

———. "Sistema e strutture nelle *Soledades* di A. Machado." *Strumenti critici* 7 (1968): 269–303.

———. "I sonetti dell'aura." In *Notizie dalla crisi*, 43–64.

Shalom Vagata, Daniela. "Appunti su alcune varianti dantesche nella tradizione estravagante della *Vita Nova*." In *Le Rime di Dante*, edited by Claudia Berra and Paolo Borsa, 377–410. Milan: Cisalpino, 2010.

Shapiro, Marianne. "The Adynaton in Petrarch's Sestinas." In *Dante, Petrarch, Boccaccio: Studies in the Italian Trecento in Honor of Charles S. Singleton*, edited by Aldo S. Bernardo and Anthony L. Pellegrini, 231–53. Binghamton: Center for Medieval & Early Renaissance Studies, SUNY at Binghamton, 1983.

———. *Hieroglyph of Time: The Petrarchan Sestina*. Minneapolis: University of Minnesota Press, 1980.

———. "The Petrarchan *Selva* revisited: *Sestina* XXII." *Neuphilologische Mitteilungen* 77, no. 1 (1976): 144–60.

———. "Spatial Relationships in Dante's *Vita Nuova*." *Romance Notes* 16, no. 3 (1975): 708–11.

Shaw, James E. *Essays on the "Vita Nuova."* Princeton, NJ: Princeton University Press, 1929.

Shepard, William Pierce, ed. *The Oxford Provençal Chansonnier: Diplomatic Edition of the Manuscript of the Bodleian Library, Douce 269.* Princeton, NJ: Princeton University Press/Paris: Les Presses universitaires de France, 1927.

Shillingsburg, Peter L. *From Gutenberg to Google: Electronic Representations of Literary Texts.* Cambridge: Cambridge University Press, 2006.

———. *Resisting Texts: Authority and Submission in Constructions of Meaning.* Ann Arbor: University of Michigan Press, 1997.

Signorini, Maddalena. "Boccaccio as Homer: A Recently Discovered Self-portrait and the 'Modern' Canon." In *Building the Canon through the Classics: Imitation and Variation in Renaissance Italy (1350–1580)*, edited by Eloisa Morra, 13–26. Leiden: Brill, 2019.

———. "Il Canzoniere Chigiano L.VIII.305: Scrittura e storia." *Segni per Armando Petrucci*, edited by Luisa Miglio and Paola Supino Martini, 222–42. Rome: Bagatto, 2002.

———. "Considerazioni preliminari sulla biblioteca di Giovanni Boccaccio." *Studi sul Boccaccio* 39 (2011): 367–95.

———. "Fortuna del 'modello-libro' *Canzoniere*." *Critica del testo* 6, no. 1 (2003): 133–56.

———. "Malpaghini, Giovanni." In *Dizionario biografico degli Italiani*, 68:266–69. Rome: Istituto della Enciclopedia italiana, 2007.

———. "La scrittura libraria di Francesco Petrarca: Terminologia, fortuna." *Studi Medievali*, s. III, 48, no. 2 (2007): 839–62.

———. "Spunti per un panorama romanzo del manoscritto antologico." *Critica del testo* 7, no. 1 (2004): 529–44.

———. "Sul codice delle *Tusculanae* appartenuto a Francesco Petrarca (Roma, BNC, *Vittorio Emanuele* 1632)." *Studj romanzi*, n.s., 1 (2005): 105–38.

———. *Sulle tracce di Petrarca: Storia e significato di una prassi scrittoria.* Florence: Olschki, 2019.

Singleton, Charles S. *Dante's "Commedia": Elements of Structure.* Baltimore: Johns Hopkins University Press, 1977.

———. *An Essay on the "Vita Nuova."* Baltimore: Johns Hopkins University Press, 1977.

———. *Journey to Beatrice.* Baltimore: Johns Hopkins University Press, 1977.

———. "The Use of Latin in the *Vita Nuova*." *Modern Language Notes* 61, no. 2 (1946): 108–12.

Smarr, Janet L. *Boccaccio and Fiammetta: The Narrator as Lover.* Urbana: University of Illinois Press, 1986.

Smith, Marc H. "Conseils pour l'édition des documents en langue italienne (XIVe–XVIIe siècle)." *Bibliothèque de l'École des chartes* 159, no. 2 (2001): 541–78.

Soldani, Arnaldo. "Un'ipotesi sull'ordinamento finale del *Canzoniere* (*RVF*, 336–66)." *Studi petrarcheschi* 19 (2006): 209–47.

———. "Osservazioni sull'ottava di Boccaccio." In *Boccaccio in versi*, Atti del Convegno di Parma, 13–14 marzo 2014, edited by Pantalea Mazzitello, Giulia Raboni, Paolo Rinoldi, and Carlo Varotti, 161–77. Florence: Cesati, 2016.

———. "L'ottava di Boccaccio e di alcuni cantari trecenteschi: Uno studio tipologico." *Stilistica e metrica italiana* 15 (2015): 41–82.

———. "Voce e temporalità nella narrazione del Canzoniere." In *Studi in onore di Pier Vincenzo Mengaldo per i suoi settant'anni*, 1:325–45. Florence: SISMEL—Edizioni del Galluzzo, 2007.

Solerti, Angelo, ed. *Rime disperse di Francesco Petrarca o a lui attribuite.* By Francesco Petrarca. Florence: Sansoni, 1909.

Sollers, Philippe. "Dante et la traversée de l'écriture." In *L'écriture et l'expérience des limites*, 14–47. Paris: Seuil, 2018.

Spaggiari, Barbara. "'Cacciare la lepre col bue.'" *Annali della Scuola Normale Superiore di Pisa*, s. III, 12, no. 4 (1982): 1333–409.

Spettoli, Letizia. "Le chiose del *Teseida* di Giovanni Boccaccio nel manoscritto più antico della tradizione (Aix-en-Provence, *Bibliothèque Méjanes*, 180)." In *Boccaccio in versi*, Atti del Convegno di Parma, 13–14 marzo 2014, edited by Pantalea Mazzitello, Giulia Raboni, Paolo Rinoldi, and Carlo Varotti, 119–31. Florence: Cesati, 2016.

Spitz, Hans-Jörg, *Die Metaphorik des geistigen Schriftsinns: Ein Beitrag zur allegorischen Bibelauslegung des ersten christlichen Jahrtausends.* Munich: Fink, 1972.

Spitzer, Leo. "The Addresses to the Reader in the *Commedia*." *Italica* 32 (1955): 143–65.

———. "Note on the Poetic and Empirical 'I' in Medieval Authors." *Traditio* 4 (1946): 414–22.

———. "Osservazioni sulla *Vita Nuova* di Dante." In *Studi italiani*, 95–146. Milan: Vita e Pensiero, 1976.

Stark-Gendrano, Rebecca. "Variorum edition." In *The Oxford Companion to the Book*, edited by Michael F. Suarez, and H. R. Woudhuysen, 2:1238. Oxford: Oxford University Press, 2010.

Stäuble, Antonio. "Dal labirinto alla solarità (*Rvf* 211–20)." In Picone, ed., *Il Canzoniere*, 463–79.

Steinberg, Justin. *Accounting for Dante: Urban Readers and Writers in Late Medieval Italy.* Notre Dame, IN: University of Notre Dame Press, 2007.

———. "The Author." In *The Oxford Handbook of Dante*, edited by Manuele Gragnolati, Elena Lombardi, and Francesca Southerden, 3–16. Oxford: Oxford University Press, 2021.

———. "Dante's First Dream between Reception and Allegory: The Response to Dante da Maiano in the *Vita nova*." In *Dante the Lyric and Ethical Poet/Dante lirico e etico*, edited by Zygmunt Barański and Martin McLaughlin, 92–118. Oxford: Legenda, 2010.

Stella, René. "La *Vita nuova* de Dante: Stratégie de la citation." *Cahiers d'études romanes* 5 (2001): 19–31.

Stierle, Karlheinz. "Paesaggi poetici del Petrarca." In *Il paesaggio: Dalla percezione alla descrizione*, edited by Renzo Zorzi, 121–37. Venice: Marsilio, 1999.

Stillers, Rainer. "L'*Amorosa visione* e la poetica della visualità." In *Autori e lettori di Boccaccio*, Atti del convegno internazionale di Certaldo, 20–22 settembre 2001, edited by Michelangelo Picone, 327–42. Florence: Cesati, 2002.

Stillinger, Thomas. *The Song of Troilus: Lyric Authority in the Medieval Book.* Philadelphia: University of Pennsylvania Press, 1992.

Storey, H. Wayne. "All'interno della poetica grafico-visiva di Petrarca." In *Commentario all'edizione in fac-simile*, Vol. 2 of *Rerum vulgarium fragmenta. Codice Vat. lat. 3195, edizione facsimilare*, edited by Gino Belloni, Furio Brugnolo, H. Wayne Storey, and Stefano Zamponi, 131–71. Padua: Antenore, 2003–2004.

———. "Boccaccio narra la vita di Dante: Dagli *Zibaldoni* alle *Esposizioni*." In *Boccaccio e la nuova* ars narrandi, edited by Piotr Salwa, 11–20. Warsaw: Sub Lupa, 2015.

———. "Il codice Pierpont Morgan M. 502 e i suoi rapporti con lo scrittoio padovano di Petrarca." In *La cultura volgare padovana nell'età del Petrarca*, Atti del convegno di Monselice-Padova (7–8 maggio 2004), edited by Furio Brugnolo and Zeno Lorenzo Verlato, 487–504. Padua: Il Poligrafo, 2006.

———. "Cultural Crisis and Material Innovation: The Italian Manuscript in the XIVth Century." *Revue belge de philologie et d'histoire* 83, no. 3 (2005): 869–86.

———. "Di libello in libro: Problemi materiali nella poetica di Monte Andrea e Dante." In *Da Guido Guinizzelli a Dante: Nuove prospettive sulla lirica del Duecento*, edited by Furio Brugnolo and Gianfelice Peron, 271–90. Padua: Il Poligrafo, 2004.

———. "Following Instructions: Remaking Dante's *Vita Nova* in the Fourteenth Century." In *Medieval Constructions in Gender and Identity: Essays in Honor *of Joan M. Ferrante*, edited by Teodolinda Barolini, 117–32. Tempe: Arizona Center for Medieval and Renaissance Studies, 2005.

———. "The Formation of Knowledge and Petrarch's Books." In *Petrarch and Boccaccio: The Unity of Knowledge in the Pre-Modern World*, edited by Igor Candido, 15–51. Berlin: De Gruyter, 2018.

———. "A Note on Boccaccio's Dantean Categories; or, What's in a Book? *libro, volume, pistole, rime*." *Philology* 1 (2015): 115–19.

———. "Petrarch's 'Original' of the *Fragmenta* 1362–1558: From Boccaccio to Rovillio's Third Printing." *Humanist Studies & the Digital Age* 1, no. 1 (2011): 28–49.

———. *Transcription and Visual Poetics in the Early Italian Lyric*. New York: Garland, 1993.

Storey, H. Wayne, and Roberta Capelli. "Modalità di ordinamento materiale tra Guittone e Petrarca." In *"Liber," "fragmenta," "libellus" prima e dopo Petrarca: In ricordo di d'Arco Silvio Avalle*, Seminario internazionale di studi, Bergamo, 23–25 ottobre 2003, edited by Francesco Lo Monaco, Luca Carlo Rossi, and Niccolò Scaffai, 169–86. Florence: SISMEL—Edizioni del Galluzzo, 2006.

Sturm-Maddox, Sara. *Petrarch's Laurels*. University Park: Pennsylvania State University Press, 1992.

———. *Petrarch's Metamorphoses: Text and Subtext in the "Rime sparse."* Columbia: University of Missouri Press, 1985.

Stussi, Alfredo. *Nuovo avviamento agli studi di filologia italiana*. Bologna: il Mulino, 1988.

———. *Tracce*. Rome: Bulzoni, 2001.

Suitner, Franco. "La fisionomia stilistica del Canzoniere e osservazioni sul testo del Contini." *Lectura Petrarce* 13 (1993): 135–47.

———. "Le rime del Petrarca e l'idea della donna 'beatrice': Convenzioni letterarie e realtà psicologica." In *Beatrice nell'opera di Dante e nella memoria europea 1290–1990*, Atti del convegno internazionale, 10–14 dicembre 1990, edited by Maria Picchio Simonelli, 261–78. Fiesole (Florence): Cadmo, 1994.

Supino Martini, Paola. "Per la storia della 'semigotica.'" *Scrittura e Civiltà* 22 (1998): 249–64.

Surdich, Luigi. *La cornice di amore: Studi sul Boccaccio*. Pisa: ETS, 1987.

Sweeney, Robert D. *Prolegomena to an Edition of the Scholia to Statius*. Leiden: Brill, 1969.

Taddeo, Edoardo. "Il tempo come tema nelle *Rime*." *Studi e problemi di critica testuale* 27 (1983): 69–108.

Tagliavini, Carlo. *Le origini delle lingue neolatine: Introduzione alla filologia romanza*. Bologna: Pàtron, 1969.

Tanselle, G. Thomas. "The Editorial Problem of Final Authorial Intention." *Studies in Bibliography* 29 (1976): 167–211.

———. *A Rationale of Textual Criticism*. Philadelphia: University of Pennsylvania Press, 1989.

Tanturli, Giuliano. "Le copie di *Vita nova* e canzoni di Dante." In De Robertis et al., eds., *Boccaccio autore e copista*, 255–60.

———. "Guido Cavalcanti contro Dante." In *Le tradizioni del testo: Studi di letteratura italiana offerti a Domenico De Robertis*, edited by Franco Gavazzeni and Guglielmo Gorni, 3–13. Milan: Ricciardi, 1993.

Tanturli, Giuliano, and Stefano Zamponi. "Biografia e cronologia delle opere." In De Robertis et al., eds., *Boccaccio autore e copista*, 61–64.

Tassinari, Maria Giovanna. "Metalingua e metadiscorso: Prospettive sulla base di un'analisi della *Vita Nuova* di Dante." *Lingua e stile* 23, no. 1 (1988): 71–94.

Tateo, Francesco. "La *nuova matera* e la svolta critica della *Vita Nuova*." In *Studi di filologia romanza offerti a Silvio Pellegrini*, 629–53. Padua: Liviana, 1971.

———. *Questioni di poetica dantesca*. Bari: Adriatica, 1972.

Tavoni, Mirko. "'Converrebbe me essere laudatore di me medesimo' (*Vita nova* XXVIII 2)." In *Studi in onore di Pier Vincenzo Mengaldo per i suoi settant'anni*, 1:253–61. Florence: SISMEL—Edizioni del Galluzzo, 2007.

———. "Il nome di poeta in Dante." In *Studi offerti a Luigi Blasucci dai colleghi e dagli allievi pisani*, edited by Lucio Lugnani, Marco Santagata, and Alfredo Stussi, 545–77. Lucca: Pacini Fazzi, 1996.

———. "La visione di Dio nell'ultimo canto del *Paradiso*." In *Dire l'indicibile: Esperienza religiosa e poesia dalla Bibbia al Novecento*, edited by Cesare Letta, 65–112. Pisa: Edizioni ETS, 2009.

———. "*Vita nuova* XXV 3 e altri appunti di linguistica dantesca." *Rivista di Letteratura Italiana* 2, no. 1 (1984): 9–52.

Taylor, Jerome, trans. *The "Didascalicon" of Hugh of St. Victor: A Medieval Guide to the Arts*. New York: Columbia University Press, 1961.

Terracini, Benvenuto. "Analisi dello 'stile legato' della *Vita Nuova*." In *Pagine e appunti di linguistica storica*, 247–63. Florence: Le Monnier, 1957.

Testa, Enrico. *Il libro di poesia: Tipologie e analisi macrotestuali*. Genoa: il melangolo, 1983.

ThLL = *Thesaurus linguae Latinae*. Berlin (formerly Leipzig): De Gruyter (formerly Teubner), 1900–.

Thompson, W. Kenneth, ed. and trans. *The Labors of Hercules*. By Pietro Andrea de' Bassi. Barre: Imprint Society, 1971.

Tissoni Benvenuti, Antonia. "L'antico a corte: Da Guarino a Boiardo." In *Alla corte degli Estensi: Filosofia, arte e cultura a Ferrara nei secoli XV e XVI*, Atti del convegno internazionale di studi (Ferrara, 5–7 marzo 1992), edited by Marco Bertozzi, 389–404. Ferrara: Università degli Studi, 1994.

———. "Le armi e le lettere nell'educazione del signore nelle corti padane del Quattrocento." *Mélanges de l'École française de Rome: Moyen Age–Temps Modernes* 99, no. 1 (1987): 435–46.

———. "Il commento per la corte." In *Intorno al testo: Tipologie del corredo esegetico e soluzioni editoriali*, Atti del convegno di Urbino, 1–3 ottobre 2001, 195–221. Rome: Salerno, 2003.

———. "Il mito di Ercole: Aspetti della ricezione dell'antico alla corte Estense nel primo Quattrocento." In *Omaggio a Gianfranco Folena*, 1:773–92. Padua: Programma, 1993.

———. "Guarino, i suoi libri, e le letture della corte estense." In *Saggi*, Vol. 2 of *Le muse e il principe: Arte di corte nel Rinascimento padano*, edited by Alessandra Mottola Molfino and Mauro Natale, 63–79. Modena: Panini, 1991.

TLIO = *Tesoro della lingua italiana delle Origini*. Edited by the Opera del Vocabolario–Consiglio Nazionale delle Ricerche. http://tlio.ovi.cnr.it/TLIO/.

Todorović, Jelena. "Boccaccio's Editing of Dante's Presumed Intentions in the *Vita Nova*." *Medioevo letterario d'Italia* 15 (2018): 155–66.

———. *Dante and the Dynamics of Textual Exchange: Authorship, Manuscript Culture, and the Making of the* "*Vita Nova*." New York: Fordham University Press, 2016.

———. "'Un'operetta del famosissimo Poeta, e Teologo Dante Allighieri': L'*editio princeps* della *Vita Nova*." *Studi danteschi* 77 (2002): 293–310.

———. "Who Read the *Vita Nova* in the First Half of the Fourteenth Century?" *Dante Studies* 131 (2013): 197–217.

Tognetti, Giampaolo. *Criteri per la trascrizione di testi medievali latini e italiani*, Quaderni della Rassegna degli Archivi di Stato, 51. Rome, 1982.

Toja, Gianluigi, ed. *Canzoni*. By Arnaut Daniel. Florence: Sansoni, 1960.

Tonelli, Natascia. *Leggere il* "*Canzoniere*." Bologna: il Mulino, 2017.

———. "Petrarca, Properzio e la struttura del *Canzoniere*." *Rinascimento* 38 (1998): 249–315.

———. "I tempi della poesia, il tempo della prosa: A proposito di alcune visioni della *Vita nuova*." In *Vita nova–Fiore–Epistola XIII*, Vol. 1 of *Atti degli incontri sulle opere di Dante*, edited by Manuele Gragnolati, Luca Carlo Rossi, Paola Allegretti, Natascia Tonelli, and Alberto Casadei, 173–94. Florence: SISMEL—Edizioni del Galluzzo, 2018.

———. "Vat. Lat. 3195: un libro concluso? Lettura di *Rvf* 360–66." In Picone, ed., *Il Canzoniere*, 799–822.

Tonello, Elisabetta. "Concerning Three Manuscripts of the *Divine Comedy* in Private Collections in New York and Milan." *Dante Notes* (2016). https://dantesociety.org/node/127.

Toniolo, Federica. "Giraldi (Ziraldi), Guglielmo." In *Dizionario Biografico degli Italiani*, 56:447–52. Rome: Istituto della Enciclopedia Italiana, 2001.

———. "Giraldi, Guglielmo." In *Dizionario biografico dei miniatori italiani: Secoli IX–XVI*, edited by Milvia Bollati and Miklós Boskovits, 305–10. Milan: Sylvestre Bonnard, 2004.

———, ed. *La miniatura a Ferrara dal tempo di Cosmè Tura all'eredità di Ercole de' Roberti*. Ferrara, Palazzo Schifanoia 1 marzo–31 maggio 1998. Modena: Panini, 1998.

Took, John. "Dante and the *Confessions* of Augustine." *Annali d'Italianistica* 8 (1990): 360–82.

Torrell, Jean-Pierre. *The Person and His Work*, Vol. 1 of *Saint Thomas Aquinas*. Washington, DC: Catholic University of America Press, 1996.

Treharne, Elaine. "Fleshing Out the Text: The Transcendent Manuscript in the Digital Age." *Postmedieval: A Journal of Medieval Cultural Studies* 4 (2013): 465–78.

Treharne, Elaine, and Claude Willan. *Text Technologies: A History*. Stanford, CA: Stanford University Press, 2020.

Troiano, Alfredo. "Strumenti scrittori in prima persona: Per un'interpretazione del sonetto XVIII di Guido Cavalcanti." *Testo: Studi di teoria e storia della letteratura e della critica* 46 (2003): 7–22.

Trovato, Paolo. *Con ogni diligenza corretto: La stampa e le revisioni editoriali dei testi letterari italiani (1470–1570)*. Bologna: il Mulino, 1991.

———. *Dante in Petrarca: Per un inventario dei dantismi nei "Rerum vulgarium fragmenta."* Florence: Olschki, 1979.

———. *Il testo della "Vita nuova" e altra filologia dantesca*. Rome: Salerno, 2000.

Trovato, Paolo, Elisabetta Tonello, Sandro Bertelli, and Leonardo Fiorentini. "La tradizione e il testo del carme *Ytalie iam certus honos* di Giovanni Boccaccio." *Studi sul Boccaccio* 41 (2013): 1–111.

Tuhoi, Thomas. *Herculean Ferrara: Ercole d'Este (1471–1505) and the Invention of a Ducal Capital*. Cambridge: Cambridge University Press, 1996.

Turner, Eric Gardner. *Greek Manuscripts of the Ancient World*. London: Institute of Classical Studies, University of London, 1987.

Ugolini, Francesco. *I cantari d'argomento classico: Con un'appendice di testi inediti*. Geneva: Olschki, 1933.

Ullman, Berthold Louis. "Petrarch's Favorite Books." In *Studies in the Italian Renaissance*, 113–33. Rome: Edizioni di Storia e Letteratura, 1955.

Vallone, Aldo. *La prosa della "Vita Nuova."* Florence: Le Monnier, 1963.

———. "*Vita Nuova* XXV e la cultura di Dante." In *Ricerche dantesche*, 75–84. Lecce: Milella, 1967.

Vandelli, Giuseppe. "Un autografo della *Teseide*." *Studi di filologia italiana* 2 (1929): 5–76.

———. "Giovanni Boccaccio editore di Dante." In *Atti della R. Accademia della Crusca*, Anno accademico 1921–1922, 47–96. Florence: Ariani, 1923.

Vanossi, Luigi. "Identità e mutazione nella sestina petrarchesca." In *Studi di filologia romanza e italiana offerti a Gianfranco Folena dagli allievi padovani*, 281–99. Modena: STEM–Mucchi, 1980.

Vattasso, Marco, ed. *L'originale del Canzoniere di Francesco Petrarca, codice Vaticano Latino 3195, riprodotto in fototipia a cura della Biblioteca Vaticana*. By Francesco Petrarca. Milan: Hoepli, 1905.

Vecce, Carlo. "Beatrice e il numero amico." In *Beatrice nell'opera di Dante e nella memoria europea 1290–1990*, Atti del Convegno internazionale, 10–14 dicembre 1990, edited by Maria Picchio Simonelli, 101–35. Fiesole (Florence): Cadmo, 1994.

———. "'Ella era uno nove, cioè uno miracolo' (*V.N.*, XXIX, 3): Il numero di Beatrice." In Moleta, ed., La gloriosa donna de la mente, 161–79.

Vecchi Galli, Paola, ed. *Canzoniere*. By Francesco Petrarca. Milan: Rizzoli, 2012.

Velli, Giuseppe. "L'apoteosi di Arcita: Ideologia e coscienza storica nel *Teseida*." *Studi e problemi di critica testuale* 5 (1972): 33–66.

———. "La memoria poetica del Petrarca." *Italia medioevale e umanistica* 19 (1976): 171–207.

Veneziani, Paolo. "Carnerio, Agostino." In *Dizionario biografico degli italiani*, 20:464–65. Rome: Istituto della Enciclopedia Italiana, 1977.

Verrier, Jean. "Le récit réfléchi." *Littérature* 5 (1972): 58–68.

Vettori, Alessandro. "Veronica: Dante's Pilgrimage from Image to Vision." *Dante Studies* 121 (2003): 43–65.

Vilella, Eduard, ed. *Al poco giorno ed al gran cerchio d'ombra* (La biblioteca de Tenzone 9). Madrid: CEMA, 2016.

Villa, Claudia. "I commenti ai classici fra XII e XV secolo." In *Medieval and Renaissance Scholarship*, Proceedings of the Second European Science Foundation Workshop on the Classical Tradition in the Middle Ages and the Renaissance (London, The Warburg Institute, 27–28 November 1992), edited by Nicholas Mann and Birger Munk Olsen, 19–32. Leiden: Brill, 1997.

———. "Due schede per *editus*." *Italia medioevale e umanistica* 31 (1988): 399–402.

———, ed. *Epistole*. By Dante Alighieri. In *Convivio, Monarchia, Epistole, Egloge*, Vol. 2 of *Opere*, edited by Gianfranco Fioravanti, Claudio Giunta, Diego Quaglioni, Claudia Villa, and Gabriella Albanese, 1417–1592. Milan: Mondadori, 2014.

———. *La "lectura Terentii": 1. Da Ildemaro a Francesco Petrarca*. Padua: Antenore, 1984.

———. "Il lessico della stilistica fra XI e XIII secolo." In *Vocabulaire des écoles et des méthodes d'enseignement au moyen âge*, Actes du colloque, Rome 21–22 octobre 1989, edited by Olga Weijers, 42–59. Turnhout: Brepols, 1992.

Villani, Gianni, ed. *Vita di Petrarca*. By Giovanni Boccaccio. Rome: Salerno, 2004.

Vitale, Maurizio. *La lingua del Canzoniere ("Rerum vulgarium fragmenta") di Francesco Petrarca*. Padua: Antenore, 1996.

Viti, Paolo, ed. *Opere letterarie e politiche*. By Leonardo Bruni. Turin: UTET, 1996.

Voigt, Eva-Maria, ed. *Sappho et Alcaeus: Fragmenta*. Amsterdam: Polak & van Gennep, 1971.

Volpe, Alessandro. "Boccaccio illustratore e illustrato." *Intersezioni* 31, no. 2 (2011): 287–300.

Warkentin, Germaine. "*Infaticabile maestro*: Ernest Hatch Wilkins and the Manuscripts of Petrarch's *Canzoniere*." In *Petrarch and the Textual Origins of Interpretation*, edited by Teodolinda Barolini and H. Wayne Storey, 45–65. Leiden: Brill, 2007.

Waugh, Patricia. *Metafiction: The Theory and Practice of Self-Conscious Fiction*. London: Methuen, 1984.

Wehle, Winfried. *Poesia sulla poesia: La "Vita Nova": Una scuola d'amore* novissimo. Florence: Cesati, 2014.

Weinrich, Harald. *La memoria di Dante*. Florence: Accademia della Crusca, 1994.

———. *Metafora e menzogna: La serenità dell'arte*. Bologna: il Mulino, 1976.

Wenzel, Horst. *Hören und Sehen, Schrift und Bild: Kultur und Gedächtnis im Mittelalter*. Munich: Beck, 1995.

Wetherbee, Winthrop. "History and Romance in Boccaccio's *Teseida*." *Studi sul Boccaccio* 20 (1991–1992): 173–84.

Wicksteed, Philip H., and Edmund G. Gardner. *Dante and Giovanni del Virgilio*. Westminster: Archibald Constable & Company, 1902.

———, trans. *Eclogues*. By Dante Alighieri. In *A Translation of the Latin Works of Dante Alighieri*, 369–85. London: Dent, 1904.

Wieck, Roger S. *Late Medieval and Renaissance Illuminated Manuscripts, 1350–1525, in the Houghton Library*. Cambridge, MA: Department of Print and Graphic Arts, Harvard College Library, 1983.

Wilkins, Ernest Hatch. *The Making of the "Canzoniere" and Other Petrarchan Studies*. Rome: Edizioni di Storia e Letteratura, 1951.

———, ed. *The Triumphs of Petrarch*. By Francesco Petrarca. Chicago: University of Chicago Press, 1962.

Wilson, W. Daniel. "Readers in Texts." *PMLA* 96, no. 5 (1981): 848–63.

Wind, Edgar. *Pagan Mysteries in the Renaissance*. New York: Norton, 1968.

Witt, Ronald G. *The Two Latin Cultures and the Foundation of Renaissance Humanism in Medieval Italy*. Cambridge: Cambridge University Press, 2012.

Wittgenstein, Ludwig. *Tractatus Logico-Philosophicus*. New York: Dover, 1999.

Wlassics, Tibor. "Le 'postille' di Dante alla *Commedia*." *Studi danteschi* 49 (1972): 115–28.

Wolf, Werner. *Ästhetische Illusion und Illusionsdurchbrechung in der Erzählkunst: Theorie und Geschichte mit Schwerpunkt auf englischem illusionsstörenden Erzählen*. Tübingen: Niemeyer, 1993.

Wolfreys, Julian. "Materialism/Materiality." In *Critical Keywords in Literary and Cultural Theory*, 143–50. Houndmills: Palgrave Macmillan, 2004.

Wood, James. *The Nearest Thing to Life*. Waltham, MA: Brandeis University Press, 2015.

Zaccarello, Michelangelo. "Filologia materiale e culture testuali per la letteratura italiana antica." In *Testo e metodo: Prospettive teoriche sulla letteratura italiana*, edited by Daniele Monticelli and Licia Taverna, 35–48. Tallinn: Tallinn University Press, 2011.

———, ed. *Le trecento novelle*. By Franco Sacchetti. Florence: Edizioni del Galluzzo, 2014.

Zaccaria, Vittorio. "Le fasi redazionali del *De mulieribus claris*." *Studi sul Boccaccio* 1 (1963): 253–332.

———, ed. *Genealogie deorum gentilium*. By Giovanni Boccaccio. Vols. 7–8 of *Tutte le opere di Giovanni Boccaccio*, edited by Vittore Branca. Milan: Mondadori, 1998.

Zacour, Norman P., and Rudolf Hirsch. *Catalogue of Manuscripts in the Libraries of the University of Pennsylvania to 1800*. Philadelphia: University of Pennsylvania Press, 1965.

Zaggia, Massimo. "Appunti sulla cultura letteraria in volgare a Milano nell'età di Filippo Maria Visconti." *Giornale storico della letteratura italiana* 170 (1993): 161–219.

Zamarra, Edoardo. "*Dolce, soave, vago* nella lirica italiana tra XIII e XVI secolo." *Critica letteraria* 46 (1985): 71–118.

Zambon, Francesco. "Il bue zoppo di Petrarca: Lettura della sestina *Là ver' l'aurora, che sì dolce l'aura* (*RVF* CCXXXIX)." *Cultura neolatina* 71, nos. 1–2 (2011): 119–39.

Zamponi, Stefano. "Il libro del canzoniere: Modelli, strutture, funzioni." In *Commentario all'edizione in fac-simile*, Vol. 2 of *Rerum vulgarium fragmenta. Codice Vat. lat. 3195, edizione facsimilare*, edited by Gino Belloni, Furio Brugnolo, H. Wayne Storey, and Stefano Zamponi, 13–72. Padua: Antenore, 2003–2004.

———. "Nell'officina di Boccaccio: Gli autori classici e medievali di una lunga iniziazione letteraria." In De Robertis et al., eds., *Boccaccio autore e copista*, 300–305.

Zamponi, Stefano, Martina Pantarotto, and Antonella Tomiello. "Stratigrafia dello Zibaldone e della Miscellanea Laurenziani." In Picone and Bérard, eds., *Gli Zibaldoni di Boccaccio*, 181–258.

Zinelli, Fabio. "Gustav Gröber e i libri dei trovatori (1877)." *Studi mediolatini e volgari* 48 (2002): 229–74.

Zingarelli, Nicola. "Il libro della memoria." *Bullettino della Società Dantesca Italiana* 1 (1893–1894): 98–101.

———. "Petrarca e i trovatori." In *Provenza e Italia*, edited by Vincenzo Crescini, 99–136. Florence: Bemporad, 1930.

Zumthor, Paul. "Autobiography in the Middle Ages?" *Genre* 6, no. 1 (1973): 29–48.

———. "Una cultura della voce." In *La produzione del testo*, Vol. 1/1 of *Lo spazio letterario del Medioevo: 2. Il Medioevo volgare*, edited by Piero Boitani, Mario Mancini, and Alberto Vàrvaro, 117–46. Rome: Salerno, 1999.

———. "La glose créatrice." In *Les commentaires et la naissance de la critique littéraire: France/Italie (XIVe–XVIe siècles)*, Actes du Colloque international sur le Commentaire, Paris, mai 1988, edited by Gisèle Mathieu-Castellani and Michel Plaisance, 11–18. Paris: Aux Amateurs des Livres, 1990.

———. *La lettera e la voce: Sulla "letteratura" medievale*. Bologna: il Mulino, 1990.

———. "Médiéviste ou pas." *Poétique* 31 (1977): 306–21.

———. *Parler du Moyen Age*. Paris: Minuit, 1980.

———. *Toward a Medieval Poetics*. Minneapolis: University of Minnesota Press, 1992.

INDEX

Pre-modern and early modern persons are indexed by their first names. Numbers in *italics* refer to textual sections and *loci* in primary sources. Page numbers for definitions are in **bold**.

FRANCESCO MARCO ARESU
is an assistant professor of Italian Studies at the University of Pennsylvania

Printed in the USA
CPSIA information can be obtained
at www.ICGtesting.com
LVHW021914131023
761060LV00009B/42